Archaeology
and the
Old Testament

Alfred J. Hoerth recently retired as director of archaeology at Wheaton College, where he taught for almost thirty years. He is coeditor of *Peoples of the Old Testament World*, and he has participated in numerous archaeological excavations.

Companion volume ──────────────────────────────
John McRay, *Archaeology and the New Testament*

Archaeology
and the
Old
Testament

Alfred J. Hoerth

Baker Books

A Division of Baker Book House Co
Grand Rapids, Michigan 49516

Published by Baker Books
a division of Baker Book House Company
P.O. Box 6287, Grand Rapids, MI 49516-6287

Fifth printing, December 2004

Printed in the United States of America

Library of Congress Cataloging-in-Publication Data

Hoerth, Alfred J.
    Archaeology and the Old Testament / Alfred J. Hoerth.
       p.   cm.
    Includes index.
    ISBN 0-8010-1129-9 (hardcover)
    1. Bible. O.T.—Antiquities. 2. Bible. O.T.—History of Biblical events. I. Title.
BS621.H56   1998
221.9′3—dc21   98-23086

For information about academic books, resources for Christian leaders, and all new releases available from Baker Book House, visit our web site:
http://www.bakerbooks.com

To my wife,

Bette,

the best thing I ever discovered in the Near East

Contents

Preface

Archaeology has become an integral part of biblical studies. Today it is fashionable for authors of Bible atlases, commentaries, dictionaries, and handbooks to assure their readers that they have incorporated the latest archaeological findings into their work. This book is designed to acquaint the beginning student in Old Testament studies with the reasons for this interest in archaeology and with some of the specific benefits that the discipline brings to the biblical text. I have structured my discussion of Old Testament history in such a way as to emphasize the individuality of the main characters. The wish is that *Simchat Torah*, "delight in studying Scripture," will result or be enhanced.

I am indebted to many people. For more than twenty years my students in Old Testament archaeology helped me learn what "works," and we have tested an in-house version of this publication. Stella Haugen proofread and polished the preliminary text, Jane Robertson Dodds drew most of its illustrations, and both greatly enhanced the ability of that edition to communicate. To Allan Fisher and Jim Weaver at Baker Book House I extend deep appreciation for their patience and encouragement along the way. My wife labored long over the several drafts through which the text evolved. Lastly, David Aiken, of Baker Book House, fine-tuned the text with meticulous attention, bringing it to this present form. The reader should thank them for the clarity of thought, and any obscure passages can be blamed on my obstinacy to emendation.

This text provides a doorway into the world of the Old Testament. The chapters ahead contain many references that will escort the interested reader beyond this threshold. Whenever possible, references are made to articles in *Biblical Archaeologist* (renamed *Near Eastern Archaeology* in 1998), *Biblical Archaeology Review*, and the more recent *Archaeology in the Biblical World*. Anyone interested in biblical archaeology would do well to keep current with these magazines. They are geared to the general public, but their articles generally contain bibliographies that point to more technical writings.

For those who delve deeper, be aware that the majority of articles and publications relevant to Old Testament archaeology treat the Bible no differently than any other ancient document. Their authors will sometimes present their conclusions as "serious" and "scholarly" and label a more conservative position as "simplistic" and "unsophisticated." At other times their critical orientation is more subtle. Such scholars consider themselves truly objective, seldom admitting that everyone brings his or her own bias to the biblical text. One should not reject such critical writings outright but should mine them for what is useful, while recognizing when their assertions are in tension with the biblical text.

I have participated in or led ten expeditions to the Near East (to Syria, Israel, Jordan, Egypt, and the Sudan). My wife and I have escorted several groups of college students on study tours into the Mediterranean and Near East. During these repeated travels I have come to feel at home in the lands of the Bible. My hope is that through this book the reader will become more at home with the message and in the world of the Old Testament.

Abbreviations

ANE 1   *Ancient Near East*, vol. 1

ANE 2   *Ancient Near East*, vol. 2

ANET   *Ancient Near Eastern Texts*

BA   *Biblical Archaeologist*

BAR   *Biblical Archaeology Review*

BASOR   *Bulletin of the American Schools of Oriental Research*

IEJ   *Israel Exploration Journal*

PEQ   *Palestine Exploration Quarterly*

Unless otherwise indicated, all dates are B.C. The abbreviations B.C.E. ("before common era") and C.E. ("common era"), coined by modern Israeli scholars to replace B.C. and A.D., may be encountered in writings about the Bible. For reactions to these alternate designations, see *BAR* 22/5 (1996): 8, 10, 12.

Sources of Chapter Epigraphs

1. W. M. Flinders Petrie 1904: 177
2. Meyer 1971: 10
3. Roux 1992: 221–23
4. *ANE* 1:7; *ANET* 19–20
5. *ANE* 1:168; *ANET* 219–20
6. Gardiner 1961: 37
7. *ANE* 1:25–26; *ANET* 31–32
8. Wenham 1958: 17
9. Archer 1964 : 190–91
10. *ANET* 487
11. John Milton, "Samson Agonistes"
12. Christie 1977: 37
13. Psalm 133 (New American Standard Bible)
14. Gordon 1959: 1.8, 18, 153, 160, 193; 2.32, 71, 124, 149
15. *ANE* 1:209; *ANET* 320
16. Roux 1992: 290–91
17. Nahum 2:1–10 (New Living Translation)
18. Psalm 137:1–6 (New American Standard Bible)
19. *ANE* 1:279–80; *ANET* 492
20. Russell 1965: 11

Archaeology

What It Is, What It Does, What It Does Not Do

Every tablet, every little scarab, is a portion of life solidified. . . . When we look closely into the work we seem almost to watch the hand that did it; this stone is a day, a week of the life of some living man. I know his mind, his feeling, by what he has thought and done on this stone. I live with him in looking into his work, and admiring and valuing it.

—W. M. Flinders Petrie

Biblical Archaeology: Illumination
   Cultural and Historical Setting
   Knowledge of People, Places, Things, and Events
   Translation and Exegesis of Biblical Passages
Biblical Archaeology: Confirmation
The Stones and the Scriptures
The Science of Archaeology
Additional Reading

Archaeology is an elusive word. It has two spellings and can be defined in numerous ways (Cleator 1976: 13–17 lists nearly three dozen definitions).[1] The 1950 edition of the *American College Dictionary* incorrectly limited archaeology to preliterate times by giving this sole explanation of the discipline: "The scientific study of any prehistoric culture by excavation and description of its remains." Robert J. Braidwood (1970: 223) composed a broader description that embraces both prehistoric and historic times, thus providing room for classical and much of Near Eastern archaeology:[2]

1. The word *archaeology* derives from Greek *archaios* ("ancient") plus *logos* ("discourse"). The alternate spelling *archeology* is normally used in the social sciences.
2. The terms *Near East* and *Middle East* refer to the same area. The latter is of more recent usage.

Archaeology is that science or art—it can be maintained that it is both—which is concerned with the material remains of man's past. There are two aspects to the archaeologist's concern. The first of these is the discovery and reclamation of the ancient remains; this usually involves field excavation or at least surface collecting. The second concern is the analysis, interpretation and publication of the findings.

Braidwood's definition correctly takes the task of the archaeologist past the digging stage. Few archaeologists are interested only in excavation; most spend much of their time analyzing what they have found and trying to fit those findings within an increasingly full picture of the past.

To many people, archaeology evokes visions of treasure hunts, of pith helmets bobbing over distant sand dunes. Field excavation might be the most romantic-sounding part of archaeology but it normally occupies only a small portion of the archaeologist's life. The bulk of an archaeologist's hours should be spent preparing the finds for publication. Furthermore, most archaeologists teach at colleges and universities or work in museums. Consequently, their fieldwork and commitments to publication are usually in addition to these other obligations.

The archaeologist is generally a rather misunderstood soul. Rock hounds often think they and the archaeologist have a similar interest in stones. In reality, the archaeologist usually knows little about geology

1.1. One of two sixty-four-feet-tall "colossi of Memnon" erected at Thebes by Pharaoh Amenhotep III in the fourteenth century. Geologists discovered that the stone from which the statues were made was quarried several hundred miles north of their present site, which prompted archaeologists to recognize that difficult logistical problems had to have been solved to transport the statues. Geology also presented archaeologists with a new question: why did the Egyptians go to such effort when they could have quarried equally good stone from nearby hills?

1.2. By studying animal bones from the excavation of Selenkihiye, Syria, paleontologist Pierre Ducos was able to determine that sheep and goats were the most abundant species in that area around 2000. He also found evidence of gazelle, deer, cattle, jackal, wolf, and perhaps horse and dog. A field archaeologist would not usually have the training to ascertain such specific data.

and is interested in rocks only when they can impart some information concerning the abilities or activities of ancient peoples. For instance, rocks can reveal regional trade activities and show the level of ability to build housing or to fashion tools. In order to recover such insights, the archaeologist will either include a geologist on staff or will record sufficient data so that a geologist can be consulted should technical analysis be needed.

Nor should an archaeologist be confused with a paleontologist. Few archaeologists have extensive training in paleontology. Fossils and mastodons date to prehistoric times. An archaeologist, whose interest is in historical periods, is generally trained to recognize certain features relative to human skeletal remains (i.e., age at death, sex, or obvious deformity) and can often recognize basic types of animals from skeletal remains. But modern excavations use specialists for more precise studies and to extract such insights as race and subsistence patterns.

Another common misconception assumes that an archaeologist's knowledge and interest has no geographical bounds. However, early on, the aspiring archaeologist finds it necessary to specialize on some specific part of the world and usually within a limited time span. There is simply too much information known, with more constantly being added, to keep current in more than one limited area. Therefore, a young person wishing a career in archaeology has to choose whether he or she wants training in prehistoric or historic periods. If the interest is primarily prehistoric or sociological, the career route is through the social sciences and into anthropology. If the focus is on historical issues, the training is more often channeled through the humanities, with its emphasis on history and languages.

Finally, there is a misconception peculiar to the Christian—namely, that biblical issues are foremost in archaeological studies. In reality,

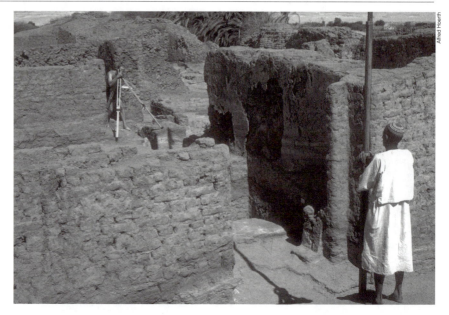

Alfred Hoerth

1.3. An architect takes measurements so that an accurate paper record can be made of an administrative center in the island fortress of Dorginarti. This fortress, in the second cataract of the Nile, was used by the Egyptians to monitor river traffic. Although important for an understanding of Egypt's military outreach in the Middle and Late Kingdoms, the excavation has no application to biblical studies.

biblical archaeology is only one of many subfields. Archaeological investigations are going on all over the world, but only in the Near East and Mediterranean areas are biblical connections going to be found. Moreover, the majority of archaeological journal articles and books published each year on the Near East and the Mediterranean have nothing to do with the Bible. In short, the typical archaeologist has no interest in biblical studies.

What then is an archaeologist? An archaeologist is a historian who is not limited to the written word, but goes beyond and literally digs out remains of ancient peoples. Through a synthesis of this additional data with the written word, the archaeologist provides a fuller history of ancient culture than is possible from written sources alone.

Biblical Archaeology: Illumination

The focus of this book is Old Testament archaeology. Together with New Testament archaeology (see McRay 1991), the two studies comprise biblical archaeology. When nineteenth-century historians began rejoicing over the wealth of information that Near Eastern archaeology was bringing to light, Christians began asking what this material from the lands of the Bible meant to their understanding of God's word. Biblical archaeology arose in response to that question.[3]

3. Since the 1960s Near Eastern archaeology has become increasingly influenced by anthropological method. This "new archaeology" has been championed by archaeologists such as William G. Dever. It should be noted, however, that Robert J. Braidwood carried out multidisciplinary excavations throughout much of the 1950s, a number of years before some proponents of new archaeology take credit for introducing such multidisciplinary staff into the Near East. In the same vein, Daniel 1981: 190–92 concludes that "new archaeology" is not really all that new. N. Davies 1986 questions the validity of the supposedly new approach, and Kempinski 1995 concludes that it has in fact had

The most important contributions of archaeology to biblical studies are the various ways it illuminates the cultural and historical setting of the Bible; adds to our knowledge of the people, places, things, and events in the Bible; and aids in translation and exegesis of biblical passages.

Cultural and Historical Setting

When the Hebrews moved into Palestine they settled on the land bridge between Egypt and Mesopotamia, the major power bases in the ancient Near East. Consequently, Israel was exposed not only to local Canaanite culture but also to the cultures and political pressures of neighboring nations. Israel did not function within a vacuum, and as the interrelationships with different cultures are further revealed through archaeological discoveries, the implications of many Bible texts may become clearer.

Just as there is an obvious danger in interpreting a Bible verse without regard to its context, a similar potential danger threatens when an episode in the Bible is separated from its cultural and historical context.[4] By way of illustration, Abraham lived in the ancient Near East. As ancient Nuzian and other texts are studied and understood, Abraham can be more readily appreciated as a living person whose actions were not only logical but conditioned by the events of his time and by the social norms in which he operated. Without such insight, one runs the risk of completely missing the thrust or purpose behind certain decisions he made (see chaps. 4–5).

Ideally, one is never content with one's present level of Bible knowledge. Thoughtful study of the biblical text often engenders questions concerning cultural attitudes and historical actions. Archaeology can provide some answers. Further, a more accurate understanding of history and culture allows deeper insight into theological issues. For instance, now that the Canaanite religion is more fully known (see chap. 10), one can better appreciate why it was so fiercely condemned in Scripture, and the consequences of a faith in violent opposition to the biblical teaching become more obvious.

Knowledge of People, Places, Things, and Events

People. Archaeology has added to the biography of dozens of Bible characters. For example, the excavation of Saul's palace sheds light on his lifestyle. Thanks to Assyrian records a new dimension can be given

a devastating effect on archaeology. Dever has also argued that the term *biblical archaeology* should be retired in favor of *Syro-Palestinian archaeology*. The ensuing battle of words over this proposed change has been spirited. Those who espouse biblical archaeology point out that it is as valid a subfield within Near Eastern archaeology as is Hittitology, Ugaritic studies, or any other specialty. The following journal articles can be consulted for a taste of the controversy over "new archaeology" vs. "biblical archaeology": Dever 1980, 1982, 1987a, 1987b; Lance 1982; E. Meyers 1984; J. Miller 1982; Rainey 1982; Sauer 1982; Shanks 1981b, 1987b; Toombs 1982; Ussishkin 1982b.

4. Several scholars correctly warn of this danger. For example, Ramm 1956: 98 argues that "historical knowledge is indispensable to the best exegesis," and R. K. Harrison 1970: 5 cautions that the "Old Testament cannot and must not be studied in isolation." Harrison repeatedly stresses how the Bible was written in the context of its time.

to the abilities of Ahab, a king the Bible rates as one of the worst rulers of Israel. Information found in Persian and Greek texts concerning Esther's husband enables us to more correctly understand the circumstances of her marriage.

Places. Most major biblical sites have been located. Consequently, travelers can glimpse what specific landscapes and cities were like in Bible times and can understand the logistics and time factors involved in various passages. The sheer size of the city of Hazor—approximately two hundred acres, compared to the normal twenty acres for other large cities in Palestine—is enough to help one better appreciate Joshua 11:10, which calls Hazor "the head of all these kingdoms."

Things. Time and time again archaeology lets us see beyond word pictures and actually touch the things of the Bible. For example, artists' drawings of horned altars often featured long steerlike horns. The reality was found to be much different when horned altars began to be recovered (see illustration 17.6). Today the material culture of the Old Testament (and the New Testament as well) is largely known. Daily life—its dress, implements, housing, and the like—can be faithfully reassembled for the various biblical periods. As the biblical characters are surrounded with these mundane items, they become more than legends in a book. We can better identify them as real human beings.

Events. Thanks to archaeology, certain biblical events are more fully understood. At several points it is possible to view a biblical event through an extrabiblical source. For example, perhaps the Amarna Letters (see chap. 10) contain Canaanite reactions to the Israelite conquest. And in the Lachish Letters (chap. 17) we read the poignant dispatches of the army of Judah as it collapsed in 586 and as Jeremiah continued to speak to "deaf" ears.

Translation and Exegesis of Biblical Passages

With the benefit of archaeological studies, hundreds of verses are more clearly understood now than they were when the translators of the King James Version finished their work early in the seventeenth century. For example, the King James Version rendering of Proverbs 26:23 contains unbalanced imagery: "Burning lips and a wicked heart are like a potsherd covered with silver dross." Only recently did Ugaritic linguistic studies allow for restoration of the correct rendering of the proverb: "Smooth words may hide a wicked heart, just as a pretty glaze covers a common clay pot" (New Living Translation). The proverb has regained its contrasting parallelism and meaningful imagery. The retrieval of this verse's intent is a small thing in itself, but it is a big thing for those interested in the accuracy of translation.[5]

Biblical Archaeology: Confirmation

Archaeology illuminates the Bible in the general ways described above. Some people mistakenly use archaeology to confirm, authenti-

---

5. Ugaritic is a Canaanite alphabetic script with close linguistic affinities to Hebrew. For a survey of how Ugaritic benefits Old Testament studies, see Craigie 1983b.

cate, or prove the Bible. This use of archaeology can be traced back to the nineteenth century when biblical archaeology arose to answer questions that Near Eastern discoveries were raising for Christian believers. The answers to some of the questions were unsettling. For instance, in 1872 George Smith translated a Mesopotamian flood story inscribed on a clay tablet. He found numerous strong parallels to the biblical story of the flood, and critics quickly concluded that the Genesis account was plagiarized rather than inspired. And when early archaeologists found no traces of the Hittites, biblical critics solemnly decided the Hittites were an imaginary people.

Conservative Christians had no easy responses to some of these attacks on the reliability of the Bible. So, toward the end of the nineteenth century, when archaeologists finally did find the Hittites, evangelicals felt a bit relieved. As biblical archaeology caused other excesses of higher criticism to be retracted, evangelicals began to feel that the discipline had vindicated their faith. Archaeology did such a good job of refuting the grosser criticisms that in 1896 J. F. McCurdy pleaded (p. 28):

> It is now in place to use the word "illustrate" almost exclusively instead of "confirm" in describing the biblical function of the monuments. The stadium of needed vindication of the historical accuracy of the Old Testament is now as good as past in our progress towards the final goal of truth and knowledge.

Eleven years later another conservative, A. T. Clay (1907: 21–22), wrote:

> It must be a source of gratification to many to know that the ruin-hills of the past have yielded so many things to prove that much which the skeptic and the negative critic have declared to be fiction is veritable history. Archeology must ever be given the greatest credit for having come to the rescue.

More turn-of-the-century references could be cited in which conservative writers put the apologetic benefits of archaeology in the past tense. Liberal scholars of that day would not have agreed to the total historicity of the Bible, but they had been taught to be more cautious when making critical statements, and they had begun to explore ways in which archaeology could be used to illuminate the Bible. Unfortunately, their evangelical counterparts were largely unaware that any shift in emphasis had taken place. That the shift was missed can be seen, for instance, in R. A. Torrey's 1907 statement: "Time and time again further researches and discoveries, geographical, historical and archaeological, have vindicated the Bible and put to shame its critics" (p. 23).

In 1934 George McCready Price asked the rhetorical question: "What did the 'critics' formerly say about the Hittites?" He answered: "They said that the classical historians of ancient Greece never mentioned them, therefore they must be a mythical people, or at least the Bible's repeated mention of them must be a mistake. Now . . . the 'critics' have to admit that the Bible was right, after all." Price (1934: 53–54) continues with the next question: "What are some other instances where archaeology has proved the 'critics' wrong and the Bible right?"

Of all the books making use of archaeology, *Halley's Bible Handbook* has probably shaped evangelical attitudes toward the discipline more than any other single work. *Halley's Bible Handbook* teaches that archaeology "authenticates"—confirms—the Bible, but unfortunately it uses old and often erroneous evidences.[6]

Until recent decades evangelical scholarship leaned toward the belief that archaeology's chief function was to confirm the Bible. Howard Vos (1968: 252) continued the argument for archaeological apologetics this way:

> Since it has been a device of enemies of the theological message of the Bible to cast doubt on that message by attacking historical and scientific references in Scripture, may it not be concluded that confidence in the spiritual message is immensely strengthened whenever archaeology demonstrates the veracity of the context of a theological dictum?

Vos's supposition seems valid, but his apologetic examples do not illustrate his premise. It is difficult to think of any archaeological discovery that would. Archaeological apologetics does not really live up to its billing. Even if every historical statement in the Bible could be proven true—confirmed—this would still not prove the theological message of the Bible.

There is the tendency by some Christians to assume too much from archaeology. Sometimes the words *confirm*, *prove*, *authenticate*, and *substantiate* can be employed. It can be proved that historical conditions were such that Solomon could have been as powerful a king as the Bible says he was; but this does not prove that God gave Solomon wisdom. It can be fairly well substantiated that there was a census when Jesus was born; but this confirmation hardly proves his divinity. No archaeological evidence will ever prove the atonement.

It must be recognized that there is a clear separation between historical and theological proof. William F. Albright, the leading biblical archaeologist of the twentieth century, claimed that archaeological discoveries led him to increasingly respect the historicity of the Bible. The positive statements that Albright made concerning the historical integrity of the Bible were reported repeatedly in evangelical publications. But these publications ignored what this leading archaeologist also clearly stated—that theologically, he was becoming increasingly more liberal. Albright illustrates the clear separation between historical and theological proof.[7]

6. Except for the addendums in recent editions, the archaeological entries seem to be no more recent than 1935. Examples of Halley's outdated and erroneous evidences are given in later chapters of this text.

7. See, for example, the interview with Albright in *Christianity Today* 7/8 (18 Jan. 1963): 3–5 and Albright's 1968 article in the same periodical. See also *BA* 56/1 (1993), an issue dedicated to an examination of Albright and his legacy. In recent years scholars intent on distancing themselves from biblical archaeology have increasingly "damned him with faint praise." One of the articles in this issue of *BA*, "Mythic Trope in the Autobiography of William Foxwell Albright" by Burke O. Long, argues that Albright always held to the substantial historicity of the Bible, and despite what he said, archaeological discoveries had no real impact on his attitude toward the Bible. Conversely, T. Davis 1995: 42–50 finds that the shift did indeed take place as Albright claimed.

In summary, archaeological apologetics was an important corrective tool in earlier decades, and it will continue to be needed as long as critics persist. However, evangelicals should recognize that the greatest value of biblical archaeology is its ability to increase understanding of the cultural and material setting within which the truths of God were given. Evangelical confidence and hope should not be built on any external proof—not even archaeology.

The Stones and the Scriptures

In his 1972 book *The Stones and the Scriptures*, Edwin Yamauchi summarizes the relationship of archaeology to the Bible and shows how archaeology has tempered biblical skepticism. He acknowledges that skepticism persists, but argues that more persists than is justified. In this regard, while evangelical scholars by and large have shifted their focus to archaeological illumination, it is now liberal scholarship that can be charged with using archaeology to prove the Bible—at least to prove what parts of it they will believe![8]

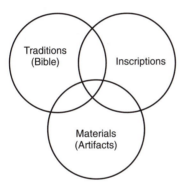

1.4. Yamauchi's circles (slightly modified). Objects or data found in written traditions (including the Bible), miscellaneous inscriptions, and materials (artifacts) can overlap or stand alone. Edwin Yamauchi (1972: 159) says: "The implication of this random distribution is that just as an object may be attested alone by excavations or alone by inscriptions, it may very often stand alone in the traditions without any necessary reflection upon its authenticity. Yet scholars have often worked under the assumption that the overlay of traditions with either inscriptional or material evidence is not only desirable but necessary."

Yamauchi's point is important. He cites examples of mistakes made by those who demanded that traditions have other support. He also notes the inconsistency with which this demand has been held. For example, no one questioned the historicity of either Pontius Pilate or Herod the Great, yet neither were found in inscriptions until the early 1960s. To paraphrase Yamauchi: it is a mistake to insist that traditions—including the Old Testament stories—must interlock with other evidences before they can be believed.[9]

Yamauchi underscores the magnitude of the mistake by illustrating the fragmentary nature of our evidence and by emphasizing how little of what once existed is now available for study. Yamauchi makes five "fractional" points: (a) very little of what was made or written in antiquity survives to this day; (b) very few of the ancient sites have been surveyed or even found; (c) probably less than two percent of the known

8. The next four paragraphs summarize Yamauchi's chapter entitled "Fragments and Circles: The Nature of the Evidence."
9. The mistaken mind-set that Yamauchi mentions continues today. For example, P. Davies 1994 prides himself on not believing anything in the Bible unless it has outside confirmation.

sites have been meaningfully excavated; (d) few of these sites have been more than scratched (many would take centuries to fully excavate); and (e) only a fraction of the fraction that has been excavated has been published and become available to the scholarly world (see also Wiseman 1990 and Shanks 1994a).

This increasing fractional improbability creates odds that are extremely heavy *against* tradition interlocking with inscriptions or materials. This being so, it is hardly damaging to the Bible that portions of its narratives and traditions cannot be externally substantiated. Yamauchi and his circles counter criticisms that demand interlocks.[10] Further, he illustrates how the Bible does repeatedly interlock with material and inscriptional remains. Despite the odds, biblical historicity is supported.

It must be acknowledged that there are cases where an inscription or material object seems to run counter to tradition. These instances need not, however, give cause for alarm. The interlocking difficulty can sometimes be harmonized if the data is weighed against a different premise. Sometimes the difficulty is resolved with the next new discovery. A case in point: Tell Beit Mirsim had long been identified with Debir despite its topography not conforming to the biblical requirements. Today Debir is recognized to be Khirbet Rabud (where the topography does agree with the biblical citations).[11] The interlocking difficulties that have not yet been so resolved do not alter the overall support of biblical historicity by archaeology.

The Science of Archaeology

As one travels through the Near East it soon becomes obvious that ancient sites are nearly everywhere. The ancient cities that dot the landscape in the Near East are usually called "khirbets" or "tel(l)s." A khirbet is an ancient site in which some of the ruins remain visible. Khirbet Qumran, where the Dead Sea Scrolls were copied in the last centuries B.C., is a well-known example of such a site. Tell (used in Arabic site names) or tel (used in Hebrew site names) is the more common designation and refers to an ancient site whose ruins were completely buried. Many tells resemble natural hills or low mesas, and it was not recognized until the nineteenth century that such formations actually concealed ancient towns and cities.

The pre-Greek inhabitants of Palestine usually founded their settlements atop a natural hill and near a source of water. With the passage of time one of many different things could happen to the site. The settlement might undergo an "urban renewal project," with older homes torn down and leveled off and new buildings erected over the old ones. When finished, a new living level—a new layer—sat atop the now slightly higher natural hill. Renewal might also follow destruction, ei-

10. Egyptologist Kenneth A. Kitchen likes to point out that "absence of evidence is not evidence of absence."

11. Compare the entry for "Debir" in the 1962 *Interpreter's Dictionary of the Bible* (1:808) with that appearing in the 1976 supplementary volume of the same set (p. 222).

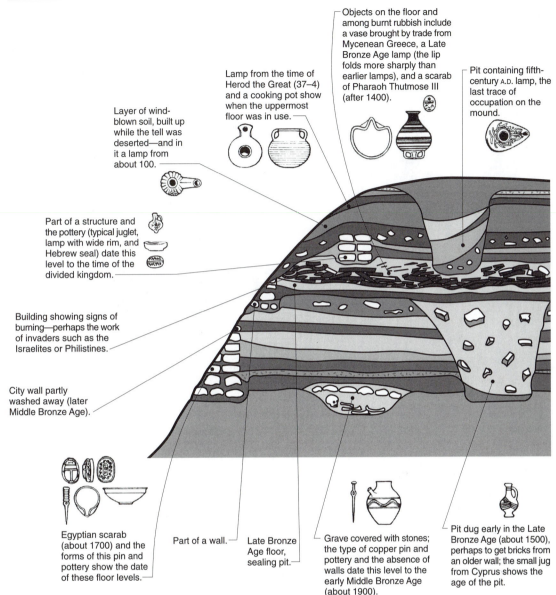

Objects on the floor and among burnt rubbish include a vase brought by trade from Mycenean Greece, a Late Bronze Age lamp (the lip folds more sharply than earlier lamps), and a scarab of Pharaoh Thutmose III (after 1400).

Pit containing fifth-century A.D. lamp, the last trace of occupation on the mound.

Lamp from the time of Herod the Great (37–4) and a cooking pot show when the uppermost floor was in use.

Layer of wind-blown soil, built up while the tell was deserted—and in it a lamp from about 100.

Part of a structure and the pottery (typical juglet, lamp with wide rim, and Hebrew seal) date this level to the time of the divided kingdom.

Building showing signs of burning—perhaps the work of invaders such as the Israelites or Philistines.

City wall partly washed away (later Middle Bronze Age).

Egyptian scarab (about 1700) and the forms of this pin and pottery show the date of these floor levels.

Part of a wall.

Late Bronze Age floor, sealing pit.

Grave covered with stones; the type of copper pin and pottery and the absence of walls date this level to the early Middle Bronze Age (about 1900).

Pit dug early in the Late Bronze Age (about 1500), perhaps to get bricks from an older wall; the small jug from Cyprus shows the age of the pit.

1.5. Cross section of a tell illustrates how the tell is formed and shows why objects found on the same horizontal level might not be of the same date.

ther nonnatural (e.g., fire or war) or natural (e.g., earthquake or a problem with the water supply that required temporary abandonment of the site). The history of a tell can be complex, but whatever the specific factors in each case, a long inhabited settlement slowly rose, layer after layer. Each living level retained distinctive fragments of its time in history. When the settlement was abandoned for the last time, the buildings left behind began to crumble and the open areas slowly silted up. Eventually, surface evidences of occupation were nearly erased, and the ancient settlement became a tell.

The excavation of an ancient site follows a fairly regular sequence. The choice of which site to dig is dependent on many factors.[12] An ar-

12. Yamauchi's estimate that less than two percent of the known sites have been adequately worked makes it clear that there is no lack of potential places to dig.

1.6. Botanist Willem Van Zeist uses water to separate carbonized seeds and charred wood from occupation debris so he can determine from the flotation samples the flora available or used in a specific time. In this excavation at Selenkihiye, Syria, botanical study found that local barley was of the two-row variety. This, and the absence of six-row barley seeds, indicates that the inhabitants were not irrigating their fields around 2000. Van Zeist also determined that carbonized olive pips and charred coniferous wood fragments were imported, not indigenous. Of the local woods, poplar was the most important for firewood and construction.

chaeologist interested in the Philistines would most likely choose a site in southwestern Palestine, in Philistia. The archaeologist interested in a specific city would choose to excavate the tell believed to contain that city.

Tells like Megiddo and Beth-shan have been excavated because of their ancient fame and the impressiveness of their mounds. Sometimes sites have been excavated because of their accessibility. Atchana, located near New Testament Antioch, was dug by Sir Leonard Woolley when his wife refused to join him for another season at then desolate biblical Ur. Tell Tayinat, near Atchana, was tested only to humor a foreman who insisted he had spotted a more important site than the one being excavated. Fortunately for biblical studies his persistence was indulged, and the Tayinat excavations provided a close parallel to Solomon's Temple.

In order to excavate in a Near Eastern country the excavator must obtain official permission (called a "concession") to dig and must convince the host country that the proposed expedition is competent to carry out the stated objectives. Generally, an inspector from the local department of antiquities is assigned to the expedition staff to insure that the interests of the host country are protected.

A modern excavation staff requires a number of trained specialists, so the archaeologist must assemble a team. A field architect is needed to transfer the architectural finds to paper. Artists are needed to draw the excavated objects. Site supervisors are needed to keep track of the artifacts and the progress of the work. Photographers, recorders, pottery specialists, botanists, geologists, and paleontologists are a few of the specialists necessary on a modern dig. As the archaeologist assembles this staff, personalities as well as expertise must be considered. Because the team will live together and work together (seasons usually last about two months and frequently under less-than-optimum conditions), it is important to have a congenial group.

Adequate funding is necessary for a successful expedition. In earlier years some important excavations were carried out through the generosity of wealthy benefactors. Megiddo (the Rockefellers) and Hazor (the Rothschilds) are two examples of this type of funding. There have also been instances of an excavator having personal financial resources. Today several European countries fund Near Eastern archaeology through allocations in their national budget. Most American expeditions to the Near East are funded through public or private foundations, research societies, or consortiums in which several schools pool their resources. Digs in Israel are often funded through fees charged to volunteer workers.

After the excavator has chosen the site, obtained the needed funds, and assembled a staff, attention must be given to gathering equipment, providing a work force, and acquiring living quarters for the staff. These last three necessities are cared for according to local conditions and customs. Equipment is obtained in the host country if possible, otherwise it is brought in by staff members. Living quarters range from tents to expedition houses, and workers may be volunteers or hired local help. These workers, divided into pickmen, shovelmen, and basket carriers, do the actual earth moving. In both Egypt and Iraq there are villages that have supported themselves for several generations by supplying skilled laborers to excavators. Some of these workers (the Quftis in Egypt and the Shergatis in Iraq) are more adept at tracing mud-brick walls and other insubstantial remains than are most trained archaeologists.

Most tells are too large to excavate completely, and the archaeologist must decide how best to use available time and resources. Generally, a "surface survey" is carried out, either randomly or by following one of

1.7. Three generations of Qufti workers assisted the excavation staff at Qustul, just south of Abu Simbel in Upper Egypt. The fifth person from the left, in the back row, Abdullah (not a Qufti), was employed for several decades as foreman on various digs conducted by the University of Chicago's Oriental Institute throughout the Near East. Dressed here in Palestinian garb to show his cosmopolitanism, Abdullah's persistence led to the excavation of Tayinat in present-day Turkey and the discovery at that site of a close parallel to Solomon's Temple.

Alfred Hoerth

several research designs, studying the pieces of pottery and other objects lying about the tell. From this survey some idea can be formed of when the site was occupied and, perhaps, where the heaviest areas of occupation were located. Traces of ancient walls might be visible on the surface, or a difference in ground cover might signal some subsurface features. Early morning shadows sometimes reveal tomb shafts by the depressions in the soil. The excavator evaluates such clues in deciding where to concentrate the work.

Before the actual digging begins, the field architect will have drawn a contour map and a grid system of the tell (illustration 1.8 shows such a map with a grid system drawn over it). Somewhere on that grid, ideally at a spot that will remain unexcavated, the architect places a "benchmark," the point of reference from which all vertical and horizontal measurements will be taken. The grid divides the site into squares, five or ten meters on a side, and each square is given its own designation. Should the excavator think, for example, that the rise in square E-3 is worth investigating, the grid will be laid out in that area by means of stakes and string. All work done in that square and all objects found there will always be designated as coming from square E-3. Any vertical or horizontal measurements necessary within the square will be related to a specific corner of square E-3, which in turn has a known relationship to the benchmark. Various measuring methods and devices are used, but the goal is to be able to re-create on paper what the archaeologist is uncovering.

A small rise on a site might signal an important area to dig, because the citadel was generally the highest point on the mound. Even without obvious signs like this, the archaeologist has come to know that the city gate will often be found either on the east side of the mound or facing an ancient road or water supply. The city dump, valuable for the cross section of material life it can provide, is usually found downwind.

When actual excavation begins, an archaeologist digs in such a way as to isolate strata. A stratum (plural strata, less frequently stratums) is

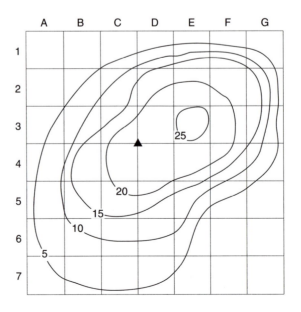

1.8. Five-meter increments in elevation are marked on a contour map of a tell with superimposed grid. The benchmark is indicated by a triangle. The individual squares are referred to by letter and number. For instance, the highest point on the tell is in square E-3. All objects found will be labeled according to the square and stratum in which they were found.

1.9. Balks used as controls by the archaeologist should not be mistaken for ancient walls. Balks are generally removed once they have served their purpose, so that a larger horizontal exposure can be made.

a "floor level or occupation surface together with the walls and debris [and objects] both above and below [it] which belong to it [in time]" (G. Wright 1962: 26). Most sites are stratified, that is, they have several levels of occupation. In some cases more than twenty living levels have been found superimposed one atop the other. The archaeologist must carefully separate the strata so that distinctive features can be studied in their own context.

That archaeology is both art and science can be demonstrated as the archaeologist follows the clues that allow accurate separation of occupation levels. For example, a floor obviously signals a specific living level. However, if the floor was too slight or is too destroyed to detect, a preserved fireplace may provide the needed evidence. When the archaeologist digs down along a mud-brick wall and reaches its stone foundation, the floor level cannot be far away. Other clues of the floor may be a doorsill in the wall or the plaster that coats the inside wall lipped out at the old floor level. The art is in being sensitive to these sometimes faint clues.

Most archaeologists working today use the "balk" method of excavation (also spelled "baulk"), which gives the site a checkerboard appearance. At first the workers leave a meter of earth between the squares. The unexcavated portion is the balk. As long as that meter width is left intact, it provides a walkway between the squares and helps keep the contents of one square from becoming mixed with objects from an adjoining square. The stratification revealed in the vertical sides (called "sections") of the balks is often drawn and analyzed.

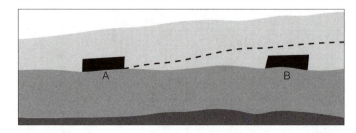

1.10. Hypothetical section illustrates how balks help determine time relationships within a site. The archaeologist looks for floor lines, burn layers, and differences in soil color or consistency to distinguish occupation levels. Two walls found on the same horizontal level are not necessarily contemporary. For example, if wall A and wall B rest on the same soil line, then the walls are contemporary; if, however, wall A rests on a soil line that runs over the top of wall B (dotted line), then wall B is from an earlier occupation.

Previously the "layer method" was in vogue. In this method a stratum was located and then followed horizontally across the excavated area. The layer method is sufficiently precise when there is ample architecture to follow from one square to the next and when the stratum is relatively flat. But it is difficult for the excavator using the layer method to span open areas and to determine which strata are contemporary when there are great differences in elevation. The artificial control provided by the balks minimizes these problems.

The archaeologist finds artifacts—objects that have survived from the past. An artifact can be small: a bead or a piece of grain; but a stone column is also an artifact. The most common artifacts an archaeologist finds are "sherds," broken pieces of pottery (called "shards" in British publications). Most sherds are eventually discarded, but the "sherd washer" must keep alert for pieces on which there is writing. In antiquity, broken pieces of pottery were used as note pads. Such a sherd is called an ostracon (the plural is "ostraca").

The archaeologist must establish the age of the artifacts as well as of the strata from which they derive. There are esoteric dating tools like dendrochronology (tree-ring dating), archeomagnetism (determining the magnetic field inherent in a pottery vessel and linking that field to a specific time and place), and radiocarbon (determining how long ago an organism died). These methods all have their uses, but pottery is the basic tool a Near Eastern archaeologist employs for dating a site. Pottery styles changed fairly rapidly, and an archaeologist learns to recognize the distinctive shapes that signal different time periods. Further, since pottery is fragile, ancient sites are strewn with the results of ancient accidents and discards. There is seldom any lack of this dating tool in an excavation. Often the archaeologist needs no more than a piece of a rim or base, a handle, or a bit of decoration to determine the shape of the original vessel and its place in time.

No matter which excavation method an archaeologist uses or whatever the motivation for digging, the archaeologist must take great care in the work. As the past is recovered, much of it is also destroyed. To reach earlier levels the archaeologist must tear down excavated strata. Since this means that no one else will ever be able to excavate that precise area again, the archaeologist has the responsibility to fully record every aspect of the work. It is essential that a "paper reconstruction" be prepared of each stratum. If properly done, a portion of human heritage has been regained and preserved.

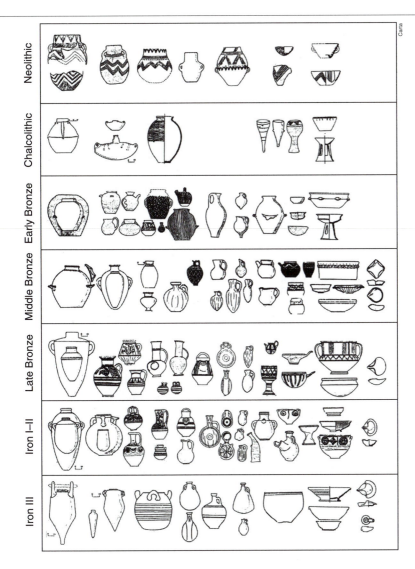

1.11. Typology (seriation) chart illustrating characteristic pottery types in Palestine beginning with the introduction of pottery around 6000 in the Neolithic period and continuing through Old Testament times. The terms used are those generally employed in archaeology in Palestine (dates are from A. Mazar 1990, except for Iron Age III, which is not covered in his book).

Period	Date	Subperiod	Date
Neolithic	8500–4300		
Chalcolithic	4300–3300		
Early Bronze	3300–2300	EBI	3300–3050
		EBII–III	3050–2300
Middle Bronze	2300–1550	MBI (= EBIV)	2300–2000
		MBIIA	2000–1800/1750
		MBIIB	1800/1750–1550
Late Bronze	1550–1200	LBI	1550–1400
		LBIIA–B	1400–1200
Iron	1200–332	Iron IA	1200–1150
		Iron IB	1150–1000
		Iron IIA	1000–925
		Iron IIB	925–720
		Iron IIC	720–586
		Iron III	586–332

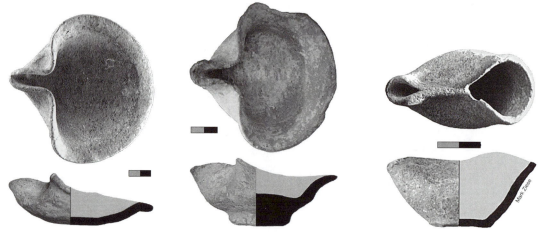

1.12. Oil lamps (left to right) from the period of the judges, late in the monarchy period, and after the fall of Jerusalem to the Babylonians, showing the development of this basic household item over a thousand-year period. These illustrations also show the way pottery is typically published in excavation reports. A centimeter scale establishes size, and the profiles (bottom row) show the outer form of the vessel (left side of each profile) and the shape of the vessel in section (right side of each profile). Such conventionalized illustrations help the archaeologist compare pottery published from different sites. These lamps, including their scales and sections, were electronically rendered. This recently developed process has an added advantage in that it allows for easy manipulation, transmittal, and study of the images.

Additional Reading

Bearman, Gregory H., and Sheila I. Spiro. "Archaeological Applications of Advanced Imaging Techniques." *BA* 59 (1996): 56–66.

Bunimovitz, Shlomo. "How Mute Stones Speak." *BAR* 21/2 (1995): 58–67, 96, 98–100.

Davis, Thomas. "Faith and Archaeology." *BAR* 19/2 (1993): 54–59.

Drinkard, Joel F., Jr., et al. (eds.). *Benchmarks in Time and Culture*. Atlanta: Scholars Press, 1988.

Eakins, J. Kenneth. "Human Osteology and Archaeology." *BA* 43 (1980): 89–96.

Eiteljorg, Harrison, II. "Reconstructing with Computers." *BAR* 17/4 (1991): 60–63.

Goldberg, Paul. "The Archaeologist as Viewed by the Geologist." *BA* 51 (1988): 197–202.

Hoppe, Leslie J. *What Are They Saying about Biblical Archaeology?* New York: Paulist, 1984.

Horn, Siegfried H. *Biblical Archaeology: A Generation of Discovery*. Washington: Biblical Archaeology Society, 1985.

Joukowsky, Martha. *A Complete Manual of Field Archaeology: Tools and Techniques of Field Work for Archaeologists*. Englewood Cliffs, N.J.: Prentice-Hall, 1980.

Levy, Thomas E. "From Camels to Computers: A Short History of Archaeological Method." *BAR* 21/4 (1995): 44–51, 64–65.

Meadow, Richard H. "The Study of Faunal Remains from Archaeological Sites." *BA* 46 (1983): 49–53.

Millard, Alan R. "The Bible B.C.: What Can Archaeology Prove?" *Archaeology in the Biblical World* 1/2 (1991): 18–39.

———. "In Praise of Ancient Scribes." *BA* 45 (1982): 143–53.

Moorey, Peter. *A Century of Biblical Archaeology*. Louisville: Westminster/John Knox, 1991.

Moyer, James C., and Victor H. Matthews. "Archaeological Coverage in Recent One-Volume Bible Dictionaries." *BA* 55 (1992): 141–51.

Peterman, Glen L. "Geographic Information Systems: Archaeology's Latest Tool." *BA* 55 (1992): 162–67.

Schoville, Keith N. *Biblical Archaeology in Focus*. Grand Rapids: Baker, 1978.

Whitehouse, Ruth D. (ed.). *The Facts on File Dictionary of Archaeology*. New York: Facts on File, 1983.

Mesopotamia before Abraham

Past things shed light on future ones; the world was always of a kind, what is and what will be was at some other time; the same things come back but under different names and colors; not everybody recognizes them, but only he who is wise considers them diligently.

—Francesco Guicciardini (ca. 1530)

The Land

"Mesopotamia," a word coined by early Greek historians, means the "land between the rivers"—the Tigris and Euphrates rivers. The Republic of Iraq is the present political designation for the same general area, but in neither case are the borders fully contained by the Tigris and Euphrates rivers. The ancient inhabitants had no encompassing name; their references to Sumer, Akkad, Assyria, Babylonia, and Chaldea designated only portions of the whole. Concerning size, one

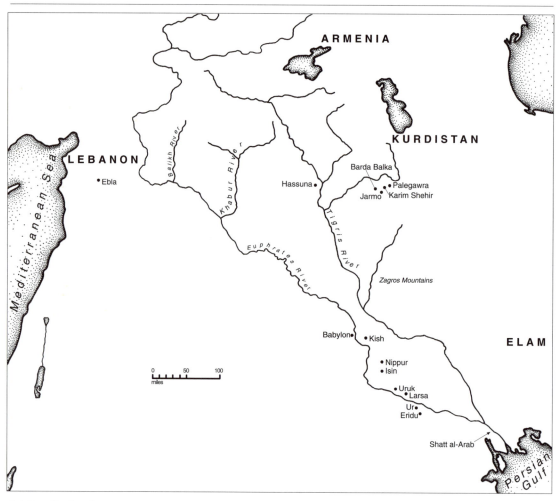

2.1. Pre-Abrahamic Mesopotamia.

estimate places the area of Mesopotamia at roughly 130,000 square miles, which makes it somewhat smaller than the state of California (159,000 square miles) and a bit larger than the state of New Mexico (122,000). Its size is close to the combined areas of the states of Illinois, Indiana, and Ohio (134,000).

The Tigris and Euphrates rivers originate in Armenia and flow southward. The Tigris is the shorter and swifter of the two waterways. At one point the longer Euphrates swings west to within one hundred miles of the Mediterranean. Finally, both rivers converge in the marshy Shatt al-Arab and then empty into the Persian Gulf.

Some maps of the ancient Near East show the coast of the Persian Gulf well north of its present position, reflecting the theory that the gulf has moved south over the centuries. This is a natural assumption since the Tigris and Euphrates can move millions of tons of material each day and because surface fossils have been found in the area north of the present gulf. Unfortunately the question is not fully settled since studies have shown that the rivers redeposit their sediment before reaching the gulf. To add to the confusion, aerial photography reveals canals and riverbeds that seem to be interrupted by the gulf—evidence that suggests the coastline has actually moved north. Archaeologists are hesitant to abandon the belief that the coastline has moved southward because cities like Ur and Eridu, presently over one hundred miles from the coastline, are referred to in ancient texts as market towns with regular access to the sea by ships. For instance, this statement was written about 2000: "Shulgi, son of Ur-Nammu, took very good care of the town of Eridu which is on the seashore" (*ANET* 266). Such declarations imply that the shores of the Persian Gulf were further north some four thousand years ago (see Beek 1962: 9–12 and Larsen 1975, the latter being an example of the technical studies done on this question).[1]

In the large plain between the Tigris and Euphrates rivers in central and southern Mesopotamia, the climate is dry and subtropical in summer (the temperature ranges from 108°F in the shade to 120°F in the sun), but in winter the temperature sometimes drops below freezing. There seems to have been no change in climate over the last six thousand to eight thousand years in Mesopotamia, so it can be assumed that civilization developed there in climatic conditions similar to today.

The southern plain receives only about ten inches of rain per year, all of it in winter. The Tigris and Euphrates flood their banks between April and June, which is too late for the winter crops and too early for summer crops. The sparsity of rain and the ill-timed flood waters led the early Mesopotamians to dig canals and build reservoirs and dikes. Using these methods they could have water when and where they needed it. The flooding that filled the ancient canals and reservoirs depended on the amount of rain or snow that fell in the faraway mountains of Armenia and Kurdistan. Flood deposits several feet thick are witness to years when too much water came, but ancient records also tell of years when too little water arrived to nurture the fields.

Another serious agricultural problem in southern Mesopotamia was caused by the slight salinity of the Tigris and Euphrates rivers. As the water table became more salt laden, the soil was adversely affected by irrigation.[2] In areas where salt was not a problem in the soil, many crops could be grown, and the land could be extremely fertile. In the fifth century the Greek historian Herodotus (1.193) reported on the richness of this land:

> Of all the countries known to us this is by far the best for producing [barley], for of trees there is no question at all, neither fig, vine, nor olive. But [barley] seed is so productive that it yields at least two hundredfold, and

1. References to cities like Eridu being coastal sites must be understood to mean (a) that the shore of the Persian Gulf was further north in antiquity or (b) that these cities were connected to the gulf by canals or other waterways.

2. This deterioration was graphically borne out by H. Helbaek's study (summarized in Jacobsen and Adams 1958: 1252) of grain impressions in excavated pottery from one southern area (since clay normally needs a binder to bring it to the proper texture for throwing pots, traces of chaff and seeds are not unusual in the more utilitarian pots). Helbaek found nearly equal proportions of wheat and barley in pottery dating to approximately 3500, but the less-salt-tolerant wheat constituted only one-sixth of the total grain impressions about a thousand years later. By 2100 wheat was down to two percent and by 1700 it was no longer present in the pottery. Ancient records reveal that salinization also adversely affected barley crops.

when it yields its very best up to three hundred, and the blades of the wheat and the barley there easily attain a width of four fingers.[3]

Barley was (and is) the chief crop in Mesopotamia. To Herodotus the land seemed extremely rich. The barrenness normally associated with modern Mesopotamia does not correctly picture the past, and the current situation could be reversed. The potential for fertile soil still exists.[4]

The northeastern foothills, lying between the Tigris and the Kurdistan Mountains, were the heart of the Assyrian kingdom. The climate is more temperate there than in the southern plain, and sufficient rainfall (between twelve inches and twenty-five inches per year) makes dry farming possible. Some land in the foothills was irrigated, but salinization never became a problem as it did in the south. On the negative side, the terrain did not allow enough land to be farmed to support the population. The resultant need to import foodstuffs was possibly a reason for Assyria's military expansion in the second and first millenniums.

In addition to the southern plain and the northeastern foothills, the steppe in northwestern Mesopotamia around the Balikh and Khabur rivers is very fertile. Its many ancient mounds attest that this has long been the case. South of the southern plain in the area of the Shatt al-Arab are marshlands with many shallow lakes and narrow waterways. Lastly, to the west is a desert and to the east the Zagros Mountains.

Prehistoric Mesopotamia

There is often the impression that, since Abraham lived so long ago, he and his world must have been rather simple. The opposite is true, for Mesopotamia already had a long and proud past by the time of Abraham. The following pages summarize the present knowledge of early Mesopotamia and sketch how God allowed this part of the world to develop before he was ready to work through Abraham. What follows is not merely a string of strange names and dates. The data allow the reader to unpack a largely neglected ancestral trunk.

There is a great deal of fluidity in the early dates for Mesopotamia. For example, the date of the early campsite of Barda Balka in northern Mesopotamia has been reduced hundreds of thousands of years from what was first thought (compare table 1 in Roux 1964: 445 with its counterpart in the revised Roux 1992: 500). It is not unusual to find

3. It is uncertain whether Herodotus ever visited Mesopotamia, but at least he reflects a belief current in his day. Lloyd 1984: 18 thinks that the reported yields are exaggerated, although Roux 1992: 8 feels that "the recently suggested overall estimate of forty- to fiftyfold . . . appears to be acceptable." Herodotus reports that there were no fig, vine, or olive trees. There were, however, extensive palm groves in ancient Mesopotamia, and by the early third millennium artificial pollination was being practiced. Utilization of date palms became so important to the economy that by the time of Hammurapi in the early second millennium there were regulatory laws concerning their production.

4. In the late 1950s the Iraqi government supported an archaeological study of ancient agriculture with the hopes that the findings could help revive the extensive irrigation networks of the past. See Jacobsen and Adams 1958 and Adams 1965.

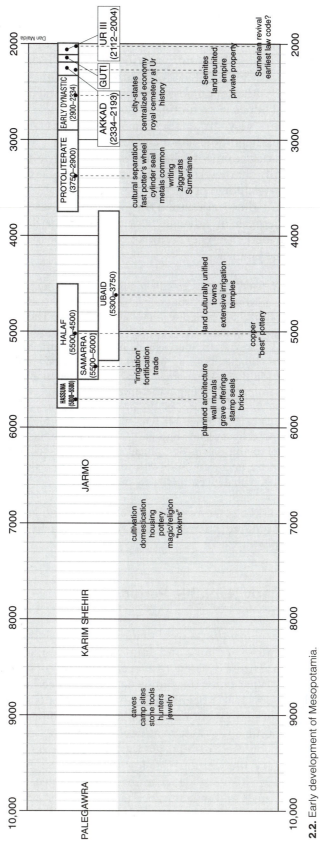

2.2. Early development of Mesopotamia.

widely differing estimates of age for these earliest periods. Cave sites like Palegawra and campsites like Karim Shehir, both in northern Mesopotamia, are currently dated in the vicinity of 10,000 and 8000 respectively. Their inhabitants were found to have used flint tools and thumbnail-sized flints called "microliths." In addition to their ground-stone industry, these people worked with shell and bone. No domesticated animal bones were found. In a material sense, the range of possessions was extremely limited, but the presence of beads, pendants, and bracelets clearly points to an esthetic need.

The development from this simple lifestyle to the more complex is generally characterized as unilinear. But Robert and Linda Braidwood, who have studied prehistoric periods in the Near East for decades, have for some time understood this development as multilinear, that is, various degrees of advancement coexisted in different places. Robert Braidwood (1960: 242) thinks our presuppositions might be clouding the true picture:

> In archaeology we are still somewhat bound by late nineteenth-century classifications, bar diagrams, neo-Grecisms such as "mesolithic" and "neolithic" for period terminology, and so on. These tend to establish an image of quick and all-pervading change from one level to another. I think the evidence increasingly instructs us otherwise: that different levels of complexity—hunting camp, village, city—integrated with one another in their development; that the hunter in effect was always there; that in the early villages the proportion of food which was actually produced by agriculture, or the proportion of other bands in the cultural spectrum that responded to this subsistence pattern, was not at all bounded by a clear horizon. . . . This picture has consequences for our understanding of geographical environment—consequences that make me a bit uncomfortable with identifying a particular type or level too closely with a given ecological cubbyhole.

It should be remembered, therefore, that while increasing complexity is encountered, there were always some nearby people living a simpler existence.

The Early Neolithic Period

The term *neolithic* is used to designate a period beginning with the domestication of plants and animals and ending with the introduction of metals. The term refers to a level of development, not to a specific time range. What clues does an archaeologist need to recognize when this development has begun? Farming implements such as sickles and evidence of permanent habitation are useful indicators but by themselves are insufficient to assure a "neolithic revolution." This is because sickles can be used to reap wild grains, and groups of people can live a sedentary life without having domesticated plants or animals. For more conclusive evidence archaeologists must turn to specialists such as botanists and paleontologists. The former examines grains found in ancient settlements and determines not only their types, but whether they were wild or domestic. The latter can likewise recognize structural differences between the bones of tame and wild animals. Insights gained from these specialists provide evidence that Mesopotamia passed into the Neolithic period about 7000 (Braidwood and Howe 1960).

Jarmo, in northern Mesopotamia, is a good example of a Neolithic village. The three-acre site contains sixteen strata, all dating early in the seventh millennium. The Braidwoods found square multiroom homes built of touf (adobe), with mud ovens and baked-in clay basins sunk in the ground. The dead were buried under the house floors, but no grave offerings were found with them. From the objects recovered at the site (illustration 2.3), it is possible to learn about the material world of that culture, as well as the skills and interests of the people. Small clay animal and human figurines, some with obvious fertility overtones, seem to indicate either religious or magic practices. Stone and bone tools

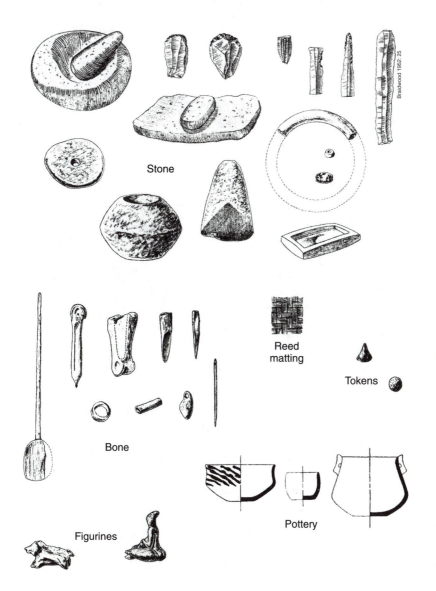

Stone

Bone

Reed matting

Tokens

Figurines

Pottery

2.3. Sampling of material remains found at Jarmo (not to scale)— objects that were once considered as necessary and natural as the possessions we take for granted today. Until the invention of writing, such objects are largely all that the archaeologist has with which to re-create the prehistoric periods. Therein lies the challenge of archaeology—to make the "stones" speak.

had expanded in variety compared to earlier sites. It was also within the course of Jarmo's occupation that pottery was introduced. This early pottery, though simple, represents a great advancement in the ability to store and transport items like food and liquids. Pottery also became an outlet for artistic abilities.

The Neolithic period was a time of profound change in human society as the focus changed from hunting and gathering to domestication and farming. Small pyramidal and other simply shaped pieces of clay found at sites like Jarmo were long assumed to be game pieces or idle bits of whimsy, but in recent years they have been identified as tokens used by farmers and merchants to keep track of which foodstuffs could be bartered, which must be kept for seed, and the like (Schmandt-Besserat 1977, 1983, and 1992).

The Hassuna and Samarra Periods (5800–5000)

The Hassuna and Samarra periods fall within the sixth millennium. Hassuna and Samarra, both in northern Mesopotamia, are "type sites."[5] At Hassuna the housing was more sophisticated than at Jarmo, the architecture was more carefully planned, and there was clear specialization in the rooms. One section of the house would be used for cooking and storage and another for other activities of daily life. Traces of murals were found on the house walls at one site.

2.4. Reconstruction of a Hassuna house (a portion of the roof is unfinished to show the method of construction). Before the end of the Hassuna period, walls were made of mud bricks rather than touf.

Adapted from Beek 1962: 42

Burial practices also changed from the seventh to the sixth millennium. By the Hassuna period the dead were buried in the corner of an unused room or in graves separated from the houses (infants were sometimes placed in jars for burial). Some of the burials contained offerings, a strong indication of belief in an afterlife.

Important "firsts" appear in the Hassuna period. One example is the prototype of the stamp seal. Pressed into mud-coated jar covers, such

5. When a distinctive culture is found, it is called by the name of the original place of discovery. Very often the type site does not prove to be the richest or most representative example known of that culture, but the initial designation is retained.

seals left a distinctive "mark of ownership" and ensured that the containers could not be broken into without discovery. Modern rubber stamps have their origin in this early sixth-millennium invention.

There is evidence that molded bricks were being used before the end of the Hassuna period. This invention might not seem overly dramatic but, as with the introduction of pottery, it brought about some very basic changes. With molded bricks it became possible to construct buildings that were stronger as well as taller, and building materials could be stockpiled. Some later architectural developments would not have been possible without bricks.

The Samarra period dates to the last half of the sixth millennium. Recent discovery suggests that a primitive form of irrigation agriculture may have begun by this time. More sobering is the finding of a settlement protected by buttressed walls and a moat. Seemingly, the need for protection had entered the communal life of Mesopotamia.

Richly decorated pottery bowls are the hallmark of the Samarra period and imply high artistic tastes. Insights can also come from less attractive finds. For example, there are only a few natural sources of obsidian in the Near East, and each source has distinctive properties. An analysis of obsidian found in ancient sites shows that Armenian obsidian was in use throughout Mesopotamia. It is unknown whether this wide distribution of obsidian points to itinerant merchants or to trading between villages. In either case, at least by the sixth millennium, Mesopotamia had begun interacting with other parts of the world.

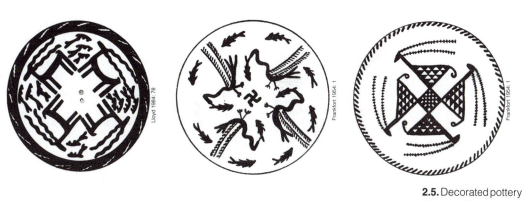

2.5. Decorated pottery from the Samarra period shows a centripetal design popular for the interior of plates and bowls. The swastika was a purely decorative motif.

The Halaf Period (5500–4500)

By the Halaf period Mesopotamia had passed into the copper age.[6] The discovery of how to smelt ores was as important as the earlier discovery that clay could be fired to produce pottery. Beginning with the Halaf period, metal slowly replaced flint and stone for tools.

While pottery is the primary dating tool, archaeologists sometimes overemphasize its chronological function to the exclusion of its other uses. As already noted, pottery sometimes exhibits artistic ability. Art historians rate Halaf-period pottery the most esthetically pleasing ever

6. The first half of the Halaf period is contemporary with the Samarra period.

2.6. Elaborately decorated bowl painted in red, black, white, and yellow. Such polychrome pottery is typical of the end of the Halaf period.

made in Mesopotamia. The Halaf potters had the skills necessary to throw extremely thin vessels and to decorate them with sophisticated painted designs. This high point in Mesopotamian ceramics was reached two thousand years before Abraham.

The Ubaid Period (5300–3750)

Until the Ubaid period only the northern portion of Mesopotamia has had anything to offer for discussion, but now the focus shifts to the south. It is not to be inferred that southern Mesopotamia was deserted before Ubaid, but the present water table in the south is so high that archaeologists are unable to adequately examine earlier periods. Ubaid began in southern Mesopotamia about the same time as Halaf did in the north, and for a few hundred years the north and south were materially distinct. Then, between 4500 and 4300, the Ubaid culture penetrated northward, and the two areas became more materially and socially unified.[7]

During the Ubaid period, southern Mesopotamia was dotted with

7. Ubaid not only covered all of Mesopotamia, it eventually reached west into parts of Syria and Anatolia and east into Iran.

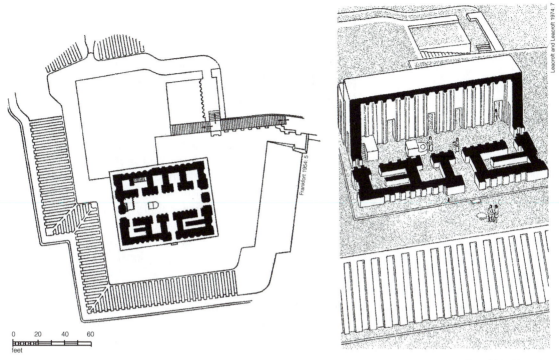

Frankfort 1954: 5

Leacroft and Leacroft 1974: 7

0   20   40   60
feet

towns sometimes containing thousands of people. Ubaid communities were normally situated along riverbanks from which more and more irrigation canals began radiating out into the landscape. At several sites toy boats with mast holes have been found, clearly showing that by this period sailboats were plying the Tigris and Euphrates rivers.

Following the invention of bricks, Mesopotamian builders became increasingly proficient. By the Ubaid period they were constructing elaborate temples built on platforms that elevated the temple above the worshipers, thus providing a physical separation between the sacred and the secular. The temples were relatively small (e.g., the interior of the temple in illustration 2.7 is only a bit over fifty feet long). Their modest size implies that temples were not intended to be group gathering places. Little more can be inferred about the mode of worship except that the figurines characteristic of earlier periods continued, suggesting that fertility remained an important religious focus.

2.7. The White Temple at Uruk during the Ubaid period (so-called because its mud-brick walls were white washed). The temple rests on a forty-foot-high platform of mud bricks. The elaborate exterior buttressing provided additional strength to the building but also gave a decorative play of lights and shadows on what would otherwise be a starkly flat, reflective surface. This ornamental niching continued as a distinctive of Mesopotamian architecture for many centuries.

The Protoliterate Period (3750–2900)

After the Ubaid period northern Mesopotamia stagnated while the south progressed to further sophistication.[8] The cultural unity between the two areas was largely lost, and a feeling of separation began that was never completely reversed and for which no fully satisfactory explanations have been found. It is especially curious that southern influence on the north faded during this period, since southern Meso-

8. Protoliterate is sometimes divided into the Uruk and Jemdat Nasr periods.

2.8. Cylinder seal impression (drawing). Seals were made of various materials; in the Protoliterate period, marble and limestone were commonly used. Until the advent of iron, designs were cut with copper chisels and drills, probably aided by emery powder for the harder stones.

Frankfort 1939: plate 4

potamia's influence was then being exerted in Iran and Egypt. Whatever the reason for the break, throughout the following centuries the south always considered itself distinct from and culturally superior to the "foreign" north. Even when the political supremacy of the south finally ended, southern Mesopotamia never willingly accepted government by the "barbarians" of the north. For their part, the northern rulers acknowledged their debt to the ancient civilization of the south.

Several important innovations appeared in southern Mesopotamia during the Protoliterate period. One was the "fast potter's wheel," which originated at the end of the Ubaid period. The fast wheel revolutionized the ceramic industry, making it possible to increase production, standardize shapes, and employ new shaping techniques. Concurrently, less attention was paid to decorating pottery. The stamp seal had been part of Mesopotamian life for many centuries, but in the Protolit-

2.9. Detail from a relief alabaster vase (over three feet tall), probably portraying the goddess Inanna, but maybe depicting a priestess in her stead. Behind the female figure are two standards (symbols later associated with the goddess). The figure presenting Inanna with gifts is variously identified as a priest, a king, or the god Dumuzi. Lower registers of the vase (not shown here) depict nude priests carrying offerings and various animals and plants. This vase provides the earliest pictures of Mesopotamian worship and may be showing part of the "sacred marriage" enacted during the Mesopotamian New Year celebration. The fertility of the land, animals, and people depended on the correct acting out of the annual "sacred marriage" in which a king and priestess reenacted the marriage of the god Dumuzi with the goddess Inanna (see Kramer 1969).

Hirmer Verlag

erate period it was replaced by the cylinder seal. While the function of a seal did not change with this adaptation, it became possible to roll out a continuous frieze. Cylinder seals continued to be a familiar part of everyday life until the days of Cyrus the Great in the sixth century.

Metals came into general use, and perhaps the chariot was invented. In architecture the first free-standing columns appeared, an innovation that made larger interior spaces possible. Sculpture also appeared. The alabaster vase in illustration 2.9 is judged to be artistically without rival in the ancient world for that time.

Writing is the most important contribution of the Protoliterate period, and the earliest examples are on small clay tablets found in a temple. These tablets were apparently used as a form of bookkeeping, to register goods given to the priesthood. The writing is pictographic, that is, a jar represents a jar. About fifteen hundred separate signs have been identified, but epigraphers have not found any meaningful order to the signs, nor do all the signs continue into later times when grammatical elements appear. Consequently these earliest texts still defy complete translation (Gelb 1969 is considered the classic introduction to the development of writing; see also Walker 1987 and Marcus 1978).

Although the signs on these earliest clay tablets are rather basic, epigraphers do not think they represent the initial stage of writing, since some were already simplified and stylized. Also, quite a few signs

British Museum

2.10. Clay tablet (roughly three inches on a side), from the end of the Protoliterate period. The linear characters are already moving away from the pictographic signs of the earliest tablets to abstract cuneiform signs. In this account of fields, crops, and commodities, circles evidently represent the number ten and lengthened circles the number one.

depict wild beasts, which would not be part of a temple inventory. Therefore, such signs must represent meanings other than their concrete objects, and writing was at least into the rebus stage.

Where then is the first stage in the history of writing to be found? Most scholars have assumed that the earliest writing was done on wood or skin that has perished and that, therefore, the beginning stages of writing are lost. Denise Schmandt-Besserat proposes, however, that small clay objects found from as early as Neolithic times are tokens and that some of their shapes can be seen in the earliest written signs. In brief, her theory is that significant changes became necessary in record keeping during Protoliterate times as cities emerged, and increased population, mass production, and other pressures put a strain on the token system. Many new token shapes appeared in response to this strain, and clay envelopes containing tokens eventually came into use. Most of the envelopes carry two different cylinder seal impressions, implying that they were used to transfer tokens. At first the surface of the envelopes were marked with the image of the enclosed tokens. Later the representative signs on the envelopes were deemed sufficient, and the original tokens were phased out in favor of the now-written record (Schmandt-Besserat 1977; but see Lieberman 1980: 339).

Three language groups can be identified in early Mesopotamia: the Sumerians, the Semites, and a "diffuse minority." These groups differ only in language, not in material culture or physiognomy. Of the three, the Sumerians became dominant, and they are generally credited with the great progress made during the Protoliterate period. Some scholars insist that the Sumerians immigrated into Mesopotamia, but most reject that theory because no distinct break with the past can be demonstrated. For example, temples remained basically unchanged in plan and decoration. However, their platforms were made higher, moving toward the staged tower or "ziggurat," which remained characteristic of Mesopotamian worship for nearly three thousand years.

The Early Dynastic Period (2900–2334)

As "Protoliterate" implied the beginning of writing, "Early Dynastic" signals the onset of a new political order in Mesopotamia. During this period kingship was spoken of as coming down from heaven and passing from one city to another. The term *dynasty* does not necessarily imply succession from father to son; rather, it refers to a succession of kings ruling over the same area for a period of time. Each time a specific city held political control over the area, scholars have assigned it a title. Ur I, for instance, refers to the first time Ur was in a superior position.

One city controlling other cities created a city-state. The city-state extended its authority to include satellite towns and villages together with their fields. To put the size of a Mesopotamian city-state into perspective, Lagash extended its city-state approximately forty miles in any direction, and its population density has been estimated at about twenty people per square mile.

2.11. Group of statues from the Abu Temple at Tell Asmar (the largest figure is about thirty inches tall). It is debated whether the two largest figures represent the god Abu and his consort or are only additional votive statues.

As expected, the king was a powerful figure, and the texts reveal that he was surrounded by an extensive bureaucracy. The texts also reflect a shift in the role of the king. At the beginning of this period he was the highest religious functionary and lived within the temple complex. Later on he moved into a separate palace and, for religious purposes, was then needed only for the New Year festival. A separate high priest and an increasingly visible priestly class appeared. One can only speculate what power struggles might have developed between the royal court and the temple.

A gradation can be discerned in the society, and some occupations were more important than others. The king and the priesthood were both definitely major powers, and together they apparently controlled much of the land. However, there was private property, more so in the north where the Semites were dominant. Temples were still too small for large congregations to gather for corporate worship, but there was a need to identify with deity. To meet this need, during Early Dynastic times worshipers placed statues of themselves in the temple to remind the deity of their allegiance. The large number of such statues that have been excavated suggests that this was a popular practice, but it did not outlast Early Dynastic times.

During the late 1920s sixteen royal tombs were excavated at Ur. The treasures found reveal the incredible wealth and power of Ur kings during the last third of the Early Dynastic period, and their discovery

British Museum

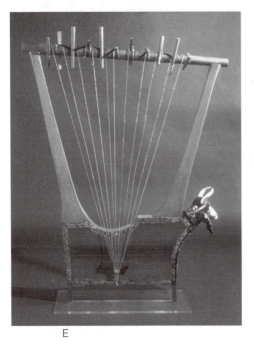

2.12. Sampling of the treasures found in the Royal Cemetery at Ur include one of the game boards discovered (A). The parade helmet (B) and the dagger and sheath (C) are only a small portion of the gold objects. The mannequin (D) displays jewelry worn by a queen. Several inlaid harps and lyres were found (E; the lyre illustrated here has been restored). One side of a two-sided inlaid plaque, called the Royal Standard of Ur (F), contains scenes of war, in which the king vanquishes an enemy, his phalanx marches out, and his war chariots roll over the dead and dying.

Hirmer Verlag

2.13. Fragment of the Victory Stele of Eannatum (also known as the Vulture Stele because another fragment of the stele depicts vultures and lions devouring naked corpses), commemorating Eannatum's victory over the nearby city of Umma in retaliation for destroying a boundary stone and occupying fields belonging to Lagash, Eannatum's city. The fragment, like the Royal Standard of Ur, shows that the phalanx as a military formation long preceded the Greek use.

caused excitement around the world. The beauty and sophistication of the objects show how far the artisans of Ur had advanced several centuries before Abraham lived in that same city.

On the negative side was the discovery of depictions of warfare and the uncovering of hundreds of people who had been sacrificed. Their remains, together with wagons and oxen, were found in "death pits" connected to the royal tombs. Sir Leonard Woolley, the excavator, suggested that these people were servants who willingly accompanied their royalty; because there is no evidence of struggle, he believed that the servants were drugged to a painless death. Another suggestion is that royalty might have been considered living gods whom people would want to continue serving in "death." Whatever the correct interpretation, these sacrifices temper our admiration for the accomplishments of the Early Dynastic period.[9]

Uses for writing expanded during this period, and much more than temple accounts were preserved. Scribal schools appeared, word lists were compiled, and history was written. For instance, texts relate that

9. This practice has been found only at Ur and only during this one phase of the Early Dynastic period.

the city of Nippur became the religious center of all Sumer, and rulers from other cities were now obliged to go to Nippur for coronation. Intercity conflicts are recorded, and one ruler named Eannatum is credited for driving out Elamites who had invaded from the east.

Other documents reveal the thoughts of rulers concerning government processes. For example, a ruler named Urukagina (sometimes rendered as Uruinimgina) thought that rulers before him had assumed too much authority. He tells how he tried to protect the poor, widows, and orphans by reducing the power of the priests and the royal officials; he declares that he is going back to the previous ways, which were of the gods. Urukagina's statements are accepted as a true attempt at social reform by a man who, even in Early Dynastic times in Mesopotamia, spoke in terms of the "good old days."

One of the last kings of Early Dynastic times was named Lugalzaggesi. He boasted that he defeated all his enemies, united the country,

Hirmer Verlag

2.14. Nearly life-size bronze head, representing either Sargon or his grandson Naram-Sin, is a beautiful example of metallurgical skill. The head was cast and then further detailed with a chisel.

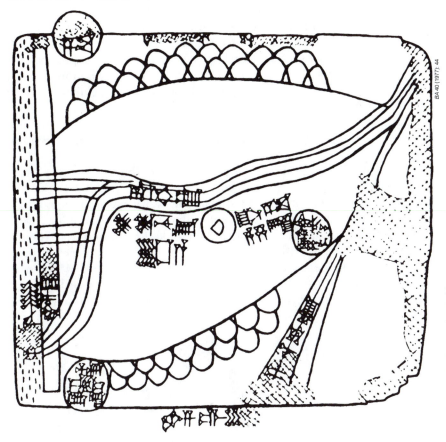

BA 40 (1977): 44

2.15. Oldest known map dates to the Akkad period. Only about two-and-one-half inches on a side, the tablet is either a road map or a record of landholding. The circle in the lower left of the tablet might represent the city of Ebla.

and ruled from the "lower to the upper sea," that is, from the Persian Gulf to the Mediterranean. While this last claim is probably hyperbole, Lugalzaggesi coined a phrase that became a favorite cry of Mesopotamian kings who followed him.

Although the data is still fragmentary, it is clear that during Early Dynastic times there were periods of peace and times of anarchy. There were invasions, internal conflicts, peace treaties, social reformers, and "empire builders." In short, if Early Dynastic history were complete, it might seem much like modern history.

Akkad (2334–2193)

While Lugalzaggesi was king of Uruk, a Semite named Sargon established himself as king further north. Under Sargon the Semites eventually took control over all of Mesopotamia. The takeover, which seems to have been quite peaceful, reunited Mesopotamia for the first time since the Ubaid period. Originally only a cupbearer to the Sumerian king of Kish, Sargon somehow overthrew his king and then attacked Lugalzaggesi and captured him. Sargon founded a new capital called Agade (which has not yet been found, but it may be in the vicinity of Babylon).

To maintain control over his emerging empire, Sargon destroyed the defensive walls of other cities to minimize the chances of rebellion, put Akkadian governors and garrisons into captured cities, and took members of local ruling families as hostages. Externally Sargon pushed east into Elam and west into Lebanon. He took control of Lebanon's wealth in timber and silver and, echoing Lugalzaggesi's boast, claimed to rule from the "upper to the lower sea." Future kings were inspired to think of the territorial limits reached by Akkad as their own rightful boundaries. Perhaps Lugalzaggesi carved out an empire, certainly Sargon did.

Sumerian civilization was largely unaffected by the Akkad period. Akkadian began to be written in cuneiform, which spread with the empire, but Sumerian continued alongside it. Neither were the gods significantly altered; Sargon's titles show that his principal deities were Sumerian. The changes made during the Akkadian period were mostly material and social. With empire there came an abundance of bronze, silver, wood, stone—commodities in short supply within Mesopotamia—and many prisoners of war who could be turned into slaves and cheap labor. Seton Lloyd (1984: 135) speaks of a "revolution in political

2.16. Victory Stele of Naram-Sin, more than six feet tall, commemorates the king's conquest of the Lullubi tribes on his eastern borders. Naram-Sin is shown advancing into a mountainous and wooded area, accompanied by his troops and with the symbols of his deities above him. Naram-Sin wears a horned headdress, one indicator that he considered himself a god.

Réunion des Musées Nationaux

ideas"; that is, the city-state was being phased out in favor of a larger centralized government. The period also marked the beginning of a shift from temple and government monopoly of the economy to private property and increased rights for the individual.

Sargon, the founder of Akkad, reigned fifty-five years. When he died his son Rimush took the throne and was able to quell the revolts that broke out in the empire. But nine years after his father's death, Rimush was killed by his own servants. Sargon's grandson Naram-Sin is the only other important king in this dynasty. Naram-Sin spent most of his thirty-six-year reign engaged in warfare, but he managed to extend the borders of Akkad a little further. Naram-Sin is, however, also blamed for bringing down the dynasty founded by his grandfather. The official reason for Akkad's fall is that Naram-Sin allowed his troops to sack the holy city of Nippur and its temple to the god Enlil. In punishment for this sacrilege "strange beings" were sent against Naram-Sin. As he fought them he was not sure if they were human, so Naram-Sin consulted an oracle for advice. The oracle told Naram-Sin to wound some of the captives, and if they bled they were human. Sure enough, when the captives were wounded, they bled. Thus encouraged, Naram-Sin continued to fight, but for each battle he was able to field fewer troops. Famine and collapse followed.

The Guti

The Guti, one of the mountain peoples living on Mesopotamia's eastern border, were Naram-Sin's enemy. They are blamed for disrupting communications and trade within Mesopotamia, upsetting the country's elaborate irrigation system, and bringing down the Akkad period. The Guti became the dominant power in Mesopotamia for approximately one hundred years. Apparently, however, they were not numerous, and many cities seem to have maintained nearly total freedom. Still, the Mesopotamians dubbed the Guti "barbarians" and characterized the period of political unrest as a time when "Who was king? Who was not king?" Finally, King Utuhegal of Uruk captured the Gutian king. Utuhegal was soon followed by Ur-Nammu (alternatively Ur-Namma), who founded a new dynasty.

Ur III (2112–2004)

Ur-Nammu founded the Ur III period, the third time the city of Ur was in political power. How Ur-Nammu achieved this takeover is not clear, but he seems to have quickly expanded his control to the previous limits of the Akkad Dynasty. After that was accomplished, Ur III experienced a time of peace.

Ur III is sometimes called a period of Sumerian renaissance. By this description it is meant that Sumerian again became the dominant language. Economically, though, the country did not revert back to the old

2.17. After Ur-Nammu founded the Ur III period, he directed a massive building program. A copper figurine depicts the king carrying the first basket of earth for a temple to the goddess Inanna, which he "restored . . . as it should be." Inscribed figurines like this one are commonly found among foundation deposits for public buildings and show the forerunners of two present-day practices: placing memorabilia in cornerstones and groundbreaking ceremonies.

British Museum

Sumerian ways. Rather, private property and private enterprise vied with the large temple holdings. Ur III was a true dynasty in that there was uninterrupted father-son succession. The kings considered themselves gods, the last time this concept is seen in Mesopotamia.

Since Ur-Nammu quickly gained political control, for most of his reign he was able to concern himself with domestic affairs. Among his accomplishments was the formulation of a law code, the oldest currently known. This law code, though poorly preserved, states in its preamble that it was written so justice might be established in the land. Ur-Nammu wanted to do away with the "duties" and with those "who by force seized the oxen, sheep, or donkeys." Ur-Nammu wanted to make sure that "the orphan was not given over to the rich, the widow was not given over to the powerful, the man of one shekel was not given over to the man of one mina" (Saggs 1988: 179; see also *ANE* 2.32; *ANET* 524; on the author of the law code, see Kramer 1983a).

Amorites had crossed the rivers to graze their flocks in the foothills of Mesopotamia as far back as Early Dynastic times, but toward the end of the Ur III period they began to threaten the political stability. By

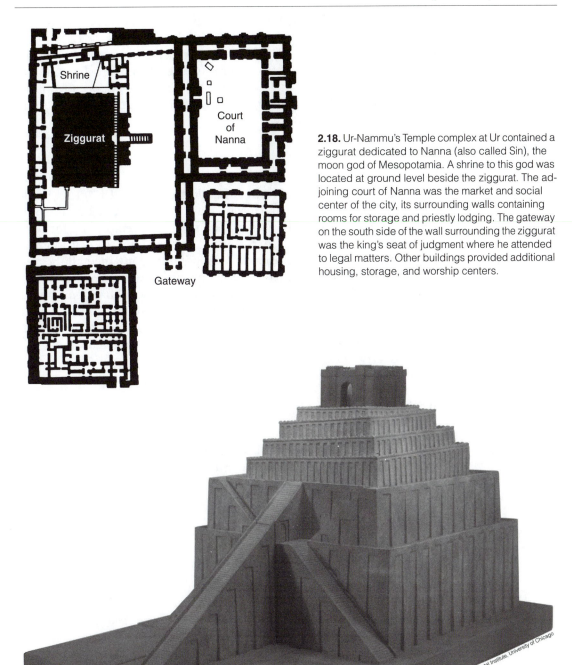

Shrine

Ziggurat

Court
of
Nanna

Gateway

2.18. Ur-Nammu's Temple complex at Ur contained a ziggurat dedicated to Nanna (also called Sin), the moon god of Mesopotamia. A shrine to this god was located at ground level beside the ziggurat. The adjoining court of Nanna was the market and social center of the city, its surrounding walls containing rooms for storage and priestly lodging. The gateway on the south side of the wall surrounding the ziggurat was the king's seat of judgment where he attended to legal matters. Other buildings provided additional housing, storage, and worship centers.

Oriental Institute, University of Chicago

2.19. Model of the ziggurat of Ur-Nammu at Ur. The ziggurat measures 150 feet by 200 feet at its base and is today preserved to about half its original height of 120 feet. The ziggurat was built solidly of sun-dried mud bricks with an eight-foot-thick outer shell of baked bricks set in bitumen.

the fifth year of Ur's King Ibbi-Sin, the Amorites had penetrated Sumer proper, and one of them had even made himself king of Larsa, only twenty-five miles north of Ur. Ibbi-Sin's problems were compounded by famine and then by one of his generals who suddenly proclaimed himself king over the city of Isin. In 2004 the Elamites swept in from the east, burned Ur to the ground, and carried Ibbi-Sin captive into Iran.

Summary

Abraham was born shortly after this destruction of Ur, into a world that already had a long and proud past.[10] He did not live in some scrubby boondocks where nothing had yet happened. Before his birth Mesopotamia had already experienced millenniums of development and achievement. Pre-Abrahamic Mesopotamia contained all the necessary components of civilized life. Its people experienced all the emotions and motivations that people feel today. Personal freedoms fluctuated but, at times, the ancient Mesopotamian had more freedom than people in parts of the world today. Our modern age has advanced over ancient Mesopotamia, but only in the spheres of technical knowledge and gadgetry.

Additional Reading

The primary specialist periodicals for Mesopotamian studies are *Iraq*, *Journal of Cuneiform Studies*, and *Sumer*. See also the bibliographical endnotes in Roux's *Ancient Iraq*.

Bodine, Walter R. "Sumerians." Pp. 19–42 in *Peoples of the Old Testament World*. Edited by Alfred J. Hoerth, Gerald L. Mattingly, and Edwin M. Yamauchi. Grand Rapids: Baker, 1994.

Crawford, Harriet. *Sumer and the Sumerians*. Cambridge: Cambridge University Press, 1991.

Finegan, Jack. *Archaeological History of the Ancient Middle East*. New York: Dorset, 1979.

Foster, Benjamin R. *From Ancient Days: Myths, Tales, and Poetry of Ancient Mesopotamia*. Bethesda, Md.: CDL, 1995.

Hallo, William W., and William K. Simpson. *The Ancient Near East: A History*. New York: Harcourt Brace Jovanovich, 1971.

Jacobsen, Thorkild. *The Treasures of Darkness*. New Haven: Yale University Press, 1976.

Kramer, Samuel N. *History Begins at Sumer*. 3d edition Philadelphia: University of Pennsylvania Press, 1981.

———. *The Sumerians*. Chicago: University of Chicago Press, 1963.

Lloyd, Seton. *Foundations in the Dust*. London: Thames & Hudson, 1980.

Michalowski, Piotr. *Letters from Early Mesopotamia*. Atlanta: Scholars Press, 1993.

10. Abraham's birth is sometimes placed within the Ur III period. The reasons for placing him later are given in the next chapter.

Nissen, Hans J. *The Early History of the Ancient Near East, 9000–2000 B.C.* Translated by Elizabeth Lutzeier and Kenneth J. Northcott. Chicago: University of Chicago Press, 1988.

Postgate, J. N. *Early Mesopotamia: Society and Economy at the Dawn of History.* London: Routledge, 1992.

Roaf, Michael. *Cultural Atlas of Mesopotamia and the Ancient Near East.* New York: Facts on File, 1990.

Saggs, H. W. F. *Everyday Life in Babylonia and Assyria.* New York: Dorset, 1965.

3
Abraham's Mesopotamia

If we push one of the doors and enter a house a pleasant surprise awaits us, for it is cool, comfortable and much larger than it appears from outside. Having washed our feet in a small lobby, we pass into the central courtyard and notice that it is paved and that a vertical drain opens in its centre, so that it can be rinsed clean and will not be flooded during the rainy season. All around us is the building. The walls are uniformly plastered and white-washed, but we know that their upper part is made of mud bricks and their lower part of burnt bricks carefully laid and jointed with clay mortar. A metre wide gallery supported by wooden poles runs around the courtyard, dividing the building into two storeys. . . . We recognize the kitchen, the workshop and store-room, the ablution room and lavatories, and that constant feature of all Oriental residences: the long, oblong chamber where the guests are entertained and eventually spend the night, the "diwan." The house furniture, now of course vanished, would consist of a few tables, chairs, chests and beds and of quantities of rugs and cushions.

The above description, valid for most houses of the Isin-Larsa and Old Babylonian periods at Ur, will sound familiar to those who have visited the Near East. It would apply word for word to any Arab house of the old style, such as can still be seen today in some parts of Aleppo, Damascus or Baghdad. Kingdoms and empires have vanished, languages and religions have changed, many customs have fallen into disuse, yet this type of house has remained the same for thousands of years merely because it is best suited to the climate of that part of the world and to the living habits of its population.

—Georges Roux

The Patriarchs in Time

To some people, history is a string of dates designed to test one's memorization skills, but dates should be seen as a tool, a framework on which the events of history can be ordered. Certainly, without chronology it would be impossible to mesh the Bible with much of the available extrabiblical information. Unfortunately, no uniform or long-range system of chronology was developed in Old Testament times. One ancient popular method was to date an event from a previous happening (e.g., Gen. 16:3), but such correlation provided only relative chronology, not a fixed date on which to hang an event. Another system used in the ancient Near East and found many times in the Bible was to date events from the beginning of a king's reign; thus, the installation of each new king brought the repetition of "year one."

Advances continue to be made in the precision of dates used, but areas of uncertainty and disagreement remain. One such area centers on the patriarchs: did Abraham live in the twenty-second or twentieth cen-

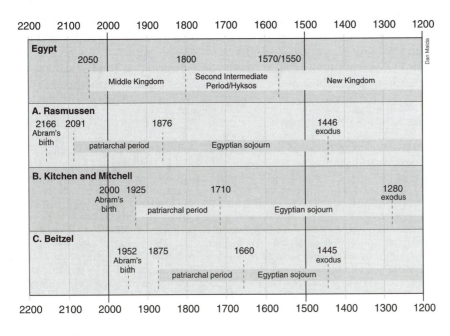

3.1. Representative evangelical viewpoints on the dates for the patriarchal period and Egyptian sojourn: (A) Rasmussen 1989: 76, (B) Kitchen and Mitchell 1980: 268–77, and (C) Beitzel 1985: 85, 208. (For Egyptian chronology, see Ward 1992.)

tury? The length of the "Egyptian sojourn" and the date of the exodus from Egypt are the two variables that create such a wide disagreement.

To establish Abraham's birth year, one must work backward from the first millennium, where firm dates are available. First Kings 6:1, the starting point, places the exodus 480 years prior to the fourth year of Solomon's reign. Solomon's fourth year can be dated to 967, and the addition of 480 results in 1447 for the exodus.[1]

Conservative scholars agree that the patriarchal period lasted 215 years, since several verses require that span of time (Gen. 12:4; 21:5; 25:26; 47:9). But they do not agree on the length of the Egyptian sojourn (see illustration 3.1). The problem is caused by a disagreement over how Exodus 12:40 should be understood. Literally translated, the verse states, "The time that the sons of Israel which dwelt in Egypt sojourned was 430 years." The Hebrew text does not require that the sojourning apply only to Egypt; it can include previous time. The Hebrews sojourned in Egypt, but the patriarchal period was also thought of as sojourning (Gen. 17:8).

Since Exodus 12:40 is ambiguous, the Septuagint (a Greek translation of the Old Testament begun in the third century) added a phrase to clarify the meaning (indicated by italics): "The time that the sons of Israel, which dwelt in Egypt *and in the land of Canaan*, sojourned was 430 years." Clearly, in the last centuries B.C., Exodus 12:40 was understood to mean that the 430 years encompassed both Egypt and Canaan. (The Samaritan Pentateuch, which also dates to the pre-Christian centuries, has a similar reading.) Conservative scholars are divided over whether this (option c in illustration 3.1) is the original intent of the verse. If 430 years refers to both Egypt and Canaan and since the patriarchal period in Canaan lasted 215 years, a similar length of time would have elapsed during the Egyptian sojourn.[2]

For those who hold to an early exodus and believe Exodus 12:40 refers only to Egypt (option *a* in illustration 3.1), Abraham will be given a birth 215 years earlier. This shift of over two centuries will obviously affect the political and economic fabric of Abraham's life in Ur. The earlier birth year will have Abraham living in the prosperous Ur III period, when the state was more in control of the economy.

Time line *c* in illustration 3.1 is the only option that puts Abraham in Mesopotamia's turbulent Isin-Larsa period, puts Joseph into Egypt

1. Minor disagreements account for the small differences in the exodus year favored by Beitzel 1985: 85, 208 and Rasmussen 1989: 76. Kitchen and Mitchell 1980: 268–77 do not take 1 Kings 6:1 to represent absolute time.

2. That both the patriarchal period and the Egyptian sojourn are to be included in this time span is further supported by Acts 13:19, in which 450 years are said to extend from the patriarchal period through the conquest of the Promised Land. Both Gen. 15:13 and Acts 7:6 refer to "slaves for four hundred years," which most scholars see as a round number (akin to our saying that Jesus came two thousand years ago). It can also be argued that the terms *slaves* and *oppressed* are broad, since the Hebrews were not slaves during the early years of the Egyptian sojourn. Scholars holding to both the long-sojourn and short-sojourn opinions put the actual oppression only toward the end of the stay. If the broad sense of *slave* and *oppression* is allowed, then the terms can also include Abraham and his descendants, who were sojourners and never owned Palestine until it was taken by Joshua. Galatians 3:16–17 is taken as another argument that the 430 years cover both Egypt and Palestine: the covenant was made when Abraham came back into Canaan from Egypt (Gen. 13:15).

during the Hyksos period, and places the exodus early enough to allow later chronological references in the Bible to stand as they are. Option *a* places Abraham in the Ur III period when private wealth was not as typical as was later the case. Joseph's rise to power is more difficult to accept in a Middle Kingdom setting. For example, the chariots of Genesis 41:43 were not part of the Egyptian scene until the later Hyksos period. A late date for the exodus (option *b* in illustration 3.1) requires that 1 Kings 6:1 (as well as Judg. 11:26) be erroneous or symbolic. A drastic condensation of the period of the judges is a further requirement. None of these adjustments are necessary in option *c*.[3]

Abraham in Ur

The Book of Genesis covers the prepatriarchal period of Abraham's life in five verses (Gen. 11:27–31). Within the span of these verses Abraham was born, grew to adulthood, took a wife, found himself in a childless marriage, and accompanied his father on a journey of several hundred miles. Archaeology lets us fill the gaps in the five verses and fit the patriarch into the context of his political, social, and material world. With these aspects in place, both Abraham's formative years and adult life in Mesopotamia take on a uniqueness and strength that could not otherwise be appreciated.

The City

Abraham probably was born in Ur of the Chaldeans.[4] Since the Chaldeans did not appear in southern Mesopotamia until many centuries later, however, the phrase *of the Chaldeans* in Genesis 11:28 is understood to be a "scribal gloss" (a phrase added by a copyist) supplied to distinguish Abraham's Ur from other cities carrying the same name.

There are occasional attempts to reject the accuracy of this clarifying phrase and to place Abraham's birthplace in northern Mesopotamia. A first reaction might be that whether Abraham was born in southern Ur or northern Ur does not really matter, that one dot on a map is as good as another, and that a scribal gloss need not be accepted as correct. If Genesis 11 were the only reference to Abraham's being born in southern Mesopotamia, such disinterest would be warranted. But Genesis 11 is only one witness; Nehemiah 9:7 and Acts 7:2–4 also place Abraham in Ur of the Chaldeans. By the time these books were written, the Chaldeans had entered and exited history. These later references

---

3. Since liberal scholars give scant credence to biblical time indicators, this weighing of evidence for the date of the patriarchs is of little relevance for them. Their debate centers on how much if any of the patriarchal narratives are true and in which millennium they could have originated. For examples of this highly critical approach to the patriarchs, see T. Thompson 1974 and Van Seters 1975; for an extended response to this approach, see Millard and Wiseman 1980. See also Kitchen 1995b.

4. The Bible does not actually state that Abraham was born in Ur, but this can be assumed from the notice that his brother Haran, who lived long enough to father Lot, died there.

3.2. Restoration and cutaway of a typical Mesopotamian house. The thick, unbaked mud-brick walls retained needed warmth during winter months, and in summer they provided natural insulation against the outside heat. (Buildings in modern Baghdad are built of more permanent materials and must resort to air conditioners to achieve similar cooling.) Because of the concern over interior summer temperatures, first-floor windows were generally small and near the ceiling so hot air could escape.

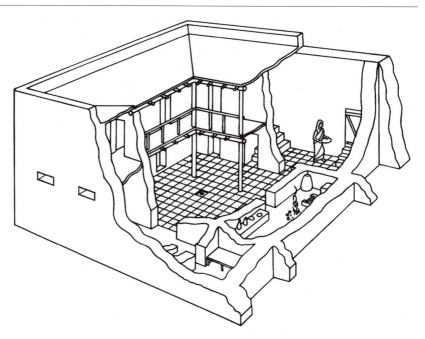

are not in the category of scribal glosses and therefore support the correctness of the location given in Genesis 11.[5]

Abraham was born shortly after 2000. Portions of Ur dating to this time were excavated by Sir Leonard Woolley, and his findings allow us to visualize some of the city as Abraham knew it. Ur was protected by a defensive wall approximately two-and-one-half miles in circumference. Its religious center was situated near the center of the city, occupied an area of two hundred yards by four hundred yards, and had changed little since the days of Ur-Nammu (illustration 2.18). The ziggurat towered over the horizon, and the adjoining court served as both the market place and religious meeting ground. The moon god Nanna was worshiped as chief deity of Ur.

By Western standards the town plan of Ur was rather haphazard. Streets meandered and in some cases suddenly came to a dead end. Housing, on the other hand, was not so casually treated. Structures varied according to space and wealth considerations, but archaeologists find the same "model house" plan repeated over several centuries (including the earlier Ur III period, in which some place Abraham). The typical house in Abraham's day was two stories tall. Its first floor was entered off the street through a single door that led into a small lobby. That room opened into a courtyard around which other rooms were arranged. The rooms surrounding the courtyard on the main floor were used as work areas and for guests. A staircase led to the balconied second floor, where sleeping and leisure rooms were located.[6]

5. Rasmussen 1989: 76 accepts southern Ur without question, and Beitzel 1985: 80 favors northern Ur. The northern-Ur theory was adequately discounted years ago by Saggs 1960.

6. Some suggestion has been made that the staircase only led to a flat roof, but such a reconstruction would not adequately account for the wooden poles ringing the open central court.

Such a house seems quite adequate and attractive. When the mud bricks were plastered and whitewashed, the walls of the house would have appeared similar to modern stucco or plastered surfaces. A drain in the center of the enclosed courtyard channeled rainwater into a cistern for storage, and evidence of running water has been discovered in some wealthy residences. Although ground-floor windows were small, the central court afforded a good source of light during the day. In the evening hours, torches or oil lamps provided needed illumination. One negative aspect of life in a Mesopotamian house is revealed by the omens of the period, which show a concern over the possibility of scorpions or snakes dropping onto one's bed at night. Later on, there were rituals to guard against collapsing walls and falling beams.

People

Westerners would be rather noticeable if they wore clothing styles of one hundred or more years ago, but in the ancient Near East styles changed very slowly. The men's clothing shown in illustration 3.3 spans 350 years with no evidence of radical change. The outer garment, which reminds one of the classical Roman toga, was sometimes decoratively fringed, but at other times plain. For ease of movement a man could wear a wrap-around kilt for work. Sandals and simple hats completed the costume. Women's clothing (illustration 3.3, right) was equally slow to change, with little more than modifications in draping. Over the centuries, variety seems to have been achieved through the use of jewelry.

Preserved statues and reliefs show that women had a variety of hairstyles. Men had fewer options: occasionally they are shown clean shaven or even bald, but a clean-shaven man risked being mocked by his peers (e.g., a Mari letter from one man to another sarcastically states, "You're not a man! You haven't a beard on your chin!"; Laessøe 1963: 48). Perhaps this explains why men are usually depicted with

3.3. Clothing typical in Abraham's Mesopotamia. Garments were most often made of wool, but sometimes goat hair, linen, or cotton.

long beards, mustaches, and full heads of hair. Assuming that Abraham followed prevailing custom, he should be visualized with this majority.

Diet

A variety of menu choices was possible for Abraham and his contemporaries. The following foods are known to have been available to the Mesopotamians:

beverages	meats, fish, nuts	fruits	vegetables	breads and cereals
beer	almond	apple	bean	barley
ghee	beef	apricot	cabbage	millet
juice	duck	cherry	chickpea	rye
milk	fish	citron	cucumber	wheat
water	goat	date	cucurbit	
wine	goose	fig	lentil	
	lamb	grape	lettuce	
	ox	lemon	onion	
	pistachio	medlar	pea	
	pork	mulberry		
	shellfish	peach		
	snail	pomegranate		
	walnut	quince		
		raisin		

Although the food groups appear both varied and adequate, not all items were available to everyone. There was a distinct difference between what the common people had on their plates and what the rich had available to them. Common people, for example, probably saw little meat except during festivals.

Politics

After the fall of Ur III in 2004, Mesopotamia moved into the Isin-Larsa period, which is characterized by several petty states vying for power. In southern Mesopotamia the most important of those powers were Isin and Larsa (see illustration 3.4); to the north Ashur and Eshnunna were dominant. Initially, Isin controlled the territory stretching north from the Persian Gulf to Babylon, and Ur was within Isin's sphere of influence. This was the political picture when Abraham was born.

When Abraham was an adult, a king named Lipit-Ishtar came to the throne of Isin. This king started a feud with the king of Larsa, but lost the struggle. Consequently, within the next decades Isin lost its hold on Ur, and "nomads" took control of the city. The nomads were pushed out by one of the early Assyrian kings, and finally Larsa added Ur to its area of influence. The political scene became even more complex as Amorites established themselves in the south and became the common enemy of both Isin and Larsa. Instability in southern Mesopotamia caused by these years of shifting power must have been difficult for people living there, and political confusion could very well have been a factor in the decision by Terah to relocate his family in the north. Other factors that might have influenced Abraham's father to relocate to the

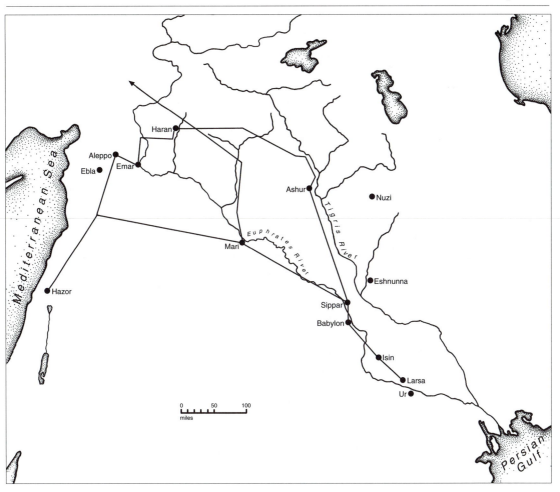

north were that the Mesopotamians could no longer grow wheat in the south and that the barley yield was declining (see p. 33 n. 2).

3.4. Abraham's Mesopotamia. Abraham's party would have traveled north from Ur along one of Mesopotamia's main roads (dark lines).

Society

When Ur III fell, the Sumerian renaissance began to fall with it. Semites began to control Mesopotamia and ruled well into the first millennium. An economic seed of change, planted years earlier by the Semitic dynasty of Akkad, came to blossom. Georges Roux (1992: 180–81) explains the economic shift this way:

> The division of the country into kingdoms erased all traces of city-states, and with the city-states disappeared most of the principles upon which they were founded. Men, land and cattle ceased to belong physically to the gods, as in proto-historic times, or to the temples and the king, as under the Third Dynasty of Ur. . . . Thus emerged a mixed society of big or medium-sized landowners and tenants who made up the bulk of the population. . . . The economic life of the country was no longer exclusively— or almost exclusively—in [the] hands [of the priests and king].[7]

7. These conclusions are supported by the many legal documents that reveal that scribes were now working for private individuals.

Two law codes are preserved from this time period. One is credited to Lipit-Ishtar and the other, called "The Laws of Eshnunna," was found in a small administrative settlement not far from Babylon. These codes give many insights into Mesopotamian society. For example, they provide a partial list of contemporary occupations: teamster, sailor, harvester, winnower, hired worker, muleskinner, moneylender, wet nurse, scribe, priest, gardener, tavern keeper.

These laws also tell us the earning power of some occupations. For instance: "The hire for a wagon together with its oxen and its driver [is one third of a shekel of silver]. . . . He shall drive it the whole day" (*ANE* 1:133; *ANET* 161). What of the muleskinner? "The hire for a donkey is one seah of barley, and the wages for its driver are one seah of barley. He shall drive it the whole day" (*ANE* 1:134; *ANET* 162). Thus, a muleskinner with his own donkey earned two seahs of barley per day (a seah of barley was equivalent to one-thirtieth shekel of silver), which means that he had to work five days to earn the same amount of buying power as the teamster earned in one day. Obviously, at least in the material sense, it was more profitable to be a teamster. Similar comparisons can be made of other occupations. For example, the hired worker labored twenty-three days for a shekel of silver. The harvester and winnower (both seasonal workers) toiled fifteen and thirty days respectively for their shekel. Knowledge of relative pay scales is not earth-shattering, but it represents the kind of detail that can be extracted and used to re-create the society in Abraham's day.

The Laws of Eshnunna not only give insight about pay, but they also provide some idea of the price structure then in force and illustrate the relative worth of certain commodities of that day. Any of the following could be purchased for one shekel of silver:

> six bushels of barley
> three quarts of "best oil" (very light oil)
> two-and-one-half gallons of sesame oil
> three gallons plus one quart of lard
> eight gallons of "river oil" (oil of bitumen)
> six pounds of wool
> twelve bushels of salt
> three pounds of copper
> two pounds of refined copper

The laws take us beyond buying power and price indexes into the very fabric of life. We learn, for example, that moneylenders were charging twenty percent yearly interest on silver, but thirty-three-and-one-third percent interest on grain. Since these interest rates were so different, it is not surprising that a creditor was prohibited from demanding repayment of the low-rate loan at the higher rate. Conversely, the creditor was protected against being repaid at the lower rate if he had lent out at the higher rate. One intriguing provision of the laws was that, should a debt not be paid, it was permissible for the creditor to seize someone from the delinquent household until payment was received. But the person sequestering another had best be able to prove the debt:

> If a man has no claim against another man, but nevertheless distrains the other man's slave-girl, the owner of the slave-girl shall declare under oath: "You have no claim against me" and he shall pay him silver in full compensation for the slave-girl (*ANE* 1:135; *ANET* 162).

In the event the slave girl died while falsely held, two slave girls had to be returned in payment. The following letter seems a bit humorous today, but that was not its tone when originally written:

> Tell Ahu-kinum: Awil-Amurrim sends the following message: Immediately after you left for the trip, Imgur-Sin arrived here and claimed: "He owes me one-third of a mina of silver." He took your wife and your daughter as pledges. Come back before your wife and your daughter die from the work of constantly grinding barley while in detention. Please, get your wife and your daughter out of this (Oppenheim 1967: 91).

As just implied, there were slaves in Abraham's world, and several laws deal specifically with them. We learn that slaves were visually marked by rings or tags worn on a chain, by rope "slave collars," or by a special hairstyle. Surprisingly, two laws prohibit slaves from financial speculation. That slaves could engage in such activity indicates more freedom than slaves are usually thought to possess.

There were wars and rumors of war while Abraham lived in southern Mesopotamia, but more personal disputes also needed attention:

> If a man throws another man to the floor in an altercation and breaks his hand, he shall pay one-half mina of silver (*ANE* 1:137; *ANET* 163).[8]

On the basis of one law it is clear that capital offenses went before the king, but most problems were handled by some kind of police court. Apparently a police court could take care of the following injuries:

> If a man bites the nose of another man and severs it, he shall pay one mina of silver. For an eye he shall pay one mina of silver; for a tooth one-half mina; for an ear one-half mina; for a slap in the face ten shekels of silver (*ANE* 1:137; *ANET* 163).

Attention to such possibilities conjures up some rather wild brawls. Less raucous, but even more serious, are some of the laws dealing with animals. The following example shows the close parallelism that can sometimes be found with later biblical statutes:

If an ox is known to gore habitually and the authorities have brought the fact to the knowledge of its owner, but he does not have his ox dehorned, it gores a man and causes his death, then the owner of the ox shall pay two-thirds of a mina of silver (*ANE* 1:138; *ANET* 163).	If, however, an ox was previously in the habit of goring, and its owner has been warned, yet he does not confine it, and it kills a man or a woman, the ox shall be stoned and its owner also shall be put to death (Exod. 21:29).

8. There are fifty shekels to the mina.

Several of the Eshnunna laws deal with various aspects of marriage.

> If a man calls at the house of his father-in-law, and his father-in-law accepts him in servitude, but nevertheless gives his daughter to another man, the father of the girl shall refund the bride-money that he received twofold (*ANE* 1:135; *ANET* 162).

> If a man has been made prisoner during a raid or an invasion or if he has been carried off forcibly and stayed in a foreign country for a long time, and if another man has taken his wife and she has borne him a son—when he returns, he shall get his wife back (*ANE* 1:135–36; *ANET* 162).

A man could divorce his wife by simply returning the bride-price or by giving her one mina of silver. But he could not divorce her if the marriage had produced children:

> If a man divorces his wife after having made her bear children and takes another wife, he shall be driven from his house and from whatever he owns and may go after him who will accept him (*ANE* 1:138; *ANET* 163).

Under the law code of the day, therefore, Abraham could easily have divorced Sarah. For many years she failed her husband in her primary duty as a wife. That Abraham did not do the legally acceptable thing, that is, divorce his barren wife, seemingly points more strongly than the Bible actually states to how deeply he loved her.

Religion

For someone living in Ur, or any other Mesopotamian city for that matter, it would have been impossible to get very far away from religion. The towering ziggurat could always be seen, and the social hub of the city centered in the square near its base. By 3000 the Mesopotamians had invented some four thousand deities. Hundreds of them might be worshiped in a given city, but each city had one chief god.

Anu was technically the chief god throughout Mesopotamian history, but even before the Isin-Larsa period he had been functionally replaced by his son Enlil. Among Enlil's many titles was "King of earth, lord of earth." Ea, another son of Anu and Innin, was in charge of the primeval deep and the sweet waters. He was also a god of wisdom ("Lord of the intelligent eye") and was good to humans ("The broad-eared one who knows all that has a name"). He was the initiator and protector of arts

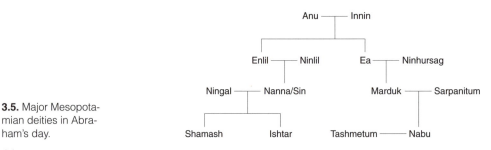

3.5. Major Mesopotamian deities in Abraham's day.

and crafts, science and literature, and also the patron of magicians. Nanna (or Sin as he was beginning to be called in Abraham's day), the moon god of Ur, is in the second rank of gods. As a moon god, Sin controlled the night, the month, and the calendar. Because of his identification with darkness he was able to read into the dark future and see the destinies of people. Marduk (sun god and god of magic) was also in the second rank of gods, but a few centuries later he rose in the pantheon until he assimilated Enlil and replaced Anu. Marduk's son Nabu was the god of wisdom and of the scribal arts. Nanna's son, Shamash, was also a sun god. As the dispeller of darkness, Shamash could see all activity, and he judged the living and the dead. The wives of deities usually had no specified function, but Ishtar, the most important of the female deities, was the goddess of war and sexuality.

The Mesopotamians believed that thousands of deities occupied their world. Martin Beek (1962: 138) states: "The collection of names of gods and the establishment of their genealogical connections . . . constituted one of the main activities of theologians in Mesopotamia." From these collections come such minor deities as Ashnan the barley god, Shumuqan the cattle god, Gula the goddess of childbirth, and Pasag the protector of travelers. Occasionally different deities had the same function; for example, there was more than one sun god, more than one war god, and two goddesses of fertility. Job descriptions sometimes changed among the lesser gods, and some syncretism existed. With such a large number of deities the theologians must have found it extremely difficult to keep track of everybody.

The Mesopotamians were expected to worship the deities, and they were taught that their purpose in life was to serve the gods. To implement worship and service, a burgeoning priesthood developed. The fol-

3.6. Cylinder-seal impression from the Akkad period depicts five Mesopotamian deities. The small figure at the lower center, Shamash (identified by his holding the sun god's saw), is flanked by Ishtar and Enki (with streams of water and fish). Behind Enki is his attendant with two faces, Usumia. On the far left is Ninurta, the warrior god.

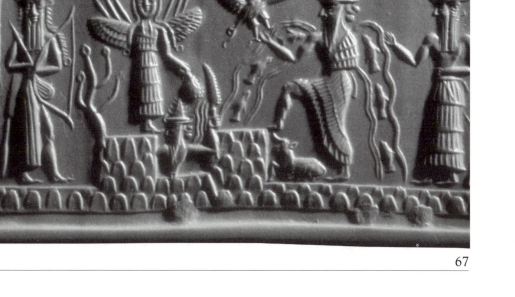

British Museum

lowing list of titles (all priests unless otherwise noted) is only a sample of the religious order and its job descriptions:

Mashmashu	performed purification rites before rituals and "worked" in the homes of afflicted people
Kalu	calmed the gods with music
Naru	sang (priest or priestess)
Nash-patri	killed sacrificial animals and symbolically cut the heads off certain evil images
Baru	diviner who accompanied the army and won honor—or disgrace—depending on the correctness of his predictions
Shailu	interpreted dreams (priest or priestess)
Kurgarru and Assinnu	acted in cult performances (possibly eunuchs)
Entu	high priestess dedicated to a god; she lived in a special section of the religious complex and was expected to remain virginal through childbearing years
Qadishtu	female ritual prostitutes

The gods had to be cared for, and that included feeding them. Priests presented food to the gods' statues each day, a "great meal" in the morning and a "light meal" in the evening. Food was placed on a table before the statue and shielded by a curtain so the god could eat and wash his hands in private. Leo Oppenheim (1977: 188–89) describes it this way:

> A number of liquid and semiliquid dishes in appropriate serving vessels were placed on the table in a prescribed arrangement, and containers with beverages were likewise set out. Next, specific cuts of meat were served as a main dish. Finally, fruit was brought in in what one of the texts takes the trouble to describe as a beautiful arrangement, thus adding an esthetic touch. . . . Musicians performed, and the cella was fumigated . . . to dispel the odor of food. Eventually, the table was cleared and removed and water in a bowl again offered to the image for the cleansing of the fingers.

Much information is preserved concerning the pantheon, priesthood, ziggurats, and temples of Mesopotamia. But it is necessary to distinguish between the systematized theology and the religious practice of the common people on the street. The New Year festival was the high point of the Mesopotamian religious calendar, but common people would have witnessed little more than a procession or two. For the remainder of the year they would bring their offerings to the temple during certain feast days, and the men would visit the temple prostitutes to ensure fertility for themselves and their property. At home, a family would have a personal shrine, normally just a niche in which rested a figure of some minor patron deity the family considered relevant to their personal life. As in the temple, this deity had to be fed, a task usually assigned to a son of the homeowner.

Mesopotamians feared attack from unseen quarters. They believed they could be afflicted by demons or witchcraft. Trouble could also result because a taboo had been broken or because some god or gods had inexplicably taken a dislike to them. To ward off demons, figurines were placed under the threshold of the house, and the people wore am-

3.7. Clay plaque of the demon Humbaba's face. In the Gilgamesh Epic (see chap. 9), Humbaba is described as fierce, his mouth fire, and his breath death.

ulets to protect themselves from the fears of the moment. Should evil get past these protections, the afflicted person then sought out the appropriate priest, who would determine the source of the difficulty and choose from a collection of spells. If demons were causing the problem, they could be exorcised, tricked into thinking the victim dead, or even trapped within some substitute for the victim. The following incantation was used to invoke Gira, one of the fire gods, against witchcraft and demons (Saggs 1988: 291):

> Flaring Gira, son of Anu, the hero, you are the fiercest amongst your brothers. You who judge cases like the gods Sin and Shamash, judge my case, make a decision concerning me! Burn my wizard and my witch! O Gira, consume my wizard and my witch! O Gira, burn them! O Gira, consume them! O Gira, bind them! O Gira, annihilate them! O Gira, send them away!

Mesopotamians were very concerned about the future, and they felt that omens gave insights into coming events. Consequently, volumes of possible situations together with their implied consequences were compiled and consulted (Saggs 1988: 275–76):

> If a snake is aggressive to a man, seizes him, bites him, hard times will reach his adversary.

> If a snake passes from the right of a man to the left of the man, he will have a good name.

> If a snake passes from the left of a man to the right of the man, he will have a bad name.

If a snake falls from the ceiling on a man and wife and scatters them, the man and wife will be divorced.

Dreams were also thought to be communications from the gods about the future, and here too all possible situations were tabulated along with an interpretation (Oppenheim 1956: 276):

If one gives him a seal of red stone: he will have sons and daughters.
If one gives him a mounted seal: he will have neither sons nor daughters.
If one gives him a seal with figures: he will have sons, peace of mind.
If one gives him a perforated seal: he will have a legitimate son.
If one gives him an unperforated seal: he will have a deaf son.
If he wears a seal and one takes it away: either his son or his daughter will die.

Should a bad prediction of the future be forecast, it could be canceled out. The following incantation is titled "A ritual 'preparation' to remove (the consequences of) evil dreams" and was to be recited with uplifted hands before Shamash (Oppenheim 1956: 300):

Shamash, you are the judge—judge my case!
You are the one who makes the decisions—decide my case!
Change the dream I had into a good one!
May I walk the straight road, may I have a companion!
Shamash, all day may they be good for me!
Shamash, all month may they be good for me!

3.8. Clay model of a sheep's liver inscribed with a number of omens. Baru priests would compare such models with the livers of sacrificed animals to discern the forecast indicated by particular features of the animal liver.

British Museum

Summary

What does this survey of Abraham's Mesopotamia do for an appreciation of the patriarch? It helps re-create the world as he knew it: the city with its winding streets and comfortable homes, his dress, his diet, and the occupations with which he would have come in contact.

Joshua 24:2 states that Abraham's father was a polytheist. It should follow, therefore, that Abraham was reared in a family that believed it imperative to serve the many gods of Mesopotamia and that any sensible person would fear the gods. Abraham's father would have believed the world was swarming with gods and was full of demons ready to do one in. Terah would have believed his neighbors were capable of witchcraft, that his house had to be guarded by protective figurines, and that his household god needed daily food. Visits would be necessary to the temple prostitutes to ensure fertility, and careful attention had to be paid to god-signs communicated through dreams or omens. Terah would have believed it was important to recognize unfavorable god-signs so they could be countered.

The Bible does not say what effect his father's polytheism had on Abraham. Some scholars become apprehensive about the religious system current in Abraham's day and argue that Abraham never lived in the city of Ur, but in a tent some distance away. They do not want to think of Abraham tending the household shrine or, as an adult participating in pagan ritual, especially consorting with the Qadishtu priestesses. Such writers argue that Abraham was always attuned to the true God.[9]

Putting Abraham in a tent outside Ur, however, would not remove him from the material and religious mind-set and obligations of his day. Perhaps Abraham never believed in the religious system of his family and his world. But perhaps he did, and God had to take Abraham not only out of Mesopotamia, but also out of a religious system totally alien to the truth. In either event, knowing the mind-set current in Abraham's day lets one appreciate the implications of Joshua 24:2 concerning Terah and the length of Abraham's step of faith.

The Move to Haran

Abraham grew to adulthood in Ur, an Ur that had been rebuilt after the destruction of 2004. The city had never regained its former stature, and it continued to be buffeted by political winds over which it had no control. Each year the priests recited the 436-line "Lamentation over the Destruction of Ur," and each year the people were expected to listen. But the glory never returned.

> O Father Nanna, that city into ruins was made. . . .
> Its people, not potsherds, filled its sides;
> its walls were breached; the people groan.

9. Jewish legends similarly attempt to separate Abraham from the polytheism of his father.

> In its lofty gates, where they were wont to promenade, dead bodies were
> lying about;
> in its boulevards, where the feasts were celebrated, scattered they lay. . . .
> O Nanna, Ur has been destroyed, its people have been dispersed (*ANET*
> 459–60).[10]

Abraham lived in an extended-family structure, and even though an adult and married, he was still subject to his father. And it was his father who decided to relocate his family, perhaps because of the unstable political climate or the deteriorating agricultural base. Whatever Terah's motivation, Abraham followed.[11] Terah would have led his family from Ur to Larsa, where the main road to the north began (see illustration 3.4 for the two main road systems in Mesopotamia). At Sippar one had to choose whether to continue along the Euphrates River or cross over to the Tigris. Since Genesis 11:31 states that their destination was Canaan but that they went only as far as Haran, it seems that they crossed to the Tigris. This "road to Emar" led north through Assyrian territory and then west toward the Mediterranean. (If they had continued along the Euphrates they would have had to divert from their stated destination to reach Haran.)

Terah stopped at Haran, but no reasons are given for his not continuing on to Canaan. Haran was an important caravan city, and politically Terah had reached a more peaceful part of the Mesopotamian world. Moreover, the principal deity at Haran was the same moon god Terah worshiped at Ur, and therefore he may have felt at home in Haran. Further, Haran was located where Mesopotamia, Syria, and Anatolia met; had Terah continued on he would have begun to edge out of the society he knew.

Ebla

A 1974 archaeological discovery in Syria generated much interest in both Near Eastern and biblical studies. Tell Mardikh (called Ebla in antiquity), a normal-looking, pottery-strewn ancient site approximately thirty-five miles south-southwest of Aleppo, had undergone excavation for several years. Portions of the outer defenses, housing, and other architecture showed that the third-millennium city contained a mixture of Syrian and Mesopotamian influences. Ebla's Syro-Mesopotamian culture was not the cause of banner headlines. The discovery of royal archives in the throne room of the palace electrified scholars because the tablets brought a third-millennium city back to life. The tablets showed that Ebla was a thriving mercantile center with contacts stretching hundreds of miles in all directions and that cara-

10. See also Kramer 1983b; Michalowski 1989; and Roux 1992: 178. "City laments" typically concluded with a prayer that the deity again show favor on its city.

11. Commentators disagree whether God called Abraham from both Ur and Haran or only from Haran. A comparison of Gen. 12:1 with Acts 7:2 shows the matter is not clear. Perhaps the call began at Ur telling Abraham to accompany his father and was made clearer at Haran. Genesis 12:1 can be translated, "Now the Lord had said to Abram."

vans were constantly moving in, out, and through Ebla. The conflagration that buried and preserved the archives has most recently been dated between 2300 and 2280 (Astour 1992).

The discoveries at Ebla generated debate on two primary levels: Near Eastern history and biblical studies. Preliminary evidence led to claims that Ebla was not only an important commercial city but also the capital of an empire stretching over much of the Near East, including Palestine and perhaps even Assyria. If true, such data would require that portions of third-millennium Near Eastern history be rewritten. Such a reappraisal would be of great importance to historians:

> 15,000 tablets, many in a previously unknown West Semitic language akin to Hebrew, reveal a lost 3rd-millennium Syrian empire as large as that of Sargon the Great. A stunning challenge to the primacy of Mesopotamia in ancient Near Eastern history and in the cultural genesis of ancient Israel.

This quotation, added as a lead-in to an article by Ebla's original epigrapher (Pettinato 1976: 44), introduces the second level of importance, the one that caused most of the stir in the newspapers and puts the discussion of Ebla in this chapter. The Ebla tablets were at first argued to have had great impact on the Bible, specifically on the patriarchs and the Book of Genesis:

> The true significance of the Ebla tablets for biblical history and our understanding of the patriarchal narratives [is revealed]. The Genesis 14 account of the punitive raid of the kings of the East upon a rebellious coalition of kings from the Cities of the Plain has long been a puzzling problem for scholars in reconstructing biblical history. The amazing correlation of the number, order, and names of the Cities of the Plain between the Ebla tablet and the biblical record indicates that the Genesis 14 narrative should be understood in the setting of the third millennium, not in the second or even first millennium as scholars have previously thought (Freedman 1978: 143).

Critical scholars have often concluded that the patriarchs were a first-millennium invention, but David Noel Freedman (1978) says that this view is incorrect. Freedman concludes that the patriarchs did not live in the second millennium; but, on the basis of information from Ebla, he argues that they should be placed in the middle of the third millennium. For the tablets to attest to the historicity of the patriarchs would be fine, but to place them so early tears at the Bible in another way. Patriarchal chronology cannot be flexed enough to fit this new proposal, and scholars who advocate such early dates favor their own efforts to find parallels in the Ebla materials, while dismissing clear biblical statements.

Many books and articles have been written on Ebla since 1974, and television specials have even been produced. A war of words developed over the tablets, with some scholars maintaining that they necessitated the rewriting of patriarchal history. Others are equally adamant that Ebla has no relevance to the Bible. Indeed, most of the alleged connections between the two have been retracted. The original excavators of

Ebla, Paolo Matthiae and Giovanni Pettinato, have taken opposite sides in this debate—a disagreement that has ended their friendship and co-operation (for an example of the bitterness that erupted, see Pettinato 1980 and Archi 1980). Politics may also have entered the fray, depending on which of these two scholarly statements is correct (the first is by Hershel Shanks, the second by Giorgio Buccellati; see Shanks 1978b: 3):

> The popular interest in Ebla stems from the light the tablets shed on the Bible. Some say they are more significant for understanding the Bible than any other archaeological discovery. But the Syrian government would like to play down this aspect of the tablets.

> Anyone suggesting that scholars working on Ebla materials might suppress Biblical connections for political reasons is either showing his gross ignorance or is guilty of bad faith. The Syrians are not concerned with any Biblical connections that the Ebla materials might reveal.

Present-day Syria has little love for modern Israel, but would this antipathy extend to information on patriarchal history? Some say yes, and claim that if Ebla proved the patriarchs did have a connection with territory belonging to modern Syria, the Israelis would use that information to claim new territorial boundaries! In the late 1970s and early 1980s Ebla was one of the "hot items" in Near Eastern and biblical archaeology. Some early conclusions have already been discarded, and presently Ebla's importance is not yet clearly understood. It may be decades before Ebla's data can be placed in proper perspective (Millard 1992).

Additional Reading

Archi, Alfonso. "Further concerning Ebla and the Bible." *BA* 44 (1981): 145–54.

Biggs, Robert. "The Ebla Tablets: An Interim Perspective." *BA* 43 (1980): 76–87, 134.

Block, Daniel I. "Chasing a Phantom: The Search for the Historical Marduk." *Archaeology in the Biblical World* 2/1 (1992): 20–43.

Hawkes, Jacquetta. *The First Great Civilizations*. New York: Knopf, 1973 (part 4).

Matthiae, Paolo. "New Discoveries at Ebla." *BA* 47 (1984): 18–32.

Pettinato, Giovanni. *The Archives of Ebla*. Garden City: Doubleday, 1981.

———. *Ebla: A New Look at History*. Translated by C. Faith Richardson. Baltimore: Johns Hopkins University Press, 1991.

Shanks, Hershel. "*BAR* Interviews Giovanni Pettinato." *BAR* 6/5 (1980): 46–52.

———. "Ebla Evidence Evaporates." *BAR* 5/6 (1979): 52–53.

———. "Syria Tries to Influence Ebla Scholarship." *BAR* 5/2 (1979): 36–47.

Shanks, Hershel, et al. "Ebla Update." *BAR* 6/3 (1980): 47–59.

Viganò, Lorenzo. "Literary Sources for the History of Palestine and Syria: The Ebla Tablets." *BA* 47 (1984): 6–16, 128.

Yaron, Reuven. *The Laws of Eshnunna*. Jerusalem: Magnes, 1969.

4

Patriarchal Palestine

Abraham and Lot

He set me at the head of his children. He married me to his eldest daughter. He let me choose for myself of his country, of the choicest of that which was with him on his frontier with another country. It was a good land, named Yaa. Figs were in it, and grapes. It had more wine than water. Plentiful was its honey, abundant its olives. Every kind of fruit was on its trees. Barley was there, and emmer. There was no limit to any kind of cattle. Moreover, great was that which accrued to me as a result of the love of me. He made me ruler of a tribe of the choicest of his country. Bread was made for me as daily fare, wine as daily provision, cooked meat and roast fowl, beside the wild beasts of the desert, for they hunted for me and laid before me, beside the catch of my own hounds. Many . . . were made for me, and milk in every kind of cooking.

—"The Story of Sinuhe"

Palestine's Geography

Bernard Ramm (1956: 97) correctly emphasizes the importance of geography to biblical studies: "To try to interpret the Bible without a basic geographical understanding of Bible lands is like trying to watch a

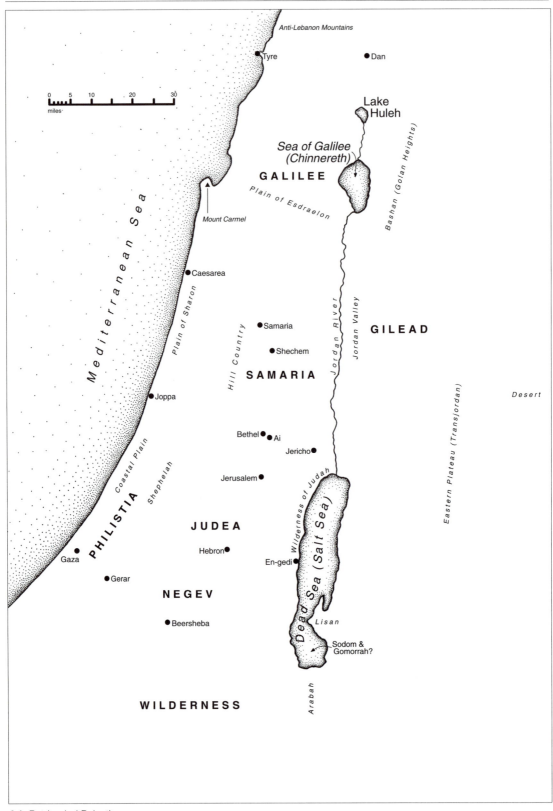

4.1. Patriarchal Palestine.

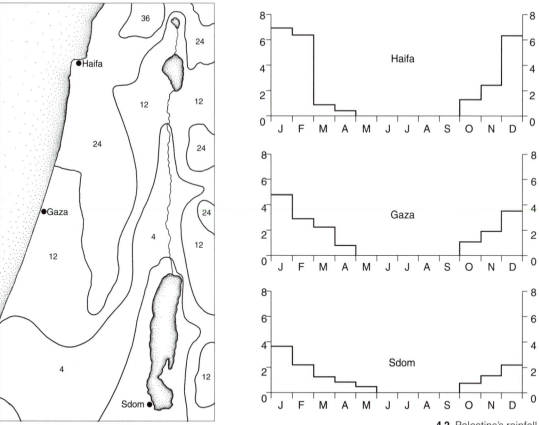

4.2. Palestine's rainfall (in inches), annually (left) and monthly (right).

drama with no scenery." The authors of the biblical drama assumed that the stage for their work was visible or at least well known. Since in our day the Bible is read all over the world, many readers are not familiar with the terrain or the location of the major cities in Palestine—knowledge that is needful for a fuller appreciation of the biblical record.

Of primary importance is the recognition that Palestine's land area is quite small. Abraham was promised the land from Dan to Beersheba, a distance of only 150 air miles (illustration 4.1). Within that limited area is a land of major contrasts. Three climatic zones are packed in: Mediterranean, steppe, and desert. The Mediterranean and desert zones are in constant tension as they influence the weather in Palestine. For example, when the morning breezes in Jerusalem are from the west (off the Mediterranean Sea), the prospects are good for a pleasant day. But if the winds are from the east (off the desert), then a hot, oppressive day can be expected.

On the whole, Palestine has a moderate climate. January, the coldest month, has an average temperature of 46°F, and summer temperatures seldom average over 90°F. But in this small land with major contrasts, cool mountain air in the Hill Country is only a few miles from the heat of the wilderness. A few inches of snow may cover the Hill Country in winter, while the coastline enjoys balmy weather.

Palestine has only two seasons: rainy and dry (illustration 4.2 shows the great variation in yearly rainfall from one region to another). When the Bible speaks of the "early rains" it refers to rains that begin before October. The term "later rains" refers to rains that continue into May. Dewfall is an important factor for Palestine since it provides moisture for vegetation during the dry season. That dewfall can be heavy is illustrated in the story of Gideon and his fleece (Judg. 6:36–40), and its importance is implied in Elijah's warning to King Ahab (1 Kings 17:1).

The land can be divided into four topographic zones: the Jordan Valley, the Eastern Plateau, the Hill Country, and the Coastal Plain. The elevation of these zones ranges from approximately four thousand feet above sea level to nearly thirteen hundred feet below sea level at the Dead Sea—the lowest point on the earth's surface.

Jordan Valley

The Jordan Valley with its river and three lakes divides Palestine into two parts. The Jordan River rises from four separate tributaries coming down from the region of Mount Hermon and descends rapidly in

4.3. Aerial view of the meandering Jordan River, clearly showing why it would not be used for boat traffic.

the short distance to Lake Huleh. In biblical times this lake measured about four miles long and two miles wide, with a maximum depth of perhaps sixteen feet. Lake Huleh and its adjacent swamps have been drained since 1948 until today only a nature park preserves a portion of the original. The remainder of the area has been put into agricultural use. In the ten air miles between Lake Huleh and the Sea of Galilee (called the Sea of Chinnereth in the Old Testament; derived from a city by that name on its northwest shore) the Jordan River drops nearly seven hundred feet. The Sea of Galilee measures thirteen miles long and seven-and-one-half miles wide and is nearly two hundred feet deep in some places.

From the Sea of Galilee the river flows through the Jordan Valley and drops another six hundred feet before reaching the Dead Sea. While it is only sixty-five air miles from the Sea of Galilee to the Dead Sea, the Jordan meanders for two hundred river miles between the two seas. Largely avoided in Old Testament times, the valley was sometimes called "the jungle of the Jordan" (Zech. 11:3 New American Bible), and it was then the habitat of lions and tigers (for a study of the Jordan Valley, see Har-El 1978).

The Jordan River finally empties its fresh water into the Dead Sea, but much of the water is then lost to evaporation. The "Salt Sea," as the Hebrews called it (Gen. 14:3), is approximately forty-six miles long and ten miles wide, but those dimensions are not constant. Today the shallow south end of the Dead Sea is drying up because water from the Jordan River is being diverted into other parts of Palestine. Continued re-channeling of the Jordan could bring that area above water, as it seems to have been during Old Testament times. Although most of the area around the Dead Sea is desolate, some freshwater springs provide pockets of habitable land. The Arabah, a mostly barren wilderness that is given little mention in Old Testament history, lies south of the Dead Sea.

Eastern Plateau

The Eastern Plateau (commonly called Transjordan) is an area of hills, valleys, and plains. Biblical Bashan, located at its north end, lies east of the Sea of Galilee. This broad plain was fertile in Old Testament times and was famed for its cattle, sheep, and oak trees (Deut. 32:14; Ps. 22:12; Isa. 2:13). The ancient area of Bashan is now called the Golan Heights. Gilead, mentioned several times in the Bible, is sometimes a reference to all the territory east of the Jordan River. At other times, however, it designated only the southern half to two-thirds of that territory. Moses gave the Eastern Plateau to the tribes of Gad, Reuben, and the half-tribe of Manasseh before the conquest.

Hill Country

The Hill Country (the primary "stage" for Old Testament history) is divided into three parts. The northern area, beginning just above Tyre and extending southward to the Valley of Esdraelon, is called Galilee. The mountains of Galilee are among the highest in Palestine, but there is some arable land, and the Valley of Esdraelon is one of the more fertile areas in the country. That valley's flat terrain has also made it an ideal battleground throughout history. The central part of the Hill Country, Samaria, is called the "breadbasket" of Palestine.[1] The topography there is characterized by rolling hills, shallow valleys, and rich soil. The southern Hill Country, extending from slightly north of Jerusalem to the region of Hebron, is called Judea. The hills of Judea are rockier, and their slopes, some of which are quite steep, are often terraced to allow farmers to cultivate vineyards and orchards.

South of Hebron, the Hill Country gives way to the Negev, "home" for part of the patriarchal period. While the biblical Negev ended a little south of Beersheba, modern Israeli usage of the term includes the land as far as the southern tip of Israel at Eilat, on the shores of the Red Sea. Although the biblical Negev appears barren in summer, it is a marginal agricultural zone that, with good management and a minimum of rainfall, can support a large population (for a study of the Negev in both the biblical and modern senses see Evenari et al. 1971).

Two other terms associated with the central Hill Country are the "Wilderness of Judah," a barren area bordering the west side of the Dead Sea, and the "Shephelah," the foothills between the Hill Country and the coastal plain (for a study of the Shephelah see Rainey 1983).

Coastal Plain

The Coastal Plain is a sandy area about twelve miles wide at its southern end, but it gradually narrows toward its northern limits. From Gaza to approximately Joppa (now within modern Tel Aviv), the plain was called Philistia and was the home territory of the Philistines. The Plain of Sharon begins at Joppa and ends just north of where Caesarea was built in New Testament times. The Bible speaks of the "rose of Sharon" (Song of Sol. 2:1) and the "majesty of Sharon" (Isa. 35:2), the latter being a reference to the forests that grew there in Old Testament times. The coastal plain is interrupted by the Carmel Range and then briefly resumes to the north, but the Anti-Lebanon Mountains soon bring it to an end.

The Effects of Geography

Much of the history covered in subsequent chapters of this book happened in the areas described above. A knowledge of the basic geographical features enables the reader to visualize the movements of people and to recognize implications that would otherwise be missed. Listed below are some examples of how the climate and geography affected the people of the Old Testament:[2]

1. The civilizations of both Mesopotamia and Egypt grew up around the river systems that brought people together for cooperative use of the water and from that initial interaction into increasingly close political union. There is no similar unifying river system in Palestine. As noted above, the Jordan River Valley with

1. The reader must distinguish whether a particular Bible text is speaking of Samaria the region or Samaria the city.
2. For a more detailed study of the land, see Beitzel 1985 or Rasmussen 1989.

its wild animals and meandering river attracted little attention; its water was not used for irrigation as was that of the Nile, Tigris, and Euphrates. The people of Palestine made minimal use of the Mediterranean Sea before late Old Testament times. Therefore, the waterways of Palestine were not conducive to bringing the inhabitants of the land into a common bond.

2. The variety of Palestine's topography and the many separate valley systems in the Hill Country tended to isolate groups of people from one another. The many Canaanite subsections, such as the Amalekites and the Perrizites, are partly a result of the isolation caused by topography.

3. Palestine's position on the land bridge between Mesopotamia and Egypt also hindered its opportunity for unification and development of a fully indigenous culture. Palestine was repeatedly subjected to foreign cultures and buffeted by armies marching in from the north or the south. There was little opportunity for Palestine to develop its own identity.

4. Palestine's varied topography included areas that were not totally desirable. For example, the Jericho oasis and the area around the Sea of Galilee were not choice locations in the heat and humidity of summer. In Old Testament times wealthy people spent their summers in the Hill Country and their winters in the lowlands. The prophet Amos criticized the rich who enjoyed their winter and summer houses while the nation was rotting socially and spiritually (Amos 3:15).

5. An understanding of Palestine's topography recovers the significance of such biblical phrases as going "up" to Jerusalem or "down" to Jericho. In either case the travel required stamina.

6. A comparison of Palestine's geography with that of Mesopotamia and Egypt leads to the realization that basic adjustments in lifestyle would be necessary for anyone coming into Palestine to live. A newcomer like Abraham could no longer think in terms of flatland distances or of waterways for transport. He had to learn to compute distances by the number of hills and valleys between him and his destination. He had to learn that it was usually easier to follow meandering ridge routes than to attempt straight-line travel. He also encountered climatic conditions that were totally new to him. People leaving Palestine had to make the adjustments in reverse.

7. The topography of Palestine might lead one to dream of a country easier to traverse. The familiar words of Isaiah 40:3–4 echo such a wish:

> Clear the way for the Lord in the wilderness;
> Make smooth in the desert a highway for our God.
> Let every valley be lifted up,
> And every mountain and hill be made low;
> And let the rough ground become a plain,
> And the rugged terrain a broad valley.

Palestine before Abraham

Like Mesopotamia, Palestine's history did not begin with Abraham. In comparison to Mesopotamia and Egypt, however, prepatriarchal Palestine was rather rustic. Because of this relatively backward condition, caused in part by factors 1–3 above, this chapter will pay less attention to the area's early years.

The Natufian period in Palestine is presently given a date range of 10,500–8500. Early evidence of these people has been found in cave

Alfred Hoerth

4.4. Neolithic tower at Jericho. A staircase (lower arrow) opens near the center of the tower's present top (upper arrow), which implies that the tower was originally not much taller. Since there were no metal tools in Neolithic times, the moat portion of the defense system may have been thermally excavated from the bedrock. In this technique, fire was used to heat the limestone, and then the area doused with cold water to cause the stone to fracture. The broken stone was then used to construct the city wall and tower(s).

4.5. Skull with facial features reconstructed in plaster. Usually found with the lower jaw missing, the chin shaped over the upper teeth, and shells inset for the eyes, similar skulls have been found at other Syro-Palestinian sites, but the practice did not outlive the Neolithic period.

sites, but more recent excavations have found them spread over much of Palestine; some even lived in simple stone-built housing. They subsisted by hunting and, along the coast, by fishing. Whether they were food producers or only food gatherers is still not clear. Like the early inhabitants of Mesopotamia these people used microliths and had an interest in personal adornment.

Neolithic Palestine is presently dated between 8500 and 4300, and Jericho is the key site for the period. Jericho has been excavated by several archaeologists, including Dame Kathleen Kenyon. She found simple mud-brick housing dating centuries before such bricks were used in Mesopotamia. The inhabitants of Jericho were farmers, and, although they had domesticated some animals, they were still hunters. Like their counterparts in Mesopotamia, they were shaping obsidian from Anatolia and Armenia into tools.

One interesting discovery at Jericho is the earliest defense system known in the world. By approximately 8000, Jericho was protected by a moat that measured nine feet deep and twenty-seven feet across. Behind the moat was a defensive wall over six feet thick and preserved to a height of twelve feet. Attached to the wall was a round stone tower thirty feet high. Certain implications can be drawn from early Jericho's defense system: (1) perhaps one thousand people lived within the protecting wall and moat, (2) obviously, there was "someone out there" to be feared, and (3) Jericho must have been an ordered society to accomplish such a building project. Kenyon thought codified law must have

4.6. Neolithic shrine at Jericho, with an interior roughly six feet by thirteen feet and coated with a red plaster. A niche was built into the wall furthest from the doorway. Near this room, excavators found a one-and-a-half foot tall flaked stone that fit (as in the illustration) atop a stone pedestal in the niche. By analogy with similar, later finds elsewhere, the stone represented deity and was therefore, a sacred pillar (Hebrew *massebah*). This is one of the earliest examples of the pagan pillars that Moses commanded the Hebrews to destroy.

been in use in order to complete such a community effort. Although "codified law" is probably too grandiose a term, the defenses do imply a complex communal life with at least some agreed-upon rules and guidelines.

The first definite evidence of religion in Palestine is found in the Neolithic period. Small animal and female human figurines suggest an interest in fertility worship. Several human skulls with plastered features were discovered under the floor of one Jericho house. Kenyon believed these skulls showed an attempt at portraiture and that they indicated a veneration of ancestors. Additionally, two religious structures were found. These religious structures and objects comprise much of what subsequent inhabitants of Palestine required for worship.[3] Therefore, almost as far back as archaeologists find human beings materially provided for, they were reaching out into the "unknown."

Chalcolithic Palestine, sometimes referred to as the Ghassulian period, has a date range of 4300–3300. Many more settlements dotted the landscape, implying a denser population by that time. The people lived in unfortified villages and were basically farmers and shepherds. Hunting apparently was not an important factor in their lifestyle. Small temples show a continuing interest in religion, and tombs with individual burials and offering vessels point to belief in an afterlife.

3. Clay statues, approximately one-half life-size, were also found at Jericho. The discovery of dozens of similar statues at Ain Ghazal in Jordan have put the Jericho examples in better perspective. Tentatively the statues are seen as a variation on the plastered skulls. See Shanks 1987d: 50–52 (with photographs on the front cover of the periodical).

4.7. Clay ossuaries from the Chalcolithic period. After the deceased's body had desiccated, the skeleton was put in a burial chest large enough to accommodate the long bones, and the ossuary deposited in a cave. Ossuaries are normally house shaped, and some apparently replicate the stilt houses used by people living in the Sharon Plain.

There are interesting regional housing differences in Chalcolithic Palestine. In some areas the people laid stone foundations and used mud bricks to build their homes. Along the coast, however, housing was sometimes raised on stilts (illustration 4.7), while in the Negev some of the people preferred underground multiroom burrows carved into the hills. Archaeologists think the stilt houses were a response to the sometimes marshy Sharon plain; but they are not agreed as to the reason for the underground dwellings. One explanation offered is that these people would have been cooler living underground; another explanation is that they were cave dwellers who migrated to southern Palestine.

Concerning the technological and artistic abilities of the Chalcolithic period, fragments of elaborate multicolored wall frescoes were found at one site (illustration 4.8). In addition to geometric designs, there are stylized "dragons," naturalistic birds, masks, and a pair of decorated shoes in what appears to be a reception scene. These complicated as well as imaginative designs are both intriguing and frustrating. They provide a glimpse into the culture, but they also emphasize the incompleteness of present knowledge of the period.

Chalcolithic Palestine, as the name implies, was using copper. When a horde of copper objects including "standards" and crowns was first found near En-gedi on the west bank of the Dead Sea, some archaeologists thought they were too sophisticated to be from this early period, but they now accept that this "astonishing evidence of the skill of the . . . metalworkers" (Kenyon 1985: 63) does indeed date to the Chalcolithic period. Additionally, rather elaborate and sometimes delicate

Pontifical Institute, Jerusalem

4.8. Part of an elaborate wall fresco found at Ghassul, a few miles northeast of the Dead Sea. The "star" is approximately six feet in diameter.

4.9. Copper "standards," mace heads, crown, and other miscellaneous copper pieces found in the Nahal Mishmar cave beside the Dead Sea. Over four hundred objects were found in the horde and may have been used ceremonially at the religious center at nearby En-gedi. The standards were probably mounted on wooden poles and carried in processions. Similar standards have been found at other Chalcolithic sites, but never in such number. The mace heads were ceremonial weapons.

ivory carvings have been found. The frescoes, copper objects, and ivory carvings indicate that sophisticated artists and artisans were at work in early Palestine.

Early Bronze Age Palestine (3300–2300) was a time of intense settlement and urbanization. One obvious change from the Chalcolithic pe-

Zev Radovan

4.10. Canaanite high place (Hebrew *bamah*) at Megiddo, built of small fieldstones, about twenty-six feet in diameter and four-and-a-half feet high. A staircase gives access to the top.

riod was that cities again had outer defensive walls. The walls were more massive than at any other time in Palestine's history, sometimes measuring more than twenty-five feet thick. What motivated this renewed need is not certain, but internal rivalries, Egyptian pressure, and waves of newcomers are some of the suggested explanations. Whatever the reason, these walls are often taken as indicators that the city-state form of government had begun. A large public building at Megiddo was perhaps the palace of one such city-state king.

Another obvious change can be seen in Early Bronze Age tombs, which exhibit a clear preference for multiple burials in caves or rock-cut tombs. One of six such tombs at Jericho contained remains of approximately 140 bodies, and another had over 400—numbers that imply the use of a tomb over several generations. The Jericho tombs measure approximately nine feet long and fourteen feet wide. When it was necessary to make room for a new burial, earlier interments were cleared from the center of the tomb, and the skulls were carefully placed around the edge of the tomb chamber.

Turning to religion, the earliest known Canaanite high place (Hebrew *bamah*) was discovered at Megiddo. At the time of excavation the area around this altar was found strewn with animal bones. Unfortunately the excavators did not analyze them to determine the types of animals used for sacrifice.

Toward the end of Early Bronze Age Palestine there seems to have been a thinning population and a general destruction and abandonment of towns. The following Early Bronze Age IV/Middle Bronze Age I (2300–2000; also more simply called Middle Bronze Age I) is currently undergoing reevaluation. The period had been characterized as a time of tribal upheaval with the diminished population nomadic. Recent excavation in Transjordan, however, has uncovered a few fortified centers. It also seems that there was some town life in Palestine proper.

In Early Bronze Age IV/Middle Bronze Age I, the tomb shapes

4.11. Toggle pin and dagger (without haft). The dagger is about nine-and-a-half inches long; its raised rib served as a blood runnel. The toggle pin was threaded through two parts of a garment, then a string through the hole in one end of the pin was wrapped around the pin, holding the garment closed.

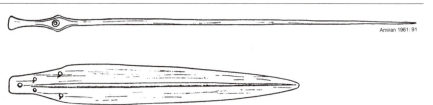

Amiran 1961: 91

changed, and instead of multiple burials, the tombs generally contained only one body. Pottery found with the skeletons includes several new shapes, and daggers and toggle pins were regularly placed with the bodies. These changes in the material culture can be traced to Syria, northwestern Mesopotamia, and perhaps even as far away as Armenia. In dispute is whether this shift in the material and social life of Palestine is due to invasion, waves of immigrants, or an internal phenomenon in which certain material changes are the result of a "cultural drift" from the north.

Scholars have been overdependent on "invasion" to explain change, but there are times in the ancient Near East when mass migrations and shifts of population appear to have actually occurred. Early Bronze Age IV/Middle Bronze Age I seems to have been one of those times, with the changes in Palestine partly the result of Amorites entering the area from the north. As the Amorites spread into new areas of the Near East, various political and economic repercussions followed. In Mesopotamia they contributed to the collapse of the Sumerian renaissance (the Ur III period). In Palestine, a period of instability intensified as the older order of city-states gave way to a less sedentary lifestyle. City-states returned, but for the three hundred years of Early Bronze Age IV/Middle Bronze Age I, such government was not characteristic of life in Palestine.

Palestine through the Eyes of Sinuhe

The Story of Sinuhe was one of the most popular pieces of literature in ancient Egypt, being copied and recopied for one thousand years. The story tells of Sinuhe, an Egyptian official, who felt so threatened by the death of the pharaoh that he thought it necessary to flee to Palestine for refuge. Whether the story is biographical or a historical novel, it nevertheless presents rich insights into ancient life in Palestine.[4]

Sinuhe's escape was filled with peril. He managed to sneak by an Egyptian border post, only to face the threat of death from thirst. Fortunately he was rescued by a group of Bedouin whose sheik had been to Egypt and recognized Sinuhe. Sinuhe was passed from group to group until he reached the vicinity of northern Palestine.[5] There he was

4. The story is set early in the Middle Bronze Age IIA (2000–1800/1750), before Abraham was in Palestine. However, the Palestine that Sinuhe presents was little changed by the time Abraham arrived there later in Middle Bronze Age IIA. For full English translations, see *ANET* 18–22 and Lichtheim 1973–80: 1.222–35.

5. Sinuhe refers to the land where he takes up residence as Upper Retenu and Yaa, terms that are understood as references to the Hill Country of northern Palestine and southern Syria.

befriended by a man named Ammi-enshi, who assured Sinuhe, "You will do well with me." As the story unfolded, Sinuhe did very well indeed (*ANE* 1:7–9; *ANET* 20):

> I spent many years, and my children grew up to be strong men, each man as the restrainer of his own tribe. The messenger who went north or who went south to the Residence City stopped over with me, for I used to make everybody stop over.[6] I gave water to the thirsty. I put him who had strayed back on the road. I rescued him who had been robbed. When the [people] became so bold as to oppose the rulers of foreign countries, I counseled their movements. This ruler of Retenu had me spend many years as commander of his army. Every foreign country against which I went forth, when I had made my attack on it, was driven away from its pasturage and its wells. I plundered its cattle, carried off its inhabitants, took away their food, and slew people of it by my strong arm, by my bow, by my movements, and by my successful plans. I found favor in his heart, he loved me, he recognized my valor, and he placed me at the head of his children, when he saw how my arms flourished.
>
> A mighty man of Retenu came, that he might challenge me in my own camp. He was a hero without his peer, and he had [beaten everyone]. He said that he would fight me, he intended to despoil me, and he planned to plunder my cattle, on the advice of his tribe. That prince discussed it with me, and I said: "I do not know him. Certainly I am no confederate of his, so that I might move freely in his encampment. Is it the case that I have ever opened his door or overthrown his fences? Rather, it is hostility because he sees me carrying out your commissions. I am really like a stray bull in the midst of another herd, and a bull of these cattle attacks him. . . ."
>
> During the night I strung my bow and shot my arrows, I gave free play to my dagger, and polished my weapons. When day broke, Retenu was come. It had whipped up its tribes and collected the countries of a good half of it. It had thought only of this fight. Then he came to me as I was waiting, for I had placed myself near him. Every heart burned for me; women and men groaned. Every heart was sick for me. They said: "Is there another strong man who could fight against him?" Then he took his shield, his battle-ax, and his armful of javelins. Now after I had let his weapons issue forth, I made his arrows pass by me uselessly, one close to another. He charged me, and I shot him, my arrow sticking in his neck. He cried out and fell on his nose. I felled him with his own battle-ax and raised my cry of victory over his back, while every[body] roared. I gave praise to Montu,[7] while his adherents were mourning for him. . . . Then I carried off his goods and plundered his cattle. What he had planned to do to me I did to him. I took what was in his tent and stripped his encampment. I became great thereby, I became extensive in my wealth, I became abundant in my cattle.

After many years in Palestine, Sinuhe received an invitation from the Egyptian court to return so that he could see the home in which he had been reared and, in time, be afforded a proper Egyptian burial. The

---

6. Messengers traveled between Byblos in the north and Egypt's capital, the "Residence City." For centuries, Egypt maintained a commercial outpost at Byblos (near modern-day Beirut) because of its interest in the cedars of Lebanon for shipbuilding and coffins.

7. Montu was the Egyptian god of war.

story relates the elaborate Egyptian funeral ritual and trappings, and then says of the simple burial in Palestine (*ANET* 21):

> It should not be that you should die in a foreign country. . . . You should not be placed in a sheepskin. . . . This is too long to be roaming the earth. Give heed to sickness, that you may return.

Sinuhe was overjoyed and responded positively to the pharaoh. Next, a delegation arrived to escort him back to Egypt (*ANE* 1:9; *ANET* 21):

> I was permitted to spend a day in Yaa handing over my property to my children, my eldest son being responsible for my tribe. My tribe and all my property were in his charge: my serfs, all my cattle, my fruit, and every pleasant tree of mine.

Sinuhe returned to Egypt and had an audience with the pharaoh and his court. The royal children were amused that the man they saw was really an Egyptian. He was called "Son of the North Wind" and dubbed a "bowman born in Egypt." Then Sinuhe was put into the house of a royal son:

> Clothing of royal linen, myrrh, and prime oil of the king and of the nobles whom he loves were in every room. Every butler was busy at his duties. Years were made to pass away from my body. I was plucked [i.e., shaven], and my hair was combed. A load of dirt was given to the desert, and my clothes to the Sand-Crossers. I was clad in fine linen and anointed with prime oil. I slept on a bed. I gave up the sand to them who are in it (*ANE* 1:11; *ANET* 22).

And so Sinuhe lived, and died, "happily ever after."

Certain insights can be drawn from the account of Sinuhe's years in Palestine. For example, Sinuhe's father-in-law, Ammi-enshi, has an Amorite name. Therefore, the Amorites had definitely arrived in Palestine by the time of the story. Further, Sinuhe is neither the first nor only Egyptian to be living in Palestine. One of the first things Ammi-enshi told Sinuhe was that he would "hear the speech of Egypt."

The story reflects a tribal society similar to that pictured in the Book of Genesis. In each account, one man controlled an extended family. When Sinuhe prepared to return to Egypt he turned his property over to his eldest son. The primacy of the eldest son is obvious in the patriarchal stories, most noticeably in the lives of Jacob and Esau.

The setting of the story was a time of tribal armies, serfs, and servants. The full story of Sinuhe reveals a Palestine in which there was crime, attack, plunder, murder, and captivity—conditions also found in the patriarchal narratives. The story of Sinuhe mentions bows and arrows, shields, battle-axes, javelins, and daggers. This array provides some idea of the weaponry available to Abraham's militia in Genesis 14. Like Abraham, Sinuhe never lost his outsider status. Abraham considered himself a sojourner in Palestine, and the people of Sodom called Lot an "alien." Later on, Jacob worried that the local populace would unite against him. The story of Sinuhe illustrates how threatening life could be for an outsider.

Institut Royal du Patrimoine Artistique-KIK, Brussels

4.12. Written on bowls or figurines of bound captives, "Execration texts" provide Egyptian insight into Palestine. The texts consist of short curses against peoples the Egyptians considered hostile and contain the earliest known mention of Ashkelon, Hazor, Jerusalem, and Shechem. Two sets of these magical texts, one shortly before the patriarchal period and the other early in that period, show an increase in the number of cities, which implies rising urbanization in Palestine.

Ancient inhabitants of Palestine were characteristically hospitable (Sinuhe was both the recipient and giver of kindness to those in need; similarly, Abraham's and Lot's hospitality to the messengers [Gen. 18:1–8; 19:1–11] was in keeping with the culture). The need to rescue someone was not unique to Abraham. Intermarriage was permitted (Sinuhe married a daughter of Ammi-enshi; Esau married foreign women). Religious tolerance was common (when Sinuhe proved himself in picked combat he gave thanks to an Egyptian god; the patriarchs openly practiced a religion that was different from that of the people around them). The story of Sinuhe describes some of the traffic that went in and out of Egypt and provides evidence that Egyptians and the Egyptian language were a part of patriarchal Palestine.

Abraham, Isaac, and Jacob—as well as Sinuhe—all lived in this land of pasture, farmland, orchards, and wells; this land plentiful in cattle, grain, fruit, and wine. The story of Sinuhe does not supply a complete picture of patriarchal Palestine and neither does the Bible. But the two complement each other and Sinuhe's story enlarges our view of the Palestine the patriarchs knew.

Abraham, Friend of God

Genesis 12 opens with the call and sevenfold promise to Abraham. These promises were not merely given and then forgotten. Rather, they are amplified and repeated several times in Scripture. Abraham heard them again (Gen. 17:4–8), and they were repeated to both Isaac (Gen. 26:2–4) and Jacob (Gen. 28:13–14). The promise was recalled in David's thanksgiving psalm (1 Chron. 16:16–19) and retained its importance even into New Testament times (Acts 3:25). In Galatians 3:8 Paul relates it to Gentiles as the spiritual descendants of Abraham.

Abraham's departure from Haran, in answer to God's call, marks the beginning of the patriarchal period. As he traveled in this early period of mobility, he was neither alone nor empty-handed. When Terah died, much of his wealth transferred to Abraham, so Abraham traveled with livestock as well as his extended family, herders, and others.

As Abraham entered Palestine, he stopped at Shechem where he built an altar, and God clarified the promise a bit more: he identified "the land which I will show you" as "this land." As Abraham moved further into the land, the Bible notes that it was already inhabited. His continuing southward migration, from Shechem to the area of Bethel and Ai and then toward the Negev (illustration 4.1), may have been an attempt to find an unclaimed area. Genesis 12 does not state how long it took Abraham to reach the Negev from Shechem, but several days would have been necessary since large groups could travel only about fifteen miles per day.

Palestine, as noted earlier, is dependent on rainfall to water its farmlands, but periodically the needed rain does not arrive. Such a shortfall seems to have occurred when Abraham had been in the Negev only a short time. The resultant famine conditions required some action, and Abraham decided to move his people into Egypt where the Nile's annual inundation made agricultural yields less capricious. The Egyptians guarded their borders, but they allowed people from Palestine to cross in times of need. For example, this thirteenth-century text, from a time when Egyptians were less inclined to act so kindly, illustrates the practice (*ANE* 1:183; *ANET* 259):

> Another communication to my lord . . . : We have finished letting the Bedouin tribes of Edom pass the Fortress of Merenptah . . .—life, prosperity, health!—which is in Tjeku, to the pools of Per-Atum . . . to keep them alive and to keep their cattle alive, through the great *ka* of Pharaoh—life, prosperity, health!—the good sun of every land.[8]

8. Tjeku is the eastern end of Goshen. Per-Atum is probably biblical Pithom. *Ka* can be translated "soul."

During Abraham's time Egypt was in its Middle Kingdom, a period of prosperity and well being. There was an emphasis on *maat* (truth) and the belief that each pharaoh was a physical child of the sun god. The Egyptians believed their country to be fully protected by their god-king, their "good shepherd." The self-confidence generated by this belief caused the Egyptians to feel benevolent toward those not fortunate enough to be Egyptians. These less fortunate people were, at times, accommodated in the largely undeveloped eastern part of Egypt's delta, the land of Goshen.

It is not necessary to infer that Abraham showed a lapse of faith by going to Egypt, but he did show such a lapse while there. Abraham's wife, Sarah, was also his half-sister, and Abraham regularly emphasized this relationship when he thought it to his advantage. Egypt was not the first place Abraham passed Sarah off as his sister rather than as his wife, nor was it the last. The practice began as soon as the two left Haran (Gen. 20:13). Technically Abraham was correct, but he intentionally misled other people. Although God never directly condemned Abraham for this policy, it is perhaps no accident that he got into serious trouble because of it.

Why did the pharaoh take a liking to Sarah? The Bible says that she was "fair," which could mean in contrast to the darker-skinned Egyptian women, or it could be a recognition that she had the idealized Egyptian complexion. It is also possible that pharaoh had no great interest in Sarah for herself and was only making a political move. Egypt was becoming more commercially interested in Canaan, and Abraham, with his entourage and livestock, would have appeared to be a wealthy man of Palestine. The Egyptian court might have concluded that friendship with Abraham would be mutually useful. In the ancient Near East, one way to cement friendship was to exchange women. According to such a plan Abraham would be expected to give his "sister" to pharaoh. In return, Hagar may have been pharaoh's gift to Abraham (Egyptian rulers never gave Egyptian princesses to foreigners). From an Egyptian's point of view Abraham should have felt honored by such an exchange. If this is a correct understanding of the episode, then Sarah's beauty, though a bonus, was not the main factor in the story.[9]

Abraham went to Egypt for help, but he took advantage of Egyptian hospitality by misleading the pharaoh. Abraham lied to a king who was much more concerned with *maat* than he was, and God had to intervene to get Abraham and Sarah out of the problem they had created for themselves. The plagues that struck pharaoh cannot be identified, but they were serious enough that he wanted them to end. Apparently someone was astute enough to link the problems with Abraham's presence. The pharaoh would have been justified to punish Abraham, but the plagues must have convinced him that some powerful "magic" surrounded Abraham. Therefore, escorting him out of the country seemed to be the safest course of action.

9. The Middle Kingdom pharaoh involved in this episode might have been Senusert III (for a brief summary of his reign see p. 141), but the linkage between this portion of biblical and Egyptian chronology is not yet sufficiently precise.

4.13. Portion of the Beni Hasan tomb painting that depicts people from Palestine entering Egypt. The men are wearing kilts or long garments that cover the chest and one shoulder. Their clothes are multicolored and fringed on the bottom, and they wear sandals on their feet. Each man is shown with a full head of hair, a short beard, but no mustache. The women also wear multicolored garments, but theirs are longer. Their footwear appears to be a type of slipper sock, and headbands decorate their long hair. The painting also depicts some weaponry: spear, bow and arrow, ax, and sword. Two of the men carry waterskins(?) on their backs, and another plays the lyre. The donkeys transport two objects, perhaps bellows, which would mean that these people worked with metal.

Within a few years of Abraham's visit to Egypt, an artist in that country completed a now-famous work (illustration 4.13). The Beni Hasan tomb painting includes a group of thirty-seven people from Palestine entering Egypt to sell eye paint. The picture is invaluable for providing insight about people in Palestine during the patriarchal period and for recreating patriarchal life.

When Abraham returned to Palestine from Egypt, his period of mobility ended. He had traveled extensively within the Near East—Ur, Haran, Palestine, Egypt—but such mobility was not exceptional. Centuries earlier, Mesopotamian kings boasted of washing their weapons in the Mediterranean, and during Abraham's time, the Assyrians maintained trade colonies in central Anatolia. Caravans linked the two areas for mutual benefit. Extensive travel was also made by private individuals and by groups such as Abraham's. A cuneiform tablet containing a rental contract written in Sippar (north of Babylon) stipulates that a wagon could not be driven to the Mediterranean coast. The wagon owner feared either damage or loss if the wagon was taken such a distance (Barton 1933: 355).

When Abraham reentered Palestine, he returned to the same area between Bethel and Ai where he had earlier pitched his tent. Others were living within walled cities, but Abraham, still a sojourner in the land, continued to use this more flexible housing style. Abraham spent only a few weeks at Gerar, then a few years between Bethel and Ai, and somewhat longer at Beersheba, but most of his life in Palestine centered in Hebron. Once back in Palestine, Abraham did not travel extensively (illustration 4.1 indicates how few miles there are between these places). Living in a tent does not necessarily mean a person is nomadic in lifestyle.[10]

10. See Gottwald 1978, who, unhappily, in the second half of his article shifts into a denial of an exodus from Egypt. The entire issue of *BA* 56/4 (1993) is devoted to "Nomadic Pastoralism: Past and Present." No occupation dating back to the patriarchal pe-

As the second millennium began, Mesopotamians had already been writing history and composing literature for several centuries. The Egyptians had long since declared their kings to be gods, and the famous pyramids of Egypt were more than five centuries old. Palestine had not been immune to developments in those countries, but some adjustments were still required on Abraham's part as he stepped into the world of Middle Bronze Age IIA Palestine (2000–1800/1750).[11] In order to fit "proper" Canaan style, Abraham would have had to adapt his dress, hairstyle, diet, and even some aspects of his social order. It is logical to assume that he adopted the material lifestyle of Palestine, but it may not have been easy.

Abraham and Lot

Lot drifts in and out of Abraham's life story. Like Abraham, Lot's early years were spent in Ur of the Chaldeans. He was the son of Haran, Abraham's younger brother, and thus Abraham's nephew. When Haran died, Abraham took responsibility for Lot, who shared Abraham's period of mobility from Ur to Haran, from there into Palestine, and then in and out of Egypt. Still, Lot was a silent participant in these events until the return from Egypt.

Both Abraham and Lot were rich in flocks and herds when they resettled near Bethel and Ai. It soon became clear that the area was unable to support all of their animals, and friction developed between their herders. Matters could understandably become tense in the dry season when grazing land became minimal. Their tension may have been compounded by the presence of Canaanite and Perrizite flocks in the same general area (Gen. 13:7). Abraham defused the problem between his and Lot's herders by allowing Lot to choose where he preferred to live. Abraham offered to go elsewhere (Gen. 13:8–9). As they stood in the Hill Country near Bethel and Ai, Abraham and Lot could see down into the Jordan Valley and the area around Jericho. Although it is near the Dead Sea, the south end of that valley is one of the lushest areas in all of Palestine. To a person interested in springs and vegetation it is a choice spot, and it was this area, "well watered . . . like the garden of the Lord" (Gen. 13:10) that Lot chose.

Most commentators conclude that Lot's choice was selfish, but it should be noted that until this moment neither man had been drawn to the Jordan Valley. The valley becomes very hot and humid during the summer; therefore, it is not as desirable year-round as is the Hill Country. Lot's choice could as easily be understood as selfless; he would

riod has been found at the normally accepted site of Beersheba. It would seem, therefore, that the patriarchal city was located at a place in the vicinity not yet identified.

11. A "terminological chaos" presently exists due to "New Archaeology" using established terms for different materials and times. It is especially confusing when some scholars use Middle Bronze Age I to designate the 2000–1800/1750 time range while others use it to refer to the 2300–2000 time frame. I follow the time sequencing found in A. Mazar 1990, a book that will guide the interested reader through the difficulties. See also illustration 1.11, where Mazar's terms and date ranges are given.

be the one to adjust to a new area, allowing Abraham to stay where he was already comfortable.

Lot moved down into the Jordan Valley and subsequently settled in the city of Sodom, usually thought to have been located in what is now the south end of the Dead Sea. Sodom and other nearby cities were later attacked by a coalition of Mesopotamian kings (Gen. 14). Numerous attempts have been made to equate the Mesopotamians named with known extrabiblical rulers, but so far all attempts have failed. When this attack took place, Mesopotamia was still politically fragmented, and so little is known about the period that it is unlikely the chapter will ever be linked to specific extrabiblical history.[12]

Genesis 14:2–4 relates that four kings served the Mesopotamian kings twelve years and then rebelled. The Bible does not explain the nature of their "serving," but archaeology provides a probable answer. The south end of the Dead Sea was a chief source for copper, which was then the primary metal for agricultural and other tools, as well as for weapons of war. Since Mesopotamia had almost no metal ores, it had to obtain this precious metal from the outside, and the supply of copper may have been the service provided by the four kings. The desire to be strong commercially and militarily would have been sufficient motivation to lead the Mesopotamian kings to invade Palestine if their supply was cut off due to rebellion. The Mesopotamian kings came south along the east side of the Jordan River, following the major route that was later called the "King's Highway." When they invaded Palestine they destroyed a few areas, defeated the rebellious kings, and looted their cities. Although the Bible does not say so, the Mesopotamian kings probably exacted a promise of renewed copper supplies before turning homeward.

By the time of this invasion Abraham had relocated to Hebron. When he learned that Lot had been captured, Abraham was quickly off to the rescue and was able to intercept the raiding party at Dan, in northern Palestine. Lot was rescued and the enemies were chased from Palestine.

The account in Genesis 14 shows that Abraham was powerful. The Hebrew word translated "trained" (v. 14) is a technical term implying that the 318 men he called out were at least militia. That Abraham was able to summon such men from his own camp to assist in the rescue of Lot also illustrates his wealth.

Extrabiblically it is known that patriarchal Palestine was a prosperous, but precarious place to live. Archaeologists find that much time was expended fortifying cities and that the cities were repeatedly destroyed and rebuilt. This precarious nature of life in patriarchal Palestine is reflected in the biblical account of Lot's rescue. Later evidence of the same uncertainty is seen when Esau approached Jacob with four hundred men. Subsequently Esau offered to leave some of his men with Jacob. Still later, Jacob was afraid that his men were "few in number" in case there was a coalition against him. So even the Promised Land

12. The occasional suggestion that Amraphel (Gen. 14:1) should be identified as the lawgiver Hammurapi is philologically weak. Kitchen 1995b: 56–57 finds that the geopolitical conditions in Gen. 14 match only the early second millennium, which supports the biblical chronology.

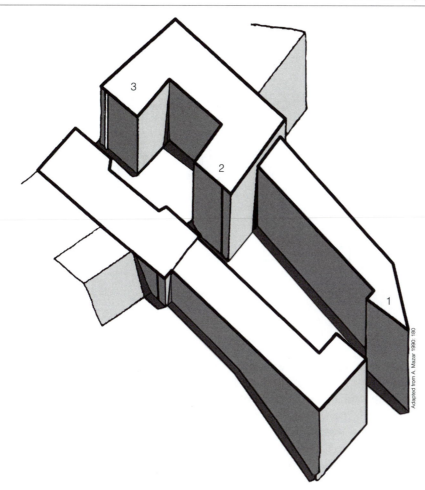

4.14. Middle Bronze Age IIA city gate at Acre. The gateway was the weakest point in a city's defense, and over the centuries many different plans were devised to protect it. During Middle Bronze Age IIA, the gate design favored by city planners had narrow, three-piered passageways (numbered), which forced an attacking force to break through that many barred doors to gain access into the city. Some gate systems even featured a "bent-axis" approach so that an attacking enemy could not make a straight run at the doorway. City life centered around the gate area, and benches were sometimes built into it to facilitate socialization, staying abreast of news and gossip, and deciding legal matters. Generally, an open area just inside the gate provided space for the city market.

Adapted from A. Mazar 1990: 180

had its problems, and the patriarchal period was a time of both wealth and worry.

Sometime later Abraham learned that Lot was again in danger; God was planning the destruction of Sodom (Gen. 18:16–33). God sent his messengers to personally assess the evil of the city, and in Genesis 19:1 they entered Sodom through its gate, which implies that Sodom was fortified. In light of Sodom's earlier problems (Gen. 14) and the general insecurity of the times, such protection seems wise.

The Genesis messengers approached Sodom in the evening before the city gates had been closed. Lot was apparently sitting alone in the gateway as they arrived, and he bowed to them in the customary greeting. When he learned they planned to spend the night in Sodom's market area, a natural expectation for travelers, Lot made the normal, hospitable offer of that era: shelter in his home.[13]

13. Lot is treated harshly by commentators, but most of the condemnation is based on inference rather than fact. For example, since Lot was found sitting in the gate it has been concluded that he must have become an official of the evil city, perhaps even its mayor! But Lot's being in the gateway, the social and legal center of a city in Palestine, implies nothing about his official status. The New Testament provides the only value judgment of the man; 2 Peter 2:7–8 thrice makes the point that Lot was a "righteous man."

4.15. Ground plan of a typical courtyard house (over forty feet across the front), excavated at Tell Beit Mirsim in the south of Palestine. When it collapsed, the ceiling debris separated the ground-floor possessions from what had been on the second floor, a division that allowed archaeologists to see that ground-floor rooms were usually storage and work areas, while the upper floor was used for leisure activity and sleeping. In the upstairs debris, archaeologists found combs, inlaid ivory boxes, and a game board.

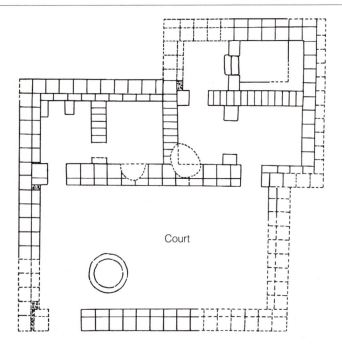

Court

Lot's home was almost surely of the "courtyard house" type. This style of housing was developed in Palestine during the patriarchal period (illustration 4.15 presents a common ground plan). The houses could be large or small, depending on the wealth of the owner, were constructed of sun-dried mud bricks generally set on a stone foundation, and featured a walled court with rooms on one or more sides. The walls and interior floors were plastered, and the courtyard was usually cobbled so that it would stay functional during the rainy season. Provision was made for storing water, ovens were placed out in the courtyard as well as inside the house proper, and a staircase gave access to the upper floor.

There is still uncertainty over the nature of Sodom and Gomorrah's destruction. Genesis 19:24 implies that the destruction came down from heaven, but some scholars infer from Genesis 19:21, 29 that an earthquake destroyed the cities. Volcanic action is also theorized, but geologists counter that active volcanoes had long since ceased in that part of the Near East. Sodom and Gomorrah have attracted a number of eccentric theories. For instance, a Russian scientist concluded that the cities were destroyed because a spacecraft landed nearby. He conjectured that the force of the subsequent liftoff devastated the cities. Erich von Daniken has a variation of this theory in his book *Chariots of the Gods?* For him the story originated when ancient astronauts decided to destroy some fissionable material and wipe out people they disliked by a nuclear explosion! The Bible presents the destruction as a punishment and as a miracle from God. Perhaps the story should be left at that.

Some improbable sightings of the cities have also been made. One was announced by a scuba diver who snorkeled north of the Dead Sea's Lisan Peninsula. His reported findings of the cities have subsequently

Adapted from Kenyon 1985: 174

4.16. Tombs at Jericho provide insight into house furnishings during the patriarchal period. Artist's reconstruction shows a bed, stool, and three-legged table (which is more stable on an uneven surface than one with four legs).

been identified by others as the remains of potash works. A more recent theory is that the cities are not under the south end of the Dead Sea as generally assumed, but rather some miles further to the south. The Bible does not demand that Sodom and Gomorrah be under the Dead Sea, but this recent suggestion requires the life of Abraham to be dated centuries earlier in order to correlate his life with the destruction of these proposed identifications. The Bible does not have enough flexibility in its chronology to accommodate such a theory. Finally, there is a revived attempt to find Sodom and Gomorrah northeast of the Dead Sea. This theory also demands a radical redating of Abraham (Shanks 1980a and Van Hattem 1981).

Additional Reading

Bar-Yosef, Ofer. "Pre-Pottery Neolithic Sites in Southern Sinai." *BA* 45 (1982): 9–12.

Cohen, Rudolph. "The Mysterious MB I People." *BAR* 9/4 (1983): 16–29.

Hess, Richard, P. E. Satterthwaite, and Gordon Wenham (eds.). *He Swore an Oath: Exploring Biblical Themes from Genesis 12–50.* Cambridge: Tyndale House, 1993. Reprinted Grand Rapids: Baker, 1994.

Levy, Thomas F. "The Chalcolithic Period." *BA* 49 (1986): 82–108.

———. "How Ancient Man First Utilized Rivers in the Desert." *BAR* 16/6 (1990): 20–31.

Mazar, Benjamin. "The Middle Bronze Age in Palestine." *IEJ* 18 (1968): 65–97.

Nakhai, Beth Alpert. "What's a Bamah? How Sacred Space Functioned in Ancient Israel." *BAR* 20/3 (1994): 18–29, 77–78.

Perlman, Isador, and Joseph Yellin. "The Provenance of Obsidian from Neolithic Sites in Israel." *IEJ* 30 (1980): 83–88.

Richard, Suzanne. "The Early Bronze Age." *BA* 50 (1987): 22–43.

Shea, William H. "Artistic Balance among the Beni Hasan Asiatics." *BA* 44 (1981): 219–28.

Wright, Mary. "Contacts between Egypt and Syro-Palestine during the Protodynastic Period." *BA* 48 (1985): 240–53.

5

Patriarchal Palestine

Abraham, Isaac, Jacob, and Esau

The tablet of adoption belonging to Nashwi, the son of Ar-shenni: he adopted Wullu, the son of Puhi-shenni. As long as Nashwi is alive, Wullu shall provide food and clothing; when Nashwi dies, Wullu shall become the heir. If Nashwi has a son of his own, he shall divide the estate equally with Wullu, but the son of Nashwi shall take the gods of Nashwi. However, if Nashwi does not have a son of his own, then Wullu shall take the gods of Nashwi. Furthermore, he gave his daughter Nuhuya in marriage to Wullu, and if Wullu takes another wife he shall forfeit the lands and buildings of Nashwi. Whoever defaults shall make compensation with one mina of silver and one mina of gold.

—Nuzi sale-adoption tablet

God's Covenant with Abraham

Genesis 15 opens as God tells Abraham his "reward shall be very great." But Abraham was concerned about the nature of this reward since he had no children. In the United States, childbearing is generally optional, and some couples choose childlessness. From such a cultural perspective it is perhaps difficult to identify with the ancient

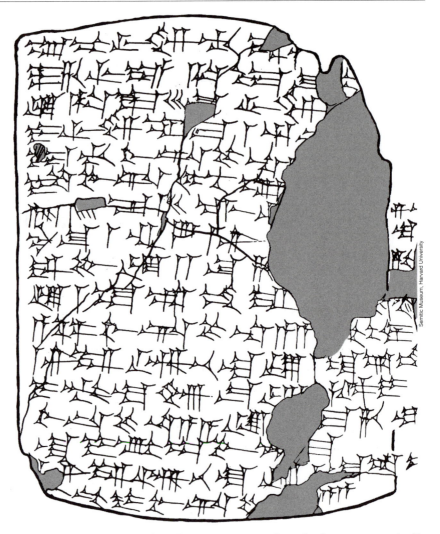

5.1. Transcription of a cuneiform tablet from Nuzi. Since cuneiform is sometimes hard to see, hand copies are normally made for study. The broken and incomplete condition of the tablet is shown, and the signs to the right indicate that the writing continued onto the side of the tablet. This tablet is a will in which Hupitaya gave his wife full authority over her sons and divided the inheritance so that the eldest son received a double share.

Near East where large families were normal and often economically necessary to the agriculturally based society. Because Sarah continued to be barren, Abraham thought that one of his servants (Eliezer) would have to carry on his family name and wealth. There is a hint of anguish and frustration when Abraham expresses this expectation to God in Genesis 15:2–3, but the full implication of what Abraham is saying long eluded commentators. When this part of Abraham's life was written down, the situation was considered too obvious to need further comment, but some of the original clarity faded with time. Then archaeologists working at the northeastern Mesopotamian city of Nuzi (see illustration 3.4 for location), found thousands of cuneiform tablets, and some of the ancient meaning was regained.[1]

A son was needed to carry on the family name—as important a consideration then as was the distribution of the family wealth. The Nuzi

1. Nuzi was excavated between 1925 and 1931. The clay tablets date to the fifteenth century, but, because of the static condition of ancient Near Eastern culture, they still closely reflect living conditions for many years on either side of their date of composition. See C. Gordon 1940.

texts reveal that a couple who had no son would adopt one. This adopted son was obligated to serve his parents as long as they lived and then bury and mourn for them when they died. In exchange for this "old-age insurance," the adopted son was made the heir. This adopted person could be anyone. In Abraham's case, as in other ancient records, it was a servant.

When God reminded Abraham that he was in the land of the promise, Abraham asked God how he might know that he would possess it. Abraham's desire for assurance is understandable because much time had passed since he left Haran. Graciously God gave Abraham a sign by participating in a covenant ceremony with him. Two basic types of covenants have been identified. The first is a parity covenant between equals (an example is found in Gen. 31 between Jacob and Laban). But in Genesis 15 the covenant is of the suzerain-vassal (king-subject) type—the form always used in the Bible for covenants between God (the suzerain) and people (the vassal). In the ceremony it was necessary to cut an animal in half and shed its blood (this action is clearer in the original language: the Hebrew verb for making a covenant is literally "to cut" a covenant). The pieces of the animals would be placed in two rows with an aisle between. The parties to the covenant walked between the rows while taking an oath invoking similar dismemberment on each other should they not keep their part of the covenant. In Genesis 15, God assumed the role of the suzerain. The specific acting out of this ceremony differs, however, from all other known examples in that God alone walked between the rows of animal pieces and took the oath only on himself.

Abraham, reassured about the covenant, knew he was mistaken to think that Eliezer had a role in God's plan. Now knowing that he would have a son, Abraham accepted Sarah's suggestion that he should father a child by one of her maids (Gen. 16:2). From the Nuzi tablets it is clear that Sarah had proposed an accepted option for that day. Surrogate mothers were permissible and the husband usually made his own choice, but in some instances an engaged girl might have to sign a prenuptial agreement promising to provide a substitute wife should she herself not have children. For example: "If Gilimninu (the bride) will not bear children, Gilimninu shall take a woman of N/Lullu-land (whence the choicest slaves were obtained) for Shennima (the bridegroom)" (C. Gordon 1940: 3).[2]

Abraham had probably given Hagar to Sarah after their troubled visit to Egypt. Now Sarah gave her to Abraham's embrace, and Hagar became pregnant. Commentators sometimes criticize Abraham and Sarah for this course of action, but Sarah had been barren for decades, and up to that point they had not yet been told that she would bear the promised son. They may have thought God wanted them to show a little initiative. The surrogate option was employed only after God made it clear that Eliezer was not the heir to the promise.

Genesis 17:15–16 finally specifies Sarah's role in the covenant promise: she would be the mother of nations and kings. Abraham laughed at this news, and his reaction cannot be understood as a laugh of joy. Gen-

---

2. Gordon's comments are in parentheses.

esis 17:17–18 makes it quite clear that Abraham doubted God's promise concerning Sarah. He thought both he and Sarah were too old to become parents. Although Abraham knew Eliezer was not the means by which the covenant would be fulfilled, he thought it would be through Ishmael. But God affirmed that Sarah would be the biological mother and that she would have a son whom Abraham should name Isaac, which means "he laughs." Each time Abraham called his son's name or saw him, he would be reminded that he had doubted God's ability.

Sarah did not learn of her predicted childbearing until she overheard Abraham's conversation with the messengers to Sodom (Gen. 18:10). The time sequence in Genesis 17–18 is not altogether clear, but perhaps Abraham had not had time to tell Sarah the momentous news. Whatever the reason, her reaction was similar to her husband's. Nevertheless, Isaac was born within a year. Genesis 21:8 mentions a feast to celebrate his weaning. Since wet nurses could be hired for as long as three years, this party was perhaps held when Isaac was already a toddler. The festivities were spoiled for Sarah when she found teenage Ishmael making fun of her little boy. Sarah angrily demanded that Abraham send Hagar and Ishmael away once and for all. Isaac's birth had already removed Ishmael from the covenant promise and from any guarantee of inheritance, but this was not enough for Sarah. She wanted the other woman and her son out of her sight and out of her life. Sarah's attitude is understandable, but her demands were diametrically opposed to ancient Near Eastern convention, which protected the old family against this natural jealousy. The same prenuptial contract quoted above contains a restraining phrase: "Gilimninu shall not send the (handmaid's) offspring away" (C. Gordon 1940: 3). God's intervention convinced Abraham to comply with Sarah's demands; Hagar and Ishmael were sent away, with God's promise that he would care for them.[3]

Several years later God tested Abraham, instructing him to sacrifice Isaac, now a teenager. Abraham did not know that God had no intention of letting the act be carried out. He did know that the Canaanites around him believed their gods sometimes required such sacrifice, and he may have been shocked that the true God was now asking for a similar offering. Abraham's emotional state is not recorded; it is not even stated whether he confided in Sarah. The Bible simply notes that Abraham took his son, two other young men, wood, and fire and traveled to the place God had specified. Possibly the men were brought along to provide protection on the trip and, if the worst happened, for companionship on the way home. Glowing pieces of charcoal or other embers would have been carried in small pottery containers and carefully nursed along until a fire was needed.

When they had reached their destination, Abraham and Isaac built an altar of rough fieldstones. Then Abraham bound his son, placed him atop the altar, and raised his knife. By that motion Abraham passed the test of obedience, and God stopped him from slaying Isaac. A ram appeared as a substitute for Isaac (see Pope 1986). How docilely Isaac let himself be tied and put atop the altar, whether the intervention by God

---

3. Muhammad claimed that all Arabs were descended from Ishmael, and Arabs still believe that today.

was audible to Isaac, and the matter of his sense of relief when the ram was substituted are left to the imagination.

Death and Burial of Sarah

Genesis 23 tells of Sarah's death and burial. Several options existed for burial of the dead in the early second millennium. Whichever type of tomb was chosen, the burial place became a kind of family vault. Each time a member of the family died, the tomb was reopened and another interment made. Remains of as many as twenty bodies have been found in such Middle Bronze Age II family tombs. In keeping with this custom, Sarah eventually shared her tomb with at least five other family members (Gen. 25:9–10; 49:29–32; 50:13).

Abraham was rich in gold, silver, and livestock, but he had no land. So when Sarah died, he went to the legal center of Hebron—its gateway—to petition for a grave site. Abraham specifically asked for the cave at the end of a field belonging to a man named Ephron. Since Ephron was among the men sitting in the city gate, the negotiations began immediately. Abraham asked for the cave of Machpelah and stated his willingness to pay full price. Ephron offered to give Abraham both the cave and its adjoining field. Ephron seems "all heart," but just as there was a code for hospitality, so too there was a code for bargaining. Perhaps Abraham was not expected to take Ephron's seeming generosity literally. In any event, Abraham declined the offer and again asked to pay full price. Commentators are divided over Ephron's response (Gen. 23:15); was he reemphasizing his generosity or was he merely starting the bargaining process? In any case, Abraham made no counteroffer, and true to his word he paid the price mentioned by Ephron. The transfer of property was made in the presence of witnesses, and the conditions of sale were carefully specified. Abraham left the gateway as owner of the cave, its adjoining field, and the trees on the land.

The agreed upon price was four hundred shekels of silver. Scales would have been borrowed from the market area near the gate, and the silver weighed out in sight of everyone. Four hundred shekels of silver would have weighed approximately ten pounds, but it is not hard to vi-

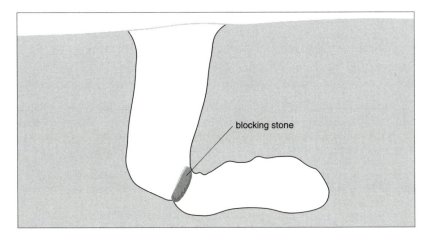

blocking stone

5.2. Section through a typical Middle Bronze Age II shaft tomb. The most common type of tomb consisted of a vertical shaft nine or ten feet deep, with a chamber approximately three feet high carved to one side. After a body was placed in the chamber, the opening from the shaft was sealed by a blocking stone, and the shaft was filled until time to inter the next family member. Other burial options included reusing tombs from earlier periods or, as in Abraham's case, using natural caves.

5.3. In 1980 the excavators of biblical Dan uncovered a portion of the city's defense system dating to the end of Middle Bronze Age IIA or the beginning of Middle Bronze Age IIB (i.e., about midpoint in the patriarchal period). A defensive wall rose more than sixty feet above the surrounding plain, and steps led from the plain up to the gate, which was flanked by projecting towers. The "basket arch" gateway (nearly twelve feet high and seventeen feet wide) is the only fully preserved gateway in Palestine dating to Old Testament times. When excavated, traces of white plaster still adhered to the mud bricks of the gate system. When the gate passageway was cleared it was found to contain three sets of piers. On the inside of the gateway, another set of stairs leads down to a street. Some defense systems found in Palestine would have required hundreds of thousands of hours to construct—another indication that the prosperity of the patriarchal period was coupled with a need for security.

sualize Abraham carrying that much weight around since he intended to buy some real estate.[4]

In the 1950s it was proposed that a Hittite law gave new insight into the bargaining process between Abraham and Ephron: "If anyone buys all the fields of a craftsman, they shall ask the king, and the buyer shall render those services which the king orders. If there remain fields in the hands of the man from whom he buys, the buyer shall not render the services" (*ANET* 191).[5] In this Hittite law, the obligation to perform "services" (Hittite *ilku*) was conferred on the buyer only when all the seller's property was passed to a new owner. Abraham asked for the cave, but Ephron was willing to sell both the cave and its adjoining field. Applying this law, the issue was over who would be responsible for the *ilku*. By deeding the field and the cave to Abraham, Ephron freed himself from this service.

Although this interpretation of Genesis 23 quickly found some acceptance, the applicability of the law to Abraham is now in question. First, exactly what the *ilku* entailed is not known, and therefore it is uncertain whether a person would try to evade it. A more serious objection is that this law comes from Hittite codes dating several centuries after Abraham. Scholars question whether Hittites in patriarchal Palestine would have been under the same legal system. Further, since there is no extrabiblical evidence of Hittite influence extending south

4. There were different shekel weights depending on whether common or royal weights were used. There were also "heavy" and "light" standards for both the common and royal weights. This transaction is the earliest biblical reference to weights and balances, which were a part of daily life throughout Old Testament times, continuing in use even after the introduction of coinage in the days of Ezra and Nehemiah. The Bible contains numerous references to honesty in the matter of weights and balances: a balance should be just (Lev. 19:36; Prov. 16:11), and false balances and weights are condemned (Prov. 11:1; 20:23).

5. For the most recent translation of Hittite laws, see Hoffner 1995.

5.4. To use a simple beam-and-balance scale, an object of known weight was placed in one pan and the substance being weighed in the other. The stone weights were often rounded or lozenge-shaped, but more elaborate shapes have also been found. Excavated examples sometimes have their weight inscribed on them (here clockwise from lower right: pim, netseph, one, two, four, eight, and twenty-four shekels), thus allowing archaeologists to determine that an ancient shekel weighed roughly four-tenths of an ounce.

of Syria, perhaps Ephron was really a Hethite, a Canaanite subgroup.[6] If Ephron was indeed a Hethite, this insight from the Hittite code is negated. Sometimes archaeological "illumination" is too quickly accepted.

The Marriage of Isaac and the Close of Abraham's Life

After Sarah's death Abraham's focus turned to a suitable marriage for Isaac. Marriages were often contracted between neighboring clans in order to form a useful alliance, but Abraham did not want his son to marry a local girl. He wanted Isaac to marry a relative from back home in Mesopotamia. Although such matchmaking is unusual in the United States, it is still normal practice in some other parts of the world. Such cultures teach that loving whom you marry, rather than the reverse, results in a stronger relationship.

Abraham's oldest servant, the one "who had charge of all that [Abraham] owned" (Gen. 24:2), was given the responsibility of finding a wife for Isaac. If this servant was Eliezer, "his loyalty is all the finer in serving the heir who has displaced him" (Kidner 1967: 146). Abraham solemnly explained to the servant what he must do. The first step was to load ten camels with "a variety of good things." These gifts, the bride-price, were transported north to the city of Nahor in Aram-Naharaim,

6. "Hittite" and "Hethite" are written identically in consonantal Hebrew. The New International Version offers Hethite as an alternate reading in Gen. 23, a reading also preferred by Hoffner 1994: 152–53. Two issues of *BA*, 52/2–3 (1989) and 58/2 (1995), are devoted to articles dealing with the current state of Hittite studies. For the traditional burial place, see N. Miller 1985.

a designation for northwestern Mesopotamia (Gen. 24:10).[7] There is no mention of the number of men accompanying the servant for protection and to help guide the camels, but even a small caravan would have needed about a month to reach its destination from southern Palestine.[8] The bride-to-be, Rebekah, was quickly found, and she and her family immediately agreed to the marriage proposal and she was on her way south. The biblical record probably omits some events, for suddenly Isaac and Rebekah are married.

In Genesis 25, Abraham's life is nearly at an end. Verse 1 of this chapter states that Abraham took another wife, but the Hebrew text is not clear whether he married Keturah while Sarah was still alive or after her death (the word translated "wife" in Gen. 25:1 can also be translated "woman"). First Chronicles 1:32 refers to Keturah as Abraham's concubine, so she might be included in the concubines mentioned in Genesis 25:6. It is possible, however, that Abraham had a plural marriage, and that Sarah had found the ability to share her husband with another woman.[9]

According to Genesis 25:6, Abraham gave gifts to the sons of his concubines and sent them east of the Jordan. Therefore Abraham was married to Keturah long enough for their sons to reach adulthood before Abraham died. These sons departed, and Isaac remained to inherit his father's wealth and promise. Then, at Abraham's death, there is the cryptic notice that Isaac and Ishmael reunited to bury their father. Abraham's remains were placed with Sarah's in the cave of Machpelah at Hebron.

Isaac

The Bible presents only snippets of Isaac's life. As a toddler he became the focus of a dispute that ended with the expulsion of Hagar and Ishmael from the extended family. The next mention of Isaac occurs when, as a teenager, he was a participant in the test of Abraham's faith. And when he was an adult, his father sent a servant to Mesopotamia to find him a bride.

A comparison of Genesis 25:20 with 25:26 reveals that Isaac and Rebekah were childless for the first twenty years of their marriage. This condition must have put as much strain on their relationship as Abraham and Sarah had experienced earlier. Isaac had to be aware of the covenant promise that Abraham's descendants would be as numerous as the sands of the seashore, and he was probably sensitive to the fact that the descendants so far could still be counted on one finger. Perhaps Abraham counseled Isaac from the strength of his own experiences, because Isaac, unlike his father, did not try to help God. Instead, Isaac

7. They went either to a city named Nahor or to the city where Nahor lived.

8. The mention of camels in connection with the patriarchs is often labeled anachronistic, but Ripinsky 1983 and 1985 has assembled evidence for the use of camels well before patriarchal times. Köhler-Rollefson 1993 attempts to explain this evidence away.

9. Compare the different conclusions reached in two editions of the same commentary: Kevan 1956: 95 and G. Wenham 1994: 77.

prayed to God "on behalf of his wife" (Gen. 25:21), and Rebekah was finally "cured" of her barrenness, and doubly so as the story unfolds.

God revealed to Rebekah that she would be the mother of twin boys and what their future relationship would be. In light of later events, it would be helpful to know whether Rebekah ever shared this knowledge with her husband. The text notes the birth of Esau and Jacob and then ignores them until suddenly they reappear as grown men with very different lifestyles. Genesis 25:29–34 relates the well-known story in which Esau exchanged his birthright for a meal. Every male child was entitled to a share of his father's estate, but the birthright (additional privileges) was customarily given to the eldest son, who then became the patriarch after his father's death.

It seems unthinkable that Esau would exchange such status for a meal. Could Jacob have been teasing his brother when he offered the food in exchange for the birthright? Could Esau's response that he was about to die be similar to the modern cliché, "I'm so hungry I could eat a horse"? When Jacob pressed his conditions for the food, Esau agreed and in so doing "despised his birthright," but later on he considered murder to reclaim the birthright. Perhaps Esau thought Jacob's demands were ridiculous and that no one would believe he had ever sworn to such a transfer. Perhaps Jacob also considered the whole episode absurd; he apparently never used the event to justify his position. The following excerpt from a Nuzi tablet supplies one insight into this story:

> On the day they divide the grove (that lies) on the road of the town of Lumti . . . , Tupkitilla shall give it to Kurpazah as his inheritance share. And Kurpazah has taken three sheep to Tupkitilla in exchange for his inheritance share (C. Gordon 1940: 5).

In this text an orchard is transferred for three sheep, an exchange that appears to be as out of balance as the episode between Jacob and Esau. The circumstances leading to the Nuzi text are unknown, but the text does show that Jacob's request was at least legal. An inheritance could be transferred to another person, however unequal such a transfer might seem.

Genesis 26 follows the birthright episode and states that famine came on the land. In patriarchal times rainfall was essential to the farmland and pastureland of Palestine (even today, with Israel's dams, deep wells, and pipelines, rainfall continues to be part of a delicate balance). When Abraham experienced the results of too little rainfall, he went to Egypt for relief. Although Egypt was still considered a place of refuge in Isaac's day, God told him to stay in Palestine. Earlier, Abraham had insisted that Isaac stay in Palestine while he sent a messenger to Mesopotamia to select a wife for him. Apparently, God wanted the heir of the covenant to remain in the Promised Land.[10]

Isaac stayed in Palestine and moved to the same city, Gerar, that his father had visited years earlier. As in Abraham's day, the city's king was

10. As the episode continues, the Bible states that Isaac stayed in Gerar a long time (Gen. 26:8). However, the inner chronology shows he stayed there less than a year. That time span, plus the good harvest Isaac experienced, shows the famine to be of short duration. God would have known that a migration to Egypt would be unnecessary.

called Abimelech. Since this name meant "My father is king," it would seem that it was either a title or a name that was passed on within the royalty at Gerar. Like Abraham, Isaac feared for his life in this city because of his beautiful wife, and so he also used the same "she's my sister" ploy, but Isaac was telling a whole lie. There was no half-sister relationship as in Abraham's case.

Abimelech's palace was likely near the city gate. Its second-story rooms would have had large windows rather than the small near-ceiling air vents used downstairs. One day Abimelech looked out a window, probably into the courtyard of the house where Isaac and Rebekah were staying (a guest house could be placed near the city gate). A rare, not fully understood Hebrew word characterizes the specific endearment the king saw taking place between Isaac and Rebekah (Gen. 26:8), and Abimelech realized the two were not brother and sister. A heated conversation followed between Abimelech and Isaac, but oddly the king did not ask him to leave until Isaac's wealth and agricultural success caused jealousy within the city.

Isaac moved to a nearby valley, where he reopened wells originally dug in Abraham's day. Residents of Gerar claimed ownership of the water from those wells, until Isaac finally relocated at Beersheba. Surprisingly, Abimelech approached Isaac at Beersheba, asking to draft a non-aggression pact with him. Abimelech's people had harassed Isaac, but they had also come to recognize that God's power was evidenced in his life. They feared that power in case Isaac should ever decide to attack them. Isaac complied with Abimelech's request, a feast was held, and oaths were exchanged.[11]

The Blessing of Jacob

Only two chapters after the record of Abraham's death, Isaac is said to be old and enfeebled. Apparently thinking that his life was nearly over, he made plans to bless Esau. Rebekah overheard the planning and immediately began preparations so that her favorite son, Jacob, would receive the blessing. Jacob raised several objections to his mother's plan but, sadly, failed to protest that her scheme was dishonest. It is unclear from the Genesis account whether Rebekah was acting out of deceit or if she was trying to help God. A proper understanding of Rebekah's motivation hinges somewhat on whether she told Isaac about the prophecy given her during her pregnancy (Gen. 25:22–23). What happened could be due to lack of communication between the parents, or it could mean that Isaac's preference for Esau left him unwilling to accept God's plan.

Rebekah camouflaged Jacob and sent him to his father with a hastily

11. On the day of the meeting with Abimelech, Isaac's men brought news that the well they had been digging yielded water. The sense of rejoicing in their report is easily missed since water is often taken for granted today in a way that was seldom possible in Old Testament times. Despite Matthews's assumption that Abraham's and Isaac's experiences at Gerar are separate redactions of a single episode, his 1986 article is useful for its insights into the interplay between herding and agricultural groups.

prepared meal. Isaac's eyes could no longer distinguish people, but he did realize it was rather soon for Esau to have finished hunting and preparing his catch. Isaac's hearing was still sufficiently sharp, but his senses of smell, touch, and taste betrayed him. Rebekah knew her husband well. It is understandable that a person's clothing could retain distinctive aromas, but how a kidskin could successfully imitate a hairy human body is less clear. The answer seems to lie in the aging process's impairment of the senses.

A careful reading of Genesis 27 shows that Jacob lied to his father four times before the smell of Esau's clothing finally convinced Isaac to convey the blessing. Understandably, Esau was incensed when he discovered what his brother had done. Isaac was equally agitated, but even though he had been duped into giving the blessing to the "wrong" son, he could not take it back. God was considered a witness in the blessing. Therefore, Isaac would not even consider changing what he had done.[12]

Esau consoled himself with the thought that he would kill Jacob as soon as his father died. Perhaps Esau vocalized his plans, because Rebekah learned of his intentions and feared she would lose Jacob. Realizing that she had to get Jacob away for "a few days" until Esau calmed down, Rebekah convinced Isaac that it was time for Jacob to go north and find a wife from among their relatives. While reasoning with her husband, Rebekah mentioned her displeasure over the two local women Esau had already married (Esau later tried to win back his mother's favor by marrying a daughter of Ishmael). This disclosure suggests that Isaac was unwise to favor Esau as the one to continue the covenant promise. It also provided further reason for Jacob to seek a wife from among his relatives.

Jacob Seeks a Wife

Isaac sent Jacob from Beersheba with a blessing and a charge that he find a wife from among the daughters of Rebekah's brother Laban. One night, while Jacob was on his way northward, he had a dream in which a stairway stretched from earth to heaven and angels were going up and down the staircase.[13] One significance of the dream is that Jacob personally heard the covenant promise for the first time. Previously God had said that Abraham's descendants would be as the stars in number. To Abraham, looking into the skies, that would have amounted to thousands. Later Abraham was told that they would be as the sands on the shore—a larger amount, but still a theoretically limited number. Now, to Jacob, they will be as dust—limitless.

12. It has long been accepted that a Nuzi court case between a certain Tarmiya and his two brothers showed an oral bequest to be valid and legally binding and that this was why Isaac could not retract his words. This text (*ANE* 1:169–70; *ANET* 220) is no longer thought applicable since the judge based his case on the testimony of witnesses and the refusal of the brothers to "take the oath of the gods" against those witnesses—not because an oral statement was legally binding.

13. Commentators reject the popular "ladder" imagery. Elsewhere the same Hebrew word carries the sense of a ramp, like that commonly built up to a city sitting on a hill.

5.5. Genesis 28:11 records Jacob's use of a stone for a pillow. There is no lack of stones in Palestine, and although Jacob may have covered his with something soft, the incident still strikes most people as strange. Over the centuries, ideas have changed regarding what constitutes proper support for the head. In fact, Somali nomads continue to use headrests much like the ancient Egyptian headrest pictured here (seven-and-three-quarter inches high).

Metropolitan Museum of Art, Rogers Fund, 1926

Jacob was fleeing a volatile situation and had shown less-than-sterling character so far. Still, God ended his promise to Jacob in a beautiful way: God promised to not forsake him (Gen. 28:15). Jacob woke up afraid and awestruck. With fieldstones he marked the spot to commemorate his meeting with God and poured out oil (perhaps some cooking oil he had brought with him) as a sign of worship. Jacob named the place Bethel, that is, "house of God."[14]

Commentators often take Jacob to task for bargaining with God. In Genesis 28:20–22 Jacob vows that if God (1) will be with him, (2) keep him on his journey, (3) give him food and garments, and (4) let him return home safely, then (a) the Lord will be his God, (b) the pillar just erected will be God's house, and (c) Jacob will tithe. However, some commentators see Jacob's words as more than a conditional commitment and argue that the "if-then" aspect of his response was the normal formula for a vow (Kidner 1967: 158). One commentator even suggests that these words indicate Jacob's conversion (Youngblood 1991: 220–21).[15]

Genesis 29 opens with Jacob reaching his destination and soon taking up residence with his uncle Laban. A few weeks later Jacob asked to marry Rachel, Laban's younger daughter. Since Jacob had no bride-price to offer for Rachel, he proposed an accepted option. In lieu of wages he would serve Laban for an agreed-upon period of time (seven

14. Genesis 28:19 reads, "And he called the name of that place Bethel; however, previously the name of the city had been Luz." This means that when Abraham earlier camped near the place it held the name Luz. Either Jacob was near Luz, a city that would later be renamed Bethel when the Hebrews occupied it, or he was in an abandoned Luz and was giving it its Hebrew name.

15. There seems to be some overlapping in the distinction between a vow and an oath, but a curse is generally implicit in an oath.

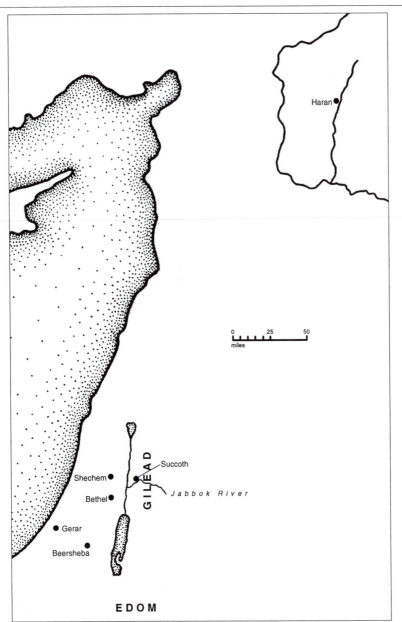

5.6. From Haran to Palestine in the patriarchal period.

years) to obtain his bride. Laban immediately accepted the offer, and it seems Rachel's opinion on the matter was not sought.[16] Strangely those seven years passed as "but a few days because of his love for her." Then Laban prepared the marriage feast; such celebrations could last seven days and were full of music, merriment, and food. The first evening Jacob was given his wife, but not the woman for whom he had contracted (Gen. 29:25).

16. Rachel is depicted as "beautiful of form and face" while Leah, the older daughter, is said to have "weak eyes," which is usually thought to mean that she could not see well or that she had some disfiguring ailment. The "pretty eyes" of the New Living Translation is unacceptable because it stretches the sense of the Hebrew and negates the contrast inherent in the verse.

Commentators speak of the deceiver being deceived and of Jacob meeting his match. How did Jacob get hoodwinked? It was dark when Leah, Rachel's older sister, was given to Jacob. Further, Laban probably ensured that Jacob drank plenty of wine before bringing him his bride. The Bible relates Jacob's feelings in this episode, but not how the women felt. Leah must have agreed to the switch, but what trepidation did she have that evening? Jacob was camouflaged when he deceived his father; was Leah disguised or did Laban make do with the wine? How must Leah have felt when Jacob dashed out the next morning? And where was Rachel during this chain of events? What were her feelings that night; was she restrained somewhere out of sight?

When Jacob found Laban he accused his father-in-law of deception. Laban explained that custom required the older daughter to be married first. In the intervening seven years Laban had probably tried to find a husband for Leah; it would have been to Laban's advantage to receive a bride-price for her. But Leah remained single and Laban chose this method of resolving his problem. Laban calmed Jacob by asking him to complete the wedding week with Leah, and then he could also have Rachel as a wife. All Jacob had to do was work another seven years to pay for her!

Marriage contracts were normally drawn up and signed by the father of the bride and the groom prior to the wedding day. Assuming such a contract existed here, Jacob had a potentially strong legal case against Laban, which could explain Laban's eagerness to mollify Jacob. Jacob agreed to the proposal; perhaps he rationalized that to go from no wives to two wives in one week could have some advantages. So one week after his morning shock, Jacob was given Rachel as his second bride.[17]

In Genesis 29:24 and 29:29 note is made that Laban gave a maidservant to each of his daughters. These maids seem like an intrusion, but their placement in the story conforms to ancient Near Eastern wedding documents. As one commentator explains, the notation in the Nuzi documents "is just as abrupt and marginal as are the present notices about Zilpah and Bilhah. . . . If our author had copied the two verses from an original contract from Harran, he could not have come any closer to the cuneiform parallel" (Speiser 1964: 227).

Marital trouble quickly became a part of Jacob's life. Old translations of Genesis 29:31 state that Jacob hated Leah, but recent translations soften this description and more correctly read that Leah was "unloved." Jacob had agreed to retain Leah as his wife, but he did not hide his preference for Rachel. The friction inherent in such a situation likely led to its later prohibition (Lev. 18:18).

The tensions in the family mounted as Leah, but not Rachel, became a mother. Leah presented Jacob with four sons. Childlessness was a disgrace for women, and after the first few years of their marriage Rachel blamed her barrenness on Jacob. Since Jacob loved Rachel he would

---

17. For laws concerning ancient marriage contracts, see *ANE* 1:135 and *ANET* 162 (laws 27–28). That Jacob did not have to wait another seven years before being married to Rachel is clear from Rachel's maid presenting Jacob with children within that time span. The polygamy noted throughout the Old Testament was due to several factors; among them was the need to guard against the high infant mortality rate and the attrition of available husbands due to warfare.

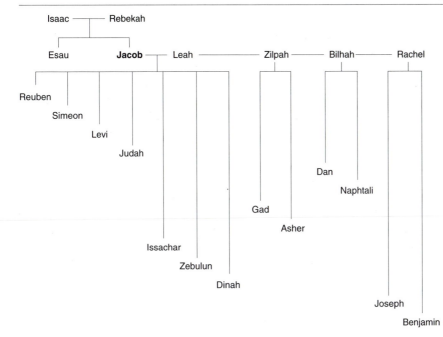

5.7. Jacob's family tree.

naturally have wanted her happy and fulfilled, and he resented the in-sinuation that he was at fault. Rachel, perhaps in desperation, suggested the same custom employed by Abraham and Sarah long before (Gen. 30:3). When Rachel wishes that her maid Bilhah "bear on my knees," Rachel is affirming that she would welcome a child born into the family by this means. Bilhah did become pregnant, and when she delivered, Rachel felt that she had been vindicated (Gen. 30:6).

Subsequently a second son was born to Bilhah. Then Leah gave her handmaid to Jacob, and Zilpah presented Jacob with two sons. Finally, after several years of frustration and three more children born to Leah, the Lord "remembered" Rachel. The Hebrew verb means that God "paid special attention to" or "lovingly cared for" her. When she gave birth to Joseph, Rachel felt her reproach fully lifted, and Jacob's family was nearly complete (illustration 5.7).

Jacob had left home for "a few days" until his brother Esau's anger subsided. Four "wives," twelve children, and several years later, but apparently soon after the birth of Joseph, Jacob began to think of home. The manner in which Jacob approached Laban and asked to be sent away, along with his wives and children, illustrates an important aspect of patriarchal life. The patriarch, Laban in this case, controlled the life of the extended family. Although an adult and himself the possessor of a large family, Jacob had to request approval of any important decision.

Laban prevailed on Jacob to stay, and the two worked out a new wage agreement. Jacob suggested that he be given the dark-colored lambs and the spotted and speckled goats.[18] Laban agreed, but before

18. Genesis 30:32 probably exhibits a scribal error in which words are accidentally repeated. The verse should most likely read, "Let me pass through your entire flock to-day, removing from there every black one among the lambs and the spotted and speck-led among the goats." This reading is supported by the specifics of Laban's action in v. 35.

115

Jacob could claim his animals, Laban cut the stipulated lambs and goats from his flocks and sent them three days' journey away. Jacob's reaction to this new deception by Laban is not recorded, but Jacob proved to be as resourceful as his father-in-law. Jacob placed striped poles at the watering troughs where the flocks came to drink and mate, and within a few years enough dark-colored lambs and spotted and speckled goats had been born for Jacob to be rich in flocks as well as in servants, camels, and donkeys. Scholars have made various attempts to understand this episode. One suggestion is that Jacob superstitiously thought the striped rods would affect the colors of the newborn animals and that God allowed it to happen for Jacob's sake (Youngblood 1991: 226). Another possibility is that Jacob put the rods in place to trick Laban into thinking his success was through magic. While Laban was thus misdirected, Jacob engaged in selective breeding to achieve his purpose.

About six years after the agreement to stay on with his father-in-law, Jacob again desired to leave.[19] Tensions were rising with Laban and his sons, and God instructed Jacob to return home (Gen. 31:3). This time Jacob decided not to ask for Laban's permission. To Rachel and Leah, Jacob poured out his frustration over the continued deception he had encountered. The two wives admitted their own frustrations (Gen. 31:14–16), and, despite the rivalry existing between them, they agreed that if God said to "go," they should go.

Jacob and his household left while Laban was away shearing sheep. Jacob took ten days to reach Gilead, and when Laban learned of their departure, it took him seven days to overtake them. Gilead is approximately three hundred miles south of Haran (illustration 5.6), so Jacob averaged thirty miles a day and Laban forty-three miles a day. Such speed seems reasonable for Laban and his men in hot pursuit, but thirty miles a day would be extremely difficult for Jacob with his flocks. Perhaps prior to his actual flight, Jacob pastured his flocks progressively further to the south. This stratagem would have reduced their distance from Gilead.

Laban should have had no trouble guessing where Jacob had headed, and he would have expected Jacob to take the well-traveled trade route south into Gilead. The night before Laban reached Gilead, God appeared to him in a dream and told him not to interfere with Jacob's plans. Therefore, by the time Laban caught up with Jacob, he had accepted his limitations, but that did not stop him from berating Jacob for leaving secretly and carrying off his daughters "like captives of the sword" (Gen. 31:26). Laban's choice of phrase calls to mind a reality of the patriarchal period: it continued to be a time of both wealth and danger.

Laban complained that, had he been informed of plans for departure, he would have sent Jacob and his family away "with joy and with songs, with timbrel and with lyre" (Gen. 31:27). Commentators generally doubt the honesty of this statement. They think it more likely that, as Jacob himself feared, Laban would have denied them permission to leave or that Jacob would have been turned out empty handed (Gen. 31:31). Laban's final protest was, "Why did you steal my gods?"

19. That Gen. 30:37–43 covers a span of six years is indicated by Gen. 31:41.

Alfred Hoerth

5.8. Baked clay statuettes, perhaps like those involved in Rachel's story (Gen. 31). The larger statuette is just over thirteen inches tall.

Jacob took great offense at the suggestion that he had taken Laban's god statues and, not knowing that Rachel had them, swore to kill the person who did. He allowed Laban to search for the god statues, but he did not find them because Rachel had hidden them in the camel saddle upon which she sat. The reason for Rachel's theft has received considerable attention over the years. Earlier studies, which used Nuzi texts to argue that the statues conferred inheritance rights on their owner, have lost favor. One recent explanation (Morrison 1983) is that Rachel felt disowned by her father, that he had "violated his responsibilities as keeper of the gods" and thus abrogated his right to them.[20] When Laban's search proved fruitless, Jacob became angry and taunted Laban to show what he had found that did not belong to Jacob. Then Jacob repeated his tale of woe:

> These twenty years I have been with you; your ewes and your female goats have not miscarried, nor have I eaten the rams of your flocks. That which was torn of beasts I did not bring to you; I bore the loss of it myself. You required it of my hand whether stolen by day or stolen at night. Thus I was: by day the heat consumed me, and the frost by night, and my sleep fled from my eyes (Gen. 31:38–40).

Jacob's words temper any tendency to see the biblical shepherd's life as an idyllic one. The Code of Hammurapi (a spelling now preferred to Hammurabi), approximately 1750, contains a law that appears to have been operative here:

20. The sale-adoption in the chapter epigraph has been used to argue that Jacob was made part of Laban's family by both adoption and marriage (C. Gordon 1940: 5–7). Although this argument is no longer accepted, this text, like Gen. 31, still illustrates the great importance attached to the god statues. Morrison also makes use of ancient herding practices to further understand the Jacob-and-Laban relationship.

> If a visitation of god has occurred in a sheepfold or a lion has made a kill, the shepherd shall prove himself innocent in the presence of god, but the owner of the sheepfold shall receive from him the stricken in the fold (*ANE* 1:166; *ANET* 177).

According to this law, when the shepherd had sworn himself innocent, the owner of the sheep incurred the loss. Jacob was pointing out that Laban had dealt illegally with him in this matter, but he had not protested. When Jacob finished speaking, Laban still claimed ownership of everything Jacob had, but he "painted" himself generous for the sake of his daughters and grandchildren. Laban also warned Jacob not to take additional wives, a prohibition regularly found in marriage contracts.

Laban suggested that he and Jacob make a covenant, and the two men erected a memorial and agreed that neither would pass that point with evil intentions toward the other. Laban's statement, "May the Lord watch between you and me when we are absent one from the other" (Gen. 31:49), is sometimes used as a benediction and as a blessing between loved ones, but Laban meant it as a curse. He was wishing evil on Jacob should he, when out of Laban's sight, violate the terms of their covenant. After this solemn threat was invoked, Laban said farewell to his daughters and grandchildren and returned to Haran.

Jacob's Reunion with Esau

Jacob was in Gilead, free of Laban, but he soon had a new problem: Esau was approaching with a force of four hundred men. Not knowing whether Esau was friendly or hostile, Jacob divided his flocks and people into two groups, in hopes that at least half of his people might escape if Esau meant to destroy him. Jacob prayed to God for help (Gen. 32:9–12), and he also tried to help himself by sending several hundred animals to the approaching Esau. Those leading the animals were to tell Esau they were a gift from Jacob. Jacob thereby hoped to appease his brother (Gen. 32:20). The whole plan was very transparent, and Esau must have seen through it.[21]

When Jacob saw Esau coming in the distance, he still did not know whether their meeting would be friendly. Therefore, Jacob assembled his children and their mothers according to his feelings for them. The handmaids and their children were placed in front, then Leah, and finally Rachel, in the most protected position. Jacob went ahead of them all—a courageous move but also the only honorable option. As Jacob approached his brother, he bowed to the ground seven times.[22]

The reunion was tearful and friendly. Esau apparently assumed Jacob would accompany him back to Edom, but Jacob excused himself

21. While Jacob awaited Esau's arrival, he had his well-known wrestling match with the angel of the Lord. There is wide evangelical opinion on the identification of this angel: Payne 1954: 45 identifies it as a Christophany (an Old Testament appearance of Christ), while Bruce 1968: 13 feels such an equation unwarranted.

22. The phrase *seven times* reflects the customary genuflection done in the presence of a superior. It is used repeatedly in the Amarna Letters (see chap. 10).

5.9. King Hammurapi of Babylon ruled during the middle portion of the patriarchal period. A strong ruler who gained control over much of Mesopotamia, he is best known today for the Code of Hammurapi, a collection of approximately three hundred laws. At the top of this diorite stele (over seven feet tall), Hammurapi faces the seated figure of the god Marduk. The remainder of the stele is covered with cuneiform inscriptions of selected Mesopotamian laws. Originally erected at Sippar (north of Babylon), this stele was taken to Susa as booty by Elamites in the twelfth century. The Elamites began to erase the laws so they could reuse the stele, but they gave up the effort. Parallel texts allow much of the erased portion to be restored. A few of Hammurapi's laws parallel later biblical law. Such similarity indicates that a "common law" existed in the ancient Near East and that some of it was incorporated, with modifications, into various local collections.

119

and said that he would follow as quickly as his flocks would permit. Jacob also declined Esau's offer to leave some men behind. Jacob clearly had no intention of going to Edom. Despite his eloquent prayer, his wrestling match, and the peaceful reunion with his brother, Jacob's old nature was still evident. As soon as Esau was out of sight, Jacob turned in a different direction and settled at Succoth. There he built a house and shelters and apparently stayed for a number of years.[23]

Eventually Jacob moved his family across the Jordan to Shechem. He bought some land near the city,[24] dug a well (see John 4), and built an altar that he called "God, the God of Israel." Jacob and his family settled into their new home. Subsequently Dinah was raped by Shechem, one of the city's influential sons. Rape, if done within one's own society was a capital offense, but this act was between two different groups so the strength of law was not clear. Although everyone could agree the crime should not have happened, there was no automatic penalty.

A range of reactions surfaced. Surprisingly, the young man wanted to marry Dinah, and his father agreed, anticipating that financial benefits would follow (Gen. 34:23). Jacob made no immediate reply because his sons were away with the livestock. When the sons heard what had happened they came home grieving and angry. Nothing is said of Dinah's feelings. Shechem's father, Hamor, begged for Dinah to be given to his son in marriage. Moreover, he recommended that there should be wholesale marriages to unite Jacob's people and the people of Shechem. Jacob's sons agreed to Dinah's marriage and apparently also to further intermarriage, but only if the men of Shechem took the sign of the covenant. Both Hamor and his son thought that was an acceptable condition and went to the city gate to convince the Shechemites. They must have been persuasive, and the prospect of a city full of happy wedding feasts was probably one of their bargaining points. They convinced the men of Shechem that much profit was worth a little pain, so the bargain was made and all the men of Shechem were circumcised in a single day.[25]

On the third day, while the men were still in pain, Simeon and Levi took their swords and slaughtered all of them. They wanted revenge, but this punishment far exceeded the original crime.[26] The other brothers followed up the slaughter by looting the town and carrying off the animals, women, and children. Jacob's reaction to this massacre and pillage was less than compassionate. He expressed no concern for the

23. The other alternative is that some years pass in Shechem before the events of Gen. 34. Dinah would have been about seven years old when Jacob left Haran. She is of marriageable age at Shechem.

24. Genesis 33:19 uses a rare Hebrew word to relate how much Jacob paid for the land. As yet nothing has been found to give the verse any precision. "Pieces of money" is only an intelligent guess.

25. Circumcision was known in the Near East prior to the patriarchal period. Sometimes it had a reproductive significance, but God had appropriated an already existing practice and dedicated it to his own purposes as the token of the covenant.

26. Simeon and Levi retrieved Dinah from the house of Hamor, but why she was there is not clear. Perhaps she was ashamed to return home or perhaps the agreement allowed her to stay in her future father-in-law's house until the actual wedding ceremony.

5.10. Representations of deities were sometimes worn as jewelry. Some of the earrings discarded in Genesis 35:4 might have been like a gold Astarte pendant found at Megiddo (shown here full-size).

victims, nor did he wonder how his sons could be so evil. Rather, he worried about his own reputation and his own safety lest other peoples in the area attacked with intent to destroy him and his family (Gen. 34:30).

Subsequently God told Jacob to move to Bethel, to live there, and to erect an altar "to God, who appeared to you when you fled from your brother Esau" (Gen. 35:1). In preparation for this move, Jacob instructed everyone to purify themselves and to dispose of any foreign gods. Jacob probably directed his order to the women and children who had been taken from Shechem, but he possibly now knew that Laban's charge of theft had been legitimate.

The distance from Shechem to Bethel is about twenty air miles. At Bethel, Jacob built an altar and called on the name of the Lord. Jacob later left Bethel and journeyed south. Either Rachel was at that time in advanced pregnancy or the travel induced early labor. In either case, her wish for another child was realized but at the expense of her life. Jacob named the baby Benjamin, which can mean either "son of the right hand" or "son of the south."[27] Jacob's life did not end here, but what follows fits better with the story of Joseph in chapter 7.

Additional Reading

Bahat, Dan. "Did the Patriarchs Live at Givat Sharett?" *BAR* 4/4 (1978): 8–11.

Biran, Avraham. "The Discovery of the Middle Bronze Age Gate at Dan." *BA* 44 (1981):139–44.

Frymer-Kensky, Tikva. "Patriarchal Family Relationships and Near East Law." *BA* 44 (1981): 209–14.

27. "Ben" means "son of," and "jamin" means "right" or "south." North has not always been the orientation for figuring direction. Early Arabic maps use a south orientation, and the Old Testament uses the east. Therefore, in Hebrew, to go to the right is to go south. When Jacob named Benjamin, he could have been referring to the right hand (i.e., the hand of honor) or to Benjamin's being born in the south, not in the north as all the other sons had been.

5.11. Basalt statue (nearly four feet tall) of the eighteenth-century King Ishtup-ilum of Mari. Mari, situated up the Euphrates River from Babylon, was the center of an important Amorite city-state during the first half of the patriarchal period. When excavated, Mari's multistoried palace was found to contain nearly three hundred rooms, courtyards, and passages. Dating centuries after the Royal Cemetery at Ur, the sprawling palace with its frescoed walls and statuary reveals that kings of Mesopotamia continued to command great wealth and power. Among the discoveries in the palace were over twenty thousand cuneiform texts containing rich detail about palace and political life. The initial excitement over their mention of people and place-names similar to those in the Bible has been tempered by the recognition that such names were then common. Still, like the Nuzi texts, customs reflected in the Mari texts illustrate life during patriarchal and later times. Mari's palace and power was destroyed by Hammurapi. (See *BA* 47/2 [1984], an entire issue devoted to Mari.)

Hirmer Verlag

Kempinski, Aharon. "Hittites in the Bible." *BAR* 5/4 (1979): 20–44.

Lemaire, André. "Mari, the Bible, and the Northwest Semitic World." *BA* 47 (1984): 101–8.

Malamat, Abraham. *Mari and the Early Israelite Experience*. Schweich Lectures 1984. Oxford: Oxford University Press, 1989.

Matthews, Victor H. "Pastoralists and Patriarchs." *BA* 44 (1981): 215–18.

Pfeiffer, Charles. *The Patriarchal Age*. Grand Rapids: Baker, 1961.

Sarna, Nahum M. "Abraham in History." *BAR* 3/4 (1977): 5–9.

Young, Gordon G. (ed.). *Mari in Retrospect*. Winona Lake, Ind.: Eisenbrauns, 1981.

Egypt before Joseph

The miserable [Canaanite], it fares ill with the place wherein he is, troublesome in respect of water and difficult on account of the many trees, its roads toilsome by reason of the mountains. He dwells not in any single place, driven abroad by want and his feet always on the move. He has been fighting ever since the time of Horus, but he never conquers, nor is he ever conquered.

—"Instruction for King Merikare"

The Land

The Greek historian Hecataeus of Miletus coined the phrase "Egypt is the gift of the Nile," which is usually credited to the later (fifth-century) historian Herodotus. The phrase emphasizes that without the waters of the Nile there would be no Egypt. The image of a lotus plant has also been used to describe this Nile: the river is the plant's stalk, the delta its flower, and the Fayum a bud on the stalk (Gardiner 1961: 27).

The headwaters of the Nile originate in Central Africa, three degrees south of the equator. The White Nile rises and flows some twenty-five hundred miles north before uniting with the Blue Nile at Khartoum. The White Nile carries a constant volume of water, but tropical rains in Ethiopia cause a great swelling of the Blue Nile in the summer months. The combined White and Blue Niles merge with the Atbara, another seasonal river, one hundred forty miles north of Khartoum. From Khartoum the Nile flows over eighteen hundred river miles and passes through six cataracts (stretches of the river containing rock outcroppings and rapids) before it reaches the Mediterranean Sea.

The Blue Nile and the Atbara cause the yearly rise in the Nile's level. The timing of the rise can vary by as much as several weeks within a single generation, but it is generally first noticed at Khartoum in the middle of May and at Aswan by the middle of June. Before the recent building of the High Dam, which blocks the Nile at Aswan, the rise reached Memphis by the end of June and crested there ("high Nile") before the end of September. About two weeks later the waters began to subside and usually left the northern fields by the end of November. By April the Nile at Memphis had returned to "low Nile."

The Egyptians were dependent on the yearly flooding and were extremely conscious that little separated a good "high Nile" (around twenty-five feet) from one that could bring destruction or famine. For instance, even a foot too much water would damage the irrigation dikes, and four feet over the ideal rise would flood out the villages. Conversely, a few feet less than an ideal rise would not sufficiently flood the fields. Because the prospect of lean years was always a possibility, the Egyptians began careful measurements of the Nile at Aswan so the northern regions could have time to properly respond to the forecast.

Year after year and century after century, the Nile rose, irrigated the land, and left its deposit of rich silt for the farmer.[1] Egypt blooms wherever the Nile water reaches its soil, but beyond that line there is desert. The contrast between "desert and sown" can be sharp, and the Egyptians expressed this reality in their references to the "black land" (the sown) and the "red land" (the desert).

Egypt is essentially a tubular-shaped country, and the area between the first and second cataracts has been wryly described as two hundred miles long by five yards wide. From the first cataract at Aswan, the Nile has another seven hundred fifty river miles until it reaches the Mediterranean Sea. For about the first six hundred of these miles the river flows through a valley at times no wider than the Nile itself, but never more than twenty miles wide.[2] "Delta" is the name the Greeks gave to the flat alluvial plain through which the Nile flows just before emptying into the Mediterranean Sea.[3] Although the delta is one of the most fertile areas of Egypt, some of its northern acreage has always been either too marshy, too salty, or too filled with lagoons to be farmed.

The climate of Egypt is usually sunny and warm, but there are regional differences due to the length of the country. The average high

1. Borings taken between Aswan and Memphis have found silt deposits from twenty-two feet to thirty-two feet thick.

2. At Aswan the cliffs fringing the Nile are sandstone, but about fifty miles north they change to limestone, the characteristic stone all the way to the delta.

3. The delta's triangular shape reminded the Greeks of their alphabet's fourth letter.

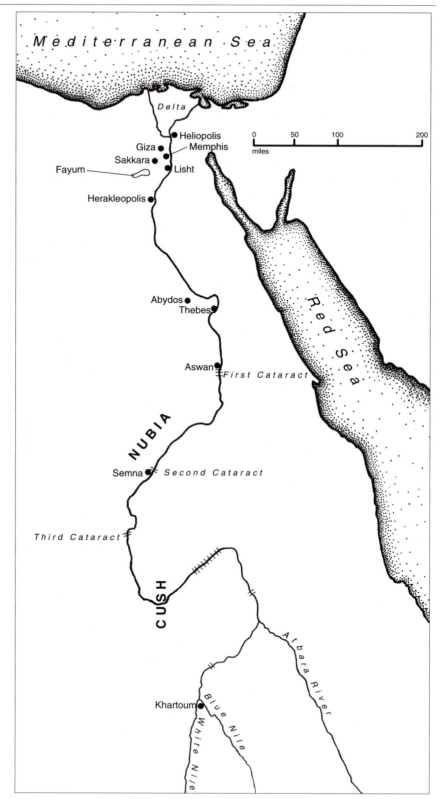

6.1. Egypt and the Nile.

temperature at Aswan is 108°F in June, but only 83°F in the delta. The entire length of Egypt experiences a noticeable cooling effect at night, and in winter Egypt can become much colder than most people suspect. The average low temperature at Aswan in January is 49°F. Rainfall in Egypt occurs mainly during the winter months, varying in amount from eight inches in the delta to less than two inches at Memphis. Further south there may be a shower every two or three years.

Egypt's size can be deceptive. The present nation covers approximately 387,000 square miles (close to the combined size of Texas and New Mexico) but almost all of that territory is desert. In 1986 the population of Egypt was fifty million people, with ninety-nine percent of that total living on three percent of the land. There are no certain figures on population in Egypt's pharaonic era but estimates range from 1.6 million to 5 million people. The ancient Egyptians also congregated along the Nile.

Ancient Egypt usually considered Aswan its southern border, but sometimes pushed its frontier to the second cataract, where it is today. The land of Cush was located south of the second cataract. The term "Nubia" refers to the area between the first and third cataracts. One ancient designation for Egypt was "the Two Lands." Then as now, "Upper Egypt," which stretches along the river south of Memphis, was recognized as distinct from the wide delta plain, "Lower Egypt," north of Memphis. The separation into two lands was so strongly perceived that a person from one of the areas could feel alien in the other. Dialectical differences developed and a person from the delta, for instance, might exaggerate that he needed an interpreter to communicate in Aswan.

Egypt's geography had an influence on communications. Traffic was convenient on the Nile, for the current carried boats north and the wind filled the sails for southern destinations. Consequently, wheels and good roads were not considered high priority until empire times (which began in the sixteenth century).

The geography of the land loosely sealed Egypt from outside contact. The Libyans could enter the country across the western desert, but only with great difficulty. The barren landscape between the first and third cataracts prevented any hostile concentration of people in the south. On the northeast, about one hundred barren miles separated Egypt from Palestine, and the Mediterranean shoreline was a natural barrier until relatively late times when maritime powers finally arose. Many Egyptologists believe that these secure borders contributed to an essentially optimistic Egyptian worldview. This optimism was further enhanced by the usually clear skies and the warmth of the sun. The regularity of the Nile inundation added to the Egyptian sense of confidence.[4]

4. There might be a "bad Nile" one year, but the prospect was that the following year would be good. The impression that the Egyptians were excessively concerned with death and the next world results from the preponderance of their materials being found in tombs and temples.

Predynastic Egypt: Egypt before Joseph

The Nile alluvium has deeply covered most of Egypt's prehistory. It is assumed the Egyptians began food production and animal domestication by 8000 and that their Neolithic period continued until about 5000. During those millenniums Egypt seems to have developed more slowly than the rest of the Near East (see Hawkes 1976: 39–59 for summaries of world development between 8000 and 5000).

Egypt's material culture, from the fifth millennium on, is more visible, but most of the evidence comes from cemeteries. The deceased were buried with personal possessions and offerings of food and drink. Some of the excavated figurines and amulets imply an interest in religion and, together with the pottery, show an artistic bent. The tomb objects also indicate that even in their early history, Egyptians believed they could "take it with them."

6.2. In a simple Predynastic burial, the body was placed in a contracted position and sometimes wrapped in matting or some other covering. Offering pots surround the body; a cosmetic palette with its rubbing stone is in front of the skull.

Burials and the little that remains of their villages show that these early Egyptians hunted, fished, farmed, and engaged in shepherding. They worked with flint and copper, and metal became increasingly important as time passed. Housing seems to have progressed from simple oval huts to flat-roofed mud-brick homes. In this period Egyptian clothing was usually made from animal skins and sometimes from wool. Linen clothing, which became traditional, was not yet common in predynastic times. A comparison of northern and southern remains

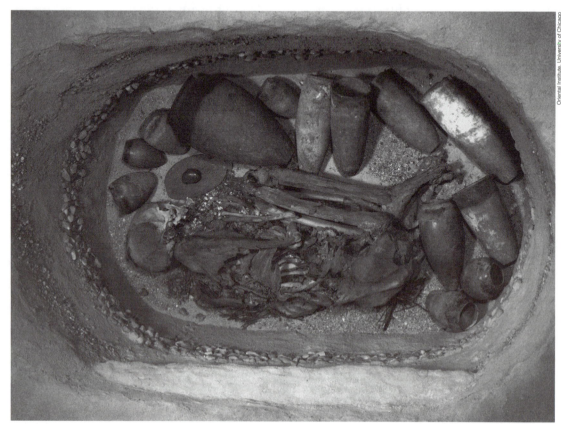

Oriental Institute, University of Chicago

British Museum

6.3. Carved palette showing cadavers being attacked by birds and a lion. The scene probably commemorates a victory by Upper Egypt over the delta region.

reveals that the Two Lands were culturally distinct and that the south was materially richer. Further, a comparison with the contemporary Ubaid period in Mesopotamia shows that Egypt's development, even in the fifth millennium, still lagged behind other parts of the Near East.

The last portion of predynastic Egypt, termed the Gerzean or Naqada III period, was a time of accelerated development, partially credited to the Nile River. Small-scale irrigation projects appear to have been carried out rather early in order to clear swamps and extend fields further into the desert. Large-scale irrigation, which began about the time Egypt moved into its historical period, demanded planning and some sort of strong governmental organization. Such organization both fostered and was maintained by the irrigation project: "It cannot be proved or disproved at present, but it is possible that the important changes in agriculture through irrigation were an immediate forerunner of historic times and, in fact, produced the historic times" (Wilson 1951: 31).

Some of the insights into the Gerzean/Naqada III period derive from commemorative slate palettes, which are similar in shape to the cosmetic palettes frequently found in the early tombs.[5] The commemora-

5. Malachite and other soft stones were ground on palettes, and the resulting powder was then applied to the eyelids and lips. Originally the application might have served as a sunscreen or magical protection, but it became primarily cosmetic.

tive palettes developed from simple functional objects to, in some cases, large carved examples on which various events (usually battles) were depicted. The commemorative palette in illustration 6.3, for example, depicts a conquering lion and anthropomorphic standards with insignia grasping bound captives. The conquering lion and bull motifs were manifestations of the king's power in dynastic times.

Toward the end of Egypt's Gerzean/Naqada III period and in Dynasty 1, elements of clearly Mesopotamian origin were introduced into the country. From Mesopotamia, then in its Protoliterate and Early Dynastic I periods, came the cylinder seal and certain artistic motifs. These evidences of contact lead some scholars to feel that Mesopotamia deserves partial credit for Egypt's development, including even the concept of writing. If true, Egypt did not imitate the Mesopotamian originals for long.[6]

Dynastic Egypt: Dynasties 1–2 (3100–2700)

Herodotus (2.99) claims that a man named Menes proceeded north from Abydos in Upper Egypt, conquered Lower Egypt, and settled in Memphis. Menes is given credit for uniting the Two Lands and beginning Egypt's Dynasty 1.[7] Egyptologists have labored long to equate Menes with one of the known early Egyptian kings, but there is still some question as to whether he was an actual person or a composite figure.

The earliest kings of Egypt left depictions of their victories in battle and of their accomplishments in peace. One king, for instance, is shown opening an irrigation canal. The Narmer ceremonial palette, just over two feet high, has reliefs on both sides. The reverse (illustration 6.4 left) shows the king, Narmer (his name is on the top center of the palette, represented by the fish [*Nar*] and the chisel [*Mer*]), wearing the white crown of Upper Egypt and brandishing a mace over another man. The glyphs beside this second man possibly signify "enemy," and the glyphs beside the two men under Narmer's feet probably identify their home areas. The papyrus plant above the fallen man is a symbol for Lower Egypt, indicating that the commemorated action took place in northern Egypt. The obverse of the palette shows Narmer wearing the red crown of Lower Egypt. There he is accompanied by standard

6. How the contact was made continues to be a puzzle, and everything from visiting artisans to invading armies has been suggested. Majority opinion prefers direct trade resulting in the transfer of crafts and ideas. The route of contact is also debated. One possibility is that Mesopotamians sailed down the Persian Gulf, up the Red Sea, and then crossed overland into southern Egypt. A less favored option is that the contact came from the north, moving either overland through Palestine or along its coast by boat. Strangely, no trace has been found of Egyptian goods or ideas reaching Mesopotamia in this same period. See Frankfort 1956 for an early discussion of this matter.

7. Some scholars include Dynasty 3 in this pre–Old Kingdom period, others even posit a "Dynasty 0." To be technically correct, the term *pharaoh* should not be used before Dynasty 18. Pharaoh means "great house" and was a synonym for the palace. During the reign of Thutmose III the term began to be applied to the king. Earlier, the Upper Egyptian king's title, *ny-swt* ("One who belongs to the sedge plant"), was used.

6.4. The Narmer Palette is one of the most famous objects from ancient Egypt. Two cow-horned heads of the goddess Hathor appear at the top of the palette, and the falcon god Horus is perched over the papyrus plant on the reverse. On each side, an official follows the king with the king's sandals.

bearers who face a series of decapitated enemies. Meanwhile a bull, representing the king, breaks down a city wall.

The palette has artistic links with the past, but it also exhibits several examples of Egyptian posturing and motifs that would be employed for many centuries. For example, the king wielding a mace over fallen enemies continued to be a common scene down into Roman times. Most importantly, Egyptologists normally take the palette to represent the forceful unification of Egypt. The southern king is shown defeating enemies in the north on one side and wearing the crown of Lower Egypt on the other. This palette is one evidence that leads most scholars to equate Narmer with the legendary Menes of Herodotus. Narmer is the earliest king to be shown wearing both crowns. Subsequently the two crowns were combined to symbolize the unification of Egypt.

Aside from the unification of the country there is little historical clarity about the first two dynasties. There is some suggestion of intermarriage between the Two Lands to strengthen the unity, and objects found bearing Narmer's name at more than one site in Palestine implies at least commercial outreach. An upheaval apparently occasioned Dynasty 2 and a new ruling family, but only scraps of information are available. The first two dynasties were seemingly preoccupied with consolidation, battle, and religious tensions.

On the other hand, the years of the first two dynasties were a time of experimentation and formulation in areas such as the arts. It was also

6.5. Model of Djoser's
Step Pyramid
complex.

the period in which Egyptians worked out their concept of divine kingship. Trends in painting and sculpture can be identified, but the process
that led to the dogma that pharaoh was a god is a subject of speculation. However, the adoption of that concept proved to have a stabilizing
effect on the country. So too did the formulation of the concept of *maat*
as a created and inherited rightness that encouraged political stability
and implicitly argued for the continuing rule of the god king. By the
end of Dynasty 2 the essentials of Egyptian culture had been established, and Egypt would remain basically unchanged in its outlook on
life for over one thousand years. The sociopolitical essential became
the assertion that Egypt was owned and ruled by a god. The spiritual

6.6. Djoser's Step
Pyramid.

essential was that Egypt was the most blessed of lands, and any setback could be only temporary (Wilson 1951: 47–50).

The Old Kingdom: Dynasties 3–6 (2700–2200)

The transition into Dynasty 3, the beginning of Egypt's classical period, seems to have been smooth. The most important pharaoh of Dynasty 3 is Djoser, the first pyramid builder. His pyramid underwent several modifications before reaching its final configuration: six stages rising to a height of 204 feet, with a base measuring 358 feet by 411 feet. This "step pyramid," like all future pyramids, was only one part of a complex. In this example, a perimeter wall over a mile in circumference clusters within it shrines, chambers, and open areas around the pyramid. The step pyramid was the first large Egyptian building made completely of stone.

Subsequent kings also constructed pyramids. The first "traditional" pyramid was built in Dynasty 4, probably by Pharaoh Sneferu. He was followed by Khufu (Hellenized as Cheops), who at Giza constructed the largest of all the pyramids: 450 feet high and 756 feet on a side.[8] The next two pharaohs built their pyramids near Khufu's; that of Khafre (Chephren) is only slightly smaller, but Menkaure's (Mycerinus) pyramid is less than half as large. After Menkaure, until Dynasty 12, few pyramids approached even that reduced size.

The pyramids at Giza are the only "ancient wonders of the world" still extant. Their size continues to amaze people and, unfortunately, to generate fables of hidden secrets, powers, and extraterrestrial builders. No lost technology was used to construct the pyramids of Egypt. The Egyptians did not then have the benefit of the wheel or the crane; but the use of ramps, ropes, sledges, levers, cradles, grease, laborers, perhaps the pulley, and patience allowed them to complete their task. The belief that they were working for a visible god, their pharaoh, also provided motivation to work.

The construction site at Giza could not have accommodated the hundred thousand workers sometimes estimated for the projects: the true figure was probably closer to one-tenth that number. Neither did the laborers toil year round. They were employed during "high Nile" when there was no fieldwork to be done and the facing blocks could be floated more easily to the site from the quarry across the river. The workers would have appreciated their rations during this otherwise idle time of year. Laudatory and apparently heartfelt expressions of pleasure were left by some of the ancient work crews.

The pyramids are the most outward evidence of the centricity that developed during Dynasties 3 and 4. The king was the state. There were no abstract words for "government" or "nation." In theory, the king was everywhere and did everything. The size of Egypt, however, did not allow the theory to work in practice. At first the centralized bu-

8. With its capstone the pyramid of Khufu was 481 feet high. One of the best books on pyramids is Edwards 1972. Tompkins 1971 contains interesting early line drawings but its text tends to the sensational.

6.7. Giza features the pyramids of Menkaure (left; with three subsidiary pyramids, probably for his queens), Khafre (center), and Khufu—the "Great Pyramid" (right). All three pyramids are solid except for their passageways and tomb chamber. Roughly six million tons of stone were used in the construction of Khufu's pyramid, the blocks averaging two-and-a-half tons. The nine ceiling slabs over its "king's chamber" weigh nearly forty-five tons apiece. The precision of the builders is impressive: the casing blocks were dressed and fitted to a tolerance of one-fiftieth of an inch, and the far ends of Khufu's thirteen-acre building site are only one inch out of level.

reaucracy was maintained by nobles, but eventually the government became too large even for their numbers, and an official class had to be developed.

Theoretically everything was under the pharaoh's control. Foreign commerce was a royal monopoly, and the king probably had a hand on or in anything that moved a great distance. He controlled the Sinai copper mines and the commercial center at Byblos where the Egyptians had an interest in the cedar trees. Commercial and military expeditions were made into Libya, the Sudan, and Palestine, but force was used only to protect the trade routes. In all this activity, the nobility and the official class aided the pharaoh and yet felt dependent on his blessings. That dependence can be seen in the way their tombs clustered around the pyramids. They believed proximity would benefit their continued identification with the pharaoh in the next world.

Mortuary texts first appeared on the tomb chamber walls of Unas, the last pharaoh of Dynasty 5, but archaisms imply they were composed earlier, probably on papyrus scrolls. The mortuary texts (at this point called "pyramid texts")[9] were a collection of spells designed to ensure the king a happy afterlife, and they show a basic way in which he differed from his subjects. At death the pharaoh became a part of the other gods; he became Osiris. His nobles also envisioned a happier afterlife, but one in which they continued to serve the king. Their relationship did not change with death.

By Dynasty 5, increasing decentralization signals that the king's magnetism was weakening. The trend has been blamed on the burgeoning number of royal children, which resulted in a blurring of the succession lines. Debate and infighting over succession could only tar-

9. Egyptologists have given different names to the mortuary texts. In the Old Kingdom they are called "pyramid texts," but from the First Intermediate period through the Second Intermediate period they are called "coffin texts." Beginning with the empire period, the mortuary texts are called the "Book of the Dead." The "Breathing Permit" is an abridgment of the "Book of the Dead."

nish the concept of a divine king followed by a divine king. Then too, the growing number of government officials weakened the centrality of the king. Pharaoh-serving job descriptions became hereditary, and government officials increasingly discovered they could act on their own initiative. One obvious evidence of the growing independence of the nobles is seen in their tombs. By Dynasty 6, nobles had begun to build their tombs in their home provinces. Nearness to the pharaoh's pyramid was no longer believed necessary for eternal life.

The priesthood also had a hand in destroying the king's absolutism. Originally a priest would also have a lay position, but in Dynasty 5 his religious duties became a full-time occupation. In the same dynasty, the priesthood at Heliopolis challenged the kings with its sun god, Re, and they seem to have imposed limitations on the kings. Evidence of their power was expressed in the kings' erecting sun temples with obelisks rising higher than their own shrinking pyramids.[10]

Toward the end of the Old Kingdom the nobles became restless, and at the same time the queen gained higher status. By the end of Dynasty 6 she was using mortuary privileges hitherto reserved for the king. Texts that only the king had used were now hers also, and afterlife was no longer dependent on her husband. She too became a god after her death.[11] The pharaoh was no longer an absolute monarch.

Various factors contributed to the collapse of the Old Kingdom at the end of Dynasty 6. Seemingly, the pharaoh could no longer control the nobles. The pyramids may have placed a mounting drain on the economy due to the expense of maintaining their temple staffs. An increasing number of temples and pyramid towns were excluded from taxation, thereby placing a heavier burden on the rest of the nation. Problems apparently developed on Egypt's borders, so that trade to the north and south was disturbed. Such disruption would have had a serious impact on Egypt and its government. Finally, Pharaoh Pepi II reigned for over ninety years, and that long length of rule by one person may have contributed to the stagnation of the country.[12]

Old Kingdom Egypt had more than pyramids and bureaucracy. Wisdom was also characteristic of the era. Fathers instructed their sons in the proper actions and attitudes for a successful life. "The Instruction of the Vizier Ptah-hotep," which dates to Dynasty 5, exhibits the extroverted and self-confident mind-set that had developed. The goals encouraged in these instructions centered on getting ahead in this world and gave little regard to spiritual values or to the future life. The text still has some commendable advice (*ANE* 1:234–35; *ANET* 412–13):

> Let not your heart be puffed up because of your knowledge; be not confident because you are a wise man. Take counsel with the ignorant as well as the wise. The full limits of skill cannot be attained, and there is no skilled man equipped to his full advantage. Good speech is more hidden

10. These kings began to add Re to their royal names, perhaps indicating some accommodation to the priesthood at Heliopolis.

11. The queen had special privileges because of her physical contact with the god-king. Daughters of kings were thought to have some divinity within them. Royal brother-sister marriages were arranged to assure the most divine strain possible.

12. The length of his reign has not been disproved.

than the emerald, but it may be found with maidservants at the grindstones. . . .

If you are one to whom petition is made, be calm as you listen to the petitioner's speech. Do not rebuff him before he has swept out his body or before he has said that for which he came. A petitioner likes attention to his words better than the fulfilling of that for which he came.[13]

These instructions or admonitions by Ptah-hotep shared more counsel that is good as well as timeless: he told his son to be just, not to be greedy, to remember his place, to keep sex in perspective, and to love his wife.

In summary, the Old Kingdom is sometimes called Egypt's classical period because the essentials of Egyptian culture were codified. The Egyptians remained basically the same in their outlook on life for the next several centuries.

The First Intermediate Period: Dynasties 7–11 (2200–2050)

The Old Kingdom rapidly disintegrated after the death of Pepi II. The short-lived Dynasties 7 and 8 continued to be based in the north, at Memphis, and claimed to rule all Egypt, but the pharaohs were weak and largely ignored. The unsettled times are further revealed in the inferior quality of the art and in the small and shoddy pyramids (e.g., the pyramid of Ibi measures only 102 feet on a side). The tomb inscriptions make allusions to hunger and killing.

One innovation can be credited to this troubled time. The Mesopotamian cylinder seal never became popular in Egypt, partly because the Egyptians did not write on clay tablets, but in Dynasty 6 the stamp seal was introduced from Syria-Palestine. In Dynasties 7 and 8 the Egyptians adapted it to the scarab shape, which became dominant by Dynasty 11 (see Ward 1994a).

With the end of Dynasty 8 the capital city was moved about fifty-five miles south to Herakleopolis. Memphis remained the symbolic seat of government during Dynasties 9 and 10, and a canal was dug linking it with the new center of power.

A Tenth Dynasty king wrote "The Instruction for King Merikare," similar in purpose to the Old Kingdom "Instruction of the Vizier Ptah-hotep" quoted above, showing a continuation of that literary form (*ANET* 415–16):

Do justice while you endure upon earth. Quiet the weeper; do not oppress the widow; supplant no man in the property of his father; and impair no officials at their posts. Be on your guard against punishing wrongfully. Do not slaughter: it is not of advantage to you. . . . A man should do what is of advantage to his soul. . . . The god is aware of him who works for him.

13. Instructions such as this one illustrate how Egyptians lived out the sometimes nebulous concept of *maat*. See Fontaine 1981.

6.8. Flat underside of a scarab (twice actual size), featuring the name of King Saankhkare (Dynasty 11).

This Tenth Dynasty text also makes mention of certain historical events. For example, it mentions that people from Syria-Palestine had moved into the delta region and established an independent government. Merikare's father was strong enough to push these intruders from Egypt. He also reestablished trade with Phoenicia, and cedar was again imported from the north.

"The Protests of the Eloquent Peasant" is set in the reign of the last Tenth Dynasty pharaoh. This rather humorous piece of literature has a serious ring: a peasant chastises an official for not only failing to render justice (*maat*) when the occasion arose, but also for not actively seeking opportunities to render justice. Justice was not simply to be maintained, it was to be sought after. This side of the story can be seen in a speech directed at the official, made by the peasant just after he had been whipped (*ANET* 409):

> So the son of Meru goes on erring! His face is blind to what he sees and deaf to what he hears, misguided of heart because of what has been related to him. Behold, you are a town that has no mayor, like a company that has no chief, like a ship in which there is no pilot, a confederacy that has no leader. Behold, you are a constable who steals, a mayor who accepts bribes, a district overseer who should punish robbery, but who has become the precedent for him that does it. . . .
>
> Do not plunder of his property a poor man, a weakling as you know him. His property is the very breath of a suffering man, and he who takes it away is one who stops up his nose. You were appointed to conduct hearings, to judge between two men, and to punish the brigand, but behold, it is the upholder of the thief that you would be. One trusts in you, whereas you are become a transgressor. You were appointed to be a dam for the sufferer, guarding lest he drown, but behold, you are his flowing lake. . . .
>
> O Chief Steward, my lord! One may fall a long way because of greed.

The Old Kingdom had been a time of stability and order, but that tranquillity had been badly shattered, and the Egyptians reacted variously to the turmoil. The eloquent peasant argued that *maat* should be rendered to everyone. Surprisingly, pharaoh could even admit to error. A shift toward equality is also evidenced in the mortuary texts of this period. Texts that had been reserved for the pharaoh were now appropriated by the nobles and, theoretically, by lower class people if they could afford the proper funeral service and inscribed coffin. The pharaoh was no longer alone as he became Osiris after his death.

There were also some negative responses to the instability. Instead of analyzing what had gone wrong, one Egyptian reaction was to make the Syro-Palestinians, who had drifted into the delta, scapegoats for all the ills of Egypt. Suicide, a very un-Egyptian act, was even weighed as an option (*ANET* 405–7). Agnosticism and hedonism were other reactions (Jacobsen and Wilson 1963: 39, 41):

> Generations pass away and others remain since the time of the forefathers. The gods who lived of old rest in their pyramids, as also the blessed dead, buried in their pyramids. And men who once built houses—their places are no more. See what has become of them! I have heard the words of Imhotep and Hordedef, those whose sayings men repeat so much—but what are their places now? Their walls are crumbled down, and their places are no more, as though they had never been! There is none who returns from over there, that he may tell us how they fare, that he may tell us what they need, that he may still our hearts, until we too travel to the place where they have gone. So give your desires free play, to let your heart forget the funeral rites for you, and follow your desire as long as you live. Put myrrh upon your head and don clothing of fine linen. Be anointed with true marvels of god's gift. Give increase to the good things of yours, nor let your heart be weary, follow your desire and your good. Fulfill your needs upon earth after the command of your heart, until there comes for you that day of mourning. The weary of heart will not hear their lamentation, nor does wailing save a man's heart from the underworld. Make holiday, and do not lag therein—see, no man can take his property with him! See, none who departs comes back again!

While Dynasties 9 and 10 ruled in the north, Thebes began to gain importance in the south. Dynasty 11, which was mostly contemporary with Dynasties 9 and 10, arose at Thebes. For a time both sides seemed willing to maintain peace, but border skirmishes sometimes occurred and became increasingly serious. Thebes began to extend its control further and further north. Sadly, the sense of individual worth and the worth of the common person was deemphasized as the pharaohs became powerful once more in the Middle Kingdom.

The Middle Kingdom: Dynasties 11–12 (2050–1800)

Egypt was reunited by force that seems to have been bloody and swift. The final kings of Dynasty 11 increased foreign trade and reopened the Sinai mines, but their reigns were beset with trouble. Dynasty 12 was established by Amenemhet, who was apparently not of royal blood. He was called the "son of someone," the term used for a person of good standing but not of princely birth. Amenemhet continued the rebuilding of Egypt, moved the capital back north (to Lisht), and declared himself pharaoh of all Egypt. He also merged the god Re with the Theban god Amon to create the sun god Amon-Re. The sprawling Karnak Temple complex dedicated to Amon-Re at Thebes was begun in Dynasty 12.

Another of Amenemhet's political moves was to make coregency a regular feature of government. He was trying to avoid the uncertainty of succession that had recently hurt the country. His son Senusert was coregent for the final ten years of his father's reign, and when Amenemhet became interested in expanding Egypt's southern border, Senusert led the army into Nubia.

By moving southward, Egypt was beginning to end its isolation. Possible reasons for this move include a desire to exploit the southern mineral wealth (either because the supply of gold was dwindling in the east or the demand for it had grown) and a wish to create a buffer between Egypt and Cush. Further, new peoples were pushing into lower (northern) Nubia, and it would have been in Egypt's best interest to monitor that influx. Whatever the exact motive(s), Egypt claimed the second cataract as its southern border.

Amenemhet, the founder of Dynasty 12 and expander of the southern borders, was killed in a palace coup. A text recording his death (and posthumously attributed to him) tells the story as if he wrote it from the grave. Amenemhet tells his son never to trust anyone completely. He also admits that he had not anticipated the attack on his life and had been unable to repel it. Such a confession places Amenemhet a great distance from the all-powerful pharaohs of the Old Kingdom.

Senusert apparently was not involved in the coup against his father; he was able to suppress it and to continue as sole ruler. (During the transition to Senusert as pharaoh, Sinuhe [see chap. 4] fled the country and took up residence in Palestine.) One of Senusert's first acts was to lead another campaign into Nubia, where he began building forts in the vicinity of the second cataract to protect his newly claimed territory. The forts were spaced along nearly one hundred miles of the Nile so one fort could signal to another. When one of these outposts, Buhen, was excavated, its battlements, slit windows, and dry moat was reminiscent of a medieval fort. Senusert was obviously serious about controlling the Nile as far as the second cataract.

The small number and usually long reigns of the Twelfth Dynasty pharaohs implies a stable Egypt. Its pharaohs revived the Old Kingdom practice of building pyramids, either as a political or a philo-

Giraudon/Art Resource

6.9. Middle Kingdom Egyptians placed models in their tombs so that the activities or people depicted would be available in the next life. This Twelfth Dynasty example shows a group of soldiers with their spears and shields.

sophical identification with the past. At Sakkara, Senusert built the largest of the Middle Kingdom pyramids: 352 feet on a side and about 200 feet high (approximately half the size of Khufu's pyramid at Giza). The main features of the Old Kingdom pyramid complexes were followed, and sometimes facsimiles of earlier tomb scenes were made. However, one change was occasioned by the plundering of Old Kingdom tombs that had already begun: burial shafts were sometimes placed outside the pyramid in an attempt to evade discovery by grave robbers.

The stability of the Middle Kingdom enabled Egypt to increase its commercial contacts with Syria-Palestine. The story of Sinuhe mentioned people from Palestine who had been to Egypt and Egyptian couriers passing through his territory. There is one record of a military force being sent into Palestine, but it was seemingly deployed to keep a trade route open. The number of Egyptian objects found in the north is taken as sign of commercial contact rather than of political control (Weinstein 1975).

As Egypt was expanding territorially to the south and commercially to the north, most of the Middle Kingdom pharaohs seem to have been enlightened leaders and genuinely concerned about their subjects. Senusert II took the throne name "He who makes justice appear," and the previous king was known as "He who takes pleasure in justice." Improved social consciousness can also be seen in the reclamation and flood-control projects undertaken at government expense. Thousands of cultivable acres were added to the delta, and records of the Nile's height were kept at the second cataract to provide the earliest possible forecasts.

The next king, Senusert III, was quite successful in reasserting the crown's authority over the nobility. Funerary texts found in nobles' tombs once more expressed the need to secure royal favor. And under Senusert III, Nubia became so fully a part of Egypt that it was con-

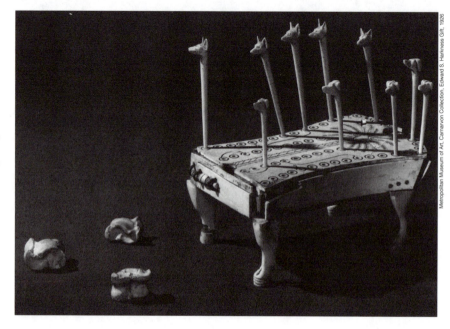

6.10. Wooden game board with ivory-and-ebony veneer from a Twelfth Dynasty Theban tomb, used for the game "Hounds and Jackals," a race game that originated in Middle Kingdom Egypt and spread through the Near East before dying out around 600 in Mesopotamia. The knucklebones to the left of the board are one form of dice used with this game. (See Hoerth forthcoming.)

Metropolitan Museum of Art, Carnarvon Collection, Edward S. Harkness Gift, 1926

sidered a province. Senusert III fortified Semna at the south end of the second cataract and erected two boundary steles to warn southerners against coming any further north unless they were on official business or interested in trading.[14] Egypt even established a trading post about one hundred miles upstream at the third cataract. The southern border began to be defended by a combination of Egyptian troops and *Medjai*, Nubian trackers and warriors. This use of *Medjai* marked the beginning of Egypt's dependence on foreign troops and became such an integral part of the country that *Medjai* became a synonym for "police."

The Middle Kingdom finally began to show signs of fatigue. The royal bloodline seems to have grown thin, and the last ruler was a queen. Apparently no appropriate male heir could be found.

The Second Intermediate Period: Dynasties 13–17 (1800–1570/1550)

The period between the Middle Kingdom and the New Kingdom is one that Egyptians wanted to forget. For example, the Abydos King List skips from Amenemhet IV of Dynasty 12 to the first king of Dynasty 18. To the Egyptians the intervening years were a time of humiliation. The breakup of the Middle Kingdom seems partly the result of weak kings, but there are also hints of competition and harem conspiracies within the royal families. A disruption of northern trade with the accompanying economic loss also seems to have been a contributing factor.

Over four dozen king names are known for the less than one hundred years of Dynasty 13.[15] This large number of rulers for that amount of time appears to be a sign of havoc and confusion, in which kings were murdering and replacing one another with extreme rapidity. It is also possible that rival claimants ruled parts of Egypt simultaneously.

Thirteenth Dynasty kings posed as legitimate successors to Dynasty 12, and they probably had nominal control of the country for a time. At least the first two kings of the dynasty managed to measure Nile heights at the faraway second cataract. Then a competing dynasty (Dynasty 14) arose in the delta. The details are sketchy, but Egypt was clearly divided when the Hyksos established Dynasty 15. Hyksos is an Egyptian word meaning "foreign rulers." There is no record of what these people called themselves. They entered Egypt from the north, and most scholars currently identify them as Canaanites. The few preserved personal names are Semitic.

The Hyksos were a minority in Egypt, but they are sometimes credited with having had superior military hardware. How much military muscle they needed to take control of Egypt is unclear. The names and

14. A stele or stela (plural steles or stelae, less frequently stelai) is an inscribed (sometimes carved) stone set up to commemorate a king's battle victory or domestic accomplishment.

15. Egyptologists are not agreed as to whether Dynasty 13 should be seen as the end of the Middle Kingdom or the beginning of the Second Intermediate period.

even the order of their kings is confusing, and their capital city (Avaris) has only recently been identified with the eastern delta site of Tell ed-Daba. Much of this lack of clarity can be blamed on the Egyptians. When the Hyksos were finally expelled, the Egyptians made a concerted effort to purge their stay from Egyptian history and landscape. The preserved documentation consists of boasts concerning how the writer had helped evict the Hyksos or had restored what they had destroyed. Little history can be pieced together from such scraps of evidence.

The Hyksos ruled Egypt for approximately one hundred years, controlling the north and allowing shadow pharaohs to continue in the south. The Hyksos themselves absorbed much of Egypt's culture, which led some Egyptians to feel their yoke was bearable. The Hyksos used Egyptian hieroglyphics and were so zealous to have earlier Egyptian texts copied that more copied documents are preserved from this period than from any other. The Hyksos kings also used such Egyptian titles as "King of Upper and Lower Egypt" and "Son of Re." They continued Egypt's commercial enterprises. Egyptian pottery distinctive to this period has been found as far south as the third cataract and as far north as Cyprus. One Hyksos king's name (Khayan) has been found on objects over much of the Near East and Mediterranean regions. They adopted the scarab seal, and what little artwork has survived from the north is better than what was being made at the same time in the south by native Egyptians. Finally, the Hyksos worshiped the Egyptian god Seth. Sir Alan Gardiner (1961: 170) sums up the Hyksos position this way: "The rare remains of the Hyksos kings point . . . to an earnest endeavour to conciliate the inhabitants and to ape the attributes and the trappings of the weak Pharaohs whom they dislodged."

Summary

Nile mud from centuries of inundation makes it impossible to trace early Egyptian history as far back as can be done for Mesopotamia. But, as with Mesopotamia, it is obvious that a complex culture had developed before the time of Abraham. By Abraham's visit, Egyptian dynasties had been in existence for a thousand years. The world-famous pyramids were already several centuries old and, to some Egyptologists, the best days of Egypt were past.[16] Abraham knew Egypt as a bustling, self-confident, and free country. After Abraham, Egypt went through a period of turmoil, but recovered. Joseph knew Egypt as a country occupied by people (the Hyksos) who tried to look the part of Egyptians but were never accepted as such by the majority of the indigenous population. This Hyksos occupation created fundamental changes in the Egyptian mind, and Egypt's relationship with its northern neighbors was never the same again.

16. To some Egyptologists, the "golden age" of the Old Kingdom is superior to the heady empire days that follow the Hyksos period.

Additional Reading

Older books by James Henry Breasted, Ernest Alfred Wallis Budge, Jean Pierre Erman, and William Matthew Flinders Petrie are still commonly available in reprints, but they should be used only in conjunction with more recent publications.

Aldred, Cyril. *The Egyptians*. 2d edition. London: Thames & Hudson, 1984.

Davies, W. V. *Reading the Past: Egyptian Hieroglyphics*. Berkeley: University of California Press, 1987.

Emery, W. B. *Archaic Egypt*. Baltimore: Penguin, 1961.

Finegan, Jack. *Archaeological History of the Ancient Middle East*. New York: Dorset, 1986.

Hallo, William W., and William K. Simpson. *The Ancient Near East: A History*. New York: Harcourt Brace Jovanovich, 1971.

Hoffmeier, James K. "Egyptians." Pp. 251–90 in *Peoples of the Old Testament World*. Edited by Alfred J. Hoerth, Gerald L. Mattingly, and Edwin M. Yamauchi. Grand Rapids: Baker, 1994.

Kemp, Barry J. Ancient Egypt: *Anatomy of a Civilization*. London: Routledge, 1989.

Knapp, A. Bernard. *The History and Culture of Ancient Western Asia and Egypt*. Chicago: Dorsey, 1988.

Lesko, Barbara S. "Women's Monumental Mark on Ancient Egypt." *BA* 54 (1991): 4–15.

Levy, Thomas E. "New Light on King Narmer and the Protodynastic Egyptian Presence in Canaan." *BA* 58 (1995): 26–35.

Smith, W. Stevenson. *The Art and Architecture of Ancient Egypt*. New York: Penguin, 1981.

Trigger, B. G., B. J. Kemp, D. O'Connor, and A. B. Lloyd. *Ancient Egypt: A Social History*. London: Cambridge University Press, 1983.

Wente, Edward. *Letters from Ancient Egypt*. Atlanta: Scholars Press, 1990.

7

Joseph and Moses in Egypt

To let you know. I was in distress on the Great Throne, and those who are in the palace were in heart's affliction from a very great evil, since the Nile had not come in my time for a space of seven years. Grain was scant, fruits were dried up, and everything that they eat was short. Every man robbed his companion. They moved without going ahead. The infant was wailing; the youth was waiting; the heart of the old men was in sorrow, their legs were bent, crouching on the ground, their arms were folded. The courtiers were in need. The temples were shut up; the sanctuaries held nothing but air. Everything was found empty. . . .

[In a dream to the pharaoh, Khnum, god of Elephantine, said:] "I know the Nile. When he is introduced into the fields, his introduction gives life to every nostril, like the introduction of life to the fields. . . . The Nile will pour forth for you, without a year of cessation or laxness for any land. Plants will grow, bowing down under the fruit. Renenut [the goddess of the harvest] will be at the head of everything. . . . Dependents will fulfill the purposes of their hearts, as well as the master. The starvation year will have gone, and people's borrowing from their granaries will have departed. Egypt will come into the fields, the banks will sparkle, . . . and contentment will be in their hearts more than that which was formerly."

—Third Dynasty text

Joseph in Palestine
Joseph in Egypt
Moses in Egypt
Additional Reading

Joseph in Palestine

Joseph was born in Haran, the first son of Rachel, the favored son of Jacob, and the most protected son in the potentially dangerous meeting with Esau (Gen. 33:2). Yet the Bible provides no details on Joseph's life until he reached the age of seventeen and the family was living in southern Canaan (the terms *Palestine* and *Canaan* are basically interchangeable).

At seventeen Joseph was old enough to be pasturing the flocks, and at one point he brought his father a bad report concerning his half-brothers, with whom he had been working. The inclusion of Joseph with these brothers may have caused tension in that group because he

7.1. Palestine and Egypt during the time of Joseph and Moses.

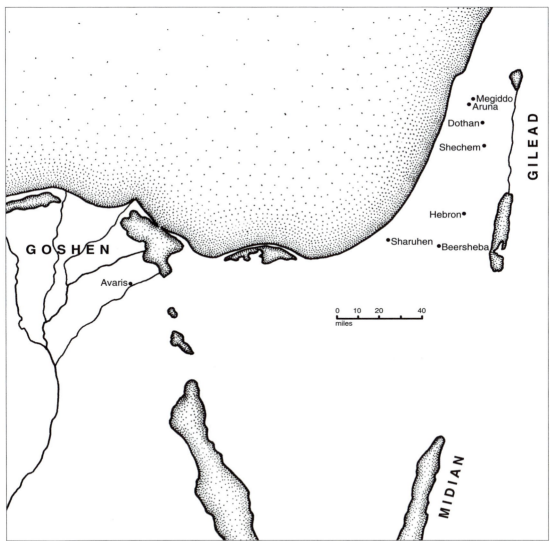

was the favorite son of the favorite wife. Also, since Joseph had lost his mother and was the youngest of his group, he could have felt particularly vulnerable.

Genesis 37:3 states that Jacob paid special attention to Joseph "because he was the son of [Jacob's] old age." Jacob may also have favored Joseph since he was a link with the deceased Rachel. Whatever the relative weights these reasons played in creating the favored position for Joseph, Jacob should have known better. He could not have forgotten the consequences of his own parents' favoritism.

As a sign of Joseph's special status, Jacob gave him a garment traditionally called a "coat of many colors," an image derived from the Septuagint translation of Genesis 37:3. More recent translations render the same phrase "long robe with sleeves" (New Revised Standard Version) or "varicolored tunic" (New American Standard Bible). The original meaning of the technical Hebrew phrase is not certain, so translators must guess at the proper image. But whatever the correct translation, the garment was a token of favoritism and became a "red flag" to Joseph's half-brothers. They could not even speak civilly to him.

Within the context of this family tension, Joseph began having dreams (Gen. 37:5–11) implying that someday he would "lord it over" his brothers and even that his father would be subservient to him. This last point was especially hard for Jacob to accept, but he kept what Joseph said in mind. Jacob had learned at Bethel to take dreams seriously.

A pivotal episode in Joseph's life began when the family flocks were taken northward for grazing. They were moved toward Shechem, a potentially dangerous area in light of earlier events (Gen. 34), and that is perhaps why Jacob sent Joseph, who had stayed home, to "see about the welfare of [his] brothers." Joseph did not reach his brothers until they were further north, at Dothan, and as he came into view his coat gave advance warning as to who was approaching. Quickly his brothers conspired to kill Joseph, threw him into a pit, and then sat down to eat. Their meal could not have been altogether peaceful, punctuated as it was by Joseph's pleadings (Gen. 42:21) and then by the arrival of a caravan en route from Gilead to Egypt.[1] The presence of the caravan prompted Judah to suggest a change of plans, namely, that they sell Joseph into slavery. In this way their brother's blood would not be on their hands and they would benefit financially. The plan was agreed to, and Joseph was bound over to the traders for twenty shekels of silver.[2]

The brothers, having kept Joseph's coat, ripped it, dipped it in the blood of a goat (Gen. 37:31), and then presented the tattered and stained garment to Jacob when they arrived home. Purposely, they let their father draw his own conclusions about what had happened; it was

1. The camels in the caravan were loaded with aromatic gum and balm and myrrh, materials that would appeal to the Egyptians. Balm was a transparent, pale yellow, fragrant gum used for incense. It could also be mixed with water and used as an ointment. Myrrh, also a fragrant substance, was used to perfume beds and garments and to embalm the dead.

2. Twenty shekels of silver weighed about eight ounces and was the going rate for a slave in the second millennium (Lev. 27:5). Joseph may have been shackled either at the time of sale or during his Egyptian imprisonment (Ps. 105:18). On the price of slaves, see Kitchen 1995b: 52–53.

not necessary to add falsehood to their deed. Jacob entered into a state of mourning and refused to be comforted by his sons and daughters.[3] His response to their attempted solace was to say, "Surely I will go down to Sheol in mourning for my son" (Gen. 37:35).[4]

Joseph in Egypt

Meanwhile, the traders brought Joseph into Egypt during the Second Intermediate period.[5] As sketched in the previous chapter, this period was politically much different from the one Abraham knew. Outwardly, however, it would have appeared quite similar.

Joseph was sold to Potiphar, captain of the pharaoh's bodyguard. Genesis 39:2 states that "the Lord was with Joseph." One way God's influence can be seen is that Joseph was not used as a field hand. Instead, Potiphar placed Joseph in the household where he was later promoted to "overseer over his house," a phrase that has been identified with a well-known title *imy-r pr* ("steward"). Such an overseer ran his master's estate so the owner could occupy himself with other matters. Joseph, although a slave, had attained a comfortable position.

Biblical authors seldom give physical descriptions of characters, but Genesis 39:6 reveals that Joseph was well built and handsome.[6] Joseph's fine appearance drew the attention of Potiphar's wife, who attempted to seduce him, but Joseph believed that to accept her advances would be a sin against God. This response indicates that a God-related moral code existed long before Moses' time. Joseph's position was extremely awkward, for he could hardly quit his job and leave. One day Potiphar's wife grew so frustrated at being scorned that she grabbed Joseph, who fled in such a hurry she was left holding part of his clothing. Lust turned to vengeance, and Potiphar's wife charged Joseph with attempted rape, using his abandoned garment as proof of her accusation. Potiphar gave Joseph no chance to defend himself, but summarily threw him into a prison reserved for the king's prisoners.[7]

3. If Dinah was Jacob's only daughter, then Gen. 37:35 refers to daughters-in-law.

4. Sheol is the place the Hebrews thought of as the destination of the dead, the "underworld." Jacob was convinced he would go to his grave mourning for Joseph. The rite of mourning consisted of any combination of tearing one's clothes, neglecting one's person, shaving the head or plucking out hair, sprinkling ashes on one's head, fasting, weeping, and lamenting. In the Near East women were (and sometimes still are) hired to weep and wail. Mourning could last for a week, a month, or up to seventy days. Jacob planned to mourn for the rest of his life.

5. See pp. 57–59 for the reasoning that places Joseph in the Hyksos period.

6. A literal translation of the Hebrew says that Joseph was "beautiful in form and beautiful in face."

7. Why did Potiphar not have his slave killed? Since Joseph had proven so trustworthy in the past, perhaps Potiphar did not entirely believe his wife, but he had to do something to appease her wrath. This story in Genesis 39 is the earliest literary example of the "woman scorned" motif. A somewhat later example exists in the Egyptian "Tale of Two Brothers" (*ANE* 1:12–16; *ANET* 23–25), which is sometimes compared to the biblical story. The Egyptian tale reads well, but has no more relationship to the Joseph story than do the numerous other examples that can be cited down into the present century. For a compilation and analysis of this literary motif through the centuries, see Yohannan 1968.

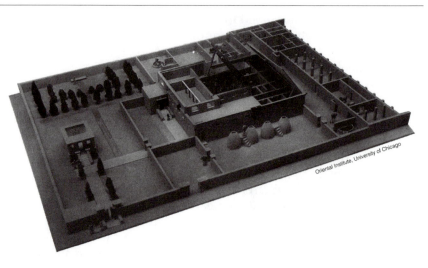

7.2. Model of villa based on an excavated estate at Tell el-Amarna, late Dynasty 18. Surrounded by grain silos, stables, servant quarters, and kitchen, the main building has air vents near the ceiling of the ground floor and windows on the second floor (most of the roofing has been left open to show construction techniques). The small building (on the far left in the model) in front of the tree-ringed reflecting pool at the back of the estate is an outdoor chapel, a feature that would not have been typical during Joseph's time in Egypt.

Oriental Institute, University of Chicago

Two of pharaoh's officials were thrown in the same prison with Joseph. These officials carried well-known Egyptian titles: "chief cupbearer" and "chief baker." One function of the cupbearer was to taste what the king drank. It is quite natural that the pharaoh also had a chief baker, since bread was so basic to the Egyptian diet (ancient Egyptians had words for dozens of different varieties). One night both officials had dreams (Gen. 40:5) and were downcast the following day because they had no one to interpret their dreams. The consternation of these two should not be minimized, because dreams were considered one way the gods informed people about what they should do and what was to happen. To understand the words of the gods was essential. This belief about dreams permeated the Near East and, as the Book of Daniel makes clear, was still operational as the Old Testament period drew to a close.

Joseph offered to interpret the dreams of these two officials. When he said, "Do not interpretations belong to God? Tell it to me, please" (Gen. 40:8), the two men would have agreed with Joseph's question, but they would have been thinking of a different deity. Joseph interpreted the dreams to signify that the cupbearer would be restored to his previous position, but that the baker would lose his life. Three days later, both of Joseph's predictions came true.

Joseph continued in jail for two more years until the pharaoh himself had a dream that bothered him.[8] Today the meaning of this dream seems clear enough, but pharaoh's wise men and magicians could offer no interpretation. Admittedly, hindsight helps the modern reader, but perhaps God clouded the minds of all but Joseph. Finally, the pharaoh's cupbearer remembered the man who had correctly told the meaning of his own dream, so Joseph was summoned, shaved, given a change of clothing, and presented to the pharaoh. The pharaoh related his dream

8. The name of this king is unknown. He would have been a Hyksos ruler, but the Egyptians destroyed the records of this period of "humiliation" so thoroughly that there is uncertainty over the names and even the order of some of the rulers.

7.3. Papyrus listing seventy-nine servants in an Egyptian household. Donald Wiseman (1958: 39) notes that forty-five of the servants are from Syria-Palestine, "probably sold into Egypt as slaves, as was Joseph about forty years after the list was written. Some of them bear good Hebrew names like Shiphrah and Menahem. In addition to the names, their office (e.g., 'chief over the house,' 'house servant') is listed in the second column and the sex of the slave is noted (third column)." The other side of the papyrus contains a prison register.

once more, this time in more detail. Joseph again prefaced his comments with the statement that God was involved in interpretations, and Genesis 41:38–39 implies that these words were not lost on the polytheistic pharaoh.

Joseph told the pharaoh the meaning of his dream and that it would be fulfilled soon. There was no divine judgment being given here as in the flood or at Sodom; this was simply one of life's irregularities. In addition to his interpretation, Joseph suggested that the wisest thing to do would be to put a good manager over the crops to store grain for the seven good years so that when the seven years of famine came, the people would not starve. The pharaoh was so impressed by Joseph's interpretation and by his reasoned approach to averting a disaster that he appointed Joseph to take charge of the preparations. Thus the stage was set for the fulfillment of Joseph's own early dreams.[9]

It should not seem strange that Egypt would gear up for seven years of preparation and that pharaoh would move a foreigner into a high position all on account of a dream. Pharaoh was himself a foreigner, and he and Joseph had similar Semitic backgrounds. Also, the Egyptians knew there was always the possibility that the Nile flooding would

9. The epigraph at the head of this chapter is set in the reign of Djoser, the builder of the famous step pyramid. It is uncertain whether this text relates an actual event or was a later forgery to support a priestly claim that certain land had been devoted to Khnum, the god of Elephantine. In any event, Egypt knew of lean years, and in the epigraph as in the story of Joseph, deity communicated via a dream.

7.4. Fragment of a Fifth Dynasty Egyptian relief showing starving people. Reliefs and written inscriptions concerning famines and food distribution "in each year of want" show why Egyptians responded to Joseph's warning as they did.

Erich Lessing/Art Resource

prove insufficient. Finally, the great importance attached to dreams coupled with the report that Joseph had already demonstrated his ability to understand the gods would encourage the people to take his words seriously.

Joseph's elevation to power contains several Egyptian touches, whether native Egyptian or acculturated Hyksos Egyptian: "Then Pharaoh took off his signet ring from his hand, and put it on Joseph's hand, and clothed him in garments of fine linen, and put the gold necklace around his neck. And he had him ride in his second chariot; and they proclaimed before him, 'Bow the knee!' " (Gen. 41:42–43). The signet ring would have consisted of a bezel into which a scarab seal had been set. The pharaoh would have had other similar rings, but because he gave one to Joseph, Joseph then possessed a visible symbol of the king's support. The garment given Joseph would have been made of the semi-diaphanous linen so familiar from Egyptian tomb paintings. The gold necklace would have been an award the Egyptians called the "Gold of Valor," given to people who made significant contributions to the state.

7.5. Steatite and gold signet ring of Hyksos King Apopy I.

Chariots were probably introduced into Egypt late in the Hyksos occupation, and Joseph's would have been little more than a wheeled platform on which he stood and held the reins of two horses. Egyptian reliefs and paintings contain frequent scenes of commoners bowing to the ground in deference to more important personages.[10]

7.6. Eighteenth Dynasty relief in which general Horemhab is awarded "Gold of Valor" collars by Pharaoh Tutankhamun.

Thirteen years removed from the time his brothers sold him into slavery, Joseph was thirty years old when he began working for the pha-

10. Joseph's title is often assumed to be that of vizier, but some scholars think it more likely that he was put in charge of a certain task, perhaps as minister of agriculture. In addition to clothing and jewelry, the pharaoh also gave Joseph an Egyptian name and an Egyptian wife. She was the daughter of the priest of On (or Heliopolis, as in some translations), and her name was Asenath, meaning "belonging to the goddess Nieth." Any qualms Joseph may have had about being married to a pagan woman would make no difference, as he had little choice but to accept the pharaoh's gifts, inanimate and animate.

7.7. Model of a granary.

raoh. As he moved about the country preparing for the lean years to come, so much grain was put into storage that the Egyptians stopped trying to record quantities. During those years of preparation, Joseph had two sons to whom he gave Hebrew, not Egyptian, names. His choice of names for his sons (Gen. 41:50–52) indicates that Joseph recognized God's help through the preceding years.

When the famine years began, Joseph opened the storehouses and sold grain from the stockpiles. As the famine extended into Palestine, people from that area came to Egypt in search of food. Egyptians were willing to share their supplies in spite of the anticipated additional lean years because the Hyksos, who controlled much of Egypt, also had some authority in Palestine. In a sense, therefore, they were sharing within the larger "family."

When the famine affected Jacob and his family, Jacob instructed his sons to travel to Egypt for grain. All the brothers went except Benjamin, because Jacob would not part with the son he believed to be the final link with his beloved Rachel. Jacob was "afraid that harm may befall him" (Gen. 42:4). Perhaps he suspected that his sons knew more about Joseph's "death" than they had told him.

When the brothers arrived in Egypt they encountered none other than Joseph. Joseph would not have personally doled out grain to everyone, but he would have made periodic inspection tours. That he was on-site when his brothers arrived could be one more instance of God "working in history" to mesh his plans. Joseph recognized his brothers immediately but the reverse was not the case. Joseph's brothers were adults when he was carried to Egypt, but Joseph was only a teenager probably struggling to grow a beard when his brothers had last seen him. Now he was in his thirties. The man they encountered did not look Hebrew, but was clean shaven and dressed in the linen garments of Egypt. Also, Joseph spoke in Egyptian and chose to work through an interpreter. As the brothers came into Egypt they may well have wondered what had become of Joseph, but not in their wildest imagination would they have thought to look for him in such a role.

Genesis 42:7 says Joseph spoke harshly to his brothers. Commentators disagree whether this attitude implies vindictiveness or if Joseph was merely probing his brothers' present character. It is not necessary that Joseph be perfect in everything he did, and perhaps this whole episode was testing his ability to forgive. When Joseph saw his brothers bowing down to him "with their faces to the ground," the realization that his dreams were coming true must have had a powerful effect.

Joseph began a "cat and mouse" game with a question for which he already had the answer, "Where have you come from?" He accused his brothers of being spies, but they protested that they were innocent. Joseph told his brothers that he would test their story by sending one of them back for the younger brother they had mentioned—while the others waited in prison for his return. Once again, Joseph's motive in so dealing with his brothers is debated. On the third day after their meeting, Joseph changed his conditions and let all but Simeon leave for home—with orders to return to Egypt with Benjamin.

When the brothers reached home, Jacob felt he had now lost two sons (Joseph and Simeon) and he refused to part with a third. Apparently no thought was given to rescuing Simeon. The grain brought back from Egypt was doubtlessly stretched as far as possible in hopes that the supply would outlast the famine. It did not, and when they had again run short of supplies Jacob relented concerning Benjamin. As the brothers traveled back to Egypt, the Bible is silent about whether they expected to find Simeon still alive. They had heard Joseph's threat that the hostage would die if they did not return with their youngest brother.

When the brothers arrived in Egypt they must have been overjoyed to find Simeon alive. Their initial meeting with the Egyptian official was also positive. But when it was time to return home again, Joseph had his silver cup planted in Benjamin's bag.[11] Soon Benjamin was charged with theft, and Joseph decreed that everyone except Benjamin was free to leave. Judah fervently pleaded—for his father's sake—that he be kept instead of Benjamin.

Whether Joseph had been toying with his brothers or had been looking for signs of repentance and unselfishness, his charade came to an end and the story reaches its turning point. Joseph suddenly announced

11. In Gen. 44:5, 15 the cup is identified as one used for divination. Joseph himself never says that he used the cup for such an activity, but this possibility provided his brothers with an "explanation" for some of the things that had been happening (e.g., seating by birth order at the banquet).

7.8. Detail from a mid–Eighteenth Dynasty Theban painted wall relief showing an Egyptian wagon. Depictions of Egyptian wagons are extremely rare.

that he wanted to be alone with the "Canaanites." The brothers would not have understood the command, but they would have watched nervously as everyone else left the room. Even the ever-necessary interpreter departed. Then Joseph started to cry "so loudly that the Egyptians heard it, and the household of Pharaoh heard of it." Very likely, some of the Egyptians peeked in to make sure their master was safe, and the brothers were probably feeling quite uncomfortable. To their amazement, the weeping "Egyptian" began to speak Hebrew, and his words both electrified and scared them: "I am Joseph! Is my father still alive?"

Joseph gathered his brothers around him and explained again that he was really their brother. He continued to calm their fears with a speech that beautifully expresses how God works in history:

> And now do not be grieved or angry with yourselves, because you sold me here; for God sent me before you to preserve life. For the famine has been in the land these two years, and there are still five years in which there will be neither plowing nor harvesting. And God sent me before you to preserve for you a remnant in the earth, and to keep you alive by a great deliverance. Now, therefore, it was not you who sent me here, but God; and He has made me a father to Pharaoh and lord of all his household and ruler over all the land of Egypt (Gen. 45:5–8).

Joseph had no way to know at the beginning of his adventures that his enslavement was for good, not bad, and it is not necessary to believe that his faith never wavered. In retrospect, however, Joseph could recognize that God knows what is best. After this emotional reunion Joseph instructed his brothers to bring their father and his extended family into Egypt where they could be cared for in Goshen. The brothers were supplied with wagons and food to speed their journey to southern Palestine and back.

It is understandable that Jacob was stunned and unbelieving when his sons reported back home. Finally though, the combination of their story and the sight of the wagons, quite possibly with Egyptian attendants, convinced Jacob of the truth. He responded, "It is enough; my son Joseph is still alive. I will go and see him before I die" (Gen. 45:28).

Jacob had most likely been living at Hebron. En route south, he stopped at Beersheba to offer sacrifices to God. That evening, in a vision, God added a new detail to the old promise of a land and a multitude of descendants: the people of Israel would grow in number not in Canaan, but in Egypt. God also assured Jacob that he would be with him in Egypt, that he would see Joseph, and that this son would be with him at his death.

Jacob continued on to Egypt with his people, property, and livestock.[12] When they entered Goshen, Joseph came out to meet them in his chariot. There was a tearful reunion and Jacob allowed that, having seen Joseph again, he was prepared to die. During all the years since Joseph had been lost to him, Jacob's mind had been bitterly centered on death, but now he spoke of that prospect in a hopeful, fulfilled manner. The reunion was a turning point for Jacob.

Metropolitan Museum of Art, Rogers Fund, 1921

Joseph coached his father and brothers on what they should say when meeting the pharaoh; namely that they were to emphasize that not only were they shepherds, but that the family had been shepherds for generations. Joseph wanted his father and brothers settled in the largely undeveloped plain of Goshen rather than with him in one of the population centers of Egypt. Goshen contained good pastureland, and

7.9. Modern replica of the chariot of Yuya (father-in-law of Pharaoh Amenhotep III), from his tomb in the Valley of the Kings.

12. Genesis 46:26–27 and Acts 7:14 give three different totals for the number of people entering Egypt. Either sixty-six or seventy people seems to be the correct figure. See Youngblood 1991: 268–69 for one way to resolve this apparent disharmony.

7.10. Drawing from a painting in the tomb of Amen-em-opet at Thebes (fourteenth–thirteenth century) showing various stages in the process of mummification.

there the family could approximate part of the lifestyle they had known in Palestine.[13] Genesis 47:7 records Jacob's introduction to the pharaoh. This encounter marks the end of the patriarchal period (which had begun 215 years earlier with Abraham's departure from Haran) and the beginning of the "Egyptian sojourn."

Joseph settled his family in the land of Goshen.[14] There, they found some differences from the life they had known. One major difference was the manner of travel, which was now easier: the hills and valleys of central Palestine kept them to the sometimes meandering ridge routes, whereas in the flat plain of Goshen they could travel in a more direct line. In Palestine they would have traveled by foot or donkey, but in the delta a boat ride was also an option. The climate was harder on Jacob and his family: in Egypt's delta they would still experience rainy and dry seasons, but they would also encounter a greater fluctuation in the yearly temperatures. Perhaps the most difficult accommodation for some of the people in the first generation was to trade their rolling hills and valleys for a landscape that was flat as far as their eyes could see.

With Genesis 47:27–28 the scene suddenly shifts to twelve years after the end of the famine. The covenantal promise began to be fulfilled; the Hebrews were becoming numerous. Jacob was still alive, but he realized the end was near. Like Sinuhe, Jacob wanted to be buried in his homeland, and he made Joseph swear to carry his body back to Palestine.

Joseph brought his sons Ephraim and Manasseh to see their grandfather. With them, Jacob reflected on the covenantal promise from God and announced that he was adopting the two young men. Jacob divided Joseph's portion of the inheritance between the two (which later on resulted in the tribes of Ephraim and Manasseh, but no tribe of Joseph). Jacob blessed the two sons of Joseph and purposely gave the primary blessing to the younger Ephraim.[15] Jacob also gathered his own sons for their final blessings, and then he died.

Joseph commanded that his father be mummified. The professional mourners began their seventy days of wailing, and the priests started the forty-day embalming process. No secret arts of embalming have been lost; today bodies can be preserved as well as or better than they were in ancient Egypt. The most important step in the mummification

13. The Egyptian disdain for shepherds need reflect no more than a city dweller's smugness toward more rural areas.

14. Genesis 47:11 says "in the land of Rameses," which represents a later editorial touch. The term *Rameses* was not used during Joseph's time but became a synonym for Egypt in later centuries.

15. The manner in which 1 Chron. 26:10 records another instance of a younger son being given first place points up the unusualness of such an occurrence.

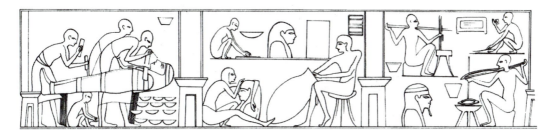

process was to dehydrate the body, to extract all body fluids. Another important step was to protect the body from future moisture and infestation (Spencer 1982).

Joseph received permission from the pharaoh to bury his father in Palestine, and a large number of people accompanied him to the cave of Machpelah, near Hebron. Jacob was laid to rest in the family burial place, bringing the number of people buried in the cave to six: Abraham, Sarah, Isaac, Rebekah, Leah, and Jacob.[16]

Joseph lived to see his grandsons and even his great-grandsons. Before he died, Joseph expressed assurance that his people would return to their land of promise and he asked that they carry his body back with them. "So Joseph died at the age of one hundred and ten years; and he was embalmed and placed in a coffin in Egypt" (Gen. 50:26). One hundred and ten may not necessarily be Joseph's age at death, since in Egypt this number was used in wishing someone a long life or to indicate that someone had lived to a ripe old age.[17]

Moses in Egypt

After Joseph's death, the Hebrews continued to live in the land of Goshen. Presumably they continued the peaceful and prosperous life started for them by Joseph. But changes were afoot, and in retrospect the Hyksos probably realized that it had been a mistake to allow a measure of local autonomy in southern Egypt. Out of southern Egypt came an Egyptian named Ahmose, and soon the Hyksos were obliged to take flight. Their delta capital of Avaris fell, and their stronghold in southern Palestine, Sharuhen, fell after a three-year siege. Ahmose, who threw the hated Hyksos out of Egypt, is often identified as the pharaoh of Exodus 1:8: "Now a new king arose over Egypt, who did not know Joseph."

Ahmose came from the south of Egypt, hundreds of miles from Joseph's sphere of influence. Ahmose would have had no sympathy for Joseph's association with the Hyksos or with the Hebrews' identification with them. Pharaoh Ahmose became worried over the foreigners still in his land, and his solution was to put those people to work on govern-

16. Rachel was buried somewhere in the Jerusalem area. There is a bit of irony in that Jacob was laid to rest beside Leah.

17. Osman 1988 argues that he found the mummy of Joseph in the Cairo Museum! This book has been scathingly reviewed by Redford 1989. For Osman to be correct, Josh. 24:32, which states that Joseph was buried at Shechem, would have to be in error.

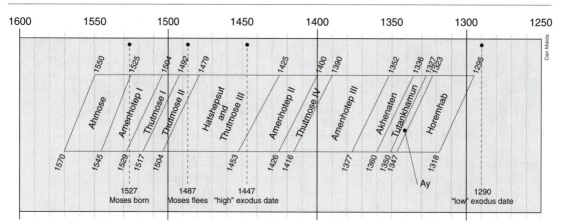

| 1600 | 1550 | 1500 | 1450 | 1400 | 1350 | 1300 | 1250 |

7.11. Two prevailing chronologies of Dynasty 18 Egypt and the life of Moses. It is not possible to correlate all phases of Moses' life with specific rulers because there is disagreement among Egyptologists over the regnal years of the Dynasty 18 pharaohs. Another factor affecting precision is that the Bible divides Moses' life into forty-year segments, which perhaps should be understood as round figures. I accept 1447 as the date of the exodus (see chap. 8) and take 1570 as the more likely beginning of Dynasty 18.

ment projects, to make them build store cities to hold the wealth of Egypt. The oppression was beginning.[18]

Before the Hyksos occupation, the Egyptians had been relatively isolated, their only outreach into the world being materially motivated. Even the shift of their southern border to the second cataract did not change that outlook on life. Egyptians had patronized foreigners both for their own good and for the good of Egypt. After the Hyksos, however, the Egyptians realized that foreigners in large numbers could not be trusted and needed to be controlled. This changed attitude toward outsiders created problems for several generations of Hebrews. The Egyptian worry that there were too many Hebrews in Goshen grew out of the fear that Egypt might again become an occupied country.

The genocide recorded in Exodus 1:16 was mandated shortly before the birth of Moses. The Hebrew midwives were ordered: "When you are helping the Hebrew women to give birth and see them upon the birthstool, if it is a son, then you shall put him to death; but if it is a daughter, then she shall live." Because of these population-control measures, Moses was placed in a basket in the Nile, where he was found by an unnamed Egyptian princess.[19]

For his first two or three years, Moses was allowed to stay with a wet nurse, his own mother (Exod. 2:7–9). But after he was weaned, Moses was brought back to the princess, who gave him his Egyptian name.[20] Acts 7:22 says that "Moses was educated in all the learning of the Egyptians," and Acts 7:23 states that he lived the first forty years of his life as an Egyptian. The earlier verse implies that Moses was taught Egypt's complex mythology and ritual and that he was expected to believe the pharaoh was a visible god.[21] Moses was surely exposed to Egyptian wis-

18. The oppression lasted over one hundred years but, regardless whether one accepts the long or short Egyptian sojourn, it by no means occupied the whole of the Hebrew stay in Egypt.

19. Since Aaron was three years old when Moses was born, it would seem that the population controls had been recently imposed. Some writers draw attention to a somewhat similar event in the life of the later King Sargon II of Assyria, but the similarity is coincidental (*ANE* 1:85–86; *ANET* 119).

20. The name *Moses* is also found in pharaonic names such as Ahmose and Thutmose.

21. Liberal scholarship has long questioned whether the Hebrews really practiced monotheism before the time of Moses. Further, it has tried to find the origin of Moses'

dom literature, such as the "Instructions of Ptah-hotep," cited in the previous chapter. And he likely would have been taught the principles of Egyptian mathematics, such as the system of "doubling" to determine sums in multiplication.[22]

During the first third of his life, Moses was part of the Egyptian court scene and saw the wealth of the world beginning to flow into a country just then flexing its military muscle. The young Pharaoh Thutmose III was pushed aside by his aunt and stepmother, Hatshepsut, who took the masculine term *pharaoh*. In reliefs, her skin is given the masculine red tone rather than the yellow shading customary for a woman. She is even depicted wearing the false beard of kingship, and in reliefs and sculpture her chest is often masculinized.

Hatshepsut held the throne of Egypt for eighteen years while Moses continued to be a Hebrew with an Egyptian veneer. Then, toward the end of her reign or early in the reign of Thutmose III, Moses tried to stop an Egyptian from harming a Hebrew. Moses killed the Egyptian and tried to hide the evidence, but the news of the murder found its way to the ears of the pharaoh.[23] Moses was forced to flee east of Sinai to Midian, where he took up residence in the clan of Jethro and married into his family. Moses' lifestyle had to undergo basic changes with this move from the courts of Egypt to the tents and flocks in Midian, but later on, Moses' experience with this different lifestyle proved to be a major asset.

When Hatshepsut died, Thutmose III reclaimed the throne of Egypt. He can be identified as the "pharaoh of the oppression," during whose reign the Hebrews began to groan and cry out for help (Exod. 2:23). Thutmose III had spent the Hatshepsut years in the army, and a little

---

monotheism in the religion of Pharaoh Akhenaten. For an evaluation of that possibility, see Redford 1987, who concludes (p. 32) that "the essential characteristics of the two monotheisms are so diverse as to exclude the possibility of influence, one upon the other." Redford's preference for the low exodus date leads him to place Akhenaten prior to the life of Moses. The high exodus date puts Moses earlier than Akhenaten, but the dissimilarities of the two religions does not warrant the suggestion of Hebrew influence on Egyptian religion.

22. For example, to multiply 35 times 20, begin doubling columns under each number and continue doubling until the column under the smaller number contains figures that can be added together to equal that smaller number (in this case, 20). Cross out the unneeded numbers in the right column (and their corresponding numbers in the left column). The remaining numbers in the left column are then added together to obtain the result:

35	20		35	20
35	1		~~35~~	~~1~~
70	2		~~70~~	~~2~~
140	4		140	4
280	8		~~280~~	~~8~~
560	16		560	16
			700	

Division was accomplished by an inverse process. By these and additional means, the Egyptians were capable of rather complex computations. For an introduction to mathematics in the ancient Near East, see Neugebauer 1969.

23. Exodus 2:15 says of the pharaoh that "he tried to kill Moses." If Hatshepsut is linked to this episode in Moses' life, then the verse is expressing official dogma, not actual gender.

7.12. Detail from a wall painting in the tomb of Menna, scribe of Thutmose IV. An overseer beats a slave while another begs for mercy.

more than two months after regaining the throne he led Egyptian forces into Palestine. Egypt was seeking security through the establishment of dependent buffer states.

Thutmose III left several texts that give insight into his personality. In the account of his routing 330 Syro-Palestinian princes gathered at Megiddo, in northern Palestine, he exhibited both his extroverted nature and feeling of superiority over non-Egyptians. According to this text, the Egyptian army marched along the coast of Palestine and then turned inland toward Aruna. At Aruna they had to decide whether to take the narrow pass from Aruna to Megiddo. Although the pass provided direct access to Megiddo, Thutmose's advisors believed it was too dangerous. They suggested the army should proceed either east or west around the intervening hills, but Thutmose III rejected their advice (*ANE* 1:177; *ANET* 235):

> I swear, as Re loves me, as my father Amon favors me, as my nostrils are rejuvenated with life and satisfaction, my majesty shall proceed upon this Aruna road! Let him of you who wishes go upon these roads of which you speak, and let him of you who wishes come in the following of my majesty!

The Egyptian army dutifully followed their pharaoh and found the Aruna pass undefended. Thutmose III easily sent the enemy coalition into inglorious rout. Garments hung from the walls of Megiddo were used to pull up into the city those fleeing the battle. Thutmose III took a large quantity of booty left in the field and then laid siege to Megiddo. The Egyptian army lived off the crops that were just coming into harvest while the people within Megiddo hung on for seven months before surrendering:

> Now the princes of this foreign country came on their bellies to kiss the ground to the glory of his majesty and to beg breath for their nostrils, because his arm was so great, because the prowess of Amon was so great . . . the princes whom the prowess of his majesty carried off, bearing their tribute of silver, gold, lapis lazuli, and turquoise, and carrying grain, wine, and large and small cattle for the army of his majesty, with one

James Hoffmeier

7.13. Wall relief of Thutmose III in which the pharaoh is smiting Syro-Palestinian prisoners, whom he holds by the hair. The prisoners hold up their hands begging for mercy. Below and beside the prisoners are the names of defeated places.

gang of them bearing tribute southward. Then his majesty appointed princes anew (*ANE* 1:180; *ANET* 237).

After his Megiddo campaign Thutmose III needed little more than dress parades into Palestine to maintain his control of the coastal highway.

Exodus 2:23 states: "Now it came about in the course of those many days that the king of Egypt died. And the sons of Israel sighed because of the bondage, and they cried out; and their cry for help because of their bondage rose up to God." About that same time, God called Moses at the burning bush to deliver Israel and to lead God's people into the Promised Land (Exod. 3). Moses was less than eager to accept the commission but finally, in the company of Aaron his older brother, he returned to Egypt. Amenhotep II succeeded Thutmose III to the throne and he, therefore, can be identified as the "pharaoh of the exodus."[24]

Amenhotep II was a famous sportsman in his youth and he left several stories of his physical abilities (*ANET* 243–45). For example, it was recorded that no one else was strong enough to draw his bow. One day he tested two hundred stiff bows and then began riding his chariot around a series of copper targets, each about three inches thick. According to the story, every shot hit the mark, and the arrows fell through the back of the targets. Amenhotep II was also reported to be a great horse trainer. Horses would not tire when he rode them nor

24. By the alternate chronology for Dynasty 18, Hatshepsut would be the king of Egypt who died, and Thutmose III would be the pharaoh of the exodus. The low date of the exodus identifies Ramesses II as the pharaoh of the exodus. In order to accept Ramesses II as the king who interacted with Moses, it is necessary to accept some biblical symbolism. See chapter 8 for more detail.

7.14. Relief from the Karnak Temple at Thebes, showing Amenhotep II shooting arrows from his chariot into a copper target and tree trunk.

would they sweat, even at a high gallop. This pharaoh was a great oarsman who did not tire, even after single-handedly rowing a barge containing two hundred people a distance of four miles. Amenhotep II also emulated his father in military exploits:

> His majesty crossed the Orontes on dangerous waters. . . . Then he . . . saw a few [of the enemy] coming furtively, adorned with weapons of warfare, to attack the king's army. His majesty burst after them like the flight of a divine falcon. The confidence of their hearts was slackened, and one after another fell upon his fellow, up to their commander. Not a single one was with his majesty, except for himself with his valiant arm. His majesty killed them by shooting (*ANET* 245).

It is necessary to see past the hyperbole, the published propaganda, to speculate at what might have been the truth. The military victories were not fabricated; the king was there, but the extent of his participation and his value in battle is problematic. In Amenhotep's mind he must have believed he had defeated other gods, and there is no reason to doubt texts that state he hanged enemy princes and displayed severed hands on his horses.[25] Amenhotep could well have been an expert with horses, but whether he really had such strength with an oar, was such a crack shot, or could make his bow penetrate what even a crossbow cannot is questionable.

Texts relate that Amenhotep II loved physical strength, and he must have staged shows of skill and muscle to give credence to his official image. But how much did Amenhotep feel he had to live a lie, how eagerly did he try to be a legend in his own time? Was Amenhotep vain and full

25. Body counts were sometimes obtained by tabulating the hands or heads of the slain. Later on, Saul demanded a variation of this practice of David (1 Sam. 18:25–27), a variation that is also depicted in Egyptian reliefs.

of bravado, or did the knowledge that he was less than his press clippings give him a sense of insecurity? Would he fear that compromise would be interpreted as weakness? However these questions are answered, the reason Moses did not want to be involved becomes more understandable. And one can appreciate the great courage Moses mustered when he confronted that pharaoh. The pharaoh's response to Moses' requests can also be seen as quite in character: "Who is the LORD that I should obey His voice to let Israel go? I do not know the LORD, and besides, I will not let Israel go" (Exod. 5:2).

Rather than attack Moses directly, the pharaoh increased the burden on the Hebrews so that they would have less time to listen to Moses and would blame him for their added labor. The Egyptians stopped supplying the straw used in making the required mud bricks. Straw is not essential to brick-making and even today some bricks are made in Goshen without it, but straw acts as a binder and prevents the bricks from breaking as they dry. Under their increased burden, the Hebrews either had to expend some of their labor force to forage for binder while meeting their same quota or else had to produce enough additional bricks to compensate for those that would not survive the drying process (Kitchen 1976).[26]

Pharaoh's heart became "hard," a description taken so literally by some that an examination of this pharaoh's mummy was once made to see whether his heart was indeed hard! But the Hebrew implies that the pharaoh was insensitive, that he maintained that attitude, and that God permitted the condition to continue. Because of the pharaoh's hardheartedness the plagues began:

1. Nile turned to "blood"
2. frogs
3. mosquitoes(?)
4. flies
5. cattle (anthrax?)
6. boils
7. hailstorm
8. locusts
9. darkness
10. death of firstborn

The first nine plagues have a somewhat natural character and order, and the Bible does not state how extensively the Egyptians were affected. Nevertheless, they demonstrated that Moses' God—not the pharaoh—was in control. These disasters might well have been regarded by the Egyptians as being directed against various Egyptian gods (Exod. 12:12), whom the Egyptians believed indwelled much of nature. Thus the first plague on the Nile could have been seen as a setback for Khnum, guardian of the Nile, and for Osiris, whose bloodstream was the Nile. The sun's being blotted out in the ninth plague could have been interpreted as an attack on Re, Atum, or Horus—all

26. Despite assuming a late exodus date, Sarna 1986 provides good insights into brick-making and other aspects of the oppression.

Art Resource

7.15. Workers in an Egyptian brickyard (from the tomb of Rekhmire, vizier of Thutmose III). The men are mixing clay (lower left), which is placed in simple rectangular molds to form bricks (upper right) and then laid out to dry (upper left). The bricks are later stacked (lower right). On the far right are a seated supervisor holding a staff (upper) and a worker transporting bricks to a building site (lower).

viewed as sun gods. The final plague has no natural explanation, but it too was directed against a god—the next king, the god-to-be. Even if natural phenomena were operative in the first nine plagues, this does not detract from their miraculous nature. Their timing and selectivity requires that they, as well as the final plague, be seen as acts of God (Hoffmeier 1992 and Stieglitz 1987).

The pharaoh vacillated whether he should allow Moses and his people to leave. When the pharaoh's eldest son died in the last plague, the king relented long enough for the trek out of Egypt to begin, thus bringing the Egyptian sojourn to a close.[27]

Additional Reading

Davis, John J. *Moses and the Gods of Egypt*. Grand Rapids: Baker, 1971.

27. There are no specific Egyptian references to the sojourn, the exodus, Joseph, or Moses. For two reasons this silence is not surprising. First, any record of Joseph was lost in the Egyptian purge of Hyksos history. It is not possible to give even a full list of Hyksos kings, let alone their viziers. Second, since the Egyptians had little interest in recording setbacks it is unlikely that the exodus and its attendant problems would have been recorded. Evidences for the exodus proposed by Hans Goedicke have found little support among other scholars. For his argument and the spirited responses that followed, see Krahmalkov 1981; Oren 1981; Radday 1982; Shanks 1981a, 1982a. Goedicke's theory received a fatal blow when the date for the eruption of the Thera volcano was put back to the late seventeenth century; see Doumas 1991.

The Exodus and Mount Sinai

The Old Testament provides objective moral standards which demand the obedience of our inmost hearts. The answer to the young man who enquired how to gain eternal life is given in the form of a series of quotations from the Ten Commandments, together with the injunction from Leviticus, "Thou shalt love thy neighbor as thyself. . . ."

When the lawyer asked the question, "Which is the great commandment in the law?", He replied with two quotations from the Pentateuch: "Thou shalt love the Lord thy God with all thy heart, and with all thy soul, and with all thy mind. This is the great and first commandment. And a second like unto it is this, Thou shalt love thy neighbor as thyself." To Him these two quotations sum up the teaching of the Old Testament. "On these two commandments," He says, "hangeth the whole law, and the prophets. . . ."

Note carefully that to our Lord these two commandments sum up, not the New Testament, but the Old. It is astonishing how many people think that these two commandments are the heart of the New Testament, forgetting that they stand in the law of Moses, dating back centuries before the time of Christ. According to our Lord they are the heart of the Old Testament. Or, to be more precise, they are the heart of the Old Testament law. There is no higher law than the Old Testament law as here expressed, and never can be. The New Testament does not reveal a higher law: it reveals the gospel.

—J. W. Wenham

En route to Mount Sinai
At Mount Sinai
    Biblical Law
    Feasts and Seasons

8.1. Clearing an enclosure wall at Tell er-Retaba, the possible site of biblical Pithom. When first excavated at the beginning of the twentieth century, it was concluded that the site lacked stratification and could not be profitably excavated due to groundwater. Even though test probes by Johns Hopkins University in the late 1970s (shown here) found the site well stratified and not endangered by groundwater, no large-scale excavation has been carried out.

When the pharaoh temporarily relented after the tenth plague, Moses led the Israelites out of Egypt (Exod. 12:37). They took with them the mummified body of Joseph (Exod. 13:19) and a "mixed multitude." The trek began at Rameses and proceeded to Pithom and Etham before reaching the "Red Sea."[1] Moses did not lead the people northeast, directly toward the Promised Land. Had they marched in that direction they would have encountered the "Wall of the Rulers," a string of forts guarding Egypt's northeastern border. This is the same

1. These three sites are in or near Wadi Tumilat, a natural corridor in and out of the eastern delta. Rameses, now generally identified with Tell ed-Daba, was called Avaris when it was founded earlier by the Hyksos. That it is called Rameses in connection with the exodus has been used as support for the late exodus date. The reasoning goes that the Hebrews could not have been forced to build a city by that name prior to 1300 when a king with that name lived. But all commentators agree that Gen. 47:11 is used retrospectively when it equates Joseph with the "land of Rameses." To be consistent, scholars should acknowledge that updating of place-names is equally plausible in both instances. Excavation has shown that Tell el-Maskhuta cannot be the site of biblical Pithom. Limited excavation at Tell er-Retaba, the only other site that has been seriously considered, suggests that it could be biblical Pithom. Etham has not yet been identified.

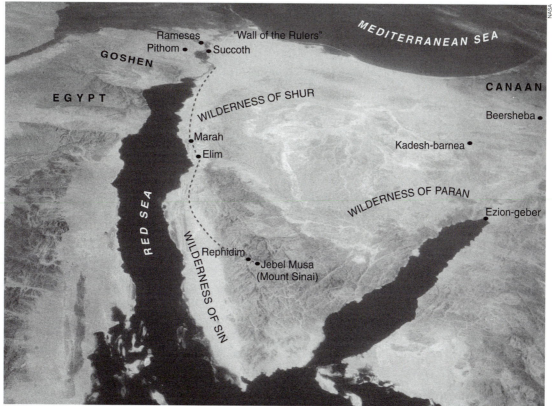

8.2. Satellite photograph of the Sinai Peninsula, on which the traditional route of the exodus to Mount Sinai has been superimposed.

military network the solitary Sinuhe managed to evade centuries before, but it would have been impossible for a large group to pass without incident.

Before the Hebrews were out of Goshen, the pharaoh changed his mind once more, and he entered the delta with over six hundred war chariots. Israel had just seen God's mighty acts in the Passover, and they were then seeing his visible guidance in the cloud and the fire. Nevertheless they panicked, so God placed his angel between Israel and Egypt and told Moses how to get his people across the sea.

Much has been written on this crossing of the Red Sea, or "reed sea," as the Hebrew puts it. The term *Reed Sea* can be applied to both the western leg of the Red Sea and to the Bitter Lakes region located between this leg of the Red Sea and the Mediterranean. The Bible does not specify where within this region the crossing took place, other than that there was a barrier of water that needed God's intervention.

Since the Hebrew text states that Moses led the people over the Reed Sea, some Bible maps show their line of march north to marshland along the Mediterranean, where there can be a physical passage through reeds. Another option prefers that the line of march be within the northern part of the western leg of the Red Sea where deep water, but no reeds, can be found. Since the term *Reed Sea* designates a large area, but not necessarily a reed-filled one, the northern line of march is unnecessary and is inconsistent with the biblical statement that a northern route was avoided (Exod. 13:17). Still, no specific point of crossing can be identified. Somewhere along the length of the Reed

Sea, God worked a miracle and there was a crossing. But not for the pharaoh's army.[2]

Once safely across the Reed Sea, Moses sang praise to God for victory and salvation (Exod. 15:1–18), and he may have then used "Reed Sea" metaphorically. In ancient Egyptian funerary texts the soul of the dead person passed over the "sea of reeds" into the next world. Moses would have been well aware of Egypt's religious jargon and might have seen a beautiful parallel in that the Hebrews were now to be set apart as holy and pure. They were "baptized," as Paul states in 1 Corinthians 10:1–2 (Towers 1959).[3]

En route to Mount Sinai

Comparatively little work has been done in the Sinai, but the few oases in the peninsula limit the possible identifications of stopping points mentioned in the text (illustration 8.2 follows the traditional routing south to Mount Sinai).[4] Marah is the Hebrew word for "bitter." Unable to drink the water of this oasis, the people complained to Moses, and God miraculously provided for their need. The distressing part of the incident is that the group was only a few days from the miracle of God's love and power at the Sea of Reeds.

From Marah they went to Elim and then to a sandy plain called the Wilderness of Sin.[5] There they became hungry, and God again provided for their need by giving them manna. The term *manna* means "What is it?" and is a pun on the Hebrews' first reaction upon seeing the bread from heaven. Although the substance was never otherwise named, God gave specific directions concerning how manna should be gathered. These instructions reminded the people of their daily dependence on God and of his continuing care for them. But the people insisted that manna was not enough; they also wanted meat. So, after God provided for their need with the manna, he also provided for their wants by giving them quail. Quails seasonally migrate through the Sinai Peninsula, and it was once the practice of local inhabitants to snare them in land nets. It may be that God timed a migration to coincide with this request.

It is occasionally claimed that manna can still be found (Keller 1981: 128–30), an assertion largely based on the modern Arab term *manna*, which describes the seasonal secretion of a certain plant found in some areas of Sinai. But there are several dissimilarities between the biblical

2. The belief that the pharaoh drowned derives from an Ethiopic fable. See Shanks 1975 concerning the finding of salt crystals in the lungs of a pharaoh once equated with the exodus!

3. This does not imply that the crossing was figurative or that it was any less miraculous, but only that Moses used a known motif to enhance the significance of the event for the people of his day.

4. See Beit-Arieh 1988b for a summary of the proposed routes and locations of Mount Sinai. Beit-Arieh concludes that the traditional routing is the most probable and that some of the other proposals are simply not viable.

5. The name *Sin* is spelled *Tsin* in Hebrew and carries no connotation of wrongdoing.

manna and this secretion: biblical manna was not seasonal, it was not similarly localized, and it spoiled quickly. Such differences preclude the correctness of the suggested identification, and the biblical declaration that manna ceased to be provided once the Israelites arrived in the Promised Land argues against the possibility of its presence at any time since then.

There were additional grumblings as God led and sustained his people in the Sinai Peninsula. He also protected them at Rephidim when the Amalekites came out for battle. Joshua entered the story at this point as the leader of the soldiers going out to face the Amalekites. For victory, Moses had to lift his hands toward heaven, and as long as he held his hands high, the battle went well. In this symbolic gesture, as with the recent miracles, God was teaching the Israelites that he was in charge of their destiny and that they could trust him for all their needs.

At Mount Sinai

Finally, three months after the crossing of the Reed Sea, Moses and the people with him arrived at their destination, Mount Sinai, where they would stay for approximately one year. Since the sixth century A.D. the traditional identification of Mount Sinai is a mountain now called Jebel Musa, "the mountain of Moses." One item in favor of the tradition's correctness is Jebel Musa's not being the tallest mountain in the area. Had this important place been identified arbitrarily, it is likely that the highest peak would have been chosen. In fact Jebel Musa's twin peak is higher. There is also a good-sized plain at the foot of Jebel Musa where the Israelites could have camped.[6]

God's chosen people became a nation at Mount Sinai. The covenant was expanded in the Ten Commandments, the laws, the tabernacle, the priesthood, offerings, feasts, and heritage. All these components were given to the Hebrews at Mount Sinai so they could serve God effectively. They were given freedom as well as responsibility. God made it clear that he expected obedience, and in return this new nation would be his treasured possession.

Biblical Law

The Hebrews already had some aspects of God's law. They knew about circumcision and tithing and that adultery was a sin. But at Mount Sinai God began to give a fuller code in terms that would be understandable and fitting for that time. The Ten Commandments, also known as the Decalogue, introduced the expanded covenant with God. The first four commandments concern duties to God, the remainder relate du-

---

6. Compare Exod. 19:1–2 with Num. 10:11–12. Some scholars make a distinction between Mount Sinai and Mount Horeb. St. Catherine's Monastery, first built in the sixth century to mark the traditional site of Mount Sinai, contains priceless mosaics, icons, and manuscripts dating to the early centuries of the church; see Agourides and Charlesworth 1978; Charlesworth 1979, 1980; Forsyth and Weitzmann 1978; and Mayerson 1983.

8.3. Small chapel and mosque sit atop 7500'-high Jebel Musa, the traditional site of Mount Sinai. Narrow passes through which the Hebrews would have had to move in this area of southern Sinai are in the distance.

ties among his people. The commandments are normally numbered in the following order:

1. one god
2. idol worship forbidden
3. use of God's name
4. keeping the Sabbath
5. honoring parents
6. murder
7. adultery
8. theft
9. false witness
10. coveting

The commandments immediately told the Hebrews that they were to be different: "You shall have no other gods before Me. You shall not make for yourself an idol, or any likeness of what is in heaven above or on the earth beneath or in the water under the earth. You shall not worship them or serve them" (Exod. 20:3–5). The Egyptians made statues of their deities, sometimes depicting them in animal form, and they wore amulets representing these same gods and goddesses. In Palestine, the Hebrews would encounter Canaanites similarly worshiping the gods of their own imagination (although not represented in animal form). But God wanted his people to worship the Creator, not things he has created. Therefore he clearly spelled out his uniqueness in the first two commandments.

The special nature of the seventh day was already implied by the regulations for gathering manna, but in the fourth commandment God gave reasons for its observance and additional instructions for keeping the day holy. Other cultures in the Near East had special days, but none of them set aside every seventh day to rest and reflect on God's provisions.

The seventh commandment condemns the taking of another person's spouse, an act considered so heinous a transgression that the death penalty was prescribed (Lev. 20:10). The eighth commandment, dealing with theft, conveyed more to the ancient Hebrew than the modern reader probably hears. To steal included finding an item and not returning it to the known owner, or not making a concerted effort to identify the owner so the property could be returned. To an ancient Hebrew "finders keepers, losers weepers" was theft.

In a compact way, the Decalogue teaches how to live in harmony with society and with God. The remainder of the Book of Exodus and the books of Leviticus, Numbers, and Deuteronomy provide the "fine print" to the commandments and to God's covenant. Portions of this material can better be understood and appreciated when compared to contemporary cultures. God told the Hebrews he did not want them engaging in prostitution, sexual perversions, and child sacrifice. It was necessary to proscribe these abominations because they were practices the Israelites would encounter in Canaanite culture. God wanted his people set apart (Lev. 18:3).[7]

The laws given at Mount Sinai are often compared with other law codes in the ancient Near East. The best known, but not the earliest, is the Code of Hammurapi, compiled nearly three centuries before the Israelites were at Mount Sinai. A comparison shows that several of the biblical laws have close parallels with extrabiblical law:

If a son has struck his father, they shall cut off his hand. (*ANE* 1:161; *ANET* 175)	And he who strikes his father or his mother shall surely be put to death. (Exod. 21:15)
If a [man] has stolen the young son of another [man], he shall be put to death. (*ANE* 1:141; *ANET* 166)	And he who kidnaps a man, whether he sells him or he is found in his possession, shall surely be put to death. (Exod. 21:16)

More similarities could be cited, which is not unexpected since the Hebrews lived in the same time and cultural context as the people who composed other law codes. Being in similar cultural milieus, they all had many of the same conditions in life: oxen or unruly children were not peculiar to any one culture. Hebrew responses to similar issues would naturally be like those of people around them.

There is a good deal of expected similarity between the law codes, but there is also some significant dissimilarity. The Old Testament law code is religiously oriented, while the others are civil. The Mesopotamians believed the god Shamash gave Hammurapi his law code so people could get along with one another. In the Bible the law code was given primarily so people could get along with God.

There is little class distinction in Old Testament law. Although punishment could be harsh, it was equally harsh for all. This equality under the law differs from the Code of Hammurapi where the severity of punishment was determined by one's social status. According to biblical law, equal punishment was to be meted out to both participants in

7. Comparisons have sometimes been made too hastily. For example, it was once thought that a Ugaritic text showed Exod. 23:19b to be a prudential rule, warning the Hebrews against a practice connected with Canaanite religious ritual. It has subsequently been found that the insight was based on a faulty translation of the Ugaritic text. See Craigie 1983b: 74–76.

cases of adultery: both were put to death. In other societies only the woman was put to death.[8] In the Bible a clear distinction was made between premeditated murder and involuntary manslaughter (Exod. 21:12–14). Elsewhere in the Near East the "blood avenger" was expected to repay one death by another, regardless of the circumstances.[9] In the Bible, provisions were made to keep people from becoming destitute (gleaning; Exod. 23:11) or eternally enslaved (the sabbatical year; Exod. 21:2). The closest parallel to such protection is found in the Egyptian "Instruction of Amen-em-opet" (*ANE* 1:243; *ANET* 424), where the son is advised to overlook the gleaning widow, but the Bible gave the practice the force of law.

The weight of these dissimilarities is significant because they show that the biblical law code was fairer and more farsighted than others contemporary with it. The laws were also farsighted in that some of the provisions spelled out at Mount Sinai covered aspects of life that Israel would not experience until it settled into the Promised Land. Rather than arguing, as some scholars have, that such aspects must be later additions to the text, they can be taken as anticipatory, as examples of God's provision for his people in advance of their needs.

Feasts and Seasons

In addition to the laws God gave to Moses, he gave instructions for the "feasts and seasons," periods of time within the year when the people would be reminded of what God had done for them and when they would have time set aside to praise God for his goodness. The sacred year began in the spring with Passover and the Feast of Unleavened Bread.[10] In this ceremony, Israel was annually reminded of God's intervention, of their redemption by the lamb's blood. The people were already familiar with Passover and the Feast of Unleavened Bread from their last days in Egypt, but new days of remembrance were added at Sinai. Fifty days after Passover, the Feast of Weeks (sometimes called Feast of Firstfruits) was celebrated. This one-day feast involved giving thanks to God for the bounty of a new year. In the fall, the Day of Atonement (Yom Kippur) was the most solemn of days, for it gave the Hebrews opportunity to clear away the accumulated sins of the year. The Feast of Tabernacles (Succoth) marked the end of the fall harvest season. Later on, Succoth also commemorated the period of wilderness wandering. Additional holidays were added to the sacred year as time went on.

Offerings

At Mount Sinai, various types of ceremonial offerings were instituted to help individuals stay in communion with God. Since the law could

8. Frymer-Kensky 1980 finds that "eye for an eye" is a formula phrase, a philosophical principle of equal retribution, not to be understood literally. She notes that biblical law is also dissimilar in that it will not allow vicarious punishment. She further argues that equal retribution is an advance over early laws in which offenses were settled by fines.

9. Hittite law also distinguishes murder and manslaughter.

10. There was also a civil year, which began in the fall. In one sense, these years are comparable to our calendar and fiscal years.

not keep people from sinning, God provided for sacrifice, then the normal method of communing with deity, to be the active means of forgiveness and rapprochement. The variety of offerings—burnt, peace, sin, trespass, and grain—might appear quite complex, but Hebrew ritual was simpler in form than contemporary practices elsewhere in the Near East. From God's point of view, the attitude, not the sacrifice itself, was always the most important aspect of any Israelite offering.

Priesthood

Moses also established the priesthood. In the past, the head of the household had handled the religious responsibilities, but at Sinai, God designated Aaron to be the high priest. His sons assisted him as priests, and the Levites were appointed to assist them in tabernacle service. The primary responsibility of the priests was to mediate between God and his people, chiefly in the offerings. They were also instructors in matters of law. As intermediaries, the priests had to be especially careful in their marriages and other aspects of life. What was permissible for other Hebrews was not necessarily allowed for priests.

Tabernacle

The tabernacle was another component of religious nationhood that originated at Mount Sinai. Fairly accurate reconstructions are possible from the elaborate instructions recorded for its construction (see illustration 8.4). Since the outer fence measured only 150 feet by 75 feet, the tabernacle was obviously not meant to accommodate a large number of people. Within the open area enclosed by the fence, there was an altar where burnt offerings would be made. There was also a laver (basin) used by the priests to wash their hands and feet before entering the sanctuary (Exod. 30:17–21). This washing symbolized the holiness of God and the need for cleanliness in his presence; without cleansing, fellowship with God was impossible.

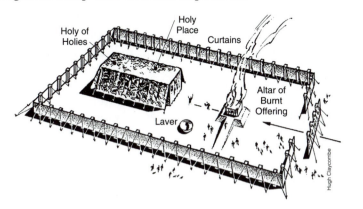

8.4. Reconstruction of the tabernacle with the altar of burnt offering and the basin.

The sanctuary floor plan was forty-five feet by fifteen feet. A veil separated the interior into two unequal parts. In the larger area, the table of showbread displayed twelve loaves of bread to symbolize that each tribe was represented before the Lord.[11] A lampstand gave light to the interior of the tabernacle, and an incense altar provided the tent with a

---

11. The table was also used for incense and libation offerings; Exod. 25:23–30.

pleasant scent. Behind the veil, within the fifteen-foot-by-fifteen-foot Holy of Holies rested the Ark of the Covenant. The ark was a portable chest that at first only contained the tablets of law Moses obtained from God. Later, Aaron's rod and a pot of manna were also placed inside.

Worship centers in the ancient Near East commonly contained statues of their deity. The Israelites had just come from Egypt where, in addition to the many temples containing such idols, the people were taught that a god dwelt on earth in the guise of the pharaoh. In part, the Israelite tabernacle was built to symbolize God's presence with his chosen people (Exod. 25:8). Uniquely, there was no representation of God in the tabernacle. In a sense, he was conspicuous by his absence.[12]

The Golden Calf

In Exodus 24:3 the people gave verbal assent to all that was taking place: "All the words which the LORD has spoken, we will do!" Although treaties were verbal, after their terms were accepted, it was customary that they be written down for a permanent record. Moses did this and the next day prepared a covenant ceremony wherein the covenant was "cut" as a blood sacrifice. Following this celebration, Moses received further instructions from God and remained on Mount Sinai for forty days. While Moses was gone, the people of the fledgling nation approached his older brother, Aaron, with the surprising request that he make them a god (Exod. 32:1).

The biblical record gives no hint as to why the people so quickly forgot the covenant they had so willingly ratified only days before. Amazingly, they requested to be led by a god of Aaron's manufacture. Equally strange is that Aaron agreed to their petition and, with the people's help, fashioned a golden calf. Aaron's role in this tragedy is difficult to understand; but since Moses later gave his brother only a tongue lashing for his part in the affair, perhaps Aaron was not quite so sinful as at first appears. In the ancient Near East, it was common practice to represent a deity standing atop an animal: the animal acted as a pedestal for the god figure. Perhaps Aaron thought to make the calf as such a pedestal; the people could worship the invisible God "standing" on the calf. If this was Aaron's thought, the plan did not work out; the people focused on the calf itself.

When Moses learned what had happened, he became so furious he shattered the law tablets God had given him. In the confrontation that followed, Moses gave the people a chance to repent, but only his own tribe, the Levites, stepped forward, and they became God's avengers for the sin that had been committed. Only after the camp had been ceremonially cleansed did Moses return to God for additional instructions and a new set of law tablets.[13] The covenant was subsequently renewed, and the organization of the people and the construction of the tabernacle finally commenced.

12. Liberal scholarship has argued that the tabernacle was a priestly fabrication from the time of the exile. Kitchen 1993, however, documents that much of its technology was second-millennium Egyptian, not late Mesopotamian.

13. Fensham 1966 parallels a Ugaritic text with Exod. 32:20 to suggest that the burning, grinding, scattering on water, and then drinking of the golden calf was a fixed ritual cursing ceremony.

British Museum

8.5. Egyptian statue of the god Apis, perhaps approximating what the golden calf looked like. (For a god standing on an animal pedestal, see p. 221.)

The Suzerain-Vassal Treaty

The laws set down at Mount Sinai spoke forcefully to God's people. Scholars recognize that even the format within which the laws were cast was particularly meaningful. J. Thompson (1982b: 281) outlines the construction of Near Eastern law codes this way (see also illustration 8.6; Kitchen 1995b: 52–56; Kline 1963; J. Thompson 1964):

> Early 2nd millennium BC law codes [left column in illustration 8.6] normally begin with title and prologue glorifying the king who had proclaimed the laws that follow, then there are blessings and curses for those who keep or break the laws. Column two shows the more complex, but very consistent pattern of late 2nd millennium treaties: the title identifies the chief partner; then comes a historical prologue to show how past benefits from the chief partner should inspire the vassal to grateful obedience to the stipulations that follow. There are provisions for the text to be preserved in the vassal's chief temple, for regular reading to his people as reminder of its terms. The gods of both parties are witnesses and guaran-

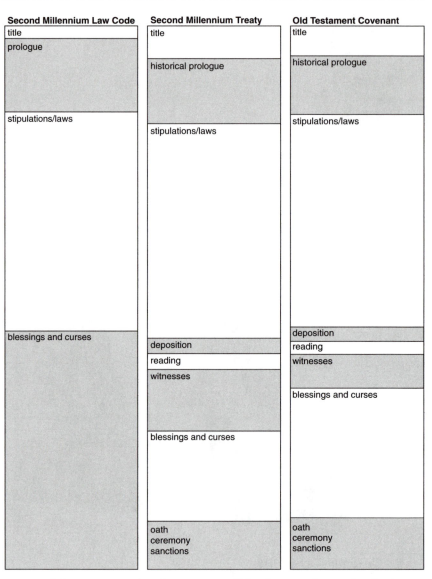

Second Millennium Law Code	Second Millennium Treaty	Old Testament Covenant
title	title	title
prologue	historical prologue	historical prologue
stipulations/laws	stipulations/laws	stipulations/laws
blessings and curses	deposition	deposition
	reading	reading
	witnesses	witnesses
	blessings and curses	blessings and curses
	oath ceremony sanctions	oath ceremony sanctions

8.6. Near Eastern law codes in the second millennium.

tors of the pact, enacting the curses and blessings on those who disobey or obey its terms. A treaty or covenant was ratified by an oath and solemn ceremony, and mention of sanctions against one who breaks it.

After c. 1200 BC this elaborate arrangement disappears. During the 1st millennium, treaties had only four elements, the title plus the terms, curses for infringement and gods of witness in no fixed order. Strikingly, the biblical covenant in Sinai, Moab and Shechem (Ex.; Dt.; Jos. 24) agree in content and form with the late 2nd millennium treaties, and not those of the 1st millennium.

This analysis undermines the argument of some that Exodus and Deuteronomy were written as late as the exile and falsely attributed to Moses. Had they been written that late, these two books would have the suzerain-vassal treaty format known in the first millennium. The second-millennium format found in Exodus and Deuteronomy argues in favor of Mosaic origin.

Summary

At Mount Sinai, God provided his people with their "constitution." In large letters God was saying, "Be separate." The law as expanded at Mount Sinai was clearly more enlightened than anything that had ever been heard. It was given in love by a God who wanted his people to know what he required in their relationship. Offerings were an accepted way to approach God, but it was clear that proper attitude, not the offering itself, was the key to pleasing God. The priesthood was established to formalize the people's linkage with God, and the tabernacle was erected to symbolize his presence with them. The feasts and seasons reminded the people of what God had done for them and gave them specific times for praise. There was a purpose in each of the components for nationhood spelled out at Mount Sinai.

The Number of People in the Exodus

There is disagreement among scholars over the number of people involved in the exodus and the conquest. Numbers 1 and Numbers 26 contain census lists of the fighting forces available to Moses. Some scholars postulate that these lists, which each record over six hundred thousand men, imply as many as six million people including women, children, and men too old to fight. Such totals seem incompatible with estimates that Egypt's population at that time was not more than three million and with the lack of physical evidence of any large depopulation of Egypt. It is also a problem to visualize such a large group of people crossing bodies of water or moving through narrow Sinai passes in any reasonable amount of time. Critical scholars often attribute such vast numbers to gross exaggeration. Some conclude that the numbers are symbolic in an as yet unrecovered way, while others put forth rather strained logistical explanations.

George Mendenhall (1958) offers a possible solution by noting that the Hebrew word *elef* (plural *alafim*), usually translated "thousand," sometimes refers instead to a tribal subsection. For example, in Judges 6:15, the word is generally translated "family," but never "thousand." Mendenhall argues therefore, that in Numbers 1 and Numbers 26 it is really an enumeration of subsections or units within each tribe that contributed soldiers. Thus, for example, according to this view Numbers 1:23, traditionally translated "the number of the tribe of Simeon was 59,300," should read "the number of the tribe of Simeon was 59 units [which contributed a total manpower of] 300." When the census lists in Numbers 1 and Numbers 26 are translated in this manner, Moses had 598 units (*alafim*) available with a total manpower of 5,550 soldiers.

Known armies of Moses' day averaged between five thousand and six thousand soldiers. Following Mendenhall's solution, a comparably sized Israelite army emerges and a "cast of millions" is no longer necessary. Moses would have had 5,550 fighting soldiers plus their wives, children, old men, and any men not conscripted—an amorphous total, but well below the commonly assumed millions. However, a problem remains. At the end of each census list there is a total of all tribal contributions (Num. 1:46; 26:51). These totals are correct only if *elef* in these lists is understood as "thousand." Mendenhall ignores this difficulty by dismissing the troubling verses as later additions to the text. But it is possible to accept Mendenhall's solution and still resolve the large totals. If Numbers 1:46 originally recorded 598 *alafim* (= units) and 5,550 *alafim* (= soldiers), a later scribe copying the passage, not realizing that *elef* had two meanings in the same sentence and thinking the verse unnecessarily cumbersome, totaled the dissimilar uses of *alafim* to get 603,550. Similarly in Numbers 26:51, a scribe might have added together 596 *alafim* (= units) and 5,730 *alafim* (= soldiers) to arrive at the total of 601,730.

Evangelicals insist on inerrancy for the Bible in its original form, that is, in the autographs. No one expects such inerrancy in the copies made through the ages, and scribal error may be the most plausible explanation for the problem under discussion. If *elef* should indeed be translated as "unit," there was still a sizable number of people who left Egypt with Moses and who fought under Joshua for the Promised Land. A reduced number diminishes neither the scope of the miracle nor the power of God as he guided his people. The lower total falls within reasonable expectations for the number of offspring that could be expected from Joseph and his extended family during their years in Egypt. Such a number could have left Egypt without making a noticeable dent in the population and could have traveled with reasonable speed through the tortuous passes of southern Sinai.

There is no easy solution to the question of the number of people who took part in the exodus, and the problem is of more importance than might at first seem the case. Some scholars have used the "cast of millions" as evidence that the Bible is nothing more than a flawed human document. That conclusion is not acceptable. Admittedly, allowances must be made whether one accepts the traditional translation or a modification of Mendenhall's solution. The probability of millions of people must be supported by explanations stronger than the evasive "God could do it," or the intrusion of scribal error into this portion of Scripture must be allowed.[14]

The Date of the Exodus

Over twenty-five years ago, Roland K. Harrison (1970: 127) wrote, "The chronology of the exodus has presented problems that are undoubtedly among the most perplexing in the whole of Hebrew history. It has been the subject of heated debate for a number of years, and the

14. J. Wenham 1967 suggests that *elef* refers to specially trained warriors, but this solution would require more freedom during the oppression than would seem to have been the case. Wenham objects to Mendenhall's proposal because tribes with many *alafim* should have more "hundreds" than tribes with less *alafim*, and that is not always the case. But if, as Mendenhall argues, an *elef* is a family unit it could not be presumed that each unit would generate equal numbers of men. Since a tribe would know the exact number of its family units, the census lists give specific *elef* numbers for units. The "hundreds," on the other hand, are round numbers, implying approximate totals. For a defense of the traditional interpretation of *elef* as thousand, see J. Davis 1968: chap. 3.

British Museum

8.7. Wall painting from the tomb of Sebek-hetep (approximately 1420) at Thebes. Showing Canaanites bringing tribute to Egypt, the painting reflects the political condition before Egypt's empire began to falter. The painting, with its white garments trimmed in red or blue, also gives insight into Canaanite fashions on the eve of the conquest.

difficulties are by no means resolved at present." This statement is no less true today. Only two of the several dates suggested for the specific year Moses led the Israelites from Egypt have found much support. These two have been termed the "high" or "early" date (approximately 1447) and the "low" or "late" date (approximately 1290).

In the preceding pages the early date of the exodus has been followed since the Bible seems rather clear on the matter. First Kings 6:1 puts the exodus 480 years before the fourth year of Solomon, who became king in 971, which points to a date of 1447 for the exodus. This date is in turn supported by Judges 11:26, where Jephthah states that Israel had already been in the land three hundred years. Jephthah's three hundred years cannot be taken literally if the exodus occurred in 1290, since that would impossibly place a judge within the united kingdom. The three hundred years, however, fit well with 1447.[15]

Extrabiblical history is also supportive of the early date of the exodus. On the death of Amenhotep II (pharaoh of the exodus according to the early date), his throne was taken by Thutmose IV, not the elder son, but a younger one who had not expected to become pharaoh. A leading Egyptologist, without regard to the Hebrews or the exodus, suggested that Thutmose IV "obtained the throne through an unforeseen turn of fate, such as the premature death of an elder brother" (Hayes 1953–59: 2.147).

Following the early date, Joshua led Israel into Canaan while Amenhotep III was ruling Egypt (1416–1377). Except for demanding tribute from certain city-states, Amenhotep III seems to have paid minimal attention to Palestine during the time Joshua was taking possession of the Promised Land. During the latter part of his reign, Amenhotep III was ill and his son, Amenhotep IV, was made coregent. Amenhotep IV was religiously preoccupied and (under his other name, Akhenaten) was busy founding the short-lived Amarna period in Egypt. Conse-

15. Proponents of the low date term 1 Kings 6:1 "artificial," and it is true that the Bible sometimes uses round numbers and forty sometimes means "generation" (480 is a multiple of 40). Judges 11:26 could equally be a round number, but it is not a multiple of 40 and therefore supports the view that the time span of 1 Kings 6:1 is not a symbolic figure that can be radically reduced.

quently, at the time that Israel was claiming Palestine, Egypt was distracted. This can account for the lack of any mention of Israel-Egypt contact during the wilderness wandering and conquest.[16]

Some of the Amarna Letters, largely correspondence between Amenhotep III and Amenhotep IV and city-state rulers in Palestine, paint a picture of turmoil in Palestine. The turmoil was caused, in part, by a people the Canaanites called Hapiru. There is reason to think the Amarna Letters and their references to the Hapiru have some connection with early Hebrew activity in Palestine (see chap. 10).

John Bright (1959: 113) allowed that the early date of the exodus was given up "chiefly because it contradicts archaeological evidence."[17] For this reason Bright and others subscribe to the low exodus date, but only two of the several arguments advanced in favor of the late date have ever carried much weight.[18] One argument resulted from a surface exploration of the Negev and Transjordan by Nelson Glueck in the 1930s. From the pottery he found, Glueck concluded that there had been a break in occupation of those areas stretching from 1900 to 1300. He reasoned, therefore, that since there were no people to harass and fight the Hebrews between those dates, the encounters recorded in the Bible pointed to a post-1300 date for the exodus.

An early rebuttal to Glueck's argument was that a settled population is not necessarily implied by the Bible and that the people who fought Israel could have been tent dwellers (e.g., the Midianites in Judg. 6–7). Indeed the Israelites themselves must have lived in tents en route to Canaan. Such reasoning argues that Edomites and other peoples who stood in Israel's way could have been Bedouin. Since nomadic people do not leave extensive evidence of occupation, Glueck could have missed their presence (Rosen 1988).

Later, Israeli archaeologists began to express skepticism over Glueck's knowledge of the pottery found in the areas he surveyed. Other archaeologists ranged from hesitant to critical over Glueck's claim that a gap in sedentary population had been found.[19] Extensive excavation still remains to be done in the Negev and Transjordan, but what has been done has uncovered occupation within Glueck's supposed time gap.[20] It is now agreed that there were people in the Negev and Transjordan throughout the second millennium and that they were not nec-

16. Excavations have found Egyptian installations in the Sinai that date to the early thirteenth century and are on the line of march taken by Moses. Proponents of the low date have not explained how Israel could have passed them without incident.

17. In the third edition of this same work (1981: 123), the same conclusion reads, "Chiefly because it is difficult to harmonize with other evidence."

18. The oft-cited mention of Rameses in connection with the exodus is not really a strong argument for the late date; see n. 1.

19. See Harding 1958 for an early suspicion that some Iron Age sites reported by Glueck really dated to the previous Late Bronze Age. G. Wright (1959a, 1959b) tried to defend the general conclusions of Glueck's surface survey, but he did not clarify whether Glueck sufficiently understood the pottery he was analyzing and using to form his conclusion.

20. Mattingly 1983 finds that Glueck's original gap hypothesis must be abandoned and that even Glueck began moving away from it. Mattingly concludes that the archaeological evidence in Transjordan is now neutral concerning the date of the exodus and conquest. See also Bienkowski 1992 and Sauer 1986.

essarily or exclusively nomadic. There is no population gap to help date the exodus—either to a high or a low date.

The second allegedly strong support for the low date of the exodus is that archaeologists found late thirteenth-century destruction levels at some of the cities conquered by Joshua. Those destruction levels, correlated with Glueck's survey date of post-1300 for the exodus, led many scholars to conclude that Joshua caused those destruction levels when he conquered Palestine about 1250. But this line of reasoning ignores destruction levels dated to about 1400, which could be used to reach a similar confirmation for the early date. Unfortunately, archaeology is not yet so precise that it can look at these two destruction levels (approximately 1400 and 1250) and prove their cause. Presently, destruction levels can "prove" either date for the exodus— and therefore they prove neither.[21]

The low date originated in the 1930s among scholars who thought extrabiblical data should take precedence over biblical data for trustworthiness. These scholars were willing to change portions of the Bible to fit archaeological evidence, but the question of date is more than a "conservative" versus "liberal" squabble. Some years ago, scholars such as Kathleen Kenyon and J. Maxwell Miller, both of whom would fall within the latter classification, moved away from accepting the archaeological evidences for the low date.[22] It is telling that the liberal focus has presently shifted from the question of date to theorizing over how much, if any, of the exodus and conquest narrative is to be believed![23]

Additional Reading

Batto, Bernard F. "Red Sea or Reed Sea?" *BAR* 10/4 (1984): 56–63 (additional comments in 10/6:10, 12, 14).
Beit-Arieh, Itzhaq. "Fifteen Years in Sinai." *BAR* 10/4 (1984): 26–54.
Bimson, John J. *Redating the Exodus and Conquest*. Second edition. Sheffield: University of Sheffield Press, 1981.
Horn, Siegfried H. "What We Don't Know About Moses and the Exodus." *BAR* 3/2 (1977): 22–31 (additional comments in 3/4:40–42).

21. If the destruction levels of 1400 are attributed to the conquest, the 1250 destructions can be variously explained as evidences of Egyptian raids, Sea People activity, and the general turmoil during the period of the judges.

22. Kenyon 1957: 256–65 allowed as many as three exoduses from Egypt. A comparison of the third (1970) and fourth (1979) editions of her book *Archaeology in the Holy Land* shows how fluid her thinking was on the exodus and that she was not convinced evidences put forth for the low date were very strong. J. Miller 1977 found that the archaeological evidence for a thirteenth-century date presented more problems than support. The exodus and the conquest dates are bound together; see chapter 10 for more data relevant to the question.

23. For a fuller presentation for the early date, see Waltke 1972 and Aling 1981: chaps. 5–6; see also Bimson and Livingston 1987 and Halpern 1987a. Halpern's vitriolic rebuttal evaded certain of Bimson and Livingston's arguments. Whether Bimson's proposal that the date range of Middle Bronze Age IIC should be lowered can be sustained (or is even necessary), his exposure of the weaknesses in the late-date evidence is important. Another cavalier dismissal of Bimson can be found in Stiebing 1985, who unfairly writes Bimson off as another follower of Velikovsky.

Perevolotsky, Aviram, and Israel Finkelstein. "The Southern Sinai Exodus Route in Ecological Perspective." *BAR* 11/4 (1985): 26–41.

Pfeiffer, Charles F. *Egypt and the Exodus*. Grand Rapids: Baker, 1964.

Roth, Martha T. (ed.). *Law Collections from Mesopotamia and Asia Minor*. Atlanta: Scholars Press, 1995.

First Things

From Creation to the Tower of Babel

Questions have been raised as to how seriously we are to take this whole narrative about Adam and Eve . . . as literal history. Many prefer to regard it as a mere myth or fable . . . in which the moral downfall of man is described by a fictitious episode designed to illustrate it. . . . No decisive objections, however, have ever been raised against the historicity of Adam and Eve either on historical, scientific, or philosophical grounds. The protest has been based essentially upon subjective concepts of improbability.

From the standpoint of logic, it is virtually impossible to accept the authority of Romans 5 . . . without inferring that the entire human race has descended from a single father. . . . There can be no question that the New Testament authors accepted the literal historicity of Adam and Eve. The origin of the human race is necessarily a matter of revelation by God, since no written records could extend back to a time prior to the invention of writing. Conceivably the true account of man's origin could have been handed down by oral tradition (and perhaps it was so handed down until Moses' time). But apart from revelation, written down as inspired Scripture, there could be no assurance as to which of the bewildering variety of legends of man's origin known to the many different cultures of earth was the true and reliable account. Here the inspired record tells of a literal Adam and Eve, and gives no indication whatever that the account is intended to be mythical. It was certainly taken as historical by Christ and the apostles.

—Gleason L. Archer

Creation
Eden
Longevity

To shape an escaped people into his chosen nation, God provided them with the necessary components for civil and religious life and with their heritage. Moses wrote down their past as recorded in the first chapters of Genesis. Lovingly, God gave the account of creation and pre-Abrahamic history that enabled Israel to ignore the polytheistic conjectures of other nations.

Creation

In Genesis 1–2 God told his people what he thought was necessary for them to know about creation. If viewed only as a creation story, Genesis is hardly unique, because references to the beginning of the universe and of our origins are common to the civilized nations of antiquity. Obviously, people were interested in "first things."

"The Memphite Theology of Creation" was composed several centuries before Abraham to justify Memphis as the ruling city in Egypt. In this document, a rationale was given for Ptah's (the god of that city) promotion to first place among Egypt's gods. The text, which was still popular in Moses' time, deals in part with creation:

> There came into being as the heart and there came into being as the tongue something in the form of Atum. The mighty Great One is Ptah, who transmitted life to all gods, as well as to their *ka's*, through this heart, by which Horus became Ptah, and through this tongue, by which Thoth became Ptah. . . .
>
> Thus all the gods were formed and his Ennead was completed.[1] Indeed, all the divine order really came into being through what the heart thought and the tongue commanded. . . . Thus were made all work and all crafts, the action of the arms, the movement of the legs, and the activity of every member, in conformance with this command that the heart thought, that came forth through the tongue, and that gives value to everything.
>
> Thus it happened that it was said of Ptah: "He who made all and brought the gods into being." . . . Thus it was discovered and understood that his strength is greater than that of the other gods. And so Ptah was satisfied, after he had made everything, as well as all the divine order. He had formed the gods, he had made cities, . . . he had put the gods in their shrines, he had established their offerings. . . . So the gods entered into their bodies of every kind of wood, of every kind of stone, of every kind of clay, or anything . . . in which they had taken form (*ANE* 1:1–2; *ANET* 5).

1. Ptah created Atum, the creator god, and other gods. *Ka* has somewhat the sense of "soul." Horus was the sky god and Thoth the moon god. The Ennead is the nine leading gods in the Egyptian religion.

Some similarity can be seen between this text and the first chapters of Genesis. In Genesis, God thought and then spoke something into being. Ptah, like God, was given ultimate credit for all creation and was satisfied after his creative acts. Human beings are assumed in the Memphite document, but not specifically mentioned as in Genesis. The similarities, however, are not meaningful. Both texts deal with the single theme of creation and it would be extremely difficult, if not impossible, to make multiple accounts of a single event or process without some resultant overlap in details.

By the time Abraham visited Egypt, the Egyptians believed that when they died they joined the gods and became part of their immortality. Egyptian mortuary texts were compiled to magically assist them in the passage from this world into the next. In the "Book of the Dead," a brief reference to creation appears: Atum "was alone on a hill at a time before the heavens had been separated from the earth. He created himself and then the other gods" (for the whole text, see Faulkner 1985). It is interesting that this text implies a time before the first god. Later, during the days of Moses, a slightly fuller reference to creation was popular in Egypt. This account, entitled "The Creation by Atum," also has Atum standing alone on a hill. Then he sneezes or spits and thereby creates two gods to which he gives life (*ANET* 3–4). "A Hymn to Amon-Re," yet another creation story, was also popular during the time of Moses (*ANET* 365):

> Hail to you, Amon-Re. . . .
> eldest of heaven, firstborn of earth,
> Lord of what is, enduring in all things. . . .
> The Lord of truth and father of the gods.
> Who made mankind and created the beasts,
> Lord of what is, who created the fruit tree,
> made herbage, and gave life to cattle.
> The [god] whom Ptah made,
> the goodly beloved youth to whom the gods give praise,
> who made what is below and what is above. . . .
> The chief one, who made the entire earth. . . .
> Jubilation to you who made the gods,
> raised the heavens and laid down the ground!

The above texts, the fullest Egyptian allusions to creation, are noticeably lacking in precision or detail. They can also be contradictory. For instance, in the last quoted text, Amon-Re is eldest of heaven and father of the gods, yet Ptah is his father! When the Egyptians did refer to creation it was usually to argue some point other than creation itself. They would use the creation motif to build the reputation or explain the importance of specific gods. In the Bible, creation is not the most important event, but is recorded to supply, for our knowledge, a beginning to the activity of God and to satisfy the natural curiosity over first things. Compared to the Egyptian treatments of creation, the Genesis account is full and overflowing with detail.

At the other end of the fertile crescent, in Mesopotamia, a more sophisticated view of creation was formulated in a major work known as *Enuma Elish* (named after its first phrase, which is translated "when on

9.1. Seven Assyrian tablets contain *Enuma Elish*, the Mesopotamian story of creation. This copy of the third tablet of the older Babylonian text (three-and-one-half inches high) was found at Nineveh and dates to approximately 650.

high"). In this epic, written shortly after Abraham left Mesopotamia, Marduk is a comparatively unknown god of the as yet insignificant Babylon. Marduk was only one among many city gods, and a main purpose of the epic was to justify the power and importance of Babylon and its god Marduk. The document thus served a function similar to that of creation stories in Egypt.

Enuma Elish begins with the gods Apsu (sweet water) and Tiamat (salt water), apparently the only two deities who have been born. Other gods are created by unexplained means, and one of them, Ea, kills Apsu. Tiamat swears vengeance against Ea and the other gods and places Kingu, one of her sons, at the head of a fearsome band of monsters. In a meeting of the threatened deities, Marduk steps forth and offers to single-handedly defeat the enemies. All he asks in return is that he be made chief god. When the other deities agree, Marduk goes out and vanquishes Tiamat, splitting her "like a shellfish into two parts" (*ANE* 1:35; *ANET* 67). After creating the constellations and the moon from Tiamat's body, Marduk addresses Ea with a plan to create the human race (*ANE* 1:36–37; *ANET* 68):

> Blood I will mass and cause bones to be.
> I will establish a savage, "man" shall be his name. . . .
> He shall be charged with the service of the gods that they might be at
> ease!

The great gods join counsel and decide that Kingu—in their view the real power behind the rebellion—should be punished:

[The great gods replied:]
"It was Kingu who contrived the uprising,
and made Tiamat rebel, and joined battle."
They bound him, holding him before Ea.
They imposed on him his guilt and severed his blood vessels.
Out of his blood they fashioned mankind.
[Ea] imposed the service and let free the gods.

There is a similarity in the sequence of creative acts in both Genesis and *Enuma Elish*: firmament, dry land, celestial luminaries, humans. Both stories begin with a watery chaos and end with God or the gods at rest. But the similarities are not meaningful; they can be explained as expected coincidences in two works on the same theme.

Archaeologists cannot excavate remains of creation, but from texts like these they know what other ancient cultures had to say about first things. Archaeology does show that while the biblical account may not be as complete as some might wish, it owes nothing to other ancient cultures or their myths. The complete *Enuma Elish* reveals many dissimilarities with Genesis. The omnipotent God in Genesis is very unlike the frightened, feuding, and foul gods of the epic. Necessarily there are similarities, but the Genesis account shows no dependence. The fledgling Hebrew nation should have been thankful when God brought them out from the "bewildering variety" of opinions on their origin and, through Moses, told the story as it happened. Viewed only as a creation story, Genesis is not unique, but viewed in comparison with these other stories, Genesis is lucid and complete.

Eden

Genesis 1 presents a summary of creation. The second chapter focuses on the first couple for whom God prepared Eden, a garden. The Bible places Eden "in the east" and in relation to four rivers: the Tigris, Euphrates, Pishon, and Gihon. Two ancient waterways in southern Mesopotamia were called the Pisanu and Guhana. Etymologically these names equate with the Pishon and Gihon and, together with the reference to the Tigris and Euphrates, would seem to locate the garden somewhere in southern Mesopotamia.[2] But several other proposals have been made, putting the location of Eden in such disparate places as the State of Ohio and the planet Mars! Critical scholars often assume that the garden is purely mythical and explain it as a projection of early Mesopotamian ideas of the world (e.g., Kraeling 1956: 41–43).

In the 1950s, after several seasons excavating on the Island of Bahrain in the Persian Gulf, Danish archaeologists identified the island as ancient Dilmun. In a Mesopotamian story titled "The Myth of Enki and Ninhursag," Dilmun is spoken of as pure, clean, bright and as both a land and a city. The translator of the text labeled it a paradise myth on

---

2. Sauer 1996 suggests that Pishon might have been found in Saudi Arabia but, for him, this does not mean the biblical story is "literally true," only that it might "preserve memories of climatic change and of early geography."

9.2. The Sumerian King List on a clay prism (dating to approximately 2000; eight inches high) records names and lengths of reign of preflood and postflood rulers. Ten "great men" ruled before the flood, with lengths of reign between 43,200 and 18,600 years. The time spans are greatly reduced for the postflood rulers.

this basis and equated Eden of the Bible with Dilmun (*ANET* 37–41). This line of reasoning led to the announcement in 1959 that "Danish archaeologists working in the British protectorate of Bahrain claim to have found the site of the biblical Garden of Eden" (*Christianity Today*, 16 Feb. 1959, p. 28). Scholars generally agree that Bahrain should be equated with Dilmun, but that Dilmun is Eden is largely one scholar's speculation. The links in this "discovery" of Eden have proven very fragile and no mention is made of Eden in the subsequent excavation report (Bibby 1969).

Wherever the garden of Eden was, it contained the "tree of life" and the "tree of the knowledge of good and evil." Adam and Eve were allowed to eat from all the trees of the garden except the latter. After eating of the forbidden tree, God took away their opportunity to eat from the tree of life by expelling them from the garden. Cain and Abel were subsequently born, and in time Cain's worship displeased God. The resulting separation seemingly precipitated the murder of Abel. Archaeology cannot provide insight into these early events. The sacred trees of Mesopotamian religion are not equatable, and seals allegedly showing Adam and Eve disconsolately leaving the garden are, in reality, Mesopotamian depictions of religious prostitution.[3]

Longevity

Archaeology can also do little with the longevity attributed to people named in the early chapters of Genesis. In the Sumerian King List (illustration 9.2), early rulers also lived abnormally long spans; perhaps the list reflects a memory of earlier longevity.[4] At least in comparison the biblical spans are modest. By the patriarchal period few people were unusually long lived by today's standards.

The Flood

Biblical Evidence of the Flood

Genesis 6:5–8 records that God "grieved in his heart" over the "wickedness of man" and purposed to "blot out" all but Noah and his family. At God's command, Noah built a large boat. Some writers have felt it necessary to prove that it was large enough to hold sufficient provisions for the time spent inside. Other writers have paid attention to the ark's appearance, and over the centuries artist re-creations have ranged from Spanish galleons to river rafts. Such disparity is due to the lack of adequate descriptive data in the biblical text.[5]

Neither does the biblical text give enough information concerning the extent of the flood to satisfy modern curiosity. Verses like Genesis 7:4, 19; 8:21; and even 2 Peter 3:6 seem to argue for a universal flood, but some conservative scholars believe it was merely local. As with much in the early chapters of Genesis, answers lie outside the realm of archaeology.

Having said that, a few decades ago an alleged archaeological evidence of the flood electrified the news media around the world. On 16 March 1929, the front page of the New York *Times* reported that proof of the flood had been found in Ur of the Chaldeans: an eight-foot-thick layer of waterborne silt. According to C. Leonard Woolley, the excava-

3. For an example of how this type of seal has been misinterpreted, see Halley 1965: 69.

4. On the connection between prepatriarchal genealogies and the Mesopotamian King Lists, see R. K. Harrison 1969: 147–52 and Walton 1981.

5. Even the statements of the ark's size are open to more than one interpretation. For a summary of the different lengths of the biblical cubit, see Scott 1959.

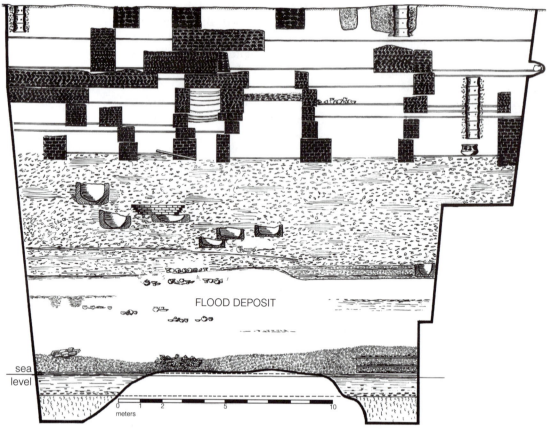

FLOOD DEPOSIT

sea
level

9.3. Sir Leonard Woolley's section drawing of Flood Pit F at Ur. The "flood deposit" dates to early in the fourth millennium. Woolley later admitted that the occupation evidence within the flood deposit actually indicated two flood layers close together in time. No similar deposit was found in Ubaid levels at nearby cities.

tor, this was convincing evidence of the biblical flood. Two days later an editorial in the same newspaper offered that the discovery helped both evangelical and liberal believers: evangelicals now had proof of the flood, and liberals had evidence that creation predated 4004.

Other archaeologists working in southern Mesopotamia questioned Woolley's conclusion, in part noting that nearby sites showed no similar flood layers. There was also suspicion, never fully resolved, that the layer in question had actually been wind laid. In his 1955 formal publication (pp. 68–69), Woolley still claimed to have found the biblical flood layer, but he acknowledged that a brief occupation level fell within the eight-foot thickness of Flood Pit F. From associated objects the deposit was dated to the end of the Ubaid period (i.e., 5300–3750; see chap. 2). Woolley's "flood layer," therefore, covered only a small area, was actually divided into two separate levels, and dated to early in the fourth millennium. These data did not dissuade Woolley, because he was not seeking evidence that would harmonize with the biblical story. What Woolley actually sought was a flood layer sufficiently large to account for the Mesopotamians to have written a flood story from which, he believed, the biblical account had derived.[6]

Evidence of the biblical flood has not been found in the silt layers of Mesopotamia. "Flood geologists" claim that the greatest geological

6. See also Mallowan 1964 for interesting observations by someone who largely follows Woolley's reasoning concerning the origin of the biblical account.

event of all time was the Noachian flood, which laid down many if not all of the rock strata in the earth's crust. To them, evidence of the flood can be seen in geology. On the other hand, geologists claim that no one trained in their discipline accepts such a theory. The bitterness that sometimes surrounds arguments for and against flood geology make archaeologists happy they are of another discipline.

For a considerable time, people have claimed that the ark itself is preserved; in fact, the first reports of alleged sightings and visits to the ark began centuries ago. The Turkish government has received hundreds of requests to explore the traditional site of Mount Ararat, near its eastern border. Liberal scholarship, which views the story as myth, has reacted with amusement and ridicule to this activity: "While we await the writing up of a variety of archaeological activities in the middle east this past summer, you will doubtless appreciate the following . . . notes . . . reminding us all how much easier it is to raise money for something other than scientific reason!" The first note concerns the "credulous people" seeking the ark (Boling 1970: 1).

Although this and similarly minded writers could be more temperate, they correctly call for caution. Over and over again, reported sightings of the ark have not been supported by fact, as the photographs taken are invariably "lost" or otherwise not available, and evidence is allegedly "suppressed" by those opposed to the claims of the Bible. The ark has reportedly been found at different locations on Mount Ararat, but rather than call some of the sightings into question, "arkeologists" formulated a split-ark theory by which portions of the ark are located in more than one place. When analyzed by Carbon-14, wood reportedly from the ark does not yield B.C. dates. Instead of accepting that the wood is not from the ark, supporters challenge the dating tool (Bailey 1977).[7]

It should be noted that Genesis 8:4 states that "the ark rested upon the mountains of Ararat." Ararat, or Urartu in Assyrian texts, is a large mountainous area (approximately where Armenia is indicated on illustrations 2.1 and 18.2). Ancient traditions suggest several landing places for the ark, and there is no evidence that Buyuk Aghri Dagh (as the Turks call the nearly seventeen-thousand-foot-tall extinct volcano) was a candidate prior to the eleventh or twelfth centuries A.D. Ark searchers could, therefore, be many miles off target.

Evangelical interest in the ark is largely centered on the belief that if found, it will prove the Bible to the unbeliever. This argument leaves in question the extent to which history can be used to prove a theological document (see again chap. 1). It also ignores the fact that certain groups in search of the ark have very nonbiblical interests. For example, to some the finding of the ark will be a proof that Atlantis truly existed; to others it will validate the lost continent of Lemuria. Thus, the finding of the ark would not be the incontrovertible proof of the Bible that some of its seekers assume.

The Flood in Ancient Extrabiblical Literature

The best extrabiblical proof of the flood is found in other ancient literature. The story of a massive flood is widespread, and several dozen

7. For a critique of "arkeology," see Hoerth 1977 and Yamauchi 1977.

different traditions are known. Before Abraham was born in southern Mesopotamia, the Sumerians had composed a flood story with Ziusudra as their "Noah" (*ANE* 1:28–30; *ANET* 42–44). In this story the flood lasted seven days and nights. Ziusudra survived the flood in a huge boat, opened a window of his boat, and made a sacrifice.

The tradition of a flood seems to have been so basic that it even rates mention in the Sumerian King List (illustration 9.2):

> In Shuruppak, Ubar-Tutu became king and ruled 18,600 years. . . . These are five cities, eight kings ruled them for 241,000 years. Then the flood swept over the earth. After the flood had swept over the earth and when kingship was lowered again from heaven, kingship was first in Kish (*ANET* 265).

According to this Mesopotamian record, after the flood, kingship was lowered to the city of Kish and then to Uruk. Gilgamesh, a priest-king, was the fifth king of the First Dynasty of Uruk, and scholars are inclined to believe there really was a king named Gilgamesh. The best known of the several versions of Mesopotamian flood stories is found in the lengthy Gilgamesh Epic. Gilgamesh is a troublemaker: he is arrogant, ruthless, and will not leave the women alone. The gods made Enkidu either as Gilgamesh's rival or to keep him from trouble. Wild Enkidu is tricked into being civilized by a temple prostitute, and he subsequently attempts to keep Gilgamesh from carrying out one of his amorous designs. The two wrestle, Gilgamesh wins, and the two become great friends. Later, Gilgamesh rejects the advances of the goddess Ishtar, and Ishtar takes out her fury on Enkidu, who becomes sick and dies. Gilgamesh now becomes fearful of death, and he sets off to see the immortal Utnapishtim to ask him how he obtained eternal life. In the course of his answer, Utnapishtim relates the following flood story (*ANE* 1:66–70; *ANET* 93–95):

> Utnapishtim said to him, to Gilgamesh:
> "I will reveal to you, Gilgamesh, a hidden matter
> and a secret of the gods I will tell you:
> Shuruppak—a city that you know . . . —
> that city was ancient, as were the gods within it,
> when their heart led the great gods to produce the flood. . . .
> [They said:] 'Man of Shuruppak, son of Ubar-Tutu,
> tear down this house, build a ship!
> Give up possessions, seek life.
> Forswear worldly goods and keep the soul alive!
> Aboard the ship take the seed of all living things.
> The ship that you shall build,
> its dimensions shall be to measure.
> Equal shall be its width and its length.
> Like the Apsu you shall ceil it.'
> I understood, and I said to Ea, my Lord:
> 'Behold, my lord, what you have thus ordered,
> I will be honored to carry out.
> But what shall I answer the city, the people, and elders?'
> Ea opened his mouth to speak,
> saying to me, his servant:

'You shall then thus speak unto them:
"I have learned that Enlil is hostile to me,
so that I cannot reside in your city,
nor set my foot in Enlil's territory.
To the Deep I will therefore go down,
to dwell with my lord Ea.
But upon you he will shower down abundance,
the choicest birds, the rarest fishes. . . ." '

"On the fifth day I laid the framework.
One whole acre was the floor space,
ten dozen cubits the height of each of its walls,
ten dozen cubits each edge of the square deck.
I laid out the contours and joined it together.
I provided it with six decks,
dividing it thus into seven parts.
Its floor plan I divided into nine parts.
I hammered water-plugs into it.
I saw to the punting-poles and laid in supplies.
Six measures of bitumen I poured into the furnace,
three [measures] of asphalt I also poured inside. . . .
Bullocks I slaughtered for the people,
and I killed sheep every day. . . .
. . . , red wine, oil, and white wine
I gave the workmen to drink. . . .
On the seventh day the ship was completed.
The launching was very difficult,
so that they had to shift the floor planks above and below,
until two-thirds of the structure had gone into the water.

"Whatever I had I laded upon it: . . .
whatever I had of all the living beings I laded upon it.
All my family and kin I made to go aboard the ship.
The beasts of the field, the wild creatures of the field,
all the craftsmen I made go aboard.
Shamash had set for me a stated time:
'When he who orders unease at night,
will shower down a rain of blight,
board the ship and batten up the entrance!'
That stated time had arrived:
'He who orders unease at night, showers down a rain of blight.'
I watched the appearance of the weather.
The weather was awesome to behold.
I boarded the ship and battened up the entrance. . . .

"For one day the south storm blew,
gathering speed as it blew, submerging the mountains,
overtaking the people like a battle.
No one can see his fellow,
nor can the people be recognized from heaven.
The gods were frightened by the deluge,
and, shrinking back, they ascended to the heaven of Anu.
The gods cowered like dogs
crouched against the outer wall. . . .
The gods, all humbled, sit and weep. . . .

Six days and six nights
blows the flood wind, as the south storm sweeps the land.
When the seventh day arrived,
the flood-carrying south storm subsided in the battle,
which it had fought like an army.
The sea grew quiet, the tempest was still, the flood ceased.
I looked at the weather: stillness had set in,
and all of humanity had returned to clay.
The landscape was as level as a flat roof.
I opened a hatch, and light fell upon my face.
Bowing low, I sat and wept,
tears running down on my face. . . .
On Mount Nisir the ship came to a halt.
Mount Nisir held the ship fast,
allowing no motion. . . .

"When the seventh day arrived,
I sent forth and set free a dove.
The dove went forth, but came back;
since no resting place for it was visible, she turned round.
Then I sent forth and set free a swallow.
The swallow went forth, but came back;
since no resting place for it was visible, she turned round.
Then I sent forth and set free a raven.
The raven went forth and, seeing that the water had diminished,
he eats, circles, caws, and turns not round.
Then I let out all to the four winds
and offered a sacrifice.
I poured out a libation on the top of the mountain.
Seven and seven cult vessels I set up,
upon their potstands I heaped cane, cedarwood, and myrtle.
The gods smelled the savor,
the gods smelled the sweet savor,
the gods crowded like flies about the sacrificer.
When at length as the great goddess arrived,
she lifted up the great jewels that Anu had fashioned to her liking:
'You gods here, as surely as this lapis
upon my neck I shall not forget,
I shall be mindful of these days, forgetting them never.
Let the gods come to the offering;
but let not Enlil come to the offering,
for he, unreasoning, brought on the deluge
and my people consigned to destruction.'
When at length as Enlil arrived,
and saw the ship, Enlil was wroth,
he was filled with wrath. . . .
'Has some living soul escaped?
No man was to survive the destruction!' "

As the story continues, Gilgamesh learns that Utnapishtim's immortality is a unique blessing and that Gilgamesh cannot attain eternal life. Gilgamesh is, however, given the opportunity to obtain new youth and virility through a certain plant. But a snake steals the plant from Gilgamesh, and he is deprived of even this benefit.

The epic's theme is essentially secular and revolves around Gil-

9.4. Tablet 11 (six inches high) of the Assyrian version of the Gilgamesh Epic, found at Nineveh and dating to the seventh century. Divided into twelve tablets, the epic's eleventh tablet contains Utnapishtim's account of the flood. Other versions of the epic date to the third millennium, and copies have been found in various parts of the Near East. A fourteenth-century fragment was found at Megiddo in Palestine.

gamesh's search for eternal life. Within that quest is the story of the flood, which contains numerous parallels to the Bible. The number of parallels cited depends in part on persistence, but unlike the creation stories, some listed below do not seem as easily explained away.

1. The flood was divinely planned.
2. The flood was connected with the defection of the human race from God/the gods.
3. A divine revelation to the hero of the deluge tells of an imminent disaster that no one else knows about.
4. A ship is built, pitched inside and out.
5. The family of the hero is saved.
6. The living creatures that are to be saved are put aboard.
7. A storm brings on the flood.
8. Everyone not on the ship is destroyed.
9. The duration of the flood is specified.
10. The ship lands on a mountain.
11. Birds are sent out to see whether the water has receded.

12. Sacrifice is offered to and accepted by the deity.
13. The hero receives a special blessing.
14. There is reference to the possibility of no future flood.

Various reactions to these similarities are possible. One response is to emphasize the differences between the two stories. Genesis is monotheistic, while the Gilgamesh Epic is polytheistic and has gods acting in very unholy ways. The purpose of the flood in Genesis is to cleanse the earth of corruption, while in the epic the reason seems to be that one god was unaccountably angry at the world. The arks are differently shaped, and Utnapishtim had to launch his boat. There are additional differences, but this emphasis cannot erase the striking similarities. The sending out of birds, for instance, seems too much alike to be accidental (raven, dove, dove in the Bible; dove, swallow, raven in the epic).

The similarities lead some scholars to conclude that the Genesis flood is a myth borrowed from the Gilgamesh Epic. For example, after referring to George Smith's translation of the clay tablets containing the epic, C. W. Ceram (1958: 220, 222) says: the tablets "established clearly that the Bible's story of the Deluge derived from a Babylonian source. The Bible could no longer be regarded only as pure revelation; it was also a history into which age-old tales had been woven." Equally plausible, if one accepts an inspired Bible, is that the similarities result from a common inheritance. Both accounts derive from the same source—the actual event. There was a flood, and both the Bible and the epic record it. As the descendants of Noah drifted apart and away from God, there must have been a long parade of human corruptions and polytheistic encrustations on the original and actual event. Some of this redaction can be seen in Mesopotamia. The Gilgamesh Epic is based on earlier stories (e.g., the Sumerian epic in which the boat builder was named Ziusudra). The builder's name and other details were changed as the story was reworked and then reworked again (see Tigay 1982 and Lambert and Millard 1969). Some of the remaining similarities are due to the sameness of the topic, while others are points that did not get erased during the various recensions. That a flood account is preserved in so many cultures shows how popular the theme was. All sophisticated cultures would be expected to need a creation story—but not a flood story—in their "beginnings." The popularity of the flood theme can be used to argue for the historicity of the event.

The Tower of Babel

The Bible says that after Noah and his family left the ark they began to spread into the world. Genesis 10, which summarizes that spread, is sometimes called the "Table of Nations." The events recorded in the first part of Genesis 11 fit somewhere into this "table."

Genesis 11:2 states that one group journeyed east and settled into the Plain of Shinar, a term for Mesopotamia's southern plain. Because Mesopotamia lacked stone, most buildings were constructed from sun-dried mud brick. Nonprivate buildings, for which permanence was deemed important, were often overlaid with baked bricks. Bitumen, found at the surface in some parts of Mesopotamia, was used as a water seal. "And they said to one another, 'Come let us make bricks and burn them thoroughly.' And they used brick for stone, and they used tar for mortar. And they said, 'Come, let us build for ourselves a city, and a tower whose top will reach into heaven, and let us make for ourselves a name; lest we be scattered abroad over the face of the whole earth' " (Gen. 11:3–4).

God was displeased with this building activity, and the city and its tower were never completed. The Hebrew says the people desired to build a *migdal.* Translated "tower," *migdal* repeatedly refers to a forti-fied tower or fortress (Judg. 8:9–17). Cities often had elaborately built defensive walls and a *migdal* to which the defenders could retreat as a last line of defense. It is probable that, as in the other Old Testament instances of the word, this is the implication in Genesis 11. This is not, however, the inference always drawn. For example, Andre Parrot (1955: 17) holds to another popular interpretation: "At all events it is recognized and admitted by all biblical scholars that the narrative in Genesis 11 had its 'starting-point' in the ruins of one of those huge tow-ers which archaeologists call *ziggurats,* and that the 'Tower of Babel' could only be the *ziggurat* erected at Babylon, in the very heart of the land of Shinar."

The scholars referred to by Parrot are those who, like him, feel the story is only another Genesis myth. They posit that Jews during the ex-ile saw either the ziggurat in Babylon or some rundown ziggurat else-where and were so impressed that they composed a fable around it. Neither these scholars nor those who take the text to be a true account are really helped in their position by archaeology. The conclusion reached here, as at so many points in Old Testament studies, is depen-dent on one's theological presuppositions.

Interestingly, in a footnote within his book, Parrot acknowledges: "It should be noted that the *ziggurat,* a sacred tower, is not to be confused with the fortified towers (*migdal*), referred to several times in Judges" (1955: 33). Parrot believes the Hebrew word should be translated "for-tified tower," except in the case of Genesis 11. He wants this sole excep-tion to the sense of the word in order to make his ziggurat–Tower of Ba-bel equation. His theological stance—his belief that the story is a myth derived from a secular source—thus leads to an expected conclusion.

For those who take Genesis 11 to be an historical account, the tower can hardly have looked like a ziggurat. Ziggurats, as noted in chapter 2, evolved from simpler religious structures, and the fully formed staged tower did not appear as a feature of Mesopotamian architecture until well into the third millennium. It is impossible to argue for a sin-gleness of language at such a late date (Gen. 11:1).[8]

8. A Sumerian reference to a time when all people "spoke in one tongue" has been found; see Kramer 1968.

Summary

The Hebrews, through Moses, received much more than the Ten Commandments at Mount Sinai. The heritage God gave them there was also an important component to their new nationhood. There is no way to know how much the Israelites knew of this early history before Mount Sinai. They could easily have retained their patriarchal history during the stay in Egypt, but whether they had knowledge concerning earlier times is less certain. Some scholars suggest that Abraham brought the information contained in the first chapters of Genesis with him from Mesopotamia, but the Bible is silent about that possibility. It is as likely that the Israelites had no account of their own "first things" until their stay at Mount Sinai.

Pre-Abrahamic Chronology

Had one asked a person listening to the first reading of Moses' fresh transcription of Genesis how long ago God had created the world, that person would probably have thought the question unnecessary, but would likely have suspected it was rather recent. In fact, both Jews and Christians have long tended to such a view. But within the last century scientific research began to assert that the time span was, in fact, much greater, and scholarly discussion began to revolve around such matters as when God began the creation process and what length of time was involved. Unfortunately for students of the Bible, the time covered by the period of beginnings is not spelled out in the Bible.

The familiar date for the creation of the world is 4004, introduced by Bishop James Ussher in the seventeenth century. He assumed that the Bible contained a complete genealogy from Adam down to New Testament times and that a simple ordering of the names and ages given established a creation date. He did not recognize that in the ancient Near East it was common to use "selective genealogies" when ordering history. This phrase refers to the habit of dropping certain names from genealogical tables to produce more balanced listings, to consciously erase "black sheep" from memory, or to trim out names that had ceased to be sufficiently important. One classic example of this selective practice can be seen in Egypt, where the ancient historians dropped the whole Hyksos period from their records. Officially the Hyksos period became a non-time, and in the Egyptian King List from Abydos, the end of Dynasty 12 is immediately followed by the first king of Dynasty 18!

Examples of similar selectivity in post-Abrahamic biblical times cast doubt over whether the early chapters of Genesis were ever meant to be considered genealogically complete. For example, Matthew 1:8 states that Uzziah was born to Joram, but in 1 Chronicles 3:10–12 three generations of kings (Ahaziah, Joash, and Amaziah) are correctly inserted between Joram and Uzziah. Joram was in fact Uzziah's great-great-grandfather. Similarly, according to Ezra 7:3 Azariah was the son of Meraioth, but in 1 Chronicles 6:6–9 six generations are listed between these two names. Clearly, the King James Version's *begat* sometimes means "ancestor of" rather than immediate "father of," and *son of* sometimes implies "descendent of." Without cross-checks like those just cited, the reader cannot be certain if a genealogical table is complete. Unfortunately, there are no cross-checks for the pre-Abrahamic period.

Writers who speak of Noah still being alive when Abraham was born or that at least one of Noah's sons outlived Abraham are working within Ussher's framework, but in recent years his chronology has sharply declined in popularity.[9] Careful examination of the biblical data and an understanding of how ancient Near Eastern genealogies were handled argues against it. Archaeology also militates against Ussher's chronology. The dates given in earlier chapters of this book for pre-Abrahamic Mesopotamia, Palestine, and Egypt have been sufficiently refined within recent decades to preclude the possibility that any radical shifts are forthcoming. The prehistory of the Near East simply cannot be compressed this side of 4004.

Paleontologists and geologists work in earlier time frames than do archaeologists. Geologic evidence has convinced some who take a conservative view of the Bible that the earth had to have been created several billions of years ago. Others of equally conservative persuasions are troubled by any suggestion that the earth could be more than ten thousand years old. This debate is outside the realm of archaeology. It would be well, however, for both sides to agree that, theologically, it makes no difference whether the world is of recent or ancient creation or whether the process took seven days or billions of years. It is unfortunate that some view one's position in this matter as a test of orthodoxy.

Additional Reading

Bailey, Lloyd. *Noah: The Person and the Story in History and Tradition*. Columbia: University of South Carolina Press, 1989.

Frymer-Kensky, Tikva. "The Atrahasis Epic and Its Significance for Our Understanding of Genesis 1–9." *BA* 40 (1977): 147–55.

———. "What the Babylonian Flood Stories Can and Cannot Teach Us about the Genesis Flood." *BAR* 4/4 (1978): 32–41.

Heidel, Alexander. *The Babylonian Genesis*. Chicago: University of Chicago Press, 1969.

———. *The Gilgamesh Epic and Old Testament Parallels*. Chicago: University of Chicago Press, 1971.

Hess, Richard S., and David T. Tsumura (eds.). *"I Studied Inscriptions from before the Flood": Ancient Near Eastern, Literary, and Linguistic Approaches to Genesis 1–11*. Winona Lake, Ind.: Eisenbrauns, 1994.

Jacobsen, Thorkild. *The Treasures of Darkness: A History of Mesopotamian Religion*. New Haven: Yale University Press, 1976 (pp. 208–15).

Kikawada, Isaac M., and Arthur Quinn. *Before Abraham Was*. Nashville: Abingdon, 1985.

9. Ussher's assumption of a continuous genealogy is not unique. Dimbleby 1902 arrived at a date of 3996, and Reese 1977: 2 puts creation on Sunday, 27 March 3976.

Kovacs, Maureen G. *The Epic of Gilgamesh*. Stanford: Stanford University Press, 1989.

Lewis, Jack P. "Noah and the Flood in Jewish, Christian, and Muslim Tradition." *BA* 47 (1984): 224–39.

Matthews, Victor H., and Don C. Benjamin. *Old Testament Parallels: Laws and Stories from the Ancient Near East*. New York: Paulist, 1991.

Stiebing, William H., Jr. "A Futile Quest: The Search for Noah's Ark." *BAR* 2/2 (1976): 1, 13–20.

Youngblood, Ronald F. *The Genesis Debate*. Grand Rapids: Baker, 1990.

The Wilderness Wandering and the Conquest

To [pharaoh] the king, my lord, my Sun-god, my pantheon, say: Thus Shuwardata, your servant, servant of the king and the dirt under his two feet, the ground on which you tread! At the feet of the king, my lord, the Sun-god from heaven, seven times, seven times I fall, both prone and supine.

Let the king, my lord, learn that the chief of the Apiru has risen in arms against the lands that the god of the king, my lord, gave me; but I have smitten him. Also let the king, my lord, know that all my brothers have abandoned me, and it is I and Abdu-Heba [of Jerusalem] who fight against the chief of the Apiru. And Prince Zurata of Accho and Prince Indaruta of Achshaph it was they who hastened with fifty chariots—for I had been robbed by the Apiru—to my help; but behold, they are fighting against me, so let it be agreeable to the king, my lord, . . . and let us make war in earnest, and let the lands of the king, my lord, be restored to their former limits!

—Letter from Prince Shuwardata (of the Hebron region)
to Pharaoh Akhenaten

Wilderness Wanderings

In the ten months spent at Mount Sinai the Israelites developed a national identity. After Passover was observed for only the second time, they began a march northward. When they reached Kadesh-barnea, the Promised Land was almost in sight, and twelve men, one representative from each tribe, were chosen to scout ahead. The men found the land to be one that "certainly does flow with milk and honey" (Num. 13:27), but they also found it inhabited by people that ten of the scouts felt were too powerful to dislodge. Of the advance party, only two, Joshua and Caleb, argued that the land could be won. The nonunanimous report nearly led to a riot.

God saw the need to rebuke the people for their lack of faith, and he decreed that everyone over the age of twenty—except for Joshua and Caleb—would finish out his or her life in the wilderness. Nearly forty years were thus added to the wilderness experience. Although the Israelites apologized to God and accepted his judgment, they then tried to circumvent his punishment by sending an army north to conquer the land. Not surprisingly, the troops were repulsed and sent reeling back to Kadesh-barnea.

Rather than constant movement over the Sinai Peninsula, it is more likely that the people of the wilderness "wandering" stayed most of the time near the springs in the vicinity of Kadesh-barnea.[1] However, these years of waiting were not uneventful. At one point Aaron's leadership was challenged, and when the authority of Moses was contested, God stepped in rather forcefully (Num. 16).

When God finally permitted Israel to continue toward the Promised Land, the passage was not without difficulty. They found themselves in a desert area containing poisonous snakes, a situation God used to test the people's faith. Another difficulty came from people living in territory through which the Israelites wished to move. In one case, Moses diplomatically petitioned the Edomites (Num. 20:17), but he was refused entry and the Israelites found another route.[2] Later on, the Amorites similarly blocked the way, but the Israelites forced their way through with military might.

Magic was an acceptable method of ancient warfare, and King Balak of Moab tried to cast a curse over the Israelites to stop their advance. Balak chose Balaam, a diviner who lived north of Moab, to handle the matter. Balaam was not particularly interested in helping the Moabites,

---

1. The identification of the oasis Ain el-Qudeirat with Kadesh-barnea is generally accepted; see Cohen 1981b. Commendably, Cohen does not take the present lack of evidence for pre-tenth-century settlement at Tell el-Qudeirat within the oasis as license to question the historicity of the Bible. Cohen cautions that only a little of the tell has been tested to virgin soil. A more popular account of his work is 1981a.

2. Numbers 21:1–3 states that the king of Arad came out to fight Israel, but extensive excavation shows that the site of Arad in the northern Negev was not then occupied. Two solutions have been proposed to resolve this problem. On the basis of Judg. 1:16–17 the king may have been ruler over an area rather than a specific city. Or, since Egyptian records speak of two Arads, the king in Num. 21 could have been ruler over the other Arad. Tell Malhatah, less than eight miles from "Greater Arad," has been tentatively identified as this second Arad.

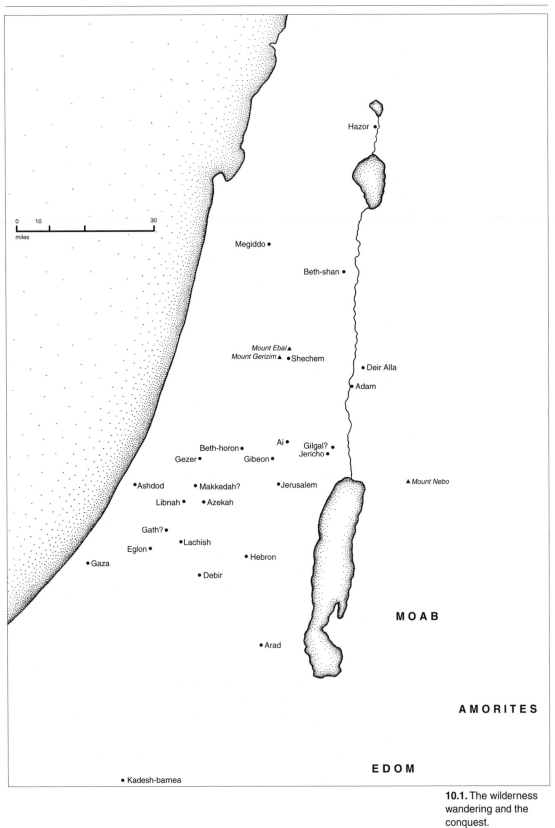

Hazor •

Megiddo •

Beth-shan •

Mount Ebal ▲
Mount Gerizim ▲ • Shechem

• Deir Alla

• Adam

Ai •

Beth-horon •   Gilgal?
Gezer •   Gibeon •   Jericho •

▲ *Mount Nebo*

• Ashdod   • Makkedah?   • Jerusalem

Libnah •   • Azekah

Gath? •

Eglon •   • Lachish

• Gaza   • Hebron

• Debir

M O A B

• Arad

A M O R I T E S

E D O M

• Kadesh-barnea

0   10   30
miles

10.1. The wilderness wandering and the conquest.

but he found the pay irresistible. As the story unfolds, however, four times Balaam uttered God's message rather than the curse for which Balak had paid. At Tell Deir Alla (perhaps biblical Succoth) in Transjordan, excavators found hundreds of fragments of a text written on plaster. After some of the fragments were joined, it was discovered that the text centers on an episode in the life of "Balaam son of Beor"—the Balaam of Numbers 22. The excavated text describes a divine vision received by Balaam: "Lo, the gods came to him at night and [spoke to] him." For some reason the Canaanites retained Balaam's memory, but not the recognition that the true God had been involved with him.[3]

The Israelites finally reached an area within sight of the eastern shore of the Jordan River.[4] There, since a military takeover of the Promised Land was anticipated, another military census was taken (Num. 26; see chap. 9 above). Also, some of the tribes (Reuben, Gad, and the half-tribe of Manasseh) requested that they be given land east of the Jordan as their inheritance share (Num. 32). Moses agreed to this request, but with the stipulation that they must help the other tribes in their battle for the land to the west.

Moses could not accompany the Hebrews into the Promised Land, but he did have the opportunity to give last words of counsel. In these parting speeches, compiled in the Book of Deuteronomy, Moses gave Israel lessons from the past. He reviewed their history since leaving Egypt, and he emphasized what God had done for them along the way. Moses also prepared Israel for the future by, among other things, elaborating on the Ten Commandments. He reviewed the laws, modifying and adapting some (compare, e.g., Exod. 22:16–17 with Deut. 22:28–29). He enjoined the people concerning various religious matters, such as remembering to tithe (Deut. 14:22). He encouraged them to thank God for everything (Deut. 8:10). And soberingly, Moses informed Israel that they were not getting the Promised Land because of their righteousness but because the present inhabitants were so wicked and because God was fulfilling his promise to Abraham and his descendants (Deut. 9:4–5).

Before his death, Moses was allowed to view the Promised Land from Mount Nebo. Then he died and was buried "in the valley in the land of Moab, opposite Beth-peor; but no man knows his burial place to this day" (Deut. 34:6). No serious attempt has been made to locate his grave, but in 1962 a small explosive charge was set off near Mount Nebo by someone who then convinced himself that the resultant damage marked the tomb of Moses (see Lissner 1963)!

Much had happened to the Hebrews since their departure from Egypt forty years earlier. The time was needlessly long, but it finally ended and the Promised Land lay ahead. The Israelites had been molded from a mass of people into a nation complete with laws, gover-

---

3. The date of the text is still not settled; opinions range from the ninth into the eighth century. Lemaire 1985 speculates that the biblical writer was familiar with the Balaam tradition and utilized part of it. It is just as plausible that the Deir Alla text is a corrupted memory of Balaam or a memory of a previous incident in his life. See also Hackett 1986.

4. For more detail concerning Israel's trek toward the Promised Land, see Herr 1993; Merling 1991; and Merling and Geraty 1994.

nors, religious system, and heritage; they were ready to claim their inheritance, the Promised Land.

The Conquest

One of Moses' last acts was to commission Joshua as his successor.[5] It became Joshua's duty to conduct the holy war, and God made his expectations clear (Josh. 1:7–8). Joshua had been groomed for his new responsibility, but it was plain that his success would hinge on his adherence to the law and to God's direction. Joshua prepared for the coming action by sending two spies across the Jordan to "view the land, especially Jericho" (Josh. 2:1). The city of Jericho, the only city in the southern Jordan Valley, sat in the plain across from the Israelites, at the gateway to the Hill Country further west. Jericho could not be bypassed, as it would then constitute a rear threat as the Israelites moved westward. Moreover, it would be wise to learn what response the people of Jericho might make to an intrusion into their oasis.

It is unlikely that any of the generation gathered at Jericho had ever seen a body of rushing water such as the Jordan River in flood stage (as it was then); any who might have swum in the Nile decades earlier had had little recent opportunity to maintain their skill. The spies probably constructed or found some means of flotation to aid their crossing.[6]

Defenses in Palestine changed over the centuries as "improved" ways kept being designed to protect a city. In Abraham's day (Middle Bronze Age II) the slopes of a tell were plastered to make it harder for an attacker to approach or hide, and sometimes a second wall was built at the base of the mound. Knowledge of fortifications from the time of Joshua (end of Late Bronze Age I and beginning of Late Bronze Age II) is rather sparse. Current evidence suggests that some cities continued to use Middle Bronze Age II defenses, others were protected by outer house walls that ringed a site, and still others actually stood unfortified. If the gate system was like the one found at Megiddo, then a six-piered gateway guarded Jericho's entranceway. That the spies were able to walk into Jericho uncontested suggests they looked similar to residents of Canaan or that strangers were a common sight in the city.

The people of Jericho were aware of the Israelites massed just a few miles away on the other side of the Jordan. The people would have been wary, and someone correctly guessed who the strangers were and why they had come. They also knew where the spies had gone to get off the street—into Rahab's house. As in patriarchal times, courtyard houses still featured flat roofs that could be used as work areas, spare rooms, and additional storage space. The story of Rahab is set in springtime when flax is harvested and dried. The flax on her rooftop would have been cut into

5. This chapter assumes the early date (approximately 1400) for the conquest. Arguments for this date were given in chapter 8, and additional evidence follows in this chapter.

6. Near the Dead Sea, the Jordan River used to be between ninety and one hundred feet across and as much as twelve feet deep. The pipelines now diverting Jordan water have reduced these figures.

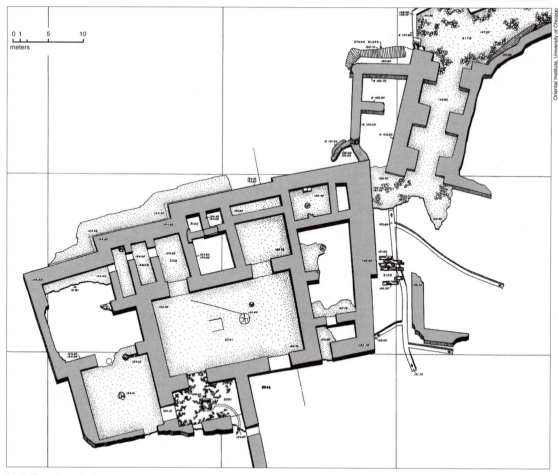

Oriental Institute, University of Chicago

10.2. The city gate (upper right) at Megiddo contained three sets of piers into which as many doors were placed. It was hoped the multiple-door system would prevent attackers from gaining entry. The palace of King Biridiya of Megiddo (who wrote the Amarna letter found on p. 218) is located beside the gateway.

approximately three-foot lengths and piled high enough, she hoped, to hide the two men. Rahab deceived the residents of Jericho into futile pursuit toward the Jordan River. She then helped the spies escape into the nearby hills, where they stayed until the search for them ended.

The spies eventually made their way back to Joshua, and after their debriefing he moved the camp to the banks of the Jordan. God was about to perform another miracle. All of Israel had heard how God parted the Reed Sea to let his people escape Egypt, but of those standing by the Jordan, only Joshua, Caleb, and those over forty years of age had been there to see it happen. Now the new generation was ready for a similar showing of God's power.

As the priests carrying the ark entered the Jordan, its waters parted and the Israelites were able to walk into the Promised Land. The Bible mentions that the water was blocked at Adam (Josh 3:16), which is usually identified as a place upstream where landslides are known to have occurred. The blocking of the Jordan River happened twice in the twentieth century, in 1906 and 1927. In the latter instance the Jordan was dammed up for twenty-one hours. Some scholars think a similar landslide was the mechanism God used for Joshua, but others prefer to understand the event as entirely supernatural. If God did choose to use a landslide, its timing still requires a miracle.

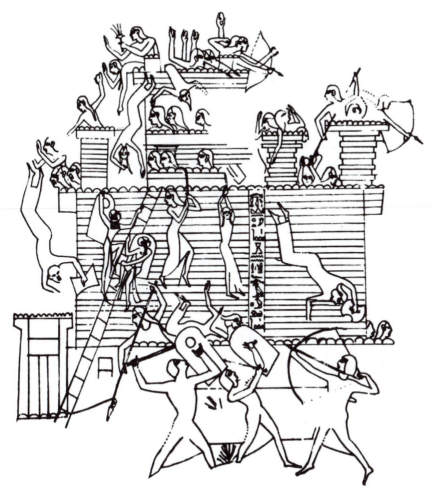

10.3. Thirteenth-century relief of Egyptian forces attacking a Syrian city, illustrating how the defenders of Jericho expected the battle to be conducted. Egyptian troops are scaling the walls, and archers are picking off defenders on the ramparts. The defenders use spears, arrows, rocks, and religion (the figure in the upper left is holding a censer) to fend off the enemy.

Safely across the Jordan, the Israelites camped at Gilgal.[7] Shortly thereafter they began the conquest with Jericho. The size of Jericho is estimated at between nine and twelve acres. Studies of ancient population density conclude that city populations averaged between one hundred and two hundred per acre, which suggests that Jericho's population was under two thousand people (Zorn 1994).

Understanding the size of Jericho and its population helps to put the confrontation into perspective. The size of the city also provides another argument for thinking that Joshua did not lead millions of Israelites across the Jordan. The men, women, and children inside the fortified walls of Jericho could not in their wildest hopes have expected to withstand millions. As soon as the inhabitants of Jericho realized the staggering odds against them, their only sensible response would have been to abandon the city. Further, Jericho would have been no more than a nuisance to be swept aside by so many Israelites, and Joshua would have had little need of the "captain of the host of the Lord" (Josh. 5:13–6:5), who commanded Joshua to take Jericho by rather unconven-

7. The Bible places Gilgal east of Jericho; it does not imply the presence of any permanent settlement, and none has been found.

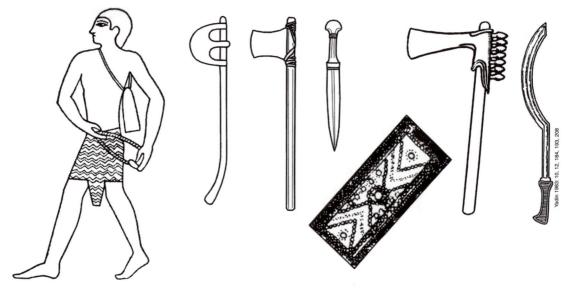

Yadin 1963: 10, 12, 184, 193, 208

10.4. Slinger depicted in an Egyptian relief, and some of the weaponry used in Palestine at the time of the conquest. An Egyptian-style ax is on the far left and a "sickle sword" (which had been recently introduced to provide cutting power through body armor) is on the far right. A typical shield is also pictured.

tional means. God wanted the people to realize that the victory would be granted by him and not achieved by their own strength. The army would not even have to fight until the city defenses were breached and the enemy was in disarray.

Presumably, the Israelites entered the Promised Land with typical Egyptian military hardware. Therefore, some of the armed force would have functioned as slingers and others as archers. For close combat, the troops would have carried axes, spears, and short swords. Some Canaanite troops would have carried Egyptian-shaped axes, while others would have used local types. Reliefs and other archaeological finds show that Canaanites carried distinctively shaped shields and wore helmets and possibly chain mail, which had been recently introduced.

None of this military hardware was used until the seventh day of the campaign. Tribal representatives simply marched around Jericho's perimeter once each day—beyond range of sling and bow, naturally—and then returned to camp until the next day's parade. One circuit of the city could have been accomplished in under an hour. The inhabitants of Jericho would have recognized the procession as a religious exercise, and they probably appealed to their gods to be stronger than the God of Israel. On the seventh day of this psychological-style warfare, the Hebrews marched around Jericho not once but seven times. The defenders of Jericho must have been extremely curious onlookers as the circling continued hour after hour. At the end of the seventh circuit, a ram's horn was sounded and the Israelites began to shout. On cue, the walls began to crumble, and the conquerors rushed in to secure the city.

It is not necessary to picture all of Jericho's outer defenses collapsing; certainly the portion containing Rahab's house did not fall. Several ingenious, but ridiculous, explanations have been offered as to how the walls of Jericho collapsed.[8] For those inclined to speculate on the me-

8. One such theory is that the daily parade kept the defenders from noticing that sappers were ripping out the foundations of Jericho's wall, with the remaining supports being pulled out when the horn sounded. Other theories are that sound waves from the

10.5. Aerial view of Old Testament Jericho. The nearby refugee houses (on both the left and right of the tell) give an idea of the relatively small size of ancient Jericho. Kathleen Kenyon presumed that Late Bronze Age Jericho almost entirely disappeared due to erosion and large-scale quarrying of the mound for soil to make bricks and to fertilize fields (when straw bricks decompose, a rich fertilizer results).

chanics God used in his miracle, an earthquake is probably the best option. Jericho is in an earthquake belt, and it has been shaken at various times in history. If God did use an earthquake, its timing makes it no less a miracle.

Archaeological Evidence for the Fall of Jericho

Archaeological evidence for the fall of Jericho has long been controversial. Beginning in 1907, Carl Watzinger excavated the site and concluded that it was unoccupied during the Late Bronze Age (1550–1200). In the 1930s John Garstang dug the site for several seasons, and he announced that he had found a collapsed double city wall and a residential area ("City IV") destroyed by fire—all dating to approximately 1400. From 1952 to 1958, Dame Kathleen Kenyon excavated Jericho. She agreed that Garstang had found tombs, some pottery, and possibly a building (Garstang's "Middle Building") all dating to Late Bronze Age IIA (1450/1400–1350/1300). But she herself found only a few Late Bronze Age wall fragments and one Late Bronze Age dipper juglet *in situ*. In addition, Kenyon's more sophisticated excavation techniques revealed that the double city wall Garstang dated to the time of Joshua really belonged to the much earlier Early Bronze Age. She put the destruction of City IV to the end of Middle Bronze Age II (approximately 1550). Kenyon concluded that there was no walled city for Joshua to conquer.

It was not until the early 1980s that final publications of Kenyon's work became available for study. Such study led Bryant Wood (1990) to concur that the double wall was indeed from a much earlier period, but he also concluded that City IV had been destroyed at the end of Late Bronze Age I (approximately 1400) as Garstang had maintained. Bas-

---

trumpets caused the collapse or that shock waves from Israel's marching in cadence collapsed the walls.

10.6. Artist's reconstruction of City IV at Jericho. Jericho was defended by a lower stone revetment wall and an upper mudbrick wall. A mud-brick wall may also have topped the lower revetment wall (as shown here). Bryant Wood places Rahab's house between the lower revetment wall and the upper city wall. City IV was destroyed by massive fire, but some of the walls seem to have collapsed prior to that conflagration. The discovery of storage jars filled with grain may point to destruction following spring harvest.

ing his analysis of City IV on pottery, scarabs, and even radiocarbon dating, Wood found that Kenyon had largely based her conclusions on the absence of certain imported pottery and that she had ignored the considerable local pottery, some of which Wood found to be Late Bronze Age in date.[9] If Wood is correct, then there is evidence at Jericho to support the early date of the exodus (see Bienkowski and Wood 1990 for a defense of Kenyon and a rebuttal by Wood).

9. There is no full agreement concerning the inner chronology or terminology of the Late Bronze Age. Depending on the chronology chosen, Late Bronze Age I ended at 1450 or 1400. The consequence of this variable is that evidence for the conquest could exist either in the transition from Late Bronze Age I to Late Bronze Age II or totally within Late Bronze Age II. To further complicate matters, the great deal of cultural continuity between these two periods sometimes makes it difficult to determine when Late Bronze Age I ended and Late Bronze Age II began. Perhaps, therefore, the life of City IV could have extended into Late Bronze Age II before its destruction.

Into the Hill Country

The defeat of Jericho gave Joshua a foothold in the Jordan Valley. One of the routes up into the Hill Country led toward Jerusalem, but Joshua sent men to scout a more northern access guarded by Ai where he could drive a wedge into the central portion of the land. The scouts returned with the positive report that only a few soldiers would be sufficient for the task. About three *alafim* were sent up into the Hill Country to remove any problem Ai might present for the larger group's passage.[10] Unexpectedly, Joshua's soldiers were routed and about three dozen of them lost their lives.

This defeat was caused by the disobedience of an Israelite named Achan. God had decreed that Jericho was under *herem* (a ban); everything in the city was to be dedicated to him as the firstfruits of the holy war. No one was to keep any spoils of Jericho. But Achan took a southern Mesopotamian robe (an imported luxury item) and about eight-and-one-half pounds of silver and gold as spoils of victory for himself. When this sin was found out, Achan was stoned to death, but commentators are divided on whether Achan's family was condemned with him.[11] Once the sinner was removed from the camp, Joshua mounted a second campaign into the Hill Country. Plans were carefully laid to lure the people of Ai into an ambush. This time the attack was a complete success, and Joshua gained his foothold in the Hill Country.

The conquest of Ai presents an archaeological problem. In the 1930s Judith Marquet-Krause identified et-Tell as a possible candidate for biblical Ai. Her initial excavation of et-Tell, however, revealed no remains dating to the time of the conquest, and subsequent archaeologists have also found et-Tell unoccupied between 2200 and 1200.[12] Thus, no one was living at et-Tell for Joshua and his soldiers to conquer. Attempts to resolve this problem usually involve redaction of the biblical record to fit the archaeological evidence. For example, one theory is that Joshua really attacked Bethel, but scribal error allowed a mistake to creep into the Bible by ascribing victory over the wrong place. Such confusion would be strange, however, because the biblical writers clearly distinguish between Bethel and Ai. Another explanation is that Ai was only an undefended outpost of Bethel and therefore too temporary in nature for archaeologists to necessarily find. Like the first theory, this one also lacks biblical support, for the Bible implies that Ai was fortified.

An obvious solution to the problem is that et-Tell has been wrongly identified as biblical Ai. To the credit of the most recent excavators of et-Tell, they did probe other likely candidates. None of the other tells,

---

10. They literally climbed into the Hill Country. Jericho is 850 feet below sea level, and Ai would be about 2,500 feet above sea level.

11. Some scholars think that Achan's family was brought out to see him punished and that their wealth was taken away. Others think the family was included in the death sentence. "Them" in Josh. 7:25 could refer to Achan's family and livestock or only to Achan's livestock. Joshua 22:20 could refer to Achan's family or to the thirty-six men who died in the first assault on Ai. If Achan's family was executed with him, that would imply they knew what Achan had done but had not tried to persuade him to repent.

12. Garstang's reported finding of Late Bronze Age pottery at the site has not been substantiated.

10.7. Modern Nablus spreads out at the base of Mount Gerizim (left) and Mount Ebal (right), illustrating the continuous importance of this junction in the north-south and east-west highway systems. Located in the small area between the bases of the two mountains, ancient Shechem controlled the highways. The proximity of the mountains and their high ground made the city vulnerable in wartime.

however, were found to contain materials within the proper time range. The solution to the "Ai problem" continues to be elusive.[13]

His entry into the Hill Country secure, Joshua led Israel about thirty miles north to Shechem, located in a saddle between Mount Gerizim and Mount Ebal. Joshua assembled the people into two groups, one on either mountain. On Mount Ebal an altar of stones was erected, offerings were made to God, and in this natural amphitheater setting Joshua read the law to the assembled people.[14] On hearing the law, the Israelites were solemnly reminded of their relationship with God and that he was granting them the land (see Crisler 1976 and Hill 1988).

The Southern Campaign

Gibeon, on the main north-south highway in the Hill Country, knew that the Israelite army would inevitably march toward it after the victories at Jericho and Ai. The Gibeonites decided that their best defense would be to trick Israel into a peace treaty, and they (along with Che-

13. Livingston 1970–71 attempts to find both Ai and Bethel a few miles southwest of et-Tell. Rainey 1970a rejects this theory but Livingston has not conceded the point; see Livingston 1994. Millard 1985b: 99 suggests that the formidable Early Bronze Age defenses could have been utilized by later inhabitants. Another possibility is that biblical Ai is under the modern village of Deir Dibwan, which is adjacent to et-Tell. Most recently, Bryant Wood's excavation of Khirbet al-Makater just northwest of et-Tell leads him to identify it as the site of biblical Ai. Zevit 1985 provides an example of how some scholars reject the historicity of a biblical episode and then try to imbue it with "higher" meaning.

14. Zertal 1985 claims to have found this altar, but its mode of construction does not accord with the biblical picture. For the acrimonious reactions that followed Zertal's article, see Kempinski 1986; Shanks 1988a; and Zertal 1986.

10.8. Amenhotep II sitting on the lap of his nurse. Potential enemies are frequently shown prostrate on footstools, with the feet of the pharaoh symbolically placed on the enemies, an imagery reflected in 1 Kings 5:3 and Psalm 110:1.

phirah, Beeroth, and Kiriath-jearim) were successful in their ruse. Kings further south realized that Gibeon's defection opened the highway to their cities. Therefore, the king of Jerusalem gathered allies from Hebron, Jarmuth, Lachish, and Eglon and advanced with their armies and besieged Gibeon in order to capture that control point. When the residents of Gibeon rushed word to Joshua, he might have enjoyed the news that those who had deceived him were in danger of annihilation. Or Joshua could have taken their plea for help as an opportune time to deal with several enemies in a single battle. But, whatever his thoughts were, Joshua had only one recourse; he had to honor his commitment no matter how it was gained. Joshua's word was his bond, and he would defend his "allies."

Joshua 10:6 says that the Gibeonites approached Joshua at Gilgal. Bible dictionaries recognize more than one site with that name, and it is likely a Hill Country Gilgal that is involved here.[15] After having just gained access to the Hill Country, it would have been unreasonable for Joshua to have retreated over 3,300 feet back down to his "beachhead" in the Jericho oasis.

A forced march from Gilgal reached Gibeon and surprised the assembled coalition. The armies of the five kings were routed, pursued westward down the steep Beth-horon pass, and chased into the foothills as far as Azekah. The "long day of Joshua," which is part of this

15. Zertal 1991: 38, 43 suggests that el-Umuq four miles from Shechem could be one of these other Gilgals.

sprawling battle, has received a great deal of attention. Various expositors have interpreted Joshua's request as a wish for more sunshine, for relief from the heat, or for strength. Since the episode is told in a poetic passage, some poetic license could be acceptable in explaining how his request was granted (Josh. 10:12–13).[16]

When the five kings who had attacked Gibeon were captured they were brought to Joshua. Before their sentencing was carried out, Joshua instructed his officers to put their "feet on the necks of these kings" (Josh. 10:24). In the ancient Near East a king showed his power over another person by putting his foot on that person (illustration 10.8).Therefore, Joshua was following Near Eastern custom.

Up to this point the biblical account of the conquest has been full of detail. But suddenly the writer disposes of six cities (Makkedah, Libnah, Lachish, Eglon, Hebron, Debir), miscellaneous towns, and one stray king in twelve verses (Josh. 10:28–39). It is as though the writer recognized that the key elements of the holy war had been spelled out and that his continued report could now be more cursory.[17]

The Northern Campaign

As Joshua was moving from victory to victory in the south, King Jabin of Hazor began to gather a northern coalition. Joshua marched on that amassing army and routed it. The biblical writer continued to give only an abbreviated account of the action, but reported that Joshua defeated some of the cities of the kings in the northern coalition and that he burned Hazor, which is described as "the head of all these kingdoms" (Josh. 11:10).[18] An average city in Palestine covered approximately fifteen to twenty acres, but Hazor occupied two hundred acres! Recognizing Hazor's great difference in size over the average gives added meaning to that city's description. Joshua never had to fight such a formidable foe in southern Palestine.

The summary account in Joshua 11 of this northern battle also contains the first reference to the Canaanites' use of horses and chariots. After the battle, in obedience to God's command, Joshua burned the captured chariots and hamstrung the horses, making them unfit for future battle. God did not want Israel to be tempted to trust in such hard-

16. The claims that astronomers or NASA scientists found evidence supporting Joshua's long day have no basis. The NASA version of this misguided attempt to prove the Bible was spread by a man who felt God had told him to make the claim.

17. The battle to relieve beleaguered Gibeon ended with the defeat of the kings and armies of three of the six cities that Joshua subsequently attacked. This can account for some of the apparent ease with which the southern campaign concluded. Further, excavation at Lachish shows that its Late Bronze Age defensive perimeter consisted of no more than an outer belt of houses. See Ussishkin 1987.

18. Yigael Yadin, following the late date of the exodus, concluded that the fiery destruction of Hazor level 13 was the result of Joshua's attack. Level 14 (and its contemporary level 1b in the upper city) date to Late Bronze Age IIA, and destructions are reported in both areas within that time frame (1400–1300). During the 1995 season, Amnon Ben-Tor, the current excavator of Hazor, found a "mighty palace" that was destroyed by fire in Late Bronze Age II (1400–1200). At the moment it seems that there were two destructions: one in the thirteenth century and one earlier. For a popular account of the excavation at Hazor, see Yadin 1975.

10.9. Hazor comprises an upper and a lower city, both of which were occupied at the time of the conquest. The ancient tell was several times larger than normal cities in Palestine and dwarfs the adjacent modern kibbutz of Ayelet Hashahar.

ware for their victories. The story of the campaign against the northern coalition finishes the account of the conquest.

The Nature of the Conquest

Joshua 12 lists dozens of kings defeated by Joshua, most of whom receive no other mention. A careful reading discloses that the conquest stretched over seven years (Josh. 14:6–10). The Book of Joshua, therefore, gives only a partial account of Joshua's military campaigns. Perhaps, if the "Book of Jashar" (Josh. 10:13) is ever recovered, more detail can be added. It is also clear that the conquest was incomplete. In the south, the major cities of Gezer and Jerusalem were still in Canaanite hands. In the north, the important city-states of Megiddo and Beth-shan continued free of Israelite control. Some of the cities that Joshua conquered were subsequently resettled by the Canaanites and needed to be regained (Judg. 1:10–15). According to Joshua 11:22, the cities of Gaza, Gath, and Ashdod remained in enemy hands, but the next verse declares that Joshua "took the whole land." The apparent discrepancy dissolves when one recognizes that Joshua isolated some strong city-states and broke two federations opposed to him. For all practical purposes Israel had firmly established itself in the land.

In recent years many critical scholars have stopped maintaining that the account of Israel's conquest of the Promised Land recorded in Joshua 1–12 is reflected in the archaeological evidence found in the transition from Late Bronze Age to Iron Age I in Palestine (approximately 1200). About the only point of agreement among critical scholars now is that the biblical text is of little or no historical value for understanding how Israel *really* made its appearance in Palestine. To accept the biblical account is now said to be naïve, and there is lively debate over whether a "peaceful infiltration" (nomadic Israelites entered Palestine in search of new pastures and gradually became sedentary) or a "peasant revolt" (the Israelites were actually lower-class Canaanites who revolted against their oppressors) is what actually happened. Variations on these two hypotheses have been proposed, and some even grant that a portion of the Israelites had been in Egypt.[19]

Although archaeological support for the late date of the exodus is ambiguous at best, some critical scholars continue to look for evidence of Israel's appearance around 1200. They fail to give serious consideration to whether the data in dispute can point to an appearance of Israel in the land some two hundred years earlier. The decrease in urban population and corresponding increase in nonsedentary people during Palestine's Late Bronze Age could reflect Israel's entrance into Palestine, the consequent disruption, the turmoil that characterizes the period of the judges, and Israel's retention of a more pastoral lifestyle. The destruction of urban centers at the end of Late Bronze Age could also reflect the turmoil during the period of the judges. Clearly, the destructions cannot be credited to a single moment in time, and at least some should be attributed to Egyptian or Sea People operations. Other destructions can be the result of inter-city warfare. The strong continuance of Late Bronze Age material culture into Iron Age I can support Israel's presence in the land prior to 1200 and their acceptance of much of the material culture. It also suggests that no new wave of people entered Palestine around 1200.[20] The proposition that certain traits distinguish Israelite from Canaanite settlements is highly questionable. The establishment of many new settlements at the beginning of Iron Age I need not signal the arrival of Israel into the land. The settlements can as well reflect Israel's transition to a more urban lifestyle in the later part of the period of the judges.

The Amarna Letters

Early in the fourteenth century, Palestine was politically unsettled. This condition is reflected in some of the nearly four hundred Amarna Letters, a collection of cuneiform tablets found at Tell el-Amarna in Egypt. The tablets are from the royal archives of Pharaoh Amenhotep III and his son Akhenaten. They were written close to the "early date" of the conquest, mainly by Canaanites to the court of Egypt.[21]

Several of the Amarna Letters mention problems caused by Hapiru (also written Habiru and Apiru). Most scholars allow that *Hapiru* and *Hebrew* are etymologically equatable, but there is little agreement be-

19. For an introduction to these hypotheses, see Finkelstein 1988; Fritz 1987a; Halpern 1983; Isserlin 1983; J. Miller 1977; and Stiebing 1989. For conservative critiques of these theories, see Hess 1993 and Waltke 1990.

20. Fritz 1987a: 98 proposes that the infiltration hypothesis should be modified to a symbiosis hypothesis. As he understands the data, it is necessary that "close relations existed between [Israelite tribes and the Canaanites] before the twelfth century." Interestingly, the scenario he paints fits nicely with the early date.

21. For the most recent collection and translation of the Amarna Letters, see Moran 1992. For a critique of whether the Amarna Letters really reflect a decline in Egypt's role in Palestine, see Several 1972.

British Museum

10.10. Letter from Prince Biridiya of Megiddo to Pharaoh Akhenaten, pleading for Egyptian help. The Amarna Letters were written in cuneiform, the diplomatic language.

yond that point. Evidence of the Hapiru is found over much of the ancient Near East, spanning the centuries before and after the time of the conquest. They were engaged in many different occupations and lifestyles. Based on what is known of them, the Hapiru do not seem to fully correspond either in activity, locale, or time with what is known of the Hebrews.

Nevertheless, in the Amarna Letters the term *Hapiru* is used by kings to describe neighbors whose armies were taking land and towns. For example, the king of Byblos assumes that anyone who takes his land is an enemy of the pharaoh, and he labels them Hapiru. Yet these same people wrote the pharaoh and swore their loyalty. G. Ernest Wright (1962: 75) probably reached the correct conclusion years ago when he theorized that Hapiru had become a pejorative term, similar to the tendency just after World War II to casually label people one disliked as Communists. The Hapiru were, more or less, a footloose, combative group, and the term *Hapiru* seems to have become a synonym for one's enemy. When Israel entered the land and began the conquest, it would have been rather natural for the Canaanites to call them Hapiru. It is possible, therefore, that at least some of the time there is a correlation between references to Hapiru and the Hebrews.

Thutmose III had begun the practice of taking Canaanite princes back with him to Egypt after military campaigns to guarantee that their fathers would behave. Egyptians attempted to acculturate these princes so their first allegiance would be to the pharaoh. Later on, when such a prince was placed on a throne in Palestine, Egypt could expect his loyalty. The plan worked with varying degrees of success, but when the Amarna Letters were being written, Egypt was distracted, and loyal princes were finding themselves without proper support. Princes pleaded for relief forces or, failing that, for safe passage back to Egypt. Local governors who were supposed to be representing Egypt were seemingly more concerned with their own interests. The few Egyptian troops that were available seem to have been moved around capriciously, and some of them proved extremely unreliable. The roads were unsafe, caravans were robbed, and people were afraid to leave their towns.

The problems revealed by the Amarna Letters cannot be equated with specific events in the Book of Joshua, but since there was much more fighting than is detailed in the Bible, perhaps some of the Amarna Letters do reflect Israel's first years in the land. At the very least, the Amarna Letters provide a glimpse of the political picture in Palestine at that time. At most, they might give actual Canaanite reaction to Israelite movements. For example, Biridiya wrote to the pharaoh (*ANE* 1:263; *ANET* 485):

> To the king, my lord, and my Sun-god, say: Thus Biridiya, the faithful servant of the king. At the two feet of the king, my lord, and my Sun-god, seven and seven times I fall. Let the king know that ever since the archers returned to Egypt, Labayu has carried on hostilities against me, and we are not able to pluck the wool, and we are not able to go outside the gate in the presence of Labayu, since he learned that you have not given archers; and now his face is set to take Megiddo, but let the king protect his city, lest Labayu seize it. Verily, the city is destroyed by death from pestilence and disease. Let the king give one hundred garrison troops to guard the city lest Labayu seize it. Verily, there is no other purpose in Labayu. He seeks to destroy Megiddo.

Biridiya was the prince of Megiddo, and he had maintained his loyalty to the pharaoh. Megiddo was threatened by Prince Labayu of Shechem who, in another letter, was accused of having gone over to the Hapiru, or Apiru. Joshua brought the Israelites to Shechem for rededication after the victory at Ai. The biblical silence regarding any conflict between Joshua and the Shechemites, coupled with the accusation from the Amarna Letters that Shechem had thrown in with the Hapiru, has led to the intriguing suggestion that the letters explain what happened when Joshua approached Shechem (Harrelson 1957).[22] Labayu also wrote to the pharaoh (*ANE* 1:266; *ANET* 486):

> To the king, my lord and my Sun-god: Thus Labayu. . . . Behold, I am a faithful servant of the king, and I have not rebelled. . . . Now they wickedly slander me. . . . Further, my crime is namely that I entered Gezer and said publicly: "Shall the king take my property, and not likewise the property of Milkilu?" I know the deeds that Milkilu has done against me. Further, the king wrote concerning my son. I did not know that my son associates with the Apiru. . . . If the king should write to me, "Plunge a bronze dagger into your heart and die!" how could I refuse to carry out the command of the king?

22. The difficulty with this theory is that it disregards Josh. 11:19, which states that only Gibeon did not resist the occupation.

Labayu pleads his innocence, but points an accusing finger at Prince Milkilu of Gezer, who in turn writes the pharaoh (*ANE* 1:267; *ANET* 486–87):

> Let the king, my lord, know the deed that Yanhamu did to me after I left the presence of the king, my lord. Now he seeks two thousand shekels of silver from my hand, saying to me: "Give me your wife and your children, or I will smite!" Let the king know this deed. . . .
>   Let the king know that powerful is the hostility against me. . . . Let the king, my lord, protect his land from the hand of the Apiru. If not, then let the king, my lord, send chariots to fetch us, lest our servants smite us.

Milkilu wanted the pharaoh either to help protect his territory or to send for him and provide safe passage to Egypt. Yanhamu, who was harassing Milkilu, was a Canaanite who seemed to have some governing power. The letters continue on with pleadings for help, with declarations that only a show of support would be sufficient to calm the situation. Florid letters of innocence and allegiance were written by those vehemently condemned as traitors in other letters. Abdu-Heba, prince of Jerusalem, wrote repeated pleas to the pharaoh (*ANE* 1:272–73; *ANET* 488–89):

> To the king, my lord. . . . Behold, I am a shepherd of the king, and a bearer of the royal tribute am I. It was not my father and not my mother, but the arm of the mighty king that placed me in the house of my father. . . . Let my king take thought for his land! The land of the king is lost; in its entirety it is taken from me; there is war against me. . . . The Apiru capture the cities of the king. . . . Let the king send archers to his land! But if there are no archers here this year, all the lands of the king, my lord, will be lost. . . . If there are no archers here this year, let the king send a commissioner, and let him take me to himself together with my brothers, and we shall die near the king, our lord!

The Egyptians seemingly left loyalists like Abdu-Heba of Jerusalem to their own devices. There is no hint in the Bible that Joshua encountered any Egyptian forces. Perhaps God timed the conquest for this moment when Egypt was preoccupied and Canaan was inwardly torn.

Canaanite Religion

One reason God gave Israel the Promised Land at that specific point in history was that the "wickedness" of the Canaanites "was complete" and they had, therefore, forfeited their claim to the land. A brief look at Canaanite religion will show what God had been tolerating and finally commanded the Israelites to eradicate.

The Canaanites were polytheists like the rest of the Near Eastern cultures. Canaanite deities were rather fluid in personality and function, but some idea of their pantheon can be gained. El, their chief god, was a rather nebulous figure who lived far away "at the source of the two rivers." He was considered the father of humans and gods and was called "Father Bull." El probably killed his father and emasculated him; he

10.11. Thirteenth-century statuette from Megiddo, presumably of the god El (approximately ten inches high and overlaid with gold leaf).

Oriental Institute, University of Chicago

killed his favorite son, cut off a daughter's head, and sacrificed another son to his dead father. El seduced, or was seduced by, two women who were subsequently driven out into the desert when they bore children.

El's wife was Asherah. She is usually associated with fertility, and a sacred pillar or tree was her symbol. Several times Moses commanded the Israelites to get rid of Asherah's pillars when they conquered the land (e.g., Deut. 7:5; 16:21). Of El and Asherah's many children, the most important, Baal, controlled the rain and therefore vegetation. Baal was the god of storm, his voice was thunder.[23] Anat, Baal's wife

23. The terms *El* and *Baal* are used in the Bible to refer to Israel's God, but this does not imply any borrowing or pagan taint. El is the generic name for god in the northwest Semitic language group, and Baal could be applied to any god.

Réunion des Musées Nationaux

10.12. Stele depicting the storm god Hadad (called Baal in Canaan) standing on the back of a bull. This use of an animal as a platform for a god might have been what Aaron had in mind when the golden calf was made at Mount Sinai.

and sister, was goddess of love and fertility, but also of war. Canaanites thought of her as both a prostitute and a virgin. In one text she rejoices as she wades in the gore of worshipers she has killed.

The Canaanites were primarily interested in ritualistic outward acts that would make their gods treat them more favorably. The Canaanites developed histories for their deities as they attempted to explain and placate the unknown, and there was a fervent attempt to "make it work." Canaanite sacrificial ritual was more diversified than Israel's; more kinds of animals were offered, and human sacrifice was sometimes required. There is no indication that Canaanite gods handed down a moral code for their people to follow. Indeed, the Canaanites were apparently much more moral than were their gods, an observation that is not especially flattering to the gods. To the Canaanite, fertility was of major importance in worship, and both male and female temple prostitution was prevalent. God inspired Moses to forewarn Israel against such practice (Deut. 23:17–18).

Palestine was dotted with Canaanite high places, sacred trees, and elaborate temples. Some of the preserved literature and cult objects reveal a strong focus on the sexual and show the great gulf that existed between the Israelite and Canaanite religions. William F. Albright (1953: 94) summed up Canaanite culture this way: "The sedentary culture which [Israel] encountered . . . seems to have reflected the lowest religious level in all Canaanite history."[24]

God had had enough. The people of Canaan were wicked in Abraham's day, but God showed mercy. The Canaanites had the witness of Abraham and his altars, and they recognized the power of the patriarch's god, but they did not forsake their own imitations. There were other opportunities and signs of the truth, but the Canaanites ignored them as well. Finally, God's mercy turned to judgment. Punishment was meted out to the Canaanites for their sins and to prevent them from leading Israel astray. In later centuries the prophets would entreat their hearers to "repent today lest tomorrow be too late." At the end of the fifteenth century many Canaanites ran out of tomorrows.[25]

Additional Reading

Curtis, Adrian. *Ugarit (Ras Shamra)*. Grand Rapids: Eerdmans, 1985.

Hess, Richard S. "Alalakh Studies in the Bible: Obstacle or Contribution?" Pp. 199–215 in *Scripture and Other Artifacts*. Edited by Michael D. Coogan, J. Cheryl Exum, and Lawrence E. Stager. Louisville: Westminster, 1994.

———. *Joshua: An Introduction and Commentary*. Tyndale Old Testament Commentaries. Downers Grove, Ill.: InterVarsity, 1996.

———. "The Southern Desert." *Archaeology in the Biblical World* 2/1 (1994): 22–33.

Hoftijer, Jacob. "The Prophet Balaam in a Sixth Century Aramaic Inscription." *BA* 39 (1976): 11–17, 87.

Krahmalkov, Charles R. "Exodus Itinerary Confirmed by Egyptian Evidence." *BAR* 20/5 (1994): 54–62, 79 (additional comments in 21/1 [1995]: 14, 16).

Lewis, Theodore J. "The Disappearance of the Goddess Anat: The 1995 West Semitic Research Project on Ugaritic Epigraphy." *BA* 59 (1996): 115–21.

Malamat, Abraham. "How Inferior Israelite Forces Conquered Fortified Canaanite Cities." *BAR* 8/2 (1982): 24–35 (correction in 8/3:6; additional comments in 8/4:64, 66; 10/2 [1984]: 12; 10/3:20–21, 74).

Yadin, Yigael. "Israel Comes to Canaan." *BAR* 8/2 (1982): 14–23.

24. Albright made this judgment with the low date of the exodus in mind, but it is equally appropriate for conditions two centuries earlier. For insights into Canaanite religion, see Coogan 1978; Gibson 1978; Gray 1964; Mullen 1980; Oldenburn 1969; Pfeiffer 1962; and Ringgren 1973.

25. For a survey of our present knowledge of the Canaanites, see Schoville 1994.

Joshua's Closing Years and the Period of the Judges

Had Judah that day join'd, or one whole Tribe,

They had by this possess'd the Towers of Gath,

And lorded over them whom now they serve;

But what more oft in Nations grown corrupt,

And by their vices brought to servitude,

Than to love Bondage more than Liberty,

Bondage with ease than strenuous Liberty;

And to despise, or envy, or suspect

Whom God hath of his special favour raised

As their deliverer? . . .

—John Milton, "Samson Agonistes"

Settlement

For a little over forty years the tabernacle had been moved along with Israel on its journeys. With the conquest over, the dismantling and reerection process came to an end. God had promised to select the

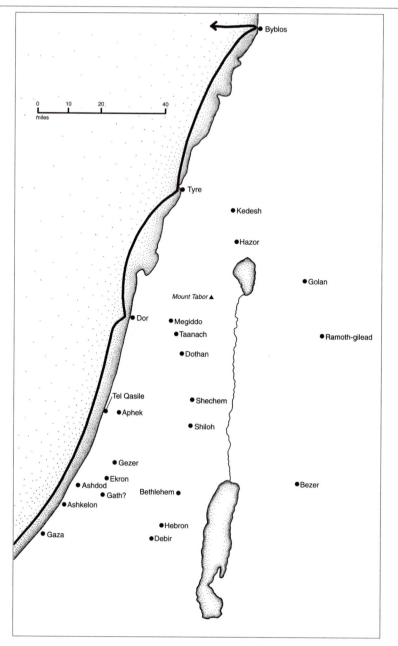

11.1. Joshua's closing years, the period of the judges, and the travels of Wen-Amon (dark line).

place where he would be worshiped (Deut. 12:11), and he now chose Shiloh in the central Hill Country for the tabernacle's permanent home. Shiloh would be the focus of Israel's worship for the next four hundred years.

Israel was established in Palestine, but Joshua found it necessary to encourage the tribes to fan out into the Promised Land (Josh. 18:3). Moses had already laid down guidelines for dividing the land (Num. 34) and had granted the tribes of Gad and Reuben and the half-tribe of Manasseh that descended from Machir (Manasseh's firstborn) land east of the Jordan (Num. 32). Joshua spelled out their territorial boundaries within Gilead in more detail and then began to carry out Moses' design by instituting a careful process to determine the land allotments for the rest of the tribes (Josh. 18:4–9).[1]

It is natural to assume that a good deal of personal preference and opinion was generated, but most importantly there was the conviction that God must affirm the decisions reached (Josh. 18:10).[2] Instead of land area, the tribe of Levi was deeded forty-eight cities scattered throughout the other tribal allotments. Clearly, this priestly tribe was to permeate the life of Israel (Josh. 21:1–42). Of those forty-eight cities, six (Kedesh, Shechem, Hebron, Bezer, Ramoth-gilead, Golan) had special function. These six were to be cities of refuge for anyone who unintentionally caused a death (Josh. 20). The careful spacing of these cities (illustration 11.1) shows how thoughtfully this provision was handled. From anywhere in the land, a person in need of such a city had only a short distance to run for protection.

The Book of Joshua also contains stories of individual settlement within the Promised Land. For example, Caleb received his long promised inheritance of the region around Hebron (Josh. 14–15), but he had to recapture Debir. Apparently some of the people who had fled before Joshua during the conquest had returned to the city. In this second battle Caleb offered his daughter Achsah in marriage as an incentive for victory, and the battle and the daughter's hand were won by Othniel. Joshua 15:18–19 is a difficult passage. It is generally understood that Achsah demanded of her father something that her new husband had been too reluctant to seek. It seems Achsah was telling her father that since he had put her in a semiarid landscape, the least he could do would be to grant some springs for the crops and flocks. In response, Caleb granted Achsah deed to "the upper springs and the lower springs" of Debir.

For many years biblical Debir was equated with a site called Tell Beit Mirsim, a site rather far from Hebron and without springs. Some scholars amended the biblical text to make the identification fit, but others showed interest in a site called Rabud whose consonants are the same as Debir, only reversed. Could Rabud be biblical Debir, the name garbled with the passage of centuries? For some years the political realities of Palestine prevented archaeologists from conducting any on-site examination of Rabud, but when such study did become possible, archaeologists found that Rabud had been occupied at the proper time in history. Additionally, they found two wells (carrying the names "the upper and lower wells") near the site that overflow in the springtime. Since the late 1960s, therefore, Bible maps show Debir close to Hebron, and scholars need no longer ponder over an alleged textual problem.

Joshua 23–24 contains Joshua's farewell addresses. He renewed the covenant at Shechem in a literary form parallel to the suzerain-vassal treaties (see chap. 8). Therefore, as Moses did at Mount Sinai, Joshua

1. Only seven divisions were necessary since Ephraim, Manasseh, Gad, and Reuben had already received their land and the Levites were not to have any specific territory. It is better to think of the "book" mentioned in Josh. 18:9 as a "scroll" since it was not until after the close of the Old Testament that the book form was invented.

2. It is not stated whether the lots employed were the Urim and Thummim used by the priests to determine God's will. Whatever they were, God's approval could be confirmed by such a process.

employed a legal outline to enhance the occasion so that the people could have no doubt as to their proper behavior toward God (J. Davis 1969: 88). If they obeyed and served God, the rest of the Canaanites would be driven from the land and Israel would have blessing and honor. But if they failed, their blessing would turn to destruction and their honor to dishonor. The people had clear examples of both contingencies in the past, and they should have had no trouble believing that, regardless of Israel's choice, God would keep his end of the covenant.

Joshua died and was buried at home. His age at death is given as 110 years but, as with Joseph, this might be a euphemism for a long life. Joshua and the other Israelites then of advanced age had been born in Egypt, and it is not impossible that the writer of the metaphor thought it a fitting tribute to Joshua's life. More important than Joshua's actual age at death is his epitaph (Josh 24:31).[3]

The Period of the Judges

Dozens of chronological charts have been devised for the Book of Judges because 1 Kings 6:1 states there were 480 years between the exodus and the fourth year of Solomon's reign. But when the various time spans in the Book of Judges are added together (i.e., the years of judging, oppression, and peace), they alone total 410 years. That total leaves only 70 years within which the following must fit:

40	years of wandering
7	years of conquest
?	years until the first judge was raised
40	years of Eli
40	years of Samuel
40	years of Saul
40	years of David
3	years of Solomon

The two most common reactions to this excess of years are either that the numbers are fanciful or that the judges partly overlap in time of service. Some overlapping can be argued between the books of Joshua and Judges, and Judges 10:7 suggests that Jephthah and Samson were almost contemporary. In any case, the writer of the Book of Judges had little interest in providing a chronology for the period. A working theory is that the major judges were consecutive and that the minor judges overlap with them.[4] Most of the judges seem limited in function to their local community or tribe and did not judge the whole territory. Two or more judges could easily be in local power at the same time (see illustration 11.2).

The history in the Book of Judges can be accepted as completely accurate. At the same time, its author has carefully selected the data so as

3. For insight into burial customs during this period, see Cooley and Pratico 1994.

4. Much information was recorded about a "major judge," in contrast to a "minor judge" for whom only a few verses of information is typically supplied. The repeated use of "forty years" also implies that that figure can be understood as a round number.

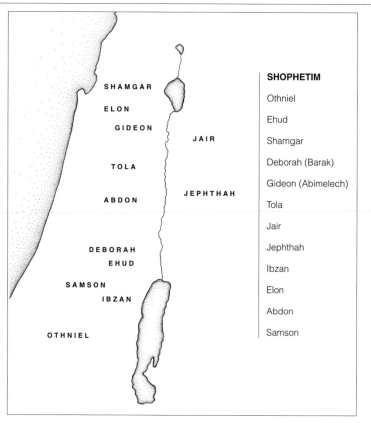

SHOPHETIM
Othniel
Ehud
Shamgar
Deborah (Barak)
Gideon (Abimelech)
Tola
Jair
Jephthah
Ibzan
Elon
Abdon
Samson

11.2. The judges according to their home areas (left) and in the order given in the Book of Judges (right). Barak and Abimelech are important personages in the book but are not judges.

to weave the history into a theological message. The recurring pattern in the book is often referred to as the "Four S's." In the first stage, the people fall into "sin," as they worship false gods or intermarry with the Canaanites. This defection from the covenant brings on a period of "servitude" in which Israel finds itself in subjection to people they were once able to control. After a term of servitude, Israel cries out to God in "supplication." A leader would then be raised up to bring the people "salvation." Because of this cyclical pattern, the Book of Judges is sometimes referred to as the book of defeat, in contrast to Joshua, the book of victory.

The English translation "judge" for the Hebrew *shophet* is somewhat misleading. The Hebrew word has a wider meaning than its English translation. In addition to judicial activity, the Hebrew word also implies defending, delivering, avenging, and punishing. However, few *shophetim* (judges) seem to have served in more than a military capacity. Their main mission was to be a military savior. As such, they were called upon to meet emergencies and could be chosen by either God or the people. There was no line of succession or continuous rule.

The Resurgence of Egyptian Power

Egypt's inattention to empire extended through the first decades of the period of the judges. Within that time span was the brief reign of the young Pharaoh Tutankhamun ("King Tut") whose fame rests on his tomb being found nearly intact and full of treasures. Then, toward the end of the fourteenth century, Seti I (1317–1304) reawakened Egypt's interest in empire. He and his successor, Ramesses II (1304–1237), began leading armies northward. Their goal was to control Palestine's coastal highway, which gave access to Syria further to the north. Centers along the coastal highway such as Gaza, Ashdod, and Aphek clearly functioned as Egyptian strongholds. However, debate continues over how far inland Egyptian control extended. Pharaoh Merenptah (1237–1227) continued the northern campaigns. The "Merenptah Stele" boasts of defeating Libyans in his fifth year, but the close of this "Hymn of Victory" contains a cryptic passage concerning a campaign even earlier in his reign (*ANE* 1:231; *ANET* 378):

> Carried off is Ashkelon; seized upon is Gezer;
> Yanoam is made as that which does not exist;
> Israel is laid waste, his seed is not.

The south-to-north alignment of the three cities (Yanoam is located somewhere in Galilee) is sometimes thought to imply that the confrontation with Israel took place in the north of Palestine, but other scholars doubt whether such an inference should be drawn. More attention has been paid to the determinatives (signs in the text that indicate the nature of the accompanying word) after each of the city names and Israel. The determinatives following Ashkelon, Gezer, and Yanoam indicate that they were city-states. The determinative for Israel, however, is one used for less-settled people. Therefore, shortly before 1200, an Egyptian scribe identified Israel as less politically established in the land—a picture in keeping with the situation reflected in the first half of the period of the judges.[5]

Merenptah's conquest of Ashkelon and Gezer probably removed the last impediments to Egypt's complete control over Palestine's southern coastal area and highway system. Gezer was a key access point into the Hill Country where the tribes of Israel were located. Could it have been there that a clash with Israelite forces occurred? We simply do not know.

An interesting confirmation of Merenptah's campaign into Palestine came to light with the reexamination of battle reliefs on a wall of the Karnak Temple in Thebes (Yurco 1990). These reliefs had been credited to Ramesses II, but it was found that they actually carried the royal cartouche of Merenptah and had been commissioned by him. Three of the battle scenes depict attacks on fortified cities, and one of the cities is identified as Ashkelon. Frank Yurco, who made the reexamination, believes that the other two cities (their names are missing) must be Gezer and Yanoam. The fourth battle scene depicts the defeat of an enemy in open terrain. This scene, Yurco argues, provides the earliest depiction of Israelites and gives, as he describes it, a "perfect match between the

---

5. Hasel 1994 weighs the various scholarly studies on this portion of the stele and concludes that "seed" should instead be translated "grain," implying that Israel was then an "agricultural/sedentary socioethnic entity." But see Hoffmeier 1997 (chap. 2), who critiques this and other analyses of the Israel portion of the stele.

Zev Radovan

11.3. The god Amon-Re is depicted twice in the top center of the Merenptah Stele (seven-and-one-half feet high, black granite): Merenptah is also shown twice, with the goddess Mut on the left and with the god Khonsu on the right. Primary attention has long focused on the next to the last line of the text, which contains the earliest extrabiblical reference to Israel. The stele provides the limit beyond which the "late date" of the exodus cannot go, but it provides no insight as to how much earlier Israel entered the Promised Land.

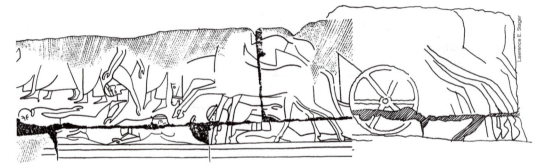

11.4. Scene 4 of the Karnak Temple relief possibly depicts Merenptah's victory over Israel as recorded on his stele. The dress is similar to the Canaanites in the three accompanying city scenes, implying that Israel had acculturated in this respect during the hundred years they had been in Palestine. Inclusion of a chariot in their fighting force may mean they had acquired such vehicles in previous engagements with the Canaanites (Yurco 1990: 33–34).

text on Merenptah's Stele and Merenptah's reliefs" (Yurco 1990: 32). Further, Yurco thinks the "reliefs provide striking confirmation of accumulating archaeological evidence that the initial Israelite settlements were in the highlands and that they were in open, dispersed villages with no substantial fortified towns" (p. 34).[6]

Deborah

If one accepts that the major judges were sequential, then Deborah and the battle against the army of Hazor (Judg. 4–5) would date about 1200, shortly after the campaign mentioned on Merenptah's Stele.[7] Deborah was one of the few *shophetim* to hold any judicial duties, but she is most readily remembered for prodding Barak to fight an army from Hazor, which had reverted to Canaanite control. The king of Hazor in Deborah's day was a man named Jabin. The name *Jabin* seems to have been popular among the kings of Hazor; in fact, a certain King Jabin of Hazor perished at the hands of Joshua during the northern conquest (Josh. 11:1–14).[8]

Barak gathered ten *alafim* of soldiers for the war from the two tribes (Naphtali and Zebulun) most affected by Hazor's dominance. One tactic of warfare is to control the high ground, so Barak marched his men

6. For Yurco, that the Israelites are dressed like Canaanites argues against the view that Israel emerged from the Shasu people, a people depicted in different dress. For the dispute over which scene actually depicts Israelites, see Rainey and Yurco 1991. The scene depicting the attack on Ashkelon shows the defenders in Canaanite dress. This is evidence that the Philistines had not yet arrived in that city.

7. One attempt to use archaeology to reach a more precise dating is no longer tenable. Judges 5:19 says the battle was fought "at Taanach near the waters of Megiddo." Since the Kishon River in the Jezreel Valley was sometimes called "the waters of Megiddo," it was theorized that this verse implied the battle was fought when Megiddo was deserted and nearby Taanach occupied. Since excavation showed Megiddo to have been destroyed about 1125, the battle was dated to the end of the eleventh century. Although such reasoning was tenuous at best, it was adopted by a number of scholars. Subsequent excavation has shown that Taanach also suffered destruction and desertion at the end of the eleventh century. All that Judg. 5:19 is declaring is that some of the battle spilled over into the area of those two well-known landmarks.

8. A cuneiform tablet fragment addressed to Jabin was found at Hazor in 1992. This royal document dates to the eighteenth or seventeenth century, implying that the name was a dynastic one, long in use. The find also undermines the suggestion that the mentions of Jabin in association with both Joshua and Deborah must refer to the same individual.

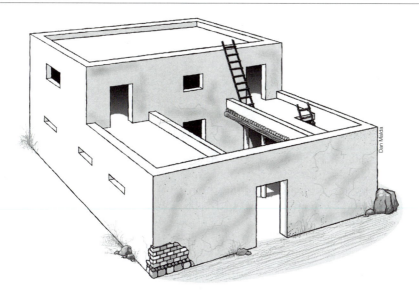

11.5. In Iron Age I, the "pillared house" became typical. Pillars on one or more sides of the interior courtyard created side aisles in which animals could be penned. The ground floor continued to be used for work and storage space, while upstairs rooms served as bedrooms and leisure areas. A wooden door would secure the entrance from the street. Curtains or doors could be used at other wall openings. (For more information on housing and other aspects of life in Iron Age I, see Stager 1985.)

to Mount Tabor, which rises one thousand feet above the surrounding plain. At least in daylight, no one could sneak up on Barak's forces. Sisera, Jabin's general, brought his army out for battle in chariots.[9] By the time the battle was joined in the Jezreel Valley, other Israelite tribes had sent support. But during the battle, it seems, God helped bring victory to Barak by sending a heavy rain that caused the Kishon River to overflow, and the enemy chariots became mired in the mud (Judg. 5:20–21).[10] Apparently, a common call to battle had been issued, and four tribes failed to answer that call. Although Deborah rejoiced in the victory, she also chided the four tribes: Reuben, Gilead (perhaps here meaning Gad), Dan and Asher (Judg. 5:15–17).[11]

Into Iron Age I

The date assigned by archaeologists for the transition from Late Bronze Age to Iron Age I is 1200 (Iron Age I lasted until 1000). Although there is no sharp break in the material culture, definite changes

9. Judges 4:13 states that Sisera had iron chariots, which means that the chariot box was iron-plated to protect the lower body of the charioteer, not that the whole chariot was made of the metal.

10. Hazor stratum 13 was destroyed near the end of the thirteenth century, a destruction level usually credited to Joshua by proponents of the "late date" exodus. It is tempting to read such destruction into Judg. 4:24, which states that "Israel pressed heavier and heavier upon Jabin the king of Canaan, until they had destroyed Jabin the king of Canaan." The Merenptah Stele's reference to Yanoam also puts Merenptah in this same area at the close of the thirteenth century, but if he had destroyed such an important city, Hazor—not Yanoam—would have been cited.

11. Aharoni 1975 attempts to place Deborah prior to Joshua's destruction of Hazor! Stager 1989 suggests that the four tribes were too economically entangled with non-Israelites to respond, but his argument is not convincing. See also Craigie 1983b: 84–86, whose alternate reading of Judg. 5:17 would remove one argument used by scholars who try to find some association between the tribe of Dan and the Danuna portion of the Sea Peoples.

11.6. Ivory inlay from Megiddo (twelfth century; ten-and-a-quarter inches long) may depict a Canaanite prince returning from battle with captives tied to his horses. The king sits on a sphinx-decorated throne and is attended by a woman, a musician strumming a lyre, and servants beside a jar and a table on which rest two cups in the shape of animal heads.

did take place. For one, surveys in the central Hill Country reveal a building explosion. The number of settlements in the central Hill Country increased from less than thirty in the Late Bronze Age to over two hundred in Iron Age I! Most Iron Age I settlements were small farming villages in contrast to the larger urban centers of the previous period. Additionally, the great majority of the Iron Age I sites had not been previously occupied. Scholars looking for the arrival of Israel around 1200 see this proliferation of new farming villages as evidence that the Israelites were then settling in. As stated in the previous chapter, it is equally likely that the settlement rise indicates that Israel was leaving a more pastoral lifestyle and finally settling down, heeding Joshua's directive to Ephraim and Manasseh (Josh. 17:14–18).

The Israelites adopted much of the material culture of Palestine, for there was no religious objection to that form of assimilation. Consequently, it is seldom possible to be sure whether an excavated site had been occupied by Israelites or Canaanites. Conversely, it is possible to examine material remains from Late Bronze Age II and Iron Age I Palestine and understand both the Israelites and the Canaanites equally well.[12]

It had been theorized that the Hill Country became densely settled in Iron Age I because a way had been found to lime plaster the interior of cisterns so that water could be collected during the rainy season and then drawn out as needed during the dry months of the year. Subsequent study has shown, however, that water cisterns are not characteristic of central Hill Country sites until later on during Iron Age II. Rather, it seems the people in the Hill Country transported water by donkey from the nearest spring or well to their villages (as is still the practice in parts of the Near East today). They stored the water in the large "collared rim" jars that were so common in Iron Age I. Such jars are capable of holding between ten and fifteen gallons each.

The Arrival of the Sea Peoples

It was also around 1200 that a large migration of people came eastward out of the Aegean. When they came in contact with Egypt, in what proved to be a last burst of glory, Ramesses III was able to hold them off (*ANE* 1:185–86; *ANET* 262–63):

> They were coming forward toward Egypt, while the flame was prepared before them. Their confederation was the Philistines, Tjeker, Shekelesh,

12. For insights into the material world of the judges see, A. Mazar 1990: chaps. 7–8.

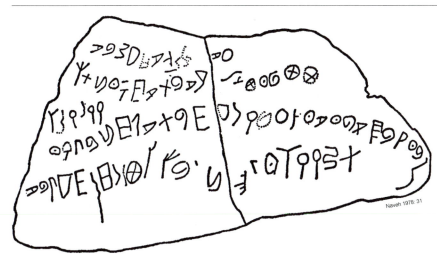

Naveh 1978: 31

11.7. Inscribed potsherd (six inches wide) found in an Iron Age I pillared house at Izbet Sarteh (just east of Aphek) and paleographically dated to the twelfth century. The ostracon contains five lines of late Proto-Canaanite letters; the bottom line is an abecedary, but no sense has yet been made of the other four lines. This West Semitic alphabetic writing was invented approximately 1700 and has been called "Canaan's greatest contribution to human culture." The Greek alphabet apparently developed from Proto-Canaanite, but when and by what manner of transmission is not yet clear. This ostracon has variously been attributed to a Canaanite, Philistine, or Israelite hand. If the latter, it could be additional proof of literacy among the Israelites in the period of the judges. If Philistine, it could be evidence that they transmitted the alphabet to the Greeks. (See Demsky 1977; Demsky and Kochavi 1978; Kochavi 1977; and Naveh 1978, 1980, and 1987.)

Denyen, and Weshesh, lands united. They laid their hands upon the lands as far as the circuit of the earth, their hearts confident and trusting: "Our plans will succeed!"

. . . I organized my frontier . . . prepared before them. . . . I have the river mouths prepared like a strong wall, with warships, galleys, and coasters . . . manned completely from bow to stern with valiant warriors carrying their weapons. The troops consisted of every picked man of Egypt. They were like lions roaring upon the mountaintops. The chariotry consisted of runners, of picked men, of every good and capable chariot-warrior. The horses were quivering in every part of their bodies, prepared to crush the foreign countries under their hoofs. I was the valiant Montu,[13] standing fast at their head, so that they might gaze upon the capturing of my hands. . . .

Those who reached my frontier, their seed is not, their heart and their soul are finished forever and ever. Those who came forward together on the sea, the full flame was in front of them at the river mouths, while a stockade of lances surrounded them on the shore. They were dragged in, enclosed, and prostrated on the beach, killed, and made into heaps from tail to head. Their ships and their goods were as if fallen into the water.

The Egyptians gave these people the name "Sea Peoples," and Ramesses III was so proud of his defense against them that he recounted his victory in both texts and temple wall reliefs. But not all the Sea Peoples died at the hands of the Egyptians; some were captured and became mercenaries in the Egyptian army. Most, however, settled along Palestine's coastal plain.[14] Of these, the Philistines are the best known—both because of their biblical connection and because they seem to have dominated the other Sea People.

A large settlement of Philistines arrived in Palestine about the time of Deborah and settled into five main cities: Ashdod, Ashkelon, Ekron, Gaza, and Gath.[15] Of the five cities, all but Gath has been confidently

13. Montu was the Egyptian god of war.

14. For whether the Egyptians settled the defeated Sea Peoples as garrison troops or whether they were conquerors of the sea coast, see I. Singer 1992 and B. Wood 1991.

15. A royal dedicatory temple inscription containing the name *Ekron* was found in the 1996 season at Tel Miqne. The inscription removed any doubt as to whether this tell was that Philistine city.

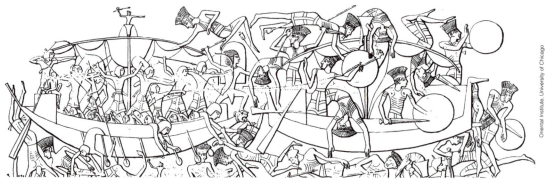

Oriental Institute. University of Chicago

11.8. Detail from a relief commissioned by Ramesses III to commemorate his victory over the Sea Peoples. An Egyptian boat on the left is defeating a Sea Peoples boat on the right. Clothing helps distinguish between the different Sea Peoples groups. The Philistines were among those who wore the "feathered headdress," but distinctively the hems of their kilts had tassels (visible only on the far left person). They also wore banded corselets.

11.9. Representative sampling of Philistine pottery.

located. Most archaeologists currently identify Gath with Tel Zafit (Tell es-Safi), but at least two misidentifications of the city have already made their way into books on biblical archaeology.

Scholars usually agree that the Philistines merged with the Canaanites and lost much of their cultural identity—but the speed with which this assimilation took place is debated. Philistine pottery shows Aegean rather than Canaanite prototypes. The Philistines had a preference for jugs and craters on which they painted swans and red and black geometric designs. Their jugs were often made with strainer spouts, possibly so they could drink barley beer from them without swallowing barley husks. Their smaller two-handled bowls were probably used for wine. William F. Albright (1971: 115) inferred from the ubiquity of the "wine craters and beer jugs" that the Philistines were "mighty carousers."

It was not until 1972 that a Philistine temple was found. In its last stage (it was rebuilt three times), the temple measured forty-seven feet by twenty-six feet. It contained benches, a storeroom, and a platform with steps leading up to it. Many cult objects were found in connection

Zev Radovan

11.10. A Beth-shan anthropoid coffin in the "grotesque style." The upper front lifted off for interment. This coffin, a type generally identified with the Sea Peoples, was adopted from the Egyptians but did not become common. The Philistines, Tjeker, and Denyen portions of the Sea Peoples wore the "feathered headdress" depicted on the lid. Compare illustration 11.8.

with the temple, and its roof was held up by two columns. The Bible states that the Philistines worshiped Dagon, and he is pictured in older books with a human body from the waist up and lower parts that tapered off into the tail of a fish. This depiction is incorrect, but the true appearance of the Philistine god is uncertain.[16]

16. For recent studies of the Philistines, see Dothan 1982a, 1982b; Dothan and Dothan 1992; Dothan and Gitin 1990; Gitin 1990; Gitin and Dothan 1987; Hindson 1971; D. Howard 1994; Karageorghis 1984; Raban and Stieglitz 1991; Sandars 1978; and Stager 1991.

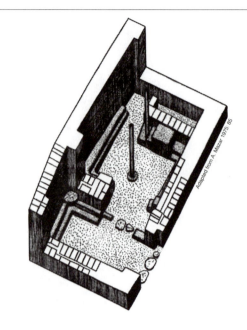

11.11. Entry to the final Philistine temple at Tel Qasile was gained by walking over threshold stones into a rectangular anteroom with low benches along three walls. A turn to the right gave access to the main room. Two columns, reminiscent of the end of Samson's life, supported the roof. The temple contained an altar to the right of the furthest column, low benches against the long walls, and a storeroom behind the altar.

Gideon

Subsequent to Deborah's judgeship the people again slipped back into sin. At one point the "servitude" was so severe that a man named Gideon was trying to thresh wheat in a winepress without being seen when the angel of the Lord approached and called him a "valiant warrior" (Judg. 6:12). Gideon must have sensed the irony in such a greeting, and he was not altogether convinced of his ability to serve as a judge.[17] That Gideon's father worshiped the Canaanite storm god and fertility goddess (Judg. 6:25) does not speak well for Gideon's religious background or for Israel's faithfulness to God.

"Gideon's fleece" is one of the better known stories from the Old Testament. Unfortunately it is often misunderstood and misapplied. A careful reading of the episode shows that Gideon put out the fleece because he was hesitant to follow God's instructions, not because he lacked a clear idea of what those instructions were. One commentator likens Gideon's requests to asking God "to do tricks" (L. Wood 1979: 132). To be faithful to the passage and to correctly make the analogy with Judges 6, a "fleece" can be "put out" only if one is questioning or seeking reaffirmation of God's clear instructions.

As Gideon prepared for battle, God had him reduce his forces to a size that could win only with God's enablement (Judg. 7:2). As the enemy was subsequently routed southeast across the Jordan, Gideon asked two Israelite cities for their assistance. Gideon was rebuffed because he had not yet fully won the battle, providing evidence that the lack of unity in Deborah's time continued into Gideon's. After the victory, some of the Israelites offered to make Gideon their king, but he declined. Later, one of Gideon's sons, Abimelech, tried to establish him-

17. When Gideon protests his inadequacy to deliver Israel (Judg. 6:15), he states that his *elef* is the least in Manasseh. In this verse *elef* is never translated "thousand."

11.12. Bronze bull figurine (seven inches long) from early Iron Age I. The figurine was found in what has been interpreted as a "high place" located near Dothan. The bull sometimes represented the storm god Baal; at other times it served as a pedestal for that god. The excavator believes the site and figurine are Israelite, but there is no clear evidence of this. If Israelite, then this is an example of the paganism into which Israel—including Gideon's father—fell during the period of the judges. If not Israelite, then the figurine and site is evidence of Canaanites who continued to dwell in the land. (See A. Mazar 1983 and 1988 and Shanks 1988a.)

self as a king and struggled for three years to maintain even the allegiance of Ephraim. Finally, during a battle he approached too closely to a *migdal* (see chap. 9), and an upper millstone thrown from its roof crushed his skull. Kingship would wait until God was ready to grant it.

Jephthah, Samson, and Ruth

Jephthah is perhaps best known because of the vow he made prior to going into battle, a vow that apparently caused him to sacrifice his daughter. Judges is a book of "defeats" in several senses of the word. Jephthah attempted to reason with the oppressing king, but when diplomacy failed, he went to war. He won the war, but his victory was marred when some Ephraimites protested that they had not been allowed to participate. Suddenly, there was civil war, and Israelite was killing Israelite. Disunity now definitely characterized the relationship between tribes. Further, as the civil war is recounted, it becomes evident that linguistic differences had even developed on either side of the Jordan (Judg. 12:5–6).

Samson, the last major judge to appear in the Book of Judges, was a one-man army rather than the leader. Samson did not have the full support of his own compatriots, showing again the disunity that characterized the period (Kelm and Mazar 1989).

Chapters 17–21 form several appendixes to the Book of Judges. They tell of the migration of the tribe of Dan to new territories in northern

Palestine and of the civil war that nearly wiped out the tribe of Benjamin. The Book of Ruth fits into a peaceful period within the days of the judges; her adventures were not appended to the Book of Judges, but stand as a separate unit. Also, it was written after the Book of Judges had been completed. Since the genealogy in Ruth stops with David, the book was likely composed then. The centuries between the events of the story and the days of David were likely spanned by oral tradition or by other written sources from which the later author drew.

The Book of Ruth contains several insights into society during the time of the judges. For example, the levitical instruction to allow the poor to glean in the harvested fields was being observed. Also certain legal proceedings were concluded by the giving of one's sandal to the other party (Ruth 4:7). This custom had ceased by the time the book was actually written, so the writer had to explain the practice to his readers. Ruth's act of going to Boaz at night, however, is not explained, so it must have still been sufficiently obvious. The reason Boaz instructed Ruth to stay the night with him is clear; since the two were at the threshing floor outside Bethlehem, Ruth would not have been able to return to her home until the city gates reopened in the morning. Finally, the story of Ruth illustrates how a city gate served as the town's legal center.

The Travels of Wen-Amon

Ramesses III successfully held off the Sea Peoples, but Egyptian fortunes went swiftly downhill thereafter, and the country split into small states. About the time of Jephthah, Wen-Amon, an official of the Temple of Amon at Karnak, was sent to Byblos to secure lumber for the ceremonial barge of his god. Wen-Amon traveled along the coast of a Palestine that was a far cry from the respectful days of Sinuhe. Inhabitants of Palestine were again feeling their independence, and the Sea Peoples had become an element of power.

Wen-Amon's travels (illustration 11.1) took him from Egypt to Dor (a Sea Peoples city) where he was given food (Stern 1993b), but his timber money was stolen. Wen-Amon waited for the thief to be caught but, apparently tiring of that, he continued on to Tyre and then to Byblos. At Byblos, Wen-Amon appropriated money and vowed to hold it until his property was returned (*ANE* 1:18; *ANET* 26):

> And the Prince of Byblos sent to me, saying: "Get out of my harbor!" And I sent to him, saying: "Where should I go to? . . . If you have a ship to carry me, have me taken to Egypt again!" So I spent twenty-nine days in his harbor, while he spent the time sending to me every day to say: "Get out of my harbor!"

Wen-Amon finally had an audience with the prince of Byblos (*ANE* 1:19–20; *ANET* 26–27):

> And I found him sitting in his upper room, with his back turned to a window. . . .

And he . . . said to me: "On what business have you come?" So I told him: "I have come after the woodwork for the great and august bark of Amon-Re, king of the gods. Your father did it, your grandfather did it, and you will do it too!" So I spoke to him. But he said to me: "To be sure, they did it! And if you give me something for doing it, I will do it! Why, when my people carried out this commission, Pharaoh . . . sent six ships loaded with Egyptian goods, and they unloaded them into their store-houses! You—what is it that you're bringing me—me also?" And he had the journal rolls of his fathers brought, and he had them read out in my presence, and they found a thousand *deben* of silver and all kinds of things in his scrolls.

So he said to me: "If the ruler of Egypt were the lord of mine, and I were his servant also, he would not have to send silver and gold, saying: 'Carry out the commission of Amon!' There would be no carrying of a royal gift, such as they used to do for my father. As for me—me also—I am not your servant! I am not the servant of him who sent you either! If I cry out to the Lebanon, the heavens open up, and the logs are here lying on the shore of the sea!"

The prince of Byblos continued to belittle Wen-Amon. Finally a letter was sent to Egypt and payment was forwarded back to Byblos. The shipment—linen, papyrus, cowhides, ropes, lentils, and fish—was much different from the precious "gifts" Egypt had once sent to Byblos. But the payment was accepted and Wen-Amon was given his timbers. Then, just as he was preparing to sail for Egypt, eleven boats from Dor appeared. Wen-Amon became frightened, and the prince of Byblos called for a meeting (*ANE* 1:23; *ANET* 29):

And he stood in their midst, and he said . . . "What have you come for?" And they said to him: "We have come after the blasted ships which you are sending to Egypt with our opponents!" But he said to them: "I cannot arrest the messenger of Amon inside my land. Let me send him away, and you go after him to arrest him."

Wen-Amon escaped the harbor and came ashore again in Cyprus where, unfortunately, the story breaks off. Although the fate of Wen-Amon is left in question, the fate of Egypt is clearly spelled out. Egypt was no longer the respected country it had once been. Already a "bruised reed," Egypt would never again be a lasting threat to the Israelites.

Additional Reading

Mazar, Amihai. "Additional Philistine Temples at Tell Qasile." *BA* 40 (1977): 82–87.

Singer, Itamar. "Merenptah's Campaign to Canaan and the Egyptian Occupation of the Southern Coastal Plain of Palestine in the Ramesside Period." *BASOR* 269 (1988): 1–10.

Smelik, Klaas A. D. *Writing from Ancient Israel*. Louisville: Westminster, 1991.

Stiebing, William H. "The End of the Mycenean Age." *BA* 43 (1980): 7–21, 133.

Wood, Leon. *Distressing Days of the Judges*. Grand Rapids: Zondervan, 1982.

The Beginnings of Kingship

Standing on the mound at Nimrud, I watched the local bird-scarer, an old Arab with his handful of stones and his sling, defending the crops from the hordes of predatory birds. Seeing his accuracy of aim and the deadliness of his weapon, I suddenly realized for the first time that it was Goliath against whom the dice were loaded. David was in a superior position from the start—the man with a long-distance weapon against the man who had none. Not so much the little fellow against the big one, as brains versus brawn.

—Agatha Christie

Samuel

The Book of 1 Samuel begins with the story of a Levite named Elkanah and his two wives. Elkanah had children by his wife Peninnah but Hannah, his other wife, was barren. First Samuel 1 tells of the continuous tensions between the two women and how Hannah asked God to grant her a child. If her request was granted, Hannah vowed to

12.1. Seven-spouted oil lamp found at Dothan. Beginning in the Middle Bronze Age in Palestine (approximately 2000), such lamps were filled with oil and a wick placed in each spout. It is suggested that these relatively rare lamps were used for religious purposes, which would, then, be the type of lamp in 1 Samuel 3.

present her offspring to God.[1] Within a year of her prayer and vow Hannah gave birth to Samuel, and in time she took him to Shiloh for dedication to the Lord for tabernacle service.[2]

When Hannah brought her son to Shiloh, Eli was having a problem with his sons. The worship of God was at an all-time low in Israel, and Eli's sons were very much a part of the apostasy (1 Sam. 2:12–17, 22). Eli scolded his sons for their behavior, but they were not receptive to correction. Finally, a "man of God" approached Eli, accused him of putting his sons above the Lord, and predicted a premature death for both of them.

The familiar story of Samuel and the voice in the night appears in 1 Samuel 3, when Samuel would have been nearly a teenager. The lamp mentioned in verses 2–3 was the "candlestick" in the tabernacle. It was lit every evening and burned until the oil was consumed the next morning. That "the lamp had not yet gone out" seems to mean that this episode in Samuel's life happened just before the dawn of a new day. The story concludes when Samuel finally admits the prediction God gave him concerning Eli's sons.

1. Hannah vowed that her son would be a Nazirite, and a fragment from the books of Samuel from Cave 4 at Qumran specifically identifies him as such. Numbers 6 spells out the specifications laid down by Moses for Nazirites, whose vows could be for a specified period of time or for life. During the evil days of Amos, Nazirites were encouraged or even forced to break their vows (Amos 2:11–12). Only Samson, Samuel, and John the Baptist are known to have been Nazirites for life.

2. Hannah also took items for sacrifice, specifically the offerings prescribed for fulfilling a vow; cf. Num. 15:8–10.

12.2. The beginning of
Israelite kingship.

At the Bible's next mention of Eli, he is already old and blind but still
judge and high priest.[3] After the Philistines won a battle against Israel
at Aphek, the Israelite forces concluded that they had lost the battle because they had not brought the ark of the covenant with them to the
conflict. Writers variously interpret this conclusion as a sign that Israel
had begun to think of the ark as a good luck charm, that they had "God
in a box," or that they had sunk into superstition if not outright idolatry
(J. Davis 1970: 37; Pfeiffer 1960: 59). In hopes of remedying the situation, Eli's sons went to Shiloh, took the ark from the tabernacle, and
brought it to the battlefield. Israel rejoiced to see the ark and launched

3. Eli's role as judge seems to have been gained through wisdom and piety rather
than by military exploit; there is no mention of his involvement in warfare.

another assault, only to lose even more decisively as the Philistines captured the ark. Eli's sons were killed in the battle, and news of the ark's capture precipitated the death of Eli.

The Travels of the Ark

The Philistines would have been exceedingly pleased to have captured a sacred object from their enemy. They took their prize to Ashdod and placed it in their temple as an offering to their chief god Dagon. But the next morning the Philistines found Dagon lying on the floor in front of the ark. They assumed the statue had fallen from natural causes so they simply put it back in place. But the following morning they were perplexed to find Dagon not only fallen but broken. They began to get suspicious because, in addition to the fallen god statue, the Ashdodites also began to have health problems.[4] They reasoned that Israel's ark might be the cause of their distress and, therefore, decided to send it to another Philistine city. The ark was taken to Gath, but the same illnesses befell the people there. Under protest, the people of Ekron had the next responsibility for the ark and, just as they feared, they too suffered. First Samuel 6:1 states that the Philistines endured these trials for seven months before their diviners advised that a test should be made to see whether the troubles were because the god of the Israelites wanted his ark back.

The Philistines chose two cows that had calves and had never been yoked. The calves were taken away and penned up, and the cows were yoked and hitched to a new cart. The ark and a box containing golden models of tumors and rats were also placed aboard. The presence of the golden objects implies that the Philistines believed in "sympathetic magic," that is, that evil or illness could be transferred to models of the problem(s) thereby effecting a cure.

The cows could be expected to balk at the yoke and refuse to leave their calves. Without a driver they would not be expected to know where to go, much less to pull together to get there. But despite these obstacles, the cows did leave their calves and pulled the cart directly to Beth-shemesh, the nearest Israelite town. The direct route the cows took and their arrival at Beth-shemesh sent the Philistines (who had followed the cart) home, convinced that their afflictions had indeed been caused by the presence of the ark in their towns.

The people of Beth-shemesh, overjoyed to find the ark returned, used the cart and the cows for a thanksgiving offering. Beth-shemesh was a levitical city and its people should have known how to care for the ark, but some of the men looked inside the chest. Perhaps they were afraid the Philistines had stolen its contents, but for this disobedience a number of the men lost their lives.[5]

---

4. The people of Ashdod were afflicted with tumors or boils. The inference of 1 Sam. 6:4 is that their town and fields were overrun by rats and consequently the people contracted bubonic plague.

5. Some translations of 1 Sam. 6:19 have 50,070, others have 70. The higher figure seems to be the result of scribal error.

12.3. Mother goddess figurine (just under seven inches high), dubbed "Ashdoda" by the excavators, found at Ashdod. A variant of Mycenean mother goddess figurines seated on thrones, this is another evidence that the Philistines were Aegean in origin. Excavations at Ashdod have not located the temple or any trace of the statue of Dagon.

Following this tragedy, Beth-shemesh petitioned the people of Kiriath-jearim to take the ark. Kiriath-jearim accepted the offer and took the ark into the Hill Country where it was stored in a house. The Bible is silent about Shiloh following Eli's death, but excavation suggests that the Philistines followed up their victory at Aphek by burning the sanctuary city (Finkelstein 1986b and A. Kaufman 1988). The only function Shiloh served in the Bible after this point was as an example of what can happen when God is disregarded.

12.4. Philistine oxcart depicted on reliefs commissioned by Ramesses III to commemorate his victory over the Sea Peoples.

Samuel as Judge, Priest, and King-Maker

Eli was dead, Shiloh was destroyed, and the ark was in storage. Within the context of this dismal picture, Samuel reappears in the biblical record. Israel recognized him as a true man of God while he was still a youth, and as an adult Samuel became the connecting link between theocracy and monarchy. Samuel was not of Aaron's lineage, so it is not certain whether he was considered high priest. However, he officiated as a priest and conducted worship at various places in the country (but not at Shiloh). Samuel was also the last of the judges, acting as a circuit-riding judge within his own tribal area of Benjamin. At least once Samuel acted in a military capacity (1 Sam. 7:7–14). The end of 1 Samuel 7 relates that during Samuel's tenure the Philistines kept their place, some territory was regained, and the Amorites kept the peace. There is much more to Samuel's life, but the Bible's emphasis shifts to a new interest—kingship—and to a new person—Saul.

In 1 Samuel 8 Samuel was old and had turned over at least part of the judicial duties to his sons. Sadly, his sons "took bribes and perverted justice," proving themselves as morally unfit as Eli's sons had been. Partly because of this and partly because of Samuel's advanced age, the elders of Israel approached Samuel with a request for a king. Samuel was initially opposed to the idea, which he took as personal rejection of himself and his leadership. After prayer, however, God informed Samuel that Israel was rejecting God's leadership, not his. He advised Samuel to listen to the elders and give them their wish, but to warn them of the consequences. Samuel did all this, and 1 Samuel 8:11–18 summarizes the predicted dangers.

Although Samuel warned the people that the price for kingship was high, the people insisted that they have their way. In their defense, however, their motivation was not entirely misplaced. They knew that God had said they would have a king one day (Deut. 17:14), and there were reasons for wanting that day "now." Samuel had grown old, and the people perhaps feared a vacuum of leadership in the face of foreign aggression. Their desire for a king may also indicate a realization that the national disunity that characterized the period of the judges called for a fresh approach.

In Samuel's day, toward the close of the second millennium, there were kings who ruled single cities, some who ruled city-states, and still others who ruled whole nations. There was, at that time, nothing that could be called an "empire." Israel did not want a city or city-state form of government. Had that been the case, they would have asked for kings, perhaps even a king for each tribe. Israel wanted a national king.

Mesopotamian kings served as agents of the gods. Before the Hittite nation fell, about 1200, its kings functioned as high priests in addition to their civil leadership duties. On occasion, they might even have to leave a battlefield if the calendar said there was a religious rite to perform back home. The Hittites believed that at his death the king became a god. In Egypt, the country was still paying lip service to the dogma that its kings were gods in life, but the humanity of the pharaohs had become all too evident.

Israel was not interested in any of these concepts. Although Israel viewed the king as an agent of God, both they and God rejected the priest-king model.[6] Nor did Israel want a deified king, either in life or after his death. Israel's unique understanding of God precluded these Near Eastern options. In 1 Samuel 8:5, when the elders of Israel first requested a king, they used a form of the word *shophet* (judge); and when the request was reaffirmed (1 Sam. 8:19–20), the elders added that they wanted their king to go before them to fight their battles. Therefore, Israel was asking for a person to continue the duties of the judges, but to carry the title *king*.

One important change implicit in this revised terminology was that their king would be a permanent head of state, and there would be uninterrupted leadership for the lifetime of the king. There was also the expectation that one day the king's son would ascend to the throne. Israel was willing to exchange the personal freedom they had under the judges for the national benefits they expected to accrue with kingship. Also, they wanted to be "like all the nations." While the people had certain expectations, God also had his. God wanted Israel's king to be obedient to his will (Deut. 17:18–19).

The First King

The story of Saul begins in 1 Samuel 9. Saul and Samuel were brought together after Saul's father lost some donkeys. In their first meeting, Saul received two rather unequal pieces of information from Samuel: the donkeys were safe and "you and your family are the focus of all Israel's hopes" (New Living Translation). Samuel seemingly paid no attention to Saul's incredulous response, and the next day the united kingdom officially began when Samuel privately anointed Saul king.

Saul was from the tribe of Benjamin, one of the lesser tribes, and that may have aided his acceptance by all of Israel. Had Saul been from an important tribe, such as Judah or Ephraim, his selection could have aroused jealousy in the fragmented society. Saul's father is described as a "mighty man of valor" (1 Sam. 9:1), a phrase generally applied to someone with a degree of wealth and influence. By extension, therefore, Saul was not from a humble background. Saul had one wife, two

6. Saul would get into trouble on that account, and centuries later so would King Uzziah.

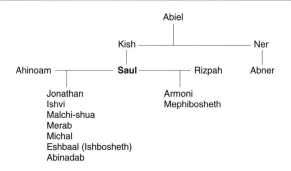

12.5. Saul's family tree.

daughters, and four or five sons.[7] He also had a concubine by whom he had two sons.

Saul's precise age at his "coronation" is not clear. First Samuel 13:1 reads literally, "A son of year was Saul when he began to reign." "Son of ——— year" is normal Hebrew idiom for expressing a person's age; obviously a copyist dropped out the number, and all known ancient manuscripts are defective at this point. Aramaic translations unconvincingly respond to the problem by paraphrasing the verse, "Saul was as innocent as a one-year-old child when he began to reign." Translations that put Saul's age at thirty are relying on some late Septuagint manuscripts. Those that put Saul's age at forty are guessing, but they seem closest to reality. Saul had to be old enough to account for Jonathan being of fighting age at the beginning of Saul's kingship (twenty was considered the minimum age for such activity; Num. 1:3). Saul also had to be young enough to reign the forty years mentioned in Acts 13:21.[8]

Saul was king of Israel only privately at first, but obviously the Israelites needed to be told. Therefore, Samuel called Israel to Mizpah, the site of an earlier revival and victory over the Philistines, for the purpose of choosing the first king. The hours spent at Mizpah must have been full of expectation, excitement, joy, impatience, and possibly twinges of personal disappointment. The time-consuming method of choosing the king would have impressed on Israel that the choice was God's, not Samuel's (1 Sam. 10:20–21). Saul's feelings during the process are not clear, and commentators disagree as to why he hid among the baggage. One inference is that he was a timid person. According to this view, an aggressive person would have been in the center of activity and an average person would at least have been part of the crowd. By a different reconstruction, Saul's behavior is a sign of modesty. Since he already knew he would be king, he did not want to feign anticipation nor did

7. There is some problem with name changes and dual names. Ishvi and Eshbaal are probably the same person, and four is probably the correct number of sons by his wife. Eshbaal is better known as Ishbosheth.

8. 1 Samuel 13:1 has a second problem, since it literally says that Saul reigned two years over Israel. Most writers assume a number has also been dropped from this part of the verse. The New American Standard Bible supplies the number thirty-two; the New International Version prefers forty-two. In either case, Acts 13:21 would then be a round figure. The New Scofield Bible offers another solution by translating the verse, "When he had reigned two years over Israel . . . ," which means that what follows in the chapter is subsequent to his first two years as king and that the forty years of Acts 13:21 need not be taken as a round figure.

he want to appear too eager. This view argues that since Saul was apart from the crowd, he may not have known when the selection process was finished, and that is why people had to look for him.

When Saul was presented to the people, most of them were delighted with the choice. Only a few "worthless men" questioned his ability to rule. Saul's physical appearance seems to have been one factor leading to his acceptance by the many, but reference to his height should not be taken to extremes. In order for Saul to be "taller than any of the people from his shoulders upward," he needed to have been only a bit over six feet tall. After the people signaled their acceptance by shouting "Long live the king," Samuel exhorted them concerning the regulations for monarchy. When the proceedings were finished, Samuel sent everyone home. King Saul also returned to his home in Gibeah, accompanied by some "valiant men" who were immediately ready to serve him.

Saul's First Act as King

One of Israel's immediate reasons for wanting a king had been concern over Ammonite pressures in Gilead (1 Sam. 12:12). The Ammonites lived east of the Jordan and controlled part of the ancient King's Highway. This control gave them some political and economic power because they could collect taxes from passing caravans. Soon after Saul's coronation ceremony at Mizpah, the Ammonite threats turned into action when they besieged the Israelite city of Jabesh (also called Jabesh-gilead). The people of Jabesh sued for peace, and King Nahash of Ammon agreed, but on condition that he be allowed to "gouge out the right eye of every one of you" (1 Sam. 11:2).

Maiming an enemy was practiced in the ancient Near East, and the taking of an eye is found in Ugaritic literature. It was not by chance that the Ammonite king specified the right eye to be lost. As in modern times, most people in those days were right handed and, therefore, most archers would close their left eyes when sighting their target. Also, during combat most soldiers would carry their shields on their left arms. Without their right eyes these soldiers would be at a disadvantage in battle as they would be forced to expose more of their heads in order to see.

The people of Jabesh felt this was a rather high price to pay even for peace. Therefore, they asked for seven days during which they would try to obtain help. The Ammonite king agreed to the truce, probably thinking he had little to fear from any of the Israelite tribes and reasoning that a seven-day wait would gain victory without danger to his troops. First Samuel 11:3 implies that messengers were sent to all the tribes of Israel. It is likely that the people of Jabesh knew of Saul's anointing, but perhaps they did not appeal exclusively to him because he had not yet demonstrated leadership.

When the messengers found Saul, he was plowing his fields (1 Sam. 11:5), an activity that implies he was not trying to establish his title in the conventional sense of the word. Initially, Saul was really no more than a judge in readiness. But King Saul rose in anger at the news and decisively demanded help from the tribes (1 Sam. 11:7). Saul ordered the tribes to meet at Bezek, about nine miles west of the Jordan, opposite Jabesh.

Because of the deadline that had been agreed to by the Ammonite king, the sounding of the alarm and the assembling of the relief forces must have proceeded at a frantic pace. After the messengers returned to Jabesh with word that help would arrive the next day, the people of Jabesh put the Ammonites off guard by making them think they were about to surrender. Saul divided his forces into three companies and attacked the Ammonite camp at the "morning watch," that is, between two A.M. and six A.M., when the Ammonites would be least prepared for battle.

Jabesh-gilead was saved, Saul had done all anyone could have asked of a king, and Israel was now ready to follow him anywhere. Some of the people wanted Saul to punish his earlier detractors, but he was gracious in triumph, and Israel gathered at Gilgal for a time of rejoicing, sacrifice, and peace offerings. First Samuel 11:15 states that Saul was made "king before the LORD in Gilgal," probably implying that he was crowned at this celebration. Installing Saul as king was Samuel's last act as a judge, ending the period of the judges. From that point on Samuel functioned as a prophet.

Saul's first task as king of Israel was to fight off an enemy. Another task, to bring the tribes together under a single banner, would be no easy matter because of the disunity that had prevailed for centuries. Israel was divided not only by hills and valleys but also by dialectical differences and memories of civil wars. A third task for Saul was to establish some structure to government. There is no evidence of an elaborate organization; the only officer mentioned in the Bible is Abner, captain of the army. Others in the court were probably, like Abner, relatives of the king. Saul held decision-making meetings but, except for Abner, it is impossible to construct an organizational chart (1 Sam. 20:24–27).

The fortress identified as Saul's residence at Gibeah gives strength to the impression that Saul never became interested in the trappings of kingship. The excavated structure was small, its outer dimensions perhaps 170 feet by 115 feet. Everything excavated from within the compound, including a plowshare, was ordinary, further emphasizing the rustic quality of Saul's kingship. There was no trace of gold or ivory inlay; everything found could also be found in a commoner's house of that time.[9]

Saul easily defeated the Ammonites to the east, but trouble with the Philistines to the west was more protracted, in part because the Philistines exercised a monopoly on iron metalworking. It seems that iron technology developed in the Aegean area and that metalworking skills came into Palestine via the Sea Peoples. The Israelites became dependent on the Philistines when they wanted to have their tools sharpened or straightened (1 Sam. 13:19–21). The charge for this service was a "pim," a reference to a specific amount of silver. Excavations have yielded pim weights (see illustration 5.4), allowing archaeologists to conclude that the Philistines were charging an exorbitant price for

9. The remains of the excavated fortress were destroyed in the 1960s by King Hussein of Jordan who began building a palace on the site. Only the shell of the new palace was completed by 1967 when Israel took control of the area after the Six Day War. A few scholars favor Jeba over Tell el-Ful as the site of Saul's Gibeah (Arnold 1990), but no excavation has been done at Jeba and no Iron Age I materials have been found in surface survey. Most scholars identify Tell el-Ful with Saul's Gibeah (Lapp 1993: 445).

Victor Lazaro, from *Great People of the Bible and How They Lived* (Reader's Digest Association, 1974)

12.6. Artist's reconstruction of Saul's palace/fortress at Gibeah.

blacksmithing. The Philistine monopoly was so complete that during the Battle of Michmash, only Saul and Jonathan on Israel's side were adequately armed.[10]

The Battle of Michmash

The Battle of Michmash is recounted in 1 Samuel 13–14. Apparently Saul kept a standing army of three thousand soldiers following the Battle of Jabesh-gilead. Saul commanded two thousand soldiers quartered in Michmash and the Hill Country around Bethel, and Jonathan commanded the remaining one thousand troops at Gibeah, Saul's capital city.

The Philistines, meanwhile, had some garrisons inside Israelite territory. Jonathan successfully attacked one of them (Geba), and Saul "blew the trumpet" in the whole land, spreading the good news. Since 1 Samuel 13:4 gives Saul credit for the victory, he and Jonathan might have worked together on the battle strategy. Having lost their outpost, the Philistines began to mobilize for a counterattack and even brought chariots up into the Hill Country. Saul then pulled his troops out of Michmash and called Israel to assemble at Gilgal. (Logistically, it seems probable that Saul regrouped at one of the Hill Country Gilgals.) Meanwhile, the Philistines moved into position at the now-vacated Michmash, an occupation that so frightened Saul's troops that some of his soldiers deserted.[11]

10. It is generally assumed that iron is involved in 1 Sam. 13; see McNutt 1990 and Muhly 1982, 1992.

11. Michmash is situated at the pass giving access to the Central Benjamin Plateau from the east, so it had strategic importance. To control the Hill Country it is necessary to control the passes, and this is why the Philistines had an interest in this seemingly remote place. The control of the Central Benjamin Plateau was also of personal importance to Saul because his hometown/capital city was on the plateau's southern edge.

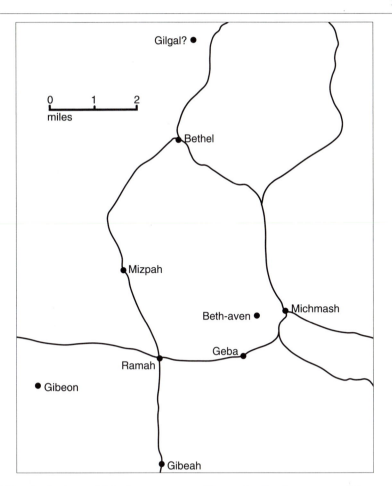

12.7. Battle of Michmash.

The depletion of his forces naturally made Saul nervous. Worse, although Samuel was expected to arrive within seven days to make offerings prior to battle, he had not arrived by the sixth day. When the seventh day had come but Samuel had not, Saul lost his patience and made the sacrifices himself so he could start the action. By personally offering sacrifices, Saul committed a grave error because, under God's law, only the priests could offer sacrifices. Just as Saul was finishing the sacrifice on the seventh day, Samuel appeared. Samuel reprimanded Saul for his transgression and announced that because of his disobedience to the law, God would not allow Saul's sons to follow him on the throne.

The judgment meted out to Saul was not overreaction on Samuel's or God's part. God had clearly drawn the lines of responsibility, and Saul by his own admission (1 Sam. 13:12) had knowingly overstepped the line. The words Samuel spoke were harsh, but he spoke them in obedience to God's instructions. This confrontation must have been distasteful for both Samuel and Saul, but God's rejection of Saul in favor of a "man after his own heart" did not signal a severing of ties between Saul and Samuel. Samuel was subsequently at Saul's side, and the two had more good years together.

At the end of the seven-day waiting period, only six hundred soldiers remained of Saul's original two thousand. Saul moved his remaining forces to Gibeah and then to Geba with Jonathan. Meanwhile the Philistines were still at Michmash, and from that outpost they sent raiding parties out in several directions. First Samuel 14 gives a glimpse of Jonathan as a man of faith, action, and independence. He decided to attack one of the Philistine raiding parties and did so without his father's knowledge. In the ensuing battle the Philistines were completely routed. Significantly, it is mentioned that some Hebrews had been working as mercenaries for the Philistines, but when the tide of battle shifted, they sided with their kin (1 Sam. 14:21). These mercenaries provide yet another evidence of how fragmented Israelite loyalties had become during the days of the judges.

Saul's Good Years

Saul was an effective military leader for the majority of his years as king, but most of his good years are compacted into two verses:

> Now when Saul had taken the kingdom over Israel, he fought against all his enemies on every side, against Moab, the sons of Ammon, Edom, the kings of Zobah, and the Philistines; and wherever he turned, he inflicted punishment. And he acted valiantly and defeated the Amalekites, and delivered Israel from the hands of those who plundered them (1 Sam. 14:47–48).

It seems evident that Saul was indeed the kind of leader the people had sought. These two verses reveal that Saul kept the surrounding enemies from exerting control over Israelite territory (illustration 12.2). The nonmilitary ramifications of these victories can only be imagined, but each success should have made the people more willing to do the king's bidding. They would also be more willing to pay the taxes imposed on them and less inclined to think in tribal terms.

Saul should be given credit for his good years, a time in which he and Samuel probably saw each other frequently. As Saul fought various battles, he must have consulted Samuel often. Unfortunately for those wanting a full biography of Saul, the details of those good years are not supplied. This silence is explained by the Bible's not being a history book in the modern sense (and neither is it a medical or psychology text to diagnose the nuances of Saul's declining years). The parts of Saul's reign that have religious significance are recorded in detail, and 1 Samuel 15 provides another such episode.

The episode recorded in 1 Samuel 15 took place over twenty years after the Battle of Michmash in 1 Samuel 13–14. In 1 Samuel 15, Samuel came to Saul with a message from God saying that Saul was to march south and fight against the Amalekites.[12] Every Amalekite was to be destroyed; no person or animal was to be left alive. Saul obediently went into battle and was victorious, but he was disobedient to God's total command (1 Sam. 15:9). In the strained meeting between Saul and Samuel that followed the battle, Samuel again communicated God's rejection of Saul as king (1 Sam. 15:22–23). Saul had shown promise in the intervening decades, but he had failed this final test (L. Wood 1979:

12. Exodus 17 and other passages show why God wanted the Amalekites punished.

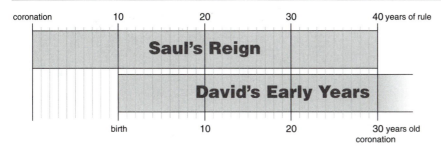

12.8. David was thirty years old when he began to rule in Hebron (2 Sam. 5:4). Accepting that Saul was king for about forty years, David was born in the tenth year of his reign. When David was anointed (immediately following Saul's second rejection by God), he was old enough to tend the family flocks by himself and to hold off wild animals, but underage for military service (1 Sam. 17:33). Fifteen would be an intelligent guess of David's age at his anointing, which added to the ten years of Saul's reign before David's birth gives a time span of about twenty-five years for Saul's successful rule and approximately fifteen years for his decline.

141–43). God wanted obedience; sacrifice was only an outward sign of one's devotion to God. Without obedience, the sacrifice was empty of meaning. God required total, not "almost" obedience. Saul's good years were over.[13]

The Transition to David as King

Israel's very first king had failed God's tests of obedience, and Samuel was called upon to anoint someone else. To anoint the person God had in mind, Samuel had to leave his hometown of Ramah and pass by Saul's Gibeah to reach Bethlehem. The biblical writer does not explain why the Bethlehemite elders were fearful of Samuel's arrival, but Samuel's trepidation that Saul would find out the purpose of his mission is understandable. If Saul discovered that someone else had been chosen king, neither that person's nor Samuel's life would be safe. God quieted Samuel's fears by giving him an ostensible reason for making the trip (1 Sam. 16:2).

At Bethlehem God revealed to Samuel that David, the youngest son of Jesse, was his choice, and Samuel anointed him to be the next king. The Bible is silent about whether anyone other than Samuel and Saul knew God had rejected the first king, neither does it say what Samuel told Jesse's family about David's future. Perhaps he only informed them that God had singled David out for a special purpose. David's brothers were not particularly pleased about being passed over. Had they known the details of their little brother's future, they might well have made his life even more difficult than they did.

Apparently, soon after David was anointed, Saul began to experience periods of depression. His depression may have been partly due to the prospect of losing his kingdom. Perhaps Samuel had made it clear that Saul's kingdom would not end until Saul died. If that were true, Saul could understandably become paranoid, suspecting an enemy lurking in every shadow. Or he may have been depressed because he may have felt less adequate for his task now that God had removed his Spirit. In any case, Saul was seemingly determined to continue to rule as long as possible, and there is no indication that God ever instructed him to abdicate.

13. 1 Samuel 15:35 seems to say that Samuel died without seeing Saul again, but that conflicts with 1 Sam. 19:24. Perhaps, therefore, 15:35 is saying that Samuel "did not go to see Saul again" (so the New International Version).

Israel Museum (IDAM), Jerusalem

12.9. Ivory horn decorated with gold bands from the fourteenth-century palace at Megiddo. The horn of oil that Samuel used to anoint David as king of Israel might have been similar.

Once, when Saul was particularly depressed, his servants suggested that music might improve his spirits. So Saul ordered a search for a suitable musician, and David, the secret king-elect, was chosen to play his lyre before the king (illustration 11.6).[14] David's music soothed the king, and at the same time it gave David the chance to experience court life and observe the workings of government before his own public coronation. His musical talent proved to be the vehicle by which David began his apprenticeship as God's servant.

Saul was greatly attracted to David's music and manner, so much so that he even appointed David his armor bearer. Moreover, Saul wrote to David's father asking that David be allowed to stay at court. Apparently, however, David continued to commute the ten to fifteen miles

14. It is generally accepted that David played a lyre, not a harp; see Avigad 1978b; Bayer 1982; Shanks 1982b. It is interesting that only in recent times has music therapy been taken seriously as a treatment for distressed people.

back and forth between his father's sheep at Bethlehem and Saul's palace at Gibeah.

David and Goliath

The Philistines had been beaten but not subdued. First Samuel 17 tells of the famous confrontation with Goliath, which enabled Saul to see David in an additional role. Warfare can be artificial, and ancient armies sometimes massed at agreed-upon places and taunted each other until one side was sufficiently exercised to initiate the conflict. A more economical way to decide the winner was to let picked champions from each side fight to the death. (The challenge to Sinuhe related in chapter 4 was of this nature.)

In 1 Samuel 17, the Philistines and Israel gathered in the low hills on either side of the Valley of Elah, which guards two approaches into the central part of the southern Hill Country. For over a month Goliath, the picked champion of the Philistines, marched into the valley twice each day and yelled taunts at Saul and his soldiers. When the biblical cubits, spans, and shekels of weight are translated into modern terms, it is obvious why Goliath was the Philistines' champion: he was abnormally tall and strong.[15] He was so intimidating that, in spite of Saul's offer of tax-free status and other riches to the family of the man who would fight, no one was willing to face Goliath. Saul should not be faulted for declining to fight Goliath himself. He, as well as Jonathan, the "heir apparent," would have been considered too important to risk in this manner. Further, Saul was beyond fighting age, and had he suggested that he go himself, his troops would have taken it as an affront to their bravery.

The older sons of Jesse were gathered with the army at Elah, but David had been kept home to care for the family flocks. After some weeks had passed, Jesse sent David with food for his older brothers and to bring back news of them. At the battle scene, David's eldest brother was less than cordial (1 Sam. 17:28–29). Such friction between the brothers may have been occurring ever since David was anointed instead of one of his elder brothers. This was probably not the first time David was at a loss for an answer.

Unexpectedly, David offered to fight Goliath and only after some persuasion did Saul agree. Possibly Saul concluded that the Philistine mocking had reached its limit, and David would break the stalemate one way or another. When 1 Samuel 17:38 states that Saul "clothed David with his garments," it probably means that Saul gave David an impressive cloak to wear. Because of Saul's height, the armor and sword mentioned probably were not his. Regardless, David felt uncomfortable with them, and he went into battle without armor and without a sword. He descended into the Valley of Elah with a staff, a pouch, and a sling; and he chose five smooth stones from the brook that runs through the valley.

15. Goliath would have been over nine feet tall and able to carry a coat of chain mail weighing 120 pounds. The tallest recorded person in the twentieth-century United States was eight feet eleven inches. The Septuagint reduces Goliath's height to somewhat over six feet.

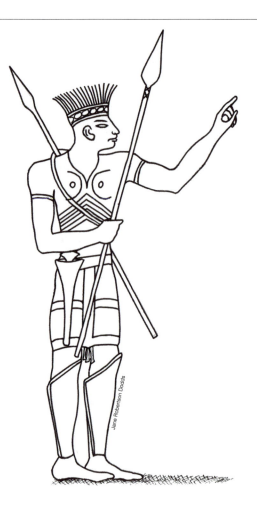

12.10. Artist's conception of Goliath's body armor and weaponry, based on the reliefs commissioned by Ramesses III and other depictions of Philistine and Aegean military personnel. Goliath wore a bronze helmet (here decorated with the "feathered" top characteristic of the Philistines), a banded corselet, and bronze greaves on his legs. Accompanied by a shield bearer, Goliath had a javelin over his shoulder, carried a spear in his hand, and wore a sword on his belt.

Jane Robertson Dodds

To use such a sling (illustration 10.4), the slinger hooks the loop end over one finger and holds the other end between thumb and index finger. He places the stone in its pouch, then whirls the sling. He releases the free end of the sling as he whips it underhand, like pitching a softball. As the free end is released, the stone is propelled toward the target at a high speed. In Old Testament times, slingers were regular components of an army and were often used together with archers; during siege warfare their role was to pick off the enemy from the besieged city's ramparts. Such slingers were capable of hurling a projectile at over one hundred miles an hour and their effective range was well in excess of one hundred yards. The Bible speaks of the amazing accuracy of the slinger (Judg. 20:16), and ancient depictions never show them wearing body armor. A slinger's mobility was his best defense (Hoffmeier 1991; Korfmann 1973).[16]

Although Goliath's body had more protection than David's, he was a more stationary target and David's sling had greater range than Goli-

16. As a result of living in the Near East, Agatha Christie, whose words appear in this chapter's epigraph, came to a more correct understanding of the David and Goliath encounter. Dame Agatha was married to Max Mallowan, who was knighted for his archaeological work in the Near East. She helped her husband on the excavations, and several of her mystery novels reflect the work and accompanying travels.

ath's spear.[17] Goliath had to know David was as lethally armed as he was, but he exuded confidence in his own abilities as he taunted David (1 Sam. 17:43–44). David's response was equally confident (1 Sam. 17:45–47): when Goliath stepped forward, David loaded and swung his sling. Suddenly one of David's stones struck Goliath in the forehead, and the Philistine champion fell to the ground dead. To seal his victory, David decapitated Goliath. Then, in keeping with the rules of picked combat, the Philistines fled the battle scene, chased by the army of Israel. Once more, the God of Israel had given victory.[18]

Additional Reading

Bierling, Neal. *Giving Goliath His Due*. Grand Rapids: Baker, 1992.

Bunimovitz, Shlomo, and Zvi Lederman. "Beth-Shemesh: Culture Conflict on Judah's Frontier." *BAR* 23/1 (1997): 42–49, 75–77.

Na'aman, Nadav. "Cow Town or Royal Capital: Evidence for Iron Age Jerusalem." *BAR* 23/4 (1997): 43–47, 67.

Younker, Randall W. "Ammonites." Pp. 293–316 in *Peoples of the Old Testament World*. Edited by Alfred J. Hoerth, Gerald L. Mattingly, and Edwin M. Yamauchi. Grand Rapids: Baker, 1994.

17. The word translated "javelin" is in some dispute. Dagger is another option (cf. the Revised English Bible), and at least one of the Sea People in the Medinet Habu reliefs carries a dagger on his chest. Goliath's spear is likened to a "weaver's beam" (1 Sam. 17:7), which is usually taken to mean that it was unusually thick. Yadin 1963: 354–55 suggests that it is instead a reference to the Aegean practice of wrapping a cord around part of the shaft. One end of the cord was held by a finger loop so that when the spear was hurled, the unwinding cord would act like rifling in a gun barrel, allowing the spear to fly further and with greater stability. Weaver's beams have loops tied to them, and Yadin thinks this was the biblical author's way of describing such an attachment.

18. In the subsequent meeting between Saul and David (1 Sam. 17:55–58), it seems as though the two had never met before, but Saul may have been using a figure of speech, or a formula, as he addressed David.

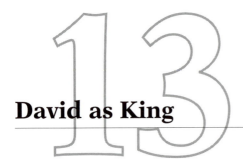

David as King

Behold, how good and how pleasant it is

For brothers to dwell together in unity!

It is like the precious oil upon the head,

Coming down upon the beard,

Even Aaron's beard,

Coming down upon the edge of his robes.

It is like the dew of Hermon,

Coming down upon the mountains of Zion;

For there the Lord commanded the blessing—life forever.

—Psalm 133

Saul's Declining Years
Two Kings and Civil War
David as King of Israel
    David's New Lifestyle
    The Fame of David
    The Shame of David
    Calamity in David's Life and Family
    The Coup
The Psalms
Additional Reading

Saul's Declining Years

After his victory over Goliath, David began to be popular within Israel. But tension also surfaced as David's abilities were lauded over those of Saul (1 Sam. 18:7–8), and Saul began to feel that David was only a step from the throne. Jonathan stood within this tightening circle of suspicion.

Oriental Institute, University of Chicago

13.1. Egyptian relief from Medinet Habu. After battle, Egyptians sometimes counted the slain enemy by heaping together a specific body part, a practice analogous to Saul's dowry request of David in 1 Samuel 18.

Jonathan initiated a friendship with David following the death of Goliath. The two shared deep faith in God (1 Sam. 14:6; 17:45–47), and both desired to rid Israel of foreign oppression. Both were brave, courageous men of action; both were popular in Israel. Toward each other, the two men were capable of deep commitment. David's commitment to Jonathan is noteworthy because of his youth. Jonathan's commitment is exemplary because of the loyalty he maintained even when it became apparent that David—not he—would accede to the throne. The friendship between David and Jonathan is also noteworthy because of the difference in the two men's ages. As noted in chapter 12 (see p. 247), Jonathan had to be at least twenty when his father became king, which was approximately ten years before David was born. To have a close friendship with someone that much younger is exceptional, and the two men show that a "generation gap" need not exist between people of greatly different years.

Saul came to realize that David, the person who had been called to soothe him, was actually part of his problem. Saul began to make attempts on David's life, on one occasion throwing his spear at him and another time trying to stab David with the same spear. Saul also sent David out to battle with only a few soldiers in hopes that he would be killed. Saul even tried to use his daughters to lure David into a trap, but this ploy only resulted in David's marriage into the royal family. Saul became obsessed with the desire to kill David, and in his frustration over Jonathan's attitude in the matter, Saul even made an attempt on Jonathan's life. Jonathan's position was extremely tenuous, and he tried unsuccessfully to bring peace between the two who meant so much to him.

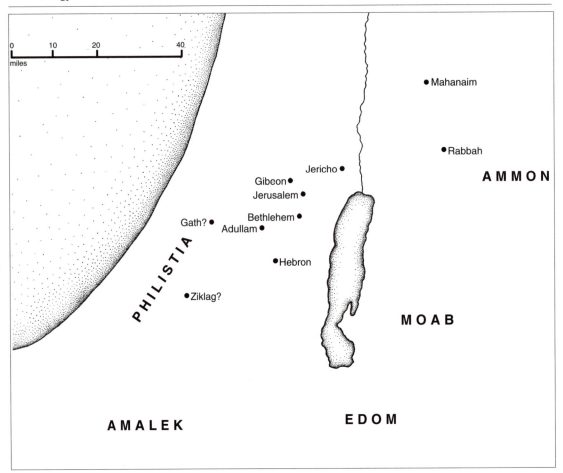

13.2. Central Palestine during the time of David.

After the several attempts on his life David finally felt it necessary to flee. He headed down the hills to the Philistine city of Gath, one place where Saul could not follow. But David soon realized the welcome accorded him was less than cordial, and he feigned madness in order to extricate himself from the city (1 Sam. 21:13). The Philistines apparently thought an insane David was neutralized as any future threat and allowed him to leave.

David returned to the Hill Country and settled at Adullam southwest of Bethlehem, where he was joined by relatives and others who were in distress, in debt, or discontented. This disparate group numbered about four hundred men, and to that total should be added some women and children. Realizing that this unwieldy group could not be moved quickly, for safekeeping David took his elderly parents east of the Jordan to Moab, another refuge out of Saul's reach.[1]

First Samuel 22–26 summarizes the flight and chase episodes that followed.[2] These chapters are rich with detail and intrigue as Saul

1. By taking in David's parents, the Moabites gained some leverage with an enemy of their enemy, Saul. The parents are never mentioned again; according to tradition, the Moabites murdered them. For information on the Moabites, see Mattingly 1994 and the several articles in *BA* 60 (1997): 194–248.
2. 1 Samuel 25:1 makes passing notice of Samuel's death and burial.

sought David. A plotting out of the locales in southern Palestine points up the desperation of both men. Although frantically searching for a proper place of refuge, David refused the opportunities to kill his tormentor. Finally, he chose to escape again into Philistine territory (1 Sam. 27:1), and this time his arrival at Gath was welcomed. Previously, David had arrived alone, with the memory of his victories over the Philistines still fresh. This time, David appeared with six hundred men and, by now, the Philistines must have known that David was a hunted man. When Saul heard what David had done, he gave up pursuit (1 Sam. 27:4).

After living some time in Gath, David asked the Philistine king for his own town. The king obliged and set David up at Ziklag, perhaps some twenty to twenty-five miles south-southwest of Gath.[3] For sixteen months David was based at Ziklag, working, or so his overlord thought, for the Philistines (1 Sam. 27:8–11). David lied to his Philistine protector to make him think he was attacking Israelites and pro-Israelite factions while he was, in reality, clearing Israel's enemies from areas of his future kingdom. David's true activities went undetected, and as far as the Philistine king was concerned, David was a trusted mercenary who could never go back to his own people (1 Sam. 27:12).

King Achish of Gath trusted David so completely that he planned to take him along in the next Philistine mobilization against Israel. When other Philistine commanders questioned David's presence, Achish assured them that David had been loyal "from the day he deserted to me" (1 Sam. 29:3). Still, the Philistine commanders wanted no part of David in their ranks. Their objection (1 Sam. 29:4) suggests that they were recalling the Battle of Michmash when Hebrew mercenaries turned on the Philistines. Achish continued to be convinced of David's loyalty, but he was forced to send him home. David, who had been deceiving Achish for over a year, protested the decision (1 Sam. 29:8), but he was probably silently giving thanks that he did not have to proceed into battle against Saul. Had David continued on with the Philistine army he would have placed himself in an untenable position. David had already shown his unwillingness to hurt Saul, and to fight against an Israelite army no matter what the outcome could only damage David's future position as king. It might well be that God intervened and saved David from this predicament.

The battle between Saul and the Philistines was to be fought in the Valley of Jezreel. This is another example of the artificiality of war as both armies had to march well north to reach this agreed-upon battlefield. Saul encamped in the city of Jezreel at the foot of Mount Gilboa and deployed his troops on its heights. The Philistines assembled on the hill of Moreh and made their base camp at Shunem. Between the two armies lay the Harod Valley, an ideal battleground.

Saul, nervous about the coming confrontation, unsuccessfully tried to make contact with God (1 Sam. 28:6) and apparently even tried fasting (1 Sam. 28:20). Finally, Saul decided to consult a "medium" for as-

---

3. Vos 1983: 90–91 conjectures that physical and religious pressures built up as David and his people stayed in the royal city. The precise identification of ancient Ziklag is still in debate; see Borowski 1988; Fritz 1993; and Seger 1984. Oren 1993 thinks Tel Sera (Tell esh-Sharia) is the most likely site.

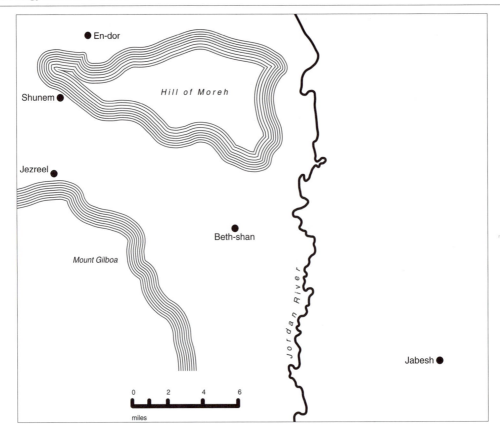

13.3. Battle of Jezreel.

sistance.[4] Years earlier, Saul had tried to rid his kingdom of such people (1 Sam. 28:3), but a woman at En-dor had escaped his purge. Saul was so desperate to know how to proceed that he was willing to risk passing through or going around Philistine positions to reach this kind of help.

When Saul reached the medium he was able to make contact with the dead Samuel—only to learn that he and his sons would die the next day (1 Sam. 28:19). A distraught Saul returned to his army, and the next day the Philistines stormed Mount Gilboa and scattered the army of Israel. Jonathan and two other sons of Saul died on the slopes, and Saul was badly wounded by an enemy archer. Rather than let himself be captured, Saul ended his life by falling on his own sword. When the Philistines stripped the dead the next day, they recognized Saul and his sons:[5]

> And they cut off his head, and stripped off his weapons, and sent them throughout the land of the Philistines, to carry the good news to the house of their idols and to the people. And they put his weapons in the temple of Ashtaroth [Ashtoreth], and they fastened his body to the wall of Beth-shan (1 Sam. 31:9–10).

4. Older translations called this woman a "witch." The Hebrew word is better translated "medium," and extrabiblical texts suggest that such people were usually elderly women.

5. It is not stated how the Philistines made the identification. Their dress could have been a sign. Another suggestion is that they wore special medallions to signal their rank.

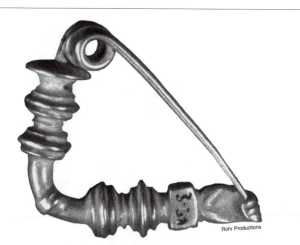

Rohr Productions

13.4. It is safe to assume that when the Philistines stripped the dead they were searching for items of value. During the period of the united kingdom, the Aegean fibula became fashionable and replaced the toggle pin (illustration 4.11) as the means for securing garments. Such "safety pins" could have been among the loot gathered by victorious Philistines.

The cryptic nature of these verses leaves unclear whether Saul's sons were also decapitated. Also unknown is where the temple of Ashtoreth was situated.[6] When the people of Jabesh-gilead heard what had happened to Saul, they remembered his earlier saving them from disgrace and repaid their debt of gratitude by retrieving his body and giving him a proper burial (1 Sam. 31:12–13).

David was back in Ziklag when a man appeared with news of Saul's death. The man bragged that he had struck the final blow to Saul's body and as proof of his claim presented David with Saul's crown and arm bracelet.[7] The man, an Amalekite, must have thought he would gain favor from David by his confession. Although possession of the crown and bracelet proved Saul was dead, it didn't prove that this man had killed him. Still, David accepted the Amalekite's story as true, but the man experienced a different outcome than he expected. After a period of weeping and fasting for Saul, David had the Amalekite executed because he could not condone the murder of the Lord's anointed by either himself or another.

Two Kings and Civil War

The biblical record gives no information about how much Samuel told David when he anointed him in Bethlehem. By the time of Saul's death, however, David had known for several years that he would be the next king of Israel. After Saul died, David asked the Lord whether

6. The assumption has been that Beth-shan was in Philistine hands, and two temples excavated there have been tentatively equated with 1 Sam. 31:9–10. The biblical text does not, however, necessarily require this conclusion. After many seasons of excavation at Beth-shan (see A. Mazar 1997), very little has been found from the time of Saul that could be called Philistine. A. Mazar 1993: 29 suggests the city was populated by Canaanites and "perhaps by groups of 'Sea Peoples'—possibly descendants of mercenaries" serving there when Egypt controlled the site. He thinks these mercenaries could have allied with the Philistines.

7. These symbols, therefore, were not available to aid the Philistines in their identification of Saul. The man must have been on the battlefield before the Philistines came to gather the spoils.

Rohr Productions

13.5. Upper part of the pool at Gibeon. The whole pool extends down some eighty feet to the water table. The original diggers removed about three thousand tons of limestone; it took modern archaeologists some twenty-three thousand hours just to clear the debris from the pool.

he should go up to Judah and to which city. When God instructed David to move to Hebron, he and his people made their home there. Soon David became king of Judah at Hebron.[8] The people of Judah were willing to submit to David since he was a Judean and had nurtured a political base there during his years as a fugitive. One way David did that, while ostensibly promoting Philistine interests, was by distributing booty from his raids to towns in southern Judah.

Meanwhile Abner, Saul's general, had escaped the defeat at Jezreel and taken Saul's remaining son, Ishbosheth (Eshbaal), to Mahanaim where he eventually made him king of Israel. The northern tribes probably found it natural that a son of Saul should be the next king, but they could not have thought Ishbosheth was an effective leader. Even after five years Ishbosheth was obliged to rule from Mahanaim in Transjordan because the territories west of the Jordan were still not free from Philistine pressures.

David's first royal act was to send a message to the people of Jabesh-gilead thanking them for caring for Saul's body. There is no reason to doubt David's sincerity in this commendation, but such action could not have hurt his standing with the northern tribes. God wanted David to be king of all the tribes, not just of Judah. By cultivating good will, David was paving the way for the fulfillment of God's purposes. However, most contacts between the two parts of Israel were not friendly. Hostility broke out, for instance, when Abner, now Ishbosheth's general, and Joab, a nephew of David who later became David's general, led soldiers loyal to their respective kings to the pool of Gibeon where a duel to the death was engaged (2 Sam. 2:14–16).

8. It has been suggested that in his early years David might have been a vassal to the Philistines. There is no real evidence for this view, but it can be assumed David was careful in his relationships with his former "allies."

Yadin 1963: 267

13.6. Tenth-century relief from the palace of Kapara at Tell Halaf (biblical Gozan) illustrates the type of "contest" described in 2 Samuel 2:16, where each man "seized his opponent by the head, and thrust his sword in his opponent's side; so they fell down together."

This combat at Gibeon was not an isolated affair (2 Sam. 3:1), but it was the prelude to a sprawling battle in which David's soldiers were victorious. Near the end of that battle, Abner killed one of Joab's brothers when he refused Abner's repeated pleas to desist from chasing him: "Therefore Abner struck him in the belly with the butt end of the spear, so that the spear came out at his back" (2 Sam. 2:23). The butt end of a spear was sometimes fitted with two prongs so it could be stuck in the ground while not being carried. As Joab's brother learned, the prongs could be as deadly as the spearhead on the other end. This incident is important in that it precipitated a blood feud between Joab and Abner.

At one point Ishbosheth thought Abner had overstepped by sleeping with Saul's concubine. Ishbosheth interpreted Abner's act as a step toward the throne. Abner became livid at such a charge and began to make overtures to David. Ishbosheth probably misread Abner's motives, but he set in motion a chain of events that would not be stopped.

Abner traveled to Hebron, met with David, and agreed to transfer Israel's allegiance to him. Joab, however, was infuriated at the meeting and killed Abner in cold blood (2 Sam. 3:27). Joab didn't trust Abner's intentions (2 Sam. 3:25) and possibly feared a potential military rival should an alliance be struck. The stated reason for Joab's action, however, was to avenge Abner's killing of his brother (even though in self-defense during battle). David's response was to declare his innocence in the matter and call down a curse on Joab and his house. David ordered everyone to mourn Abner's passing and gave him a respectful burial.

The news of Abner's death unsettled both Ishbosheth and his followers. Soon, two commanders in Israel's army assassinated their king, beheaded him, and brought this trophy to David. They probably thought they were delivering good news to David, and they might well have expected a reward, but David reacted just as he had with the Amalekite messenger who brought news of Saul's death: he ordered their execution. David's political instincts would prevent him from wanting to offend anyone who supported Saul's house, much less to give the impression that he condoned the assassination of Saul's son. Moreover, David had earlier vowed to Saul that he would not harm any of his offspring (1 Sam. 24:20–22). Still, the death of Ishbosheth occasioned David's ascension to the throne of a unified Israel (2 Sam. 5:1–3).[9]

David as King of Israel

It would not be wise to rule a united Israel from Hebron, deep within the tribal territory of Judah, so one of David's first priorities was to choose a new capital city.[10] He chose a site that was more central, that was a border town between two tribes, and that had never before been occupied by Hebrews. He chose a small site (variously estimated as being between nine and twelve acres) possessed of good natural defenses and situated near major east-west and north-south trade routes. Jerusalem, David's choice for his new capital, had long been occupied by Canaanites (specifically Jebusites). Although Saul's palace-fortress at Gibeah was approximately four miles away, he apparently never tried to oust the Jebusites.

Deep valleys enhanced Jerusalem's defenses on the east, south, and west sides (illustration 13.7). Only the northwest perimeter of the city required any elaborate fortification. The water supply was the major weakness in Jerusalem's defense: it had only a single spring in the eastern valley. The Jebusites had cut a tunnel to channel spring water into Jerusalem; although the Jebusites boasted that even "the lame and the blind" would be sufficient to hold off an enemy, it seems that David was able to take the city through this water system.

The most popular understanding of 2 Samuel 5:8 is that David sent soldiers into the water tunnel and then up its shaft into Jerusalem. The shaft (today called Warren's shaft) is difficult to climb, so the Jebusites would not have had it heavily protected. Joab (1 Chron. 11:6) could have led a few men into the tunnel at night, overpowered any guards at the top of the shaft, and then opened the city gates to allow more attackers to swarm in.[11] First Chronicles 11:6 reports that Joab was the first man up the water shaft and that David rewarded him by making him chief of Israel's army.

9. 2 Samuel 5:5 states that David was king over Judah alone for seven-and-a-half years and over a united Israel for thirty-three years.

10. The Philistines would have naturally preferred a divided Israel. Two battles between David and the Philistines are recorded in 2 Sam. 5, and in both instances David asked God for direction and was obedient to what he was told to do. God and David were victorious. It may be, though, that this Philistine problem was solved before David took Jerusalem; see L. Wood 1979: 228–29.

11. Abells and Arbit 1995 mistakenly think the text requires that siege was laid to the city. It is as likely that David withdrew and Joab made his move when the Jebusites were again relaxed. Cole 1980 offers a fine survey of water tunnels, but alternative scenarios concerning their development are just as likely. Shiloh's 1981 proposal that Warren's shaft be dated post-David is based on a misunderstanding of the nature of the shaft (see Gill 1994). It is as possible that Jerusalem's water system served as the inspiration for the water systems constructed later in other major cities in the country. Some scholars translate the key word in 2 Sam. 5:8, *tsinnor*, to mean that David encouraged his men to attack the city with hooks, tridents, or other weapons. A Ugaritic cognate supporting the water shaft reading has hopefully put these and other speculations to rest (see Kleven 1994).

13.7. Topographic map of Jerusalem. The heavy line is the city's perimeter in the reign of David. Gihon Spring, outside the northeast corner of the city, is connected to Jerusalem via the Jebusite tunnel. David's city is outside the present "old city" walls, the lighter straight lines near the top of the illustration.

David's New Lifestyle

King David was more inclined toward the grandeur of royalty than Saul had been and therefore contracted with the Phoenicians, the master builders of the Near East, to build a palace in Jerusalem. Phoenicians were skilled in working with stone, and they had a monopoly on the best wood to be found in the Near East, the cedars of Lebanon. David wanted the best.[12]

David took on another mark of Near Eastern kingship when he began to use foreigners as his bodyguards (2 Sam. 8:18).[13] It was custom-

12. E. Mazar 1997 believes she has identified the location of David's palace.

13. The Cherethites were Cretans who apparently settled alongside the Philistines in Palestine. The Pelethites were Philistines.

ary for Near Eastern rulers to surround themselves with mercenary bodyguards who, being foreigners, could hardly be expected to kill the king and take the throne for themselves. Kings hoped the mercenaries would remain loyal to them, and in David's case they did.

David wanted to bring the ark of the covenant into Jerusalem to make the city Israel's religious, as well as political, capital. The Bible does not state whether David consulted the Lord about his desire, but the ensuing difficulties (2 Sam. 6) seem to imply that he acted hastily. Kings of other lands liked to build temples for their gods, and David, recognizing the inequity of his life in a palace while the ark of God rested in a tent in Jerusalem, wanted to build a house for the Lord. Although his desire was worthy and God was pleased with David's thoughtfulness (1 Kings 8:18), because of David's militarism, he was not allowed to carry out his plan (1 Chron. 22:7–10).

God did not disapprove of David's wars; in fact, God blessed him and helped him in his battles. But the Lord wanted to be thought of in the context of peace, and had David built the temple other nations might have inferred that Israel's god was a god of war. Although David must have been very disappointed, he was gracious in accepting God's will. And David found something useful to do concerning the future temple: he gathered necessary materials (1 Chron. 22:14–16) and drew up the architectural plans (1 Chron. 28:11–12). By making these preparations, David could feel that he had at least a part in building a house for his God.

The Fame of David

Saul had been a defensive king whose efforts were continually aimed at trying to keep enemies out of his territory. David, on the other hand, went on the offensive. He "defeated . . . and subdued" the long troublesome Philistines (2 Sam. 8:1), even Gath, the city where he had once lived. David garrisoned Edom to the southeast, neutralized the Moabites to the east, and garrisoned the city of Damascus to the northeast.[14] David even reached the Euphrates, where he conquered Zobah. The king of Hamath, at least, was glad for David's northern expansion because it removed one of his neighboring enemies.

After David defeated the king of Zobah, 2 Samuel 8:4 states that he hamstrung the enemy's chariot horses, keeping only enough for one hundred chariots, perhaps in response to Moses' guideline that Israel's kings should not have many horses (Deut. 17:16). Horses were a prestige item, and too many could make a king proud. David apparently decided one hundred chariots was an acceptable number. Solomon is usually thought of as the king who put the army of Israel on wheels, but the transition clearly began with David.

14. 2 Samuel 8:13 is a classic example of a scribal error. The verse states that David killed eighteen thousand Arameans in the vicinity of the Dead Sea. But a parallel passage, 1 Chron. 18:12, identifies the slain as Edomites. Edom was located near the Dead Sea; Aram was not. There is very little difference between the way *Aramean* and *Edomite* are written in Hebrew; some ancient scribe carelessly miscopied a single consonant in the 2 Samuel passage, and his mistake was perpetuated. The error has long been recognized, but the deep respect for the received text keeps some modern translations from making a correction. For a survey of the Edomites, see Hoglund 1994.

The Bible portrays David as a strong ruler in the ancient Near East. In fact there are reasons to believe he was the strongest ruler of that era. Specifically, to the south Egypt continued to be a badly "broken reed," and to the north Mesopotamia was preoccupied with internal troubles. Temporarily, Palestine, the "land between," had less need to worry about these powers. David's strength was also enhanced when he broke the Philistine's iron monopoly and gained control of the iron and copper resources in Edom. Consequently, iron, an important military material that was scarce in the days of Saul, was by Solomon's reign so abundant it was being put to casual use.

David, the mighty king, was willing to be friendly to neighboring nations. Second Samuel 10 records the death of the king of Ammon and how David sent a delegation to greet the new ruler. Unfortunately, the new king misjudged David's motive and disgraced the delegation. David responded by sending Joab and the army into Ammon. Joab was forced to fight on two fronts, but the Ammonites were humbled. David personally participated in a second battle across the Jordan. All in all, through a combination of military conquest and skillful diplomacy, David became a famous king.

The Shame of David

Shame entered David's life in 2 Samuel 11. On a spring evening, perhaps unable to sleep, David took a stroll around the flat roof of his palace. As he looked into an adjoining courtyard, he saw a beautiful woman bathing. That David saw the woman was an accident—but what followed was not. David ordered the woman, Bathsheba, brought into the palace, where he slept with her. There is no information about Bathsheba's feelings in the affair, whether she resisted his advances or encouraged him. Certainly David was guilty.

Bathsheba was married to a mercenary named Uriah, who was then with Israel's army besieging Rabbah, the Ammonite capital. Therefore, when Bathsheba found herself pregnant, it was obvious that Uriah was not the father. As soon as Bathsheba informed David of her condition, he set about trying to cover up his guilt. David called Uriah back from Rabbah, ostensibly to give him a report on the war, but really so he would spend time with his wife. After Uriah proved too dedicated a soldier to visit Bathsheba (2 Sam. 11:11), David sent him back to Joab carrying, unknowingly, his own death sentence (2 Sam. 11:14–15). In a short time Bathsheba was widowed.[15]

From the human standpoint, David's sins of adultery and virtual murder were close to a perfect crime. Only David and Bathsheba necessarily knew of their affair, and only David and Joab needed to have known the real cause of Uriah's death. But David had not reckoned on

15. Uriah is identified in 2 Sam. 11:3 as a Hittite. Although the Hittite nation collapsed about 1200, during the period of the judges, acculturated people in the southeastern provinces of the fallen empire maintained aspects of the Hittite culture for several centuries. Uriah, as well as the Hittites with whom Solomon dealt, belong to this "afterglow" and have been labeled "Neo-Hittites" in the scholarly literature. Most military letters were delivered orally so that, if the messenger were caught, the information would not be as easily available to the enemy. In this instance the Ammonites would have had little use for the contents of Uriah's message.

God's view of his sin nor on God's methods of punishment. The prophet Nathan forecast disastrous consequences to David's family (2 Sam. 12:10–14).

Calamity in David's Life and Family

Bathsheba's baby died, just as Nathan had prophesied, and David's sin began to spread into his family. David's oldest son, Amnon, raped his half-sister Tamar. Another son, Absalom, brooded over the act for two years, and then, when he found occasion, killed Amnon. Did Absalom kill Amnon solely for the wrong done to Tamar or were his motives more self-serving? Amnon was the oldest son of David. Since David's second son, Chileab, is mentioned only once (2 Sam. 3:3), it is assumed that he died at a young age. Absalom was David's third son. With both Chileab and Amnon dead, Absalom was next in line for the throne. If Absalom did not think of that consequence before killing Amnon, he did soon after.

Absalom was forced to flee to Geshur, an area northeast of the Sea of Galilee.[16] There was no city of refuge in Geshur, but it was the home of Absalom's maternal grandfather and that relationship seems to have afforded sufficient security. Second Samuel 14:1 lacks a second verb in the Hebrew, and translators have to guess at David's feelings for Absalom at that point. Whatever they were, Joab plotted to get Absalom back home. Perhaps Joab was trying to do David a favor or perhaps he was trying to do himself a favor; it would not hurt to build a friendship with the heir apparent.

After three years, Absalom was finally brought back to Jerusalem, but David refused to see him for another two years. Because Jerusalem was so small, there must have been times when it was difficult to avoid each other. Certainly, life became difficult for Absalom, and he began to think that he would have been better off staying in Geshur. Twice Absalom tried to get Joab to intercede for him with David, but Joab would not respond; perhaps when David refused to see the newly returned Absalom, Joab realized that he should not become more involved in their estrangement. Joab interceded for Absalom only after Absalom took extreme action to motivate him (2 Sam. 14:30–32). His effort was successful, and after five years of separation, Absalom and his father were finally reunited.

The Coup

As soon as Absalom was again a part of David's household, he began to ride around Jerusalem in a chariot accompanied by runners who made way for him. Of more consequence, Absalom began the practice of standing beside Jerusalem's city gate each day and speaking with people who came to the capital with legal problems. The city gate was still the judicial center of a city, and Jerusalem's gate probably had a special seat built into it for the king to occupy at designated times. Ab-

16. Kochavi et al. 1992 suggest that Tel Hadar, on the northeast shore of the Sea of Galilee, with its massive fortifications, storage facilities, and imported luxury items, could have been the city to which Absalom fled.

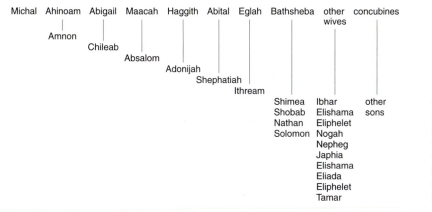

Michal	Ahinoam	Abigail	Maacah	Haggith	Abital	Eglah	Bathsheba	other wives	concubines
	Amnon								
		Chileab							
			Absalom						
				Adonijah					
					Shephatiah				
						Ithream			

Shimea	Ibhar	other
Shobab	Elishama	sons
Nathan	Eliphelet	
Solomon	Nogah	
	Nepheg	
	Japhia	
	Elishama	
	Eliada	
	Eliphelet	
	Tamar	

13.8. David's wives and children (based on 2 Sam. 3:2–5 and 1 Chron. 3:5–9; see 1 Chron. 3:1–3 and 2 Sam. 5:14–16 for slightly different listings).

salom fawned over the people he met in the gateway and openly wished that he were king so that he could dispense justice.

Absalom fostered his own popularity for four years, and by the end of that time he had stolen the hearts of the people.[17] With this base of support, Absalom made his move for the throne. First, he lied to his father about why he wanted to go to Hebron. Then, as Absalom proceeded to his father's first seat of government where he must have expected strong Judean support, messengers fanned out into the land announcing, "As soon as you hear the sound of the trumpet, then you shall say, 'Absalom is king in Hebron' " (2 Sam. 15:10).

The trumpet sounded and suddenly the coup was on. Several reasons have been suggested to explain the willingness of the people to revolt against David. Perhaps the affair with Bathsheba had become public knowledge, and respect for David had eroded. Further, some may have suspected that Uriah's death had been planned. This reasoning would account for Ahithophel (2 Sam. 15:12), one of David's advisors, joining the revolt. Ahithophel seems to have been Bathsheba's grandfather; perhaps he never forgave David for seducing his granddaughter and getting rid of her husband. Absalom's activity at the gateway must have won over some of the people, and the way he behaved there perhaps implies that David had been neglecting internal affairs. There could also have been dissatisfaction over some of Joab's actions. Finally, it is obvious from the text that some people still preferred the house of Saul to David and wished for a Benjaminite rather than a Judean king.

Whatever the relative weights to these suggestions, David seems to have been caught off guard and to have panicked. Jerusalem was a strong city, and the first report of trouble might have been overblown. Still, David took his six-hundred-man mercenary force and quickly fled Jerusalem. The priests Zadok and Abiathar also left the city and carried the ark out with them, but David sent them back into Jerusalem. He wanted them to remain in the city as spies. David told the priests that he would wait down near the Jordan for news; he must have had total trust in them to tell them where he could be found. David also told a man named Hushai to stay in Jerusalem to be his "ears" and to try to

---

17. In some translations, 2 Sam. 15:7 reads that Absalom promoted himself for forty years, but all commentators agree that this has to be a scribal error, and that four is the correct figure. Internal chronology makes that clear; David's whole reign in Jerusalem did not exceed thirty-three years.

thwart Absalom's plans. David's trip to the Jordan River was even more unpleasant; before he had proceeded very far he was lied to (2 Sam. 16:3) and had curses, stones, and dirt thrown at him (2 Sam. 16:13). David and those with him were understandably weary when they finally arrived at the Jordan River.

Absalom entered Jerusalem. With him was Ahithophel, who advised Absalom to establish himself as the new king by sleeping with the ten concubines David had left behind. Therefore, a tent was pitched on the palace roof and Absalom took the concubines of his father "in the sight of all Israel." In so doing Absalom appropriated one of the marks of kingship—his predecessor's women—but he also fulfilled part of Nathan's earlier prophecy (2 Sam. 12:11–12).

Ahithophel wanted troops to go in hot pursuit of David. Such an action would have been wise, but Hushai, who had quickly worked his way into Absalom's inner circle, appealed to the new king's vanity. He advised Absalom to call a general mobilization and then personally lead an army of thousands against the smaller numbers of his father. Absalom elected to follow Hushai's advice. Ahithophel, apparently recognizing that such delay would be fatal, returned home and committed suicide. Since Ahithophel had been David's advisor, he probably anticipated how David would treat a traitor.

After David was informed of the events in Jerusalem, he crossed the Jordan and found a welcome in Mahanaim. Because Absalom followed Hushai's advice, David had time to gather help from various parts of Transjordan (2 Sam. 17:27). However many soldiers David specifically mustered, they were probably fewer in number than the force that came against him under Absalom's banner. But at least the core of David's army (i.e, the mercenary bodyguards) were probably better fighters than the conscripts gathered for Absalom.

David divided his forces into three groups led by Joab, Joab's brother, and the mercenary commander who had sworn allegiance to David when the coup began. These commanders and their troops would fight for David, but they refused to let him fight because, as they said, if any of them died, the battle would continue, but if David died, it was finished.[18] David complied with the wishes of his generals and watched them march out to battle while he stayed behind to wait and worry. The battle was out of David's hands, but he demanded one thing of the three leaders within the hearing of the soldiers, "Deal gently for my sake with the young man Absalom."

The battle was fought in the vicinity of Mahanaim, but the details are glossed over with little more information than that David's soldiers won.[19] More attention is paid to Absalom's fate. Absalom was riding a

18. Winning a battle by capturing the enemy king is a strategy much older than the game of chess (see also 2 Sam. 18). A more obvious example occurred about 125 years later when King Ahab went to battle against the Syrians (1 Kings 22). This strategy was also the decisive factor when Alexander the Great was battling the Persian Empire. In two of the three battles that Alexander fought against the Persians, the tide turned when the Greeks zeroed in on the Persian king and he fled.

19. The battle was fought in the "forest of Ephraim." For some reason a forest east of the Jordan had been given this designation, perhaps as a result of the slaughter in Judg. 12.

mule (a mark of royalty), and while he was in the forest his head became caught in the branches of an oak tree.[20] When Joab heard of Absalom's predicament, he was incredulous that he had been left alive. While the soldiers respected David's caution about his son, Joab ignored their reminder and murdered Absalom as he hung from the tree. Then Joab blew the trumpet to signal victory.[21]

David was sitting in the court between Mahanaim's two gate systems when news reached him of Absalom's death.[22] David's sorrow put a pall over the returning troops, and when Joab returned to Mahanaim he was incensed at David and spoke sharply to his king (2 Sam. 19:5–7). Joab's remonstrance jarred David into reality, and he agreed to meet with the victorious troops. Soon afterward, however, David replaced Joab with Amasa, the general who had just led the losing army against him! Commentators variously interpret David's appointment of Amasa as a sign of senility (David would have been about sixty-five years old), as a way of ridding himself of Joab's dominance, or as an emotional impulse rather than a rational move. But David, who would never forgive Joab for killing Absalom, could as well have been making a shrewd attempt to heal the wounded country. By placing Amasa over Joab, David could be signaling his forgiveness toward everyone who had sided with Absalom.

The coup had been put down, but there was now the matter of restoring David to the throne. Second Samuel 19:9–10 provides a taste of the indecision over his reinstatement, and David was apparently bothered that the groundswell for his return was coming from Israel while nothing was being heard from Judah, his home tribe. Because of this silence, David sent word to the priests in Jerusalem and had them ask the elders of Judah why they were the "last to bring back the king."

When the decision to restore David became unanimous, he moved south from Mahanaim to a point on the Jordan River, possibly opposite Jericho. An official reception committee numbering in the thousands formed on the opposite bank, and the emotions at welcoming David back ranged from joy to fear (2 Sam. 19:16–30). The reception must have lasted for several hours before David finally crossed to the west bank of the Jordan, but before he could proceed further, an argument erupted over why Judah should take responsibility for the king's return when Israel had been the first to suggest it.

Some scholars fault David for insensitivity when he allowed Judah to assume the primary role in his return, and there is no record that David tried to quiet the dissension. The arguing came to an end when

20. Absalom is usually pictured hanging by his hair in the tree, but the not-always-reliable ancient historian Josephus was the first to so describe the incident. Some commentators think him correct and assume that this is why his copious hair is made mention of in an earlier chapter. Other commentators adhere to the literal meaning of 2 Sam. 18:9 and feel that Absalom would have been wearing a helmet, not a crown as Saul seems to have done in the Battle of Jezreel, and that his hair would not have been flying around.

21. Absalom was brought down from the oak tree and buried in a pit. There is no record that he was ever reburied.

22. Mahanaim has not been positively identified. Reading 2 Sam. 18:24–19:8 with the artist's reconstruction of a double gate in mind (illustration 14.7) will add to the reality of the episode as David learned of Absalom's death.

a man named Sheba blew his trumpet, declared further talk to be a waste of time, and urged Israel to continue its break with David (2 Sam. 20:1). Suddenly David was again without the allegiance of Israel.

David proceeded up to Jerusalem with his remaining supporters, took care of his concubines, and gave orders for the capture of Sheba. Amasa, David's new general, proved unable to raise an army within the set time so David appointed Abishai, Joab's brother, to see to the matter. Abishai set out immediately with forces that included David's mercenaries and Joab. En route north they met Amasa. Joab put Amasa off guard, murdered him, and left his body lying beside the road.

David's troops found Sheba in Abel Beth-maacah, a city four miles northwest of Dan. The city was put under siege, but since its people were not allied with Sheba's position, they killed him and threw his head over the wall. The siege was then lifted and the rebellion was finished. David was again in full control of Israel—and he reinstated Joab as general over the whole army!

In David's few remaining years he would experience the trauma of another son trying to usurp the throne, but he would also feel the joy of seeing the son of his choice become king. Second Samuel 21–24 forms an appendix in which various memorable events of David's life and reign are collected; for example, the famine in the land caused by sin, pestilence caused by a census having been illegally taken, numerous battles, and feats of heroism. It is difficult to tell where these events fit chronologically within David's reign.

The Psalms

David was a musician in his youth, expert enough to play for King Saul. In addition to making music, David composed songs and may even have invented new instruments.[23] Six different authors can be identified in the Book of Psalms, but nearly half of the 150 compositions are credited to David. While David was king, he appointed four thousand priests for musical roles (listed according to their instruments in 1 Chron. 16:4–6; 23:5; 25:1, 6–8). The reference in 1 Chronicles 25:8 to "the teacher as well as the pupil" implies that David intended the pattern he established to continue—and it did (2 Chron. 23:18; 29:25–26, 30; Ezra 3:10; Neh. 12:24). David, though king of Israel, could not build the temple. He did, however, build much of the liturgy—a more lasting edifice.

It was not long after the discovery of the Ugaritic tablets in 1929 that scholars began finding parallels in language and thought between these texts and the Book of Psalms. Psalm 29, attributed to David, is perhaps the classic example that Canaanite literary forms had an influence on the writers of some biblical psalms. Scholars speculate that Psalm 29 was originally a hymn lauding the Canaanite storm god and that little more was done to the original beyond substituting God's name. Whether Psalm 29 is really so fully based on a Canaanite original, it is

23. Compare the translations of Amos 6:5 in the New American Standard Bible and the New Revised Standard Version.

13.9. Carved ivory box (just over 2.5 inches high) found at the Assyrian capital of Kalhu (biblical Calah) and probably part of the treasures taken from Syro-Palestine in the eighth century. A group of musicians are depicted (from left to right) playing string, percussion, and wind instruments.

possible that the psalm is doing more than declaring God the Lord of nature. By deliberately imitating Canaanite expressions, it could be arguing to the world of that day that God, not Baal, is truly the lord of nature (Craigie 1983b: 68–71).[24]

Psalm 104 is another psalm for which outside influence has been speculated. In older works Psalm 104 is compared with the fourteenth-century Egyptian "Hymn to the Aton" (*ANE* 1:226–31; *ANET* 369–71), with a direct link between the two sometimes posited. Similarity in thought and structure between the two works was even used to argue that Hebrew monotheism derived from the Amarna period in Egypt. Subsequently, similarities with texts from various parts of the Near East have led scholars to see Psalm 104 as a cosmopolitan psalm whose "words would create a sense of recognition in the ears of Egyptians and Canaanites, but its message focused firmly on the one true God" (Craigie 1983b: 79).

24. Craigie's 1983a summary comment concerning Psalm 29 led some readers to charge him with blasphemy and with disparaging the reliability of the Bible (see *BAR* 10/1 [1984]: 82; 10/3 [1984]: 75). A professor from a decidedly evangelical seminary subsequently came to Craigie's defense (*BAR* 11/1 [1985]: 76), pointing out that "language and literary genre were commonly shared" in the Near East and that to "utilize a magnificent piece of literature to honor the true God is not reprehensible. Could not the author of Psalm 29 be correcting a false notion that Baal was the god of storms by asserting, in the very same way, that the storm-god was not Baal but the very God of creation that Israel praised?"

The Book of Psalms gives insight into the liturgy of Old Testament worship. A good number of ancient musical instruments have been found, and numerous depictions of people playing musical instruments are also known. The Hebrew names for musical instruments are more precisely understood than was true a few decades ago. All this evidence allows us to more correctly visualize Old Testament worship (Bayer 1982 and Mitchell 1992). But, despite occasional claims to the contrary, the actual sound of the music that accompanied the psalms is still lost. The best possibility to "hear" ancient Hebrew music derives from a fourteenth-century clay tablet found at Ugarit. The tablet contains a cult song with musical notation for lyre accompaniment. After scholars deciphered the notation, they built replicas of ancient lyres, consulted Babylonian musical texts that described how to tune a lyre, and produced a recording entitled "Sounds from Silence" (Kilmer, Crocker, and Brown 1976). Assuming there would have been a similarity with Hebrew music, perhaps we can gain some idea of the sound of Hebrew praise (Shanks 1980b).

Additional Reading

Bahat, Dan. *Carta's Historical Atlas of Jerusalem*. Jerusalem: Carta, 1983.

Barnett, Richard D. "Polydactylism in the Ancient World." *BAR* 16/3 (1990): 46–51.

Broshi, Magen. "Estimating the Population of Ancient Jerusalem." *BAR* 4/2 (1978): 10–15.

Meyers, Carol L. "Of Drums and Damsels: Women's Performance in Ancient Israel." *BA* 54 (1991): 16–27.

Shanks, Hershel. "Has Jerusalem's Millo Been Found?" *BAR* 8/4 (1982): 6–7.

Shiloh, Yigael, and Mendel Kaplan. "Digging in the City of David." *BAR* 5/4 (1979): 36–49.

Solomon as King

*"Let what is mine remain unused, let me use up what is yours!"—will this
endear a man to the household of his friend?*

Possessions are sparrows in flight which can find no place to alight.

*He who does not support either a wife or a child, his nose has not borne
a leash.*

Marrying several wives is human; getting many children is divine.

Conceiving is pleasurable, being pregnant irksome!

The poor are the silent ones of the land.

Tell a lie and then tell the truth: it will be considered a lie!

For his pleasure—married! On his thinking it over—divorced!

*He was made to dwell near the water, but he looks toward the uplands
without looking at their rigors!*

—Mesopotamian proverbs

David's Successor

David appointed Solomon to be the next ruler but, when David was old and sick, Adonijah, the eldest living son, decided it was time to declare himself king.[1] Adonijah swung two influential officials to his side: Abiathar the high priest and Joab, commander of the army. He invited these two and some other people to a banquet at En-rogel just outside the southern wall of Jerusalem. Pointedly, Solomon of David's sons, Zadok (a priest who seems to have been second to Abiathar), Nathan the prophet, and Benaiah (the commander of David's foreign bodyguard) were among those excluded from the invitation. Adonijah obviously knew who would not be sympathetic to his cause.

Nathan rushed to Bathsheba to inform her that both her life and Solomon's were in danger. Nathan and Bathsheba then hurried to alert David to what was happening.[2] David recognized the urgency and ordered an immediate anointing of Solomon as king. Therefore, in the company of David's supporters, Solomon rode on the royal mule down to Gihon Spring east of Jerusalem, where Zadok anointed him king (1 Kings 1:38–40).[3]

David gave thanks to God: "Blessed be the Lord, the God of Israel, who has granted one to sit on my throne today while my own eyes see it" (1 Kings 1:48). Since Saul had forfeited his son's opportunity to succeed him, David was the first king of Israel to be able to say these words. In the centuries to come, many kings of Israel and Judah would wish for a similar experience, but not all would realize it.

The banquet was still in progress about a quarter of a mile south of Gihon Spring when word reached the party that Solomon had been crowned. The guests immediately realized their danger and "each went on his way." Adonijah panicked and fled to the horns of the altar that David had built in Jerusalem. The altar was considered a place of refuge (Exod. 21:14), much like the cities of refuge established by Moses, and from that spot Adonijah pleaded for his life. Solomon forgave his elder brother, and after Adonijah prostrated himself before the new king, Solomon sent him home.

Solomon was about twenty years old when he became king, and he already had a wife and a one-year-old son.[4] The length of the coregency of David and Solomon is uncertain, but estimates range from a few months to as much as three years. During David's remaining time he counseled the young Solomon in the ways of kingship and in the proper attitude toward God. He urged Solomon to be strong, to show himself

1. Adonijah became the eldest son because of the events and circumstances related in the previous chapter. God had chosen Solomon, before he was born, to be the next king; 1 Chron. 22:9–10.

2. Ellison 1956: 303 posits that, since Abishag the Shunammite was with David when Bathsheba and Nathan appeared, she was party to the plot. She was to keep David from learning what was happening, but she was unable to prevent a queen from seeing the king. This speculation was dropped from the revised edition (Bimson 1994: 339).

3. Solomon was later given a more formal coronation; 1 Chron. 29:22–25.

4. David had arranged a marriage between Solomon and Naamah, an Ammonite princess. That this happened prior to Solomon's coronation is seen from Rehoboam's being forty-one years old when Solomon died after a forty-year rule (1 Kings 14:21).

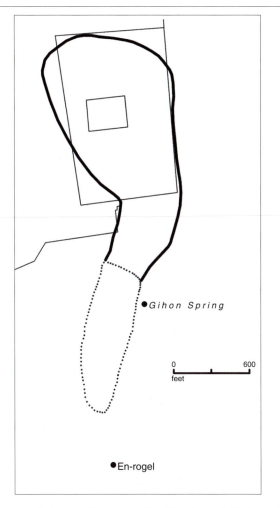

14.1. Features of Jerusalem during Solomon's reign: the extent of David's city (dotted line), its expansion under Solomon (heavy solid line), the temple area (small rectangle), and the "old city" walls (light solid line). The Haram esh-Sherif (large rectangle) indicates where the Dome of the Rock presently stands.

Gihon Spring

0   600
feet

En-rogel

a man, and to walk in God's ways. Finally, David died and was buried in the capital city.[5]

David left Solomon with a kingdom stretching from the Euphrates to the land of the Philistines and to the border of Egypt. All parts of the kingdom were offering tribute. But Solomon was not a mere caretaker, only reaping the rewards of his father's reign. He was active both internally and externally to improve his nation.

Solomon Establishes His Kingdom

First Kings 2:12 states that "Solomon sat on the throne of David his father, and his kingdom was firmly established." Certain early actions on Solomon's part helped him gain this firm control. One such action occurred when Adonijah appealed to Bathsheba to intercede with Solomon on his behalf. Adonijah wanted the hand of Abishag the

5. Concerning the nonauthenticity of the present "tomb of David" in Jerusalem, see *BAR* 9/4 (1983): 72–73; 9/6 (1983): 20, 80–81. For another suggested location of the tomb, see Shanks 1995.

Shunammite, the woman who had attended David toward the end of his life. Bathsheba agreed to his request and asked Solomon to give the woman to be Adonijah's wife. Solomon was furious at the suggestion (1 Kings 2:22–24).

There is not enough information given in the story to confidently say what was in the mind of the three participants in this incident. It does seem obvious, however, that Solomon considered his brother's request to be treasonous, a step toward the throne. Adonijah may indeed have had renewed designs on the crown (and that would explain why he did not go before the king himself), but it is also possible that he only desired the girl because she was beautiful (1 Kings 1:4). Bathsheba should have recognized that Adonijah's request could be interpreted as a wish to appropriate one of the marks of kingly succession, but she may have also believed that Solomon was too firmly in power to be harmed by her "small request." On the other hand, she might have anticipated Solomon's violent reaction and felt it was an ideal way to remove a potential threat to her son. Whatever the individual motivations, Solomon ordered Adonijah's immediate execution.[6]

Another of Solomon's early moves was to remove Abiathar from the priesthood. He was sent to his hometown and is never heard of again (1 Kings 2:26–27). When Joab heard of Adonijah's execution and Abiathar's exile, he knew his life was in danger, so he fled to the altar in Jerusalem. Unlike Adonijah's earlier experience, the altar did not afford refuge for Joab. This is partly because, on his deathbed, David had asked Solomon to see that Joab did not die in peace (1 Kings 2:5–6). David said he wanted Joab punished for the deaths of Abner and Amasa, but the death of Absalom was probably uppermost in his mind. Joab was executed and buried at home, apparently in respect for his past importance (1 Kings 2:28–34).

On his deathbed, David also asked Solomon to punish Shimei, to find a way for him to die "with blood" (1 Kings 2:8–9). This Benjaminite had cursed David when he fled Jerusalem (2 Sam. 16:5–13), but upon his return David had promised not to slay him (2 Sam. 19:16–23). Solomon restricted Shimei to Jerusalem with the warning that he would die if he ever left the city. Three years later Shimei went down into Philistia to retrieve some runaway servants. When Solomon heard of this, Shimei was executed (1 Kings 2:36–46).

These punishments seem out of character with the "man of peace" image usually associated with Solomon, but each time Solomon was technically correct. Further, from a political standpoint, he was strengthening his hold on the throne. No brother would again contest his right to rule, and some potential rivals to his authority were neutralized. Even the restriction on Shimei can be seen in political terms. Forbidden access to his hometown or to any part of Benjamin, there was little chance he could stir up support for a rival ruling family. And fi-

6. Palace intrigue would have been known to Solomon. The rape of Tamar happened when he was a youth, and he could not have been oblivious to the resulting turmoil and the death of the offender. Teenage Solomon surely accompanied his father in his flight from Jerusalem during Absalom's coup attempt. The execution of Adonijah probably quelled all thoughts any remaining brothers may have had concerning the throne.

nally, in some of these acts Solomon proved himself an obedient son who respected his father's deathbed requests.

Solomon's Internal Affairs

The First Temple

King David commissioned Solomon to build the temple for the Lord, and in preparation for this task David had gathered some of the building supplies and prepared the architectural plans (1 Chron. 22:2–16; 28:10–20). The ground plan was similar to the tabernacle, but its overall size was twice that of the previous structure. The temple had a close parallel in plan and size in a nearly contemporary sanctuary found at Tell Tayinat in Syria (Haines 1971).[7]

In the second month of Solomon's fourth year, construction began on the temple (2 Kings 6:1). Additional cedars of Lebanon were purchased, cut, and made into rafts for easy transport south along the Mediterranean coast. At Joppa the rafts were dismantled, and the timbers floated up the Yarkon River and then transported overland into the Hill Country for delivery to Jerusalem. Solomon hired Phoenician workers, the master builders in the Near East, to help in the construction.

Several chapters in both 1 Kings and 2 Chronicles tell of the care and attention to detail that went into building the temple.[8] One departure from the tabernacle was the porch and the two pillars that stood at the front of the building. By analogy with Syrian sanctuaries, the pillars in Solomon's Temple should have functioned as supports for the porch roof, but they are often reconstructed as free standing. Several scholars have conjectured about these pillars and the names they were given (Jachin and Boaz; 2 Kings 7:21–22). Two of the more implausible theories are that the pillars were fire altars or phallic symbols. More likely they were part of either the temple's decoration or its structural needs.

The Holy of Holies in the temple, as in the tabernacle, had equal dimensions in height, width, and depth. In the case of the temple that measurement was thirty feet, but the temple building stood forty-five feet tall. The Bible is silent as to how the remaining fifteen feet of height were accounted for. One possibility is that the Holy of Holies was raised above the rest of the temple and reached by means of a staircase. (In illustration 14.4 a "false ceiling" is offered as the probable solution.)

Rooms were built against the sides and back wall of the temple for storage of the equipment necessary for worship.[9] In the court around

7. These parallels and Solomon's use of Phoenician artisans (2 Chron. 2:13–14) and decoration is not troubling; the architecture itself is neutral. A temple excavated in recent years at Ain Dara in northern Syria is even more comparable; like Solomon's temple, it had chambers on three sides. As yet, no English report is available for the Ain Dara temple.

8. Fritz 1987b is a well-illustrated article, but the author implies more guesswork than is needed because he takes some of the biblical description to be later insertions. For an example of attention paid to detail, see Millard 1989b.

9. Kitchen 1989a finds that Solomon's Temple fits the common Near Eastern practice of having more storage and service space than worship space.

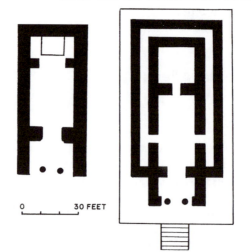

14.2. Ground plans of the Syrian sanctuary at Tell Tayinat (left) and Solomon's Temple (right).

0   30 FEET

British Museum

14.3. Wheeled metal stand from Cyprus would have held a basin and is similar to the biblical water stands located in the courtyard of Solomon's Temple.

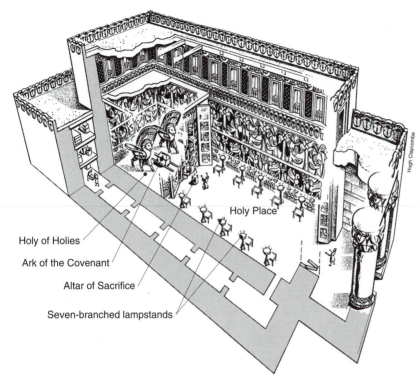

Holy Place

Holy of Holies

Ark of the Covenant

Altar of Sacrifice

Seven-branched lampstands

Hugh Claycombe

14.4. Artist's reconstruction of Solomon's Temple.

the temple was an altar and a basin (bronze sea), just as there had been in the tabernacle (Zuidhof 1982). The same type of equipment was placed within the temple as had been used in the tabernacle, though some pieces were expanded in number. For example, in the tabernacle there was only one lampstand, in the temple ten (C. Meyers 1979); and a second set of cherubim, each with wingspans of fifteen feet, was placed in the Holy of Holies. Some new equipment was added, such as the portable water stands used in the court.

The temple took seven years to complete, but sometimes Solomon is faulted for spending about twice that much time to build his palace. This is hardly a valid criticism because the Bible makes it quite clear Solomon did his best to make God's temple the finest structure in the world and that God was pleased with the results (1 Kings 8:10–11). Certainly Solomon spared no expense on the precious woods and gold overlay used in building and outfitting the temple. Moreover, the structure was not large (temple size was not necessarily an indication of devotion to deity), the main building measured only ninety feet long by thirty feet wide by forty-five feet high. Seven years seems a generous length of time to build such a small edifice.[10]

10. It has long been held that Solomon's Temple (and later Herod's) was built on or near where the Dome of the Rock now stands in Jerusalem. A. Kaufman 1983 presents a detailed argument for siting the temples approximately 330 feet north of the dome—findings that led some to believe that a new temple could be built on the Temple Mount without disturbing Islam's third most holy shrine. Riots broke out in Jerusalem in 1990, with many people killed, when it was rumored that an attempt would be made to lay the cornerstone for a new temple. Ritmeyer 1992 reexamines the evidence and concludes that the temples were, as previously thought, where the Dome of the Rock now rests.

When the temple was ready for dedication and the leaders of Israel had assembled, the priests brought the ark up from the tent in David's city to the temple area and placed it in the Holy of Holies beneath the cherubim (Ritmeyer 1996). When the ark was in place, God gave evidence of his pleasure by sending fire and a cloud (1 Kings 8:10–11; 2 Chron. 7:1–3). Solomon stood atop the temporary platform raised in the courtyard and addressed Israel, reminding the people of God's role in their history. He ended the service with a prayer of dedication and a benediction. Days of sacrificing, feasting, and celebration followed the ceremonies.[11]

Other Buildings in Jerusalem

Solomon extended the limits of Jerusalem both north and slightly west in order to construct the temple and his palace. Jerusalem occupied about thirty-two acres by the end of Solomon's reign, which made it roughly three times the size it had been in David's day. Several names identify structures built for Solomon in Jerusalem—House of the Forest of Lebanon, Hall of Pillars, Hall of the Throne—but whether they are separate buildings or portions of his sprawling palace is unclear (2 Kings 7:2–7). One enigmatic reference to the building technique, though, is now understood:

> So the great court all around had three rows of cut stone and a row of cedar beams even as the inner court of the house of the LORD, and the porch of the house (1 Kings 7:12).

The practice of putting beams in the coursing of a wall originated in Anatolia, where earthquakes are a constant threat. The wall beams act as a shock absorber in the event of an earthquake. The Phoenicians carried this building technique with them into Palestine (H. Thompson 1960).

The biblical writer gives hints of the extravagant way the new building(s) in Jerusalem were outfitted. Solomon commissioned five hundred gold-plated shields to be placed in the House of the Forest of Lebanon. And according to the detailed description in 1 Kings 10:18–20, Solomon's throne was inlaid with ivory and gold. Finally, all of Solomon's drinking vessels were made of gold because silver was considered too common (1 Kings 10:21). However fantastic this display of gold might seem today, it is in accord with the known practices of the ancient world, both in the use of gold and in the records of quantity (Millard 1989a, 1994).

"Solomon's Stables"

Solomon also commissioned a great many building projects in other parts of Israel (1 Kings 9:15–19). First Kings 9:19 mentions cities for chariots and horsemen. David had made a first step toward mechaniz-

---

11. 2 Chron. 5:12–13 gives some idea of the pageantry associated with the temple dedication.

14.5. Proto-Aeolic capitals, like this one found at Megiddo, were used in royal centers during the monarchy. Most were set atop pilasters. It is reasonable to assume that similar capitals were used to decorate some of Solomon's constructions in Jerusalem. The decoration represents a stylized palm tree, an architectural design from which the classical Ionic capital developed.

ing the army, but it was Solomon, the man of peace, who introduced war chariots in large quantities. Although 1 Kings 9:15 does not specifically say that Hazor, Megiddo, and Gezer were Solomon's chariot cities, they would have been logical choices. All are located in terrain over which chariot maneuverability could be exploited. Further, Hazor guarded the main northern route into Israel, Megiddo commanded the strategic Aruna Pass that linked northern and central Israel, and Gezer watched the nearby border with Philistia.[12]

When the site of Megiddo was excavated in the 1930s, archaeologists found structures that they identified as stables built to house some of Solomon's chariot force. The buildings were divided by pillars into three aisles, and the excavators assumed that horses had been quartered in the outer two rows. Mangers found in the buildings strengthened this theory, and the identification continued in favor until similar structures were found at Hazor, Beersheba, and elsewhere. At Beersheba the buildings contained clear indications that they had been used as storehouses. Therefore, a countertheory is that all such structures were storehouses and not stables. The mangers, then, served to quiet pack animals during loading and unloading. The issue is even more confused since subsequent excavation at Megiddo has led some archaeologists to redate the structures there to the time of Ahab (Currid 1992; Herr 1988; Shanks and Yadin 1976).

For many years "Solomon's Stables" have been a famous example of the way archaeology illuminates the Bible. But such a simple building plan could have served as either stables or storehouses. Neither is it necessary that such a plan function the same way at every site. At Megiddo, the single access door and the narrowness of the side aisles

12. There is evidence that the south of the country was also guarded (e.g., with the building of a fort at Arad). The date and function of other constructions in the Negev is not so certain. Cohen 1985 argues that over forty "fortresses," small settlements, and isolated farmsteads in the central Negev should be attributed to widespread settlement and fortification of the area during the reign of Solomon (a view subsequently emended; see Cohen 1986). For an alternate interpretation of the evidence, see Finkelstein 1986a. See also Haiman 1994 and Meshel 1994.

14.6. "Solomon's Stables" (area 364) as pictured in the Megiddo excavation report (top), with a model (bottom). From left to right: the buildings restored, partially restored to show the interior, and as actually found by excavators. The function and date of the structures are in question, but it is accepted that clerestory roofs, as shown here, would have been necessary to provide light and ventilation for the interior.

makes the storehouse identification more probable. If the buildings found at Megiddo date to the time of Ahab, then stables dating to Solomon's day could still be awaiting excavation. Such structures could be similar to what has already been found, but additional doorways and wider side aisles enabling grooms to easily move individual horses would make the buildings more functional (G. Davies 1994).

Solomon's Gate Systems

The excavators of Megiddo also found a gate system that they dated to the time of Solomon. Its finely cut stones show the quality of workmanship available. Subsequently a similar gateway was uncovered at Hazor and also dated to the reign of Solomon. When Yigael Yadin, the excavator of Hazor, recognized the similarity of Hazor's and Megiddo's gateways, he recalled the record in 1 Kings 9 that Solomon fortified Hazor, Megiddo, and Gezer. Gezer was first excavated at the turn of the century when methodology and pottery chronology were not yet fully developed. But Gezer's architectural records were kept carefully enough that when Yadin reexamined the excavation reports, he was able to recognize part of a Solomonic gateway within a level the original excavators had dated to be centuries later.

Further study and renewed excavation at Gezer showed that in all

MEGIDDO

HAZOR

GEZER

0   10 METERS

14.7. Gate plans (right) of three of Solomon's major cities. Each set of piers held doors through which an enemy would have to force its way. Double walls connected by cross-walls (known as casemate walls) were popular for defense during the Solomonic period and can be seen attached to the gateways at Hazor and Gezer. Casemate walls gave the appearance of great strength while saving in labor and material. The resultant rooms could serve various functions and could be filled in at whatever point the wall might be attacked. Artist's reconstruction of the Megiddo gate system (top) shows the ramp into the city blocked by an outer gateway. Inside that gateway an open area was ringed by battlements. A second towered gateway then gave access through the defensive wall into the city. Remains of the main gate system at Gezer (bottom), seen from inside the city, show a large drain, now uncovered, under the entryway street to keep the area dry.

three sites the type of construction, the material used, and the dimensions of the gates are similar and in some cases identical. This similarity led Yadin to believe that the three gate systems had not only all been built by Solomon but by a single architect working for Solomon (Fargo 1983; Yadin 1958; Yadin 1975: 193–205).[13]

The Mining Industry

Solomon also had an interest in expanding the mining industry. Archaeologists have found ample evidence of copper mining and open-air smelting activity in the vicinity of the eastern leg of the Red Sea. Some of the ancient operations found there were first attributed to the time of Solomon, but subsequently redated to an earlier period. It is extremely difficult to date slag deposits or mining operations, and at this time it is not possible to say which of the known remains can be safely credited to Solomon (S. Singer 1978).

Between 1938 and 1940, Nelson Glueck excavated Tell el-Kheleifeh near the shore of the Red Sea and reported finding an elaborate copper refinery dating to Solomon's reign. He interpreted holes in the walls of the complex's central building as flues designed to channel wind currents from the Red Sea into the refinery blast furnaces. Despite the reservations of other archaeologists, the discovery of Solomon's copper refinery began to be reported in books on biblical archaeology. In 1965, Glueck finally admitted he had erred. A wall surrounding the central building in which the so-called flues were found would have blocked wind currents from the sea—which dissenting archaeologists had long pointed out. The holes in the wall of the central building were simply open spaces left after the wood used in the building's construction had decayed. It now seems that the structure was a fortress, but that its initial phase was Solomonic is in question.[14]

Maintaining Government

Solomon enlarged the bureaucracy. Abner is the only official named in Saul's reign, David had several more, but Solomon exceeded even his father's needs (1 Kings 4:1–19). David may have neglected some of his judicial duties, but Solomon became famous for his wisdom in such matters (1 Kings 3:16–28). Additionally, Solomon increased the allegiance of at least two of his top officials by giving his daughters to them in marriage (1 Kings 4:11, 15).

Largely for tax purposes, Solomon divided the country into twelve districts (1 Kings 4:7). The divisions generally followed the old tribal boundaries, but they were not exactly the same because new territories had been added and also because a main purpose of the redistricting was to insure provisions for the king and his household. Each district

13. Work has resumed at Megiddo. In part, the current excavators are restudying the gate system at the site and claiming radically new conclusions that have found little acceptance (Shanks 1998).

14. For an unreserved acceptance of "Solomon's refinery," see Albright 1971: 127–28. But then see Pratico 1986.

was obligated to supply the king with foodstuffs for one month of each year; and the old tribal boundaries would not have been equal in that ability.[15]

Solomon's External Affairs

Trade

Outside his own borders, Solomon engaged in a mixture of trade and diplomacy. His trading ventures were greatly aided by the Phoenicians, who were just then beginning what would become a far-ranging maritime trade. With Solomon, the Phoenicians built a fleet of ships that sailed south from Israel's Red Sea port at Ezion-geber (1 Kings 9:26–28; 2 Chron. 8:17–18) to Ophir.[16] Solomon probably exported his surplus grain, wine, oil, metals, and luxury items such as dyed cloth from Phoenicia.[17] The ships took three years to make a round-trip, so they must have stopped at several ports along the Arabian and African coasts. Returning ships were laden with gold, silver, precious stones, ivory, special woods, and monkeys.[18]

Solomon's fleet probably docked for trade purposes at ports controlled by the kingdom of Saba. Scholars place Saba (Sheba) at the southwest end of the Arabian Peninsula, more than one thousand miles from Israel. The ruler of Saba may have worried that Israel's shipping would damage his caravan trade, and so he sent his wife to meet with Solomon. Assyrian records show that Arabian queens played prominent political roles early in the first millennium. Therefore, the Queen of Sheba had more in mind than Solomon's wealth and wisdom when she visited Jerusalem.[19] The queen went home dazzled by all she had seen and heard in Solomon's court, but very likely his diplomatic skills also played a part in the success of the visit.[20]

15. For the possibility that Egypt adopted this tax plan, see A. Green 1979.

16. The location of Ophir is still uncertain; one of several possibilities is that it is located midway between Mecca and Medina on the Arabian Peninsula; see Berkowitz 1977. Tell el-Kheleifeh has long been considered to be Ezion-geber, but it is now recognized that further excavation is necessary to maintain that identification. Flinder 1989 reexamines the problem and thinks that Tell el-Kheleifeh might be Elath (Eloth). He proposes that the island of Jezirat Faron, seven miles from the north end of the Red Sea, should be identified as Ezion-geber.

17. Reference to "ships of Tarshish" in 1 Kings 10:22 and 2 Chron. 9:21 need not mean that Solomon was also plying the Mediterranean shipping lanes. Rather, this may be a designation for a class of ships capable of transporting copper ingots from refineries on Sardinia and Cyprus. This designation may imply that copper was one of Solomon's major exports from his Red Sea port; see L. Wood 1979: 294–95.

18. The "peacocks" of 1 Kings 10:22 in some translations is now understood to mean baboons (so the New English Bible and the Jerusalem Bible). Baboons and monkeys were used much like court jesters.

19. Kitchen 1995a: 19 notes that after 700 "Arabia's queens disappear almost completely from public political roles" and therefore "she cannot be some imaginary 'deuteronomic' or other later invention of the sixth to fourth centuries B.C."

20. Concerning the alleged affair between Solomon and the Queen of Sheba, see L. Wood 1979: 328.

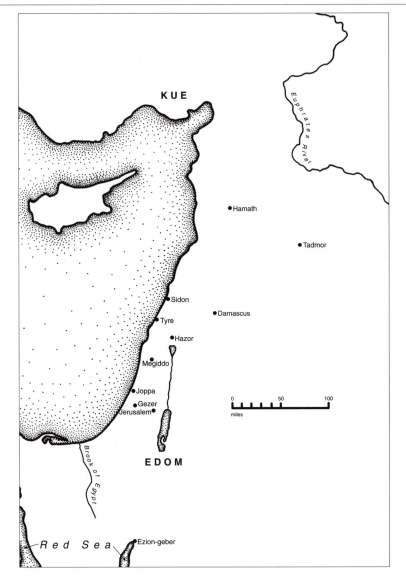

14.8. Palestine and neighboring areas during the time of Solomon.

Solomon imported horses and chariots from Egypt and additional horses from Kue, an area near the northeast corner of the Mediterranean. First Kings 10:26 states that Solomon had fourteen hundred chariots (each would have been pulled by two horses). Solomon obviously retained sufficient numbers for his own army and then sold his surplus to the "Neo-Hittites" and Arameans based east of Kue (1 Kings 10:28–29).[21]

21. Egypt is spelled *Misraim* in Hebrew (with a plural ending because Egypt was thought of as the Two Lands, the flat delta region and the Nile Valley). First-millennium Assyrian texts refer to Egypt as *Musur* and use the same designation for an area north of Kue. From the similarity of consonants, some scholars conclude that 1 Kings 10:28 refers to that northern region rather than to Egypt (Tadmor 1961). A footnote at 1 Kings 10:28 in the New International Version allows the possibility for this reading here and in the next verse. For an opposing view, see Patterson and Austel 1988: 104–5. Arameans are usually called "Syrians" in English translations. For a survey of these people, see Pitard 1994.

Diplomacy

Diplomacy was one of Solomon's strengths, and he was able to forge friendships with several neighboring nations. Many of the women in Solomon's ever-expanding harem no doubt came to Jerusalem as part of successful treaties between Israel and their countries. Solomon's friendship with Hiram of Tyre probably led to his marriage to a princess(?) from Phoenicia (1 Kings 11:1).[22] But Solomon's contact with Egypt is most noteworthy: "Then Solomon formed a marriage alliance with Pharaoh king of Egypt, and took Pharaoh's daughter and brought her to the city of David, until he had finished building his own house" (1 Kings 3:1). The Bible gives no details of this marriage, but several references to it imply that Israel thought it quite important. By correlating the chronologies of Israel and Egypt, it is possible to identify the pharaoh as Siamun, the next-to-last ruler in Egypt's Dynasty 21 (Kitchen 1986: 280–83; Malamat 1958, 1979). The marriage of Solomon and the pharaoh's daughter was especially important because it represents a break in Egyptian tradition. For centuries Egyptian state policy allowed a prince—but not a princess—to be given in marriage to another country. For example, years before Solomon, the king of Babylon had forged a friendship treaty with Egypt, and he expected to receive a princess as part of the agreement. Instead, he was told in a letter that Egyptian policy did not allow a king's daughter to be given to other rulers. The Babylonian king wrote back (Steindorff and Seele 1957: 111):

> If, my brother,[23] you write that you will not permit your daughter to marry, saying, "Never has the daughter of an Egyptian king been given to anyone," why not then? You are the king and able to act according to your own will. If you desire to give her, who can say anything?

The Babylonian king went on to say that he would settle for another beautiful woman because he could pass her off as a king's daughter (Steindorff and Seele 1957: 112):

> But if as a matter of principle you will send none at all, then were you not taking consideration of brotherhood and friendship when you wrote of forging closer relations with each other by a marriage? . . . Why, then, has my brother not sent to me even one woman? Well, you have not sent a woman to me; shall I then, like yourself, withhold a woman from you?

Solomon's marriage to the pharaoh's daughter took place at a time when Egypt was divided by two rival dynasties; one pharaoh ruled from Tanis in the delta and the other from Thebes in Upper Egypt. Political marriages were made between these broken pieces of once-mighty Egypt, but the ancient policy against sending a princess

---

22. Hiram was king of Tyre, but it is likely that he was also king over all of Phoenicia. That he had access to the cedars of Lebanon and that Solomon thought ceding him twenty cities bordering Phoenician territory might complete their business transaction (1 Kings 9:10–13) implies more influence than a mere city king would have had. Concerning Solomon's cash-flow problem and the possible reason for Hiram's reaction, see Gal 1990, 1993 and Heltzer 1975.

23. "Brother" was used as a diplomatic term.

abroad had been maintained. It is apparent that Siamun, the pharaoh based in the delta, found it necessary to break the centuries-old article of foreign policy when, for the first time, Egypt was faced with the reality of a superior power on its northern border. This new situation called for a new response. This insight from Egyptology amplifies the Bible's statement that Solomon was a mighty ruler.[24]

Solomon was a statesman rather than a military figure, as Saul and David had been, but there is one record of Solomon using force to further Israel's fortunes: "Then Solomon went to Hamath-zobah and captured it. And he built Tadmor in the wilderness and all the storage cities which he had built in Hamath" (2 Chron. 8:3–4).[25] When David conquered the area known as Zobah, the king of Hamath sent presents of gratitude to Israel because Zobah had been oppressing him. But during Solomon's reign, Zobah must have gotten out of line, and the good relations with Hamath must have been broken. The few words of these verses show that Solomon's military force was ready and able to do battle when diplomacy failed.

The Sources of Israel's Wealth

The trade Solomon engaged in added to the wealth of his kingdom, but so too did the gifts and tribute that came in from all sides (1 Kings 10:25). Solomon's wealth was also partly at the expense of his own people. He used the corvée and levy, common ways in the ancient Near East to further government projects, and Israelites as well as Canaanites supplied the government with free labor for the designated periods (1 Kings 5:13–18; Rainey 1970b). Additionally, Solomon's subjects were required to pay taxes. As mentioned earlier, each district was charged with the responsibility of supporting the government one month out of each year. These payments abetted Solomon's lavish treatment of himself, his family, and his guests. The food bill alone was staggering:

> And Solomon's provision for one day was thirty kors of fine flour and sixty kors of meal, ten fat oxen, twenty pasture-fed oxen, a hundred sheep besides deer, gazelles, roebucks, and fattened fowl (1 Kings 4:22–23).[26]

These needs could have become a definite burden on the country. Certainly this taxation, plus the corvée and levy, created the tensions within Israel that reduced the kingdom to a fragile condition by the time of Solomon's death.[27]

24. For an interesting exchange concerning the credibility of the Bible's account of Solomon, see Millard 1991a, 1991b; and J. Miller 1991.

25. Hamath-zobah is a reference to Hamath in the area of Zobah. Tadmor was an important caravan city linking Syria-Palestine with Mesopotamia.

26. One kor is roughly equivalent to ten bushels.

27. Judah is not mentioned in the redistricting established by Solomon, but Judah could have been under some other tax structure. If Judah had some special position, such favoritism would also have contributed to the unrest in Israel. The corvée and levy became a breeding ground for discontent. It was one of the prices Samuel had long ago warned the Israelites they would have to pay for kingship (1 Sam. 8:10–18). He also warned them that God would not listen to their complaints.

Solomon's Last Years

Solomon dedicated the temple to God in the eleventh year of his reign. There is no reason to think he was anything but true to the Lord during those early years or, for that matter, for the majority of his reign. But with the passage of time, Solomon flagrantly ignored Moses' warning that future kings of Israel should not "multiply wives for himself, lest his heart turn away" from God (Deut. 17:17). Saul had only one wife and one concubine, David had about eight wives and somewhere over ten concubines, but Solomon amassed one thousand wives and concubines! Perhaps the majority of these women were the result of intermarriage between royal families (and the entourage that accompanied each princess). Even if Solomon had no real contact with most of the women, they were still a source of his downfall.

It is hard to escape concluding from 1 Kings 11:4–8 that in his later days Solomon had fallen so far he actually engaged in idol worship. Ashtoreth was a fertility goddess whose worshipers engaged in ritual sexual acts. High places to Chemosh and Molech were built on what is now called the Mount of Olives. The followers of Molech believed that infant sacrifices were sometimes required. Hopefully, such practice is not implied in the statement that Solomon's "wives burned incense and sacrificed to their gods."[28]

The immediate result of Solomon's apostasy was that the Lord allowed a man named Rezon to conquer Damascus in the north and begin to pull that territory from Israel's control (1 Kings 11:23–25). To the southeast, Hadad returned from refuge in Egypt (where he had fled from David) and began to cause trouble for Solomon in Edom (1 Kings 11:14–22, 25). Within Israel, the prophet Ahijah prophesied that Jeroboam, one of Solomon's officials, would become king over ten of the twelve tribes after Solomon's death (1 Kings 11:26–40). When Solomon heard of this, he tried to have Jeroboam assassinated, but the king-elect fled to Egypt for safety. On this tragic note, after forty years as king of Israel, Solomon died and was buried in the city of David (1 Kings 11:41–43).

The Wisdom of Solomon

In the days of Solomon, the copying and compiling of proverbs was a court activity or pastime. First Kings 4:32 says that Solomon spoke three thousand proverbs, and most of those collected in the Book of Proverbs are attributed to him. The Book of Proverbs contains 915 proverbs, but certain verses clearly indicate that some proverbs were added after Solomon, perhaps as late or later than the reign of Hezekiah (cf. Prov. 30:1; 31:1). That the Book of Proverbs is a collection is perhaps best shown by the duplication of two identical proverbs (18:8; 26:22).

28. Concerning the question of child sacrifice, see Stager and Wolff 1984 and Day 1989.

Israel's fascination for proverbs did not begin with Solomon; for example, David recited an "old saying" in 1 Samuel 24:13. God inspired Solomon and others to collect and compose the proverbs contained in the Book of Proverbs, and Israel was aware of the wisdom literature from other parts of the Near East. The Mesopotamian proverbs and maxims in the chapter epigraph give an example of the thoughts from that part of the ancient world. Because wisdom is timeless, some of these proverbs have modern counterparts. The last two proverbs in the epigraph may be rendered: "Marry in haste, repent in leisure" and "The grass is always greener on the other side of the fence."

The Book of Proverbs was compiled that its readers may "know wisdom." Practical, as opposed to intellectual, wisdom is taught in the book. It promotes a wisdom for living in the world. Tenets of Israel's faith underlie the guidelines for successful living, and in that respect the book is distinct from other collections known from the ancient Near East.[29] The Book of Proverbs can be used to formulate models for present-day living. The book has important guidelines concerning subjects such as diligence and laziness, marriage, and friendship. For example, with regard to friendship, the Book of Proverbs stresses the quality, not the quantity, of friendship. Ancient proverbs can also give rich insight into life in former days:

> [Proverbs] are the safest index to the inner life of a people. With their aid we can construct a mental image of the conditions of existence, the manners, characteristics, morals and [worldview] of the community which used them. They present us with the surest data upon which to base our knowledge of [a people's philosophy] (E. Gordon 1959: 1).

The Song of Songs (also called the Song of Solomon or Canticles), though attributed to Solomon, may not be from his pen; some anonymous poet might have written it in critique of Solomon. Most modern scholars reject the idea that the Song of Songs is an allegory about God and Israel (a typical Jewish viewpoint), God and the Virgin Mary (a typical Catholic viewpoint), or Jesus and the Church (a typical Protestant viewpoint). Rather, they understand it as speaking to the ever-important issue of keeping physical love in its proper context.

There is even less agreement over whether Solomon authored the Book of Ecclesiastes. The book's opening statement—"The words of the Preacher, the son of David, king in Jerusalem"—does not necessarily provide an identification. Although the writer asserts that he was king over Israel (Eccles. 1:12), he never specifically says he is Solomon.[30] And, at least in its present form, the Hebrew style dates later than the united kingdom. If, however, the book was written by Solomon, its last chapter implies that he repented of the error of his later years. In essence, the "preacher" argues the folly of any worldview that reaches no

---

29. Mesopotamian proverbs were also intended to impart a practical wisdom, but they lacked the religious dimension of the biblical proverbs.

30. The word translated "preacher" is *qohelet* in Hebrew, but the sense of the word is not clear. Since it was a fairly common practice to attribute a book to a famous person, some scholars think that is the case here.

higher than the human condition and preaches against the belief that personal happiness should be the chief goal of life.

First Kings 4:29–34 extols the great wisdom of Solomon. He began his life with so many more advantages than Saul, yet for all his wisdom he fell perhaps even further than Saul. Saul neither condoned nor fell into false worship as Solomon did. Most unhappily, because of his great fall, Solomon's death occasioned the death of the united kingdom.

Additional Reading

Gonen, Rivka. "Was the Site of Jerusalem's Temple Originally a Cemetery?" *BAR* 11/3 (1985): 44–55 (additional comments in 11/5:24–25).

Ishida, Tomoo (ed.). *Studies in the Period of David and Solomon*. Winona Lake, Ind.: Eisenbrauns, 1982.

Laperrousaz, Ernest-Marie. "King Solomon's Wall Still Supports the Temple Mount." *BAR* 13/3 (1987): 34–44.

Pritchard, James B. (ed.). *Solomon and Sheba*. London: Phaidon, 1974.

Ritmeyer, Leen. *The Temple and the Rock*. Harrogate: Ritmeyer Archaeological Design, 1996.

Ussishkin, David. "Building IV in Hamath and the Temples of Solomon and Tell Tayinat." *IEJ* 16 (1966): 104–10.

———. "King Solomon's Palace and Building 1723 in Megiddo." *IEJ* 16 (1966): 174–86.

The Early Divided Kingdom (931–841)

The House Divided
King Jeroboam of Israel
King Rehoboam of Judah
King Abijah of Judah
King Asa of Judah
Kings Baasha, Elah, Zimri, and Omri of Israel
King Ahab of Israel and King Jehoshaphat of Judah
The Close of the Early Divided Kingdom
The Early Divided Kingdom in Review
The Chronology of the Kings of Israel and Judah
Additional Reading

The House Divided

Rehoboam was forty-one years old when his father, Solomon, died (1 Kings 14:21). There had been no coregency as with David and Solomon, but Rehoboam was first in line for the throne. For some reason, Shechem was selected as the site for his coronation, and the people

Zev Radovan

15.1. The Gezer calendar (just over four inches high) is small enough to be held in the hand. Inscribed in paleo-Hebrew, it is thought to be a schoolboy's writing exercise. The text dates from either the reign of Solomon or, more likely, the reign of his son Rehoboam. When first found in 1908 the calendar was among the earliest Hebrew inscriptions known. It no longer holds that distinction, but it does provide an interesting example of an ancient memorization drill. This agricultural calendar specifies periods for planting, pruning, harvesting, and the like. Most people probably thought of their year in terms of such activities; see Talmon 1963.

who assembled there promised allegiance to Rehoboam on condition that he "lighten the hard service of your father and his heavy yoke which he put on us" (1 Kings 12:4).

The people's request reflects the dissatisfaction that had grown during Solomon's rule, and the provisional acceptance of Rehoboam shows how fragile the united kingdom had become. Rehoboam consulted with the elders who had been in Solomon's service, and they recommended that Rehoboam agree to the people's request. They believed that in so doing he would bind the nation together. However, Rehoboam also sought the advice of young men who had grown up with him

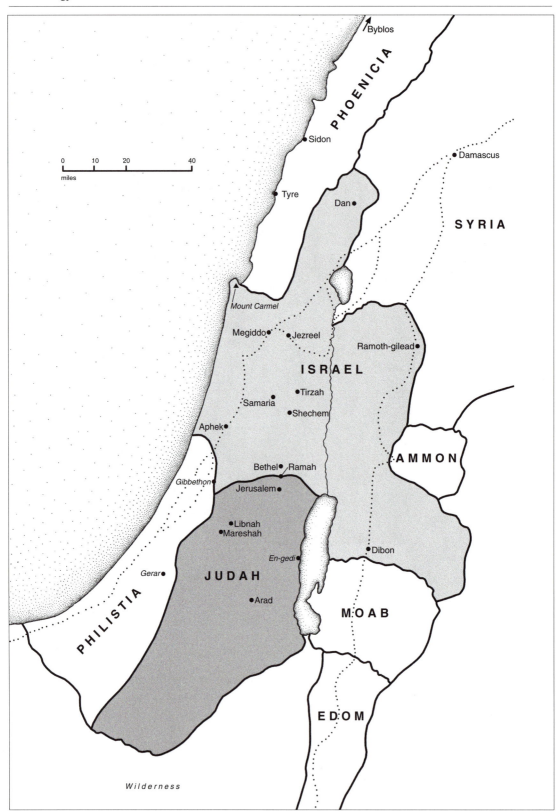

15.2. The early divided kingdom (trade routes are indicated by dotted line).

and were already in his service.[1] They apparently thought that, as a new king, Rehoboam should assert his authority; perhaps they also had visions of their own rise in power. In any event, they advised Rehoboam to rebuke the people for their temerity and to promise even harsher controls. Rehoboam unwisely chose the latter advice (1 Kings 12:14).

Rehoboam probably felt secure since the line of David had ruled a united Israel for over seventy years, since he represented the third generation in that line, and since he had the backing of a strong army. But Jeroboam had returned from Egypt after the death of Solomon, and he was present during the confrontation at Shechem. The biblical author gives no indication that Jeroboam promoted himself or whether Israel knew of Ahijah's prophecy (1 Kings 11:30–31), but somehow the northern tribes came to see Jeroboam as the man to support their position. When Rehoboam rejected the plea of the people, the refrain from the lips of Sheba (2 Sam. 20:1) was heard again (2 Chron. 10:16).

Rehoboam did not immediately recognize the seriousness of the moment, as he sent his royal official in charge of forced labor to meet with the people. Such an official, representing what the populace was protesting, could only aggravate the situation further. When the crowd stoned the official to death, Rehoboam finally realized his own danger and fled back to Jerusalem. At home, Rehoboam began to assemble an army to quell the revolt, but God sent the prophet Shemaiah to stop such preparations (1 Kings 12:24). The mobilization was ended, and Rehoboam accepted the fact that he would be king of only Judah. Nothing more is known about Shemaiah, but he must have been recognized as a true prophet of the Lord, and he illustrates the increasing role prophets play in the centuries that followed.

King Jeroboam of Israel

Jeroboam was made king over Israel (see illustration 15.2 for the boundaries of the two new nations).[2] Not only did Israel control more of Palestine's land area than did Judah, but that land area comprised the best pasturage and farmland—the region of Samaria and the Esdraelon Valley stretching east from Mount Carmel. Israel, but not Judah, had access to the Mediterranean and its increasing commercial traffic. Moreover, the major land trade routes between Egypt and Syria ran through Israel, but none through Judah. Finally, Israel had the larger population. To its advantage, Judah retained Jerusalem with its accumulated wealth and, most importantly, the temple where God had specified he would be worshiped.[3]

---

1. 1 Kings 12:8 might imply that instead of weighing the different opinions, Rehoboam immediately rejected the advice of Solomon's elders. For a study of these "young men," see Fox 1996.

2. Ahijah prophesied that Jeroboam would become king over ten tribes. The border of the resulting kingdoms of Judah and Israel ran through the territory of Benjamin, placing part of it in each nation. Compare 1 Kings 12:20 with 12:21, 23.

3. The mineral resources in Edom were lost at the end of Solomon's reign.

While Rehoboam maintained the southern capital at Jerusalem, Jeroboam established his capital at Shechem, the scene of the united kingdom's collapse. But Jeroboam was worried about the religious requirement for his people to visit the temple in Jerusalem each year. He believed his subjects would, in time, be wooed away and his life would be placed in danger. Therefore, after consultation, Jeroboam had golden calves set up, one in Dan and the other at Bethel. Then he declared the border with Judah closed (1 Kings 12:28).[4]

Scholars are divided over whether Jeroboam meant the golden calves as a break from true worship or whether he was trying to set up alternate places for worshiping God. His announcement is similar to that of Aaron at Mount Sinai (Exod. 32:4, 8), and it is possible that Jeroboam felt the calves could be acceptable pedestals for the worship of the Lord. If Jeroboam's placement of golden calves at Dan and Bethel was "innocent," his other religious innovations were not. Illegally, he began acting as high priest, and he allowed other non-Levites to enter the priesthood. He also set up high places within Israel and shifted the Feast of Tabernacles within the religious calendar (1 Kings 12:31–33).

Jeroboam's activities caused Levites and others faithful to the Lord to emigrate into Judah. Jeroboam's actions also caused the Lord to send a prophet from Judah to condemn his apostasy (1 Kings 13). When Jeroboam tried to seize the prophet, the Lord intervened in a forceful manner. Jeroboam's failure is especially tragic in light of the covenant God had made with him (1 Kings 11:37–38). God spelled out his condemnation through the same Ahijah who had prophesied to Jeroboam that he would become king (1 Kings 14:7–11).

King Rehoboam of Judah

Although Rehoboam was restrained from sending troops into Israel, he did engage in a military buildup (2 Chron. 11:5–12), presumably to guard against incursions from Philistia and Egypt, as well as from any designs Jeroboam might have. Rehoboam wisely spread some of his sons about the kingdom, giving them responsibility over fortified cities. Initially, Rehoboam served the Lord, and the religious fervor caused by the faithful flocking in from the north during his early years undoubtedly helped (2 Chron. 11:16–17). After only three years, however, Rehoboam began to fall away from God; high places, sacred pillars to the sex goddess Asherah, and other false deities began to dot the landscape of Judah (1 Kings 14:22–24). Even male cult prostitution, a part of the Canaanite religion Moses had specifically condemned, was allowed.

For two more years God showed mercy, allowing both Rehoboam and Jeroboam to continue in their apostasy. Then Egypt, which had been friendly in Solomon's reign, no longer found it necessary to continue that policy, and God's judgment came in the form of Shishak,

4. Avraham Biran, who has excavated for many years at Dan, found what he believes are the remains of the high place built by Jeroboam. See Laughlin 1981 and Shanks 1987a.

James Hoffmeier

15.3. Detail from a relief in the Karnak Temple at Thebes in Upper Egypt commemorating Pharaoh Shishak's raid into Palestine five years after the death of Solomon. Shishak holds a sword in one hand and in the other ropes, which are connected to 156 cartouches, ovals (each containing the name of a place Shishak claims to have defeated) to which bound bodies are added.

founder of Egypt's Dynasty 22 (2 Chron. 12:2, 4, 9; Kitchen 1989b). Pharaoh Shishak (sometimes transliterated Sheshonk or Shoshenq) was so proud of his campaign into Palestine that he had a relief commemorating his action carved on a wall of the Karnak Temple in Thebes. The relief shows Shishak subduing Palestine and names 156 places that he claims to have conquered in the raid. Almost 70 of the 156 names are in the Negev, including Arad, where level 11 came to a fiery end.[5] One explanation for this emphasis on the Negev is that Egypt was trying to cut Judah's link to the Red Sea so as to regain Egyptian control of trade with Arabia and Africa.

Shishak's Karnak relief claims that the Egyptian forces invaded Israel as well as Judah (see the left portion of illustration 15.4). The Bible

5. A shrine is associated with Arad's level 11, and it naturally raises the question of how a religious structure could have been permitted in addition to the one in Jerusalem. Perhaps it reflects conditions in the last years of Solomon's reign when he allowed pagan features within Jerusalem itself. For a survey of Arad's Solomonic and later history, see Herzog, Aharoni, and Rainey 1987.

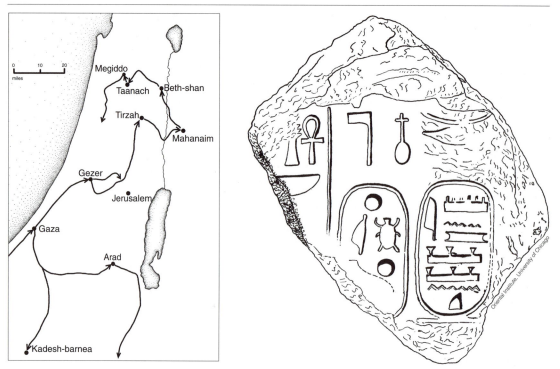

15.4. In 926 Pharaoh - Shishak marched his army into Palestine and invaded Israel and Judah (left). Fifteen-inch fragment of an Egyptian victory stele (right) found at Megiddo contains the birth name of Pharaoh Shishak on the right. The left cartouche containing his throne name distinguishes him from other pharaohs who had the same birth name.

does not mention any attack on the northern kingdom, and it is surprising that Shishak would harass Jeroboam, for whom he had recently provided refuge from Solomon. Even though by this time Egyptian kings had the habit of padding their accomplishments, corroborating evidence shows that Shishak did indeed sweep into northern Israel.

On the temple wall at Karnak, Shishak lists northern cities such as Taanach, Beth-shan, and Megiddo, and at Megiddo the excavators found remains of an Egyptian victory stele that Shishak had placed in that city. Although only a portion of the stele was recovered, it is sufficient to determine which part of the original monument it had been. More importantly, the temple relief and the stele fragment show that, although Egypt was reduced to a nuisance role among world powers, five years after the death of Solomon it was able to terrorize both fragments of Israel's once-united kingdom. The Bible mentions only the attack on Judah, but archaeology reveals that sin brought sorrow to Israel as well.[6]

King Abijah of Judah

Rehoboam died and was succeeded by his son Abijah (1 Kings 15:1) while Jeroboam was still king in Israel.[7] While Rehoboam was alive,

6. Since it was an earlier native Egyptian pharaoh who gave Solomon a princess for a wife, that Egyptian princess and political tie meant nothing to Shishak, who was Libyan by ancestry. See Kitchen 1986: 432–47 for a study of Shishak's campaign.

7. Abijah (also called Abijam) was not the oldest son but was the firstborn of Rehoboam's favorite wife.

there was "war . . . continually" between him and Jeroboam (1 Kings 14:30). These clashes were probably only border skirmishes, but at least by the time of Abijah it is obvious that conditions had become more serious and that Judah had emerged as the stronger of the two nations. This state of affairs is clear from the large-scale battle begun when Abijah invaded Israel and walked into an ambush (2 Chron. 13). Abijah escaped the larger army of Israel with God's help and then took possession of several cities belonging to the northern kingdom. Most telling, Abijah captured Bethel, the southern cult city of Israel.

King Asa of Judah

Asa, one of Abijah's sons, began his reign in very godly fashion (1 Kings 15:11–13). He did away with the foreign altars, high places, the male cult prostitutes, and the idols—including an image of Asherah belonging to his mother.[8] For these acts God gave peace to his nation, and during that time Asa built walled and towered cities to fortify Judah. Second Chronicles 14:1 states that Asa had peace for ten years, but no trouble is recorded until his fourteenth year. In that year Asa was attacked by a large Egyptian army whose general was Zerah (2 Chron. 14:9–15; 16:8). Zerah was an Ethiopian, probably commanding the army of Egypt for Pharaoh Osorkon I, son of Shishak. Osorkon would have been trying to duplicate his father's successful raid into Palestine. Outnumbered, Asa faced the Egyptians at Mareshah (later called Marisa), where he called on the Lord for help before he engaged the enemy. God routed the Egyptian army, and Asa's army pursued them as far as Gerar.

In his fifteenth year Asa began to feel pressures from the north. King Baasha of Israel began to fortify Ramah near the border with Israel. Second Chronicles 15:9 states, "Many defected to [Asa] from Israel," and Baasha wanted to curtail such traffic. Asa clearly believed that more than a closed border was implied, and, since Ramah is south of Bethel, Baasha might have also been trying to recover that religious center. The previous year, Asa had relied on God for aid, but this time he used gold and silver from his own treasury and from the temple to induce the king of Syria to break his treaty with Israel and forge a new one with Judah (1 Kings 15:18–19).

The results of Asa's treaty with Syria were threefold. First, the Syrian king sent his armies south into Israel where they conquered cities in the vicinity of the Sea of Galilee (1 Kings 15:20). This foray awakened Syrian interest in the lands to its south, and Israel experienced several decades of struggle with its northern neighbor.[9] Second, the intrusion of Syrian forces led Baasha to break off his fortification of Ramah (1 Kings 15:21). Presumably Baasha redirected his attention to his

8. Maacah was either Asa's mother or grandmother (1 Kings 15:13). Her apostasy caused Asa to remove her from being queen mother.

9. The initial conclusion drawn from the inscription on a stele fragment found at Dan in the summer of 1993 was that Ben-Hadad of Damascus held the city of Dan. Further fragments found in 1994 necessitated a different understanding; see chapter 16.

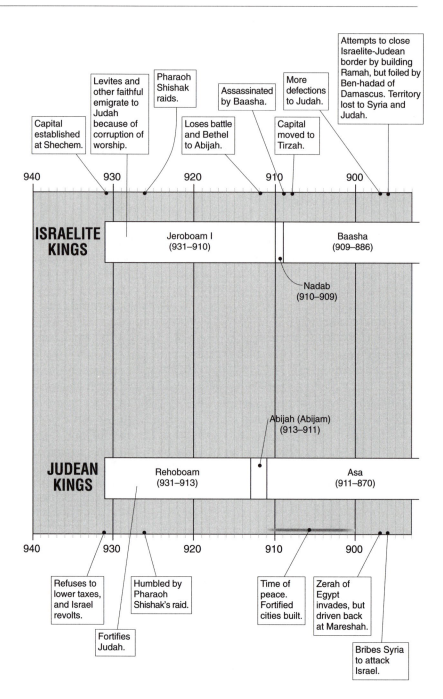

15.5. The early divided kingdom.

northern border. This distraction enabled Asa to mobilize the Judeans to enter Israel and carry off the stones and timber that had been put into Ramah. The appropriated materials were taken a short distance north and used to fortify Geba and Mizpah as outposts for a newly aligned border.[10]

Asa's involvement with Syria maintained Judah's strength over Israel

10. 2 Chron. 15:8 also states that Asa captured cities in the Hill Country of Ephraim.

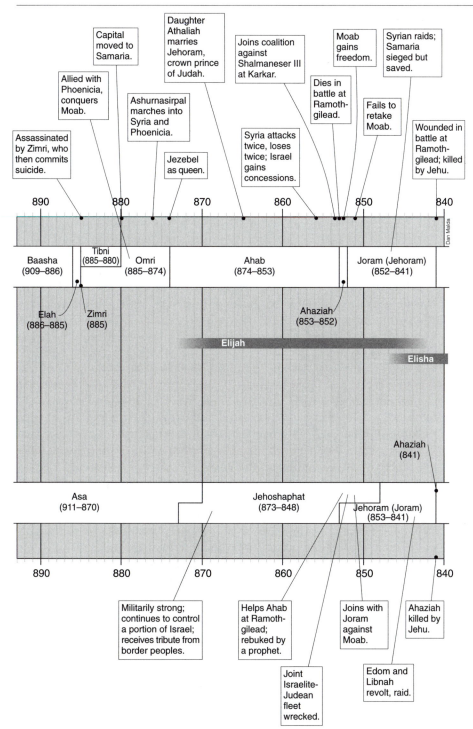

Assassinated by Zimri, who then commits suicide.

Allied with Phoenicia, conquers Moab.

Capital moved to Samaria.

Daughter Athaliah marries Jehoram, crown prince of Judah.

Ashurnasirpal marches into Syria and Phoenicia.

Jezebel as queen.

Joins coalition against Shalmaneser III at Karkar.

Syria attacks twice, loses twice; Israel gains concessions.

Dies in battle at Ramoth-gilead.

Moab gains freedom.

Fails to retake Moab.

Syrian raids; Samaria sieged but saved.

Wounded in battle at Ramoth-gilead; killed by Jehu.

890   880   870   860   850   840

Baasha (909–886)

Tibni (885–880)

Omri (885–874)

Ahab (874–853)

Joram (Jehoram) (852–841)

Elah (886–885)   Zimri (885)

Ahaziah (853–852)

Elijah

Elisha

Ahaziah (841)

Asa (911–870)

Jehoshaphat (873–848)

Jehoram (Joram) (853–841)

890   880   870   860   850   840

Militarily strong; continues to control a portion of Israel; receives tribute from border peoples.

Helps Ahab at Ramoth-gilead; rebuked by a prophet.

Joins with Joram against Moab.

Ahaziah killed by Jehu.

Joint Israelite-Judean fleet wrecked.

Edom and Libnah revolt, raid.

and benefited his country materially, but his advantage had been gained at a price. The third consequence of Asa's misplaced trust was that it cost him the support of the Lord (2 Chron. 16:7–10). The Bible says little about Asa's remaining twenty-six-year reign in Jerusalem. If

2 Chronicles 16:12 is representative, Asa's allegiance to God was a thing of the past.[11]

Kings Baasha, Elah, Zimri, and Omri of Israel

All of Baasha's reign as king of Israel falls within Asa's years in Judah and, although 1 Kings 15:32 says there was continual hostility between the two, their only recorded contact is the one described above. Baasha was not from the family of Jeroboam, but had usurped the throne by assassinating Jeroboam's son, Nadab, while both were at the siege of Philistine Gibbethon (1 Kings 15:27).[12] When Baasha took the throne he carried out a slaughter that would prove all too typical for Israel (1 Kings 15:29). The Bible says little more about Baasha's years as king except that he moved Israel's capital to Tirzah.

While Asa continued his long reign over Judah, Israel experienced continued dynastic upheaval. Elah, son of Baasha, ascended to the throne when his father died, but his reign was cut short when Zimri, the commander over half of the nation's chariotry, assassinated him and declared himself ruler over Israel. Predictably, a bloodbath followed (1 Kings 16:11).

Zimri's coup may have been on impulse, or perhaps he had not sufficiently cleared his intentions with others. Israel was again besieging the Philistine city of Gibbethon when word of Elah's death reached the army. The army immediately proclaimed Omri, their commander, king of Israel. Omri then withdrew the army from Philistia and besieged Tirzah instead. The city fell and Zimri, after only seven days as king, committed suicide by burning the palace down on himself (1 Kings 16:18).[13] Zimri's suicide did not, however, give Omri a clear claim to the throne. Part of Israel sided with another claimant named Tibni, and for five years there was conflict between the two factions. The Bible gives no details beyond saying that Omri's people "prevailed" and that he became king of all Israel when Tibni died (1 Kings 16:21–22).

The Bible supplies little data on the life or reign of Omri, but it does say that he built a new capital at the more strategic Samaria. Samaria was the third and last city to serve as Israel's capital. Another detail given is that Omri's son, Ahab, married the Phoenician Princess Jezebel. The Bible is silent about any war between Omri and Judah, an omission that might reflect actual circumstances and foreshadow the rapprochement that soon became obvious between the two nations.

11. Archaeological evidence shows that the fortress at Arad destroyed by Shishak was rebuilt (level 10) during the reign of either Asa or Jehoshaphat, and its shrine reactivated. Such a rebuilding would fit the latter years of Asa's reign. Level 10 is said to have continued in operation until the last years of the early divided kingdom, but it would be very strange if worship at Arad was not terminated earlier, during one of Jehoshaphat's religious revivals.

12. All that is said of Nadab, Jeroboam's son, is that he continued his father's evil (1 Kings 15:26). The Davidic line continued throughout the life of Judah, but Israel repeatedly experienced coups, bloodbaths, and new ruling houses.

13. Level 7b at Tirzah (Tell el-Farah North) was assigned to this assault, but the palace was not found in the excavated portion of the site.

British Museum

15.6. Statue of Ashurnasirpal II found at Nimrud, now in the British Museum (approximately forty-one inches high). Ashurnasirpal, the first Assyrian king to make mention of Israel (referring to it as the "land of Omri"), holds a mace and a sword (not visible in this view). The appearance of the king gives little insight into his personality, but texts like the epigraph in chapter 16 reveal his brutality.

During Omri's reign, still another foreign nation edged into Israel's history. In 876 Assyrian King Ashurnasirpal marched westward out of Nineveh. He crossed the Euphrates River and received heavy tribute from Carchemish, controlled at that time by Neo-Hittites (*ANET* 275):

> I took over the chariot corps, the cavalry, and the infantry of Carchemish. The kings of all surrounding countries came to me, embraced my feet, and I took hostages from them, and they marched with me toward the Lebanon.[14]

Ashurnasirpal continued west, receiving more tribute, adding more local people to his army, and settling some of his people into surrendered towns. When towns would not surrender, he adopted the following policy (*ANET* 276):

> I destroyed them, tore down the walls, and burned the towns with fire; I caught the survivors and impaled them on stakes in front of their towns. At that time I seized the entire extent of the Lebanon mountain and reached the Great Sea. . . . I cleaned my weapons in the deep sea and performed sheep offerings to all the gods. The tribute of the seacoast—from the inhabitants of Tyre, Sidon, Byblos, . . . —their tribute I received and they embraced my feet.

14. For typical propaganda by Ashurnasirpal II, see the epigraph to chapter 16. Propaganda was used by the Assyrians to frighten many cities into submission. For the siege tactics of Ashurnasirpal II and subsequent Assyrian kings, see Albenda 1980 and Bleibtreu 1990, 1991.

15.7. Line drawing of an orthostat from the palace of Ashurnasirpal II at Nimrud. The Assyrians became masters of siege warfare, and this scene depicts the various ways they defeated a city. From left to right: armored sappers tear out the base of a wall, tunnelers undermine the city wall, a mobile tower batters down the wall. The defenders have caught the ram with a chain and are trying to pull it up, and at the same time Assyrian soldiers are pulling down on the ram to break it free from the defenders' chain. Archers, protected by coats of mail or by partners holding shields, fire arrows into the besieged city. An adjoining panel depicts Assyrians storming over the battlements by means of scaling ladders.

I ascended the mountains of the Amanus and cut down there logs of cedars, stone-pines, cypresses, and pines and performed sheep offerings to my gods. I had made a sculptured stele commemorating my heroic achievements and erected it there.[15]

Ashurnasirpal's foray into northern Syria and Phoenicia did not extend Assyria's borders in that direction; it was little more than a raid, albeit a costly one to Jezebel's father and other kings to the north of Israel. The campaign did, however, put the Near East on notice that Assyria was awakening from its long slumber. Israel itself was not affected by this first incursion of Assyrian troops, but Assyria had become aware of that nation's existence. From the ninth to the seventh centuries, Assyrian records often called Israel *mat-Omri* ("land of Omri") or *bit-Omri* ("house of Omri").

The Moabite Stone (also called the Mesha Stele), one of the earliest archaeological finds relating to the Bible, adds to the information available on the reign of Omri. The stone was found at Dibon in southern Transjordan in 1868. The opening lines read (*ANE* 1:209–10; *ANET* 320):

I am Mesha, son of Chemosh[16] . . . , king of Moab, the Dibonite—my father had reigned over Moab thirty years, and I reigned after my father—who made this high place for Chemosh . . . because he saved me from all the kings and caused me to triumph over all my adversaries. As for King Omri of Israel, he humbled Moab many years, for Chemosh was angry at his land. And his son [Ahab] followed him and he also said, "I will humble Moab." In my time he spoke thus, but I have triumphed over him and over his house, while Israel has perished forever! Now Omri had occupied the land of Medeba, and Israel had dwelt there in his time and half the time of his son Ahab, forty years; but Chemosh dwelt there in my time.[17]

15. As mentioned in chapter 2, Mesopotamia was deficient in certain metals and wood. Assyria now began a conquest to acquire these commodities.

16. Chemosh was the national Moabite god.

17. The Moabite Stone was probably carved early in the late divided kingdom, but it reflects the reign of Omri. Note that the title of Horn's 1986 article is misleading, since the stele was not actually blown to pieces.

Réunion des Musées Nationaux

15.8. The Moabite Stone (black basalt; three feet three inches high), now in the Louvre, commemorates King Mesha's successful revolt against Israel's control. The stele was shattered shortly after its discovery, and some of the pieces were never recovered. Fortunately, an impression of the whole stele was made before this tragedy.

When the Moabite Stone was found, it gave the solution to a question that had gone unanswered for centuries. The Bible states that David conquered Moab, that Solomon held Moab, and that Moab broke free at the outset of the divided kingdom. But in the next biblical reference to Moab, 2 Kings 3:4, Ahab is receiving tribute from Moab. Nowhere does the Bible state how or when Moab was reclaimed for Ahab to be receiving such tribute. The Moabite Stone provides that information, telling, as it does, of Omri's conquest from the Moabite point of view. The Bible authors were not particularly interested in the material accomplishments of evil kings, but archaeology reveals that Omri was a more important figure than we would have otherwise known.[18]

King Ahab of Israel and King Jehoshaphat of Judah

Ahab succeeded his father to the throne of Israel in 874. He so surpassed his father and the previous kings of Israel in his apostasy that 1 Kings 16:33 declares he "did more to provoke the LORD God of Israel, than all the kings of Israel who were before him" (see Stern 1993a). Specifically, Ahab worshiped the god Baal (an altar and temple to that god were built in the capital city) and erected a pillar to the sex goddess Ashtoreth. First Kings 21:25 states that Jezebel incited her husband to evil, and she would have been eager to introduce Baal-Melqart (the Sidonian form of Baal worship) into her new land. Indeed, Jezebel was so zealous for her Phoenician deity that she even caused the death of the prophets of the Lord (1 Kings 18:13). Further, as a Phoenician princess, Jezebel had grown up to believe that royalty was not to be denied.[19] Therefore she could not understand why, when Ahab was rebuffed by Naboth (1 Kings 21), her husband simply went off and sulked. Thoughtful wife that she was, Jezebel had Naboth murdered to obtain the vineyard for her husband.

Because of such wickedness, the prophet Elijah declared to Ahab that both rain and dew would cease in Israel until he spoke the word to restore them. A famine resulted and lasted three years, severely hurting Israel (1 Kings 18:5). In a religious context, the famine attacked Baal, the god of vegetation and rain. King Ahab went to great lengths (unsuccessfully) to find Elijah, in hopes of persuading him to restore the rainfall. Finally, in obedience to God, Elijah met King Ahab and proposed a test of strength between Elijah and the prophets of Baal. Ahab accepted the challenge, so Elijah, 450 prophets of Baal, 400 prophets of Asherah, and a large crowd assembled on the eastern edge of the Carmel ridge. There, overlooking the plain of Esdraelon, Elijah criticized the people for their religious wavering (1 Kings 18:21). Elijah suggested that he and the prophets of Baal each be supplied with wood and an ox for sacrifice so that a test could be made to see who was following the true god (1 Kings 18:24–29).

Elijah shows himself versed enough in Canaanite religion to know that it contained prayers designed to awaken gods, to summon them back from a journey, and the like. Aware of their theology, Elijah jokingly suggested they try some of its foolishness.[20] After the prophets of Baal had failed, Elijah called on the Lord "that this people may know

18. Lemaire 1994 claims to have found reference to the "House of David" on the Moabite Stone. This reading has been rejected by P. Davies 1994, but supported by Rainey 1994b.

19. The Tale of Aqhat (*ANE* 1:118–32; *ANET* 149–55) gives an example of the "might equals right" mind-set that would have been programmed into Jezebel. For an introduction to the Phoenicians, see Ward 1994b.

20. For works dealing with Canaanite religion, see n. 24 in chapter 10.

that you, O Lord, are God," and suddenly his altar began to blaze. The crowd, struck by the futility of the day-long worship of Baal compared to God's immediate response to Elijah, at least momentarily acknowledged that "the Lord, he is God; the Lord, he is God." A short, poignant story relates how Elijah then restored rain to Israel (1 Kings 18:41–45).

Most of Elijah's ministry took place during the kingship of Ahab, but his activity cannot be dated to specific years within the king's reign. Neither can all of Ahab's activities be safely plotted out. Ahab was married to Jezebel when he took the throne, so the references to his apostasy possibly reflect an early attitude. The incident with Naboth probably occurred late in his reign.

Ahab continued the construction his father, Omri, had begun at Samaria, and the small portion of the palace that has been excavated there reveals a quality of building equal to that of Solomon's day. First Kings 22:39 makes passing reference to Ahab's house of ivory, an allusion to inlaid palace furniture. Ivory inlays were popular with wealthy families in Syria-Palestine, and the Assyrians coveted such decorations when they began to ravage the area in the late divided kingdom.[21]

Jehoshaphat was coregent with his father for three years, and when he became sole king of Judah he began to improve both the political and religious climates of his country. The army was deployed in fortified cities and garrisons within Judah, as well as in the cities that Judah still controlled in southern Israel (2 Chron. 17:2).[22] Jehoshaphat's military power compelled Philistines to the west and "Arabians" to the east to send tribute to Jerusalem. Jehoshaphat removed the high places and Asherim; but even more important, he sent officials, Levites, and priests throughout Judah to teach the people from the "book of the law of the Lord" (2 Chron. 17:9). Jehoshaphat "took great pride in the ways of the Lord" (2 Chron. 17:6).

The thaw between Judah and Israel, which seems to have begun in the days of Omri and Asa, became complete when Athaliah, daughter of Ahab and Jezebel, married Jehoram, crown prince of Judah (2 Kings 8:18). This intermarriage between the two royal families took place about 865 and was destined to cause great harm to Judah.[23]

Little specific information is available about the middle years of either Jehoshaphat or Ahab. The Moabite Stone indicates that Moab believed itself free of Israel's control about midway through Ahab's reign. A weakened Israel is also implied later on when King Ben-Hadad of Syria was so emboldened that he brought his army south to besiege Samaria. When Ahab refused the tribute demanded by Ben-Hadad, the two kings traded epigrams (1 Kings 20:10–11).[24] With the armies

21. Little of Ahab's palace remains because Herod the Great's builders destroyed most of it when they put down deep foundations for their own constructions. For a survey of ivory in the ancient Near East, see Shanks 1985.

22. The stratum 5 fortress at En Haseva (alternately Hatzeva) south of the Dead Sea might have been built by Jehoshaphat; see Cohen and Yisrael 1995.

23. The marriage had to be early enough for their son, Ahaziah of Judah, to be twenty-two years old in 841.

24. The basalt monument known as the Melqart Stele was erected by a Bir-Hadad, a name equivalent to Hebrew Ben-Hadad. Debate has long centered on which of the three kings of Damascus mentioned in the Bible should be credited with the stele. Pitard 1988 argues that the Bir-Hadad in question has no relationship to those kings.

poised for battle, a prophet approached Ahab and announced that the Syrians would be defeated by the Lord. Both Ahab and Israel were apostate, but God reached out and provided them with evidence that "I am the Lord." As predicted, the Syrians were routed.

At the beginning of the next year the Syrians, thinking that Israel's "gods are gods of the mountains," brought their army into the plains around Aphek (located somewhere near the southeast end of the Sea of Galilee) where "surely we shall be stronger than they" (1 Kings 20:23). However, the Lord again gave Ahab the victory to impress upon him that "I am the Lord" and to convince the Syrians that they were not opposing some localized deity. In this second battle, Ahab captured the Syrian king, but spared his life in return for trading rights in Damascus and the return of cities that Syria had captured earlier. This treaty between Israel and Syria left Ahab in a dominant position, but God was not pleased (1 Kings 20:35–43).

Ahab was becoming a strong king, which is evidenced in his playing an important role in one of the famous battles of antiquity. In 858, the year he took the throne of Assyria, Shalmaneser III marched west, killing and plundering en route to the Mediterranean where he erected a stele and tabulated the tribute received from his campaign. In 853 Shalmaneser III marched west once more. Tribute, but no resistance was offered him until he reached the vicinity of Karkar (sometimes transliterated Qarqar) in northern Syria. There Shalmaneser records that a coalition of twelve kings opposed his advance (*ANE* 1:190–91; *ANET* 278–79):

> I destroyed, tore down, and burned down Karkar. . . . [Its king] brought along to help him 1,200 chariots, 1,200 cavalrymen, 20,000 foot soldiers of [Hadadezer] of Damascus; 700 chariots, 700 cavalrymen, 10,000 foot soldiers of Irhuleni from Hamath; 2,000 chariots, 10,000 foot soldiers of Ahab, the Israelite; 500 soldiers from Que; 1,000 soldiers from Musri; 10 chariots, 10,000 soldiers from Irqanata; 200 soldiers . . . from Arvad; 200 soldiers from Usanata; 30 chariots, 10,000 soldiers . . . from Shian; 1,000 camel-riders . . . from Arabia; . . . soldiers . . . from Ammon—all together these were twelve kings. They rose against me for a decisive battle. I fought with them with the support of the mighty forces of Ashur[25] . . . and I did inflict a defeat upon them. . . . I slew 14,000 of their soldiers with the sword, descending upon them like Adad when he makes a rainstorm pour down. I spread their corpses everywhere, filling the entire plain with their widely scattered fleeing soldiers. During the battle I made their blood flow. . . . The plain was too small to let all their souls descend into the netherworld, the vast field gave out when it came to bury them. With their corpses I spanned the Orontes before there was a bridge. Even during the battle I took from them their chariots, their horses broken to the yoke.

Shalmaneser's claims acquire a hollow ring when studied together with other documents pertaining to his reign. He left unsaid that the Assyrian army proceeded no further than Karkar, and there is none of the usual boasting about pursuing the enemy. There is only passing mention of booty, and none of tribute. The Assyrians were confronted with a coalition fielding approximately twice their number of chariots;

25. Ashur was the chief god of Assyria.

British Museum

15.9. Portion of a bronze band from the main palace gate at Balawat. The Assyrians nailed thin bands to the wooden leaves of their gates to prevent successful torching of the entryway. This band (eleven inches high) is only one of many that Shalmaneser III commissioned to cover doors over twenty feet high. Like orthostats (illustration 15.7), they carry the story of the king's wars. Although Shalmaneser III was stopped at Karkar, these bands portray the success he had in the west twelve years later. The upper register shows tribute from the island city of Tyre being transported ashore; below left, the Assyrian army leaves its camp to subdue another city.

if Shalmaneser was correct in claiming victory, it could well have been only Pyrrhic in nature.

In biblical studies the Battle of Karkar is important for two reasons. First, in the fifty-to-sixty-thousand-man coalition that opposed the Assyrians, Ahab is given credit for fielding the second largest army and over half the chariots; only the Syrian contingent was larger. This battle report suggests that, although Ahab was evil in God's eyes, he had probably become the most powerful king the northern kingdom had yet known (Elat 1975).[26] Second, the Battle of Karkar represents the first physical contact between Israel and Assyria.

The Battle of Karkar was fought in 853, and when it ended Ahab apparently kept his troops under arms because he had another military engagement in mind for that same year. Ahab proposed to end the three-year peace between Israel and Syria by recapturing the important trading city of Ramoth-gilead. Jehoshaphat joined forces with Ahab in this campaign and, after the ominous forecast given by a prophet, even agreed to lead the enemy into mistaking him for Ahab (1 Kings 22:30).

Jehoshaphat had to be aware that opposing forces often made a concerted effort to kill the enemy king. That he was willing to act as a decoy to protect the life of Ahab probably implies that he had no other choice. Ever since the days of Abijah there had been clear indications that Judah was stronger than Israel, and even in the opening days of Jehoshaphat's reign that superiority was evident. But only a few years after the fateful intermarriage between Israel and Judah, the weight of power seems to have shifted. Jehoshaphat's action in the Battle of Ramoth-gilead and his continued cooperation with Israel seem to signal the beginning of Israel's superiority over Judah. Still, Israel failed to capture Ramoth-gilead from Syria, and the prophecy was fulfilled. De-

---

26. It is also to be remembered that some scholars believe the "stables" at Megiddo date to the time of Ahab.

spite Ahab's strategy, a stray arrow mortally struck him down (1 Kings 22:31–35).[27]

The Close of the Early Divided Kingdom

Jehoshaphat seems to have been extremely busy after the Battle of Ramoth-gilead. Second Chronicles 19:4–11 reports that he began judicial reform and another religious revival; perhaps his zeal was in response to a prophet's rebuke for his entanglement with Ahab (2 Chron. 19:2–3). In the same year, a coalition of Moabites, Ammonites, and Edomites massed at En-gedi in preparation to attack Jehoshaphat (2 Chron. 20).[28] Fearfully, Jehoshaphat called on the Lord and learned to his relief that God would handle the enemy. Judah was saved when the Moabites and Ammonites conspired against the Edomites, and then, after slaughtering the Edomites, they fell into bloody dispute among themselves.

Unfortunately, in the same year (assuming that the events in 2 Chron. 19–20 are sequential), Jehoshaphat formed another alliance with Israel—this time with Ahaziah, son of Ahab and the new king of Israel. The two countries together began to build a commercial fleet at Ezion-geber on the Red Sea, but their goal was never realized. God was displeased with such an association, and the "ships were broken," perhaps by a storm (1 Kings 22:48).

Ahaziah of Israel died childless and Joram, another of Ahab's sons, took his place.[29] One of Joram's early goals was to try to reclaim Moab; 2 Kings 3:4–5 states that the Moabite King Mesha paid tribute to Israel, but rebelled following the death of Ahab. In the Moabite Stone, Mesha claimed that he had been subservient to Israel only half the days of Ahab. From the Moabite perspective, therefore, the break took place earlier than Israel was willing to admit. Joram asked Jehoshaphat of Judah to aid him in his attack on Moab. Amazingly, Jehoshaphat was again cooperative and even brought Edom (again subject to Judah) into the coalition. Moab lost the battle, but Israel apparently did not regain the territory.[30]

Elisha took Elijah's place as a prophet about midpoint in Joram's reign.[31] Several episodes in Elisha's life seemingly date to the reign

27. Ahab was quite likely hit in the armpit; body armor would have protected the entire torso but provision had to be made for the arms to have full range of motion.

28. Edom was in revolt against Judah. 1 Kings 22:47 refers to that nation having a deputy rather than a king.

29. Joram was also called Jehoram, the two names being used interchangeably (cf. 2 Chron. 22:5, 7). I use Joram as the name for the king of Israel and Jehoram for that of the king of Judah.

30. The closure of this campaign, where the Moabite king sacrificed his son and Israel broke off its siege, is much debated; see Horn 1986: 56 and Margalit 1986. To add to the stream of suggestions: the sacrifice could have caused contention in the coalition concerning what their response to the act should be. The Edomite allies could have become upset and frightened. Israel could have been pressured to accept that the siege was going to be too protracted to be worth the effort.

31. Elijah was still functioning when Jehoram became sole ruler in Judah. When Elisha asked for a double portion of Elijah's spirit (2 Kings 2:9), he was asking to be Elijah's successor in the same way the eldest son received a double portion of his father's estate.

of Joram and reveal strong Syrian pressures on Israel. In one incident, the commander of the Syrian army was able to freely wander about in Israel (2 Kings 5). In another story, the Syrian army besieged the capital city of Samaria, and mothers were reduced to eating their own sons (2 Kings 6:24–7:20). In this latter narrative, the Lord showed his continuing love for wayward Israel by frightening the Syrians away. If these incidents date to the reign of Joram, they reflect how unstable Israel had become only a few years after the strong rule of Ahab.

Jehoram had been coregent with his father Jehoshaphat for several years, but he had not absorbed his father's devotion to God. Perhaps Jehoram was even instrumental in some of Jehoshaphat's unwise decisions during their joint reign. Second Kings 8:18 implies that Jehoram's apostasy resulted from his marriage to Athaliah, daughter of Ahab. Certainly, when Jehoram became sole ruler over Judah, he behaved in a way all too typical of kings in his wife's home country. It was Judah's turn to witness a bloodbath (2 Chron. 21:4).

Jehoram's reign was hardly successful, either politically or religiously. Edom to the southeast revolted and set up its own king, and the city of Libnah also declared its freedom (2 Kings 8:20–22). Even worse, the Philistines formed a coalition that invaded Judah, sacked Jerusalem, and killed all of Jehoram's family except his youngest son. In the king's last two years he suffered a painful illness that finally killed him. Second Chronicles 21:20 candidly concludes that when he died it was "with no one's regret" and that he was not buried "in the tombs of the kings."

Twenty-two-year-old Ahaziah (not to be confused with the slightly earlier King Ahaziah of Israel) succeeded his father to the throne of Judah in 841, but he had little opportunity to occupy it. That same year, his uncle, King Joram of Israel, was waging war for the control of Ramoth-gilead.[32] Ahaziah accompanied his uncle to battle and to the fateful event that ended the early divided kingdom.

During the conflict for Ramoth-gilead, Joram was slightly wounded and retired to the city of Jezreel to recuperate. Subsequently, Ahaziah left the battle to visit his uncle, thus placing both kings together in Jezreel. About that same time Elisha commissioned a prophet to go to Ramoth-gilead and meet with Jehu, one of Israel's army captains. The prophet privately anointed Jehu as new king over Israel and charged him to end the "house of Ahab" because of its sins (2 Kings 9:4–10). When Jehu reluctantly told the other captains what had transpired, they declared him king (2 Kings 9:13). Jehu then took a company of soldiers, and they quickly drove their chariots toward Jezreel. The detailed account of Jehu's arrival and the killings that followed marks the end of the early divided kingdom (2 Kings 9:17–27).[33]

32. They fought against Hazael, who had recently usurped the throne of Damascus as Elisha had predicted (2 Kings 8:13).

33. Recent excavations have found that Jezreel was an elaborately fortified site. See Williamson 1996.

The Early Divided Kingdom in Review

At the outset, political relations between Judah and Israel were hostile. Although Israel would seem to have had more advantages in land, commerce, and population, Judah was the stronger nation for most of the period. Their shift to weaker status seems to become evident at the Battle of Ramoth-gilead in 853 and can be attributed to Judah's earlier intermarriage with Israel.

Foreign powers became increasingly involved in the fortunes of the early divided kingdom. Egypt troubled both nations in the early years and attacked Judah once during the reign of Asa. In spite of those two raids, however, Egypt was not a great threat. In the last half of the early divided kingdom, Assyria came more and more into view, even pitting its army against a coalition that included Ahab at the Battle of Karkar. But Assyria's dominance over Israel had not yet begun. Phoenicia continued the friendly relations with Israel that had been established during the united kingdom. Other neighboring nations played minor roles, sometimes by bringing tribute to Judah and Israel and other times by declaring their freedom. Of the foreign nations, Syria posed the major threat in the early divided kingdom, but primarily to Israel since it was a buffer for Judah.

The biblical authors rate all the kings of Israel as evil. While that is true in the religious history of the nation, some kings were powerful and good in the secular realm. Ahab was probably the most successful northern king from the standpoint of material gain. The kings of Judah were a mixture of good and evil. Jehoshaphat, although not always wise, was the best from both the religious and the secular point of view. Elijah and Elisha were the prominent prophets of the period, and it is not incidental that God placed both of them in apostate Israel.

The Chronology of the Kings of Israel and Judah

Beginning with the first millennium there is suddenly a wealth of chronological data available. All the kings of Israel and Judah are listed, together with the length of their individual reigns (e.g., 1 Kings 14:20) and with synchronisms between Israel and Judah (e.g., 1 Kings 15:1), and the accession age of the Judean kings is often given (e.g., 1 Kings 22:42). Sometimes the exact time is recorded for an event that took place during a king's reign (e.g., 2 Kings 25:1), or the number of years between one event and another is given (e.g., 2 Kings 14:17). Some events are recorded in both Old Testament and extrabiblical history (e.g., 2 Kings 15:19, which is also recounted in the annals of Tiglath-pileser III; see *ANE* 1:193–94; *ANET* 283–84) and with synchronisms between the reigns of Hebrew and other kings (e.g., Jer. 25:1).

This abundance of data is markedly different from earlier periods, where little information exists for establishing dates.[34] Still, when an

34. Critical scholarship generally takes the position that premonarchial history is largely a first-millennium assemblage of folklore and embellished memory. It does not

attempt is made to draw together all the varieties of information noted above, it is soon obvious that not all the interlocking figures agree with each other. The apparent disharmony is so marked that charges of "obvious error" have been made against the biblical text.

The alleged errors take various forms. For example, 2 Kings 8:25 and 9:29 differ by one year in their synchronisms between the kings of Israel and Judah. Another disharmony is brought to light when the reigns of kings are added up. Jeroboam and Rehoboam became kings at the same time, and the later kings Joram and Ahaziah died together. It must follow therefore that as much time elapsed from the beginning of Rehoboam's reign to the end of Ahaziah's reign (two kings of Judah) as elapsed from the beginning of Jeroboam's reign to the end of Joram's reign (two kings of Israel). But, simple addition shows that ninety-eight years elapsed between the coronation of Jeroboam and the death of Joram, but only ninety-five years between the crowning of Rehoboam and the murder of Ahaziah. A third example of the problems encountered in the chronology of the kings is found when 2 Kings 13:10; 14:1–2, 23; and 15:1 are plotted out: there appears to be a period of twelve years in which Judah had no king.

Problems such as these have long been recognized, and the Septuagint translators seem to have altered some verses to "correct" certain of the glaring discrepancies. Through the centuries scholars have worked out various systems in an attempt to reconcile the apparent problems. Unfortunately, several of their systems take extrabiblical data to be more trustworthy than the biblical. Other writers have proclaimed their discovery of hidden chronological codes that can penetrate the "veil of magic numbers" (the phrase is from Stenring 1965: 25, an example of the mystic treatment sometimes given to Bible chronology).

In 1951, Edwin R. Thiele published his study on the chronology of the kings (now in its third revised edition; 1983). Thiele discovered that the biblical chronology made sense and fit with the extrabiblical data and that the alleged discrepancies were resolved when the fundamental principles of biblical and nonbiblical ancient Near Eastern chronology were understood. He found the following five principles governing ancient chronology:

1. The years of a king's reign were credited according to accession or nonaccession years (see illustration 15.10 for how the two systems differ). In the accession-year system, a king was given credit for the year in which he died. His successor treated the remainder of that calendar year as his accession period and began to count his own reign at the onset of the new year. Under the nonaccession-year system, the king was still given credit for the year in which he died, but his successor would count the remainder of that same year as his first year of reign. When the next full year began, the new king began his second year. Obviously, each time

---

seem reasonable, however, that such great interest was paid to detailed first-millennium chronology, while an elaborate supporting chronology was not fabricated for premonarchial history. It would seem more plausible that the premonarchial history was written, as it claims, prior to this emphasis on chronological detail.

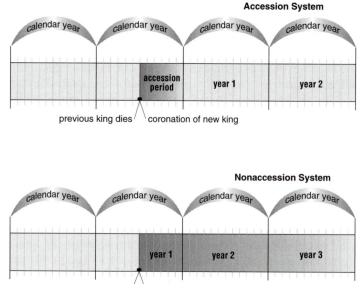

15.10. Accession and nonaccession systems for computing a king's reign.

there was a new king under the nonaccession-year system, an artificial year was implanted in the chronology.

2. Israel and Judah alternated between the accession and nonaccession systems during the course of their history. These changes were not capricious, but usually resulted from the king's desire to conform to whichever system was in use by the country then most powerful in the Near East. To correctly understand biblical chronology in "real time" it is necessary to know when these changes in system took place.

3. Kings could start their regnal year in either the month of Nisan (in the spring according to the Hebrew calendar) or Tishri (in the fall). Partly on the basis of the Gezer Calendar, which begins in the fall, Thiele concludes that Judah counted from Tishri and Israel from Nisan.[35] This difference makes synchronisms between the two countries more difficult to calculate and in its simplest form (without factoring in the accession systems) means that the regnal years of the two countries could only agree with each other six months of any given year.

4. The kings of both Judah and Israel sometimes had their sons rule with them as coregents, with both coregents being given full credit for the years of overlapping reign. Therefore, coregencies created years, sometimes decades, of artificial time that have to be identified to remove "error."

5. When a scribe of one country referred to events in another country he used his own chronological system, even if it differed from the way the other country marked its time. It is therefore neces-

35. The text cited in the epigraph to this chapter was found on a small piece of limestone at Gezer and has become known as the Gezer Calendar. The two months of olive harvest in the first line correspond roughly to the last half of September through the first half of November. The succeeding lines of the inscription continue through the year.

sary to determine whether chronological citations in the Bible are from the perspective of Judah or Israel.

The five principles recovered by Thiele are quite simple and do not demand strained explanations. They do demand careful inspection of each chronological citation so it can be translated into real time. One difficulty not resolved by Thiele (nor by any other proposed chronology) has to do with the years of Hezekiah's reign. In this one instance, Thiele was forced to conclude that the data suffered scribal error in its transmission. Despite this one puzzle, Thiele's chronology has found good acceptance among scholars of all theological persuasions.[36] Happily, if a chronological "error" is found in the time of the kings, it can be labeled as only "seeming" and Thiele's study can be consulted to resolve the apparent problem.

Thiele's dates are closely followed in this chapter and in chapters 16–17 to the fall of Judah in 586. Biblical events did not happen in a vacuum, or a time warp. While chronology is not an end in itself, it should be obvious that without firm dates it is impossible to correctly integrate Bible history into extrabiblical history. In the first millennium there was much contact between Israel and the rest of the Near East, and the prophets in the next chapters were pointing to various world powers as the tools of God. The exegesis of whole chapters in their books depends on proper historical setting. With the historical setting illuminating their lives and ministries, the prophets move from the shadows of the past to the light of the present.

Additional Reading

Finegan, Jack. *Handbook of Biblical Chronology*. Princeton: Princeton University Press, 1964.

Pfeiffer, Charles F. *The Divided Kingdom*. Grand Rapids: Baker, 1967.

Yeivin, Ze'ev. "The Mysterious Silver Hoard from Eshtemoa." *BAR* 13/6 (1987): 38–44 (additional comments in 14/2 [1988]: 59; 14/3:58).

36. At the 1994 national meetings of the Society of Biblical Literature and the American Schools of Oriental Research, Anson F. Rainey roundly rebuked scholars who do not accept Thiele's chronology.

The Late Divided Kingdom (841–722)

I built a pillar over against his city gate, and I flayed all the chief men who had revolted, and I covered the pillar with their skins; some I walled up within the pillar, some I impaled upon the pillar on stakes, and others I bound to stakes round about the pillar; . . . and I cut off the limbs of the officers, of the royal officers who had rebelled. . . .

Many captives from among them I burned with fire, and many I took as living captives. From some I cut off their hands and from others I cut off their noses, their ears, and their fingers, of many I put out the eyes. I made one pillar of the living, and another of heads, and I bound their heads to posts (tree trunks) round about the city. Their young men and maidens I burned in the fire. . . .

Twenty men I took alive and upon stakes I impaled them. . . . The rest of them I consumed with thirst in the desert of the Euphrates.

—Ashurnasirpal II

King Jehu of Israel

The friendship and cooperation that had developed between Judah and Israel was completely and permanently shattered when Jehu killed kings Ahaziah and Joram, but he did not stop with those two. (See illustration 16.3 for an outline of subsequent history.) Jezebel, Joram's mother, was at Jezreel. She knew that she too was about to die, but she purposed to do so in style and with a curse on her lips (2 Kings 9:30–35).[1]

Jehu exceeded his instructions from Elisha concerning the house of Ahab, and there was a typical northern kingdom bloodbath before he was satisfied. Jehu was clearly not a follower of the Lord, since he did not dispose of the golden calves nor was he "careful to walk in the law of the LORD" (2 Kings 10:31). Even Jehu's purging of Baal worship can be seen as a political move against a dangerously powerful priesthood, rather than as a religious exercise.

When the killing was over, Jehu had secured his hold on the throne of Israel, but at the price of friendship with surrounding nations. The death of Jezebel and her house harmed the long-standing friendship between Israel and Phoenicia. Judah could hardly have taken as a friendly gesture the loss of their king and his relatives by Jehu's command. And even worse for the relations between the two countries was the usurping of Judah's throne by Athaliah, mother of the dead Ahaziah and daughter of the dead Jezebel. To further compound Jehu's isolation, at the time of his anointing he had been fighting against the Syrians for control of Ramoth-gilead.[2]

Jehu became king of Israel in 841, and in that same year the Assyrian King Shalmaneser III came west again. No coalition opposed him as had occurred twelve years earlier at the Battle of Karkar. Instead King Hazael of Damascus fought the Assyrians alone and lost 16,000 soldiers, 1,121 chariots, and 470 riding horses. Damascus withstood the subsequent siege, but its surrounding landscape was devastated. Shalmaneser III then proceeded further west, pillaging and collecting booty, including "tribute of the inhabitants of Tyre, Sidon, and of Jehu, son of Omri" (*ANE* 1:191; *ANET* 280; see illustration 15.9). This tribute payment is not mentioned in the Bible, but it is recorded on the Black Obelisk of Shalmaneser (*ANE* 1:192; *ANET* 281):

> The tribute of Jehu, son of Omri; I received from him silver, gold, a golden *saplu*-bowl, a golden vase with pointed bottom, golden tumblers, golden buckets, tin, a staff for a king, and wooden *puruhtu*.[3]

1. The word *officials* in this passage is sometimes translated "eunuchs." The Hebrew word *saris* has both meanings. Dictionaries disagree as to which is the primary use or whether both are implied. In this passage, most translations choose "eunuch." Such officials were used in court as early as David's reign (1 Kings 22:9; 1 Chron. 28:1) and continued in service for the last kings of Judah. Their duties were not limited to the harem, as they also served close to the king. As with the use of foreign bodyguards, a eunuch would be less likely to plan a coup since he had no prospect of establishing a dynasty.

2. As Schniedewind 1996 recasts the biblical account, Jehu and King Hazael of Damascus were in collusion, and Jehu was a vassal of Hazael.

3. As noted in the previous chapter, the Assyrians often called Israel the "land/house of Omri." "Son" could be used loosely in both Hebrew and Assyrian texts, and here

16.1. Black Obelisk of Shalmaneser III (six feet six inches high), found in the Northwest Palace at Nimrud and now in the British Museum, commemorates Shalmaneser's campaigns during several years of his reign. The enlarged detail shows Jehu kneeling before Shalmaneser (dated via other records to 841); both figures are flanked by two attendants. The Assyrians had a great fondness for collecting animals and plants from afar, and an elephant, camels, monkeys, apes, and perhaps a rhinoceros are among the tribute depicted from other kings. Kyle McCarter (1974) attempts to identify the figure on the Black Obelisk as Joram rather than Jehu, an identification rejected by Edwin Thiele (1976) and Baruch Halpern (1987b). It is also suggested that the kneeling figure is an Israelite official and not the king himself, but Assyrian reliefs depict rulers and not their subordinates doing obeisance.

Jehu began his reign by alienating neighboring nations and by paying the first of many tributes that Israel would provide the Assyrians. Although Jehu enjoyed a relatively long reign, he was never a strong ruler. He was harassed by the Syrian armies of Hazael, and he lost all of Transjordan to that nation.

---

would signify only that Jehu was an Israelite (although Tammi Schneider 1995 attempts to show that Jehu was a descendant of Omri). The meanings of *saplu* and *puruhtu* are unknown.

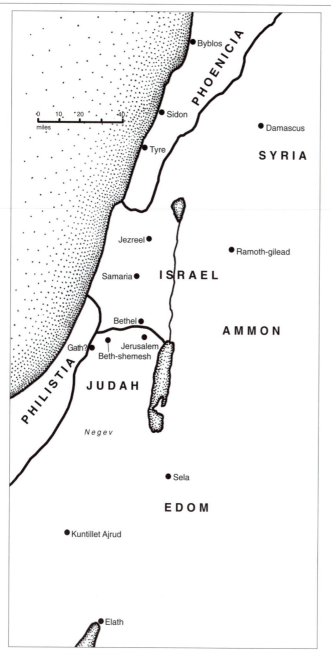

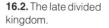

16.2. The late divided kingdom.

Queen Athaliah and King Joash of Judah

Jehu's coup had serious repercussions for Judah. When Athaliah heard that her son Ahaziah was dead, she seized the throne of Judah for herself. Her intrusion into the Davidic line of kings was a direct consequence of Jehoshaphat's unfortunate marriage alliance with Israel, and, being a princess from Israel, it is not surprising that she immediately "rose and destroyed all the royal offspring" (2 Kings 11:1). Only one male grandchild survived Athaliah's purge—and only because

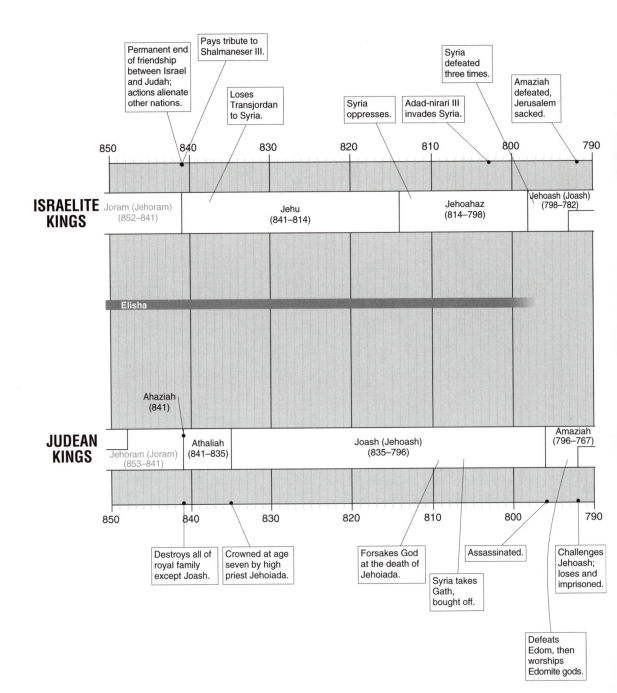

16.3. The late divided kingdom.

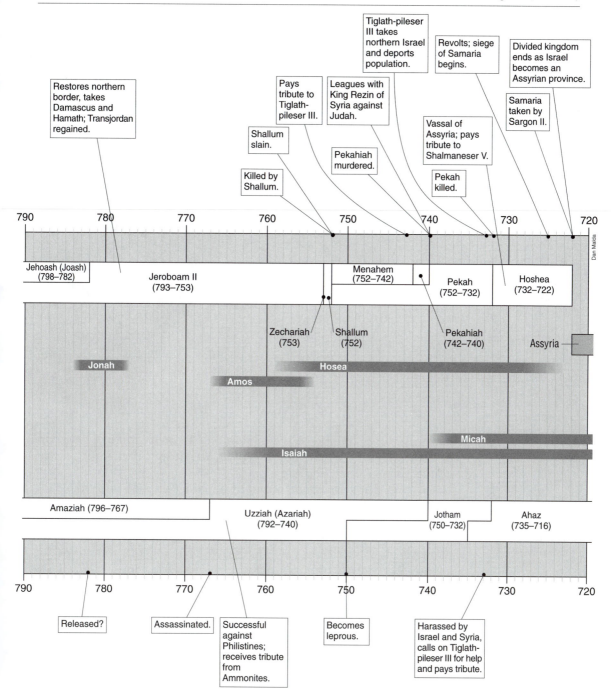

Restores northern border, takes Damascus and Hamath; Transjordan regained.

Pays tribute to Tiglath-pileser III.

Leagues with King Rezin of Syria against Judah.

Tiglath-pileser III takes northern Israel and deports population.

Revolts; siege of Samaria begins.

Divided kingdom ends as Israel becomes an Assyrian province.

Shallum slain.

Vassal of Assyria; pays tribute to Shalmaneser V.

Samaria taken by Sargon II.

Pekahiah murdered.

Killed by Shallum.

Pekah killed.

790 780 770 760 750 740 730 720

Jehoash (Joash) (798–782)

Jeroboam II (793–753)

Menahem (752–742)

Pekah (752–732)

Hoshea (732–722)

Zechariah (753) Shallum (752)

Pekahiah (742–740)

Assyria

Jonah

Hosea

Amos

Micah

Isaiah

Amaziah (796–767)

Uzziah (Azariah) (792–740)

Jotham (750–732)

Ahaz (735–716)

790 780 770 760 750 740 730 720

Released?

Assassinated.

Successful against Philistines; receives tribute from Ammonites.

Becomes leprous.

Harassed by Israel and Syria, calls on Tiglath-pileser III for help and pays tribute.

Dan Malda

16.4. Fragments of a basalt stele found at Dan in 1993 and 1994. The large fragment on the right is just over twelve inches high; two smaller fragments (left) were joined after their discovery. One line of the Aramaic inscription (here highlighted) contains the phrase *house of David* and is the first known extrabiblical reference to King David (Shanks 1994b). The stele was erected by King Hazael of Syria, possibly after his attacks on Israel during the reign of Jehu (2 Kings 10:32–33). It is proposed that the stele was subsequently smashed by Jehoash of Israel. Excavators are hoping to recover more of the stele. The initial conclusion drawn from the thirteen-line largest fragment was that the stele was set up by Ben-Hadad of Syria after his attack on northern Israel (1 Kings 15:20), but the smaller fragments, with their reference to the later Syrian King Hazael, corrected this view (Biran and Naveh 1993, 1995). The correctness of the "David" reading was challenged by P. Davies 1994 (see Rainey 1994b for response).

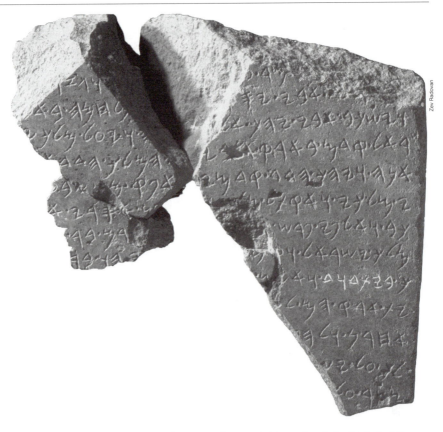

Ahaziah's sister hid the baby in Solomon's Temple. Athaliah held control of Judah for six years but, except for the desecration of the temple, no record is given of her reign.

The infant Joash, son of Ahaziah, remained hidden with Ahaziah's sister and her husband, Jehoiada the high priest, for six years.[4] When Joash was seven years old, Jehoiada, apparently unable to wait any longer, exacted an oath (of silence?) from some key people and showed them Ahaziah's son. Next, Jehoiada carefully arranged a coup to rid the country of the evil queen (2 Chron. 23:1–15). Following her death, the young Joash was placed upon the royal throne, although he was of such a tender age he could not have provided leadership to Judah. No direct information is available as to who ran the government until he reached his majority, but 2 Kings 12:2 hints that Jehoiada might have assumed this role.

Seemingly the first thing done in Joash's reign was to cleanse Jerusalem of Baal worship. Later on, but still early in his reign as a young adult, Joash decided to restore Solomon's Temple, which had been neglected since the days of Jehoshaphat. Joash gave instructions for the repair, but the work still had not been done by his twenty-third year as king. Therefore, about 812, Joash implemented a new and more successful plan for accomplishing the work.

Sometime after the temple restoration was completed, Jehoiada

---

4. This is the only known instance where the priesthood and the royal house were linked by marriage.

died and, sadly, Joash's goodness did not outlive the burial. Joash was led to abandon the temple and serve "the Asherim and the idols" (2 Chron. 24:17–18).[5] Prophets spoke out against Joash's apostasy, but they were ignored. When the son of Jehoiada condemned what was happening, his protests only led Joash to order him put to death (2 Chron. 24:21–22).[6] Within a year, Judah paid for the king's sin when the army of Syria swept into Judah, captured Gath, and threatened Jerusalem. They forced Joash to deplete his own treasuries, as well as the wealth of the temple, to raise sufficient tribute. Joash's last years provide a striking contrast to the early part of his reign, and he was never forgiven for murdering Jehoiada's son. Some years after the Syrian attack, he became the victim of a conspiracy and 2 Chronicles 24:25 states pointedly that he was buried in Jerusalem, but not "in the tombs of the kings."[7]

King Jehoahaz of Israel

Syria's interest in Judah did not mean that Israel was any freer from northern threats. In fact, Jehu's son Jehoahaz seems to have been even harder pressed by the Syrians than his father had been (2 Kings 13:7). Jehoahaz continued the evil religious pattern of all the kings of Israel, but the northern pressures troubled him so much that he actually called upon the Lord for help. Second Kings 13:5 simply states that in response "the Lord gave Israel a deliverer, so that they escaped from under the hand of the Syrians." Archaeology seems to have filled in the details of this verse, identifying the deliverer as King Adad-nirari III of Assyria. In approximately 803 this king brought his armies into Syria (*ANET* 281–82):

5. Asherah (plural Asherim) was the Canaanite mother goddess. King Abijah had earlier disposed of an Asherah image made by the queen mother Maacah (1 Kings 15:13), while a later king, Manasseh, set up such an image in Solomon's Temple (2 Kings 21:3, 7). Such lapses into apostasy were not limited to royalty, which is perhaps evidenced by inscriptions and folk art (dated in the vicinity of 800) found at Kuntillet Ajrud in the wilderness south of Kadesh-barnea. Kuntillet Ajrud seems to have been a caravan stop between Judah and the Red Sea. Fragmentary wall inscriptions that make reference to Baal, El, and Yahweh could imply religious syncretism or pluralism. Most attention has been paid to inscriptions found on jars, one of which is translated, "Yahweh of Samaria and his Asherah." One interpretation of an amateurishly painted scene is that it depicts Yahweh with the Egyptian deity Bes and Asherah. All conclusions derived from the scene and the inscriptions need to be handled with caution, as there is not yet a scholarly consensus on the material. See Dever 1984; Hestrin 1991; Lemaire 1984b, 1985; Meshel 1979; Meshel and Meyers 1976; and Taylor 1994. Scholars who attempt to use this material as evidence that the Hebrew religion did not fully evolve into monotheism until well into the first millennium choose to believe that the biblical picture of revealed monotheism (from which segments of God's people repeatedly defected) is a redacted version of reality.

6. Jesus referred to this murder in Luke 11:51, expecting that his listeners would know such a relatively minor event in their history.

7. There is some difficulty meshing the data given in Kings and Chronicles for the final events of Joash's life. One reconstruction reports a second attack by Syria in which Joash was badly wounded and soon after assassinated.

> I marched against the country. . . . I shut up [the] king of Damascus in Damascus, his royal residence. The terror-inspiring glamour of Ashur,[8] overwhelmed him and he seized my feet, assuming the position of a slave of mine. Then I received in his own palace in Damascus, his royal residence, 2,300 talents of silver corresponding to 20 talents of gold, 5,000 talents of iron, garments of linen with multicolored trimmings, a bed inlaid with ivory, . . . and countless other objects being his possessions.

For once, the hated and feared Assyrians did Israel a good turn. Adad-nirari III's attack on Syria forced that country to relax pressure on Israel in order to protect its own lands. Israel was saved, but apparently neither Jehoahaz nor his compatriots recognized Adad-nirari III's campaign as God's answer to the king's prayer for help (2 Kings 13:6).

King Jehoash of Israel and King Amaziah of Judah: Syrian Decline Begins

Not since the days of Jehoshaphat and Ahab had either Judah or Israel been particularly powerful; each had suffered from revolts, invasions, and royal assassinations. However, at the beginning of the eighth century, the political fortunes of both countries improved. Israel's political upswing was prophesied early in the reign of Jehoash by a terminally ill Elisha. The Bible makes no mention of any activity by Elisha during the rule of either Jehu or Jehoahaz, but he met with Jehoash and predicted that Israel would defeat the Syrian armies three times (2 Kings 13:14–19). Elisha died shortly thereafter, and so too did Hazael, the Syrian king who had terrorized Israel and Judah. Hazael was succeeded by his less capable son, Ben-Hadad (2 Kings 13:24), and soon the Syrians were beaten, as prophesied, by the armies of Israel. Jehoash was able to reclaim cities that had been taken by Syria.[9]

At the same time that Israel was regaining some of its past power, Amaziah took the throne of Judah. One of his first acts was to execute his father's assassins. Also early in his reign he successfully invaded Edom and was able to take the nearly impregnable Sela (2 Kings 14:7; 2 Chron. 25:7–12).[10] Then, inexplicably, Amaziah, who had been obedient to a prophet of the Lord concerning the dismissal of mercenaries from Israel, began worshiping the gods of the Edomites he had just defeated!

Whatever Amaziah's rationale, it is hardly surprising that a prophet came to warn him that he would regret such worship. Amaziah discounted the criticism and, perhaps seeing himself as a strong militarist,

8. Ashur was the chief god of Assyria.

9. A stele of Adad-nirari III reveals that Jehoash paid tribute to Assyria in 796. Assyrian power was about to go into a decline, but at least early in his reign, Jehoash found it expedient to placate the king who had "helped" his father. See Page 1968 and Malamat 1971.

10. Most scholars accept that Sela is the site known today as Petra. This fortress city of the Edomites was ringed by mountains and could be reached only by a narrow and easily defensible pass. For a dissenting voice on the identification, see Haran 1968.

issued a challenge to Israel that their two nations meet in battle.[11] King Jehoash of Israel responded to Amaziah with a parable warning him to withdraw his challenge or be defeated (2 Chron. 25:18–19). Amaziah refused to withdraw, so a battle was fought at Beth-shemesh, in the territory of Judah. Judah was defeated and Amaziah was captured. Jehoash ordered that the north wall of Jerusalem be torn down to symbolize Judah's helplessness against Israel, and treasures and hostages were taken to Samaria (Jerusalem has no natural defenses on its northern side). Amaziah apparently was one of those hostages, and his imprisonment would have been the reason for his son Uzziah to begin his long coregency. Clearly, Amaziah's worship of Edomite gods was costly to both him and his country (2 Chron. 25:20).

King Jeroboam II of Israel and King Uzziah of Judah: The Days of Power Return

Israel's renewed strength did not diminish when Jehoash's son took the throne. On the contrary, Jeroboam II expanded the boundaries of Israel past those his father had won and as far as David and Solomon had pushed them:

> He restored the border of Israel from the entrance of Hamath as far as the Sea of the Arabah. . . . He recovered for Israel, Damascus and Hamath (2 Kings 14:25, 28).

The "entrance of Hamath" probably refers to a valley east-southeast of Byblos and north of Damascus; the Sea of the Arabah is a reference to the Dead Sea; the Arabah is the valley running from the Dead Sea to the Red Sea. Unfortunately, the means by which Jeroboam II achieved this expansion are not provided, but political conditions were certainly right: Assyria was weakened and preoccupied with Armenia, and Syria had not yet recovered from Adad-nirari III's earlier attacks.

As mentioned in an earlier chapter, broken pieces of jars and bowls were sometimes used as notepads. Several dozen such sherds were found scattered in the fill beneath the floor of an administrative building at Samaria. Archaeological and paleographic evidence dates these "Samaria Ostraca" within the eighth century, and they can be understood as temporary records for the arrival of wine and cosmetic oil into the capital city. Detailed study leads most scholars to place them during the reign of Jeroboam II, a time when Israel was preoccupied with these facets of the "good life" (Amos 6:4–6).

The ostraca provide insights into Israel's administrative and fiscal procedures. Since nearly all the clans of the tribe of Manasseh are men-

---

11. The phrase *come, let us face each other* in 2 Chron. 25:17 is a euphemism used by Amaziah to announce his military intentions. Amaziah might have acted out of a sense of pride over his recent victory, but it is more likely that he wanted to redress the wrong done to him by the Israelite mercenaries he had dismissed. The mercenaries retained the money given them by Amaziah, but they were angry at being cheated of the prospect of going into battle and winning booty. Therefore, as they marched homeward they plundered cities in Judah (2 Chron. 25:13).

tioned, we learn that such distinctions were still meaningful. The ostraca also supply the names of settlements (and people) not mentioned in the Bible, revealing a dense agricultural population in the region of Samaria. Altogether, the data allows greater understanding of the prosperity that developed in Israel (see I. Kaufman 1982 and Rainey 1988).

One detail of Israel's political revival is often overlooked, namely that Jonah had predicted its recovery (2 Kings 14:25). Jonah, the earliest of the literary prophets, came from a town about fifteen miles west of the Sea of Galilee. His message of a reviving Israel would naturally have pleased the people of that country and made him a popular individual. Such popularity could have added to his reluctance to leave Israel and carry a message of doom to faraway Nineveh, but Jonah's reservations were stronger than that. Assyria had become much feared and much hated, and other nations would have been pleased over the internal difficulties Assyria was experiencing at that time. Jonah was among those not eager to have Assyria recover. Moreover, he feared that if the Assyrians repented, God would forgive them (Jonah 4:2).

Jonah's perspective clashed with the Lord's for some time, and even when the prophet went to the sprawling capital of Assyria he hoped his message would be ignored. On the contrary, the polytheistic Assyrians were temporarily attracted to (as they would have understood it) one more god who, perhaps, could relieve them of their current problems.[12]

In 767 Uzziah became sole possessor of the throne in Judah.[13] He moved against the Philistines and claimed some of their territory, and the Ammonites thought it politic to send him tribute. The weakness of Edomites and Arabs to the south and east allowed Uzziah to build Elath on the Red Sea and to restore the territory to Judah (2 Kings 14:22). Uzziah fortified Jerusalem, equipped his army, and engaged in programs designed to improve Judah's agricultural base (2 Chron. 26:9–15).

Judah's prosperity is reflected in archaeological surveys that reveal that settlements expanded into most of the Negev during Uzziah's reign. Thus, by the time of Uzziah and Jeroboam II, the two kingdoms jointly controlled as much territory as David and Solomon had possessed. Scriptural silence suggests that the two countries did not openly fight with each other while this prosperity prevailed.

The Prophets Amos and Hosea

The prophets Amos and Hosea ministered in Israel during this period of peace and prosperity, but their books indicate that it was also a time

12. Plagues hit Nineveh in 765 and 759, and there was a total eclipse of the sun on 15 June 763. One theory is that these events conditioned the Assyrians for the message of judgment. If correct, this suggestion would put Jonah's time line well within the reign of Jeroboam II. It is as possible, however, that the plagues and eclipse explain why the Assyrians did not continue to acknowledge God. On Jonah and Nineveh, see Wiseman 1979.

13. Uzziah's father, Amaziah, was probably released from imprisonment in Samaria as a gesture of goodwill when Jeroboam II took sole possession of Israel's throne. Nothing more is known about Amaziah's reign except that he fled from a conspiracy in Jerusalem and was killed at Lachish; 2 Kings 14:19.

16.5. Collection of seals dating from the eighth and seventh centuries. Glyptic (i.e., seal stones) was one of the artistic mediums in which Hebrew artisans became quite skilled. Seals could be set in ring mountings or hung around the neck as pendants. Usually carrying the owner's name, such stones were used to seal documents or containers. To prevent tampering, a scroll would be rolled or folded, tied with a string to which a lump of clay would be affixed, and the seal pressed into the clay before it hardened. Such seals (known as bullae, singular bulla) can be seen in illustrations 17.17 and 18.1. A jasper seal (A) depicts a worship scene and is inscribed "Amoz the scribe." Another seal (B) pictures a fighting cock and reads "Belonging to Jehoahaz, son of the king." It is not clear whether the title *son of the king* was always meant to be understood literally. A third seal (C) carries the inscription "Ahiyahu." The impression of the jasper seal (D) was excavated in 1904 at Megiddo but subsequently lost in Istanbul. "Belonging to Shema" is written above the roaring lion, and his title below the ground line: "Servant [i.e., official] of Jeroboam." Paleographically, the seal can be dated to the reign of Jeroboam II. The Bible does not mention Shema as Jeroboam's official, but the semiprecious stone and the skill of the engraver implies that he held a prominent position. The last seal still in its copper setting (E) was excavated at Elath. Above the figure of a horned ram is the inscription "Belonging to Jotham." Second Kings 14:22 states that Uzziah "built Elath and restored it to Judah." This ring could have belonged to Uzziah's son Jotham, who became coregent and subsequently king of Judah.

Smithsonian Institution, Department of Anthropology

of moral decline and religious indifference. Amos was a Judean shepherd and a caretaker of sycamore trees.[14] Although an unlikely spokesman for the Lord, he was commissioned to travel to Israel's cult center at Bethel. There he spoke against the sins of the faltering Syrians and other neighboring countries and cities. Amos did not exclude his own country of Judah from condemnation, and had that been the end of Amos's preaching he would have been well received in Israel. However, Amos directed most of his criticism against the social and religious ills of Israel.

The rich in Israel benefited from the expanded borders and the peace of Jeroboam II's reign, but they could not see beyond their own profit margin. Amos made note of the rich who could afford both winter houses along the warm Mediterranean coast or shores of Galilee and summer houses up in the cooler Hill Country. While their own houses were decorated with expensive ivory inlays and filled with other luxury items, they were indifferent to the welfare of the poor (Amos 6:4–7; see Beach 1993 and King 1988b).

Not surprisingly for the northern kingdom, the religious ritual of the rich was empty of substance; they were only going through motions and holding to outward observances. In addition, their rituals were a mixture of Mosaic law and foreign cults. To say the least, God was displeased (Amos 5:21–27). Since Amos was an outsider, a Judean, denouncing the sins of Israel, it is probable that he quickly provoked the high priest at Bethel to action. The high priest informed Jeroboam II of what was happening and demanded that Amos return to Judah (Amos 7:13). Amos responded sharply to the high priest, but how much longer he was permitted to speak or what then happened to him is left to speculation. Suggestions for Amos's fate range from expulsion to imprisonment to martyrdom. Most scholars think he merely returned home, dictated his book to a professional scribe, and resumed his previous occupations.

Unlike Amos, Hosea was a citizen of Israel. Hosea's ministry continued until the fall of Israel, but the first three chapters of his book fit within the reign of Jeroboam II. In those chapters Hosea's wife and children illustrate the increasing separation of God from Israel; the years of mercy were ending, and judgment was imminent. In his remarriage Hosea symbolized God's attitude toward adulterous Israel; God did not cease to love and would, in time, restore his people.[15]

There is much more to be gleaned from the books of Amos and Hosea, and it is important to recognize that the messages of these prophets, as well as of those that follow, come into sharper focus when seen in their historical context. The prophets help "flesh out"

14. Amos is called a *noqed*, a word generally translated "shepherd." The Hebrew word is only used one other time in the Old Testament (2 Kings 3:4), but from the several occurrences of the root *nqd* in Ugaritic texts some scholars suggest that Amos held a more prominent position. Craigie 1983b: 71–74, for example, concludes from the Ugaritic evidence that Amos "probably owned, or managed, large herds of sheep and was engaged in the marketing of their products."

15. The remainder of Hosea's book represents a collection of sermons preached during the closing decades of Israel.

the historical scene. Separately, neither the prophets nor the history can be fully appreciated.[16]

The Fall of Israel

Like all kings of Israel, Jeroboam II failed to properly honor God.[17] In the secular sense, however, he had a long and successful reign. Jeroboam II was one of the last kings of Israel to die a natural death, but when he died Israel quickly sank into a period of bloodshed and confusion from which it never recovered. Only six months after Jeroboam II died, his son and successor, Zechariah, was assassinated. His assassin, Shallum, fared even worse; within a month he was murdered at the hands of Menahem. These events and the troubled years that followed must have been difficult for those who had known only the peaceful and prosperous reign of Jeroboam II.

Israel and Judah had been able to enjoy a period of prosperity partly because of the weakness of Assyria. But as Israel's King Menahem soon learned, that weakness was ended. Assyria had found a strong leader in Tiglath-pileser III and was about to carve out an empire larger than anything the Near East had ever known. In 743 that empire began to form as the Assyrian army marched out to the Mediterranean, receiving homage and tribute from many local princes along the way. Tiglath-pileser III boasted (*ANE* 1:193–94; *ANET* 283–84):

> I received tribute from . . . Rezon of Damascus, Menahem of Samaria, Hiram of Tyre, Sibittibili of Byblos, . . . to wit: gold, silver, tin, iron, elephant hides, ivory, linen garments with multicolored trimmings, blue-dyed wool, purple-dyed wool, ebony wood, boxwood wood, whatever was precious enough for a royal treasure; also lambs whose stretched hides were dyed purple and wild birds whose spread-out wings were dyed blue, furthermore horses, mules, large and small cattle, male camels, female camels with their foals. . . .
>
> As for Menahem I overwhelmed him like a snowstorm and he . . . fled like a bird, alone, and bowed to my feet. I returned him to his place and imposed tribute upon him, to wit: gold, silver, linen garments with multicolored trimmings.

The pillage of the Near East had begun with a new intensity, and Menahem became one of the unwilling contributors to the coffers of Assyria. The Bible records that, by exacting fifty shekels of silver from each wealthy man, Menahem was able to raise sufficient tribute to cause the Assyrian king to depart (2 Kings 15:19–20).[18] On the basis of seventh-century Assyrian records, some commentators con-

---

16. For numerous insights into the lives and ministries of these prophets, see King 1988a.

17. In naming his son Zechariah ("the Lord has remembered"), however, Jeroboam II implies some acknowledgment of God.

18. Pul (used in 2 Kings 15) was the alternate Babylonian name for Tiglath-pileser III.

16.6. Portion of an audience scene from the palace at Til Barsip. The seated king is identified as Tiglath-pileser III. Such paintings are a reminder of the richness of costume detail that was part of Assyrian life.

clude that each man was being asked to contribute the standard price for a slave in order to stay free (Wiseman 1993: 255). Assyria had never been stronger, and this tribute marked only the first phase of its future domination of Israel.

Menahem died about a year after he bought off the Assyrians, and his son Pekahiah ruled only briefly before joining the list of assassinated kings. This time it was Pekah, one of the men who rode with the king in the royal chariot, who murdered his way to the throne.[19] Then King Pekah together with King Rezin of Syria made a fatal mistake: they believed that with additional help they could withstand Assyrian pressures.

When the kings of Israel and Syria tried to enlist Judah in a common defense against Assyria, Judah would have none of it. Consequently, Israel and Syria attempted a military takeover of Judah to force its cooperation. Judah was hurt by their attacks, but in the end Assyria totally destroyed Syria and annexed the northern portion of Israel (2 Kings 15:29; 16:9). Pekah could not stand against the might of Assyria. As the several place-names in 2 Kings 15:29 relate, he found himself with little more than Ephraim and the land northward as far as the Esdraelon Valley (approximately Jezreel in illustration 16.2) and no longer in control of the coastline. What had been northern Israel became an Assyrian province.

Tiglath-pileser III seems to have been the first Assyrian king to employ mass deportation. By not killing the defeated peoples the Assyrians could exact continuing tribute. By relocating populations to distant portions of the empire the Assyrians hoped to dilute national feelings and thus lessen the chance of future revolts. The practice would have been most successful with people who believed their gods were limited to their particular homeland.

It was not too long before Pekah was murdered by the next man to lust after the throne (2 Kings 15:30), and Tiglath-pileser III's annals record the accession of the final king of Israel (*ANE* 1:194; *ANET* 284):

19. Chronological references may indicate that Pekah had an independent government east of the Jordan following Shallum's death.

They overthrew their King Pekah and I placed Hoshea as king over them. I received from them ten talents of gold, one thousand talents of silver as their tribute, and brought them to Assyria.

Whatever involvement Tiglath-pileser III might really have had in Hoshea's coup, Hoshea certainly began his reign as a vassal to the Assyrians. But when Tiglath-pileser III died in 727, most of the subject nations revolted, including Hoshea, who hoped that the next king would not be strong enough to reassert control. However, the new king, Shalmaneser V, was stronger than anticipated, and Hoshea was soon pulled back into line (2 Kings 17:3). Shortly afterward, Hoshea sought military aid from Egypt and again stopped paying tribute to Assyria. Nothing came of this contact with Egypt, but the cessation of tribute brought the Assyrian army down on what remained of Israel.[20] The city of Samaria endured a siege for three years; this time there was no intervention by the Lord, and the capital fell. Shalmaneser V is the Assyrian king who actually brought his armies into Israel, but victory was claimed by the next ruler, Sargon II. The details are not presently clear; Sargon may have been a general in the army in charge of the siege, or perhaps Shalmaneser V died just before Samaria fell. In either event Sargon took credit for the fall of Samaria (*ANE* 1:195; *ANET* 284–85):[21]

I besieged and conquered Samaria, led away as booty 27,290 inhabitants of it. I formed from among them a contingent of 50 chariots and made [the] remaining inhabitants assume their social positions. I installed over them an officer of mine and imposed upon them the tribute of the former king.

As of 722 the country of Israel ceased to exist. Whenever possible the Assyrians divided conquered land into administrative districts and placed native "puppets" over them. This policy was carried out in 732 when Syria, northern Israel, and southern Israel were formed into separate districts. Ten years later Hoshea's repeated disloyalty caused the Assyrians to reorganize the three areas into a single new province. Hoshea's disloyalty also caused more of the people of Israel to be deported to distant lands (2 Kings 18:11). Also in accordance with Assyrian policy, people who had proved troublesome elsewhere were brought into the new province.

In the early days of the divided kingdom, the prophet Ahijah had prophesied that Israel would be exiled beyond the Euphrates (1 Kings 14:15–16). The Assyrians were the instrument by which this prediction was realized. And as this chapter of history closed with the fall of Israel, the importation of foreign populations into the same area gave birth to a new people—the Samaritans (2 Kings 17:24–41).

20. 2 Kings 17:4 calls the Egyptian ruler Pharaoh So, who has been identified as Tefnakht or, more likely, Osorkon IV; see Kitchen 1986: 371–76. Lemaire 1995 reports on an Egyptian-style seal with Hoshea's name, which belonged to one of that king's high-ranking officials.

21. For Shalmaneser V's and Sargon II's roles in the fall of Samaria, see Hayes and Kuan 1991.

16.7. Artist's reconstruction (top) of the palace area of Sargon II at Dur-Sharrukin (Khorsabad) in northern Mesopotamia. The city stretches one mile on a side, but had not been completed or even occupied when Sargon died; it was abandoned by his successor. Still, Khorsabad evokes a strong impression of the man and the nation that destroyed Israel. Massive twenty-five-ton bull-man-god (center) is one of several that guarded the entrance into the throne room at the Khorsabad palace. Among the small finds from Khorsabad is a bronze band (bottom) that had been wrapped around a doorpost in the temple to the sun god Shamash. Sargon II is depicted "mastering" two bulls, a common Assyrian motif probably intended to symbolize the power of the king.

Judah during the Dying Days of Israel

Shortly after Menahem murdered his way to the throne of Israel, calamity of a different nature befell Judah. Uzziah, who had greatly strengthened his country and with respect to religion had been doing well, for some reason now decided to intrude on priestly prerogatives. When the priests opposed him, Uzziah became angry and would have persisted, but the Lord struck him with leprosy. For the rest of his life, Uzziah was separated from the temple and his family. He was forced

16.8. Ivory pomegranate (under two inches high) carries an inscription, which has been read as "Belonging to the temple of the Lord, holy to the priests." Paleographically the inscription is dated to the eighth century and possibly topped a scepter carried by priests in the Jerusalem Temple. The artifact was first seen in a Jerusalem antiquities shop and purchased by the Israel Museum for $550,000! (See Artzy 1990; Avigad 1990; Lemaire 1984a; and Shanks 1988b, 1992, 1993a: 10–30.)

to live in a separate house, and his son Jotham was brought in as co-regent to act on his behalf.[22]

The year 740 was an eventful one. In Israel, Pekah murdered Pekahiah, and in Judah, Uzziah died. That same year, Jotham became king in his own right and the prophet Isaiah received his call to the ministry (Isa. 6:1). The Bible regards Jotham as a good king and credits him with strengthening Judah and even with receiving tribute from the Ammonites. Little information is given of his reign, however, and there is no mention of contact between him and Isaiah. The latter silence may be due to Jotham's goodness and because he was forced to relinquish his power about five years after his father's death. For the remainder of Jotham's reign, he seems to have been only a figurehead ruler.

By 735 the political waters had become troubled. Israel and Syria had leagued together in common defense against Assyria and sought the addition of Judah to their cause. But a pro-Assyrian political party in Judah pushed Jotham's son Ahaz into power. To this party, it was better to pay tribute than to risk the consequences of losing to Assyria. Since Ahaz would not join with Israel and Syria, those nations decided to conquer Judah and install their own puppet as ruler. Judah suffered severe losses but Jerusalem did not fall.[23] Within that tense setting, God

22. A badly damaged text of Tiglath-pileser III mentions a battle against "Azriau of Iuda" at Arpad in northern Syria (*ANET* 282). Some scholars believe this record refers to Uzziah and dates after he was stricken with leprosy—therefore showing that he continued as effectual ruler of Judah. Other scholars believe the reference is to a local Syrian king. For an introduction to the debate, see Thiele 1983: 141–42. Naʾaman 1974 proposes that the document dates to 701 and should be ascribed to Sennacherib and Hezekiah.

23. The Edomites and Philistines took military advantage of this situation; 2 Chron. 28:17–18.

commissioned Isaiah to meet King Ahaz, whom he found at the south end of Jerusalem inspecting the city's water supply. Isaiah gave the king words of encouragement and even offered him the opportunity to check Isaiah's credentials as a true prophet (Isa. 7:4–11).

Ahaz refused to accept Isaiah's counsel. He instead stripped the palace and robbed Solomon's Temple of treasures dedicated to God, which he sent off to Tiglath-pileser III of Assyria with a plea for help (2 Kings 16:7).[24] The Assyrians rescued Ahaz and (as already noted) destroyed Syria and reduced Israel's size and strength. The tribute that Ahaz sent to Assyria spared Judah, but he had an even higher price than gold and silver to pay for his protection—he had to acknowledge religious dependence on Assyria (2 Kings 16:10–14). In matters of religion Ahaz was unlike his father. Not only did Ahaz erect an Assyrian altar in Jerusalem's temple area, he also closed Solomon's Temple and destroyed vessels dedicated to God. Ahaz erected shrines and altars everywhere in Jerusalem and the Judean countryside, he made "molten images for the Baals," and he burned incense to false gods. Possibly he even sacrificed some of his children in pagan worship. Spiritually, the king was dead.

The meeting between Ahaz and Isaiah took place about 735, and it seems to have been the only contact the two men ever had.[25] As the late divided kingdom drew to a close, Ahaz, Isaiah, and all the people of Judah must have been looking north at the death throes of Israel. There must have been great agitation as the Assyrian Empire moved to the borders of Judah.

The Late Divided Kingdom in Review

For the entirety of the late divided kingdom, there was no friendly contact between the nations of Judah and Israel. When there was contact it was hostile, and Judah suffered. The small nations surrounding Palestine continued to be subservient or belligerent depending on the strength of Israel and Judah. Egypt had been only an occasional nuisance during the early divided kingdom and was almost totally absent during the late divided kingdom. Of the major powers, Syria continued its dominant role in Palestine, then weakened, and finally allied itself with Israel just before totally collapsing in 735. In the first year of the late divided kingdom, Assyria exacted tribute from Israel. Assyria's fortunes ebbed, allowing a period of peace and prosperity for Palestine, but then Assyria returned, more formidable than ever, and began the process of subjugating Israel. In 722 Israel ceased to exist and its people were scattered. Judah survived, but without Israel as a buffer against pressures from further north.

Of the kings of Israel, Jeroboam II was good at least in a material sense. Of the kings of Judah, Uzziah ranks first from the standpoints of

24. A building inscription includes "Jehoahaz of Judah" (a long form of Ahaz's name) in a list of kings who brought tribute to Tiglath-pileser III; *ANE* 1:193; *ANET* 282.

25. The prophet Micah's ministry also spans the reigns of Jotham and Ahaz. Micah seems to have had a rural ministry; like the earlier Amos, he called for social justice and true worship of God.

religion and economy. During the late divided kingdom, God's messengers began to come more prominently into play. In Judah, the prophets Isaiah and Micah started their ministries. In Israel, God continued to send witnesses to those who had rejected him: Jonah, Amos, and Hosea. Once God even used the Assyrians to rescue Israel, but his mercy finally passed to judgment. For Israel it was a judgment coupled with the promise of restoration.

Additional Reading

Astour, Michael C. "841 B.C.: The First Assyrian Invasion of Israel." *Journal of the American Oriental Society* 91 (1971): 383–89.

Bordreuil, Pierre. "A Note on the Seal of Peqah the Armor-Bearer, Future King of Israel." *BA* 49 (1986): 54–55.

Gwaltney, William C., Jr. "Assyrians." Pp. 77–106 in *Peoples of the Old Testament World*. Edited by Alfred J. Hoerth, Gerald L. Mattingly, and Edwin M. Yamauchi. Grand Rapids: Baker, 1994.

Saggs, H. W. F. *The Might That Was Assyria*. London: Sidgwick & Jackson, 1984.

Shanks, Hershel. "Three Shekels for the Lord." *BAR* 23/6 (1997): 28–32.

Judah Alone (722–586)

Nineveh, you are already surrounded by enemy armies! Sound the alarm! Man the ramparts! Muster your defenses, and keep a sharp watch for the enemy attack to begin! For the land of Israel lies empty and broken after your attacks, but the LORD will restore its honor and power again.

Shields flash red in the sunlight! The attack begins! See their scarlet uniforms! Watch as their glittering chariots move into position, with a forest of spears waving above them. The chariots race recklessly along the streets and through the squares, swift as lightning, flickering like torches. The king shouts to his officers; they stumble in their haste, rushing to the walls to set up their defenses. But too late! The river gates are open! The enemy has entered! The palace is about to collapse!

Nineveh's exile has been decreed, and all the servant girls mourn its capture. Listen to them moan like doves; watch them beat their breasts in sorrow. Nineveh is like a leaking water reservoir! The people are slipping away. "Stop, stop!" someone shouts, but the people just keep on running.

Loot the silver! Plunder the gold! There seems no end to Nineveh's many treasures—its vast, uncounted wealth. Soon the city is an empty shambles, stripped of its wealth. Hearts melt in horror, and knees shake. The people stand aghast, their faces pale and trembling.

—Nahum 2:1–10 (New Living Translation)

Hezekiah

Manasseh

Amon

Josiah

Jehoahaz, Jehoiakim, and Jehoiachin

Judah survived the Assyrian takeover of the northern kingdom, and King Ahaz managed to rule for another six years. Ahaz had to stay at least outwardly subservient to the Assyrians during those final years, but he apparently had freedom to exert some control over Philistia. This seems clear because, when he died, the Philistines were pleased, and Isaiah was led to caution them that their rejoicing was premature (Isa. 14:28–31).

Hezekiah

Hezekiah was twenty-five years old when he replaced his father Ahaz as king of Judah.[1] Ahaz had closed Solomon's Temple, but on the very first day of Hezekiah's reign the building was reopened. Hezekiah did not stop with simply opening the temple; he also ordered it cleansed, replenished, and rededicated. Sacrifice was made to the Lord, and the ceremony was carefully carried out to conform to the pattern established earlier by David and others (2 Chron. 29:25–30). No statement is given as to how Hezekiah became so different from his idolatrous father, but recent political developments may have impressed a sense of urgency on the young king to be right with the Lord (2 Chron. 29:6–11).

Still Hezekiah was not finished. Although it would be late in the religious calendar, it was decided that Passover should be celebrated. Hezekiah even extended the call for celebration to those in the north who had escaped exile (2 Chron. 30:1–9). The appeal to join in worship met with mixed response in occupied Israel, but it was more wholeheartedly accepted in Judah, and a great gathering formed in Jerusalem.[2] The Feast of Unleavened Bread was held with "great joy," so much so that when it was over, the whole assembly decided to immediately do it all over. And they did! When the celebration finally ended, the enthusiasm generated in the people led them to destroy pagan pillars, Asherim, high places, and altars throughout Judah.[3] And the worshipers who returned to occupied Israel did the same in their territories.

---

1. There are chronological problems with Hezekiah's reign, and some writers assume an initial period of coregency for Hezekiah. I follow Thiele, who does not allow for such a shared time.

2. The couriers did not go into Naphtali, Dan, or east of the Jordan River (2 Chron. 30:10–11, 18). Perhaps those areas were closed to outsiders or their Jewish populations had been fully relocated.

3. According to 2 Kings 18:4 the bronze serpent made by Moses had become an object of worship. Hezekiah had the serpent destroyed. Although there is no mention of Isaiah's interaction with the king in these opening weeks, it must have been an encouraging time for the prophet. Isaiah was already middle aged, had been commissioned decades earlier by the Lord, and in the intervening years had had only one unsuccessful meeting with King Ahaz. Isaiah would have repeated access to Hezekiah, and he would find the godly king attentive, though not always wise.

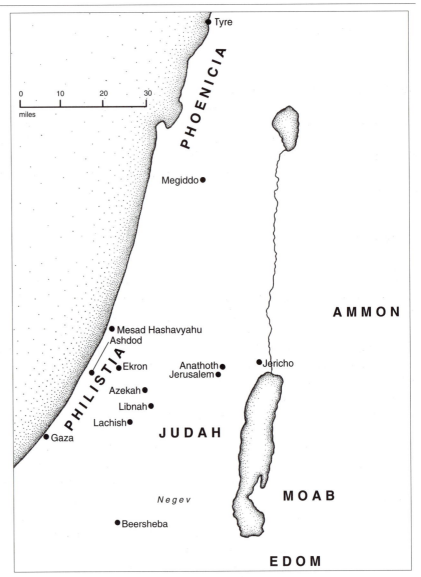

17.1. Judah and neighboring states.

Hezekiah began his reign under the shadow of an Assyria ruled by Sargon II, the king credited with the destruction of Israel. The western part of the Assyrian Empire became restive in Hezekiah's early years, and Egypt seems to have incited portions of it to revolt. Indeed, in either 712 or 711 Pharaoh Shabako of Egypt joined with Philistia and other areas against Assyria. Sargon II reported the plotting this way (*ANE* 1:198; *ANET* 287; translation from Luckenbill 1926–27: 2.§195):

> Philiste (Philistia), Iaudi (Judah), [Edom], Moab . . . payers of tribute [and] tax to Ashur, my lord (they sent) numberless inflammatory and disdainful (messages) to set them at enmity with me, to [pharaoh], king of Egypt, a prince who could not save them, they sent their presents (bribes) and attempted to gain him as an ally.

Isaiah reports that an Assyrian army was sent into Palestine and at Ashdod scored a victory over the uprising (Isa. 20:1). Sargon II listed

Judah as a participant in the rebellion, but perhaps Hezekiah was only a bystander. Whatever Judah's participation, for the next three years Isaiah encouraged Judah not to trust Egypt for salvation (Isa. 20:2–4). Isaiah gave a consistent message to his contemporaries: they were not to trust in people or nations for their strength; they were to trust in God the Holy One of Israel for help. Isaiah was not preaching pacifism, but he was warning against collaboration with those who did not honor God.

Sargon II died in 705. Typically, revolt broke out within the Assyrian Empire, and the new king's power was tested. Hezekiah joined in the revolt and even used the occasion to expand into Philistia, where he took control of Gaza (2 Kings 18:7–8).[4] In Palestine only three kings remained loyal to Assyria. One of them was King Padi of Ekron, but his own subjects deposed him and carried him to Jerusalem. Ignoring Isaiah's position on such entanglements, Hezekiah imprisoned Padi, an action recorded in the annals of Sargon II's son and successor, Sennacherib (*ANE* 1:199; *ANET* 287; Luckenbill 1924: 31):

> The officials, the patricians, and the common people of Ekron—who had thrown Padi, their king, into fetters because he was loyal to his solemn oath sworn by the god Ashur, and had handed him over to Hezekiah, the

17.2. Detail from a "seascape" found in Sargon II's palace at Khorsabad. The whole relief is over nine feet tall. Ships are shown both laded with and towing timbers. One of Assyria's purposes in campaigning west was to gain control of Lebanese cedar, which was then the finest wood in the Near East.

4. Borowski 1995 fails to credit Hezekiah with any real religious zeal. Rather he sees all the reforms as parts of a "grand scheme" to revolt against Assyria. Borowski attempts to make the several evidences fit that scenario.

17.3. Two examples of hundreds of stamped jar handles found at various sites in Judah. Prior to firing, the jars were stamped with seals picturing either a "winged sun disk" (as in these examples; the symbol has been alternately identified as a "flying scroll") or a "four-winged beetle." The inscriptions on such handles read *lmlk* ("belonging to the king") plus one of four city names: Sochoh (top), Ziph, Hebron, and *Mmst* (bottom; possibly a title for Jerusalem). At more than one site, *lmlk* jar handles were found in destruction levels dating to Sennacherib's invasion in 701. Since the handles are from jars of differing sizes, the seals could not have been indicators of capacity. Rather, royal officials seem to have had the seals put on storage jars used to gather provisions as the country prepared to withstand Assyrian incursions. (For an introduction to the *lmlk* jar handles, see Aharoni 1979: 394–400; A. Mazar 1990: 455–58; Ussishkin 1976.)

Jew—and Hezekiah held him in prison, unlawfully, as if Padi were an enemy.[5]

Hezekiah knew Sennacherib would not passively watch the western portion of the empire secede. In preparation for the expected Assyrian response, Hezekiah seems to have consolidated Judah into four administrative districts and to have stored food supplies for his army in specially marked containers. Hezekiah also began preparing Jerusalem should the city come under siege. Some of the city wall was repaired and strengthened, towers were built, and a new line of wall erected.[6] The springs outside the city were stopped up (to prevent the Assyrians from making use of them), and Gihon Spring was redirected into a new pool made at the south end of Jerusalem (2 Chron. 32:3–5, 30).

Of Hezekiah's preparations to defend Jerusalem, his work in connection with Gihon Spring is best known. "Hezekiah's tunnel" meanders

5. Ashur was the chief god of Assyria. In the 1996 excavations at Ekron, Padi's name was found on an inscription that places him fourth in a line of five kings who ruled over the city. Padi was followed to the throne by his son Achish.

6. Excavators have uncovered a section of city wall 130 feet long and 23 feet wide dating to this activity; see Rosovsky 1992.

Israel Museum (IDAM), Jerusalem

1,748 feet from Gihon Spring south to the pool of Siloam (illustration 17.5). The tunnel, cut through the limestone bedrock of Jerusalem, was dug from opposite ends. As the crews progressed toward each other it must have become increasingly difficult to keep sufficient air inside the tunnel; the workers would have been competing with their oil lamps for the same oxygen. Various theories have been advanced to explain the less-than-direct route of the tunnel, with some concluding the diggers were incompetent. A countertheory, that the workers were following and enlarging a natural water channel, now has geologic support (so Gill 1994; earlier studies include Amiran 1976; Cole 1980; Shaheen 1976). When the work was completed, gravity fed the water from Gihon Spring outside Jerusalem into the Siloam pool within newly built city walls. As long as the Assyrians did not discover the exterior Gihon Spring, Jerusalem could not be forced to surrender for lack of water.

About twenty feet inside the pool end of the tunnel, an inscription describing the project was cut in the tunnel wall. The inscription was subsequently forgotten and not rediscovered until 1880 by Arab boys bathing and playing in the water. When found, the inscription was partly submerged, so the tunnel floor was cleaned to lower the water

17.4. The Siloam Inscription. Turkey was in control of Palestine when this inscription was discovered and recovered. It was subsequently taken to the Istanbul Archaeological Museum, where it now resides (see Shanks 1991 and 1993b).

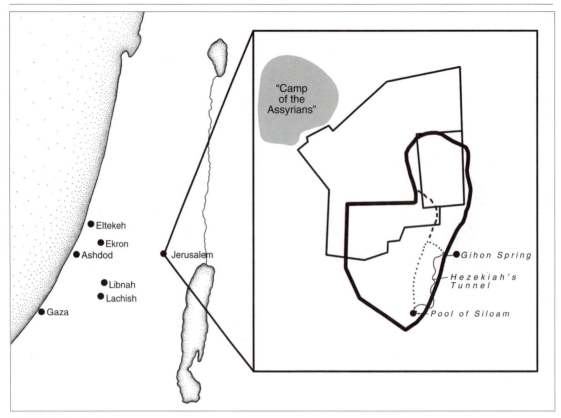

17.5. Cities involved in Sennacherib's 701 campaign into Palestine. The inset shows features of Jerusalem at this time: Hezekiah's city walls (solid heavy line), the "old city" walls (solid light line), and the city's size under David (dotted line) and Solomon (dashed line) (see illustrations 13.7 and 14.1).

level and acids applied to remove lime deposits obscuring part of the text. Finally six lines of text were revealed. Fortunately, several casts were made of the inscription, because one night it was clumsily cut from the tunnel wall and secretly carried away. The inscription was recovered, but broken. The beginning of the inscription was missing before this act of vandalism, and the centuries of flowing water obscured some of the preserved lines. Still, the following translation gives insight into the project carried out at Hezekiah's behest (*ANE* 1:212; *ANET* 321; see also Parker 1994 and Shanks 1984a):

> . . . when the tunnel was driven through. And this was the way in which it was cut through: While . . . were still . . . axes, each man toward his fellow, and while there were still three cubits to be cut through, there was heard the voice of a man calling to his fellow, for there was an overlap in the rock on the right and on the left. And when the tunnel was driven through, the quarrymen hewed the rock, each man toward his fellow, ax against ax; and the water flowed from the spring toward the reservoir for twelve hundred cubits, and the height of the rock above the heads of the quarrymen was one hundred cubits.[7]

The thousands of hours that went into cutting the tunnel must have produced many a backache and blister, but Hezekiah believed the project essential if Jerusalem was to stand against an Assyrian attack.

7. Rogerson and Davies 1996 contested the date of this inscription and, therefore, of the tunnel. Their conclusions were quickly refuted; see Hendel 1996 and Cahill 1997.

Alfred Hoerth

17.6. Horned altar (just over five feet tall) from Beersheba is made of cut stones, contrary to biblical law (Exod. 20:25). Charred stones forming the top of the altar show that it had been used for burnt offerings. This altar, which could have been known to the prophet Amos (Amos 5:5; 8:14), was reused to repair a storehouse wall, a dismantling that probably took place during Hezekiah's religious reforms. The Arad altar (see p. 301 n. 5 and p. 306 n. 11) was apparently terminated at the same time (see Rainey 1994a).

Although the western part of Assyria's empire went into revolt when Sennacherib took the throne in 705, local problems prevented him from immediately responding to this breakaway. In Babylonia a Chaldean ruler named Merodach-baladan had harried Sennacherib's father until the Chaldean was finally chased into Elam. With Sargon's death, Merodach-baladan returned to southern Mesopotamia and declared himself king of Babylon. Two years later, Sennacherib was finally able to send Merodach-baladan fleeing back into the swamps of Elam, and then Sennacherib began preparations for a western campaign. In 701 he marched out of Nineveh, and one by one the cities in Phoenicia were brought back into line. Sennacherib moved down the coast of Palestine, defeated a coalition that included Egyptian troops, and began the reclamation of Philistia (*ANE* 1:200; *ANET* 288):

> I assaulted Ekron and killed the officials and patricians who had committed the crime and hung their bodies on poles surrounding the city. The common citizens who were guilty of minor crimes, I considered prisoners of war. The rest of them, those who were not accused of crimes and misbehavior, I released. I made Padi, their king, come from Jerusalem and set him as their lord on the throne, imposing upon him the tribute due to me as overlord.

The Assyrian forces next moved up into the Hill Country of Judah and began simultaneous attacks on several of Hezekiah's fortified cities. Sennacherib took personal interest in the key city of Lachish, and it was probably when that city came under siege that Hezekiah thought

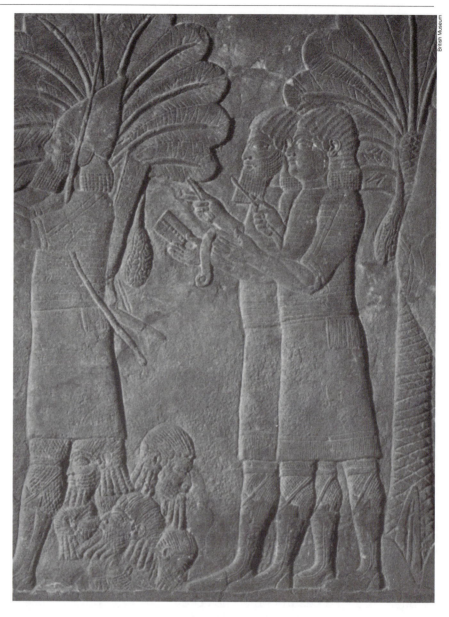

17.7. Relief depicting scribes of Sennacherib counting the heads of the enemy dead (see illustration 13.1 for a similar Egyptian practice). One scribe is writing on a scroll, while another is using a hinged writing board coated with beeswax into which cuneiform was written (see Wiseman 1955 and M. Howard 1955).

he would be wise to release Padi from imprisonment. At least it is while Sennacherib was at Lachish that Hezekiah tried to placate him with tribute (2 Kings 18:14–16). Sennacherib's report adds detail to the biblical account and the way he pressed his attack (*ANE* 1:200; *ANET* 288):

> As to Hezekiah, the Jew, he did not submit to my yoke, I laid siege to forty-six of his strong cities, walled forts, and the countless small villages in their vicinity and conquered them by means of well-stamped earth-ramps and battering rams brought near to the walls, combined with the attack by foot soldiers, using mines, breeches, as well as sapper work. I drove out of them 200,150 people, young and old, male and female, horses, mules, donkeys, camels, big and small cattle beyond counting, and considered them booty. Himself I made a prisoner in Jerusalem, his royal residence, like a bird in a cage. I surrounded him with earthwork in

Oriental Institute, University of Chicago

17.8. Sennacherib Prism, a six-sided baked clay prism (fifteen inches tall) found at Nineveh. One of the more famous archaeological finds relating to the Bible, this cuneiform text deals with Sennacherib's military campaigns, including his 701 invasion of Hezekiah's Judah. This prism is in the University of Chicago's Oriental Institute. Another with much the same text, the Taylor Prism, is in the British Museum in London.

order to molest those who were leaving his city's gate. His towns that I had plundered I took away from his country and gave them to King Mitinti of Ashdod, King Padi of Ekron, and King Sillibel of Gaza. Thus I reduced his country, but I still increased the tribute and the . . . presents due to me as his overlord, which I imposed later upon him beyond the former tribute, to be delivered annually. Hezekiah himself, whom the terror-inspiring splendor of my lordship had overwhelmed and whose irregular and elite troops which he had brought into Jerusalem, his royal residence, in order to strengthen it, had deserted him.

Sennacherib went on to list additional precious metals and jewels that became his. The tribute and booty also included ivory inlaid couches and chairs, elephant hides, precious woods, concubines, male and female musicians, and more. Hezekiah failed to heed Isaiah's advice against foreign entanglements, and Judah paid dearly. Sennacherib makes it clear just how dearly.

Second Kings 18 (also 2 Chron. 32 and Isa. 36) states that while Sennacherib was still besieging Lachish, he sent a delegation and some of his army to Jerusalem (Ussishkin 1979b; see illustration 17.5 for the location of the Assyrian camp). Perhaps Sennacherib thought the tribute he had received indicated that more direct pressure would humble Hezekiah. At Jerusalem, Assyrian officers tried to impress on the defenders the futility of relying on Egyptian aid and of the way none of the other national gods had been able to protect their people from attack. The Assyrians asked Jerusalem to surrender (2 Kings 18:31–32). Distraught when he learned of the Assyrian delegation and their terms, Hezekiah appealed to Isaiah, and the prophet encouraged Hezekiah not to fear; the Lord would deal with Sennacherib. Then, according to 2 Kings 19:8, the head of the delegation returned to Sennacherib and found him "fighting against Libnah, for he had heard that the king had left Lachish."

Second Kings 19:8 implies that Lachish had fallen and Sennacherib had moved over to the still stubborn Libnah. That Lachish did fall in Sennacherib's campaign is a certainty. Sennacherib was so proud of that victory that nearly seventy linear feet of wall reliefs commemorating his assault on the city were found at Nineveh.[8]

The excavation of Lachish has provided its own graphic story of Sennacherib's attack. At the southwest corner of the city, archaeologists uncovered a ramp built by the Assyrians in order to bring up their siege towers. They also discovered a counterramp inside the same corner of the city by which the defenders tried to neutralize the Assyrian thrust (Ussishkin 1984). One crest from an Assyrian helmet was found during excavation, implying that Assyrians also died. But largely it was the people inside Lachish who suffered; archaeologists found a mass grave into which the dead had been placed when the city was being cleared. Over fifteen hundred skeletons filled the grave, vividly illustrating the consequences of being in Lachish in 701.[9]

The Assyrian officers and undoubtedly the rest of the task force had returned to Sennacherib because word was received that Pharaoh Taharqa was bringing the Egyptian army into Palestine. The Assyrian

---

8. The reliefs lined some two-thirds of one room in a ceremonial suite. Originally, the entire room was probably decorated. See Ussishkin's several works (1979a, 1980, 1982a, 1988) and Shanks 1984b.

9. Three of the skulls had evidence of trepanning, an operation in which an opening is cut through the skull to relieve pressure on the brain. One of the skulls had signs of healing, showing that one of the three people survived the operation—but not the politics of King Hezekiah.

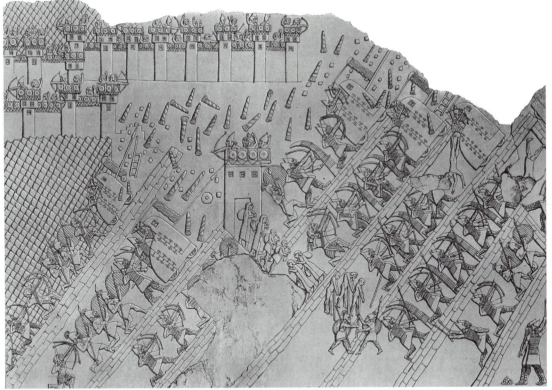

forces were spread thin, and it was necessary to regroup to meet this new enemy. Although the Assyrians were redeploying, they kept pressure on Hezekiah to surrender. Hezekiah fervently prayed to God (2 Kings 19:15–19), and Isaiah again reassured his king of the Lord's protection. Isaiah also declared that Jerusalem would not come under siege, indicating that Sennacherib's account exaggerates the pressure put on Judah's capital. The Egyptian army was defeated at Eltekeh, but Sennacherib's campaign was almost over.[10] Suddenly an "angel of the Lord" decimated his army, and Sennacherib returned to Nineveh to console himself with wall reliefs of glorious triumph and annals freighted with lists of tribute. Exactly how the Assyrian army was afflicted is not clear, but the loss was sufficiently severe to cause Sennacherib to suspend his campaign. It is noteworthy that his annal's account of battle suddenly breaks off and has Sennacherib heading home. His scribes chose not to record all that had transpired. Sennacherib had a successful western campaign, but only so far as the Lord permitted him.

In 703 Sennacherib had chased Merodach-baladan from southern Mesopotamia, but in 700 he was back, again trying to foment rebel-

17.9. Line drawing of one of the Lachish reliefs depicting the successful assault on that city in 701. Sennacherib attacks with slingers, archers (some protected by companions holding large shields), and siege towers wheeled up ramps to batter the city wall. Assyrians pour water over the towers' leather coverings to douse fire arrows that hit them. The city fell, and in this compressed time scene, some of the inhabitants are shown being led away into exile or impaled on poles. In other Lachish reliefs, some of the defenders are decapitated or have their legs broken at the knees.

10. Until Kitchen's analysis of the data (1986: 154–61, 383–86; 1983), some scholars thought it necessary to divide the accounts in 2 Kings 18–19; 2 Chron. 32; and Isa. 36–37 into two campaigns, the second being just before the end of Hezekiah's reign. At issue was the Bible's identification of Taharqa as pharaoh, a title he did not hold until well after 701. As Kitchen recognized, the Bible was following a practice that is still common in our day—that of referring to people by their most important titles without implying that they were always in that position. It is now clear that such an awkward division of the texts is unnecessary and that Sennacherib's only campaign in Palestine was in 701.

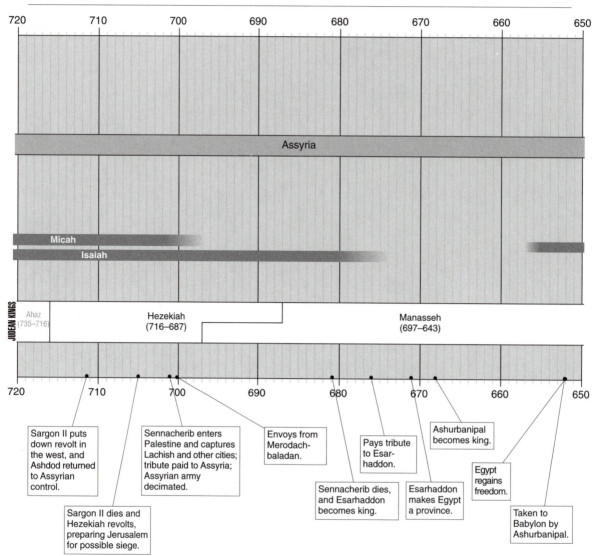

17.10. Judah.

Timeline labels:

Assyria

Micah

Isaiah

JUDEAN KINGS

Ahaz (735–716)

Hezekiah (716–687)

Manasseh (697–643)

Sargon II puts down revolt in the west, and Ashdod returned to Assyrian control.

Sargon II dies and Hezekiah revolts, preparing Jerusalem for possible siege.

Sennacherib enters Palestine and captures Lachish and other cities; tribute paid to Assyria; Assyrian army decimated.

Envoys from Merodach-baladan.

Sennacherib dies, and Esarhaddon becomes king.

Pays tribute to Esar-haddon.

Esarhaddon makes Egypt a province.

Ashurbanipal becomes king.

Egypt regains freedom.

Taken to Babylon by Ashurbanipal.

lion.[11] Merodach-baladan sent letters and a present to Hezekiah (Isa. 39:1). Perhaps he had learned that Sennacherib failed to conquer all of Judah and thought of Hezekiah as a potential ally. Merodach-baladan would be interested in learning whether Judah could distract Sennacherib sufficiently to allow Babylonia to again break free of the empire. Hezekiah was flattered at the attention shown him by the envoys, and Isaiah was once more frustrated at the short-sightedness of his king. Fortunately for Judah, nothing seems to have come of the Chaldean overtures because, before the year 700 was over, Sennacherib advanced into Babylonia and Merodach-baladan fled into Elam for the final time.

Hezekiah lived his remaining years with no severe pressures from Assyria. Second Chronicles 32:23, 27–29 reflects a period of prosperity, possibly in this last part of his reign. Perhaps Judah even experienced

11. The reappearance of Merodach-baladan in Babylonia could have been the "rumor" mentioned by Isaiah; 2 Kings 19:7.

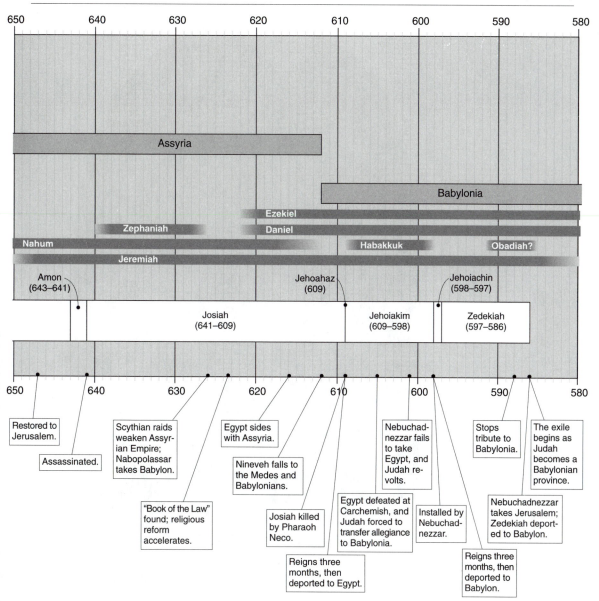

some expansion, thanks to its neighbors having been weakened by Assyria. Archaeological evidence certainly indicates increased settlement in the Negev during the days of Hezekiah. It was also within the reign of Hezekiah that Jerusalem spread its boundaries the furthest to the west (see illustration 17.5; Broshi 1974–75).

Manasseh

Coregent with his father for ten years, Manasseh was still in his early twenties when Hezekiah died. Manasseh reigned as sole king of Judah for forty-four years, but the biblical writers had little interest in his political or administrative abilities during those decades. They empha-

17.11. Black marble boundary stone (eighteen inches high). Merodach-baladan (left) is conferring a land grant to an official (right). Emblems of four Babylonian deities on pedestals are above the two men.

sized that Hezekiah's godly attitude was not shared by his son, that Manasseh rebuilt the high places and altars and allowed the worship of Baal and "all the host of heaven." Altars to these false deities were placed in the courts of the temple, and even worse a statue of the sex goddess Asherah was placed within Solomon's Temple. Manasseh "made his sons pass through the fire" and engaged in other apostate activities. In short, the king led "Jerusalem to do more evil than the nations whom the LORD destroyed before the sons of Israel" (2 Chron. 33:2–9).

Isaiah and Hezekiah had been close associates, but there is no mention of any contact between Manasseh and the prophet. Isaiah seemingly lost contact with the court and increasingly turned his attention to the coming fall of Judah, exile, and restoration. Although Isaiah apparently was not in touch with Manasseh, 2 Chronicles 33:10 states that God spoke to both the king and the people of Judah. Sadly, no one listened, and God withdrew his mercy and allowed Assyria to be his means of judgment. Assyrian annals record that in 676 Manasseh paid

Bildarchiv Preussischer Kulturbesitz, Vorderasiatisches Museum

17.12. Assyrian practice of puncturing an enemy's nose or lip, putting a ring or hook through the hole, and tying a rope to the ring or hook assured compliance. Relief of King Esarhaddon with ropes attached to Pharaoh Taharqa of Egypt and possibly King Baalu (Balu) of Tyre is reminiscent of Manasseh's treatment at the hands of Ashurbanipal.

tribute to Sennacherib's son, King Esarhaddon of Assyria (*ANE* 1:201–2; *ANET* 291):

> I called up the kings of [Syria] and of the region on the other side of the Euphrates River, to wit: King Balu of Tyre, King Manasseh of Judah, King Qaushgabri of Edom, King Musuri of Moab, King Sillibel of Gaza . . . to-

17.13. Sampling of reliefs lining the walls of Ashurbanipal's palace at Nineveh. *Top:* A lion is released into the king's game preserve. *Bottom:* The king fires from his chariot, while lions he has already killed lay strewn about. A wounded lion is held at bay by men in the king's chariot. *Facing page, top:* Ashurbanipal offers libation at the conclusion of a lion hunt. An offering table and incense stand are in front of the king, fan bearers behind him. *Facing page, bottom:* The king and queen relax in a garden. A harpist, fan-bearers, and servants bringing food populate the scene. Near the harpist, the head of King Teuman of Elam dangles from a tree.

gether twenty-two kings. . . . All these I sent out and made them transport under terrible difficulties, to Nineveh, the town where I exercise my rulership, as building material for my palace: big logs, long beams, and thin boards from cedar and pine trees, products of the Sirara and Lebanon mountains, which had grown for a long time into tall and strong timber, also from their quarries.

Assyria became increasingly convinced that Egyptian meddling was responsible for its continuing problems controlling Syria-Palestine. Therefore, a few years after Manasseh paid his tribute to Esarhaddon, the Assyrian armies reached into Egypt and made that country another province within the empire. Less than twenty years later however, in 652 Egypt declared itself free again. Ashurbanipal, who was by then king of Assyria, planned to reclaim the country and was concerned that Manasseh might entertain similar ideas of revolt. These considerations seem to have been the reason that the Assyrians "captured Manasseh with hooks, bound him with bronze chains, and took him to Babylon"

British Museum

(2 Chron. 33:11).[12] It was perhaps this highly humiliating treatment that awakened the king to his religious senses: "And when he was in distress, [Manasseh] entreated the LORD his God and humbled himself greatly before the God of his fathers" (2 Chron. 33:12). Within a few years Manasseh was allowed to return to Jerusalem, where for the remainder of his reign he tried to strengthen his country and to correct the religious errors of his earlier years (see Beit-Arieh and Cresson 1991 and Tatum 1991).

Amon

Little can be said of Amon, Manasseh's son, except that he had just become a teenager when his father was taken to Assyria. Amon must have married shortly thereafter, while his father was still in captivity,

12. Ashurbanipal was probably in Babylon rather than Nineveh because a rebellion in the south had just been crushed.

because when Amon was sixteen he had a son, Josiah. Amon was old enough to be crowned coregent but for some reason, perhaps the knowledge that Manasseh would soon be released, this was not done. Although Amon had a few years with Manasseh after the latter's return from Assyria, his father's new godliness did not turn him from the teachings of his childhood. Amon was twenty-two years old when he took the throne of Judah, and although he reigned only two years it was sufficient time to sweep away his father's recent reforms. Amon was assassinated. What was behind the murder is unknown, but since the "people of the land" then killed the assassins, it was likely some palace intrigue rather than a popular revolt.

Josiah

Josiah was only eight years old when he was crowned king to replace his murdered father. No mention is made of how the youth was assisted in his role until he became an adult or of the factors that caused him to increasingly seek the Lord (2 Chron. 34:3). The prophet Jeremiah was born about the same year as Josiah, into a priestly family from Anathoth, a village approximately three miles northeast of Jerusalem. Jeremiah's parentage and proximity to Jerusalem make it virtually certain that he and his family were at the temple for all the feast days and celebrations and were aware of the increasing devotion of the king. Josiah was twenty years of age when he began his religious reforms, and Jeremiah 1:2 records that the very next year God called Jeremiah to be a prophet.[13]

Beyond stating that Josiah was able to carry out some of his religious reforms in occupied Israel, neither Kings nor Chronicles make any mention of the political scene during the first half of Josiah's reign. Extrabiblically, it is known that two years after Josiah began his reforms (and thus one year after Jeremiah was called to be a prophet) the mighty Assyrian Empire suddenly began to break up. The western portion of the empire fell away in 626 when the seminomadic Scythians[14] and Cimmerians swept down out of Armenia, stormed through Syria and northern Palestine, and badly frightened the Egyptians. Scythians either fought on their own or hired out as mercenaries to other nations; they were little concerned about whose side they were on, as long as there was the prospect of plunder. Their raids in 626 accomplished a sudden and final end to Assyrian hold on land west of the Euphrates.

To further compound its problems, also in 626 a Chaldean named Nabopolassar conquered Babylon and declared southern Mesopotamia free from Assyrian control.[15] Without warning, both ends of the Assyrian Empire had dropped away. This set of historical events explains how King Josiah was freed from having to pay tribute to Assyria and

13. For insights into the ministry and world of the prophet Jeremiah, see King 1993.

14. Scythians were so called by the Greeks. See Rolle 1989 and Yamauchi 1982, 1983.

15. Chaldea, Babylonia, and Neo-Babylonia are synonyms. I use "Babylonia" from this point on in the book.

17.14. The final years of Judah.

how Judah was able to experience one final period of freedom from outside control.

In the eighteenth year of his reign, as Josiah was having Solomon's Temple cleared and repaired, "the book of the law of the LORD given by Moses" was found (2 Kings 22:8). Whatever portion of Scripture was discovered in the temple, when it was read to Josiah he decided that his reforms had not been extensive enough.[16] The people rededicated themselves to God and increased their zeal in ridding Judah of pagan religions. False priests were done away with, houses of prostitution were razed, and centers of pagan worship were torn down and defiled.[17] Even the high place at Bethel was finally destroyed. From Solomon's Temple itself, presumably from the storage areas that ringed the building on three sides, several objects of false worship were brought out and destroyed. Among the objects done away with were vessels made for Baal, Asherah, and other false gods; an image of Asherah; horse images dedicated to the sun; and chariots of the sun.[18] The renewed reforms of Josiah, which extended north as far as the Galilee, can be dated about 621.

16. The book is traditionally identified as Deuteronomy.

17. This is when the shrine at En Haseva was apparently dismantled and its cult vessels smashed; Cohen and Yisrael 1995 and 1996. See also Beit-Arieh 1988a and 1996.

18. For a possible representation of horses dedicated to the sun, see Shanks 1978a. The temple at Arad was destroyed some time in Josiah's reign. Bitter arguments developed, however, between certain archaeologists over whether the excavators of Beersheba uncovered evidence that Josiah desecrated a pagan worship center in that southern city. See Rainey 1977; Shanks 1977; and Yadin 1977–78.

17.15. Archaeology often provides intriguing insights from ordinary finds. This ostracon (almost eight inches high) was found at Mesad Hashavyahu, a fort on the Mediterranean coast. On the basis of stratigraphy and paleography, it was dated to the last half of Josiah's reign. Found in a guardroom of the fortress gate, the city's legal center, this potsherd records a harvester's complaint over the taking of his cloak, a garment that could be taken in pledge but not kept overnight (Exod. 22:25–27; Deut. 24:10–13). With its Jewish names, reference to the Sabbath, and allusion to Jewish law, this potsherd leads to the conclusion that the fort was under Jewish control and that Josiah laid claim to that coastal region and the important highway that ran through it (see Amusin and Heltzer 1964; Dobbs-Allsopp 1995; and Naveh 1960, 1964). Also of interest was the large quantity of Aegean pottery found at Mesad Hashavyahu, implying that Josiah staffed the fort with Greek mercenaries.

Josiah was a godly king, and he and Judah benefited from the prophets who lived during his reign. Of God's messengers, 2 Kings 22 and 2 Chronicles 34 imply that the prophetess Huldah was important to Josiah. Zephaniah records that his ministry took place during the reign of Josiah; the religious problems he condemned most likely fit early in Josiah's reign, before the king's reforms were fully underway. Some scholars credit Zephaniah with stimulating the reform movement, but there is no convincing evidence of contact between the two men.[19] Little is recorded of Jeremiah's life during the reign of Josiah. But, since his and Josiah's interests were so similar, it is safe to assume that Jeremiah must have actively supported the king. It is also safe to conclude that not everyone in Judah was affected by the religious reforms. At least once Jeremiah was called by God to speak out against false worship (Jer. 3:6–10).

While reforms were underway in Judah, Assyria continued to disin-

19. Zephaniah's prophesy regarding the fall of Assyria was fulfilled within the reign of Josiah, thus giving another reason for placing Zephaniah early in the reign of the king. Zephaniah predicted the end of Judah, but he also declared that judgment could be avoided (Zeph. 2:1–3). Because of the widespread reforms instituted by Josiah, the punishment was at least delayed (2 Chron. 34:27–28).

tegrate, and a Near Eastern "world war" began to shape up. On the one side was the faltering Assyria, which surprisingly found at least token support from Egypt. Although once subjugated by Assyria, Egypt now felt Assyria the lesser of potential evils. A weakened, but friendly Assyria could serve as a buffer against the Scythians and the emerging power of Babylonia, and it could allow Egypt to realize its dream of expanding once more into Syria and Palestine. On the other side, the Babylonians found allies in the Medes, who were becoming powerful in northwestern Iran.

In 612 the Medes and the Babylonians marched on Nineveh, the capital of Assyria. On the third assault the city fell, a fall vividly described by the prophet Nahum.[20] A poorly preserved chronicle of the Babylonian Nabopolassar also gives detail as to the way Nineveh fell (*ANE* 1:202–3; *ANET* 304–5):

> The king of Akkad [i.e., Babylonia] called up his army and King Cyaxares of the Medes marched toward the king of Akkad, . . . they met each other, . . . ferried across, and they marched upstream on the embankment of the Tigris and . . . pitched camp against Nineveh. . . . Three battles were fought, then they made a great attack against the city. In the month Abu . . . , the city was seized and a great defeat he inflicted upon the entire population. On that day, King Sinsharishkun of Assyria fled to . . . , many prisoners of the city, beyond counting, they carried away. The city they turned into ruin-hills and heaps of debris. The king and the army of Assyria escaped.

Although remnants of the Assyrian army fled westward and regrouped at Haran, they lost that position in 610. For all practical purposes, Assyria had collapsed in 612. The Babylonians took control of Nineveh and began assuming control over the areas that had been within the Assyrian Empire.[21]

It is unclear whether Egypt paid more than lip service to its Assyrian allies until it was too late, but Egypt did pose an obstacle to Babylonian expansion. Each year an Egyptian army marched north, perhaps with hopes of reviving some fragment of Assyria, but more likely with thoughts of restoring its own long-past glory. In any case, Judah found itself between the emerging Babylonian Empire and an increasingly expansionist Egypt. In 609 Pharaoh Neco of Egypt marched north to face the Babylonian armies at Carchemish. Various explanations have been used to explain Josiah's refusal of peaceful passage for Neco. Possibly Josiah did not want aid to reach the fragmented Assyria, or perhaps (implied by the location of their confrontation) he was trying to expand into the former territory of Israel and felt that the Egyptians would con-

20. Nahum's account of Nineveh's fall is predictive. Since Nahum refers to Assyria's destruction of Thebes in Egypt as a past event (it was destroyed in 663), he must have prophesied somewhere between 663 and the fall of Nineveh in 612. Nahum does not identify the destroyers of Nineveh. By putting the prophet and his message into history, by recognizing the fierce hatred the Jews and the rest of the Near East had for Assyria by this time, the "good news" of Nahum, as a seventh-century Judean would have heard it, can be appreciated.

21. The Medes were primarily interested in holding the important trade center of Haran. They carried their loot back into Iran and largely left the field open for Babylonian takeover.

test such a move. Whatever the reason, Josiah was mortally wounded in the ensuing battle (2 Chron. 35:22–24).[22]

Second Kings 23:25 rates Josiah as the best king in the long history of Judah. However, his confrontation with Egypt soon cost Judah its freedom. Josiah's death also pushed Jeremiah into a new phase of his life. Called to be God's messenger some twenty years earlier, Jeremiah began a more vocal and visible ministry in Judah. He began to emerge as a political commentator to his people and to earn the title *weeping prophet*.

Jehoahaz, Jehoiakim, and Jehoiachin

After Josiah's death, his son Jehoahaz was placed on the throne of Judah. Three months later Jehoahaz was called to Riblah in Syria (where Neco was laying claim to territories), and from there he was put in chains and carried off to Egypt. Egypt had pretensions of grandeur again and hoped to make Judah one of its steps to a revived empire. The news of Jehoahaz's imprisonment must have shocked the people of Judah, who had hardly recovered from the tragedy of Josiah's death. The increasingly vocal Jeremiah advised the Judeans that their new king would never return (Jer. 22:11–12).

Pharaoh Neco exacted tribute from Judah and selected another son of Josiah, Joahaz, to rule as Egypt's puppet king. As a mark of vassalage the son's name was changed to Jehoiakim. This son was very different from his father: Jehoiakim raised taxes and made use of forced labor to further his own interests—policies that led Jeremiah to direct some scathing commentary toward this son of Josiah (Jer. 22:13–19).

Without Josiah's influence, foreign idols again dotted Judah's landscape, and Jeremiah found himself without godly political support. He began to be persecuted by his own people (Jer. 26:1–8), and he was forced to communicate through Baruch, his secretary (Avigad 1978a, 1979; Tsvi Schneider 1988, 1991; Shanks 1987c, 1996; Shiloh 1986; Shiloh and Tarler 1986). Jeremiah continued to speak against the evil in Judah, even though similar condemnation had led to the death of another prophet (Jer. 26:20–24). Jeremiah probably had to keep reminding himself of God's commissioning promise of protection (Jer. 1:18–19).[23]

Judah had become part of Egypt's hoped-for revived empire, but that hope was dashed in 605 when the Egyptian army was crushed by the Babylonians in battle at Carchemish. (Jeremiah supplied political commentary to the event; Jer. 46.) The Babylonian army subsequently swept through Palestine (Stager 1996), and Jehoiakim was forced to become a puppet ruler for a new power—the Babylonians led by King Nebuchadnezzar II (also called Nebuchadrezzar). Tribute was taken from Jerusalem, and some Judeans, including Daniel, were selected for deportation.

22. The fort at Mesad Hashavyahu, near the coastal highway that Pharaoh Neco would have taken north, seems to have been abandoned as a result of this Egyptian campaign.

23. Jeremiah was not alone in Judah. The ministry of the prophet Habakkuk is generally dated within the reign of Jehoiakim, and Obadiah may have ministered in the closing days of Judah.

17.16. Carved proto-Aeolic capital (above) found at Ramat Rahel, just south of Jerusalem (for a similar capital from the time of Solomon, see illustration 14.5). The finely constructed and decorated palace/fortress found at the site has been attributed to Jehoiakim. Jeremiah condemned Jehoiakim's use of unpaid labor to build himself "spacious upper rooms" painted bright red and paneled with cedar. Balustrades once adorned the windows of an upper floor (below). When found, remains of red paint were visible.

Despite all the turmoil swirling around him, Jehoiakim never heeded Jeremiah's warnings. Even when Jeremiah wrote a scroll calling king and country to repentance (Jer. 36), Jehoiakim showed contempt for it and the prophet. Jeremiah became a hunted man, but he refused to keep silent. In 601 Nebuchadnezzar failed in an assault on Egypt. That failure, plus Egyptian encouragement, was probably the reason Jehoiakim unwisely stopped paying tribute to Babylonia. At first, local Babylonian garrisons and vassal troops harassed Judah,[24] but later the Babylonian army was sent westward and Jerusalem came under siege. At some point in these military maneuvers, Jehoiakim died and his son Jehoiachin took the throne—in time to surrender to Nebuchadnezzar three months later.

Zedekiah

When Jerusalem fell, Jehoiachin and thousands of his people, including Ezekiel, were carried off into exile. Nebuchadnezzar then ap-

24. The fortress at Arad was apparently destroyed by these bands of raiders; see Rainey 1987a.

17.17. Bulla stamped "Belonging to Berekhyahu son of Neriyahu the scribe." This lump of clay (here greatly enlarged), used to close a papyrus document, was sealed by none other than "Baruch son of Neriah" (Jer. 36:4). Baruch's name here carries a suffix abbreviation for God, indicating that his full name meant "blessed of God." ("Neriah" in Jeremiah 36 and "Neriyahu" on the seal are the same individual.) One of the inferences drawn from this bulla is that Baruch was an official royal scribe before he became involved with Jeremiah. Additional bullae found in Jerusalem and environs contain further names of biblical personages involved with Jeremiah and his times (see Shanks 1987c; Shiloh 1986).

Zev Radovan

pointed Josiah's youngest son, Zedekiah, to be his vassal king.[25] Conditions improved slightly for Jeremiah, at least he once again had contact with the king. At one point in his reign Zedekiah was called to Babylon, possibly to assure Nebuchadnezzar of his loyalty (Jer. 51:59). If such assurance was indeed given, it was short lived, for in 588, Zedekiah withheld tribute. As expected, Nebuchadnezzar led his army westward but, since the Ammonites were also in rebellion, he was uncertain which country to attack first. He consulted his gods for direction (Ezek. 21:21–29)[26] and was encouraged to direct his armies into southern Palestine, where Judah tried desperately to prepare for defense.

Twenty-one ostraca found in a gate room at Lachish give testimony to the mounting tension within the army of Judah. Most of the letters were written by a man named Hoshaiah to Yaosh.[27] The following letter (number 3) contains hints of inner disputes, but it also implies that contacts were being made with Egypt in hopes that that country would

25. Zedekiah's Hebrew name had been Mattaniah. Like Jehoiakim it was changed as a sign of vassalage.

26. On the practice of using arrows to discern the will of the gods, see Iwry 1961.

27. Scholars debate both the role and location of these two men: Hoshaiah was either commander of Lachish or just someone stationed at a military outpost; Yaosh was either a Jerusalem resident or commander of Lachish. Borowski 1984 finds Yadin's interpretation attractive, but it was rejected by Rainey 1987b. Barstad 1993 sees the ostraca as the written records of orally delivered messages.

send aid. Even to the very end, Judah looked toward people, not God, for support (*ANE* 1:213; *ANET* 322):

> Your servant Hoshaiah has sent to inform my lord Yaosh: May the Lord cause my lord to hear tidings of peace! And now you have sent a letter, but my lord did not enlighten your servant concerning the letter that you sent to your servant yesterday evening, though the heart of your servant has been sick since you wrote to your servant. And as for what my lord said, "Do you not understand?—call a scribe!" As the Lord lives, no one has ever undertaken to call a scribe for me; and as for any scribe who might have come to me, truly I did not call him nor would I give anything at all for him!
>
> And it has been reported to your servant, saying, "The commander of the host, Coniah son of Elnathan, has come down in order to go into Egypt; and unto Hodaviah son of Ahijah and his men has he sent to obtain . . . from him."
>
> And as for the letter of Tobiah, servant of the king, which came to Shallum son of Jaddua through the prophet, saying, "Beware!" your servant has sent it to my lord.

Jeremiah 34:7 refers to the attacks of Nebuchadnezzar's armies on the cities of Judah and mentions that besides Jerusalem only Lachish and Azekah were still holding out (Rainey 1987a).[28] Another ostracon (number 4) makes mention of a fire-signal system by which cities could communicate (Shanks 1983b; R. Wright 1982). Either the writer was not in position to see Azekah or the letter was written subsequent to Jeremiah 34:7 and the city had already fallen (*ANE* 1:213; *ANET* 322):

> May the Lord cause my lord to hear this very day tidings of good! And now according to everything that my lord has written, so has your servant done; I have written on the door according to all that my lord has written to me. And with respect to what my lord has written about the matter of Beth-haraphid, there is no one there.
>
> And as for Semachiah, Shemaiah has taken him and has brought him up to the city. And as for your servant, I am not sending anyone there today, but I will send tomorrow morning.
>
> And let my lord know that we are watching for the signals of Lachish, according to all the indications that my lord has given, for we cannot see Azekah.

These and other Lachish letters provide some of the dying words of Judah as it tried to survive the onslaught of Babylonia. The cities of Lachish and Azekah fell, and then in January 587 Nebuchadnezzar began his siege of Jerusalem (Jer. 52:4). God sent Jeremiah to speak to Zedekiah, to tell the king that Babylonia was acting out God's will (Jer.

---

28. The fort at Arad was rebuilt during the reign of Zedekiah, and Eliashib (see Rainey 1987a) resumed command. Vouchers and letters found in the excavation add to our knowledge of the military movements during the last years of Judah. Some vouchers deal with Kittim, apparently indicating that Zedekiah employed Greek mercenaries in the Negev. One ostracon pleads that troops be sent to reinforce Ramat Negev "lest Edom should come." Arad's fort was destroyed by fire, probably the work of Edomites who took advantage of faltering Judah. See the prophet Obadiah's condemnation of Edom's attitude as Judah suffered.

17.18. Reverse of La-
chish letter 4.

Israel Museum (IDAM), Jerusalem

27; 34:2–7). The king and the prophet had several meetings, and Zedekiah seems to have been wracked with indecision. He was hoping for
aid from Egypt, and surprisingly some came, forcing Nebuchadnezzar
to lift the siege of Jerusalem long enough to chase the Egyptians back
home. But then the siege resumed, and conditions became even more
desperate. Even then Zedekiah could not bring himself to act on Jeremiah's advice. Consequently Jerusalem did not surrender. Charred
wood, ashes, and arrowheads found during excavation speak to the intensity of the city's destruction when it fell in 586. Solomon's Temple
was destroyed, the ark lost, and more treasure and people sent into
captivity (S. Singer 1976).[29]

Jeremiah had advised Zedekiah to surrender the city, both to save it
and his family from destruction. But the king refused, and as the Babylonians broke through Jerusalem's defenses, Zedekiah fled and tried to
escape across the Jordan into Ammonite territory. He reached the
plains of Jericho, but there he was caught and brought before Nebuchadnezzar for sentencing. Zedekiah was forced to witness his sons'
execution, then was blinded, bound, and carried to Babylon. The manner of his own death is not recorded. In 586 the fire signals were all ex-
tinguished, and there were no more kings of Judah. Judah had ceased
to exist.

29. The probability is that the ark, like the rest of the temple and its objects, would
have been stripped of its precious metals and then left to burn. 2 Macc. 2:4–8 states that
Jeremiah hid the ark on Mount Nebo, while other traditions have it hidden away by
priests. More than one attempt at its recovery have been made, but most such searches
have been based on mystic or intuitive grounds. For recent claims that the ark has been
found, see Shanks 1983a and 1983c. For the tradition that the ark was taken to Ethiopia, see Hoberman 1983; Isaac 1993; and Porten 1995.

Additional Reading

Albenda, Pauline. "Western Asiatic Women in the Iron Age: Their Image Revealed." *BA* 46 (1983): 82–88.

Brown, Shelby. "Perspectives on Phoenician Art." *BA* 55 (1992): 6–24.

Cahill, Jane, et al. "It Had to Happen—Scientists Examine Remains of Ancient Bathroom." *BAR* 17/3 (1991): 64–69 (additional comments in 17/5:18, 20; 18/6 [1992]: 22).

Gitin, Seymour. "A Royal Dedicatory Inscription from Ekron." *IEJ* 47 (1997): 1–16.

Larue, Gerald A., *Babylon and the Bible*. Grand Rapids: Baker, 1969.

Malamat, Abraham. "The Last Kings of Judah and the Fall of Jerusalem." *IEJ* 18 (1968): 137–56.

McKay, John, *Religion in Judah under the Assyrians*. Naperville: Allenson, 1973.

Porten, Bezalel. "The Identity of King Adon." *BA* 44 (1981): 36–52, 197–98.

Russell, John. *Sennacherib's Palace without Rival at Nineveh*. Chicago: University of Chicago Press, 1991.

Shanks, Hershel. "Letter from a Hebrew King?" *BAR* 6/1 (1980): 52–56.

Yadin, Yigael. "The Mystery of the Unexplained Chain." *BAR* 10/4 (1984): 65–67 (additional comments in 10/6: 16, 18).

The Exile

By the rivers of Babylon,

There we sat down and wept,

When we remembered Zion.

Upon the willows in the midst of it

We hung our harps.

For there our captors demanded of us songs,

And our tormentors mirth, saying,

"Sing us one of the songs of Zion."

How can we sing the Lord's song

In a foreign land?

If I forget you, O Jerusalem,

May my right hand forget her skill.

May my tongue cleave to the roof of my mouth,

If I do not remember you,

If I do not exalt Jerusalem

Above my chief joy.

—Psalm 137:1–6

Jeremiah's Final Days
Ezekiel
Daniel
The Babylonian Empire after Nebuchadnezzar
Daniel and the End of the Babylonian Empire
The Nature of the Exile
Additional Reading

Kristine S. Henriksen

18.1. Gedaliah came from a line of Judean officials: his grandfather was Shaphan, scribe to King Josiah (2 Kings 22:3). A seal impression (illustrated here at nearly four times actual size) reading "Gedaliah who is over the house" was probably made by the biblical Gedaliah, indicating that at one point in his career he had been in charge of a royal estate.

With the fall of Jerusalem, Judah was turned into a Babylonian province, and a Judean named Gedaliah was appointed governor over the new territory. Because Jerusalem was burned out, Gedaliah made his administrative headquarters at Mizpah, a few miles north of the ruined capital (2 Kings 25:22–24).

Archaeology shows that—unlike the Assyrians who had brought in foreigners to repopulate Israel—the Babylonians left Judah in a depleted state. Some sites were totally destroyed, and some of these were resettled, but only after a space of time. Moreover, the population governed by Gedaliah largely comprised the poorer people of the land, the ones Babylon had not been inclined to deport (2 Kings 24:14). The Bible notes that those left in the land were given vineyards and fields and that they became "vinedressers and plowmen" (2 Kings 25:12; Jer. 52:16). These Judeans were in service to the Babylonians (Jer. 40:9), and the Babylonians expected to receive some portion of Judah's commodities as tribute (Graham 1984).

Jeremiah's Final Days

Jeremiah was one of the more prominent people remaining in occupied Judah. The Babylonians had released Jeremiah from detention and given him the option to remain or accompany the other deportees into exile. It is possible that the Babylonians learned of Jeremiah's political stance (i.e., to accept the Babylonian takeover) from the people deported in 597 or from deserters before Jerusalem fell (Jer. 39:9). They could also have heard of Jeremiah's moderating advice to those in exile (Jer. 29). Whatever the reason for this Babylonian deference to Jeremiah, he elected to stay in Judah with Gedaliah.

As news of Gedaliah's appointment became known, some of the soldiers who had escaped the fall of Judah filtered back home and were allowed to remain on the condition that they support the Babylonian occupation. News of Gedaliah's governorship also encouraged Jews who had fled into neighboring countries to return to their homeland. But word of a plot against the governor's life, instigated by the Ammonites who undoubtedly hoped to gain some political advantage for themselves, also surfaced. Unwisely, Gedaliah refused to believe the rumor, and only two months after his appointment he and those about him (including a token force of Babylonians) were assassinated. The assassins were led by Ishmael, identified as part of the royal family of Judah. Hostages were taken, but they were rescued and Ishmael escaped into Ammon.

There was understandable fear concerning how the Babylonians would respond to the death of Gedaliah and his bodyguards. Jeremiah's counsel was sought, and he advised the people to stay in occupied Judah, that God would support them, that Nebuchadnezzar need not be feared, but that going into Egypt would have serious consequences (Jer. 42:7–22). The prophet's advice was rejected, and a group fled to the supposed safety of Egypt. Jeremiah and his faithful secretary Baruch were part of this migration, undoubtedly against their will.[1]

Ezekiel

Ezekiel's life bridged the decades on both sides of the fall of Jerusalem. He was born into a priestly family when Judah was free from Assyrian control and during a time of religious revival. Ezekiel grew up in Jerusalem and would have been familiar with the city and its temple area. He would probably have been too young during Josiah's reign to be impressed with the collapse of Assyria or with anything Jeremiah may have been doing. Ezekiel would have taken the peaceful times for granted.

Ezekiel was approximately twelve years old when King Josiah made his fatal mistake, trying to stop the Egyptian army. Within about a four-month period, young Ezekiel experienced the death of the only king he had known, his state funeral, the coronation of a new king, the imprisonment of that new king by the Egyptians, and the imposition of a puppet king.

A few years later the Babylonians turned Jehoiakim into their puppet ruler and took hostages from Judah for good measure. One teenager named Daniel was taken, while another teenager named Ezekiel was left to live on in Jerusalem. Ezekiel, therefore, became an adult during the reign of Jehoiakim. Assuming that Ezekiel's father was a godly priest, Ezekiel's family could not have been happy with the apostate king. By then Jeremiah was coming under strong attack, and Ezekiel was old enough to understand the issues involved; perhaps he even witnessed some of the confrontations and visual aids of the older prophet.

By 597 Nebuchadnezzar had lost patience with Jehoiakim and marched on Jerusalem, taking the city and appointing Zedekiah as his new puppet king. Some of the population was again carried off into exile, this time including the young adult Ezekiel. Ezekiel was resettled in a town called Tel-abib, not far from Babylon. The Chebar River men-

---

1. Jeremiah 43–44 was written in Egypt. Jeremiah prophesied an attack on Egypt by Nebuchadnezzar (he made a punitive attack in 568) and condemned false worship by Jews in Egypt. Nothing is definitely known concerning the remainder of the prophet's life or death.

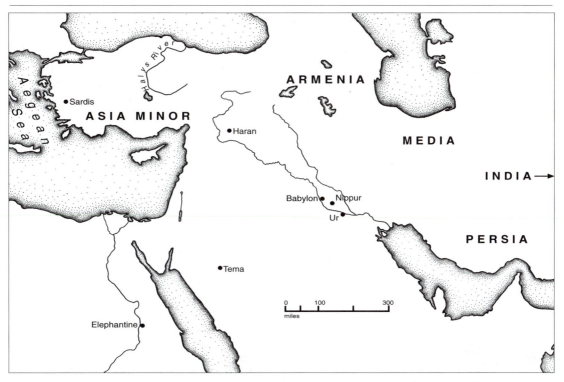

18.2. The exile.

tioned in relation to his town was actually one of the large irrigation canals that laced southern Mesopotamia. This one began just north of Babylon, coursed through Nippur, and ended south of Ur.

Ezekiel and those exiled with him were forced to begin new lives in a very different setting. They had to live in a flat terrain; hills and valleys such as they had known were nowhere to be seen. Southern Mesopotamia's climate was much hotter than that of Judah, and there was even less rainfall than in Palestine. The exiles had to learn new building techniques since there were no stones with which to build houses or fences, and farmers had to learn the intricacies of irrigation.

Ezekiel's call to be a prophet came five years after he arrived in Babylonia.[2] He was commissioned to preach essentially the same message that Jeremiah was preaching in Judah: that Jerusalem would fall and the exile would not soon be over. Ezekiel 8–11 records the prophet's vision of the sin of Jerusalem and God's abandonment of the city. Ezekiel was shown the false worship that was then being practiced in Jerusalem, and Ezekiel 8 provides additional insight into the sin Jeremiah was combating.[3]

For seven years Ezekiel prepared those in exile for the collapse of Judah, and when it happened his message shifted to one of hope and restoration. The dry bones of Ezekiel 37 and the vision of a new temple

2. The reference to thirty years in Ezek. 1:1 is debated, but it most probably means that Ezekiel was thirty years old when he was called by God.

3. Ezekiel never directly mentions Jeremiah, but there are parallels between Ezek. 8–11 and the language used by Jeremiah. It is possible that Ezekiel occasionally expanded and developed some of Jeremiah's messages for his own audience.

in Ezekiel 40–48 are probably the most familiar of Ezekiel's prophecies. The last dated message in his book was given in 571, when Ezekiel was about fifty years old, but nothing is known concerning the remainder of his life. Half of his fifty recorded years were spent in Judah, the rest in exile. Ezekiel was separated from Jerusalem, but not from God. He provided a witness to those in exile, showing that despite the necessary judgment God still loved his people.[4]

Archaeology has shed little light on the book or life of Ezekiel beyond putting the prophet in his proper historical setting. Archaeology does, however, explain one peculiarity in the Book of Ezekiel. Scholars have thought it strange that the prophet used the exile year of King Jehoiachin as his reference point rather than the years of Zedekiah's reign (Ezek. 1:2). Seal impressions reading "Eliakim, Steward of Jehoiachin" have been found at two sites in Judah, leading to the conclusion that after the deportation of 597 an official named Eliakim continued to manage the royal estates. For many Judeans, Jehoiachin was still considered the legitimate king (Albright 1942).

Daniel

Daniel was born approximately the same year as Ezekiel. He was of noble birth, but nothing else is recorded concerning his early years. Still, like Ezekiel, he would have experienced the good years of King Josiah and the series of traumas beginning with Josiah's death in 609. Four years later, while still a teenager, Daniel found himself among the tribute and population being carried back to Babylonia in the first Judean deportation.

Daniel and three of his friends were among the young men selected for three years of training to become scribes for the sprawling Babylonian Empire. Since the Babylonians were in control of many different ethnic and linguistic groups, it was necessary that the government have scribes proficient in both the court language and the various local languages. Bilingual scribes would be able to translate official edicts into whichever local languages were necessary before sending them out into the empire. Likewise, when communications arrived in a local language, a scribe would translate the document for the Babylonians.

Daniel lived centuries after Joseph, but dreams and their interpretations were still important in the Near East. King Nebuchadnezzar must have had cause to mistrust the diviners in his court because, after an especially troubling dream, he placed an additional condition on them. Nebuchadnezzar wanted to know not only what his dreams meant, but he also demanded that he be told what he had dreamed. The interpreters naturally protested, in part because they were schooled to explain a dream through study of its components (Oppenheim 1977: 206–27). In

4. Various misuses and misunderstandings of Ezekiel have unfortunately attracted a following. One "biblical scholar" claimed to have discovered a coded message in the book that described the precise location of treasures from Solomon's Temple. The resultant attempt to unearth this wealth was disastrous (Silberman 1980). See also Yamauchi 1983: 96–97.

Mesopotamia, thousands of ominous signs, including dreams, had been compiled and catalogued together with their interpretations. Nebuchadnezzar's wise men would have searched entries such as the following to help them in their analysis (Oppenheim 1956: 258, 271, 279):

> If a man carries a sprout in his lap and kisses it repeatedly this man will acquire barley and silver. But if it grows out of his lap whatever he owns will be lost.
> If a man is clad in the hide of a goat an important person will be removed and will die.
> If a man flies repeatedly whatever he owns will be lost.
> If a man takes off and flies once for a subject it means loss of good things, for a poor man loss of poverty, he will see his good wishes fulfilled.
> If a man flies from the place he is standing on and rises toward the sky: to this man one will restore what he has lost.
> If he eats meat he knows peace of mind.
> If he eats meat he does not know peace of mind.
> If he eats the flesh of his friend he will enjoy a large share.
> If his friend eats his face he will enjoy a large share.
> If he eats the flesh of his hand his daughter will die.
> If he eats the flesh of his foot his eldest son will die.
> If one gives him a door he will grow old.
> If one gives him a bolt the secret will not leak out.
> If one gives him a wheel he will have twins.

The above list is only a small sampling of the hundreds of dreams that were catalogued. Sometimes the reasoning behind their interpretations is clear, but just as often it is not. Nebuchadnezzar was not rejecting this collected lore, but he was seeking definite proof that his diviners had contact with the gods. He knew what he had dreamed, but he thought that if his diviners were wise enough, they could learn this as well. The heated confrontation ended with Nebuchadnezzar ordering the execution of all his wise men. For some reason Daniel and his friends were to be included in this purge, but they escaped when God revealed the dream and its interpretation to Daniel, who then took the information to the king. Whether Nebuchadnezzar fully understood the interpretation, he was so impressed with Daniel's ability to tell him what his dream had been that he elevated the young man (still a teenager) to higher governmental status. Just as in the days of Joseph in Egypt, it was important to reward and keep such a person close.[5]

If the Septuagint correctly dates Daniel 3, the story of Nebuchadnezzar's golden image, then Daniel's three friends were thrown into a fiery furnace in 586, the same year that Jerusalem fell. The furnace involved was almost certainly one of the many large kilns used for firing the facing bricks needed to make important structures more durable.[6] Jeremiah 29:22 records another instance where two men were burned to death at Nebuchadnezzar's command, and there are also extrabiblical references to such a practice in Mesopotamia. In this episode, however,

5. At this point Ezekiel was still maturing in Jerusalem, while Jeremiah was undergoing persecution in the same city.

6. So many bricks were made that for centuries nearby villagers have been constructing their buildings with baked bricks taken from ancient Babylon!

18.3. The Euphrates River flowed through Babylon and bisected the inner city. Triple walls protected this portion of Babylon, and a wet moat fed by the Euphrates provided additional protection. Procession Street (A) passed through the Ishtar Gate (B), beside which the palace (C) was located. A massively walled fortress (D) was situated on the west side of the palace. The Hanging Gardens (one of the seven wonders of the ancient world) was presumably near the palace, but the long-held assumption that it was within the northeast corner of the palace is no longer accepted. The city's ziggurat (E) and temple to Marduk (F) are to the south. The façade of the Ishtar Gate (facing page, top), nearly forty-seven feet high, as reconstructed in the Berlin Museum. The colorfully glazed bricks alternately depict a bull (symbolizing the god Adad) and dragon (symbolizing the god Marduk). The walls of the Procession Street were decorated with dozens of glazed tile lions symbolizing the goddess Ishtar (facing page, bottom).

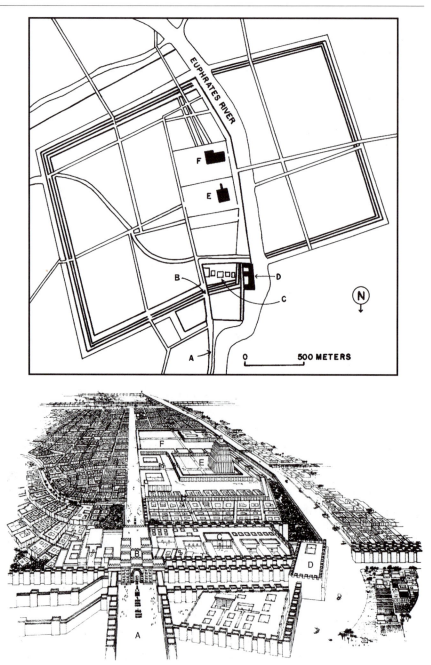

Nebuchadnezzar was unsuccessful in his attempt to punish Daniel's friends; for a time, the king was willing to acknowledge the power of Daniel's god.[7]

7. Some passages in Daniel are sometimes taken as evidence that Nebuchadnezzar converted to Judaism. Unfortunately they only illustrate that he, like other peoples in the ancient Near East, accepted a plurality of gods and believed that some had to be treated carefully. Note that Dan. 2:47 is prior to the "golden image" of Dan. 3. Dan. 3:28–29 was probably uttered around the time Nebuchadnezzar burned Jerusalem and its temple to the ground. Dan. 4:34–37 cannot be chronologically placed, but extrabiblical texts clearly reveal Nebuchadnezzar's zeal for the gods of Babylonia: "Trusting in the

18.4. Building brick from Babylon, just over twelve inches square, stamped with the name of Nebuchadnezzar and recording his restoration of the temples to Marduk and Nabu within the city.

Nebuchadnezzar, the builder of the Babylonian Empire, was also occupied with strengthening and beautifying Babylon, a city whose ruins today spread over hundreds of acres. Daniel 4:30 reflects Nebuchadnezzar's pride in Babylon, but extrabiblical texts are much more expansive (J. Thompson 1982a: 191–93):

> A great wall which like a mountain cannot be moved I made of mortar and brick. . . . Its foundation upon the bosom of the abyss . . . its top I raised mountain high. I triplicated the city wall in order to strengthen it, I caused a great protecting wall to run at the foot of the wall of burnt brick. . . .
>
> Upon the . . . great gates strong bulls . . . and terrible serpents ready to strike, I placed. . . . A third great moat-wall . . . I built with mortar and brick. . . .
>
> The produce of the lands, the products of the mountains, the bountiful wealth of the sea, within [Babylon] I gathered. . . . The palace . . . I rebuilt in Babylon with great cedars I brought from Lebanon, the beautiful forest to roof it. . . .

power of my lords Nebo and Marduk. . . . Marduk, my king. . . . O Marduk, my lord, do remember my deeds favorably" (*ANET* 307). That Nebuchadnezzar was not a convert to Judaism may also be seen in the name of his son and successor: Evil-Merodach, which means "Man of Marduk" (the first part of this name is not a description of his personality; it can also be transliterated "Awil").

Huge cedars from Lebanon, their forest with my clean hands I cut down. With radiant gold I overlaid them, with jewels I adorned them.

Procession Street was sixty-two feet wide and paved with imported stone; it was called *Aibur-Shab* ("the enemy shall never pass") and must have supported many a triumphal parade when the empire ruled the Near East. Nebuchadnezzar was proud of what he had done for Babylon. Many bricks that went into Nebuchadnezzar's building projects were stamped with dedicatory messages, and bricks bearing his name can even now be picked up in the ruins of the city. Such stamped bricks were originally used structurally rather than as face bricks; their inscriptions were intended only for the eyes of the gods.

Daniel 4 contains the account of Nebuchadnezzar and another dream. Daniel interpreted the dream, but the king ignored Daniel's advice. The interpretation was subsequently fulfilled, and Nebuchadnez-

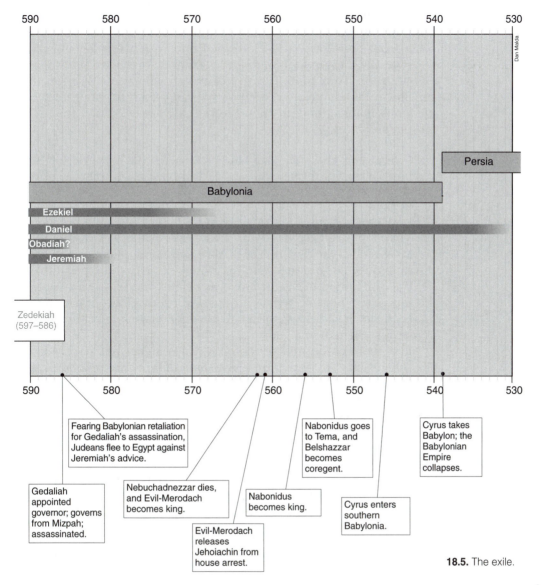

18.5. The exile.

zar found himself stricken with boanthropy, a form of insanity in which the afflicted person believes he is a bull. During the term of his illness, Nebuchadnezzar would have been treated well because the Babylonians would have considered him to be god possessed. The timing of the episode within Nebuchadnezzar's reign is not given, but it must have been long after the dream that catapulted Daniel to high position. Presently there are almost no Babylonian records for the final two-thirds of Nebuchadnezzar's reign, but there seems to have been a time of internal problems, which could have derived from an interim government.

The Babylonian Empire after Nebuchadnezzar

The Babylonian Empire, which Nebuchadnezzar had done so much to build, began to diminish after his death in 562. The throne was briefly taken by his son Evil-Merodach who, in his first year, released Jehoiachin from house arrest and provided him with a regular allowance (2 Kings 25:27–30). Evil-Merodach's kindness received unexpected amplification from administrative documents found at Babylon. The cuneiform tablets involved are poorly preserved, but more than one mentions Jehoiachin with regard to the delivery of oil and foodstuffs for him and his sons:

> For Jehoiachin king of the land Judah, for the five sons of the king of the land of Judah, and for eight Judeans, each one half sila of grain (adapted from Saggs 1988: 132).

Evil-Merodach ruled for only two years before he was assassinated. Then two kings reigned briefly before a high royal official named Nabonidus ascended the throne in 556. Although Nabonidus was already in his sixties when he began to rule, his mother seems to have had a strong influence on him until she died nine years later. She was a worshiper of the moon god Sin and apparently passed on that devotion to Nabonidus. In fact, Nabonidus appears to have had more interest in Sin than in Marduk, the national god.

Nabonidus's career and personality are an enigma, and widely different conclusions are drawn from the same data. Some scholars argue that Nabonidus's strong identification with Sin and the city of Haran indicates that he was not even a true Babylonian and that he never really had a chance to gain lasting acceptance as king. Conversely, regardless whether he was a Babylonian, some argue that his interest in Sin was a statesmanlike attempt to unite the empire under a common moon god.[8]

Because of his interest in the moon god, Nabonidus wanted to restore Sin's temple in Haran. Since his wishes were blocked by the Medes who had controlled the city since the fall of Assyria, Nabonidus

8. By this reasoning, not all vassal nations in the empire worshiped a deity analogous to the sun god, the god of magic, Marduk, but almost all had a moon god by one name or another.

Bildarchiv Preussischer Kulturbesitz, Vorderasiatisches Museum

18.6. Fragmented cuneiform tablet from Babylon containing reference to Jehoiachin.

reached out for assistance to a Persian named Cyrus. At that moment the Persians were under Median authority, but they were becoming restless. Nabonidus encouraged Cyrus's desire for power, and the Persian generated so much trouble that the Medes removed their troops from Haran to bolster the home front. This redeployment won Nabonidus his immediate goal, and he was able to occupy Haran and rebuild its Sin temple.[9] In the long run, however, Nabonidus's brief alliance with Cyrus proved Babylonia's undoing.

Nabonidus was unable to halt the flow of history set in motion in Persia—a motion that he abetted when he temporarily allied himself with Cyrus. In the next few years Cyrus launched campaign after campaign until the Persians eventually took control not only of the Medes, but also of much of the Near East. Nabonidus's response to this burgeoning Persian power provides yet another subject for scholarly debate. In 553 Nabonidus left his son Belshazzar as regent in Babylon while he took an army and moved to Tema.[10] This move into an oasis in the Arabian Desert five hundred miles from Babylon has been vari-

9. Because Nabonidus did a great deal of temple restoration and searching for foundation deposits, he has whimsically been called the "first archaeologist."

10. Belshazzar represents a classic case of critical scholarship's premature denial of Bible history. Since ancient Greek historians identified Nabonidus as the last ruler of the Babylonian Empire and made no mention of Belshazzar, nineteenth-century scholarship concluded that Belshazzar was a fictitious biblical invention. Subsequently, inscriptions were found that made reference to Belshazzar as Nabonidus's eldest son and crown prince. It is true that Belshazzar is never referred to as king in any of the documents, but there are indications that he held a special status, and one document has him entrusted with both the kingship and the army. Therefore, the Bible's reference is to Belshazzar's functional governmental role. See also n. 12.

18.7. Stele (nearly twenty-three inches high) depicting Nabonidus holding a staff in one hand and his other hand raised toward symbols of the gods Sin, Shamash, and Ishtar.

ously judged as "totally inexplicable," the whim of a religious recluse, or as a strong move designed to secure the profitable incense trade routes.[11]

Whatever Nabonidus's motivation, he was not in Babylon at a time of increasing need. His son Belshazzar became the effectual, but not an effective, ruler of the empire. One important example of Belshazzar's ineffectiveness concerns the annual New Year festival. The Babylonians believed that the celebration ensured the favor of the gods for the coming year and that, if the ceremonies were not performed properly, the sun would stop shining and floodwaters would cover the housetops. At one point within the several-day-long event, the ritual required the king of Babylon to sleep with a selected priestess. Belshazzar, as regent, could not participate in this sacred marriage. Each year that this portion of the festival was not consummated only increased the ire of the priesthood and the populace against their rulers.

11. Beaulieu 1989: 178–85 sees the move as one of voluntary exile due to differences between father and son. Beaulieu thinks Belshazzar might have been the dominant figure throughout Nabonidus's reign.

Daniel and the End of the Babylonian Empire

Already in his sixties when Nebuchadnezzar died, Daniel lived through the years of increasing tension and, in the first year of Belshazzar's coregency, had a dream that greatly bothered him (Dan. 7). Two years later another dream agitated him even more (Dan. 8) as God revealed to Daniel that the Babylonian Empire was about to be destroyed by the Medes and the Persians. Daniel would have been well aware of these countries to the east, especially of the Persians, who had already expanded beyond their borders. Daniel might have wondered what the rise of Persia meant for Babylonia, but through God's revelations he knew it meant the end of the empire he had served for almost fifty years. He was about to see his second "homeland" overthrown.

As the years went on, Belshazzar continued on the throne in place of his absent father. The Persians under Cyrus encroached more and more on territories outside their homeland, and Persian banners were flown over Media, northern Mesopotamia, Armenia, India, and Asia Minor as far as the Halys River. After another campaign, Persian control extended all the way to the Aegean, where Sardis was made the new empire's western capital.

The Babylonian Empire shrank as Persian power grew. By 546 the Persians were in control of southern Babylonia, and by 539 little more than the city of Babylon and its environs were left of the old empire. By this time Nabonidus had returned from Tema, but his response to the empire's collapse was to gather various god statues into Babylon for their collective powers of protection.

While the armies of Cyrus were on the outskirts of Babylon, Belshazzar held his famous banquet. With some justification Belshazzar believed that Babylon could never fall. The city occupied hundreds of acres; its outer wall was over seventy feet wide, so broad that chariots could pass each other along its top; it had towers and wide, wet moats. The inner city was protected by three sets of defensive walls, moats, and towers and a fortress with massive walls beside the palace.

The palace was comprised of hundreds of rooms and several open courts—ample space for the throng Belshazzar invited to his banquet (illustration 18.8). Belshazzar's throne room, just off the central court, would be where the undecipherable handwriting suddenly appeared. Belshazzar became alarmed—especially when none of his diviners could deal with this inscription. This was outside the realm of their omen volumes. Then the queen came into the hall, and from the conversations that followed, it becomes clear that Daniel had been only a minor official since Nebuchadnezzar's death. Daniel came into Belshazzar's presence for the first time.

Daniel was in his eighties when he explained the handwriting to Belshazzar. Belshazzar had promised that anyone who could read and interpret the inscription would be made "third ruler in the kingdom" (Dan. 5:7).[12] Although Daniel predicted doom for the king and the

12. When it was found that Belshazzar was actually second ruler in the kingdom, it became clear why he specified "third ruler" as his reward; it was the highest position that could be offered to the person successfully deciphering the handwriting.

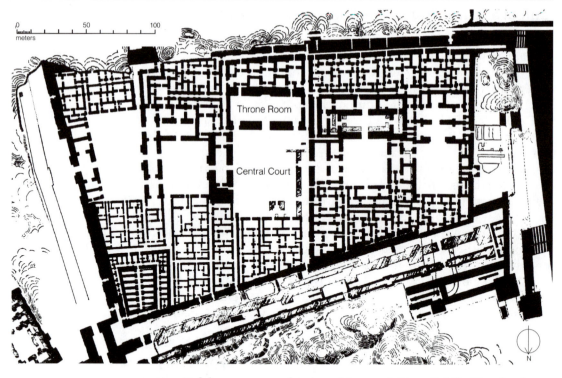

country, Belshazzar proved true to his word (Dan. 5:29). Shortly thereafter, Belshazzar was dead and the last of the Babylonian Empire fell (Millard 1985a).

As Cyrus the Persian marched through southern Mesopotamia, most of the cities greeted him as a liberator. They were tired of Belshazzar and his negligent father, and they had heard positive reports of the way Cyrus respected people in his new territories. Cyrus was a master of propaganda; he cast himself as a just man to those he ruled, as a ruler with happy subjects, as a benefactor to the needy, and as a king over kings. Cyrus also promoted himself as properly religious, and he wanted the Babylonians to believe that their god Marduk had elected him to rule. The following excerpts from one of Cyrus's inscriptions illustrates the image he wanted to convey (*ANE* 1:206–7; *ANET* 315–16):

> Marduk . . . scanned and looked through all the countries, searching for a righteous ruler willing to lead him in the annual procession. Then he pronounced the name of Cyrus. . . . Marduk, the great lord, a protector of his people, beheld with pleasure Cyrus's good deeds and his upright mind and therefore ordered him to march against his city Babylon. He made him set out on the road to Babylon, going at his side like a real friend. His widespread troops . . . strolled along, their weapons packed away. Without any battle, he made him enter his town Babylon, sparing Babylon any calamity. He delivered into Cyrus's hands Nabonidus, the king who did not worship Marduk. All the inhabitants of Babylon as well as of the entire country . . . bowed to Cyrus and kissed his feet, jubilant that he had received the kingship, and with shining faces. . . . They worshiped his very name.
>
> I am Cyrus, king of the world, great king, legitimate king, king of Babylon . . . king of the four rims of the earth. . . .

Bildarchiv Preussischer Kulturbesitz, Vorderasiatisches Museum

18.8. Plan of the palace of Nebuchadnezzar (facing page) and portion of the south wall of the central court as reconstructed in the Berlin Museum (left). The wall is just under forty-one feet high. Anyone standing in the court could look past its central door to the king seated in the far niche. Anton Moortgat (1969: 161) describes the wall decoration as "part of one of the greatest compositions in glazed brick of the Neo-Babylonian period, and its symbolical-decorative meaning is undoubtedly connected with the concept of the Neo-Babylonian kingdom. A long row of stylized, slender trees with volute capitals supports a continuous frieze of palmettes, and is suspended above another frieze of lions pacing along on a band decorated with rosettes. There can be no reasonable doubt about the meaning of the whole decoration: tree and palmette, symbol of life, as old as Mesopotamian culture, suspended above the lions, the symbol of the Underworld, from which life is bursting forth. In the centre of this sits the king enthroned, the protector and renewer of life."

When I entered Babylon as a friend and when I established the seat of the government in the palace of the ruler under jubilation and rejoicing, Marduk, the great lord, induced the magnanimous inhabitants of Babylon to love me. . . . My numerous troops walked around in Babylon in peace, I did not allow anybody to terrorize any place. . . . I strove for peace. . . . I abolished the corvée. . . . I brought relief to their dilapidated housing, thus putting an end to their main complaints.

According to Herodotus, the Persians gained entry into Babylon by diverting the Euphrates and coming in through its riverbed. They met little resistance. The Bible says that Belshazzar was slain; Babylonian

British Museum

18.9. Baked-clay Cylinder of Cyrus (nine inches long) records his capture of Babylon without a battle.

records report that Nabonidus was spared and treated as a harmless person who should be humored. Soon Cyrus was able to make a triumphal entry (*ANE* 1:204; *ANET* 306):

> Cyrus entered Babylon, green twigs were spread in front of him—the state of "Peace" was imposed upon the city. Cyrus sent greetings to all Babylon. Gobryas, his governor, installed subgovernors in Babylon.

One historical difficulty with the fall of Babylon still has not been resolved. Daniel 5:31 says that "Darius the Mede" took the kingdom, but no such person has been found outside the Bible. Various attempts have been made to identify this Darius with known historical figures, and some scholars equate him with the above-mentioned Gobryas. In cuneiform records and according to Greek historians, Gobryas played a key role in the capture of Babylon and its subsequent administration. Therefore, one working hypothesis is that Cyrus appointed Gobryas subruler over Babylon and that Gobryas took on the trappings of royalty. The name *Darius* was possibly an old Persian royal title such as "Caesar" or "Augustus" in the Roman Empire.[13]

During the administration of "Darius the Mede," Daniel received a new and high position (Dan. 6:1–3). Persian policy was to rule through local people whenever possible, and Belshazzar's reward, though short lived, perhaps gave Daniel the exposure necessary for the Persians to include him in their new government. For some reason, however, the elderly Daniel soon became so unpopular with other officials that they could not wait for him to die naturally. Instead, the officials succeeded in having Darius the Mede innocently pass an edict by which Daniel could be accused and sentenced to death.[14] The ploy worked and

13. It is also theorized that "Darius the Mede" was another designation for Cyrus. For a summary of attempts to resolve the problem, see Yamauchi 1990: 58–59. As with the conundrum over Belshazzar, it can be expected that Darius the Mede will be solved in time.

14. This edict of Darius the Mede was not in line with Persian policy. Perhaps he went along with the religious demands because the Babylonians insisted that local norms be carefully followed. The ecumenically minded Persians would see the logic in such an argument.

Daniel was thrown into a lion's den. Game preserves with their penned animals (see illustration 17.13) were evidently still a feature of Mesopotamian life, and this is the type of "den" into which Daniel was thrown.

God protected Daniel from the lions, and Darius the Mede was happy to throw those who plotted against Daniel into the den—to a different fate. Daniel's life was spared but, because of his advanced age, he probably did not live much longer. God told him the exile was ending, and he may have seen the first group leave for Palestine, but he would have been too old to make such a journey. He was also too important both to the Persians and to his own people where he was.

The Nature of the Exile

The populations of Israel and Judah were not completely deported when their countries fell. Those left behind in Israel soon found themselves amid imported neighbors, and in time there was intermarriage and a blurring of religious values. The Samaritans eventually emerged from this mixture. In Judah there was some attempt to continue worship among the ruins of Solomon's Temple (Jer. 41:5). Their life does not seem to have been easy, as neighboring peoples filtered in and claimed land in previously Judean territory.

Many thousands were uprooted in the various deportations and forced to make new beginnings in distant lands. These people must have had a wide spectrum of emotions, from hatred of God to a recognition that they had merely become the ones to experience the long-heralded punishment. The Bible provides several insights into the life of those in exile and indicates that their lot was not as severe as is sometimes imagined. For example, families were not torn apart in exile; when they finally returned home, the Bible records they did so by families and by groups still identified with specific cities in Palestine. To have done so implies that their communities and family structures stayed intact throughout captivity.

That Jeremiah addressed a letter to those in exile during the reign of Zedekiah shows that people in faraway lands were not completely cut off from home. And the lifestyle that Jeremiah thought they could and should assume does not sound like one of suffering or deprivation (Jer. 29:4–7). Of greatest importance, especially to the religious, the exiles were allowed freedom of worship. This privilege can be inferred from the false prophets that Jeremiah's letter also addressed, the repeated access that people had to Ezekiel, and Ezra's later being recognized for his knowledge of the Jewish faith. Also, the synagogue emerged during the Babylonian exile as a replacement for the distant and destroyed temple. Both Ezra and Ezekiel state that study of the law could be an acceptable substitute for sacrifice, and this is what began to take place within synagogues. Later, when people returned from exile, they brought the synagogue concept with them—not to replace the temple, but to coexist with it.

18.10. Silver amulet, pictured here unrolled (just over one-and-one-half inches long), and another (slightly more than twice that length) were discovered in 1979 in tombs at Ketef Hinnom just across the Hinnom Valley from Mount Zion in Jerusalem. The initial excitement generated over these amulets was due to the presence of the name *Yahweh*, the first time God's divine name had been found in the Jerusalem area. The fragile nature of the amulets has thus far stymied their full decipherment, but each has an abbreviated version of the priestly benediction of Numbers 6:24–26 and contain, therefore, the earliest biblical texts known. The tombs and the amulets provide additional insights concerning Palestine during the beginning of the exile. The tombs show, for example, that the environs of Jerusalem were not as deserted as some have supposed; the wealth of objects in the tombs reveals that not all those who stayed behind were indigent (Jer. 39:10). These artifacts attest to the practice of wearing amuletic texts in Old Testament times and indicate personal use of the priestly blessing at least this early (Barkay 1983 and 1986).

The exiles were possibly allowed a form of local government. The repeated visits of elders to Ezekiel suggest that some form of the old patriarchal system had been reinstituted. Without a functioning Jewish king, the elders may have served to bond the people together. It is quite clear that one could become both rich and important while in exile. So much freedom must have been allowed, or at least winked at, that by the time the exile was over, many of the Jews had become wealthy (cf. Ezra 2:68–69). Some had become goldsmiths and pharmacists, hardly menial occupations in Babylonian society (Neh. 3:8). Daniel and his friends provide obvious examples of the upward mobility at least a few came to enjoy.

The negative side of exile probably included some of the people being put to work on government projects, and all would have been required to pay taxes to their imposed rulers. False prophets with their deluding words of soon return would have created tensions, especially when their prophecies were found to be hollow. Adjustment must have been most difficult for the first generation of exiles, those with strong attachments to the homeland, and those who longed to worship God in Jerusalem. Psalm 137 expresses the cry of such a person, but such sentiments were in the minority at least by the time it was permissible to return home. As each successive generation was born in exile, it would have been harder to maintain strong cultural and religious ties with the homeland.

Archaeological data supports the conclusion that exile was not an entirely distasteful experience. In the last half of the fifth century, long after forced exile was over, there was a large mercantile center in Nippur, a city sixty miles southeast of Babylon. A number of the hundreds of business documents recovered from this activity contain Jewish names like Benjamin, Gedaliah, and Hananiah. These clay tablets show that some Jews in Nippur were quite successful and stayed in their adopted country even when they had the opportunity to return to Palestine (Coogan 1974 and Stolper 1976).

This disinclination to return home can also be demonstrated in Egypt, the country to which Jeremiah was forcibly taken. Several Jewish communities established themselves in Egypt, and one of these was situated at Elephantine (part of modern-day Aswan) on Egypt's southern border. After the Jerusalem Temple had been rebuilt, the community at Elephantine began to correspond with those who had returned to Judah. From the preserved letters, it is clear that the Jews in Egypt had specific problems and needs, but there are no hints that they considered returning to Palestine (Kraeling 1952; see also the epigraph to chap. 19).

Additional Reading

Arnold, Bill T. "Babylonians." Pp. 43–75 in *Peoples of the Old Testament World*. Edited by Alfred J. Hoerth, Gerald L. Mattingly, and Edwin M. Yamauchi. Grand Rapids: Baker, 1994.

Avigad, N. "Seals of Exiles." *IEJ* 15 (1965): 222–32.

Dougherty, Raymond P., *Nabonidus and Belshazzar: A Study of the Closing Events of the Neo-Babylonian Empire*. New Haven: Yale University Press, 1929.

Freedy, K. S., and Donald B. Redford. "The Dates in Ezekiel in Relation to Biblical, Babylonian and Egyptian Sources." *Journal of the American Oriental Society* 90 (1970): 462–85.

Herr, Larry G. "The Servant of Baalis." *BA* 48 (1985): 169–72.

Wiseman, Donald J. *Nebuchadrezzar and Babylon*. Schweich Lectures 1983. Oxford: Oxford University Press, 1985.

Yamauchi, Edwin M. "Babylon." Pp. 32–41 in *Major Cities of the Biblical World*. Edited by Roland K. Harrison. Nashville: Nelson, 1985.

———. "Persians." Pp. 107–24 in *Peoples of the Old Testament World*. Edited by Alfred J. Hoerth, Gerald L. Mattingly, and Edwin M. Yamauchi. Grand Rapids: Baker, 1994.

Younker, Randall W. "Israel, Judah, and Ammon and the Motifs on the Baalis Seal from Tell el-ʾUmeiri." *BA* 48 (1985): 173–80.

Zorn, Jeffrey. "Mizpah: Newly Discovered Stratum Reveals Judah's Other Capital." *BAR* 23/5 (1997): 28–38, 66.

From the Restoration to the Close of the Old Testament

To our lord Bagoas, governor of Judah, your servants Yedoniah and his colleagues, the priests who are in the fortress of Elephantine. May the God of heaven seek after the welfare of our lord exceedingly at all times and give you favor before King Darius and the nobles a thousand times more than now. May you be happy and healthy at all times. Now, your servant Yedoniah and his colleagues depose as follows: . . . the priests of the god Khnub . . . conspired . . . to wipe out the temple of the god Yaho from the fortress of Elephantine. . . . Coming with their weapons to the fortress of Elephantine, they entered that temple and razed it to the ground. . . . Now, our forefathers built this temple . . . back in the days of the kingdom of Egypt, and when Cambyses came to Egypt he found it built. . . . [When our temple was destroyed] we and our wives and our children wore sackcloth and fasted and prayed to Yaho the Lord of heaven. . . . We have also sent a letter . . . to our lord and to the high priest Johanan and his colleagues the priests in Jerusalem and to Ostanes the brother of Anani and the nobles of the Jews.

—Letter from Elephantine Jews to the governor of Judah

Xerxes and Esther
Ezra and Nehemiah
Additional Reading

The year 539 marks the close of the Babylonian period and the beginning of the Persian period in Near Eastern history. In at least three important ways Persian rule differed from that of the previous empires. Assyrian and to a lesser extent Babylonian practice had been to rule by fear. The harsh Assyrian treatment of rebellious nations was broadcast as an incentive to others to remain passive. The Persians could be equally harsh with their enemies, but their propaganda attempted to instill gratitude and contentment among their subjects. Their policy was to hold the empire through "love not war." It had also been Assyrian policy to belittle the gods of other nations and perhaps to impose a portion of Assyrian religion on the subject nations.[1] The Persians, on the other hand, were ecumenically minded. Their own chief god was Ahuramazda, but the depth of their devotion to this deity seems minimal. The Persians went out of their way to acknowledge the deities of subject nations, and they encouraged other peoples to properly worship their gods. They even provided assistance to those who needed to restore their god statues or temples.

The Assyrians began and the Babylonians continued the practice of deporting people from their homeland and resettling them in distant reaches of the empire. This uprooting of peoples probably lessened the ability of some to revolt, but it also cultivated a hatred for the regime that never fully dissipated. Although the Persians relocated some populations, they largely encouraged people to live where they chose in the empire, and if they wished to return to their ancestral homeland they could even expect help in their resettlement.

In short, the Persians tried to rule with a "velvet glove." They wanted happy subjects, and to that end they allowed freedom of movement within the empire, as well as freedom of religion. The impact of these new attitudes on the Jews was immediate, and the Book of Ezra preserves two copies of the proclamation made specifically for them in 538 (Ezra 1:2–4; 6:3–5).[2] Some conclude from this decree that Cyrus had converted to Judaism, but there is absolutely no warrant for such an assumption. Cyrus must have made the same general acknowledgment to dozens of local deities. His proclamation should be seen in context with the fawning pro-Marduk remarks made when he overthrew Babylon (see pp. 382–83).

Ezra 2 reports that fifty thousand Jews responded to the proclamation, a number that indicates that no great groundswell developed to return home. They set out for a homeland that had changed. Palestine, along with Phoenicia, Syria, and Cyprus, was now grouped into a Persian district (satrapy) called "The Land beyond the River" (i.e., the Euphrates) with its capital in Damascus. Palestine itself was divided into four provinces: Galilee, Samaria, Judah, and Idumea. The densest population and most prosperous area was now along the coastline where the towns were controlled by either Tyre or Sidon (Katzenstein 1979). The prevalence of Greek pottery is just one of several indications of the growing cosmopolitan character of the coastal cities. The great amount of pottery found there for transporting commodities signals the increased importance of the Mediterranean and its shipping lanes.

---

1. For example, Ahaz was forced to build an Assyrian altar within the precincts of Solomon's Temple; 2 Kings 16:10–16.

2. One copy is in Aramaic (Ezra 6:3–5) and is the record that would have been kept in a Persian legal library. The other copy (Ezra 1:2–4) is in Hebrew and is the version proclaimed directly to the Jews. It should be recalled that some years earlier the Babylonians trained Daniel to be a scribe to handle some of the multilingual needs of the empire. Those needs continued with the Persians. In that regard, note that a trilingual inscription accompanies the relief on the Behistun monument (illustration 19.3).

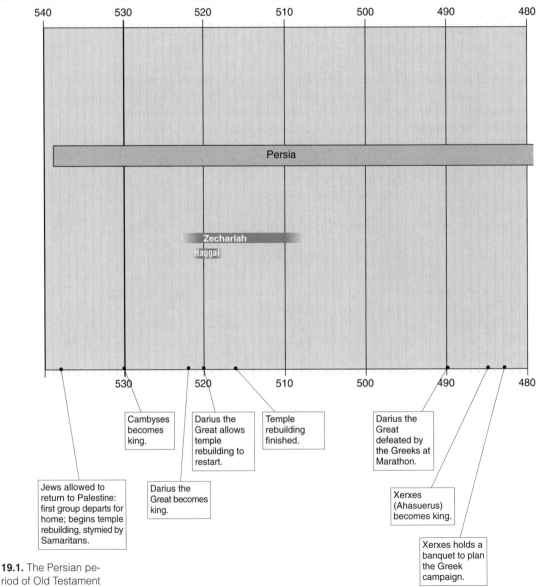

19.1. The Persian period of Old Testament history.

Within the figure:

540 530 520 510 500 490 480

Persia

Zechariah
Haggai

530 520 510 500 490 480

Cambyses becomes king.

Darius the Great allows temple rebuilding to restart.

Temple rebuilding finished.

Darius the Great defeated by the Greeks at Marathon.

Jews allowed to return to Palestine: first group departs for home; begins temple rebuilding, stymied by Samaritans.

Darius the Great becomes king.

Xerxes (Ahasuerus) becomes king.

Xerxes holds a banquet to plan the Greek campaign.

Months later, when those who elected to return arrived in the Jerusalem area, some probably felt they had made the wrong decision. They found little land that was not claimed by others, and they soon began to fear for their own safety. They quickly reinstated worship in Jerusalem and set about rebuilding the temple. There was both praise to God and tears shed by "old men who had seen the first temple" (Ezra 3:1–13). This bittersweet gathering was approached by Samaritans from northern Palestine with offers of aid (Ezra 4:2). The Samaritans had grown prominent in the affairs of the land, and they naturally wished to participate in a project of such importance. However genuine their offer of assistance, those in charge of the rebuilding felt the Samaritans were not sufficiently orthodox to participate.

The rebuffed Samaritans reacted by frightening the returnees into

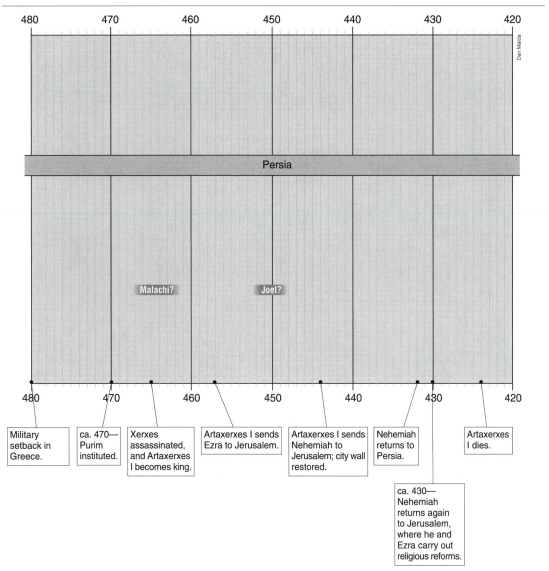

480 470 460 450 440 430 420

Persia

Malachi? Joel?

480 470 460 450 440 430 420

Military setback in Greece.

ca. 470— Purim instituted.

Xerxes assassinated, and Artaxerxes I becomes king.

Artaxerxes I sends Ezra to Jerusalem.

Artaxerxes I sends Nehemiah to Jerusalem; city wall restored.

Nehemiah returns to Persia.

Artaxerxes I dies.

ca. 430— Nehemiah returns again to Jerusalem, where he and Ezra carry out religious reforms.

discontinuing construction, and the urgency to finish the work slowly waned. In time Cyrus died and was succeeded by his son Cambyses II. Cambyses is not mentioned in the Bible, but extrabiblically it is known that he passed through Palestine in 525 and conquered all of Egypt, something the Assyrians and Babylonians had not been able to do.[3] Three years later Cambyses was hurrying back home to put down a rumored revolt when he died in northern Palestine or Syria. The Jerusalem Temple still had not progressed beyond the new foundations.

3. The epigraph heading this chapter is from a letter written in 407 (*ANE* 1:279–80; *ANET* 492). As noted in the letter, these Elephantine Jews had become part of the Diaspora some time before the reign of Cambyses. Over one hundred years after the completion of the Jerusalem temple, their letters give no hint that they wished to emigrate to Palestine. This Darius is Darius II (423–405). Khnub is the Egyptian ram-god. Yaho might be a variation on the divine name for God, or it might signal, along with their building a temple in Egypt, that these Jews were no longer orthodox in their worship. A high priest named Johanan is mentioned in Neh. 12:22–23.

John McRay

19.2. Tomb of Cyrus at Pasargadae, about fifty miles north of Persepolis. In 530 Cyrus, nearly seventy, personally led a battle in the far northeast part of his empire. He was mortally wounded and died three days later. Set in a garden, the doorway into the tomb is only four-and-one-half feet high and has two swinging doors. The outer door had to be closed before the inner door could be opened. The tomb is long since empty, but it is reported to have had a tublike sarcophagus of gold resting on a couch.

Cambyses left no son. Darius, an uncle from another branch of the royal family, became one of the claimants for the throne. Darius held a high position in the Immortals, the elite corps within the Persian army, and within two years he had quieted all opposition to his assumption of kingship. Then he began to earn his title: "Darius the Great."[4]

As Darius was solidifying his claim to the Persian throne, the Lord raised up the prophet Haggai in Jerusalem. Little is known about Haggai's background, but the opening verse to his book indicates that he began his ministry to the people of Judah in late August 520. Haggai condemned his listeners for having lost their enthusiasm for God's house and for being preoccupied with their own homes (Hag. 1:2–4). In various ways the Lord had been trying to make the people rethink their priorities (Hag. 1:5–6), but they had not responded. In Haggai, the Lord must have chosen an extremely persuasive speaker because, within a month, work had resumed on the temple.[5]

The rebuilding had barely begun when Tattenai, a governor from the district of Samaria, visited Jerusalem. He and his colleagues began to assert their authority, and they dispatched a report to Darius concerning the work and asking whether they should allow the project to continue (Ezra 5:7–17). This action of the governor and his colleagues must have been devastating to the people in Jerusalem. They had just

4. He is not to be confused with Darius the Mede who earlier controlled Babylon.

5. With work renewed, Haggai reminded the people of how unfulfilled their lives had been, and he predicted that their faithfulness would bring a change (Hag. 2:15–19). Haggai (as well as Amos 4) taught that hardship can be from God, designed to bring a person back to him.

19.3. The Behistun monument, about seventy miles southwest of Ecbatana, was carved high on a cliff where it could not be defaced. In the relief portion Darius (third from the left) is the largest figure at five feet eight inches and faces the captured leaders who contested his becoming king. The trilingual inscription is fifty-nine feet wide and extends on both sides and beneath the relief. The inscription is written in Old Persian, Elamite, and Babylonian (the three languages used for formal inscriptions) and provided the key to deciphering Mesopotamian cuneiform.

responded to Haggai, believing they were finally doing God's will, and suddenly their effort was only bringing them grief. What, they must have worried, would be Darius's response? To their credit, they did not halt work on the temple (Ezra 5:5), but their enthusiasm must have dropped, and some must have questioned Haggai's credentials. Into this time of consternation the Lord sent Zechariah, who began to work with Haggai to bolster the morale of the people (e.g., Zech. 8:3–9).[6]

Tattenai's letter duly arrived at the Persian court and a memorandum from Cyrus was located in the Ecbatana archives directing that the temple be built (Ezra 6:1–5). Bureaucracies in that part of the Near East were famous for their record-keeping systems. The Persians kept tablets and scrolls on shelves, in baskets, and in jars, and they used tags and other labeling devices to hasten retrieval of documents. Their system was so good that Alexander the Great later adopted it for his library in Alexandria.

Following the retrieval of the Cyrus document, Darius the Great dictated a reply and sent it on its way to Palestine. Some Bible readers may assume the people in Jerusalem waited and worried for many months, even years for the reply, but that is not the case. Darius the Great introduced several changes in the way the empire was administered, and the highway system was one of his high priorities. The Persian Royal Road stretched some seventeen hundred miles from Susa through Arbela (near Nineveh) to Sardis (illustration 19.4). The road was carefully maintained, and rough stretches were paved. It was the Persians who invented horseshoes to facilitate mail moving over this Royal Road. Post stations were positioned on average every fifteen miles so Persian couriers could mount fresh horses. This communication network functioned so well that a letter written in Susa would reach Sardis in one week.[7] Fifth-century Greek historian Herodotus was so impressed by the efficiency of the Persian mail system that he coined the well-known saying in praise of Xerxes's system of mounted couriers (8.98):

> Neither snow nor rain nor heat nor gloom of night stays these couriers from the swift completion of their appointed rounds.

6. Like Haggai it is uncertain whether Zechariah grew up in Palestine or returned to that land in 538. He was a priest as well as a prophet.

7. A courier could average about 240 miles a day. A caravan took ninety days to cover the same distance, an average of nineteen miles a day.

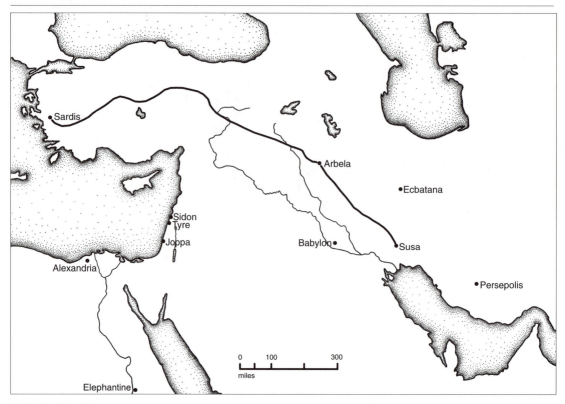

19.4. The Near East between the restoration from exile to the close of the Old Testament. The exact route of the Persian Royal Road between Susa and Sardis is not certain. The dark line indicates the "northern route."

Secondary routes branched off the Royal Road, but no precise time figures have been preserved for the courier service connecting Jerusalem with the Persian capitals. Assuming the road system was fully operational early in Darius's reign, the whole episode could have been resolved in a month or two at the most. And, since Haggai began his ministry in late August 520 and had finished before the end of that same year, less than four months must be the outside time span.

Wildly different emotions can be imagined as Darius's letter was read in Jerusalem (Ezra 6:6–12). Darius felt that the earlier edict of Cyrus should be honored and that the favor of another god could not hurt him. In return for allowing the work to proceed, he expected that prayers be said on his and his sons' behalf. Tattenai probably expected commendation, if not reward. Now, not only would the temple construction proceed, but he and his colleagues had been saddled with expenses for its completion and use! For the Jews there must have been the realization that the trouble had been only a prelude to a blessing. God had provided the necessary expenses, and the work could continue without worry or need.[8]

The rebuilding of the temple was completed in 516, the sixth year of King Darius, (Ezra 6:15), and with its dedication it can be said that both God and his people had returned home. The hope of restoration and the prophecies of regathering were now realized. As Hosea, Jere-

8. There is an echo in this episode of Joseph's earlier observation that God can work out for good what others intended for evil.

19.5. In the treasury scene at Persepolis (just over twenty feet wide; limestone), Darius is seated on his throne, receiving a report from his Median commander. Xerxes, at that time crown prince, is on the dais with his father. Behind him are two court officials; spearmen balance the scene on either end.

miah, and other prophets had stressed, God had to divorce himself from evil, but his love and mercy would outlast his judgment.

There were disturbances when Darius died in 485, and a number of destructions in central Palestine coincide with this time. Regrettably, the archaeological record for the Persian period in Palestine is less than for earlier centuries (although Stern 1982 finds the situation not as meager as has often been assumed). Later Roman builders put down deep foundations, often destroying Persian-period levels in the process. At other sites Persian levels were so near the surface that they suffered from weather and erosion.

Xerxes and Esther

Following the completion of the temple, the biblical record is silent until 483. Then the focus becomes the Persian homeland, where the empire was being ruled by Khshayarsha (Hebrew Ahasuerus), son of Darius the Great. This new king was known to the Greeks as Xerxes I, and this is the form of his name most commonly used. The Book of Esther opens with Xerxes holding a lavish banquet (Esth. 1:3–9). One purpose of this banquet might have been to bring together the command elements of the Persian military in order to plan a campaign against Greece. Xerxes had spent his opening years as king regaining Egypt, which had revolted after learning of his father's defeat at Marathon, and punishing Babylon for an uprising. Now there was time to avenge Marathon.[9]

There is approximately a three-year interval between Esther 1 and Esther 2, during which Xerxes was involved with his campaign to conquer Greece (compare Esth. 1:3 and 2:16). The Persian army marched

9. Darius was defeated by the Athenians in the plains of Marathon in 490. Athenian forces then rushed home because their city was debating whether to surrender to a Persian fleet. When the Athenian forces reached Athens the Persian fleet retired. The marathon race, which was introduced into the modern Olympic Games in 1896, commemorates the legend that a courier ran over twenty miles from the battle to Athens to proclaim victory and then dropped dead from the exertion.

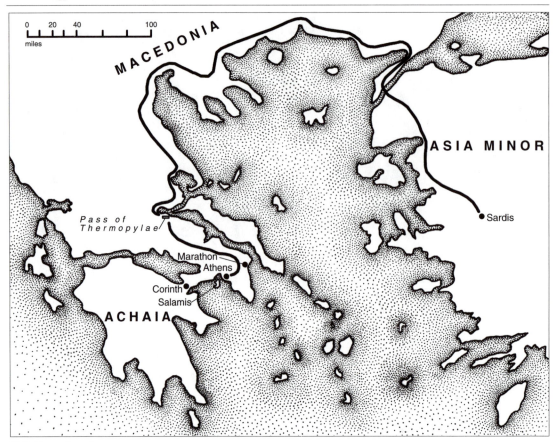

19.6. Campaign of Xerxes into Greece. During his army's march from Sardis to Athens (heavy line), the Persian fleet followed offshore.

across Asia Minor and into Macedonia, and a fleet composed largely of Egyptian and Phoenician ships sailed west along the coastlines (illustration 19.6). Xerxes had the advantage of numbers in both his army and navy, and he met little resistance as his army poured into Greece.

The Persians met their first serious obstacle at Thermopylae, where a pass about fifty feet wide was flanked by the sea on one side and mountains on the other. There, a few thousand defenders successfully stalled the whole Persian army until a traitor revealed the presence of a path leading up into the mountains and then down behind the Greek positions. Xerxes sent his Immortals up the path, and when Leonidus the Spartan commander learned of the flanking movement, he allowed most of his allies to retire. But instead of pulling back with his own three hundred soldiers, Leonidus chose to stand and buy time for the evacuation of Athens. He and his Spartans perished, but their sacrifice is immortalized in Greek history.

Xerxes pushed past Thermopylae, marched on Athens, and captured the acropolis. The Persian king seemed very much in command of the situation when he moved on the Greek fleet located in the nearby bay of Salamis. Xerxes had his portable golden throne set atop a hill overlooking the bay. Not all the details of the ensuing battle are certain, but by all accounts the Persian ships sailed into a trap and were forced into shallow waters where they could not maneuver. As Xerxes watched, his fleet was decimated (P. Green 1970). Xerxes then pulled out of Greece

19.7. Gold rhyton (just under four inches tall) found at Ecbatana. This drinking cup illustrates the wealth and artistic ability available to Persian nobility.

with most of his army and wintered at Sardis. While there, his attempted seduction of his sister-in-law failed. Xerxes's mood when he returned home the next spring, and the beauty contest of Esther 2 was conducted, can be well imagined.

The Persians had several capitals. The three main ones were Ecbatana (where Cyrus's decree concerning the Jerusalem Temple was found), Persepolis the treasury city, and Susa. Xerxes spent the remainder of his years moving from one to another of his capitals, amusing himself with building programs and women. He never again accompanied his army to war.[10]

Esther's story is set in Susa, but she would have been equally familiar with Ecbatana and Persepolis.[11] As queen she would have moved with Xerxes from one capital to another. Many beautiful treasures have been recovered in the excavation of Susa. Unfortunately, poor excavation technique destroyed much of the character of the ancient city, and the objects have to be appreciated apart from their original context. Enough is known of the three capitals, however, to recognize that all were architecturally similar. The treasury city of Persepolis affords better insights into a Persian palace in the days of Xerxes and Esther.

A plot on Xerxes's life was foiled by Mordecai, the uncle who had reared Esther (Esth. 2:20–23).[12] This attempt on Xerxes's life was not an isolated incident, for there was much intrigue in the Persian court. In one convoluted episode Xerxes's brother and sister-in-law fled from

10. The Persian general left in Greece with the remaining forces died in battle the next year. After his death the Greek campaign completely collapsed.

11. Esther is the name given her by the Persians after she had won the beauty contest. Her Hebrew name was Hadassah.

12. Mordecai could be the extrabiblical Marduka, one of Xerxes's high officials. It is clear from the Bible that Mordecai had access to the court at least by the time Esther became part of it and that he received an official position some years later.

Réunion des Musées Nationaux

19.8. Life-size procession of Persian royal guards from the palace of Darius the Great at Susa. Created by Babylonian artisans, the friezes recall the decorative technique used earlier at Babylon (see illustrations 18.3 and 18.8).

19.9. Persepolis (facing page, top left) was set on an artificial terrace, and entrance was gained by means of a monumental staircase (A). Darius the Great began and Xerxes finished the Apadana or audience room (B), with columns nearly seventy feet high. Darius commissioned a treasury building at the site (C), and Xerxes added another (D) to accommodate the tribute flowing in from all corners of the empire. Xerxes's palace (E) has a private staircase leading into the harem (F); the size of the harem was more than doubled when he returned from Greece. Little of the site's elevation remains (facing page, center) because much of it was constructed in mud brick to provide cool interiors. Reliefs at Persepolis show an eclectic art, with Mesopotamian, Egyptian, and even Greek elements. The central scene (facing page, lower right) on the façade of the Apadana's eastern stairway depicts Persian (wearing fluted crowns and ankle-length robes) and Median Immortals (wearing rounded hats and short tunics). The Immortals were based at Persepolis. The "stacked folding" on the Persian costume is attributed to Greek artisans who worked at the site. Dozens of tribute scenes decorate the staircases of the Apadana (facing page, lower left), each depicting tribute bearers in their native costume and presenting tribute characteristic of their country. On the right, a Persian escorts Syrians carrying vessels of gold and silver and leading a chariot drawn by two horses. A "royal hero" from a doorway in Xerxes's harem plunges a dagger into the belly of a griffin with scorpion tail (facing page, top right).

the court to try to set up opposition to the crown. They were captured, and Xerxes subjected them to tortured deaths.

The story of Esther centers on an official named Haman, who hated Mordecai. Haman used divination for nearly a year before he felt he had received the proper sign to make his move. A decree written by Haman (with authority from Xerxes) then announced that in eleven months all Jews were to be annihilated. The time lag likely derives from the use of divination in search of a propitious day for such slaughter. Understandably, the Jews went into mourning and began fasting, but Mordecai also went into action and urged Esther to make appeal to the king. He suggested to Esther that God had placed her within the court for just such an emergency. By this time, Esther had been married to Xerxes for more than five years, and tellingly she notes that she has not been summoned by her husband for a month (Esth. 4:11). Her novelty had worn off. Esther appealed to Xerxes, and soon Haman was hanging from the gallows he had prepared for Mordecai.

In commemoration of the deliverance from Haman, Purim, a new annual celebration, was added to the Hebrew religious calendar. To Jews, the Book of Esther has come to be an assurance of their survival. To them, as well as to Christians, it is also an example of how God protects his people.[13] In 465 the protection around Xerxes failed and the king was murdered. Esther would have still been relatively young, but nothing further is known about her.

Ezra and Nehemiah

When Xerxes died, several intrigues and deaths played out before the throne was secured by Artaxerxes I, a younger son of Xerxes. The biblical account resumes in the seventh year of Artaxerxes (457) when Ezra traveled to Jerusalem (Ezra 7:6). Ezra possibly held a position in the Persian court that put him in charge of Jewish affairs. As such he was commissioned to promote the worship of the Lord in the Jerusalem Temple and to ensure that the judicial system in that area was sound (Ezra 7:11–26). Artaxerxes's decree to Ezra shows that the Persian policies of religious freedom and movement within the empire were still operative. Ezra left for Jerusalem in the company of about eighteen hundred men and their families. Three-and-one-half months later the group arrived in Jerusalem, and Ezra was appalled to find religious laxity. The Jews who had rebuffed the Samaritans had developed some unorthodox descendants of their own.[14]

The sending of Ezra to Jerusalem had a motive not recorded in the

13. Over the centuries the Book of Esther has been badly maligned. Critical scholarship originally treated it as pure fiction. When historians, philologists, and archaeologists began demonstrating the accuracy of the book's local color and compatibility with known history, the scholarly position shifted to calling the book a "historical novel." In this way, it could still be maintained that the plot and all the characters except Xerxes were imaginary.

14. Ezra 1–6 records events largely before Ezra's time. Ezra 7–10 relates Ezra's own story, but the events need not have taken more than one year. Following his reforms, Ezra reported back to the Persian court.

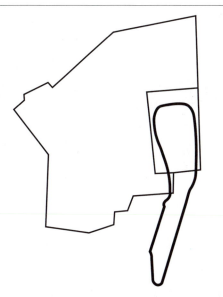

19.10. Jerusalem's city wall in the days of Nehemiah (dark line) and the present "old city" walls (light line).

Bible. Egypt, this time aided by Athenian forces, had again revolted. A struggle with the Greeks for control of the eastern Mediterranean had begun, and the Persians wanted their land bridge into Egypt to remain secure. Ezra's presence in Jerusalem would help monitor the situation. The next year a Persian fleet and army moved south from Syria and began putting down the Egyptian uprising.

Thirteen years after Ezra instituted reforms in Jerusalem, another imperial official for the Persians became exercised over his people's homeland. This official was Nehemiah, a cupbearer to King Artaxerxes and possibly a eunuch. As early as Jeremiah's rescue by an Ethiopian eunuch (Jer. 38:7), the term *saris* could be used as a title or as a physical description, but the Persians normally rendered their food tasters eunuchs in order to reduce the temptation for men in such sensitive positions to kill the king and start their own dynasty.[15]

Nehemiah's concern over the security problems in Jerusalem led to his appointment as governor of Judah.[16] Nehemiah was sent to Jerusalem with letters of passage and a letter instructing that he be given timbers from the "king's forest" for the work he had in mind. Nehemiah was accompanied on his journey by army officers and cavalry troops. This show of strength and authority naturally alarmed governors of provinces surrounding Jerusalem, because the power structure was being altered. In Jerusalem, Nehemiah privately inspected the walls of the city. Then he organized the people to rebuild the defenses.

Despite numerous attempts against Nehemiah and the project, in fifty-two days the city walls had been restored and new doors had been hung in the gateways. Jerusalem was again a walled city. During this same time (mid-fifth century), fortresses began dotting coastal Palestine and the Hill Country. This refortification of Jerusalem can also be

15. For the debate on whether Nehemiah was a eunuch, see Yamauchi 1990: 260–64.

16. There is no evidence for Nehemiah's housing in Judah, but a substantial palace/residence found at Lachish could provide an idea of what would have been provided him in Jerusalem.

19.11. Tombs (left to right) of Darius II (the ruler following Artaxerxes I), Artaxerxes I, and Darius the Great at Naqsh-I Rustam, three miles north of Persepolis. Persian religion did not permit in-ground burials. Following Cyrus's entombment (illustration 19.2), Persian kings were placed in cruciform-façaded tombs cut into living rock. The simple interiors were large enough to accommodate only the king and his immediate family. Two later (Sasanian) reliefs are near the base of Darius's tomb.

viewed as part of Persia's move to tighten its grip on the west (Hoglund 1992: 165–205).

Until recent years, Nehemiah's description contained the most detailed information available on the configuration of ancient Jerusalem, but this can now be supplemented by recent excavation. Nehemiah's walled city (illustration 19.10) covered approximately the same space as did Solomon's city, but it was only about one-fourth the size it had been in Hezekiah's day (compare illustrations 14.1 and 17.5). Much of Nehemiah's repairs followed lines established in Solomonic and later times. That little work had to be done from the foundation up helps explain why the project could be completed in under two months' time.[17]

Nehemiah returned to Artaxerxes in 432 and stayed in the Persian court for perhaps two years before making a second trip to Jerusalem. When he arrived back in Jerusalem he found that religious laxity had crept in again and that one of his previous enemies had even been given a room in the temple court. Exactly when Ezra returned to Jerusalem is not clear, but he and Nehemiah began working together on needed religious reforms.[18]

17. At some point Ezra had begun restoration of the city walls (Ezra 4:6–23). Note also that Neh. 3 speaks of "repairs" plural. The Water Gate mentioned in Neh. 3:26 and 8:1–3 has perhaps been found; see E. Mazar 1989.

18. As an archaeological aside, in the books of Ezra and Nehemiah, gifts to the temple were assessed in terms of coins—the earliest biblical reference to coinage, a medium of exchange probably invented about 550 by King Croesus of Sardis in Asia Minor. The Persians learned of the innovation when they swept into that area with their armies, and coinage began to spread within the empire. It is generally stated that coins first appeared in Palestine in the fifth century, but one coin found at Ketef Hinnom outside Jerusalem in 1983 pushes that beginning date back into the sixth century.

Zev Radovan

19.12. Persian coin bearing the figure of a falcon spreading its wings. It is inscribed in Aramaic with *Yehud* ("Judah").

Additional Reading

Avi-Yonah, Michael. *The Holy Land from the Persian to the Arab Conquest*. Grand Rapids: Baker, 1977.

Ellison, H. L. *From Babylon to Bethlehem: The People of God between the Testaments*. Grand Rapids: Baker, 1976.

Fennelly, James M. "The Persepolis Ritual" *BA* 43 (1980): 135–62 (see also *BA* 44 [1981]: 72–74).

Ghirshman, R. *The Art of Ancient Iran*. New York: Golden, 1964.

———. *Iran*. New York: Penguin, 1954.

Hallo, William W. "The First Purim." *BA* 46 (1983): 19–29.

Hendin, David, *Guide to Biblical Coins*. New York: Amphora, 1987.

Herr, Larry G. "What Ever Happened to the Ammonites?" *BAR* 19/6 (1993): 26–35, 68 (additional comments in 20/2 [1994]: 16, 18, 20).

Hicks, Jim. *The Persians*. New York: Time-Life, 1976.

Meshorer, Yaʾakov. "The Holy Land in Coins." *BAR* 4/1 (1978): 32–38.

Millard, Alan R. "The Persian Names in Esther and the Reliability of the Hebrew Text." *Journal of Biblical Literature* 96 (1977): 481–88.

Olmstead, A. T. *History of the Persian Empire*. Chicago: University of Chicago Press, 1948.

Porten, Bezalel. "A New Look: Aramaic Papyri and Parchments." *BA* 42 (1979): 74–104.

Schmidt, Erich F. *Persepolis*. 3 volumes. Chicago: University of Chicago Press, 1953–70.

Stern, Ephraim. "The Persistence of Phoenician Culture." *BAR* 19/3 (1993): 38–49.

———. "What Happened to the Cult Figurines?" *BAR* 15/4 (1989): 22–29, 53–54 (additional comments in 15/6:12, 15).

Wapnish, Paula, and Brian Hesse. "Pampered Pooches or Plain Pariahs? The Ashkelon Dog Burials." *BA* 56 (1993): 55–80.

Into the New Testament

In most Bibles the period between the Old and the New Testaments is represented by a single blank page which, perhaps, has symbolic significance. "From Malachi to Matthew" has for long remained vague and unfamiliar to many readers of the Scriptures. Many mysteries remain, but in recent times much light has been cast on this whole period. Exciting new insights have been given by the writings of numbers of scholars and by some remarkable archaeological discoveries.

—D. S. Russell

From Persian Rule to the Death of Alexander the Great
Ptolemaic Rule of Palestine
Seleucid Rule of Palestine
Hasmonean Rule of Palestine
Roman Rule of Palestine
Additional Reading

The centuries between the Old and the New Testaments were years of great change for the Near East. The changes had impact on the whole fabric of life, and aspects of the political, social, and religious setting of the first century A.D. were shaped by the developments of the last centuries B.C. Knowledge of these intertestamental centuries provides a needed bridge from Old Testament times into the world of the New Testament.

20.1. Rulers of Palestine in the last centuries B.C.

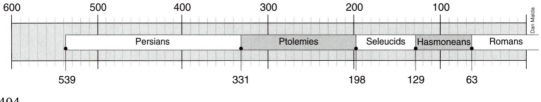

From Persian Rule to the Death of Alexander the Great

Persia was in control of the Near East as the Old Testament closed, and it continued that dominance for some decades longer. Following Artaxerxes I, the ruler in the days of Ezra and Nehemiah, the Persian Empire repeatedly struggled with Greece over western Asia Minor (Ionia). The Persians became adept at pitting Athens and Sparta against each other in order to maintain control of the region, and some of the Greek cities in Ionia came to believe Persian control was preferable to "freedom" under Athens or Sparta. Philip of Macedon eventually entered the picture and endeavored to unite all of Greece against Persia. He had little initial success, however, because southern Greece distrusted Philip and felt itself superior to Macedonia. In 338 Philip finally resorted to force and defeated Athens in battle despite Persian aid to Athens. That same year, the Persian king, Artaxerxes III, was poisoned in a palace power struggle, and his assassination sparked a Greek dream of a crusade against the Persians. The dream was not entirely based on the desire for revenge for past incursions. The Greeks were also galled because the "barbarians" were richer than the Greeks.

Toward the end of 337 Philip had been chosen to lead the crusade. The first step in his strategy was to demand that Persia pay reparations for the aid it had extended Athens. The new Persian king naturally refused, but his response gave Philip an excuse for war. By the next year Philip's troops were in Asia Minor liberating Ionia, but the crusade stalled when Philip was assassinated. Just a month earlier, another poisoning had felled the king of Persia. By mid-336, therefore, two new rulers came on the scene.

The new Persian king was Darius III, and Alexander succeeded his father in Macedonia. Alexander found that many Greeks were glad to see Philip gone and were not interested in continued Macedonian rule.

20.2. For many years the Persians contributed to Greek disunity by using gold coins to buy the friendship of first one and then another Greek city. At one point, a Spartan complained that he had been driven from Ionia by Persia's "ten thousand archers," gold coins like the ones pictured here (shown about three times actual size), bearing the image of the archer king.

Rohr Productions

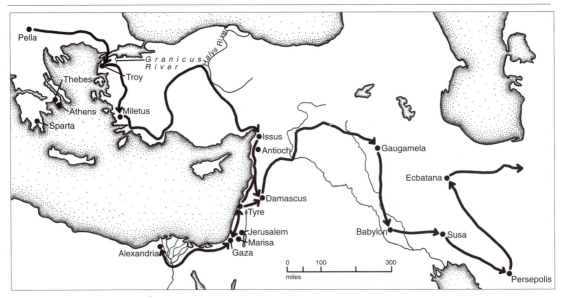

20.3. The intertestamental period. Alexander's line of march is indicated by the heavy black line.

Athens went so far as to ask Persia for money to revolt against Macedonia. Thebes (north of Athens) revolted and killed its Macedonian garrison without waiting for any Persian gold. Greek opinion seems to have been divided into two schools of thought. One was that the Greeks in Asia Minor had to be freed from Persia no matter who accomplished the task. The other was that the Persian yoke was preferable to Macedonian control.

Alexander was determined to continue the crusade, and he met the Greek reluctance with force. Since Thebes had killed its Macedonian garrison, Alexander burned that city and sold its people into slavery as a warning to others. With that show of strength, the twenty-year-old Alexander assumed he had subdued, if not united, the Greeks. In 334 he marched toward Asia Minor with an army of about thirty-five thousand troops, including a token force of seven thousand Greeks. The real strength of Alexander's army lay in its Macedonian infantry and its phalanx formation. His cavalry was largely composed of conscripts gathered along the way, and for a time he was supported by a small fleet. Interestingly, Alexander's army also included scholars. Historians, surveyors, botanists, and geographers marched with him into Asia Minor.

The records indicate that early in his career Darius III had proven both brave and forceful. Now, as a forty-five-year-old king, he followed typical Persian strategy and sent three hundred talents of gold into Greece to increase dissension against Alexander. The money was accepted by both Sparta and Athens.

Alexander marched from Pella, seemingly oblivious to the unrest the Persians were encouraging behind him (illustration 20.3). He crossed into Asia Minor, captured the village of Troy, and then paid homage to the tomb of Achilles. According to ancient Greek historians, the Persians met Alexander with a vastly larger army, but not all modern scholars are willing to accept that claim. Some allow for slightly superior numbers, while others contend that Alexander's forces were much larger in this first battle (Frye 1963: 157). Either way, Darius believed

Alexander to be less a nuisance than Philip had been, and he ordered that Alexander be taken alive and brought to Susa.

Darius III erred in his evaluation of Alexander's strength, but his problems were not all his own doing. Over the years the Persians had evolved the practice of sending satraps along with the army, and regardless whether those governors knew anything about military strategy they were the supreme commanders. The Persian generals proposed to pull back into Asia Minor, scorching the earth as they retired, thus rendering Alexander unable to feed his army. However, the Persian satrap accompanying the army refused to have his lands burned and demanded that the army engage the enemy. Overruled, the Persian generals were forced to confront Alexander at the Granicus River.

The first Greek assault was beaten back, but Alexander himself led the next charge, turned the battle, and defeated the Persians. The Persian cavalry fled but was not pursued, and the Persian foot soldiers who surrendered were sent home. Greek mercenaries with the Persians, however, were charged with treason; nine-tenths of them were executed, and the remainder were sent off to Macedonia as slaves. Having won a foothold in Asia Minor, Alexander began to "free" the Ionic cities. Those cities that chose not to be freed were burned to the ground. Alexander worked his way south and sent his Greek fleet home after reaching Miletus. From there Alexander turned east toward his next goal. As he did so, the Persian navy sailed to Ionia and began to retake part of the western coast.

By this time Darius III was quite aware of how serious a threat Alexander was, and he personally accompanied his army into a position west of Alexander. This position effectively cut Alexander's supply line[1] but, instead of waiting Alexander out, Darius moved to the less-strategic Issus where their two armies met. Alexander attacked the Greek mercenaries with Darius and made a direct assault on the Persian king. The Persian line broke, Darius fled, and Alexander's army quickly swept toward Damascus, where they captured the Persian baggage train. With the baggage train was the Persian royal family, Darius's mother, wife, children, and, tellingly, ambassadors from Sparta, Athens, and Thebes. The ambassadors' presence indicates how little support the crusade had in Greece. The Persian royal family was treated kindly, the ambassadors were not.[2]

Alexander continued south and laid siege to Tyre, Persia's only naval base in Phoenicia. Twice Darius proposed terms for peace, but Alexander rebuffed him each time. Tyre fell after a seven-month siege, and Alexander moved south to Gaza, which was taken within two months. In 332 Palestine and its Jewish population passed from Persian to Greek control. The Near East was poised for change.

When Alexander marched into Egypt, that country, with its hatred of Persian control and its commercial and cultural contacts with Greece, welcomed him as a liberator. Alexander was even crowned pharaoh, and the Egyptians fabricated a story to convince themselves that Alex-

---

1. Five thousand infantry and eight hundred cavalry had just reached Alexander, but no additional reinforcements could join him while the Persians maintained their position.

2. Darius's wife died while in Alexander's custody, and she was given a royal burial.

20.4. The Alexander Mosaic from the House of the Faun at Pompeii (over eleven feet high). A second-century copy of an earlier Greek painting, the mosaic depicts the pivotal moment in the Battle of Issus as Alexander (on the left) charges toward Darius III who is about to bolt from the conflict in his chariot.

ander was part of their royal line. The site for a new city, Alexandria, was marked off, partly to replace the recently destroyed port cities of Tyre and Gaza.

Alexander left Egypt, passed again through Palestine, and advanced on Persia. Unwisely, Darius III made no attempt to hold either the Euphrates or the Tigris, and the two armies faced each other at Gaugamela. Alexander commanded approximately forty-seven thousand soldiers in this battle, and it is assumed the Persian army was much larger. Details are sketchy on the actual tactics, but it seems that Darius III's chariots and elephants failed in a flanking movement while Alexander succeeded in breaking through the line that protected the Persian king. Once more Darius III fled the battlefield; in his absence, the victory was finally won by Alexander.[3]

With this third victory over Darius III, in October 331 Alexander became known as "Alexander the Great" and the Persian Empire came to an end. Alexander was greeted in Babylon with flowers and hymns as the Babylonians welcomed the end of Persian rule and the heavy taxes levied since the days of Xerxes. The capital cities of Susa and Persepolis offered no resistance, and all the wealth of the treasury city became Alexander's. Four months later, while Alexander was still in the city, Persepolis burned to the ground. The cause of the conflagration is not clear, but it left piles of burned beams and rain-washed wall stubs for archaeologists to find. Since excavations at Persepolis yielded little in the way of portable treasure, its looting was apparently extensive.

Alexander continued north and then east from Persepolis, and by the spring of 326 he had crossed the Indus River. At the Battle of Jhelum, his forces were victorious, but they were no longer willing to continue fighting. Alexander had a near mutiny on his hands before he agreed to

3. Darius was held captive by an eastern satrap and then stabbed to death.

Israel Museum (IDAM), Jerusalem

20.5. The "Alexander hoard" was found in this small jug. Alexander used images of the deities Hercules and Athena, rather than his own portrait, on the coins he issued.

turn back. A series of small battles and other obstacles attended the long march westward, but by the spring of 324 Alexander arrived again at Susa. Alexander dreamed of uniting the world into a single nation and culture (though not a purely Greek culture) and of making Babylon a capital of his new world. Alexander began to assume certain Persian customs, and in a mass wedding he forced dozens of his generals and ten thousand of his Greek soldiers to marry Persian women; he himself married Stateira, daughter of Darius III. Unrest developed within Alexander's Macedonian ranks over his "Persian ways," but they did not have to tolerate his dream for long. In the spring of 323, while Alexander was at Babylon, he became sick and died before he attained his thirty-third birthday.

Alexander's conquests inaugurated a process of change in the Near East. Aramaic had become the lingua franca under the Persians, but its use had never spread to the extent that Greek would. For the first time, a common language began to link the Near East with the Mediterranean world. Greek art, literature, and philosophy had reached their peak prior to Alexander, and these cultural gifts now began to spread eastward with the new language. The Persians had had little interest in making everyone culturally Persian, so under their rule ethnic differences remained. The infusion of Hellenism into the Near East, on the other hand, began to generate more uniformity in lifestyles.

The struggle for control of Alexander's empire lasted for several years after his death. In the Near East, one of his generals, Seleucus, rose to power in southern Mesopotamia but slowly shifted his base westward and founded the Antioch of New Testament fame. Another general, Ptolemy, was in command of Egypt when Alexander died, and he began to tighten his control over that territory. For the most part, Alexander's dream of one nation and one merged culture was rejected. Arnold Toynbee (1969: 44) states it this way:

> Like present day Westerners, the Greeks assumed that mankind's coming common civilization would, as a matter of course, be theirs. They resented and resisted Alexander's attempt to impose an amalgam of the Greek and the Iranian ways of life on the conquered and the conquerors alike. Alexander's generals objected to mixed marriages as decidedly as Ezra did. After Alexander's death, all of them, with the one notable exception of Seleucus, repudiated the Iranian wives whom Alexander had wished on to them.

Ptolemaic Rule of Palestine

To the south of Palestine the Ptolemies ruled Egypt, and to the north the Seleucids ruled Syria. Both powers coveted Palestine (at first controlled by the Ptolemies). The Ptolemies continued the previous Persian policy of religious freedom and did not try to force a new culture upon the inhabitants of Palestine:

> The Greeks had no temptation to be coercive; for they were confident that Hellenism was so superior to all other ways of life, and therefore so attractive, that it would be adopted voluntarily, sooner or later, by all non-Greeks who had the good fortune to have access to it (Toynbee 1969: 44).[4]

Many Jews did accept the "good fortune," especially those thousands who were taken from Palestine and resettled in Alexandria to help populate the new city. There were occasional unpleasantries, but largely the Jews in Egypt were treated as full citizens. It seems Ptolemy II commissioned a Greek translation of the Old Testament (the Septuagint), an increasing necessity for transplanted Jews who became less and less familiar with Hebrew.

The Jews left in Palestine were more resistant to the cultural and social pressures of Hellenism, largely because of the proximity of the temple and the lifestyle it fostered, but they definitely felt the pressure of

---

4. Robert Harrison 1994 attempts to show that Judaism was not thoroughly Hellenized before the middle of the second century.

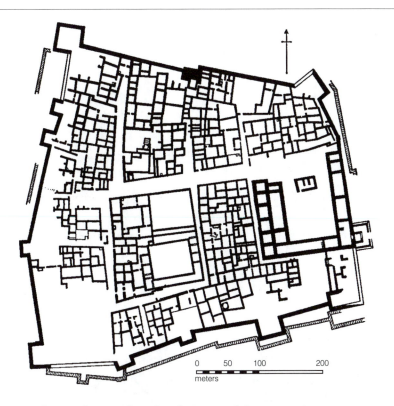

20.6. Plan of the upper city at Marisa, with an apparent city gate on the right. The U-shaped area just inside the gate served as the religious precinct, with the marketplace located in the northern of the two large rectangles near the center of the city.

new peoples settling in their land. Many of these immigrants were mercenaries brought in (with their families) by the Ptolemies for use as garrison troops and as reinforcements for their repeated battles with the Seleucids for control of Palestine.

The Seleucids also sought to settle mercenaries on the soil they controlled. Both sides preferred Greeks, especially Macedonians, and by bringing these people to live in the lands for which they were expected to fight, the governments hoped to maintain adequate troop strength and foster increased allegiance. Immigrants were sometimes settled into new sites organized on the Greek model, and at other times they were integrated into already existing towns. A population estimate made of Seleucid territory suggests that within a few decades ten percent of Syria's population were foreign-born Greek (Jones 1969: 117). Since the Seleucids and the Ptolemies were continually at odds with one another, the same percentage can perhaps be applied to Ptolemaic Palestine. In any case, Greek colonization was keenly felt in Palestine, and it created strong cultural tensions.

The site of Marisa (called Mareshah before the exile), twenty-one miles southwest of Jerusalem, provides an example of Hellenism being grafted into Palestine's culture. Marisa's towered defensive wall seems to continue the typical model (illustration 20.6). And the grid system of its streets is not as novel as was once believed, because new findings indicate that toward the end of the Old Testament, cities in Palestine were becoming more planned. But one basic departure from Old Testament times concerned the marketplace, which had always been an open space just inside or outside the city gate. At Marisa, in keeping with the

20.7. Plan of Tomb I at Marisa (top) has a short flight of stairs leading into an underground antechamber (A) from which three side chambers extend (B, C, D). Forty-one burial slots extend from the side chambers, and three larger burial vaults were cut on the east end of the tomb. Looking east from the antechamber into side chamber D (bottom), low benches line the sides of the chamber and the far wall contains elements of a Greek temple shrine. The painted decorations were vandalized after discovery but are shown here as restored in 1993.

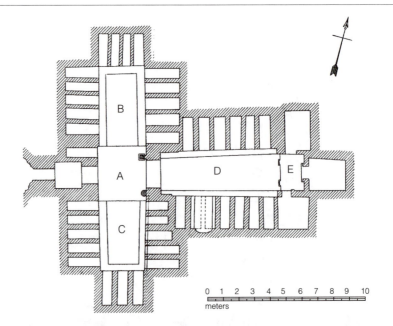

```
0  1  2  3  4  5  6  7  8  9  10
meters
```

Greek plan, a central area within the city was set aside to serve that purpose. For a Jew to live in such a city meant a significant change in this aspect of life. Since the commercial and legal center was no longer within and near the traffic flow of the gateway, people could not as easily congregate and feel the pulse of their city.

During the excavation of Marisa, a Greek inscription was found that described a man as the "agora official." The inscription shows the intrusion of a new language into daily life, and the beginning of more "orderliness" in business matters. Greek decorative styles, including Ionic and Corinthian capitals, were also found at Marisa (Horowitz 1980).

Change can also be appreciated by the way Marisa's inhabitants cared for their dead. Marisa's tombs dotted the area and are most famous for their painted wall decorations: garlands, offering urns, people in Greek dress, and a hunting scene in which a variety of animals are depicted (illustration 20.7). After studying the paintings, excavators concluded that the work showed Greek training, but was of provincial quality. John Peters and Herman Thiersch (1905: 91–92) have this to say concerning the hunting scene:

> The unmistakable delight in the animal world is, as is evinced by the preference for the Egyptian fauna, evidently something connected with the Grecian culture in the kingdom of the Ptolemies. . . . In one way or another this animal frieze may be regarded as a radiation of the thoughts and interests centered at that time in Alexandria, an unexpected reflection in the provinces which illuminates the culture of the capital from a new side.

Funerals and burials are very tradition bound, but the Marisa tombs represent a new model—one that became the preferred option by New Testament times. The people who settled into intertestamental Marisa looked to the Mediterranean world (as opposed to the Near East) for their lifestyle and ideology. Marisa illustrates the type of cultural changes that developed subsequent to Alexander's invasion of the Near East.

Seleucid Rule of Palestine

The Seleucids, in Syria, repeatedly tried to annex Palestine to their own territories. As Ptolemaic and Seleucid armies fought over control of Palestine, the Jews in the land divided into pro-Ptolemaic and pro-Seleucid factions. There was no Jewish unhappiness over Ptolemaic rule as such, but the heavy taxation necessary to continue the war effort led some to wish for an end to the hostilities. Some Jews believed the Seleucids would not tire until they reached their goal.

In 198 the Seleucid king, Antiochus III the Great, won a decisive battle north of the Sea of Galilee, and Ptolemaic control of Palestine came to an end. Antiochus III was welcomed into Jerusalem by pro-Seleucid Jews, who even helped him overcome a Ptolemaic garrison still within the city. In appreciation of the Jewish aid, Antiochus III issued two proclamations supporting continued religious freedom for the Jews. Therefore, the political transfer of power caused no change in the religious life of the Jews; as long as their religion was left alone, they re-

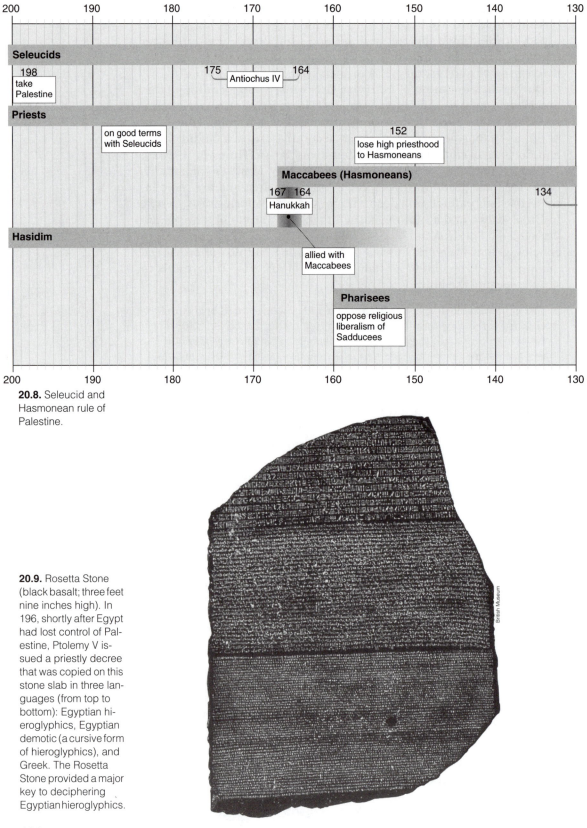

20.8. Seleucid and Hasmonean rule of Palestine.

20.9. Rosetta Stone (black basalt; three feet nine inches high). In 196, shortly after Egypt had lost control of Palestine, Ptolemy V issued a priestly decree that was copied on this stone slab in three languages (from top to bottom): Egyptian hieroglyphics, Egyptian demotic (a cursive form of hieroglyphics), and Greek. The Rosetta Stone provided a major key to deciphering Egyptian hieroglyphics.

British Museum

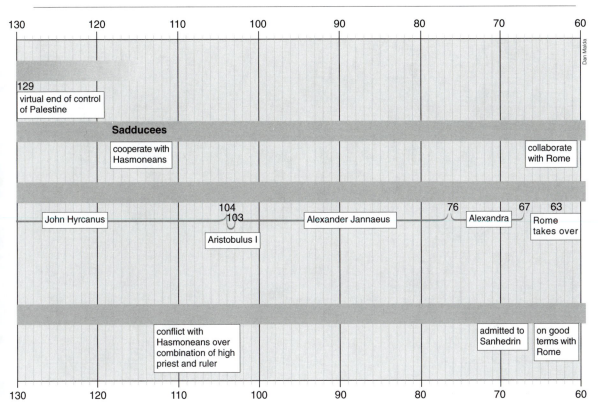

130	120	110	100	90	80	70	60

129
virtual end of control of Palestine

Sadducees

cooperate with Hasmoneans

collaborate with Rome

| | | **104** **103** | | | **76** | **67** **63** |

John Hyrcanus — Alexander Jannaeus — Alexandra — Rome takes over

Aristobulus I

conflict with Hasmoneans over combination of high priest and ruler

admitted to Sanhedrin

on good terms with Rome

mained politically passive. Acculturation—what to do about Hellenism—was their main struggle.

In 188 Antiochus III was soundly defeated by Rome in Asia Minor, and another power loomed into the politics of the Near East. Antiochus was forced to pay Rome a heavy indemnity and to promise that he would no longer recruit mercenaries from the west. Antiochus needed to pay off the Romans, and one of several priestly families vying for the office of high priest offered him a large sum of money. They had come

20.10. Coin of Antiochus IV.

20.11. Artist's reconstruction (right) of the façade of the main building at Iraq el-Emir (or Araq el-Emir) in Transjordan and during excavation (above). Iraq el-Emir was built by the Tobiads—Ammonites who figure in Old Testament history when Ezra and Nehemiah were active in Jerusalem—and two large halls in nearby cliffs have the name *Tobiah* cut in Aramaic characters beside their entrances. Commissioned early in the second century by a Tobiad named Hyrcanus, this building is an example of how a native of Palestine was attracted to Hellenistic architecture. The function of the building has been debated, with temple or manor house being the conclusions drawn by recent excavators.

to believe that God was unconcerned with what they did culturally and were therefore willing to give Antiochus III the money and a promise that Hellenism would be promoted in return for the office. Antiochus declined the offer, but the episode demonstrates that all was not well in Jewish religious circles.

When Antiochus IV Epiphanes took the Seleucid throne in 175, the indemnity to Rome had still not been fully paid. When a priestly group again offered money in return for the high priesthood, Antiochus IV accepted the bargain. Three years later, another group made an even more lucrative offer, and a new high priest was installed. This appointment of the high priest by a pagan ruler did not bother Jews sympathetic to Hellenism, but it infuriated pious Jews.

Antiochus IV had ambitions of conquering Egypt. In his second campaign against that country, in 168, he encountered Roman officials who were also becoming interested in that land. They rudely told him to leave and to renounce any idea of conquest. Humiliated, Antiochus IV returned north and took his frustration out on Jerusalem. His armies attacked the city, plundered the temple treasury, and killed many Jews. Centuries of religious freedom for the Jews were coming to an end, and religious persecution was about to begin.

Antiochus IV dreamed of a pan-Hellenic league against Rome and believed his realm would be strengthened if all his subjects followed Greek ideals and customs. To that end Antiochus began to put strictures on the Jewish religion. The observance of the Sabbath and circumcision were forbidden, and Jews were forced to eat ceremonially unclean foods. Anyone found in possession of a biblical scroll could be executed. The Jerusalem Temple was desecrated, and ritual prostitution was performed within the temple precincts. On 15 Kislev 167 (late November–early December), the supreme desecration took place. An altar dedicated to Zeus was erected on the old Jerusalem Temple altar, and pigs were sacrificed to Zeus on the new altar.

The religious persecution triggered the Maccabean Revolt. Jewish guerrilla warfare was so successful against the Seleucid armies that the Jews were able to reclaim Jerusalem. After the temple was cleansed and rededicated, the festival of Hanukkah was celebrated for the first time (25 Kislev 164). Shortly thereafter a truce was called in which the Seleucids guaranteed religious freedom, but now a large number of Jews wanted political freedom as well.

Hasmonean Rule of Palestine

Following the rededication of the temple, the next decades were filled with warfare and death as the struggle for political freedom was led by the Hasmoneans, the name by which the descendants of the Maccabees were known. The years were also filled with tension between various Jewish factions. The priesthood cooperated with the Hasmoneans, even though they had been forced to relinquish the office of high priest to them. Those Jews who believed any concession to Hellenism might lead to complete abandonment of the faith formed a pious (Hasidic) movement. When Antiochus IV tried to wipe out the Jewish faith, the Hasidim felt their fears were vindicated and that acculturation had been proven wrong. The Hasidim participated in the successful revolt against the Seleucids but then, for reasons not presently clear, they broke with the Maccabees. About 160 a group that would become known as the Pharisees split away from the Hasidim. As can be assumed from their origin, the Pharisees were opposed to Hellenism and, by extension, to the attitudes of the priests and their supporters, including the Sadducees.

By 129 the Hasmoneans under John Hyrcanus had virtually freed Palestine from Seleucid control, and there was once again a Jewish ruler in Jerusalem. Hyrcanus expanded his authority to the south, where he gave the Idumeans the choice of converting to Judaism or

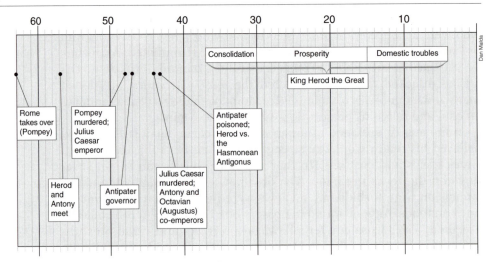

20.12. Roman rule of Palestine.

leaving. To the north he destroyed both the Samaritan temple on Mount Gerizim and, later, the city of Samaria.[5] Toward the end of his reign, Hyrcanus became embroiled in a heated dispute with the Pharisees over the position of high priest. The Pharisees demanded that the high priesthood be given back to the Sadducees. The Pharisees were fighting for the law, not out of any love for the Sadducees but, since the position of high priest was technically above that of ruler, there was no way Hyrcanus would accede to their demands. The dispute, however, marks the beginning of the Pharisees as a political party—much of the time as a dissident political party.

Alexander Jannaeus followed the brief reign of Aristobulus I as Hasmonean king. More territory was added to the realm, but Jannaeus's brutalities led to much internal opposition. After his death the kingdom passed to his widow, Alexandra. Under Alexandra the Pharisee's fortunes rose, and for the first time they were admitted to the Sanhedrin, the Jewish high court. At her death in 67 there was great turmoil about her successor, so much so that various factions asked Rome to step in. Rome obliged in 63, and for all practical purposes the Hasmonean monarchy ended.

Roman Rule of Palestine

Roman rule in Palestine began in 63 when Pompey entered Jerusalem and Judea became part of the Roman province of Syria-Palestine. The takeover was beneficial in that it gave Jews the prospect of Roman

5. The Samaritans probably built their temple on Mount Gerizim around the time of Nehemiah. When Antiochus IV began his persecution of the Jews the Samaritans claimed to be Sidonians and offered to dedicate their temple to Jupiter. That response is only one of several aggravations that generated the great bitterness between Jews and Samaritans by New Testament times. Hyrcanus's act of destroying the Samaritan temple accounts for John 4:20 being in the past tense. By the time of Jesus it had been gone for over a century. Current excavation has reportedly found evidence of the temple (*BAR* 21/5 [1995]: 24, 85).

John Trever

20.13. Isaiah Scroll from Qumran Cave 1 (ten inches high and twenty-four feet long unrolled), open to Isaiah 38–40. One of the most famous archaeological discoveries of all time, the Dead Sea Scrolls date between the second century B.C. and the early first century A.D. When first discovered in 1947, the Dead Sea Scrolls pushed the date of the oldest known manuscripts of the Old Testament approximately one thousand years closer to the autographs. Almost every book of the Old Testament has been found, plus commentaries, intertestamental psalms, religious orders, and apocryphal works. Added to the already known Apocrypha and Pseudepigrapha (also from the intertestamental period), they provide additional insight into the history and religious life of Judaism as it moved toward New Testament times. (For an introduction to the Dead Sea Scrolls, see Bruce 1966; for the Apocrypha, see Metzger 1957; for the Pseudepigrapha, see Charlesworth 1976. Additionally, since 1989, *Biblical Archaeology Review* has had a continuing interest in the scrolls.)

roads, aqueducts, fine buildings, and hopefully peace. One aspect the Jews would not have thought positive, however, was the way it reduced their influence. The Hasmoneans had conquered Hellenized cities along the coast and in Transjordan. Rome freed those cities from Jewish control and grouped those in Transjordan into a confederation called the Decapolis. The Jews were left to govern only those areas where they were in the majority. The heady days of Jewish kingship and control were again over.

The Nabateans, southeast of the Dead Sea, resisted Pompey's takeover until an Idumean named Antipater persuaded them to pay tribute and become vassals to Rome.[6] By this action, Antipater ingratiated himself to Rome, and his family began a loyalty to that empire that would span five generations.

Antipater's favors to Rome continued. For example, when Rome was attacking Egypt, Antipater supplied food and water to the emperor's army as it marched south through Judea. Still later, Antipater quelled a threatened Jewish revolt. As a reward for his many kindnesses, Antipater became de facto ruler of Judea. When Pompey was murdered in 48 and Julius Caesar became the new emperor of Rome, Antipater was ready to serve him as well. At one point Caesar needed help in Egypt so Antipater sent three thousand Jewish troops and persuaded still more Jews to help. This aid led to more than de facto con-

6. The Idumeans and Nabateans took their respective places on the playing board for the roles they would play in New Testament history in this way: after Jerusalem fell in 586, the Edomites exploited the situation by expanding into part of southern Judah. Shortly afterward, their homeland east of the Dead Sea was overrun by Nabateans. Some Edomites were absorbed by these Nabateans; others fled into southern Judah to join the Edomites already there. In southern Judah, Edomites were called Idumeans. As mentioned above, John Hyrcanus forced the Idumeans to either accept Judaism or move on.

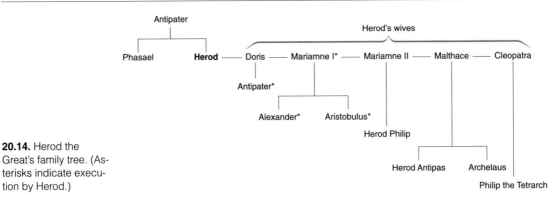

20.14. Herod the Great's family tree. (Asterisks indicate execution by Herod.)

trol of Palestine. About 47 Caesar exempted Antipater from taxation, made him a Roman citizen, and appointed him governor of Judea, Samaria, and Galilee.

To consolidate his position, Antipater made his son Phasael ruler of Jerusalem and another son, Herod, governor of Galilee. In Galilee, Herod began to have difficulties with "bandits," many of whom he caught and executed without trial. Jewish writers identify the bandits as Zealots—"freedom fighters" who resisted the Roman takeover that the Idumean Herod represented. According to prevailing law, Herod did not have the authority to execute anyone—that was the Sanhedrin's function. Therefore the Sanhedrin summoned Herod to Jerusalem to stand trial for his life. The accounts of what happened differ, but all versions agree that the Sanhedrin discovered Herod to be above local law. A ruler with Rome's backing could do as he pleased.

Julius Caesar was assassinated in 44, and Antipater was poisoned the following year. Herod then began to vie with a Hasmonean named Antigonus for the throne of Judea. Both men appealed to Rome, at that time jointly ruled by Antony and Octavian. Not surprisingly, in light of Herod's friendship with Antony, in 41 Herod was chosen to govern Judea.[7] Herod had won the political infighting, but Antigonus played on the antipathy between Rome and Parthia by bribing the Parthians to invade Judah on his behalf.[8] Antigonus pledged one thousand talents of silver and five hundred Jewish women to be chosen from the defeated enemies in return for aid.

The Parthians invaded Palestine in 40 when Rome was too distracted elsewhere in the empire to respond. Antigonus took the throne in Jerusalem, and again a Hasmonean was declared king. Herod's brother Phasael died in the Parthian invasion, but Herod fled all the way to Rome, where he was crowned king of Judea by Antony and Octavian. In 37 Rome was finally able to spare troops and lay siege to Jerusalem. During the siege, Herod married a Hasmonean princess named Mariamne, thus becoming part of the Jewish royal family.

7. Herod and Marc Antony met and became friends in 57 when Rome was putting down a Hasmonean rebellion.
8. The Parthians lived to the east in Mesopotamia and Persia. Rome repeatedly broke treaties and promises with them, and by this time Parthia had become hostile to Rome.

When Jerusalem fell, Antigonus was taken prisoner and beheaded. Herod finally occupied the throne.

Herod's reign can be divided into three phases. The years between 37 and 30 can be called his period of consolidation. During that time he eliminated those who had sided with Antigonus (one writer charges Herod with instituting a "reign of terror in the country"; Schalit 1969: 72). Herod also had great difficulty because of Cleopatra of Egypt. As a Ptolemy, she wanted Ptolemaic Palestine back. Her friendship with Antony caused Herod to lose territories to Egypt, and if it had not been for Herod's own friendship with Antony, Herod would probably have also lost his life. When Antony and Cleopatra committed suicide in 31, Herod was able to convince Octavian that his primary loyalty was to Rome. Octavian allowed Herod to continue as king of Judea, and the lands Cleopatra had annexed were returned to him.

The second phase of Herod's reign lasted from about 30 to 15. During these years Herod enjoyed a relative peace and earned his title: "Herod the Great." Herod was the great builder. He is best known for his rebuilding of the temple in Jerusalem, but he also dotted the southern part of his country with fortresses such as Masada and Herodium. He turned Samaria into a Greco-Roman showplace, complete with theater, racetrack, pagan temple, and streets lined with colonnades and statuary. On the coast he built the similarly lavish port city of Caesarea. Herod's interest in architecture even extended outside his own land. He commissioned buildings and other constructions in distant places such as Antioch on the Orontes and the Island of Rhodes.

The final phase of Herod's reign extended from about 15 to his death in 4, during which he was plagued by a series of domestic troubles. Court intrigue, plot, and counterplot filled the air as his sons contended against one another. At one point Herod charged two of his sons with treason. They were acquitted by Rome, but after a subsequent trial both were strangled. These executions caused Octavian to remark that he would rather be Herod's pig than his son! Another son became impatient for the crown, but Herod learned of his plot in time to also have him put to death. The crown never sat easily on Herod's head, and events such as these make his reaction to the news brought by the wise men more understandable.

The intertestamental period was one of political change for Palestine—from Persian to Ptolemaic to Seleucid to Hasmonean and then to Roman rule. Within this period Jewish culture was buffeted by the Greco-Roman world. Jewish factions responded differently to the new order, and their diverse responses created some of the tensions so evident within New Testament times.

Additional Reading

Anderson, Robert T. "Mount Gerizim: Navel of the World." *BA* 43 (1980): 217–21 (errata in *BA* 44 [1981]: 72).

Berlin, Andrea M. "Between Large Forces: Palestine in the Hellenistic Period." *BA* 60 (1997): 2–51.

Betlyon, John W. "Archaeological Evidence of Military Operations in Southern Judah during the Early Hellenistic Period." *BA* 54 (1991): 36–43.

Boardman, John, *The Greeks Overseas: Their Early Colonies and Trade*. London: Thames & Hudson, 1980.

Cate, Robert L. *A History of the Bible Lands in the Interbiblical Period*. Nashville: Broadman, 1989.

Ellison, H. L. *From Babylon to Bethlehem*. Grand Rapids: Baker, 1976.

Eshel, Hanan. "How I Found a Fourth-Century B.C. Papyrus Scroll on My First Time Out!" *BAR* 15/5 (1989): 44–53.

Geraty, Lawrence T. "The Khirbet el-Kôm Bilingual Ostracon." *BASOR* 220 (1975): 55–61.

Lapp, Paul W. "Bedouin Find Papyri Three Centuries Older than Dead Sea Scrolls." *BAR* 4/1 (1978): 16–24 (additional comments in 5/6 [1979]: 11; 6/3 [1980]: 15).

Linder, Elisha. "Excavating an Ancient Merchantman." *BAR* 18/6 (1992): 24–35.

McCullough, W. Stewart. *The History and Literature of the Palestinian Jews from Cyrus to Herod, 550 B.C. to 4 B.C.* Toronto: University of Toronto Press, 1976.

Moeller, Henry R. (ed.). *The Legacy of Zion: Intertestamental Texts Related to the New Testament*. Grand Rapids: Baker, 1977.

Rappaport, U. "Gaza and Ascalon in the Persian and Hellenistic Periods in Relation to their Coins." *IEJ* 20 (1970): 75–80.

Ronen, Yigal. "The First Hasmonean Coins." *BA* 50 (1987): 105–7.

Scott, J. Julius, Jr. *Customs and Controversies: Intertestamental Jewish Backgrounds of the New Testament*. Grand Rapids: Baker, 1995.

Stone, Michael E. "Why Study the Pseudepigrapha?" *BA* 46 (1983): 235–43.

Reference List

Abells, Zvi, and Asher Arbit
  1995   "Some New Thoughts on Jerusalem's Ancient Water Systems." *PEQ* 127:2–7.
Adams, Robert M.
  1965   *Land behind Baghdad: A History of Settlement on the Diyala River.* Chicago: University of Chicago Press.
Agourides, S., and James H. Charlesworth
  1978   "A New Discovery of Old Manuscripts on Mt. Sinai: A Preliminary Report." *BA* 41:29–31.
Aharoni, Yohanan
  1975   "Hazor and the Battle of Deborah—Is Judges 4 Wrong?" *BAR* 1/4:3–4, 26.
  1979   *The Land of the Bible: A Historical Geography.* Revised edition. Translated and edited by Anson F. Rainey. Philadelphia: Westminster.
Albenda, Pauline
  1980   "Syrian-Palestinian Cities on Stone." *BA* 43:222–29.
Albright, William F.
  1942   "King Joiachin in Exile." *BA* 5:49–55. Reprinted in *The Biblical Archaeology Reader,* vol. 1 / pp. 106–12. Edited by G. Ernest Wright and David Noel Freedman. Garden City, N.Y.: Doubleday, 1961.
  1953   *Archaeology and the Religion of Israel.* Baltimore: Johns Hopkins University Press.
  1968   "Archaeological Discoveries and the Scriptures." *Christianity Today* 12 (June 21): 3–5.
  1971   *The Archaeology of Palestine.* Gloucester: Peter Smith.
Aling, Charles F.
  1981   *Egypt and Bible History: From Earliest Times to 1000 B.C.* Grand Rapids: Baker.

Amiran, Ruth
  1961   "Tombs of the Middle Bronze Age I at Ma'ayan Barukh." *'Atiqot* 3:84–92.
  1976   "The Water Supply of Israelite Jerusalem." Pp. 75–78 in *Jerusalem Revealed: Archaeology in the Holy City, 1968–1974.* Edited by Yigael Yadin. Translated by R. Grafman. New Haven: Yale University Press.
Amusin, J. D., and M. L. Heltzer
  1964   "The Inscription from Meṣad Ḥashavyahu: Complaint of a Reaper of the Seventh Century B.C." *IEJ* 14:148–57.
ANE 1   *The Ancient Near East*, vol. 1: *An Anthology of Texts and Pictures.* Edited by James B. Pritchard. Princeton: Princeton University Press, 1958.
ANE 2   *The Ancient Near East*, vol. 2: *A New Anthology of Texts and Pictures.* Edited by James B. Pritchard. Princeton: Princeton University Press, 1975.
ANET   *Ancient Near Eastern Texts Relating to the Old Testament.* Edited by James B. Pritchard. 3d edition with supplement. Princeton: Princeton University Press, 1969.
Archer, Gleason L., Jr.
  1964   *A Survey of Old Testament Introduction.* Chicago: Moody.
Archi, Alfonso
  1980   "Archi Responds to Pettinato." *BAR* 6/6:42–43.
Arnold, Patrick M.
  1990   *Gibeah: The Search for a Biblical City.* Sheffield: Academic Press.
Artzy, Michal
  1990   "Pomegranate Scepters and Incense Stand with Pomegranates Found in Priest's Grave." *BAR* 16/1:48–51.

Astour, Michael C.
1992   "The Date of the Destruction of Palace G at Ebla." *Bibliotheca Mesopotamica* 25:23–39.

Avigad, Nahman
1978a   "Baruch the Scribe and Jerahmeel the King's Son." *IEJ* 28:52–56.
1978b   "The King's Daughter and the Lyre." *IEJ* 28:146–51.
1979   "Jerahmeel and Baruch: King's Son and Scribe." *BA* 42:114–18.
1990   "The Inscribed Pomegranate from the 'House of the Lord.'" *BA* 53:157–66.

Bailey, Lloyd R.
1977   "Wood from 'Mount Ararat': Noah's Ark?" *BA* 40:137–46.

Barkay, Gabriel
1983   "The Divine Name Found in Jerusalem." *BAR* 9/2:14–19.
1986   *A Treasure Facing Jerusalem's Walls*. Jerusalem: Israel Museum.

Barstad, Hans M.
1993   "Lachish Ostracon III and Ancient Israelite Prophecy." *Eretz Israel* 24:8–12.

Barton, George A.
1933   *Archaeology and the Bible*. Sixth edition. Philadelphia: American Sunday School Union.

Bayer, Bathja
1982   "Ancient Musical Instruments: The Finds That Could Not Be." *BAR* 8/1:20–33.

Beach, Eleanor Ferris
1993   "The Samaria Ivories, *Marzeaḥ*, and Biblical Text." *BA* 56:94–104.

Beaulieu, Paul-Alain
1989   *The Reign of Nabonidus, King of Babylon 556–539 B.C.* Yale Near Eastern Researches 10. New Haven: Yale University Press.

Beek, Martin A.
1962   *Atlas of Mesopotamia: A Survey of the History and Civilisation of Mesopotamia from the Stone Age to the Fall of Babylon*. Translated by D. R. Welsh. Edited by H. H. Rowley. New York: Nelson.

Beit-Arieh, Itzhaq
1988a   "New Light on the Edomites." *BAR* 14/2:28–41.
1988b   "The Route through Sinai: Why the Israelites Fleeing Egypt Went South." *BAR* 14/3:28–37.
1996   "Edomites Advance into Judah—Israelite Defensive Fortresses Inadequate." *BAR* 22/6:28–36.

Beit-Arieh, Itzhaq, and Bruce C. Cresson
1991   "Ḥorvat ʿUza: A Fortified Outpost on the Eastern Negev Border." *BA* 54:126–35.

Beitzel, Barry J.
1985   *The Moody Atlas of Bible Lands*. Chicago: Moody.

Berkowitz, Lois
1977   "Has the U.S. Geological Survey Found King Solomon's Gold Mines?" *BAR* 3/3:1, 28–33.

Bibby, Geoffrey
1969   *Looking for Dilmun*. New York: Knopf.

Bienkowski, Piotr (ed.)
1992   *Early Edom and Moab: The Beginning of the Iron Age in Southern Jordan*. Sheffield Archaeological Monograph 7. Sheffield: Collis.

Bienkowski, Piotr, and Bryant G. Wood
1990   "Battle over Jericho Heats Up." *BAR* 16/5:45–49, 68–69.

Bimson, John J.
1994   "1 and 2 Kings." Pp. 334–87 in *New Bible Commentary: Twenty-first Century Edition*. Fourth edition. Edited by D. A. Carson et al. Downers Grove, Ill.: InterVarsity.

Bimson, John J., and David Livingston
1987   "Redating the Exodus." *BAR* 13/5:40–53, 66–68 (additional comments by Bimson in 14/4 [1988]: 52–55 and 14/6:22, 74).

Biran, Avraham, and Joseph Naveh
1993   "An Aramaic Stele Fragment from Tel Dan." *IEJ* 43:81–98.
1995   "The Tel Dan Inscription: A New Fragment." *IEJ* 45:1–18.

Bleibtreu, Erika
1990   "Five Ways to Conquer a City." *BAR* 16/3:36–44.
1991   "Grisly Assyrian Record of Torture and Death." *BAR* 17/1:52–61, 75 (additional comments in 17/3:12).

Boling, Robert G.
1970   *American Schools of Oriental Research Newsletter* 3.

Borowski, Oded
1984   "Yadin Presents New Interpretation of the Famous Lachish Letters." *BAR* 10/2:74–77.
1988   "The Biblical Identity of Tel Halif." *BA* 51:21–27.
1995   "Hezekiah's Reforms and the Revolt against Assyria." *BA* 58:148–55.

Braidwood, Robert J.
1952   *The Near East and the Foundations for Civilization: An Essay in Appraisal of the General Evidence*. Condon Lectures. Eugene, Ore.: Oregon State System of Higher Education.
1960   "Concluding Address." Pp. 224–46 in *City Invincible: A Symposium on Urbanization and Cultural Development in the Ancient Near East*. Edited by Carl H. Kraeling and Robert M. Adams. Chicago: University of Chicago Press.
1970   "Archaeology: Introduction." Vol. 2 / pp. 223–26 in *Encyclopaedia Britannica*. Chicago: Benton.

Braidwood, Robert J., and Bruce Howe
1960 *Prehistoric Investigations in Iraqi Kurdistan*. Studies in Ancient Oriental Civilization 31. Chicago: University of Chicago Press.

Bright, John
1959 *A History of Israel*. Philadelphia: Westminster.
1981 *A History of Israel*. Third edition. Philadelphia: Westminster.

Broshi, Magen
1974–75 "The Expansion of Jerusalem in the Reigns of Hezekiah and Manasseh." *IEJ* 24:21–26 (additional comments in 25:192).

Bruce, F. F.
1966 *Second Thoughts on the Dead Sea Scrolls*. London: Paternoster.
1968 *The New Testament Development of Old Testament Themes*. Grand Rapids: Eerdmans.

Cahill, Jane M.
1997 "A Rejoinder to 'Was the Siloam Tunnel Built by Hezekiah?'" *BA* 60:184–85.

Ceram, C. W.
1958 *The March of Archaeology*. Translated by Richard Winston and Clara Winston. New York: Knopf.

Charlesworth, James H.
1976 *The Pseudepigrapha and Modern Research*. Missoula, Mont.: Scholars Press.
1979 "St. Catherine's Monastery: Myths and Mysteries." *BA* 42:174–79 (additional comments in 44 [1981]: 133–35).
1980 "The Manuscripts of St. Catherine's Monastery." *BA* 43:26–34.

Christie, Agatha
1977 *An Autobiography*. New York: Dodd, Mead.

Clay, Albert T.
1907 *Light on the Old Testament from Babel*. Second edition. Philadelphia: Sunday School Times.

Cleator, P. E.
1976 *Archaeology in the Making*. New York: St. Martin.

Cohen, Rudolph
1981a "Did I Excavate Kadesh-Barnea?" *BAR* 7/3:20–33.
1981b "Excavations at Kadesh-barnea, 1976–1978." *BA* 44:93–107.
1985 "The Fortresses King Solomon Built to Protect His Southern Border: String of Desert Fortresses Uncovered in Central Negev." *BAR* 11/3:56–70.
1986 "Solomon's Negev Defense Line Contained Three Fewer Fortresses." *BAR* 12/4:40–45.

Cohen, Rudolph, and Yigal Yisrael
1995 "The Iron Age Fortresses at ʿEn Ḥaṣeva." *BA* 58:223–35.
1996 "Smashing the Idols: Piecing Together an Edomite Shrine in Judah." *BAR* 22/4:40–51, 65.

Cole, Dan
1980 "How Water Tunnels Worked." *BAR* 6/2:8–29 (additional comments in 7/1 [1981]: 20, 62 and 7/2 [1981]: 64).

Coogan, Michael D.
1974 "Life in the Diaspora: Jews at Nippur in the Fifth Century B.C." *BA* 37:6–12.
1978 *Stories from Ancient Canaan*. Philadelphia: Westminster.

Cooley, Robert E., and Gary D. Pratico
1994 "Gathered to His People: An Archaeological illustration from Tell Dothan's Western Cemetery." Pp. 70–92 in *Scripture and Other Artifacts*. Edited by Michael D. Coogan, J. Cheryl Exum, and Lawrence E. Stager. Louisville: Westminster.

Craigie, Peter C.
1983a "The Tablets from Ugarit and Their Importance for Biblical Studies." *BAR* 9/5:62–73 (additional comments in 10/1 [1984]: 82; 10/3:75; 11/1 [1985]: 76).
1983b *Ugarit and the Old Testament*. Grand Rapids: Eerdmans.

Crisler, B. Cobbey
1976 "The Acoustics and Crowd Capacity of Natural Theaters in Palestine." *BA* 39:128–41.

Currid, John D.
1992 "Puzzling Public Buildings." *BAR* 18/1:52–61 (additional comments in 18/3:66–68, 70).

Daniel, Glyn
1981 *A Short History of Archaeology*. Ancient Peoples and Places 100. London: Thames & Hudson.

Davies, Graham I.
1994 "King Solomon's Stables: Still at Megiddo?" *BAR* 20/1:44–49 (additional comments in 20/3:74 and 20/4:61).

Davies, Nigel
1986 "The 'New' Archaeology." *Intercollegiate Review* 22/1:27–32.

Davies, Philip R.
1994 "'House of David' Built on Sand: The Sins of the Biblical Maximizers." *BAR* 20/4:54–55.

Davis, John J.
1968 *Biblical Numerology*. Grand Rapids: Baker.
1969 *Conquest and Crisis: Studies in Joshua, Judges, and Ruth*. Grand Rapids: Baker.
1970 *The Birth of a Kingdom: Studies in I–II Samuel and I Kings 1–11*. Grand Rapids: Baker.

Davis, Thomas
1995 "Albright and Archaeology: The Search for Realia." *Archaeology in the Biblical World* 3/1:42–50.

Day, J.
1989 *Molech: A God of Human Sacrifice in the Old Testament*. Cambridge: Cambridge University Press.

Demsky, Aaron
1977   "A Proto-Canaanite Abecedary Dating from
        the Period of the Judges and Its Implica-
        tions for the History of the Alphabet." *Tel
        Aviv* 4:14–27.
Demsky, Aaron, and Moshe Kochavi
1978   "An Alphabet from the Days of the Judges."
        BAR 4/3:22–30.
Dever, William G.
1980   "Archeological Method in Israel: A Con-
        tinuing Revolution." *BA* 43:40–48.
1982   "Retrospects and Prospects in Biblical and
        Syro-Palestinian Archeology." *BA* 45:103–7.
1984   "Asherah, Consort of Yahweh? New Evi-
        dence from Kuntillet ʿAjrûd." *BASOR*
        255:21–37.
1987a   Letter to the Editor. *BAR* 13/4:10–11.
1987b   "The New Archaeology." *BA* 50:150–51.
Dimbleby, J. B.
1902   *The Date of Creation*. London: Nister.
Dobbs-Allsopp, F. W.
1995   "The Genre of the Meṣad Ḥashavyahu Os-
        tracon." *BASOR* 295:49–55.
Dothan, Trude
1982a   *The Philistines and Their Material Culture*.
        New Haven: Yale University Press.
1982b   "What We Know about the Philistines."
        BAR 8/4:20–44 (additional comments in 8/
        5:58, 62 and 8/6:16).
Dothan, Trude, and Moshe Dothan
1992   *People of the Sea: The Search for the Philis-
        tines*. New York: Macmillan.
Dothan, Trude, and Seymour Gitin
1990   "Ekron of the Philistines: How They Lived,
        Worked, and Worshiped for Five Hundred
        Years." *BAR* 16/1:20–36.
Doumas, Christos G.
1991   "High Art from the Time of Abraham." *BAR*
        17/1:40–51.
Edwards, I. E. S.
1972   *The Pyramids of Egypt*. New York: Viking.
Elat, M.
1975   "The Campaigns of Shalmaneser III
        against Aram and Israel." *IEJ* 25:25–35.
Ellison, H. L.
1956   "I and II Kings." Pp. 300–338 in *The New
        Bible Commentary*. Edited by F. Davidson.
        Grand Rapids: Eerdmans.
Evenari, Michael, et al.
1971   *The Negev*. Cambridge: Harvard University
        Press.
Fargo, Valerie M.
1983   "Is the Solomonic City Gate at Megiddo
        Really Solomonic?" *BAR* 9/5:8, 10, 12–13
        (additional comments in 10/2 [1984]: 94,
        96).
Faulkner, Raymond O.
1985   *Book of the Dead*. Revised edition. London:
        British Museum.

Fensham, F. Charles
1966   "The Burning of the Golden Calf and
        Ugarit." *IEJ* 16:191–93.
Finkelstein, Israel
1986a   "The Iron Age Sites in the Negev High-
        lands—Military Fortresses or Nomads Set-
        tling Down?" *BAR* 12/4:46–53.
1986b   "Shiloh Yields Some, But Not All, of Its Se-
        crets." *BAR* 12/1:22–41.
1988   "Searching for Israelite Origins." *BAR* 14/
        5:34–45, 58.
Flinder, Alexander
1989   "Is This Solomon's Seaport?" *BAR* 15/4:30–
        43.
Fontaine, Carole R.
1981   "A Modern Look at Ancient Wisdom: The
        Instruction of Ptahhotep Revisited." *BA*
        44:155–60.
Forsyth, George H., and Kurt Weitzmann
1978   "Saving the Mt. Sinai Mosaics." *BAR* 4/
        4:16–31.
Fox, Nili
1996   "Royal Officials and Court Families: A New
        Look at the ילדים (*yĕlādîm*) in 1 Kings 12."
        BA 59:225–32.
Frankfort, Henri
1939   *Cylinder Seals: A Documentary Essay on the
        Art and Religion of the Ancient Near East*.
        London: Macmillan.
1954   *The Art and Architecture of the Ancient Ori-
        ent*. Pelican History of Art. Harmonds-
        worth, Middlesex: Penguin.
1956   *The Birth of Civilization in the Near East*.
        Garden City: Anchor.
Freedman, David Noel
1978   "The Real Story of the Ebla Tablets: Ebla
        and the Cities of the Plain." *BA* 41:143–64.
Fritz, Volkmar
1987a   "Conquest or Settlement? The Early Iron
        Age in Palestine." *BA* 50:84–100.
1987b   "Temple Architecture: What Can Archaeol-
        ogy Tell Us about Solomon's Temple?" *BAR*
        13/4:38–49.
1993   "Where Is David's Ziklag?" *BAR* 19/3:58–61,
        76.
Frye, Richard N.
1963   *The Heritage of Persia*. New York: Mentor.
Frymer-Kensky, Tikva
1980   "Tit for Tat: The Principle of Equal Retribu-
        tion in Near Eastern and Biblical Law." *BA*
        43:230–34 (additional comments in 44
        [1981]: 135).
Gal, Zvi
1990   "Khirbet Roš Zayit—Biblical Cabul: A His-
        torical-Geographical Case." *BA* 53:88–97.
1993   "Cabul: A Royal Gift Found." *BAR* 19/2:38–
        44, 84 (additional comments in 19/4:8, 10–
        11).
Gardiner, Alan
1961   *Egypt of the Pharaohs*. Oxford: Oxford Uni-
        versity Press.

Gelb, Ignace J.
1969   *A Study of Writing*. Chicago: University of Chicago Press.

Gibson, J. C. L.
1978   *Canaanite Myths and Legends*. Second edition. Edinburgh: Clark.

Gill, Dan
1994   "Jerusalem's Underground Water Systems: How They Met." *BAR* 20/4:20–33, 64.

Gitin, Seymour
1990   "Ekron of the Philistines: How They Lived, Worked, and Worshiped for Five Hundred Years." *BAR* 16/2:32–42, 59.

Gitin, Seymour, and Trude Dothan
1987   "The Rise and Fall of Ekron of the Philistines: Recent Excavations at an Urban Border Site." *BA* 50:197–222.

Glueck, Nelson
1965   "Ezion-geber." *BA* 28:70–87.

Gordon, Cyrus H.
1940   "Biblical Customs and the Nuzu Texts." *BA* 3:1–12. Reprinted as "Biblical Customs and the Nuzu Tablets" in *The Biblical Archaeology Reader*, vol. 2 / pp. 21–33. Edited by Edward F. Campbell Jr. and David Noel Freedman. Garden City, N.Y.: Doubleday, 1964.

Gordon, Edmund I.
1959   *Sumerian Proverbs: Glimpses of Everyday Life in Ancient Mesopotamia*. Philadelphia: University Museum.

Gottwald, Norman K.
1978   "Were the Early Israelites Pastoral Nomads?" *BAR* 4/2:2–7.

Graham, J. N.
1984   " 'Vinedressers and Plowmen': 2 Kings 25:12 and Jeremiah 52:16." *BA* 47:55–58.

Gray, John
1964   *The Canaanites*. New York: Praeger/London: Thames & Hudson.

Great People
1974   *Great People of the Bible and How They Lived*. Pleasantville, N.Y.: Reader's Digest.

Green, Alberto R.
1979   "Israelite Influence at Shishak's Court?" *BASOR* 233:59–62.

Green, Peter
1970   *Xerxes at Salamis*. New York: Praeger.

Hackett, Jo Ann
1986   "Some Observations on the Balaam Tradition at Deir ʿAllā." *BA* 49:216–22.

Haiman, Mordechai
1994   "The Iron Age II Sites of the Western Negev Highlands." *IEJ* 44:36–61.

Haines, Richard C.
1971   *Excavations in the Plain of Antioch II*. Oriental Institute Publications 95. Chicago: University of Chicago Press.

Halley, Henry H.
1965   *Halley's Bible Handbook*. Twenty-fourth edition. Grand Rapids: Zondervan.

Halpern, Baruch
1983   *The Emergence of Israel in Canaan*. Chico: Scholars Press.

1987a   "Radical Exodus Redating Fatally Flawed." *BAR* 13/6:56–61 (additional comments in 14/2 [1988]: 12–13, 58).

1987b   "Yaua, Son of Omri, Yet Again." *BASOR* 265:81–85.

Har-El, Menashe
1978   "The Pride of the Jordan: The Jungle of the Jordan." *BA* 41:65–75.

Haran, Menahem
1968   "Observation on the Historical Background of Amos 1:2–2:6." *IEJ* 18:201–12.

Harding, G. Lankester
1958   "Recent Discoveries in Jordan." *PEQ* 90:10–12.

Harrelson, Walter
1957   "Shechem in Extra-biblical References." *BA* 20:2–10. Reprinted in *The Biblical Archaeology Reader*, vol. 2 / pp. 258–65. Edited by Edward F. Campbell Jr. and David Noel Freedman. Garden City, N.Y.: Doubleday, 1964.

Harrison, Robert
1994   "Hellenization in Syria-Palestine: The Case of Judea in the Third Century BCE." *BA* 57:98–108.

Harrison, Roland K.
1969   *Introduction to the Old Testament*. Grand Rapids: Eerdmans.

1970   *Old Testament Times*. Grand Rapids: Eerdmans.

Hasel, Michael G.
1994   "Israel in the Merneptah Stela." *BASOR* 296:45–61.

Hawkes, Jacquetta
1976   *The Atlas of Early Man*. New York: St. Martin.

Hayes, John H., and Jeffrey K. Kuan
1991   "The Final Years of Samaria (730–720 BC)." *Biblica* 72:153–81.

Hayes, William C.
1953–59 *The Scepter of Egypt: A Background for the Study of the Egyptian Antiquities in the Metropolitan Museum of Art*. 2 volumes. [New York:] Metropolitan Museum of Art.

Heltzer, M.
1975   "On Tithe Paid in Grain in Ugarit." *IEJ* 25:124–28.

Hendel, Ronald S.
1996   "The Date of the Siloam Inscription: A Rejoinder to Rogerson and Davies." *BA* 59:233–37 (additional comments on inside front cover of this issue).

Herr, Larry G.
1988   "Tripartite Pillared Buildings and the Market Place in Iron Age Palestine." *BASOR* 272:47–67.

1993   "The Search for Biblical Heshbon." *BAR* 19/6:36–37, 68.

Herzog, Ze'ev, Miriam Aharoni, and Anson F. Rainey
1987   "Arad: An Ancient Israelite Fortress with a
         Temple to Yahweh." *BAR* 13/2:16–35.
Hess, Richard S.
1993   "Early Israel in Canaan: A Survey of Recent
         Evidences and Interpretations." *PEQ*
         125:125–42.
Hestrin, Ruth
1991   "Understanding Asherah: Exploring
         Semitic Iconography." *BAR* 17/5:50–59.
Hill, Andrew E.
1988   "The Ebal Ceremony as Hebrew Land
         Grant." *Journal of the Evangelical Theologi-
         cal Society* 31:399–406.
Hindson, Edward E.
1971   *The Philistines and the Old Testament*.
         Grand Rapids: Baker.
Hoberman, Barry
1983   "The Ethiopian Legend of the Ark." *BA*
         46:113–14.
Hoerth, Alfred J.
1977   "In Search of Noah's Ark: A Critical Re-
         view." *Near East Archaeological Society Bul-
         letin* 9:4–23.
forth-   "The Egyptian Game of Hounds and Jack-
coming   als." In *Board Games in Perspective*. Edited
         by I. L. Finkel. London: British Museum.
Hoffmeier, James K.
1991   "The Aftermath of David's Triumph over
         Goliath." *Archaeology in the Biblical World*
         1/1:18–23.
1992   "Egypt, Plagues in." Vol. 2 / pp. 374–78 in
         The Anchor Bible Dictionary. Edited by
         David Noel Freedman et al. New York:
         Doubleday.
1997   *Israel in Egypt*. New York: Oxford Univer-
         sity Press.
Hoffner, Harry A., Jr.
1994   "Hittites." Pp. 127–55 in *Peoples of the Old
         Testament World*. Edited by Alfred J.
         Hoerth, Gerald L. Mattingly, and Edwin M.
         Yamauchi. Grand Rapids: Baker.
1995   "Hittite Laws." Pp. 213–47 in *Law Collec-
         tions from Mesopotamia and Asia Minor*.
         Edited by Martha T. Roth. Atlanta: Schol-
         ars Press.
Hoglund, Kenneth G.
1992   *Achaemenid Imperial Administration in
         Syria-Palestine and the Missions of Ezra
         and Nehemiah*. Society of Biblical Litera-
         ture Dissertation Series 125. Atlanta:
         Scholars Press.
1994   "Edomites." Pp. 335–47 in *Peoples of the
         Old Testament World*. Edited by Alfred J.
         Hoerth, Gerald L. Mattingly, and Edwin M.
         Yamauchi. Grand Rapids: Baker.
Horn, Siegfried H.
1986   "Why the Moabite Stone Was Blown to
         Pieces." *BAR* 12/3:50–61 (correction in 12/
         5:75).

Horowitz, Gabriel
1980   "Town Planning of Hellenistic Marisa: A
         Reappraisal of the Excavations after
         Eighty Years." *PEQ* 112:93–111.
Howard, David M., Jr.
1994   "Philistines." Pp. 231–50 in *Peoples of the
         Old Testament World*. Edited by Alfred J.
         Hoerth, Gerald L. Mattingly, and Edwin M.
         Yamauchi. Grand Rapids: Baker.
Howard, Margaret
1955   "Technical Description of the Ivory Writing-
         Boards from Nimrud." *Iraq* 17:14–20.
Isaac, Ephraim
1993   "Is the Ark of the Covenant in Ethiopia?"
         BAR 19/4:60–63.
Isserlin, B. S. J.
1983   "The Israelite Conquest of Canaan: A Com-
         parative Review of the Arguments Applica-
         ble." *PEQ* 115:85–94.
Iwry, Samuel
1961   "New Evidence for Belomancy in Ancient
         Palestine and Phoenicia." *Journal of the
         American Oriental Society* 81:27–34.
Jacobsen, Thorkild, and Robert M. Adams
1958   "Salt and Silt in Ancient Mesopotamian Ag-
         riculture." *Science* 128 (Nov. 21): 1251–58.
Jacobsen, Thorkild, and John A. Wilson
1963   *Most Ancient Verse*. Chicago: University of
         Chicago Press.
Jones, A. H. M.
1969   "Hellenism in Syria and Palestine." Pp.
         117–22 in *The Crucible of Christianity: Ju-
         daism, Hellenism, and the Historical Back-
         ground to the Christian Faith*. Edited by Ar-
         nold Toynbee. London: Thames & Hudson/
         New York: World.
Karageorghis, Vassos
1984   "Exploring Philistine Origins on the Island
         of Cyprus." *BAR* 10/2:16–28.
Katzenstein, H. Jacob
1979   "Tyre in the Early Persian Period (539–486
         B.C.E.)." *BA* 42:23–34.
Kaufman, Asher S.
1983   "Where the Ancient Temple of Jerusalem
         Stood." *BAR* 9/2:40–61 (see 9/4:5, 14, 72 for
         corrections).
1988   "Fixing the Site of the Tabernacle at
         Shiloh." *BAR* 14/6:46–52.
Kaufman, Ivan T.
1982   "The Samaria Ostraca: An Early Witness to
         Hebrew Writing." *BA* 45:229–39.
Keller, Werner
1981   *The Bible as History*. Translated by William
         Neil. Second edition. Revised by Joachim
         Rehork. Translated by William Neil and
         B. H. Rasmussen. New York: William Mor-
         row.
Kelm, George L., and Amihai Mazar
1989   "Excavating in Samson Country." *BAR* 15/
         1:36–49.

Kempinski, Aharon
 1986 "Joshua's Altar—An Iron Age I Watch-tower." *BAR* 12/1:42, 44–49.
 1995 "Two Recent Books on the Archaeology of Early Palestine." *IEJ* 45:55–64.
Kenyon, Kathleen M.
 1957 *Digging up Jericho: The Results of the Jericho Excavations, 1952–1956*. New York: Praeger.
 1985 *Archaeology in the Holy Land*. Fifth (= fourth) edition. Nashville: Nelson.
Kevan, Ernest F.
 1956 "Genesis." Pp. 75–105 in *The New Bible Commentary*. Edited by F. Davidson. Grand Rapids: Eerdmans.
Kidner, Derek
 1967 *Genesis: An Introduction and Commentary*. Tyndale Old Testament Commentaries. Downers Grove, Ill.: InterVarsity.
Kilmer, Anne D., Richard L. Crocker, and Robert R. Brown
 1976 *Sounds from Silence*. Berkeley: Bit Enki.
King, Philip J.
 1988a *Amos, Hosea, Micah—An Archaeological Commentary*. Philadelphia: Westminster.
 1988b "The Marzeaḥ Amos Denounces." *BAR* 14/4:34–45.
 1993 *Jeremiah: An Archaeological Companion*. Louisville: Westminster–John Knox.
Kitchen, Kenneth A.
 1976 "From the Brickfields of Egypt." *Tyndale Bulletin* 27:137–47.
 1983 "Egypt, the Levant and Assyria in 701 B.C." *Ägypten und Altes Testament* 5:243–53.
 1986 *The Third Intermediate Period in Egypt (1100–650 B.C.)*. Second edition. Warminster: Aris & Phillips.
 1989a "Two Notes on the Subsidiary Rooms of Solomon's Temple." *Eretz Israel* 20:107–12.
 1989b "Where Did Solomon's Gold Go?" *BAR* 15/3:30 (additional comments in 15/5:16).
 1993 "The Tabernacle—A Bronze Age Artifact." *Eretz Israel* 24:119–29.
 1995a "Ancient Arabia and the Bible." *Archaeology in the Biblical World* 3/1:16–24.
 1995b "The Patriarchal Age: Myth or History?" *BAR* 21/2:48–57, 88, 90, 92, 94–95.
Kitchen, Kenneth A., and T. C. Mitchell
 1980 "Chronology of the Old Testament." Vol. 1 / pp. 268–77 in *The Illustrated Bible Dictionary*. Edited by J. D. Douglas et al. Wheaton: Tyndale.
Kleven, Terence
 1994 "Up the Waterspout." *BAR* 20/4:34–35 (additional comments in 20/6:12, 14 and 21/1 [1995]: 78).
Kline, Meredith G.
 1963 *Treaty of the Great King*. Grand Rapids: Eerdmans.

Kochavi, Moshe
 1977 "An Ostracon of the Period of the Judges from ʿIzbet Sartah." *Tel Aviv* 4:1–13.
Kochavi, Moshe, et al.
 1992 "Rediscovered! The Land of Geshur." *BAR* 18/4:30–44, 84–85.
Köhler-Rollefson, Ilse
 1993 "Camels and Camel Pastoralism in Arabia." *BA* 56:180–88.
Korfmann, Manfred
 1973 "The Sling as a Weapon." *Scientific American* 229/10:35–42.
Kraeling, Emil G.
 1952 "New Light on the Elephantine Colony." *BA* 15:50–67. Reprinted in *The Biblical Archaeology Reader*, vol. 1 / pp. 128–44. Edited by G. Ernest Wright and David Noel Freedman. Garden City, N.Y.: Doubleday, 1961.
 1956 *Rand McNally Bible Atlas*. New York: Rand McNally.
Krahmalkov, Charles R.
 1981 "A Critique of Professor Goedicke's Exodus Theories." *BAR* 7/5:51–54.
Kramer, Samuel Noah
 1968 "The 'Babel of Tongues': A Sumerian Version." *Journal of the American Oriental Society* 88:108–11.
 1969 *The Sacred Marriage Rite*. Bloomington: University of Indiana Press.
 1983a "The Ur-Nammu Law Code: Who Was Its Author?" *Orientalia* 52:453–56.
 1983b "The Weeping Goddess: Sumerian Prototypes of the *Mater Dolorosa*." *BA* 46:69–80.
Laessøe, Jørgen
 1963 *People of Ancient Assyria: Their Inscriptions and Correspondence*. Translated by F. S. Leigh-Browne. London: Routledge & Kegan Paul.
Lambert, Wilfred G., and Alan R. Millard
 1969 *Atra-ḫasīs: The Babylonian Story of the Flood*. Oxford: Clarendon.
Lance, H. Darrell
 1982 "American Biblical Archeology in Perspective." *BA* 45:97–101.
Lapp, Nancy L.
 1993 "Fûl, Tell el-." Vol. 2 / pp. 445–48 in *The New Encyclopedia of Archaeological Excavations in the Holy Land*. Edited by Ephraim Stern. New York: Simon & Schuster.
Larsen, Curtis E.
 1975 "The Mesopotamian Delta Region: A Reconsideration of Lees and Falcon." *Journal of the American Oriental Society* 95:43–57.
Laughlin, John C. H.
 1981 "The Remarkable Discoveries at Tel Dan." *BAR* 7/5:20–37.
Leacroft, Helen, and Richard Leacroft
 1974 *The Buildings of Ancient Mesopotamia*. Leicester: Brockhampton.

Lemaire, André
1984a   "Probable Head of Priestly Scepter from Solomon's Temple Surfaces in Jerusalem." *BAR* 10/1:24–29.
1984b   "Who or What Was Yahweh's Asherah?" *BAR* 10/6:42–51 (additional comments in 11/2 [1985]: 77–78 and 11/3:79).
1985   "Fragments from the Book of Balaam Found at Deir Alla." *BAR* 11/5:26–39.
1994   " 'House of David' Restored in Moabite Inscription." *BAR* 20/3:30–37 (see 20/5:70 for corrections).
1995   "Name of Israel's Last King Surfaces in a Private Collection." *BAR* 21/6:48–52.
Lichtheim, Miriam
1973–80   *Ancient Egyptian Literature*. 3 volumes. Berkeley: University of California Press.
Lieberman, Stephen J.
1980   "Of Clay Pebbles, Hollow Clay Balls, and Writing: A Sumerian View." *American Journal of Archaeology* 84:339–58.
Lissner, Ivar
1963   "The Tomb of Moses Is Still Undiscovered: Excavation Sensation in Jordan." *BA* 26:106–8.
Livingston, David
1970–71   "Location of Biblical Bethel and Ai Reconsidered." *Westminster Theological Journal* 33:20–44 and 34:39–50.
1994   "Further Considerations on the Location of Bethel at el-Bireh." *PEQ* 126:154–59.
Lloyd, Seton
1984   *The Archaeology of Mesopotamia*. Second edition. London: Thames and Hudson.
Luckenbill, Daniel D.
1924   *The Annals of Sennacherib*. Oriental Institute Publications 2. Chicago: University of Chicago Press.
1926–27   *Ancient Records of Assyria and Babylonia*. 2 volumes. Chicago: University of Chicago Press.
Malamat, Abraham
1958   "The Kingdom of David and Solomon in Its Contact with Egypt and Aram Naharaim." *BA* 21:96–102. Reprinted in *The Biblical Archaeology Reader*, vol. 2 / pp. 89–98. Edited by Edward F. Campbell Jr. and David Noel Freedman. Garden City, N.Y.: Doubleday.
1971   "On the Akkadian Transcription of the Name of King Joash." *BASOR* 204:37–39.
1979   "The First Peace Treaty between Israel and Egypt." *BAR* 5/5:58–61.
Mallowan, Max E. L.
1964   "Noah's Flood Reconsidered." *Iraq* 26:62–82.
Marcus, David
1978   *A Manual of Akkadian*. Lanham: University Press of America.
Margalit, Baruch
1986   "Why King Mesha of Moab Sacrificed His Oldest Son." *BAR* 12/6:62–63, 76 (addi-

tional comments in 13/2 [1987]: 12, 14–15, 60–61 and 16/3 [1990]: 62, 67).
Matthews, Victor H.
1986   "The Wells of Gerar." *BA* 49:118–26.
Mattingly, Gerald L.
1983   "The Exodus-Conquest and the Archaeology of Transjordan: New Light on an Old Problem." *Grace Theological Journal* 4:245–62.
1994   "Moabites." Pp. 317–33 in *Peoples of the Old Testament World*. Edited by Alfred J. Hoerth, Gerald L. Mattingly, and Edwin M. Yamauchi. Grand Rapids: Baker.
Mayerson, Philip
1983   "Codex Sinaiticus: An Historical Observation." *BA* 46:54–56.
Mazar, Amihai
1975   "Excavations at Tell Qasîle, 1973–1974 (Preliminary Report)." *IEJ* 25:77–88.
1983   "Bronze Bull Found in Israelite 'High Place' from the Time of the Judges." *BAR* 9/5:34–40 (additional comments in 10/1 [1984]: 20, 22).
1988   "On Cult Places and Early Israelites: A Response to Michael Coogan." *BAR* 14/4:45.
1990   *Archaeology of the Land of the Bible, 10,000–586 B.C.E.* New York: Doubleday.
1993   "Beth Shean in the Iron Age: Preliminary Report and Conclusions of the 1990–91 Excavations." *IEJ* 43:201–29.
1997   "Four Thousand Years of History at Tel Beth-Shean: An Account of the Renewed Excavations." *BA* 60:62–76.
Mazar, Eilat
1989   "Royal Gateway to Ancient Jerusalem Uncovered." *BAR* 15/3:38–51.
1997   "Excavate King David's Palace!" *BAR* 23/1:50–57, 74.
McCarter, P. Kyle, Jr.
1974   "Yaw, Son of 'Omri': A Philological Note on Israelite Chronology." *BASOR* 216:5–7.
McCurdy, J. F.
1896   "Oriental Research and the Bible." Pp. 3–28 in *Recent Research in Bible Lands: Its Progress and Results*. Edited by Herman V. Hilprecht. Philadelphia: Wattles.
McNutt, Paula M.
1990   *The Forging of Israel: Iron Technology, Symbolism, and Tradition in Ancient Society*. Sheffield: Sheffield Academic.
McRay, John
1991   *Archaeology and the New Testament*. Grand Rapids: Baker.
Mendenhall, George E.
1958   "The Census Lists of Numbers 1 and 26." *Journal of Biblical Literature* 77:52–66.
Merling, David
1991   "Heshbon: A Lost City of the Bible." *Archaeology in the Biblical World* 1/2:10–17.

Merling, David, and Lawrence T. Geraty (eds.)
1994 *Hesban: After 25 Years*. Berrien Springs: Andrews University Press.

Meshel, Zeᵓev
1979 "Did Yahweh Have a Consort?" *BAR* 5/2:24–35 (additional comments in 22/4 [1996]: 12).
1994 "The 'Aharoni Fortress' Near Quseima and the 'Israelite Fortresses' in the Negev." *BASOR* 294:39–67.

Meshel, Zeᵓev, and Carol L. Meyers
1976 "The Name of God in the Wilderness of Zin." *BA* 39:6–10 (see also 40 [1977]: 66–68).

Metzger, Bruce M.
1957 *An Introduction to the Apocrypha*. New York: Oxford University Press.

Meyer, Karl E.
1971 *The Pleasures of Archaeology*. New York: Atheneum.

Meyers, Carol L.
1979 "Was There a Seven-Branched Lampstand in Solomon's Temple?" *BAR* 5/5:46–57.

Meyers, Eric M.
1984 "The Bible and Archaeology." *BA* 47:36–40.

Michalowski, Piotr
1989 *The Lamentation over the Destruction of Sumer and Ur*. Mesopotamian Civilizations 1. Winona Lake, Ind.: Eisenbrauns.

Millard, Alan R.
1985a "Daniel and Belshazzar in History." *BAR* 11/3:72–78.
1985b *Treasures from Bible Times*. Tring: Lion.
1989a "Does the Bible Exaggerate King Solomon's Golden Wealth?" *BAR* 15/3:20–29, 31, 34 (additional comments in 15/5:13, 16 and 16/1 [1990]: 66; corrections in 15/5:12–13).
1989b "The Doorways of Solomon's Temple." *Eretz Israel* 20:135–39.
1991a "Solomon: Text and Archaeology." *PEQ* 123:117–18.
1991b "Text and Archaeology: Weighing the Evidence: The Case for King Solomon." *PEQ* 123:19–27.
1992 "Ebla and the Bible—What's Left (If Anything)?" *Bible Review* 8/2:18–31, 60, 62.
1994 "King Solomon's Shields." Pp. 286–95 in *Scripture and Other Artifacts*. Edited by Michael D. Coogan, J. Cheryl Exum, and Lawrence E. Stager. Louisville: Westminster.

Millard, Alan R., and Donald J. Wiseman (eds.)
1980 *Essays on the Patriarchal Narratives*. Leicester: Inter-Varsity. Reprinted Winona Lake, Ind.: Eisenbrauns, 1988.

Miller, J. Maxwell
1977 "Archaeology and the Israelite Conquest of Canaan: Some Methodological Observations." *PEQ* 109:87–93.
1982 "Approaches to the Bible through History and Archeology: Biblical History as a Discipline." *BA* 45:211–16.
1991 "Solomon: International Potentate or Local King?" *PEQ* 123:28–31.

Miller, Nancy
1985 "Patriarchal Burial Site Explored for First Time in 700 Years." *BAR* 11/3:26–43.

Mitchell, T. C.
1992 "The Music of the Old Testament Reconsidered." *PEQ* 124:124–43.

Moortgat, Anton
1969 *The Art of Ancient Mesopotamia*. London: Phaidon.

Moran, William L.
1992 *The Amarna Letters*. Baltimore: Johns Hopkins University Press.

Morrison, Martha A.
1983 "The Jacob and Laban Narrative in Light of Near Eastern Sources." *BA* 46:155–64.

Muhly, James D.
1982 "How Iron Technology Changed the Ancient World and Gave the Philistines a Military Edge." *BAR* 8/6:40–54.
1992 Review of *The Forging of Israel* by Paula M. McNutt. *BA* 55:153–54.

Mullen, E. Theodore, Jr.
1980 *The Divine Council in Canaanite and Early Hebrew Literature*. Chico: Scholars Press.

Naᵓaman, Nadav
1974 "Sennacherib's 'Letter to God' on His Campaign to Judah." *BASOR* 214:25–39.

Naveh, Joseph
1960 "A Hebrew Letter from the Seventh Century B.C." *IEJ* 10:129–39.
1964 "Some Notes on the Reading of the Meṣad Ḥashavyahu Letter." *IEJ* 14:158–59.
1978 "Some Considerations on the Ostracon from ᶜIzbet Ṣarṭah." *IEJ* 28:31–35.
1980 "The Greek Alphabet: New Evidence." *BA* 43:22–25.
1987 *Early History of the Alphabet*. Jerusalem: Magnes.

Neugebauer, Otto
1969 *The Exact Sciences in Antiquity*. New York: Dover.

Newberry, Percy E.
1905 *Ancient Egyptian Scarabs*. Reprinted Chicago: Ares, 1979.

Oldenburn, Ulf
1969 *The Conflict between El and Baᵓal in Canaanite Religion*. Leiden: Brill.

Oppenheim, A. Leo
1956 *The Interpretation of Dreams in the Ancient Near East*. Philadelphia: American Philosophical Society.
1967 *Letters from Mesopotamia: Official, Business, and Private Letters on Clay Tablets from Two Millennia*. Chicago: University of Chicago Press.

1977 *Ancient Mesopotamia: Portrait of a Dead Civilization.* Revised edition. Completed by Erica Reiner. Chicago: University of Chicago Press.

Oren, Eliezer D.
1981 "How Not to Create a History of the Exodus—A Critique of Professor Goedicke's Theories." *BAR* 7/6:46–53.
1993 "Tel Seraᶜ (Tell esh-Shariᶜa)." Vol. 4 / pp. 1329–35 in *The New Encyclopedia of Archaeological Excavations in the Holy Land.* Edited by Ephraim Stern. New York: Simon & Schuster.

Osman, Ahmed
1988 *Stranger in the Valley of the Kings: The Identification of Yuya as the Patriarch Joseph.* San Francisco: Harper & Row.

Page, Stephanie
1968 "A Stela of Adad-Nirari III and Nergal-eres from Tell al Rimah." *Iraq* 30:139–53.

Parker, Simon B.
1994 "Siloam Inscription Memorializes Engineering Achievement." *BAR* 20/4:36–38.

Parrot, Andre
1955 *The Tower of Babel.* Translated by Edwin Hudson. London: SCM.

Patterson, R. D., and Hermann J. Austel
1988 "1, 2 Kings." Vol. 4 / pp. 1–300 in *The Expositor's Bible Commentary.* Edited by Frank E. Gaebelein. Grand Rapids: Zondervan.

Payne, J. Barton
1954 *An Outline of Hebrew History.* Grand Rapids: Baker.

Peters, John P., and Herman Thiersch
1905 *Painted Tombs in the Necropolis of Marissa (Mareshah).* London: Palestine Exploration Fund.

Petrie, W. M. Flinders
1904 *Methods and Aims in Archaeology.* Reprinted New York: Blom, 1972.

Pettinato, Giovanni
1976 "The Royal Archives of Tell Mardikh–Ebla." *BA* 39:44–52.
1980 "Ebla and the Bible—Observations on the New Epigraphic Analysis." *BAR* 6/6:38–41.

Pfeiffer, Charles F.
1960 *An Outline of Old Testament History.* Chicago: Moody.
1962 *Ras Shamra and the Bible.* Grand Rapids: Baker.

Pitard, Wayne T.
1988 "The Identity of the Bir-Hadad of the Melqart Stela." *BASOR* 272:3–21.
1994 "Arameans." Pp. 207–30 in *Peoples of the Old Testament World.* Edited by Alfred J. Hoerth, Gerald L. Mattingly, and Edwin M. Yamauchi. Grand Rapids: Baker.

Pope, Marvin H.
1986 "The Timing of the Snagging of the Ram, Genesis 22:13." *BA* 49:114–17.

Porten, Bezalel
1995 "Did the Ark Stop at Elephantine?" *BAR* 21/3:54–67, 76–77 (additional comments in 21/5:14, 16).

Pratico, Gary D.
1986 "Where Is Ezion-geber?" *BAR* 12/5:24–35 (additional comments in 13/3 [1987]: 66).

Price, George McCready
1934 *Modern Discoveries Which Help Us to Believe.* New York: Revell.

Raban, Avner, and Robert R. Stieglitz
1991 "The Sea Peoples and Their Contributions to Civilization." *BAR* 17/6:34–42, 92–93.

Radday, Yehuda T.
1982 "A Biblical Scholar Looks at BAR's Coverage of the Exodus." *BAR* 8/6:68–71 (additional comments in 9/2 [1983]: 66).

Rainey, Anson F.
1970a "Bethel Is Still Beitin." *Westminster Theological Journal* 33:175–88.
1970b "Compulsory Labour Gangs in Ancient Israel." *IEJ* 20:191–202.
1977 "Beer-Sheva Excavator Blasts Yadin—No Bama at Beer-Sheva." *BAR* 3/3:18–21, 54–56.
1982 "Historical Geography—The Link between Historical and Archeological Interpretation." *BA* 45:217–23.
1983 "The Biblical Shephelah of Judah." *BASOR* 251:1–22.
1987a "The Saga of Eliashib." *BAR* 13/2:36–39.
1987b "Watching out for the Signal Fires of Lachish." *PEQ* 119:49–51.
1988 "Toward a Precise Date for the Samaria Ostraca." *BASOR* 272:69–74.
1994a "Hezekiah's Reforms and the Altars at Beer-sheba and Arad." 333–54 in *Scripture and Other Artifacts.* Edited by Michael D. Coogan, J. Cheryl Exum, and Lawrence E. Stager. Louisville: Westminster.
1994b "The 'House of David' and the House of the Deconstructionists." *BAR* 20/6:47, 68, 70, 72 (additional comments in 21/2 [1995]: 14, 16, 18, 20, 22, 30–31, 78–79, 100; 21/5:20, 22).

Rainey, Anson F., and Frank J. Yurco
1991 "Can You Name the Panel with the Israelites?" *BAR* 17/6:54–61, 93.

Ramm, Bernard
1956 *Protestant Biblical Interpretation.* Boston: Wilde.

Rasmussen, Carl G.
1989 *Zondervan NIV Atlas of the Bible.* Grand Rapids: Zondervan.

Redford, Donald B.
1987 "The Monotheism of the Heretic Pharaoh: Precursor of Mosaic Monotheism or Egyptian Anomaly?" *BAR* 13/3:16–32.
1989 Review of *Stranger in the Valley of the Kings* by Ahmed Osman. *BAR* 15/2:8.

Reese, Edward
 1977 *The Reese Chronological Bible*. Minneapolis: Bethany.
Ringgren, Helmer
 1973 *Religions of the Ancient Near East*. Translated by John Sturdy. Philadelphia: Westminster.
Ripinsky, Michael
 1983 "Camel Ancestry and Domestication in Egypt and the Sahara." *Archaeology* 36/3:21–27.
 1985 "The Camel in Dynastic Egypt." *Journal of Egyptian Archaeology* 71:134–41.
Ritmeyer, Leen
 1992 "Locating the Original Temple Mount." *BAR* 18/2:24–45, 64–65 (additional comments in 18/4:16–18).
 1996 "The Ark of the Covenant: Where It Stood in Solomon's Temple." *BAR* 22/1:46–55, 70–73 (additional comments in 22/3:18, 20, 66–68).
Rogerson, John, and Philip R. Davies
 1996 "Was the Siloam Tunnel Built by Hezekiah?" *BA* 59:138–48.
Rolle, Renate
 1989 *The World of the Scythians*. Berkeley: University of California Press.
Rosen, Steven A.
 1988 "Finding Evidence of Ancient Nomads." *BAR* 14/5:46–53, 58–59.
Rosovsky, Nitza
 1992 "A Thousand Years of History in Jerusalem's Jewish Quarter." *BAR* 18/3:22–40, 78.
Roux, Georges
 1964 *Ancient Iraq*. First edition. New York: Penguin.
 1992 *Ancient Iraq*. Third edition. New York: Penguin.
Russell, D. S.
 1965 *Between the Testaments*. Philadelphia: Fortress.
Saggs, H. W. F.
 1960 "Ur of the Chaldees." *Iraq* 22:200–209.
 1988 *The Greatness That Was Babylon: A Survey of the Ancient Civilization of the Tigris-Euphrates Valley*. Second edition. London: Sidgwick & Jackson.
Sandars, Nancy K.
 1978 *The Sea Peoples*. London: Thames & Hudson.
Sarna, Nahum M.
 1986 "Exploring Exodus: The Oppression." *BA* 49:68–80.
Sauer, James A.
 1982 "Syro-Palestinian Archeology, History, and Biblical Studies." *BA* 45:201–9.
 1986 "Transjordan in the Bronze and Iron Ages: A Critique of Glueck's Synthesis." *BASOR* 263:1–26.
 1996 "The River Runs Dry." *BAR* 22/4: 52–57, 64.

Schalit, Abraham
 1969 "A Clash of Ideologies: Palestine under the Seleucids and Romans." Pp. 47–76 in *The Crucible of Christianity: Judaism, Hellenism, and the Historical Background to the Christian Faith*. Edited by Arnold Toynbee. London: Thames & Hudson/New York: World.
Schmandt-Besserat, Denise
 1977 "An Archaic Recording System and the Origin of Writing." *Syro-Mesopotamian Studies* 1/2:31–70.
 1983 "Tokens and Counting." *BA* 46:117–20.
 1992 *Before Writing*. 2 volumes. Austin: University of Texas Press.
Schneider, Tammi
 1995 "Did King Jehu Kill His Own Family?" *BAR* 21/1:26–33, 80, 82.
Schneider, Tsvi
 1988 "Azariahu Son of Hilkiahu (High Priest?) on a City of David Bulla." *IEJ* 38:139–41.
 1991 "Six Biblical Signatures." *BAR* 17/4:26–33 (additional comments in 18/1 [1992]: 16).
Schniedewind, William M.
 1996 "Tel Dan Stela: New Light on Aramaic and Jehu's Revolt." *BASOR* 302:75–90.
Schoville, Keith N.
 1994 "Canaanites and Amorites." Pp. 157–82 in *Peoples of the Old Testament World*. Edited by Alfred J. Hoerth, Gerald L. Mattingly, and Edwin M. Yamauchi. Grand Rapids: Baker.
Scott, R. B. Y.
 1959 "Weights and Measures of the Bible." *BA* 22:22–40. Reprinted and revised in *The Biblical Archaeology Reader*, vol. 3 / pp. 345–58. Edited by Edward F. Campbell Jr. and David Noel Freedman. Garden City, N.Y.: Doubleday, 1970.
Seger, Joe D.
 1984 "The Location of Biblical Ziklag." *BA* 47:47–53.
Several, Michael W.
 1972 "Reconsidering the Egyptian Empire in Palestine during the Amarna Period." *PEQ* 104:123–33.
Shaheen, Naseeb
 1976 "The Siloam End of Hezekiah's Tunnel." *PEQ* 108:107–12.
Shanks, Hershel
 1975 "Did the Exodus Pharaoh Die with Salt in His Lungs?" *BAR* 1/3:28–29.
 1977 "Yigael Yadin Finds a Bama at Beer-Sheva." *BAR* 3/1:3–12.
 1978a "The Mystery of the Horses of the Sun at the Temple Entrance." *BAR* 4/2:8–9.
 1978b "The Politics of Ebla." *BAR* 4/3:2–6 (over the pseudonym Adam Mikaya).
 1980a "Have Sodom and Gomorrah Been Found?" *BAR* 6/5:26–36.

1980b   "World's Oldest Musical Notation Deciphered on Cuneiform Tablet." *BAR* 6/5:14–25.

1981a   "The Exodus and the Crossing of the Red Sea, according to Hans Goedicke." *BAR* 7/5:42–50 (additional comments in 7/6:14–16; 8/1 [1982]: 12, 14; 8/2:12, 50, 52–54).

1981b   "Should the Term 'Biblical Archaeology' Be Abandoned?" *BAR* 7/3:54–57.

1982a   "In Defense of Hans Goedicke." *BAR* 8/3:48–52 (additional comments in 8/5:63–64, 66; 8/6:21).

1982b   "What Did David's Lyre Look Like?" *BAR* 8/1:34–35.

1983a   "The Ark That Wasn't There." *BAR* 9/4:58–61 (additional comments in 9/6:18, 20).

1983b   "Network of Iron Age Fortresses Served as Military Signal Posts." *BAR* 9/2:6, 8.

1983c   "Tom Crotser Has Found the Ark of the Covenant—or Has He?" *BAR* 9/3:66–69 (additional comments in 9/4:5 and 9/5:30–31).

1984a   "Clumsy Forger Fools the Scholars—But Only for a Time." *BAR* 10/3:66–72.

1984b   "Destruction of Judean Fortress Portrayed in Dramatic Eighth-Century B.C. Pictures." *BAR* 10/2:48–65.

1985   "Ancient Ivory." *BAR* 11/5:40–53.

1987a   "Avraham Biran—Twenty Years of Digging at Tel Dan." *BAR* 13/4:12–25.

1987b   "Dever's 'Sermon on the Mound.' " *BAR* 13/2:54–57.

1987c   "Jeremiah's Scribe and Confidant Speaks from a Hoard of Clay Bullae." *BAR* 13/5:58–65.

1987d   "1986 Annual Meeting." *BAR* 13/2:50–53.

1988a   "Two Early Israelite Cult Sites Now Questioned." *BAR* 14/1:48–52.

1988b   "Was *BAR* an Accessory to Highway Robbery?" *BAR* 14/6:66–67.

1991   "Please Return the Siloam Inscription to Jerusalem." *BAR* 17/3:58–60.

1992   "The Pomegranate Scepter Head—From the Temple of the Lord or from a Temple of Asherah?" *BAR* 18/3:42–45.

1993a   *The Temple of Solomon and the Tomb of Caiaphas*. Washington: Biblical Archaeology Society.

1993b   "Turkey Goes for the Gold (But Keeps the Stone)." *BAR* 19/6:22.

1994a   "Archaeology's Dirty Secret." *BAR* 20/5:63–64, 79.

1994b   " 'David' Found at Dan." *BAR* 20/2:26–39 (additional comments in 20/5:68, 70).

1995   "Is This King David's Tomb?" *BAR* 21/1:62–67.

1996   "Fingerprint of Jeremiah's Scribe." *BAR* 22/2:36–38.

1998   "Where Is the Tenth Century?" *BAR* 24/2:57–60.

Shanks, Hershel, and Yigael Yadin
1976   "Megiddo Stables or Storehouses?" *BAR* 2/3:1, 12–22 (additional comments in 3/1 [1977]: 43–44, 48).

Shiloh, Yigael
1981   "Jerusalem's Water Supply during Siege—the Rediscovery of Warren's Shaft." *BAR* 7/4:24–39.

1986   "A Group of Hebrew Bullae from the City of David." *IEJ* 36:16–38.

Shiloh, Yigael, and David Tarler
1986   "Bullae from the City of David: A Hoard of Seal Impressions from the Israelite Period." *BA* 49:197–209.

Silberman, Neil A.
1980   "In Search of Solomon's Lost Treasures." *BAR* 6/4:30–41.

Singer, Itamar
1992   "How Did the Philistines Enter Canaan?" *BAR* 18/6:44–46.

Singer, Suzanne
1976   "Found in Jerusalem: Remains of the Babylonian Siege." *BAR* 2/1:7–10.

1978   "From These Hills. . . ." *BAR* 4/2:16–25 (additional comments in 4/3:48–49).

Speiser, Ephraim A.
1964   *Genesis*. Anchor Bible 1. Garden City: Doubleday.

Spencer, A. J.
1982   *Death in Ancient Egypt*. New York: Penguin.

Stager, Lawrence E.
1985   "The Archaeology of the Family in Ancient Israel." *BASOR* 260:1–35.

1989   "The Song of Deborah: Why Some Tribes Answered the Call and Others Did Not." *BAR* 15/1:50–64.

1991   "When Canaanites and Philistines Ruled Ashkelon." *BAR* 17/2:24–37, 40–43.

1996   "The Fury of Babylon: Ashkelon and the Archaeology of Destruction." *BAR* 22/1:56–69, 76–77 (corrections in 22/2:66; 22/3:68).

Stager, Lawrence E., and Samuel R. Wolff
1984   "Child Sacrifice at Carthage—Religious Rite or Population Control?" *BAR* 10/1:30–51 (additional comments in 10/3:20).

Steindorff, George, and Keith C. Seele
1957   *When Egypt Ruled the East*. Second edition. Revised by Keith C. Seele. Chicago: University of Chicago Press.

Stenring, Knut
1965   *The Enclosed Garden*. Stockholm: Almqvist & Wiksell.

Stern, Ephraim
1982   *Material Culture of the Land of the Bible in the Persian Period, 538–332 B.C.* Warminster: Aris & Phillips.

1993a   "How Bad Was Ahab?" *BAR* 19/2:18–29.

1993b   "The Many Masters of Dor." *BAR* 19/1:22–31, 76, 78.

Stiebing, William H., Jr.
1985   "Should the Exodus and the Israelite Set-
        tlement be Redated?" *BAR* 11/4:58–69 (ad-
        ditional comments in 11/6:19, 72, 74 and
        12/1 [1986]: 75–76; corrections in 12/1:10).
1989   *Out of the Desert? Archaeology and the Exo-
        dus/Conquest Narratives*. New York:
        Prometheus.
Stieglitz, Robert R.
1987   "Ancient Records and the Exodus Plagues."
        BAR 13/6:46–49.
Stolper, Matthew W.
1976   "A Note on Yahwistic Personal Names in
        the Murašû Texts." *BASOR* 222:25–28.
Tadmor, Hayim
1961   "Que and Musri." *IEJ* 11:143–50.
Talmon, Shemaryahu
1963   "The Gezer Calendar and the Seasonal Cy-
        cle of Ancient Canaan." *Journal of the
        American Oriental Society* 83:177–87.
Tatum, Lynn
1991   "King Manasseh and the Royal Fortress at
        Ḥorvat ʿUsa." *BA* 54:136–45.
Taylor, J. Glen
1994   "Was Yahweh Worshipped as the Sun?"
        BAR 20/3:52–61, 90–91 (additional com-
        ments in 20/5:16–18).
Thiele, Edwin R.
1976   "An Additional Chronological Note on
        'Yaw, Son of ʿOmri.'" *BASOR* 222:19–23.
1983   *The Mysterious Numbers of the Hebrew
        Kings*. Third edition. Grand Rapids:
        Zondervan.
Thompson, H. C.
1960   "A Row of Cedar Beams." *PEQ* 92:57–63.
Thompson, J. A.
1964   *The Ancient Near Eastern Treaties and the
        Old Testament*. London: Tyndale.
1982a   *The Bible and Archaeology*. Third edition.
        Grand Rapids: Eerdmans.
1982b   "Deuteronomy, Book of." Pp. 280–84 *New
        Bible Dictionary*. Second edition. Edited by
        J. D. Douglas et al. Downers Grove, Ill.: In-
        terVarsity.
Thompson, Thomas L.
1974   *The Historicity of the Patriarchal Narratives:
        The Quest for the Historical Abraham*. Ber-
        lin: de Gruyter.
Tigay, Jeffrey
1982   *The Evolution of the Gilgamesh Epic*. Phila-
        delphia: University of Pennsylvania Press.
Tompkins, Peter
1971   *The Secrets of the Great Pyramid*. New York:
        Harper & Row.
Toombs, Lawrence E.
1982   "The Development of Palestinian Archeol-
        ogy as a Discipline." *BA* 45:89–91.
Torrey, R. A.
1907   *Difficulties and Alleged Errors and Contra-
        dictions in the Bible*. Chicago: Bible Insti-
        tute Colportage Assoc.

Towers, John Robert
1959   "The Red Sea." *Journal of Near Eastern
        Studies* 18:150–53.
Toynbee, Arnold
1969   "The Mediterranean World's Age of Agony:
        The Historical Antecedents." Pp. 19–46 in
        *The Crucible of Christianity: Judaism, Helle-
        nism, and the Historical Background to the
        Christian Faith*. Edited by Arnold Toynbee.
        London: Thames & Hudson/New York:
        World.
Ussishkin, David
1976   "Royal Judean Storage Jars and Private
        Seal Impressions." *BASOR* 223:1–13.
1979a   "Answers at Lachish." *BAR* 5/6:16–39.
1979b   "The 'Camp of the Assyrians' in Jerusalem."
        IEJ 29:137–42.
1980   "The 'Lachish Reliefs' and the City of La-
        chish." *IEJ* 30:174–95.
1982a   *The Conquest of Lachish by Sennacherib*.
        Tel Aviv: The Institute of Archaeology.
1982b   "Where Is Israeli Archeology Going?" *BA*
        45:93–95.
1984   "Defensive Judean Counter-Ramp Found at
        Lachish in 1983 Season." *BAR* 10/2:66–73.
1987   "Lachish Key to the Israelite Conquest of
        Canaan?" *BAR* 13/1:18–39.
1988   "Restoring the Great Gate at Lachish." *BAR*
        14/2:42–47.
Van Hattem, Willem C.
1981   "Once Again: Sodom and Gomorrah." *BA*
        44:87–92.
Van Seters, John
1975   *Abraham in History and Tradition*. New Ha-
        ven: Yale University Press.
Vos, Howard F.
1968   "Archaeology." Pp. 249–68 in *Christianity
        and the World of Thought*. Edited by Hud-
        son T. Armerding. Chicago: Moody.
1983   *1, 2 Samuel*. Grand Rapids: Zondervan.
Walker, C. B. F.
1987   *Reading the Past: Cuneiform*. Berkeley: Uni-
        versity of California Press.
Waltke, Bruce K.
1972   "Palestinian Artifactual Evidence Support-
        ing the Early Date of the Exodus." *Biblio-
        theca Sacra* 129:39–47.
1990   "The Date of the Conquest." *Westminster
        Theological Journal* 52:181–200.
Walton, John
1981   "The Antediluvian Section of the Sumerian
        King List and Genesis 5." *BA* 44:207–8.
Ward, William A.
1992   "The Present Status of Egyptian Chronol-
        ogy." *BASOR* 288:53–66.
1994a   "Beetles in Stone: The Egyptian Scarab."
        BA 57:186–202.
1994b   "Phoenicians." Pp. 183–206 in *Peoples of
        the Old Testament World*. Edited by Alfred
        J. Hoerth, Gerald L. Mattingly, and Edwin
        M. Yamauchi. Grand Rapids: Baker.

Weinstein, James M.
1975   "Egyptian Relations with Palestine in the
        Middle Kingdom." *BASOR* 217:1–16.
Wenham, Gordon J.
1994   "Genesis." Pp. 54–91 in *New Bible Com-
        mentary: Twenty-first Century Edition*.
        Fourth edition. Edited by D. A. Carson et
        al. Downers Grove, Ill.: InterVarsity.
Wenham, J. W.
1958   *Our Lord's View of the Old Testament*. Lon-
        don: Tyndale.
1967   "Large Numbers in the Old Testament."
        Tyndale Bulletin 18:19–53.
Williamson, Hugh G. M.
1996   "Tel Jezreel and the Dynasty of Omri." *PEQ*
        128:41–51.
Wilson, John A.
1951   *The Burden of Egypt: An Interpretation of
        Egyptian Culture. The Culture of Ancient
        Egypt*. Chicago: University of Chicago
        Press. Reprinted in 1975 as *The Culture of
        Ancient Egypt*.
Wiseman, Donald J.
1955   "Assyrian Writing-Boards." *Iraq* 17:3–13.
1958   *Illustrations from Biblical Archaeology*.
        Grand Rapids: Eerdmans.
1979   "Jonah's Nineveh." *Tyndale Bulletin* 30:29–
        51.
1990   "The Bottleneck of Archaeological Publica-
        tion." *BAR* 16/5:60–63.
1993   *1 and 2 Kings: An Introduction and Com-
        mentary*. Tyndale Old Testament Commen-
        taries. Downers Grove, Ill.: InterVarsity.
Wood, Bryant G.
1990   "Did the Israelites Conquer Jericho?" *BAR*
        16/2:44–58.
1991   "The Philistines Enter Canaan." *BAR* 17/
        6:44–52, 89–90, 92.
Wood, Leon J.
1979   *Israel's United Monarchy*. Grand Rapids:
        Baker.
Woolley, C. Leonard
1955   *Ur Excavations*, vol. 4: *The Early Periods*.
        London: British Museum.
Wright, G. Ernest
1959a   "The Achievement of Nelson Glueck." *BA*
        22:98–100.
1959b   "Is Glueck's Aim to Prove That the Bible Is
        True?" *BA* 22:101–8.
1962   *Biblical Archaeology*. Revised edition. Phila-
        delphia: Westminster/London: Duckworth.
Wright, Rodney
1982   "Lachish and Azekah Were the Only Forti-
        fied Cities of Judah That Remained (Jere-
        miah 34:7)." *BAR* 8/6:72–73.

Yadin, Yigael
1958   "Solomon's City Wall and Gate at Gezer."
        IEJ 8:80–86.
1963   *The Art of Warfare in Biblical Lands in the
        Light of Archaeological Study*. Translated by
        M. Pearlman. New York: McGraw-Hill.
1975   *Hazor: The Rediscovery of a Great Citadel of
        the Bible*. New York: Random.
1977–78 "Yadin Answers Beer-Sheva Excavator—
        Reply to Rainey's 'No Bama at Beer-
        Sheva.'" *BAR* 3/4:3–4 (additional com-
        ments in 4/2 [1978]: 46–47).
Yamauchi, Edwin M.
1972   *The Stones and the Scriptures*. Grand Rap-
        ids: Baker.
1977   "Critical Comments on the Search for
        Noah's Ark." *Near East Archaeological Soci-
        ety Bulletin* 10:5–27.
1982   *Foes from the Northern Frontier: Invading
        Hordes from the Russian Steppes*. Grand
        Rapids: Baker.
1983   "The Scythians: Invading Hordes From the
        Russian Steppes." *BA* 46:90–99.
1990   *Persia and the Bible*. Grand Rapids: Baker.
Yohannan, John D. (ed.)
1968   *Joseph and Potiphar's Wife in World Litera-
        ture*. New York: New Directions.
Youngblood, Ronald F.
1991   *The Book of Genesis: An Introductory Com-
        mentary*. Second edition. Grand Rapids:
        Baker.
Yurco, Frank J.
1990   "3,200-Year-Old Picture of Israelites Found
        in Egypt." *BAR* 16/5:20–38 (additional
        comments in 17/1 [1991]: 18, 21, 62–63, 72,
        74).
Zertal, Adam
1985   "Has Joshua's Altar Been Found on Mt.
        Ebal?" *BAR* 11/1:26–43 (see 11/4:10 for cor-
        rections).
1986   "How Can Kempinski Be So Wrong!" *BAR*
        12/1:43, 49–53 (additional comments in 12/
        4:64–66; 12/5:16; 13/2 [1987]: 67–68).
1991   "Israel Enters Canaan: Following the Pot-
        tery Trail." *BAR* 17/5:28–47.
Zevit, Ziony
1985   "The Problem of Ai." *BAR* 11/2:58–69.
Zorn, Jeffrey R.
1994   "Estimating the Population Size of Ancient
        Settlements: Methods, Problems, Solu-
        tions, and a Case Study." *BASOR* 295:31–
        48.
Zuidhof, Albert
1982   "King Solomon's Molten Sea and (π)." *BA*
        45:179–84.

Scripture Index

Italic page numbers refer to illustration captions.

Subject Index

Italic page numbers refer to illustration captions.